The Psychoanalytic Study of the Child

VOLUME TWENTY-SEVEN

The Psychoanalytic Study of the Child

VOLUME TWENTY-SEVEN

QUADRANGLE BOOKS

A New York Times Company

Library of Congress Catalog Card Number: 45:11304

International Standard Book Number: 0–8129–0322–6

Designed by Ruth Smerechniak

Manufactured in the United States of America

CONTENTS

Seymour L. Lustman

ALBERT J. SOLNIT, M.D.

SEYMOUR L. LUSTMAN DIED AT THE AGE OF 51 AT THE HEIGHT OF HIS personal and intellectual capacities. As a child he had been encouraged by his parents to develop his artistic interests. Although he never lost his love for and appreciation of the graphic arts, he gave up this early interest in painting and sketching as he became increasingly fascinated by the psychological and psychosomatic questions posed by adults and children.

He had majored in psychology at Northwestern University, but was not clear about his primary interests when he graduated in 1941. While mulling over his future plans he accepted a job in personnel, clearly foreshadowing his interest in personal relationships

Sterling Professor of Pediatrics and Psychiatry; Director, Child Study Center, Yale University, New Haven.

and in personality development. Indeed, Dr. Lustman's chairmanship of the Task Force on Research and Manpower for the Joint Commission on Mental Health of Children many years later (1966–1968) reflected his interest in personnel as well as in personality.

When the United States entered World War II, Dr. Lustman volunteered because he felt deeply about the issues and values in-' volved, deferring his career choice and development, although he had decided to go to graduate school at the University of Chicago to study psychology. During his military service of four years, he became an officer and was attached to the Medical Corps in order that his skills as a psychologist could be utilized. Several psychiatrists were impressed by his analytic mind and as they became friends, they urged him to go to medical school to become a psychoanalyst. These friendships characteristically persisted and in the postwar period several members of this group became colleagues in psychoanalysis.

After the war Dr. Lustman first obtained his Ph.D. in psychology at the University of Chicago in 1949 and then his M.D. at the University of Illinois in 1954. Now the pattern of intellectual and scientific interests became clearer. From the beginning, nature and nurture would be viewed as complemental in their influence on personality development.

Beginning his career at Yale University in 1955 as a Commonwealth Fellow in Psychiatry, he completed his training in general and child psychiatry at Yale University and his psychoanalytic training at the Western New England Institute for Psychoanalysis in 1962. His talents as a clinical teacher, theoretician, and investigator were acknowledged when he was appointed to full professorial rank in 1964, receiving an honorary M.A. from Yale in that same year. A training and supervising psychoanalyst at the Western New England Institute for Psychoanalysis, he had recently completed two years as President of the Western New England Psychoanalytic Society, had served as Chairman of the Task Force on Research and Manpower of the Joint Commission on Mental Health of Children, and a Councilor-at-Large of the American Psychoanalytic Association. Prominently involved in the professional and scientific activities of the American and International Psychoanalytic Association, he also had a special interest in the role of the American Academy of Child Psychiatry in stimulating and supporting research and scholarly activities. This was demonstrated by his Chairmanship of its Committee on Research and by serving on the Editorial Board of its Journal. He played a leading role on the editorial boards of several other distinguished journals, and, in 1969, he became an editor of *The Psychoanalytic Study of the Child.*

His earliest work, starting with his Ph.D. thesis, examined the relationships of psyche and soma, starting with a focus on repression in symptom formation. During his medical student days he reported on a study of headaches as a psychosomatic phenomenon (1951). In most of his scholarly work, Dr. Lustman was simultaneously interested in the content of the study, the methodological criteria of the investigation and the scientific philosophical implications of the research.

In the opening statement of his 1951 paper on headaches, Dr. Lustman wrote: "The purpose of this preliminary report is threefold: 1) to present an experimental method by which the meaning of neurotic symptomatology such as headache can be studied; 2) to demonstrate the relationship between rage and the symptom of headache; and 3) to shed some light on the relationship between repression and symptom formation."

Often Dr. Lustman expressed his philosophical concerns in papers dealing with medical education, but in all of his work his extraordinary capacities for incisiveness and synthesis characterized his scientific questioning and thinking. Searching for basic assumptions he began in his medical student days to probe for the earliest evidence of a body-mind relationship in brilliantly conceived experimental studies of autonomic functions in neonates that he carried out with Dr. Julius Richmond and his colleagues (1953–1955).[1] Later he used these studies to make basic contributions to psychoanalytic theory in two articles (1956, 1957) published in *This Annual.* In the second paper, "Psychic Energy and Mechanisms of Defense," he stated, "This discussion will address itself to three problems facing psychoanalytic theory today. These

[1] See The Writings of Seymour L. Lustman.

are questions of quantity and source of neutralized energy, and the basic mechanisms of defense."

Typically, his research and writings could not be absorbed in one hearing or reading because of the several levels of inference that were tightly interwoven. In "Rudiments of the Ego" he concluded:

> Inherent autonomic endowment is thought of as one of the nuclear apparatuses from which the primitive ego emerges, and upon which subsequent formative influences impinge, and with which they interact in the ultimate development of first body ego, and then mental ego. This is in keeping with Freud's (1937) postulated inborn, inherited ego factors; it seems to corroborate Hartmann's concepts of an "undifferentiated stage" and of a "conflict-free sphere of ego development"; and it seems to support the autonomy of the ego as formulated by Hartmann.

He quickly understood the research potentials of child analysis, as well as its limitations. I often thought of him as a tapestry designer, though I knew he was artistically a painter. As an investigator he wove his theoretical syntheses from experimental, clinical and theory building efforts into a tightly reasoned, scientifically elegant and original fabric with vivid imagery and an illuminating perspective. In his 1962 paper, "Defense, Symptom, and Character," for which he received the David Rapaport Prize of the Western New England Institute for Psychoanalysis, he indicated these capacities when he stated:

> With the technical and theoretical development of child analysis as a field, the danger of "easily misunderstood material" has sharply diminished. Hartmann and Kris have repeatedly stated that the field of direct observation of children has become an ever-increasing source of live data of increasing import. This has been misunderstood by some to mean that with children observational techniques can replace psychoanalysis. Hartmann and Kris had reference to the child prior to the age at which child analysis could be used. From then on, the techniques of child analysis differ considerably from those of experiment and observation—even when the latter are carried out by psychoanalytically trained or sophisticated experimenters

and observers. It is precisely the inextricability of the *three-fold* function of psychoanalysis as a theory, therapy, and research "instrument" which makes child analysis the richer source of research data [p. 218].

Dr. Lustman was a brilliant behavioral scientist, known nationally and internationally for his psychoanalytic and psychosomatic research, as well as for his gifted clinical and theoretical teaching. He was a compassionate master clinician and therapist of children, youth, and adults. His high standards of scholarship were evident not only in his teaching and his statesmanship in the service of basic research, but especially in his own original studies, some of which were still in the planning stage.

Although it would not be apparent at any but the most sophisticated level, his interests when he died formed the outlines and preliminary sketches of a large creative canvas that contained several major and minor themes converging into an integrated composition of scientific investigation. The major theme was the psychoanalytic inquiry into impulse control, with children and adolescents occupying the central focus. On the side, with distant perspectives, could be seen the derivatives of the ethical and moral implications of biological control (genetics), and of impulse regulation and expression. The texture of the painting seemed to be foreshadowed in a few samples, indicating a profound concern with methodology, also suggested by the experimental sketches on proportions and perspectives. The preliminary presentations implied that color would have been in the service of the themes, with lightness and darkness in an uncertain balance. Perhaps the clearest emotion conveyed is that connected with the imagery of the children in motion. They are active, spirited, durable, and impish. They are sad and joyous. They are abiding.

Seymour L. Lustman
The Early Professional Years

JULIUS B. RICHMOND, M.D.

I FIRST MET SEYMOUR LUSTMAN IN 1950 WHEN HE WAS A FRESHMAN in medical school. I had lectured to his class on child development and discussed some of our observations of newborn infants.

He appeared at my office the next morning with a reprint of his recently published paper on "Headache as an Internalized Rage Reaction." This paper reflected, even in his earlier studies for his doctorate in psychology, his deep interest in the relationships between biological and psychological phenomena. We immediately plunged into a discussion of mind-body relationships (and contin-

Professor of Child Psychiatry and Human Development, and Professor and Chairman, Department of Preventive and Social Medicine, Harvard Medical School; Psychiatrist-in-Chief, Children's Hospital Medical Center; Director, Judge Baker Guidance Center, Boston, Mass.

ued this discussion over his entire lifetime). He showed surprise that anyone in a medical setting would have any familiarity with factor analysis and the then popular Stephenson Q-sort technique. This first meeting began a collaboration that lasted for many years.

These were the years when the field of psychosomatic medicine was blossoming. Franz Alexander and Thomas French were providing leadership in bridging psychoanalytic and medical concepts at the Chicago Institute for Psychoanalysis. Dr. Alexander conducted a weekly psychosomatic conference at the University of Illinois College of Medicine. Dr. Lustman became a regular attendant at these sessions, even though he was not yet into his clinical studies and had to absent himself from his classwork in order to attend.

The focus of this work was on the "specificity hypotheses," which attempted to define the personality constellations associated with specific disorders and which became for many years the major research commitment of the Chicago Institute for Psychoanalysis. There also was a group of child analysts, among them Margaret Gerard and Irene Josselyn, who were concerned with the problems of children manifesting psychosomatic disorders.

Dr. Lustman immersed himself in the studies of children. We had become concerned with the issue that Freud referred to as the "equipment" that the patient brought to the adaptational problems he faced. Alexander had defined this as the X factor. We had determined that research into children's problems should move closer to issues of innate differences in both the constitution of the child and his predisposition to psychosomatic disorders. We turned to studies of differences in autonomic regulatory reactivity in newborn infants in an effort to identify these differences at the earliest possible time. Because cardiac rate could be measured readily without creating disturbance in the infant, we focused our attention on this function.

Dr. Lustman quickly saw the relevance of such studies for child development and plunged into this work with great imagination and vigor. During the period immediately following World War II, studies in high altitude physiology were in their ascendancy. The University of Illinois had established a laboratory for studies in aviation physiology, which had developed an elaborate technology for the study of human physiology. With his usual resourcefulness, Dr. Lustman found his way to these laboratories and received authorization to adapt their facilities to the study of newborn infants. He sensed that the decompression chambers that were available offered a ready-made setting for standardized observations (in later years it took much work to establish comparable facilities in laboratories for newborn studies). Those who came to know Dr. Lustman later were probably unaware of his talents at adapting electronic instrumentation for specific studies. He jerry-built a crude polygraphic recording system for skin temperature, cardiac, respiratory, and behavioral recordings, which in later years became commercially available as the sophisticated polygraphic recording instruments that we know today. His approach was one of consistent problem solving; he always defined clearly the hypothesis to be tested and then set out very pragmatically to develop the appropriate instrumentation and to collect the necessary data.

In contrast to many medical students who define their career goal as psychiatry and psychoanalysis, Dr. Lustman retained a deep interest in clinical medicine and was fascinated by surgery. He worked hard on the wards and every patient piqued his curiosity. For those who knew him, it was no surprise that he wrote a paper on hip fracture in the aged when he graduated from medical school. In addition to his clinical and research interests, Dr. Lustman was even then deeply concerned with the many problems of medical education (a curriculum change had been introduced at the Case-Western Reserve Medical School at this time) and contributed many ideas for proposals which our curriculum committee was formulating.

In 1954 he helped me develop a paper on "Total Health: A Conceptual Visual Aid." We were concerned with the heavy emphasis on disease and pathology in the teaching of medical students and were aware of the difficulty in defining health and conceptualizing it. Thus we came to focus on the functional capacity of the individual and the many simultaneously interacting factors that determine it. In our effort to show the person in the light of his development, we arrived at a series of diagrams to depict the person over time and to introduce a quantitative concept of functional capacity (Figs. 1 and 2) . This paper was adapted for teaching by others and became the most widely reproduced and quoted in our respective bibliographies. Its scheme, moreover, was very useful for our growing concerns with problems in psychosomatic medicine. The summary states:

> To balance the trend toward specialization and compartmentalization fostered by rapid advances in the medical sciences, it is desirable to emphasize a comprehensive approach to the understanding of man and his relationship to his environment in health and disease. With this in view, a quantifiable, graphic schema is presented which permits a presentation of the dynamic relationships among the multiplicity of types of forces operative upon and within the organism at any given moment. This technique has been found useful in teaching and for the graphic recording of our understanding of individual patients and disease processes [Richmond and Lustman, 1954, p. 29].

Dr. Lustman's interests were also being shaped by his association and friendship with Dr. David Shakow, whose extensive knowledge of research and psychoanalysis and high standards of scholarship have influenced many of us. It was in the context of discussions with Dr. Shakow that Dr. Lustman decided to apply to Yale for psychiatric training, since, in addition, there was the Child Study Center, where Dr. Milton J. E. Senn had developed an interdisciplinary training program in child development and child psychiatry, and where he and Dr. Ernst Kris were conducting a longitudinal study of child development. Dr. Lustman was accepted for these programs and at the same time enrolled in the Western New England Institute for his psychoanalytic training. A fellowship from the Commonwealth Fund enabled him to complete his varied training.

Throughout his medical school years, Seymour Lustman pursued the study of autonomic response patterns in the newborn. These studies resulted in a series of joint publications. Our first paper on "Autonomic Function in the Neonate: Implications for Psychosomatic Theory" started as follows:

A theory to explain the genesis of psychosomatic disorders should be capable of explaining at least the following three factors: (1) the process of physiologic alteration; (2) organ specificity; and (3) individual specificity. That the autonomic nervous system would play a central role as the final common pathway in mediating somatic reactions to emotional stimuli has been generally accepted since the classic work of Cannon. It is no longer tenable to speak of a "language of organs" in a symbolic sense without considering underlying physiological processes [Richmond and Lustman, 1955, p. 269].

After presenting data on such varied autonomic reactions as reflex vascular and pupillary dilatation, which illustrated the highly individual response patterns that had been hypothesized, the paper concluded: "The results of these studies indicate that there are qualitative and quantitative individual differences in autonomic function apparent within the first days of life. These differences are both in terms of autonomic-system endowment and rate of maturation" (p. 274).

These studies were extended to include cardiac rate regulation in the newborn period and were continued by our group over a number of years.

Although his move to Yale separated Dr. Lustman from our group, he continued to be fascinated by behavior in early life. His studies in psychoanalysis stimulated him to think of the integration of empirical physiological findings with psychoanalytic thought. Thus, a few years later, drawing on the data collected while a member of our group, he wrote the paper "Rudiments of the Ego" (1956). The extension of his thinking is apparent in the following quotations:

In his discussion of the import of psychoanalytic ego psychology, Kris (1950) points out that it ". . . re-emphasized the character of psychoanalysis as a psychology of adaptation, of learning, and clinical data have implemented these general assumptions as far as the child's earliest experiences are concerned." Actually, clinical data are most inadequate in terms of origins of ego function. Kris indicates this in noting the increasing research concern with the development of the ego, and the acceptance of the tendency to integrate observational data into the general flow of psychoanalytic thought. It thus appears that the earliest factors of ego development are beyond the powers of reconstructive psychoanalytic techniques, as they exist today [p. 89].

[Lustman then presents data on individual difference in response to stimulation of erogenous zones and concludes that] this paper highlights the necessity for longitudinal studies of an experimental as well as an observational nature. We would like to emphasize that our discussion has been, in the absence of longitudinal data, a purely speculative attempt at integrating our cross-sectional findings into pertinent psychoanalytic concepts. We feel such speculation is warranted only if it is clearly recognized as such, and if its purpose is to stimulate further research. We conclude that inherent autonomic endowment (including corticoautonomic relations), demonstrable in the three-day-old neonate, is one of the factors making up the autonomous conflict-free sphere of ego development, and as such participates in and markedly influences subsequent ego development. We feel that our data give suggestive evidence for the phase concept by indicating that in the neonate the oral area is the primary erogenous zone, as analytic theory predicts. The finding of individual hyperreactors in other areas such as the anal zone adds perspective to reported clinical variations in phase sequence [p. 97].

By the time this paper was published, Dr. Lustman was deeply immersed in psychoanalytic thought and practice. While he wistfully talked of returning to observations of the infant, on the many occasions of our meeting, his other responsibilities were too demanding. The rapid advances in this field would have required virtually a full-time commitment to it.

His interest in medical education continued and we had many discussions over the years. It seemed fitting, therefore, on the occasion of the publication of a *Festschrift* in honor of Dr. Milton J. E. Senn, that we would collaborate on a paper entitled "On the Acceptance of Realistic Goals in Medicine" (Lustman and Richmond, 1963). Dr. Lustman's concerns were with the internship as a transitional period. The paper stated the problem as follows:

As constituted today, it is usually the internship period during which the young physician comes to grips with the frustrations of the realistic limitations of what can be done as contrasted to what one *should be able* to do. In the transition from training to practice, the problem may be stated as coming to grips with what can be done as contrasted to what ideally *could or should* be done [p. 559].

This paper highlighted the growing dissatisfaction with the internship experience. Almost a decade later certain specialties, led by psychiatry, were to abolish the internship requirement. The reordering of clinical experiences for the student in recent years was forecast by the following:

It is in many ways unfortunate that the intern's first professional responsibility for patients is in the hospital, where the very seriously ill and the most perplexing diagnostic problems are to be found. It is a paradox that it is the intern, the man in the hospital who is least prepared in terms of skill, age, experience, emotional maturity, and confidence, who spends the most time carrying out the most intimate procedures to the painfully ill and dying. It is a little reminiscent of the "sink or swim" philosophy of education. It is no wonder that under these circumstances therapeutic "nihilism" can become an important implicit or explicit concern to the young physician [p. 563].

The greatest satisfactions in medicine depend on a concept of the acceptance of realistic, although limited, goals in terms of oneself and one's own profession. This is never to be misunderstood to mean not trying all within one's ability and within the scope of one's profession to aid the patient [p. 569].

In more recent years Dr. Lustman's concerns broadened from those of medical education to those of the university. The high standards with which he had been imbued caused him to worry about the dilution of opportunities for scholarship and research in the face of pressures for community service. The dialogues he stimulated had a wholesome effect on all who would read or listen to his presentations. The richness of his background as psychologist, physician, psychiatrist, and psychoanalyst made him an eloquent spokesman. We can honor his memory by pursuing his values.

The Writings of Seymour L. Lustman

1943
Malingering on the G. T. Test. Hq. 8th Service Command.

1951
The Headache as an Internalized Rage Reaction: A Preliminary Report. *Psychiatry*, 14:433–438.

1953
(with J. B. Richmond & J. J. Grossman) A Hearing Test for Newborn Infants. *Pediatrics*, 11:634–638.

1954
Hip Fracture in the Aged.

(with J. B. Richmond) Total Health: A Conceptual Visual Aid. *Journal of Medical Education*, 29:23–30.

1955

(with J. B. Richmond) Autonomic Function in the Neonate: I. Implications for Psychosomatic Theory. *Psychosomatic Medicine*, 17:269–275.

(with E. L. Lipton & J. B. Richmond) Autonomic Function in the Neonate: III. Cardiac Rate and Skin Temperature Responses in Newborn Infants. *Psychosomatic Medicine*, 17:475–476.

(with E. L. Lipton & J. B. Richmond) Autonomic Function in the Neonate and Psychosomatic Disease. *American Journal of Diseases of Children*, 90:491.

1956

Rudiments of the Ego. *This Annual*, 11:89–98.

1957

Psychic Energy and Mechanisms of Defense. *This Annual*, 12:151–165.

1959

Libido Updated. Review of *Erogeneity and Libido: Some Addenda to the Theory of Psychosexual Development of the Human*, by Robert Fliess. *Contemporary Psychology*, 4:18–20.

1960

Emotional Problems of Children as They Relate to Orthodontics. *American Journal of Orthodontics*, 46:358–362.

1962

Defense, Symptom, and Character. *This Annual*, 17:216–244.

1963

(with J. B. Richmond) On the Acceptance of Realistic Goals in Medicine. In: *Modern Perspectives in Child Development: Essays in Honor of Milton J. E. Senn*, ed. S. A. Provence & A. J. Solnit. New York: International Universities Press, pp. 558–574.

Some Issues in Contemporary Psychoanalytic Research. *This Annual*, 18:51–74.

1964

Discussion remarks in Panel on Child Analysis at Different Developmental States, rep. G. McLean Abbate. *Journal of the American Psychoanalytic Association*, 12:135–150.

1965

Split Custody: A Clinical Evaluation. In: *The Family and the Law*, by J. Goldstein & J. Katz. New York: Free Press, pp. 325–328.

1966

Behavior Disorders in Childhood and Adolescence. In: *The Theory and Practice of Psychiatry*, by F. C. Redlich & D. X. Freedman. New York: Basic Books, pp. 676–704.

Impulse Control, Structure, and the Synthetic Function. In: *Psychoanalysis—A General Psychology: Essays in Honor of Heinz Hartmann*, ed. R. M. Loewenstein, L. M. Newman, M. Schur, & A. J. Solnit. New York: International Universities Press, pp. 190–221.

1967

The Scientific Leadership of Anna Freud. *Journal of the American Psychoanalytic Association*, 15:810–827.

The Meaning and Purpose of Curriculum Planning. *Journal of the American Psychoanalytic Association*, 15:862–875.

1968

The Economic Point of View and Defense. *This Annual*, 23:189–203. Reprinted as Introduction to Panel on the Use of the Economic Viewpoint in Clinical Psychoanalysis. *International Journal of Psycho-Analysis*, 50:95–102, 1969.

Book Review: *The Technique and Practice of Psychoanalysis*, by R. R. Greenson. New York: Behavioral Science Book Service.

1969

Mental Health Research and the University: A Position Paper for the Joint Commission on Mental Health of Children. *Archives of General Psychiatry*, 21:291–301.

1970

Discussion remarks in Panel on The Use of the Economic Viewpoint in Clinical Psychoanalysis, rep. K. T. Calder. *International Journal of Psycho-Analysis*, 51:245–249.

Cultural Deprivation: A Clinical Dimension of Education. *This Annual*, 25:483–502.

Editor, Volume IV, Report of the Joint Commission on Mental Health of Children.

1972

Yale's Year of Confrontation: A View from the Master's House. *This Annual*, 27:57–73.

A Perspective on the Study of Man. *This Annual*, 27:18–54.

A Perspective on the Study of Man

SEYMOUR L. LUSTMAN, M.D., PH.D.

IN SPEAKING OF MAN, IT IS MOST USEFUL TO MAINTAIN A CLEAR DIS-
tinction between mankind in the aggregate and individual men.
Although there are those few, wondrous men who experience true
pleasure in knowledge for the sake of knowledge, knowledge for
mankind in the aggregate has never been far from the question,
"Can man survive?" Sometimes asked directly, most often tangentially, it is an ageless, anxious query. In epochs past it has been
addressed most specifically to the not-understood, usually discreet,
but threatening circumstance of the moment. Accordingly, in the
study of myths and primitive religions, it is clear that man created
deities and rites which were projections of his fears and confusions,

---

This paper is published posthumously. Dr. Lustman had not yet undertaken its
final revisions. The editors have made no basic changes in his draft.

(18)

and gave him the illusory comfort that he *could* survive; or that he could, at the least, be reincarnated. This was accomplished by circumventing terror-filled ignorance and impotence via the creation of magic ritual, or devising codes of conduct, both of which he could control.[1]

Such early created religious fictions were projections. Man's so-called knowledge of himself and his world were cast in the image of his concerns and in the service of his desperate needs for security. He attempted to avoid impotence by turning passive experience into active participation, and, in addition, preserved a longed-for superhuman, divine spirit which looked after him. The same is true in the evolution of graphic, musical, and literary art forms. It is also apparent in the evolution of philosophies, and now in man's latest and certainly most sophisticated attempt to understand and control via his highest level intellectual activity—science. Perhaps the best statement of this projective element in science is Bronowski's (1958) description of the theorizing of Newton: "The world of speculation [i.e., Newton's speculation] is suddenly seen to chime with the real world, with a triumphant note like a peal of bells. . . . The laws are not a deduction from experiment in any obvious sense. Their success is not that they follow from the real world, but that they predict a world which is essentially like ours" (p. 36). The same is true of Einstein's speculations.

Self-knowledge, called by Cassirer (1944) "the highest aim of philosophical inquiry" (p. 1), has been approached through a variety of methods other than philosophical. There are several interesting and important aspects of this. The first is the essential relatedness in spite of an apparent hierarchy of methods. The second is the wedding of knowledge to man's effort to control himself and his fate. Wisdom became power, in both a magical and a real sense. The third is an increasing sense of objectivity and freedom in the search for knowledge, moving from magic to science.

If one follows Cassirer, there is great value in studying myth and

---

[1] One cannot help but be impressed with how old and how persistent is man's fear of helplessness. In current psychoanalytic theory the danger of passive helplessness remains central to its theory of psychic trauma. The shift from a passively experienced danger to an actively reproduced "game" wherein the victim is now the perpetrator is the central hypothesis in the psychoanalytic theory of play.

religion, the development of language, art, history, philosophy, and science. Cassirer's is perhaps the richest of several schemata which give an overall sense of the ways in which experiencing and thinking man has attempted to examine himself. As a scientist, I would consider science the most reasoned and fruitful of the available techniques for such self-study. At the same time, I would agree with Cassirer that science has given us a wealth of presumed "facts" which are in no way necessarily a wealth of thoughts. I remain particularly concerned with the elaboration and proliferation of disconnected and disparate data and theories which seem to lack any conceptual unity and are, accordingly, most difficult to utilize. Nor can I accept the notion of a "science of man" divorced from philosophy.

The nature of this essay does not require any extensive review of these ways of "knowing." It is abundantly clear, however, that the urge to know, the urge to dispel doubt and to feel certainty, has put the source of knowledge not in the physical world, but as a projection of man himself. This is particularly true of man's attempt to find meaning in life, as well as to participate in his fate. The uses of religions to explain, to lead, to inspire, and to protect, remain evidence for this point. The effort of religion to turn passive obedience into passionately active inspiration and aspiration; its effort to channel man's motives, to reinforce societal taboos, are further vivid demonstrations of man's urge to know—and, by knowing, to survive, and to control and direct his destiny. To those who think "human engineering and management" is a new field, much can be learned from the methods whereby religions, such as the Semitic, are organized around the enforcement of societally conceived taboos. Restraint is burdensome, if not onerous. In the effort to avoid oppression, the religious experience of turning passive obedience to active inspiration and aspiration resulted in control being experienced (by many) as a new, positive, and gratifying freedom.

If we accept this relationship of man's efforts to know with the multiplex issues of survival, the needs of our age are magnified as never before. All conflict and dissonance have presumably seemed awesome to those who lived through them. However, the particular burden of our civilization and generation is the omnipresent awareness of multiple, unremitting conflicts with catastrophic potential, taking place simultaneously and interacting with each other. As Arthur Schlesinger (1969) poignantly put it, the velocity of history has changed. The complexity of our bewildering, capricious, overwhelming world has multiplied with ever-increasing and disconcerting speed. With these ominous developments, the question, "Can man survive?" may be said to have assumed greater urgency and clarity. Addressed to limited problems, questions can still be asked in terms of can man survive pestilence, heat, cold, a hostile environment, a desert, a swamp, disease, war, violence, passionate aggression, overpopulation, pollution, and the host of problems that small groups and large groups of men face.

However, the overwhelming evidence of the degree to which mankind contributes to the creation of his problematic state makes it a reasonable assumption that the essence of man's survival lies in the question, "Can man survive himself?"

Given the incredible complexity of man as an animal, it is quite likely true that almost everything that has been said on the issue of survival has a certain degree of relevance, if not validity. Nevertheless, for the purpose of bringing to bear the most important asset man has for survival, I would like to focus on what I consider the single most unique characteristic of man. Although man is a biological animal, he is different from all other forms, and this difference between man and the next highest animal form is greater than the difference in the rest of the animal species. This is not primarily due to his marvelous hand or his upright posture, but directly due to his extraordinary, thoroughly unequaled mind and intelligence—his ability to learn, his ability to abstract, symbolize, and communicate. The mind of man is his most unique characteristic.

It is this essence of man that makes him unusual and incomparable among all animal forms. It is his mind that made Cassirer define man as an "animal symbolicum" (p. 26). By this he meant that, compared with other animals, man lives not merely in a broader reality; he lives in a new dimension of reality. He must adapt to more than a physical universe; he must live and adapt to a symbolic universe. Language, myth, art, religion, and science are parts of this universe. By virtue of this tangled web of human experience, the symbolic net, man does not live in a physical world of hard facts, he lives in the midst of emotions, in hopes and fears, in illusions and disillusions, in fantasies and dreams. In language, religion, art, and science, man can do no more than to build up his own universe—a symbolic universe that enables him to understand and interpret, to articulate and organize, to synthesize and universalize his human experience. Although man and other animal forms share similar physiological processes, and although other animals have intelligence, only man can create and communicate a symbolic universe.

I do not take issue with those who feel that man's survival is related to issues of aggression and destruction, as put forth in certain human analogues of ethological theory, or psychoanalytic theory, or philosophical and sociological concepts. Nevertheless, I would like to advance the concept that man's ability to survive or to destroy himself rests primarily on his incredible quality of intelligence. I do not mean this in the sense of supreme rationalism; any theory of man must take cognizance of his irrationality. What I refer to is the difference between problem solving and planning.

If we continue to make a clear distinction between individual men and mankind as a species, the ability to survive or to destroy rests in mankind as a species. The crucial difference between the two is that individual man can use his intelligence in an anticipatory or planning mode, whereas his wondrous intelligence has forced him (in the aggregate) to act as a problem-solving animal, rather than as a planning animal. This is due to the speed and variety with which hosts of individual men, acting alone, increase all dimensions of mankind's world and proliferate problems.

The difference between problem solving and anticipatory planning is that the latter is dedicated to the prevention of the appearance of problems, whereas the former is brought to bear only after a problem has been delineated with such force that it can no longer be ignored.

I can think of no period in history when mankind has been able to plan. This was not apparent as long as there was space which permitted him to expand, to flee, and to avoid confrontation. Now that there appears to be no place to go, it becomes clearer that in concert, as a species, we address conflict after it pre-empts our attention and then can only act as a problem-solving animal. At the moment, there seem to be too many of us, with too diverse hopes and values to permit us to anticipate common problems and to operate as planning animals. This was never more apparent or inescapable than today when there are no readily available escape hatches, no longer places to run to hide from the ever-increasing complexity of life.

As long as man continues to address survival in a problem-solving way, after the problem has emerged and been elaborated, I suspect that his possibility for survival as a species is low. His creative intelligence makes it impossible to catch up with the prodigious proliferation of problems. It may well be that we shall not be able to plan in concert until all issues other than physical survival are dwarfed by a threat so pointed, so universal, so relentlessly inescapable, that mere survival becomes the only dominant, shared value. There are many who feel the bomb has presented us with this threat. True or not, it has not made all men fear imminent death. Of course, there are other aspects of survival than physical survival. However, values such as freedom, intellectual and artistic richness are too varied, too idiosyncratic, to command universal prominence.

Perhaps I can make this clearer by concrete examples. Given the complicated problems of our age, the simplest to tackle should be such concerns as air traffic over our large cities or the pollution of our streams by detergents. At the same time that individual men, or small clusters of men, begin to recognize that these are problems of destructive potential, other men, by virtue of their creative intelligence, amplify and elaborate the forms of the problem so that by the time a solution is reached for one area, the overall boundaries of the hazard have been massively extended. The problems of air traffic are being heroically increased at the same time that the most rudimentary aspects of safety are being resolved. It is said that our airports would now be safe for piston engine traffic and limited jet traffic while we are already elaborating massive jet and supersonic planes. By the time we were capable of chemically breaking down the first detergent, we had already developed numerous other forms.

War, as a problem-solving solution, remains as terrifying evidence of our inability to plan. And yet, we know that war is hardly the only destructive force that we have created to cope with the urgencies of immediate problems. Although ecology, as a scientific discipline, was established almost a hundred years ago, we are much farther from coping with the destructive imbalances now than we were then. We may be buried in garbage before our technologists and scientists can figure out how to do away with the disposable bottle. Mankind, as a species, may yet perish in a sea of garbage, overpopulated, wtihout food, air, inundated by noise and a host of noxious elements, chemically and physically irradiated, and possibly incinerated.

Nevertheless, we remain remarkably complacent in spite of the fact that many of our finest scientists fear that we are rapidly approaching an irreversible ecological nadir. Our people have been led to a great trust in American technology; to the degree that most would never worry about the diminishing water supply of our land and would rest assured that before the absence of water threatened our survival, our chemists will have synthesized a substitute. Our faith in technology is distressingly similar to early man's need for benevolent deities. It is as if technology has replaced religion for many.

I know of no contemporary problem which is not being complicated a hundredfold by man's creative, active intelligence during the period when its simplest forms are undergoing the problem-solving techniques of civilization. Yet these problems are relatively simple compared to those of the biological-behavioral and social science areas.

If man cannot bring to bear his remarkable intelligence in anticipatory understanding and controlling of *himself,* rather than on corrective, ameliorative solutions to those *"things"* and *"circumstance"* which his inventiveness has created, our plight remains crucially dangerous.

If we are, indeed, to survive as a species, our finest scholars and our greatest universities must be dedicated to some kind of reassessment of the innumerable ways independently working scholars proliferate knowledge in increasingly specialized spheres. We must resynthesize these pieces of knowledge into some kind of conceptual unity, rather than continue this massive multiplication of discontinuous and unrelated data. Only when we have put together our understanding of mankind will it be possible to bring this knowledge to bear on the survival of our species. I again quote Ernst Cassirer, "our wealth of facts is not necessarily a wealth of thoughts. Unless we succeed in finding a clue of Ariadne to lead us out of this labyrinth, we can have no real insight into the general character of human culture; we shall remain lost in a mass of disconnected and disintegrated data which seems to lack all conceptual unity" (p. 22).

The Conflict in Science

Our men of letters are beset by an astonishing lack of humility, all clinging to one toe of the elephant and all firmly convinced that each has the entire beast within his grasp. We seem to have lost the perspective that the scientific enterprise is a loose federation of man; a loose compilation of knowledge of which no one man has ever known more than the tiniest fragment. The simplest capitulation for the scientist would be his acceptance of the idea that science is not the only avenue by which man has attempted to understand himself. Science is only the last, although the most promising and sophisticated, approach. It supplements, rather than supplants, other avenues such as philosophy, the arts, religion, and primitive myths. Hopefully, it can integrate other avenues. Of greater complexity is the integration of diverse areas within science itself.

In a simplified way, if we address ourselves to science and philosophy, there seem to be two broad currents of thought which are in conflict with each other and which demonstrate, perhaps, the major need for the development of conceptual bridges. These two basic views of man, both critical, both of inordinate value to each other, are not yet integrated, but locked in conflict. This not only is true on an ideological and theoretical level, but does in fact pit scientist against scientist and philosopher against philosopher in endless, petulant, unproductive, but thoroughly mortal feuds.

In an engaging essay, Gordon W. Allport traces the current dichotomy in psychology through its philosophical precursors, focusing on the Lockean tradition as opposed to the Leibnitzian tradition. As Allport (1955) puts it, "The Lockean point of view . . . has been and is still dominant in Anglo-American psychology. Its representatives are found in associationism of all types, including environmentalism, behaviorism, stimulus-response (familiarly abbreviated as S–R) psychology, and all other stimulus-oriented psychologies, in animal and genetic psychology, in positivism and operationism, in mathematical models—in short, in most of what today is cherished in our laboratories as truly 'scientific' psychology" (p. 8). He continues to point out that this group holds what is external and visible as more fundamental than what is not, and considers concepts of causality as external to the organism. Of major import is the fact that preoccupation with molecular units brings with it a strong belief in the equivalence of species and leads scientists to theorize about the mind of man from the behavior of lower forms.

In short, the fundamental postulate is that man is a *tabula rasa* and that experience writes upon the wax of the mind. What this has resulted in is an attempt of a significant part of American psychology to relate itself only to those problems, and to work only on those organisms that yield to acceptable operations, i.e., the reduction of abstract concepts to the data of observation or to the processes of observation itself. This has resulted in the fragmentation of man or the attempt to study man's affective, cognitive, creative life through the "scientism" of the rat and the pigeon. It has led to a worship of physics as the best, if not the only, scientific method. By such a limited definition of method, the most significant aspects of man are precluded from scientific observation.

On the other hand, the Leibnitzian tradition maintains that the person is neither a collection of acts nor merely the locus of acts, but the person is the source of acts. This is purposive, motivational, and in keeping with Kant's view of inherent categories. The list of men who attempted to reach beyond the mechanics for synthesized cohesiveness is great. Concepts of organization, hierarchy, *Prägnanz*, insight, all speak to the inherent activity of the mind that molds, arranges, and interprets sensory data in ways not allowed for by the elementarist theories.

That this conflictual dichotomy is not merely a problem of psychology is made abundantly clear by George Gaylord Simpson

(1967) in his essay, "The Crisis in Biology." He reviews the splitting of biology into physical, chemical, or molecular biology on the one hand, and organismic or evolutionary biology on the other. Dramatic successes in the microbiological studies of nucleic acids have further intensified and made difficult achievement of a harmonious bridge. On one side are those who feel that the detailed working of the living organism is amenable to exploration by physical and chemical probing, and that the properties of living organisms are *totally* comprehensible in chemical terms. Those on the other side believe that living things do exhibit phenomena that cannot be reduced to chemical terms, particularly the purposefulness of organisms, all of which are clearly, intricately adapted to their environment and their ways of life. Evolutionary, organismic biology is not reducible to a philosophy taking account only of the physical, nonbiological aspects of the universe.

It is worth briefly reviewing Simpson's concepts of the differences between the two views. First, nonliving systems studied by physicists and chemists are *simple*. They involve few kinds of materials and few variables. They are further simplified in the laboratory by restricting the variety of materials and thereby controlling the variables. Living organisms, particularly man, are infinitely more *complex,* and are *organizational.* It is the complexity and the kind of structural and functional assembly in living organisms that differentiate them from nonliving systems. Simpson further maintains that there is a hierarchy of complexity in which each level of the hierarchy includes the one below it. He concludes that knowledge of included levels is necessary, but not sufficient, for complete understanding of those that are more inclusive. This results in interactions which cannot be inferred from any amount of knowledge of the separate parts.

Obviously, one must agree with Simpson's view that knowledge of molecules is necessary, but not sufficient for understanding of organs. Yet, the same perplexing problem exists when one moves in the other direction of complicated hierarchy; knowledge of cells is also necessary, but not sufficient for understanding of the molecules in them.

Simpson's second contrast is that the physical sciences are for the most part *typological* and *idealistic,* i.e., they usually deal with objects and events as invariant types, not as individuals with differing characteristics. Organisms, on the other hand, are not only types, but are individuals, and no two are likely ever to be exactly alike. The diversity is not incidental, nor interpretable as deviations from a norm or type. It is part of their nature as organisms. If organisms had not varied for some billions of years, then by evolutionary doctrine, they would not exist at all. As Bertalanffy points out, any student of elementary genetics learns that there are some 500 mutations or races of the fruit fly. In this regard, I would agree with Allport's speculation that all of the animals in the world are psychologically less distinct from one another than one man is from other men.

The third major contrast is in the fact that the physical sciences are *nonhistorical* and, accordingly, *repeatable*. Gravity, for example, has no history and a chemical reaction is also devoid of a history. Biology, as a study of living things, inevitably and always has historical factors, and the physical factors of repeatability, predictability, do not apply to the historical aspects of biology. No two organisms, not even identical twins, are exactly alike, and for each the history is somewhat different from the other. Both would be unique and inherently unrepeatable. Simpson concludes with the philosophical question, "That DNA is 'the secret of life' is less true . . . than that life is the secret of DNA" (p. 374).

Complexity

That the above state of affairs is the result of the complexity of phenomena is abundantly clear. To return to psychology, all theoreticians within the field have suffered from an attempt to create a "general psychological theory of man" out of the particular fragment with which they deal. The so-called information explosion has contributed to the problem, since it pierces some disciplinary barriers, but makes massive correlations, integrations, and synthesis a larger problem. The idea of a "general psychological theory" of man has become a limiting, rather than a broadening concept. It is a contradiction in terms, since on "general theoretical" grounds man can no longer be considered primarily a psychological animal—although he can for specific theoretical purposes.

Even within psychology itself, appropriately or inappropriately, there have been massive shifts toward biology (neurophysiology and pharmacology) and sociology. There is no "general theory of man" available as yet. The most reasoned, even if excessively ambitious, effort at a general theory is embodied in L. von Bertalanffy's General Systems Theory, to which I shall return.

Stripped of pretentious expansionism, all scientists continue to work in the only way that science can: that is, to struggle with overwhelming complexity. As a core problem of science, this is characterized by man-made compartmentalizations of all science (as a complex unity) into separate, specific disciplines. The same process of delineation and compartmentalization characterizes each discipline.

In a schematic sense, the process seems to be one of coping with complexity by progressive simplification and delineation, which then leads to resynthesis with extension of the boundaries of the original circumscribed areas, with further simplification and resynthesis in a progressively spiral fashion. This occurs on a conceptual level, although it must be borne in mind that the process depends on its ability to open new areas of empirical research and to respond to the findings of such efforts. Of course, the conceptual resynthesis of areas with contiguous borders tends to blur such artificial boundaries. This is apparent at the moment in many areas of physics, chemistry, and biology. In a microscopic sense, such scientific fragmentation is not without its dangers. In a macroscopic sense, such division of labor not only is productive, but actually represents the only possible way of going about the task.

When faced by overwhelmingly complex systems, the scientist —sometimes aided by circumscribed interest, sometimes by deliberate plan, and always by the absence of more adequate conceptualizations—breaks the phenomena into smaller, more easily comprehended and manageable areas. This *tactic* of crisp delineation emphasizes the *process* aspects of science, and demands a sophisticated and purposeful creative simplification. The crucial compo nent is that each choice permits further work—not that it is "right" or "wrong." Humility can be most helpful—loss of perspective remains the greatest danger.

In those areas, e.g., physics, where the phenomena more readily permit this segmentation, progress has been greatest. In phenomena which resist meaningful partition of complex interrelationships, the work is slower, and the conceptual problems greater.

Man, as his life is lived, is just such an area of study where innumerable variables resist meaningful control. One always struggles between overwhelming complexity and irrelevant minutia. How far the fragment can be studied out of the context of the whole without losing relevance is a constant scientific-methodological problem. This is the problem of organization in excessively complex biological systems. Because of the complexity, the study of man has spawned more independent scientific disciplines than any other area. This, too, adds immeasurably to the problem. As Boulding (1956) has put it, "we have the separate disciplines and sciences, with their separate bodies of theory. Each discipline corresponds to a certain segment of the empirical world, and each develops theories which have particular applicability to its own empirical segment" (p. 197). More than that, each profession and scientific discipline has necessarily developed a technical or theoretical language of its own, a system of values, and a preferred way of working. While this language of professional subculture may facilitate the accomplishment of professional tasks, they are a handicap to interprofessional or interdisciplinary communication. Words and concepts change their meaning from one profession and discipline to another, and, of course, each has terms that are exclusively its own.

Models and Theories

One characteristic of work in complicated systems—particularly biological ones—is the use of models. Models are theoretical constructs, which by and large have little relationship to structural reality, but are hypothetically devised to aid in the comprehension of function. Their structure is an attempt to relate function to structure—since autonomous function implies, and can be dealt best with theoretically, as an aspect of structure. This is particularly true when we speak of structures of the mind where we are not speaking of the anatomical structures of the brain. It is, again, a creative scientific fiction—a construct in the mind of the investigator. Accordingly, as described by Beckner (1959), "Scientists have recourse to model explanation when the phenomena under consideration present complexities that, for whatever reason, defy analysis adequate for explanatory purposes on the basis of the existing theory of the field" (p. 38). Models are used because they demonstrate a way to simplify a complex subject matter without naïve oversimplification; they suggest ways for applying theoretical concepts and principles of demonstrated fruitfulness in one region of science to a region where they have not been applied; and they formulate possible mechanisms underlying a phenomenon.

The scientist who tried to understand man is confronted with Norbert Wiener's (1948) mind as a "black box" problem. Unable to see into the black box, he must create a model which will account for the phenomenon that concerns him. With the exception of B. F. Skinner, all theoreticians work this way. They construct a nonexistent abstraction, inferred from whatever phenomena they can observe which *might* account for the phenomena.

The number of models available for the mind of man range from the naïve oversimplification of a stimulus-response model—even naïve when an "O" is put in the middle to represent the organism—though quite complicated models such as engineering models and cybernetic models, computer models, neuronal nets, the psychoanalytic model of a mental apparatus, through the most ambitious, but complicated models of systems theory.

Prior to looking again at man and a perspective to the study of man, I feel impelled to review briefly the function of such models and theories. It is quite clear to the philosopher and to the philosopher of science, as well as to most broad-ranging scientists—although obviously not so clear to the empiricist and the positivist—that no perception, recording, organization, and presentation of data are possible without an implicit or an explicit theory. Science goes nowhere without theory, and the instances in which explicit theory was in advance of empiric substantiation and discovery are many. The difference seems to lie between an implicit, intuitive, or a purposefully deceptive "atheoretical" statement, and a clearly, explicitly, articulated set of theoretical propositions and models. It is quite possible to confuse these two issues (implicit vs. explicit theory) with the issues of the relationship of empiricism to theory construction. Theory is always related to a specific phenomenological domain—but usually precedes and guides empiricism. There are those empiricists who insist that the universal scientific methods start with the empirical collection of data. That is one way, but hardly the only, nor even the most important. I would agree with Conant (1952), who notes, "The history of science demonstrates beyond a doubt that the really revolutionary and significant advances come not from empiricism but from new theories" (p. 30).

Within a historical context, in retrospect, it is possible to find some theories which were "wrong." In a contemporary sense, rightness and wrongness tend more to be value judgments of individual scientists, and are not descriptive of theory as such. Theory is much better judged along the dimension of utility or usefulness, which always raises the next question of "Useful for what?" These two components of *utility* and *relevance* are the most valuable ways of assessing theory because they address themselves to such issues as phenomenology, purpose, heuristic impact, the state of the field.

To return to man: for scientific purposes, man is as complicated or as simple as the questions asked; as complicated or as simple as the phenomenon delineated for study; as complicated or as simple as the relationship of part phenomena to whole phenomena; as complicated or as simple as the breadth or limited scope of conceptualization. For practical purposes, if by that we mean child rearing, teaching and learning, living, loving, and medically treating human beings, man is never simple, but is always complicated. We do not have a simple phenomenological field if we deal with man, but we do, unfortunately, have simplistic scientists. It is obviously not yet, if indeed it will ever be, possible to view the total phenomenon of mankind. Yet, at the same time, it is possible to assume an intellectually broader stance and to be less opportunistic and expansionistic in our presumed understanding of those bits and pieces of man that we have been able to glean. Economics, political science, biology, all branches of psychology, psychiatry, law, psychoanalysis, anthropology, etc., have something clearly valid to say about that portion of men with which they concern themselves. This is true because man is all of these things—and even more. What seems to be sorely needed is some humility and less of the aggrandized territoriality which characterizes our scientific debates.

Laboratory and Clinical Research

It is quite possible to retain an overall awareness of interrelationships and complexity, while at the same time working productively in one's own area. The view of man from the microscopic laboratory is quite different from the view of man in the clinic. Neither is wrong; both have elements of correctness. However, it is noteworthy that the theories about man which arise from the clinic differ dramatically from the theories about man which arise from the laboratory.

All areas of medicine share the centuries-old responsibility for the care and well-being of mankind. To this end, they have developed a uniquely reciprocal relationship with more basic scientific disciplines, which via technological development has made, and continues to make, available for physicians methods of treatment. The physician, particularly the psychiatrist, is in the position to feed back the richness and complexity of life as viewed from the consultation room.

To use this opportunity in a scientific way demands another conceptualization of the process of science than that afforded by the experiment. The experiment is but one way of working in science, and arises primarily out of physics because it is made possible by a phenomenology which permits the delineation and control of a few variables. This is not possible within the clinic, and with a field as complicated as the lives that men live. For example, if a physicist were asked how long this book might last, he would tell you that he could take it into the laboratory, and, after performing certain tests, would give you the temperature, the pressure, etc., necessary for its destruction. If you were to tell him you didn't mean that, but you were going to put the book out on a street corner, and not even know which street corner, perhaps to move it about at random, the physicist would tell you that you are mad—that this is not a scientific question, that it can't be answered, etc. He would point out that it depends on such random unpredictable things as, will a truck hit it, or lightning, or a flash flood, or will it be stolen or burned, etc. Yet the latter is the case with human beings and the human state. It is this complicated richness of man's inner and outer life which the clinician shares with only one other avenue of man's probing of himself—the humanities, particularly great literature.

There are several other basic assumptions which must be made in order to utilize the clinic contact as scientific. The first is that within the clinical paradigm, the closest one can come to experimental manipulation is to take advantage of the "experiments in nature." Catastrophe, maternal deprivation, sensory deprivation, are all examples of experiments in nature of a sort that man can never do to himself—but which can be explored when they present themselves.

In addition, since the clinic is organized essentially around varying degrees of pathology, one must postulate something about the relationship of pathology to normality. To the mechanistic laboratory worker, pathology is usually a special case which has no relevance to studies in normal development. To the organismic biologist, the situation was well stated by Paul Weiss (1961) : "changes in the standard pattern of formative processes lead to deviations from the standard form: deformations end up as 'deformities.' In this sense, 'deformities' become valuable clues to the inner workings of formative processes" (p. 134). "Pathology and developmental biology must be reintegrated so that our understanding of the 'abnormal' will become but an extension of our insight into the 'normal,' while, *pari passu,* the study of the 'abnormal' will contribute to the deepening of that very insight" (p. 150) .

This fundamental, biological way of working (at varying stages of research development) leads one to use the absence, or the distortion, of a structure as a primary way of determining the structure's function. While this is obviously in itself a simplification, since it does not take into account the interaction of varieties of other structures, the ablation experiment (possible in physiological work with animals) has been very rich. The use of the same kind of experimental situation described above as "experiments in nature" has been equally rich. For example, if one wants to know the importance of mothering on personality development, one can get enormous insight via the study of those children who have been deprived of mothers. If one wants to know the impact of vision on personality development, one can get more vivid leads via the study of the blind than one can in setting up a normal distribution curve of various degrees of visual acuity (Anna Freud, 1969). Going directly to the motherless child, to the blind child, is the same principle that Weiss spoke of in terms of the relationship of normal and abnormal growth and developmental processes. In assessments of such research, one must apply concepts of *appropriate* rigor and *appropriate* systematization—appropriate to the complexity of the phenomena, the stage of the science, or the stage of the specific substantive area.

In clinical work with man, particularly psychiatric work, one rarely assumes, if ever, that things are there or absent. One knows that all things are to some degree present in all men, but that the intensities and patterning of interaction may be what makes for illness. It is, for example, assumed that the ability to empathize with another human being depends in part on the mechanism of projection. One must be able to "put oneself" in the position of the other, to feel what he feels. It is further assumed that a degree of benevolent paranoia, or usual suspiciousness, is a crucial adaptive aspect in living. To be without this is a serious handicap which makes one prey to all manner of ulterior manipulations by others. This is not to be confused with the more mature aspects of the ability to trust. Yet, it is these same mechanisms of projection and suspiciousness which, in the extreme, can be part of a paranoid condition which is not vaguely benevolent.

There are but two more aspects of the clinical situation which should be mentioned since they represent major advantages which more than offset the presumed lack of precision. The first of these is that the clinic counts regularly on the motivation of seeking relief to overcome the superficiality so characteristic of most experiments. The second, and perhaps the most important, is that it gives the caretaking scientist *unique access*. The three clearest examples of this come from the localization of brain function as a by-product of brain surgery in the hands of scientists like Penfield; the classical work of William Beaumont in contributing to the understanding of human digestion by taking advantage of just such a clinical, caretaking experiment in nature; and the work of Freud.

I would like to turn now to some examples of the directions in which the dichotomy of microunits vs. organismic thinking leads. I shall ultimately focus on the question of self-control, since it remains an increasingly prominent problem in our world.

I shall start with the Skinnerian model, not because I consider it a significant model, but because it is the simplest. Starting from what he considers common sense, and making a rather spurious insistence that he has no theory about the nature of man, Skinner does, in fact, build a theory of behavioral control on the basis of a simple operant conditioning mechanism.

If one looks at the work of Skinner (1953), it becomes almost a caricature of Allport's "Lockean position." He works with a simple learning mechanism which is predicated on the idea that the organism is reactive only to external stimulation. All of learning is reduced to learning via reward or punishment (positive or aversive reinforcement). Accordingly, motivation remains external and molecular, and behavior is "cue" determined. Since man as well as animals such as the rat or pigeon can "learn" by such conditioning, Skinner assumes species equivalence as a valid mode for attacking such learning. Accordingly, the operant conditioning model is drawn primarily from work with the rat and pigeon in Skinner boxes. From this simplistic analogue, Skinner rests his basic assumptions of man on this work with the pigeon.

Yet it is a fact that a simple operant learning model does not explain the pigeon. In an interesting article, Michener and Walcott (1966) demonstrate that landmarks and training, for the homing pigeon, are operative within 10 miles of the loft. At the same time, it seems quite clear that other mechanisms of navigation operate as far as 87 and 100 miles away from home. The conclusion is that the homing pigeon does not use landmarks alone. How he finds his loft remains obscure, but can hardly be based on an exclusive operant training model. It has, as a species, other intelligence or perhaps innate or instinctual resources. A mechanism by which a pigeon can learn, but which does not explain this presumed simple animal, can hardly be a basis for a psychology of man.

However, Skinnerian logic dictates that since similar statistical operant schedules can be drawn for man and pigeon, the nature of man and pigeon are the same. Accordingly, the future of man, i.e., child rearing, education, the learning of language, social intercourse, love, are all reduced to the building of habit chains through "human engineering."

There are a number of reasons why this simplistic view of man has exasperated men of science such as Conant (1952), who said, "The universe is not constructed along the lines of an automatic machine distributing rewards and punishments—at least not in this world of mortals" (p. 88f.).

Although many scientists have expressed concern about the anthropomorphizing of animals, i.e., endowing animals with human characteristics and reasoning from lower to higher forms via species equivalence, it took a humanist, a gifted writer, Arthur Koestler, to indicate that the greater danger was not in the anthropomorphism of an animal, but in the "ratomorphism" of man. Koestler (1967) traces the history of the decline of the conditioned reflex as *the* fundamental unit of behavior in physiology, but says, "That did not unduly worry the behaviourists. They shifted their terminology from conditioned reflexes to conditioned responses." Koestler continues:

> Behaviourism is indeed a kind of flat-earth view of the mind. Or, to change the metaphor: it has replaced the anthropomorphic fallacy—ascribing to animals human faculties and sentiments—with the opposite fallacy: denying men faculties not found in lower animals; it has substituted for the erstwhile anthropomorphic view of the rat, a ratomorphic view of man. It has even re-named psychology, because it was derived from the Greek work for 'mind,' and called it the 'science of behaviour.' It was a demonstrative act of semantic self-castration, in keeping with Skinner's references to education as 'behavioural engineering.' Its declared aim, 'to predict and to control human activity as physical scientists control and manipulate other natural phenomena,' sounds as nasty as it is naïve. Werner Heisenberg, one of the greatest living physical scientists, has laconically declared: 'Nature is unpredictable'; it seems rather absurd to deny the living organism even that degree of unpredictability which quantum physics accords to inanimate nature [p. 17].

Koestler joins Cassirer in emphasizing the uniqueness of human language. Many, Chomsky (1959) for one, have pointed to the fact that the Skinnerian account of how man acquires language takes the meaning out of thought and speech. In Koestler's view, if we labor the point with the methods of S–R theorists, we risk arriving at the conviction that human speech is an impossibility. Koestler concludes by saying, "It is impossible to arrive at a diagnosis of man's predicament . . . by starting from a psychology which denies the existence of mind, and lives on specious analogies derived from the bar-pressing activities of rats" (p. 18).

Ludwig von Bertalanffy (1967) sees this work moving toward a sociology of "robot man." Bertalanffy speaks to the need not for some new hypothetical mechanism better to explain peculiarities in behavior of the laboratory rat, but a new conception of man. He is quite in agreement with Koestler when he states that in fleeing its anthropomorphic fallacy, behaviorism has established a zoomorphic fallacy, making man no different than an animal. Bertalanffy insists that man as an organism is characterized by "primary activity" in contrast to the conception of its "primary reactivity." He concluded that there is such a thing as human culture with its myriads of manifestations and that there is no such *human culture* in pigeons and monkeys. As Jakob von Uexküll said, in the world of the fly we find only "fly things"; in the world of a sea urchin we find only "sea urchin things." Bertalanffy's scientific humanism leads him to the same exasperation with Skinner that was expressed by Koestler. He sees the danger of "ratomorphism" as "robot man," constricted by a "behavioral engineering" tantamount to "functional decerebration." We cannot make a rat feel or act like a human. However, because of man's dependence on complex processes of learning in his development, it is possible to limit man's essentially human experiences by turning to Skinner. If we permit this, we may commit what Bertalanffy calls "menticide."

Thus, from the view of comparative theory, the issue of how man controls himself, or how man can bring to bear what he knows about himself in the service of control, ranges from a Skinner operant model through a hierarchy of disciplines, ending up in the Law as a theory of man's attempts at external control of himself.

Central to most considerations about man's internal control of himself, as well as his response to societal sanctions in the form of ostracism or legal action, is the concept of guilt. I assume that in the world of man, we find "human things" and among the most unique aspects of humanness is the phenomenon of guilt.

Let us look for a moment at the laboratory paradigm of guilt. Mowrer (1969) quotes the work of Salama as follows, "Hungry rats were taught, individually, to eat small quantities of damp mash stuck to the end of a small wooden stick or spatula poked up through the metal grill that constituted the floor of the box-like apparatus in which the experiment was performed. Each rat learned to take the stick in its front paws, eat the food, and then drop the stick back through the grill for 'reloading' " (p. 546). After this procedure had been well learned (it required only 15 or 20 trials), a "rule" was made that the rat should not touch the stick or eat the food when it was offered. And whenever this rule was violated, the rat was punished in the following way: 10 seconds after the rat had eaten the food and dropped the stick, electric shock was applied from the grill floor and left on until the rat "turned it off" by leaping into the air. It took only 3 or 4 repetitions of this procedure to produce the expected index of "guilt"; after eating the now-forbidden food and dropping the stick, the rat would become very quiet, its eyes would protrude, it might urinate or defecate, it would look up, and then it would leap, within the 10-second delay period, before any shock was applied. The rat thus "indicated" that it had become "guilty."

This description concludes with the point that, interestingly enough, "No rat was ever able to be sufficiently fearful in advance of eating and dropping the stick to inhibit, i.e., to resist the temptation" to eat (p. 546).

This seems a far cry from the guilt described in Shakespeare as revealed in the speech of Richard III after his dreams before the final battle:

Have mercy, Jesu! Soft! I did but dream.
O coward conscience, how dost thou afflict me!
The lights burn blue. It is now dead midnight.
Cold fearful drops stand on my trembling flesh.
What! do I fear myself? there's none else by:

Richard loves Richard; that is, I am I.
Is there a murderer here? No. Yes, I am:
Then fly: what! from myself? Great reason why:
Lest I revenge. What! myself upon myself?
Alack! I love myself. Wherefore? for any good
That I myself have done unto myself?
O! no: alas! I rather hate myself
For hateful deeds committed by myself.
I am a villain, Yet I lie; I am not.
Fool, of thyself speak well: fool, do not flatter.
My conscience hath a thousand several tongues,
And every tongue brings in a several tale,
And every tale condemns me for a villain.
Perjury, perjury, in the high'st degree:
Murder stern murder, in the direst degree;
All several sins, all us'd in each degree,
Throng to the bar, crying all, 'Guilty! guilty!'
[V, iii, 179-200]

Other concepts of the development of control include the concept of human morality. Two approaches can be made through the developmental psychologies of Piaget and Freud. Piaget, a most sophisticated theoretician, has concerned himself with the concept of "moral development." One can contrast the Piaget and the Freudian concepts as follows: Since Piaget (1932) is concerned with thought, he arrives at a beautiful developmental progression of what children consciously *think about* moral values and judgments. Since he is a marvelous epistemologist, his theoretical constructs are models of theory construction. His phenomenological field is clear, circumscribed, and legitimate. However, it is only tangentially related to the empirical base of psychoanalytic superego theory (Freud, 1921, 1923; Hartmann, 1960; Hartmann and Loewenstein, 1962). Piaget is not concerned with how people behave, or where they get their values or controls from; nor is he concerned with guilt and shame. Psychoanalysis is concerned with these things. The correlation of abstract thought in the Piaget sense to inner control of behavior is not easily established. The clinician, whether he be a psychoanalyst or a clinical psychiatrist, knows that our jails are filled with people who know and can abstract all the rules. As a matter of fact, to be a certain type of confidence man, one must know all of the rules.

One can only say that the two systems, each a legitimate area of inquiry, are addressed to different areas of phenomenology. If one follows the Piaget concept of morality—as was recently (1968) done in a conference on "The Acquisition and Development of Values," one is astonished to find that for some scientists it is possible to devote an entire conference on morality with no reference to the phenomenon of guilt. The major research reported is based on interviews of children and young adults who were asked to react to 10 hypothetical moral dilemmas. In a Piaget-style sequence, these dealt with problems such as whether a man has a right to steal a drug or food which will save his wife's life if he has exhausted every other means of obtaining it. Through the study of the answers to these dilemmas, it is possible to establish a developmental sequence of the conscious abstraction of moral development. The relationship of this to human behavior is essentially ignored, although it was held to have implications for phenomena as complicated as student riots. Perhaps one can call this "cognitimorphism" of man.

The only direct statement about guilt in the entire conference came from the essentially philosophical proposition by the psychiatrist, Lifton. Using a clinical base, Lifton put forth his concept of "protean man who suffers considerably from guilt, but often without awareness of what is causing his suffering. He feels a vague, but persistent self-condemnation related to the symbolic disharmonies of his life—a sense of having no outlet for his loyalties, and no symbolic structure for his achievements" (p. 44). To Lifton, this is the guilt of social breakdown, which included various forms of historical and racial guilt, and leaves a residue of a nagging sense of unworthiness, all the more troublesome for its lack of clear origin. By and large, this is a psychoanalytic description of guilt, although, for Lifton, the concept has other sources.

Psychoanalysis, as a discipline, postulates a difference between motives and causes of behavior. Motives are ultimately conceptualized as drive-derived. Causes of behavior can be brought about by many things, such as reality events or by ego defenses. Much of psychoanalytic theory deals with control, primarily from within man or self-control, and this is abstracted as part of a conflict or a facilitating theory.

Psychoanalytic theorists struggle with the identical Wiener

"black box" problem which plagues all students of man. As stated above, some scientists find it helpful to put a computer in the black box, although they know there is not a computer there—or a servomechanistic, feedback loop. In the same manner, psychoanalysis constructs a model of the mind consisting of id, ego, and superego. These are not morphological entities that exist. They are scientific fictions, models that help the scientist. At its base, the psychoanalytic model of a "psychic apparatus" is a classification of function. The id, ego, and superego are groupings of similar functions of the human mind as seen primarily in the consultation room, but also in the direct observation of developing children.

The utilitarian relevance of psychoanalytic theory varies with the distance any incorporated phenomenon is from the conceptual intrapsychic structure of man as analysis conceptualizes it. As it extends from this intrapsychic conflict and facilitating theory of man, the problems become those of redefining the phenomenological field. Accordingly, psychoanalytic propositions are most congruent with what psychoanalysis postulates as intrapsychic processes; their applicability becomes less specific and less useful as the field is shifted. For example, as one shifts from the individual to small group phenomena—with the exception of the family—to nations, etc., the congruence between empiricism and psychoanalytic theory deteriorates. Scientists who deal with large group phenomena, such as societies and nations, have less use for psychoanalytic concepts precisely because they are intrapsychic concepts. At the same time, it should be stated that psychoanalytic theory does have fruitful concepts dealing with reality and adaptation in man. Further, it has had both heuristic and substantive value to sociology and anthropology—chiefly around superego theory.

What analysis calls superego theory is the internalization of prohibitions, demands, ideals, values, and judgments taken over from parents and the significant social others. This can facilitate moral behavior which leaves the individual with a sense of pride and well-being. If an impulse or an act is in conflict with this "agency," the individual experiences that uniquely human emotion— "guilt." In human affairs, the relationship between conscious and unconscious moral values and man's ability to experience guilt is very close. If one studies children, one can discern stages from the point where a young child is stopped from taking, or acting, or doing by parental prohibition. In the absence of the parent, the deed is done. Control and its specific content are external to the child. The developmental progression is then to shame and ultimately to the experience of guilt. The content of what makes different children feel shame may vary—but some cultural values are obviously shared and transmitted by the adults of any similar group. Shame still implies an external referent and there are many things we feel comfortable doing alone but would feel a distinct sense of shame if we were observed. The acceptance of cleanliness would be a case in point.

The capacity to feel guilt is a much higher stage of development since it implies an autonomous, unconscious quality of self-judgment quite apart from whether others have knowledge of the thought, the impulse, or the act. It most frequently occurs around the content of an internal conflict of which there may be *no* self-knowledge. I have seen, as have many psychiatrists, men in war incapacitated by this vague guilty remorse and self-condemnation who know consciously and intellectually that there is no reason to justify the feeling. A particularly painful and frequent example is "the guilt of the survivor"—the lucky one, who for no reason other than luck was not killed with his crew mates. I recently saw a nationally decorated hero, who had saved the life of one of two children at risk of his own—overcome with vague guilt and dread, and obsessed with thoughts of his own daughter. Men can neither experience nor unravel such complexities in laboratory experiments or in such studies as answering a standardized set of moral dilemmas. It can best be studied in the unique access of the clinical situation where guilty, tormented men come for help. Those whose development does not progress this far have a great tendency toward delinquency. There is a vast body of primarily psychoanalytic data on that troublesome group of amoral, guiltless delinquents who plague society.

Since this large group has no control from within, they become a legal as well as a societal problem. It is my firm conviction that the richest theory of man's external control of himself lies in the Law. I refer to the Law as a complex body of underlying social science and behavioral science, as well as legal science. Collaborative work between legal scholars and psychoanalysts, between the Law and the social sciences has only but begun—but is a most vigorous and exciting area.

We have now come a great distance from the excessively simplistic concepts of Skinner's species equivalence and are more in line with Polanyi's statement (1966), "Yet, however greatly we may love an animal, there is an emotion which no animal can evoke and which is commonly directed toward our fellow men. I have said that at the highest level of personhood we meet man's moral sense, guided by the firmament of his standards" (p. 51). This is congruent with Polanyi's feeling that man is not only liable to a far greater range of errors than animals are, but by virtue of his moral sense, he also becomes capable of evil.

It would seem to me that where there is *genuine* effort to conceptualize and theorize about the nature of man, it may be counterproductive to pit one theory against the other. For example, to pit Piaget against Freud, or Freud against legal scholars or sociologists, is not necessarily productive, since these theories relate to different aspects of man. Few of the existing theories are "wrong" or "right." In its complexity, except for the issue of excessive simplicity, each theoretical domain has its own view of man, and each has useful and relevant theories for its own tiny segment of man. The problem with incorporating contributions from theories such as Skinner's lies not in that they do not apply to man— scientifically, it rests on their excessively simplistic and expansionistic qualities; philosophically, it rests on their dehumanizing man.

For example, consider the idea of man as a learning animal. There can be no doubt that one of the principal characteristics which has moved man above other animal forms is his ability to learn. The problem is in trying to define learning theory in terms of those simple mechanisms which can be studied with precision in the laboratory. It would seem to me that this is Skinner's error. There can be no doubt that men can learn via operant conditioning or Pavlovian conditioning, and I would venture the guess that man is capable of learning by every mechanism used by lower forms. On the other hand, there are other more complicated ways that man learns, which are, for example, present in Gestalt theories, or in psychoanalytic theory. What psychoanalysis calls identification and internalization are essentially learning propositions. In developing children, one can see this process start as imitation and ultimately result in someone who is unconsciously "a chip off the old block." It is most unfortunate that no one has been skillful enough to evolve a learning theory addressed to this complicated model of learning. Yet, insight itself, in Gestalt psychology and in psychoanalysis, is a learning theory term. As a matter of fact, the relationship of any psychotherapeutic endeavor, from psychoanalysis through human engineering, can be conceptualized as a re-education of an educational form—if one uses education and learning in its broadest sense.

Epilogue

One is then left with the problem of how to bring together the isolated, but useful facets of man learned by the many differing disciplines. The most ambitious, but not fully realized, attempt has been that of general systems theory as generated by Ludwig von Bertalanffy. The idea has aroused great interest and great resistance—in part because of the fact that it is so abstractly theoretical, and secondly, the model makers in this field have turned more to machine analogies than biological analogies. For example, one of the central aspects of all living organisms is that of homeostasis or equilibrium. This concept goes back as far as Cannon and was already implied in the work of Claude Bernard. Much of current systems theory uses the cybernetic or servomechanism feedback analogy as the model for this mechanism in man. There is some question of why this is more useful than other more biological models, but that is not important in this discussion.

I think the most crucial aspect of systems theory is not the specific attempts which have been made—for there have been many—but an attitude: one which recognizes the multidimensional aspects of science which must ultimately be placed into a cohesive whole. Our divisions are man-made and we are becoming aware of the fact that we have sliced up an indivisible universe.

As I have indicated earlier in this essay, the need for a unified theoretical perspective arose from the continued problems of reductionism vs. vitalism; the increment of information in specialized areas of science which, on the one hand, increases compart-mentalization, but also increases disciplinary overlap on the other; and the breakdown of the so-called "classic" divisions of science with the loss of authoritative arbiters of "truth."

Although speaking as a philosopher to the historic loss of a needed neutrality, an intellectual cement, a frame of reference, Cassirer (1944) also spoke for science when he said:

> Every philosopher believes he has found the mainspring and master-faculty—*l'idée maîtresse,* as it was called by Taine. But as to the character of this master-faculty all the explanations differ widely from, and contradict, one another. Each individual thinker gives us his own picture of human nature. All of these philosophers are determined empiricists: they would show us the facts and nothing but the facts. But their interpretation of the empirical evidence contains from the very outset an arbitrary assumption—and this arbitrariness becomes more and more obvious as the theory proceeds and takes on a more elaborate and sophisticated aspect. . . .
>
> Owing to this development our modern theory of man lost its intellectual center. We acquired instead a complete anarchy of thought. Even in the former times to be sure there was a great discrepancy of opinions and theories relating to this problem. But there remained at least a general orientation, a frame of reference, to which all individual differences might be referred. Metaphysics, theology, mathematics, and biology successively assumed the guidance for thought on the problem of man and determined the line of investigation. The real crisis of this problem manifested itself when such a central power capable of directing all individual efforts ceased to exist. The paramount importance of the problem was still felt in all the different branches of knowledge and inquiry. But an established authority to which one might appeal no longer existed. Theologians, scientists, politicians, sociologists, biologists, psychologists, ethnologists, economists all approached the problem from their own viewpoints. To combine or unify all these particular aspects and perspectives was impossible. And even within the special fields there was no generally accepted scientific principle. The personal factor became more and more prevalent. . . . every author seems in the last count to be led by his own conception and evaluation of human life [p. 21].

My felt need is to fill this vacuum, not with other arbiters, but with a perspective. I think this is what Boulding (1956) had in mind when he pointed out that this current state of science has led to the felt need for a body of systematic theoretical constructs which could discuss the general relationships within the empirical world. General systems theory does not seek to establish a single, self-contained "general theory of practically everything" which would replace specific theories of particular disciplines. It seeks, rather, to point to similarities in theoretical constructions of the different scientific areas and to develop theoretical models having applicability to different fields of study, and hopes ultimately to develop a "spectrum" of such theories.

The major impetus toward a general systems theory came from Bertalanffy, who, as a young biologist, forced to cope with the mechanism-vitalism controversy, found he was led to advocate the so-called organismic viewpoint. By this he meant that organisms were organized and that this organization was more than the sum of the components which constitute it. He clearly articulated the concept of "primacy of activity," demonstrating that in evolution, neurophysiology, and embryonic development, spontaneous activity, primitive but subsequently adaptive activities and spontaneous mass movements precede reaction to stimuli (and learned behavior). Although the wealth of his knowledge of biology, psychology, mathematics, engineering, and other sciences is never far from his theory construction, Bertalanffy recognized the need for a theoretical conceptualization of relationships.

In a general way, there seem to be two directions one could move in such a theoretical task. The first is to seek for general phenomena found in many different areas of science. Some of these are felt to be the fact that all sciences address themselves to a population, and all populations change and interact. For example, ecology is such a concept in biology, whereas capital and capital goods are such concepts in economics. Another is that the individual of each scientific area interacts with, and is adapted to, his environment. This leads to concepts of behavior, homeostasis, and equilibrium. A third is that all such systems demonstrate growth and slow maturation along a time dimension. A fourth is the interchange of information or communications. At this point, most of the model makers have turned to mechanical analogues, and this area, through the use of scientific analogy, has been inundated with models deriving from cybernetics, computers, information theory, game theory, decision theory, topology, or mathematical inference, etc.

The other approach to a general systems theory is one which takes advantage of the degree of learning present in the current disciplines and attempts not only to arrange them in a hierarchy based on complexity of organization but also to restate an appropriate level of abstraction at each step. This is made quite explicit by Simpson (1967) when he speaks of the element of organization in organismic function. He stresses the complexity and the kind of structural and functional assemblage in living organisms that differentiate them from nonliving systems. "There is a hierarchy of complexity that runs from atoms through molecules, cells, tissues, organs, individuals, specific populations, communities and comprehensive ecological systems to the whole realm of the organic and its environments in space and time. The lowest level that has all the basic properties of life is the cell, and biology, strictly speaking, covers the levels from there onward. . . . Each level of the hierarchy included that below. Knowledge of included levels is necessary but is not sufficient for complete understanding of those more inclusive" (p. 367).

Such a concept as hierarchy of organizational complexity has implicitly characterized medical school curricula for a very long period of time. Yet, in no curricula is the additive, rather than the synthesized, aspect of interrelationships easier to see. In no curriculum is the need for a unification and consolidation of theory clearer.

Meir (1969) arbitrarily divides the attempts at developing a system approach into four efforts. The first is called "the biological-humanistic approach," best exemplified by von Bertalanffy. Seeking isomorphic laws in diverse scientific disciplines and studying similarities with a view toward "wholeness," "organizations," "dynamics," "primary activity," and "equifinality," Bertalanffy (1968) ultimately defines system as a complex of elements in mutual interaction in which each element is a system in and of itself, but part of a larger system, all showing the same characteristics listed above.

Meir calls the second approach "the empirical or multidisciplinary approach," characterized by several groups—perhaps the best known being that of James G. Miller started in Chicago in 1949. The search for a unified theory of human behavior in this group began with the consideration of whether a sufficient body of empiric knowledge existed to justify developing an empirically testable general theory. The group attempted to merge into a single framework the thinking of psychodynamic psychiatry, projective techniques of psychology, neuropathology, endocrinology, biochemistry, and neurophysiology, and the concept of the social sciences.

A second group, started by Roy Grinker, Sr. (1956), was a more classically organized interdisciplinary group which attempted to develop an interdisciplinary common language. There are thus basic aspects of the person comprising the system *person,* then the group, then society and culture. This group used an impressively wide range of the social and behavioral sciences as its stratified components of a large system.

The third group, called "the experimental or mechanismic approach," relies very heavily on electronic and computing devices as model constructions to simulate functions of living organisms. This approach was generated by Norbert Wiener, and, although vigorous, seems, by the nature of its model building, to be concerned with simpler systems than those which exist in nature. The fourth, called "the formal or mathematical approach," also derives as a direction from cybernetics and is developing new and quite complicated mathematical models for the study of systems.

Obviously, Meir's classification is arbitrary and serves the purpose of discussion. Many aspects of these four directions are interrelated, and many concepts are shared.

As I indicated above, no single aspect of this endeavor has as yet reached its most significant degree of substantive fruition. For me, its major value lies in a scientific stance, an attitude, which forces upon the individual (however immersed he is in his own area) an awareness of a broader and interrelated spectrum. To accept this, seems to me a great step and one that minimizes the strident and painful debate which ensues from fiercely held commitments to one or another set of concepts. It should also make collaborative research easier.

Where and how can this occur, and in what way will it be of utility to mankind? To answer the first of these questions, I think it would be wisest to describe what is needed. We need a large group of well-trained scholars who are immersed in their own specialties, but who work in an atmosphere which promotes communication and contact. We need biophysicists with their increasing knowledge of genes; we need physiologists, all forms of biologists, biochemists, psychologists such as Piaget with an interest in intellectual growth and development; psychoanalysts; and dynamic psychiatrists, sociologists, anthropologists; and more than anything else, humanists from the arts and philosophy. Obviously, this is nothing new, but is just a description of the self-determined faculty of a great university. I do not think this can occur in a "think tank" because it does not permit individual scientists sufficient immersion with their own colleagues in their own specific areas. It is my impression that even interdisciplinary men need this sense of rootedness. Although changes in the university have forced the development of many "think tanks" to carry specific aspects of work, they further lack the reciprocal stimulation between faculty and students and are for the most part too small to encompass the intellectual excitement of the great universities.

There is, however, an aspect of my thought about the university which is related to the underlying principle of my entire discussion. This is an architectonic principle of the relationship between structure and function. This principle is amply demonstrated in all of biology, as well as the arts and architecture, but it is equally applicable to social institutions. A physician does not fashion a prosthetic foot to replace a hand. Nor is the appearance of a prosthetic hand as important as the function of the device. It would be less than wise to build a bank building if the intent was to have a functioning hotel.

I cannot think of restructuring universities without first conceptualizing the functions of universities. I believe that our society requires many different kinds of institutions, and I seriously question how many functions one particular institution can fruitfully encompass. I have stated elsewhere (1969) my conviction that the great vitality of the American university system has come from its heterogeneity in the sense that it consists of a large number of very different kinds of institutions, each with its own specific charge. This has ranged from the extremely practical mission of certain agricultural colleges, to the freest kind of scholarly tradition as has been represented by schools such as Yale, Harvard, the University of Chicago, and others. The use, or the relevance, of these few great universities to society's needs can best be viewed in terms of the large university system in its responsibility for short-term and long-term needs of the country and the world. Forcing all universities to respond to short-term needs is humanistically helpful and of immediate ameliorative aid. On the other hand, if this concern sacrifices the long-term uses and superimposes a monotonous mediocrity, we may have done ourselves a great disservice. We do need different kinds of institutions, and we do need different kinds of universities. Among our most striking needs are those free, self-determined faculties which in the history of science have served us so well.

As an example, I would like to refer to medicine with the heavy demand for care, or the delivery of health services, from the people of America. Many of our great universities have moved massively into accepting the full responsibility for patient care in their local communities. I do not for a moment question the need for health services. I merely question the wisdom of using one kind of institution for something that another kind of institution could do better—especially if the shift detracts from the services of the first institution.

If I were given the task of providing health services for a community, the model of the university would be the very last model I would use. It is costly, inefficient, and by and large does not deliver care as well as other kinds of institutions because it was structured for other functions, i.e., education, research, as well as patient care. I would turn, instead, to other models, such as Kaiser-Permanente, a National Health Service, a variety of different clinics that exist as models. On the other hand, if I were asked to develop a great university which would train teachers and scientists, and which would preserve the long-range health needs of the country, a National Health Service, or Kaiser-Permanente, would be the last model I would use. I would use the model of the few existing great universities.

It seems short-sighted not to recognize that the needs of the citizenry may be best serviced by the establishment of different kinds of institutions, as well as different kinds of universities— some of whose functions may overlap—but whose primary responsibility to the country can be divided into short-range and long-range needs. In the historically free heterogeneity of our great universities, whether by intrigued interest or irritated awareness, multidisciplinary teaching goes on. It is in this atmosphere that interdisciplinary and innovative thinking is most likely to emerge. If the badly needed synthesis and further extensions of our knowledge of man do not occur in this setting, I wonder where they can. I think Robert Maynard Hutchins (1969) stated it very well in his prophetic statement, "There can be no objection to a community's setting up institutions to reflect what it thinks it wants at any given time. What it wants it should—or at any rate, it will —try to get. The university, I suggest, is the institution that performs its highest, its unique, service to society by declining to do what the society thinks it wants, by refusing to be useful in the common acceptance of that word, and by insisting, instead, that its task is understanding and criticism. It is a center of independent thought" (p. 4) .

The nation, science, and the university will each lose something very important if the ideal of a community of free scholars, the innovative people it attracts, the opportunities made available to them, and the communication made possible within the university, is significantly altered. The future interdependent development of all begs for a tolerant re-evaluation by men of vision.

As to the utility of mankind, I think it is clear that I have placed the entire idea of the university system in a system theory. By preserving centers which produce an interdisciplinary perspective of the universe—because of the fact that man sees his world as extensions of himself, man will remain the center of such a system. But he will remain the center of an interrelated system. For our short-range survival, we desperately need scientists and technologists who can purify our lakes and streams, and quickly. For the long-range survival of the species, we need those centers where men worry about mankind—where they try to understand the nature of this animal who, by his own creative, intelligent qualities of mind, brings himself to the edge of disaster.

BIBLIOGRAPHY

ALLPORT, G. W. (1955), *Becoming*. New Haven: Yale University Press.
BECKNER, M. (1959), *The Biological Way of Thought*. New York: Columbia University Press.
BERTALANFFY, L. VON (1967), *Robots, Men and Minds*. New York: Braziller.
— (1968), *General System Theory*. New York: Braziller.
BOULDING, K. E. (1956), General Systems Theory: The Skeleton of Science. *Management Science*, 2:197–208.
BRONOWSKI, J. (1958), *The Common Sense of Science*. Melbourne, London, Toronto: William Heinemann.
CASSIRER, E. (1944), *An Essay on Man: An Introduction to a Philosophy of Human Culture*. New Haven: Yale University Press.
CHOMSKY, N. (1959), A Review of B. F. Skinner's "Verbal Behavior." *Language*, 35:26–56.
CONANT, J. B. (1952), *Modern Science and Modern Man*. Garden City: Doubleday Anchor.
CONFERENCE (1968), The Acquisition and Development of Values: Report of Conference, May 15–17. Bethesda: National Institute of Child Health and Human Development.
FREUD, A. (1956–1965), *Research at the Hampstead Child-Therapy Clinic and Other Papers* [*The Writings of Anna Freud*, Vol. 5]. New York: International Universities Press, 1969.
FREUD, S. (1921), Group Psychology and the Analysis of the Ego. *Standard Edition*, 18:67–143. London: Hogarth Press, 1955.
— (1923), The Ego and the Id. *Standard Edition*, 19:3–66. London: Hogarth Press, 1961.
GRINKER, R. R., JR., ed. (1956), *Toward a Unified Theory of Human Behavior*. New York: Basic Books.
HARTMANN, H. (1960), *Psychoanalysis and Moral Values*. New York: International Universities Press.
— & LOEWENSTEIN, R. M. (1962), Notes on the Superego. *This Annual*, 17:42–81.
HUTCHINS, R. M. (1969), Remarks on the Inauguration of President Edward H. Levi. *Univ. Chicago Mag.*, 61 (4), Jan./Feb.
KOESTLER, A. (1967), *The Ghost in the Machine*. New York: Macmillan.
LUSTMAN, S. L. (1969), Mental Health Research and the University: A Position Paper to the Joint Commission on Mental Health of Children. *Arch. Gen. Psychiat.*, 21:291–301.
MEIR, A. Z. (1969), General System Theory: Developments and Perspectives for Medicine and Psychiatry. *Arch. Gen. Psychiat.*, 21:302–310.
MICHENER, M. C. & WALCOTT, C. (1966), Navigation of Single Homing Pigeons: Airplane Observation by Radio Tracking. *Science*, 154:410–412.
MILLER, J. G. (1965), Living Systems: Basic Concepts. *Behav. Sci.*, 10:193–237.

MOWRER, O. H. (1969), Too Little and Too Late. *Int. J. Psychiat.*, 7:536–556.

PIAGET, J. (1932), *The Moral Judgment of the Child.* Glencoe, Ill.: Free Press, 1948.

POLANYI, M. (1966), *The Tacit Dimension.* Garden City: Doubleday.

SCHLESINGER, A., JR. (1969), *The Crisis of Confidence.* Boston: Houghton Mifflin, p. 240.

SHAKESPEARE, W. (1597), *The Tragedy of King Richard the Third. The Histories and Poems of Shakespeare.* Oxford: Oxford University Press, 1925.

SIMPSON, G. G. (1967), The Crisis in Biology. *Amer. Scholar*, 36:363–377.

SKINNER, B. F. (1953), *Science and Human Behavior.* New York: Macmillan.

WEISS, P. (1961), Deformities as Clues to Understanding Development of Form. *Perspectives in Biology and Medicine*, 4:133–151.

WIENER, N. (1948), *Cybernetics.* New York: Wiley.

PROBLEMS OF

DEVELOPMENT—

ADOLESCENCE

Yale's Year of Confrontation

A View from the Master's House

SEYMOUR L. LUSTMAN, M.D., PH.D.

THIS HAS BEEN AN EXTRAORDINARY AND TUMULTUOUS DECADE FOR
the Academy. Nor is there any reason to assume that the current
lull in activity marks the end of discord on campus. One of the
consequences has been a burgeoning corps of campus watchers and
a voluminous increase in the literature dealing with students and
the campus.

This paper was presented at the Panel Discussion on "Youth and the Campus,"
held at the Annual Meeting of the Association for Child Psychoanalysis, in Williams-
burg, Virginia, March 21, 1971. It is published posthumously in the form it was
presented. The editors have made no attempt to prepare a detailed bibliography or
to attach a concluding statement.

Dr. Lustman was Professor of Psychiatry, Yale University, Child Study Center and
Department of Psychiatry; Chairman, Task Force IV, Joint Commission on Mental
Health of Children; and Master of Davenport College, Yale University.

(57)

It is with some reluctance that I join this swell of "campusolo-
gists" and "studentologists." The hesitancy I feel is focused around
two factors. The first is that I am in agreement with the critic who
said that the massive literature of this field does not need yet one
other "I was bravely there when the excitement happened" paper.

My second reluctance stems from the fact that I remain critical
of the literature on youth. It is a presumably scientific literature—
most of which is found in the daily press and popular magazines.
It is essentially a polemic literature, one filled with exhortations,
one that I would describe as scientists writing editorials. I have no
quarrel with scientists trying to inform the general public of their
scientific work; I consider that their duty. I have no quarrel with
polemic among scientists, but I question scientists cloaking their
editorial opinion in a spurious and misleading sense of scientism.

In this literature, students in general and radical students in
particular are at one and the same time described as sick or sane;
alienated or involved; arrogant or humble; immoral or religious;
amoral or endowed with a supermorality which goes beyond the
conventional morality; obscene or pure; selfish or generous; violent or gentle; cynical or idealistic.

There can be but four factors accounting for such a bewildering mass of contradictions. First: we are dealing wih a heterogeneous student population which, in the aggregate, is precisely that
different; second, for many students, adolescence is such a kaleido-
scopic, erratic, and fluid enough stage of life that an individual,
over a period of time, can be all of these things; third, the tunnel
vision, bias, or confusion of the observer; fourth, the relative heat
or calm of the moment—on and off campus; and fifth, the interaction of these four.

These have long been recognized as core problems for the social and behavioral sciences. They have yielded a methodological
concern which is focused primarily on sampling and observer bias.
Into these problems, a more impassioned ideology with its resultant partisanism has now been introduced which goes far beyond
the subtle issues heretofore encountered.

One must, in addition, note the complexity of the field itself;
one which permits no adequate methodological way of interdisciplinary study. We all see that part we have been trained to see and

we measure what we think we can measure. As Boulding (1956) put it, "we have the separate disciplines and sciences, with their separate bodies of theory. Each discipline corresponds to a certain segment of the empirical world, and each develops theories which have particular applicability to its own empirical segment" (p. 197) . My segment, i.e., the one in which I have been trained, is the clinical and normal developmental area. It is one which has attracted much attention and is the one to which I shall primarily address myself. I do not for one moment mean to deny the importance of the others—nor would I minimize the significance of all acting in concert on any individual or group, including the shifts that occur. Yet, the normal, as well as the abnormal, clinical dimension warrants attention since the phenomenon of adolescence is the substrate upon which all the other forces impinge.

The whole problem could be finessed by saying that everything everyone has said has some bearing on the situation—and this would be correct. But the matter of balance, interaction, hierarchy would be lost, and we would lose the benefit of debate. Nonetheless, everyone clinging to one hair and insisting that he has the whole elephant in his grasp presents a rather astonishing loss of perspective and loss of humility on the part of presumably well-trained scientists.

I would like to focus for just a moment on some aspects of this clinical literature. Given the fact of the breadth and complexity of the problem and the obvious heterogeneity of the population— sampling becomes a crucial variable. This is a quagmire into which some of our best people have strayed—some with more disastrous consequences than others. Indeed, the most frequently quoted books and articles in this area have been justifiably criticized as being based on the simplest sampling errors available in the literature.

For example, Keniston's oft-quoted volume *Young Radicals* is based on from 1 to 8 hours of interview and observation with but 11 committed radical students. These were completely self-selected leaders functioning over one summer as a "steering committee." In addition, Keniston readily admits that he shared the same bias as his small sample, a matter to which I shall return.

To generalize from such minimal data, gathered from a handful of self-selected leaders who shared a pre-empting purpose demands several basic assumptions: first, that all radical students are the same and share the same motivation—thus the sample is representative; second, that the students *know* what motivates them—this seems a scientific regression to a purely conscious psychology; and third, that they bear objective witness to the complex vicissitudes of their development and are capable and willing to tell it undistorted, in spite of their fervent, participatory absorption. This seems a lot to ask of a passionately engaged adolescent—no matter what his area of involvement might be. Granting face-validity would give any clinician—with a normal or abnormal populace—pause. To accept such assumptions is *at best* in the service of a search for a simplistic specificity of causation. On that level it is not a new problem—it plagued psychosomatic medicine which searched (in vain) to define "an ulcer personality" or a "specific conflict for asthma." Now, some search for the same developmental formula to define "a radical personality." At *its worst* it is propaganda.

Perhaps I can make this clearer by an example. The literature which dominated the press prior to the campus turmoils was on the hippie phenomenon. The same sorts of problems were apparent in the front pages covering that crisis. When the hippies were in their affluent days in the Haight, the Joint Commission on Mental Health for Children, spurred by national and Congressional concern, went to look. Given our usual scientific "categorimania," it appeared sensible to us that there were at least five, if not more, broad groups of the young people involved in the hippie movement. There were the intellectuals, from whom the music, philosophy, and caretaking emanated. There were the proletariat, who were the followers. Among these youngsters there were very few who dropped out—but many who had been dropped, with a prominent sprinkling of schizoid and schizophrenic youngsters. There were the curious and the drifters, who moved in and out without commitment or duration. There were the weekend hippies, who were essentially middle-class students or employed young people, who dropped into the Haight on weekends for kicks. In addition, there were the exploiters, those who took advantage commercially, sexually, and otherwise of the hippies. The point is that, *by the nature of the phenomenon*, the wary or the unwary, by intent or inadvertently, could prove whatever they wanted to prove about hippies based on the sample they selected. They could all be generalized as schizophrenic, they could all be generalized as brilliant, they could all be generalized as criminal—and indeed they were so characterized.

Having teethed on that scientific debacle, it is somewhat curious to find the same errors repeated. This stems from the fact that for most of us the detachment of which we academicians were so proud in the '50s has become difficult, if not impossible. The crucible in which we live is either a collective adventure or a collective tragedy. Some authors have chosen the course of idealizing adolescent romanticism, and they present us with events and analyses through a seemingly privileged subjectivity. Others focus on baser formulations from no less privileged subjectivity, and some, like Bettelheim, from no data at all—not that such theoretical formulations do not have some possible utility.

It is obvious that one of the major problems remains the problem of objectivity. Students arouse much in academicians. The superheated atmosphere and the issues themselves have such a personal impact that it is most difficult to maintain the perspective and distance we like to believe we usually have. Such intensely personal issues as how and what we teach, political values, sexual behavior, drug use, and particularly violence, strain our precarious objectivity.

As a matter of fact, so concentrated has been our response to the *political values* expressed by students that most of the literature reflects little more than increasingly subtle—sometimes not so subtle—sophisticated and sometimes unsophisticated ways of applauding or denouncing those values we individually cherish. It is an astonishingly idiosyncratic group of pseudoscientific papers which seems to have been markedly affected by the very political rhetoric and passion it seeks to describe and explain. Although the major, if not only, classification that has been superimposed on students is political, of particular note is the extent to which the clinical continuum has been used (or abused) to contaminate judgment of political or ethical matters. This permeates method and content.

Some, like Lifton (1970), try to make a virtue out of what most consider a methodological hazard. He states, psychohistory "seems to require . . . a considerable ethical concern with the problems being investigated. Erik Erikson has hardly been neutral in his feelings about Luther's achievements or about what Gandhi's legacy may still mean for the world. Nor has Keniston been neutral about student radicals, Coles about minority-group aspirations, nor I about Hiroshima and its legacy. Rather, all of us have been struggling toward ways of acknowledging our involvements and exploring their relationship to our findings, toward making conceptual use of these very involvements" (p. 295).

Since this group was stimulated by the thought of Erik Erikson, the major concepts that guide it are derived from psychoanalytic theory. In that light, a word must be said about this mode of working. Intuition and empathy have always been the key tools of the artist, the humanist, and the historian. Degrees of intuition and empathy are present in all men, but are particularly sought, trained, and sharply honed in the psychoanalyst. He regularly accepts their urgings as tentative hypotheses in his daily work. However, this is quite different from the use, by the observer, of current circumstance to solve or resolve his own inner conflicts or dilemmas. Lifton's is a curious misapplication of the psychoanalytic concept of countertransference. This is regarded as a hazard to understanding—not a benefit—and is quite likely no more valuable to a behavioral scientist than to a therapist.

For this reason, psychoanalysts and most behavioral and social scientists would agree with Hirsch (1970) who states:

> Where the conservative defender of academic freedom is naive to think that inquiry based upon choices can be ethically neutral, the radical activist is naive to suppose that inquiry as such can be bound to an ideology. Only the *choice* of a question is in the province of moral or ideological commitment. Once the choice is made, the results of inquiry are determined by evidence and by logic. It is an intellectual scandal to confuse relevance with inquiry by assuming that a particular social, moral, or political commitment must predetermine the results of an inquiry. . . . There is no doubt that ideology *can* predetermine the results of inquiry and is more likely to do so if the inquirer assumes that the fusion is inevitable [p. 344f.].

Again, as a clinician, as well as a behavioral scientist, it would seem to me that a dialogue or interview between two equally biased participants who share the same convictions is precisely the kind of interaction that can produce a *folie à deux*. If they share opposite bias, the likelihood is stalemate or a war of rhetoric or action.

One major impression I have after reading this literature is that much of it is less directed toward understanding youth than a matter of adult factions talking *through* youth to each other. It puts me in mind of estranged or divorced parents who use their children as a continuing vehicle for interaction. They blame, they wheedle, they threaten, they cajole through the major avenue of communication left to them—their children. To continue the analogy one step further, they try to win or threaten the children and turn them against each other. Sometimes blatantly, sometimes subtly, they fight each other.

As but one example, I would like to cite the following: Leon Eisenberg (1970), writing on "Student Unrest: Sources and Consequences," is concerned with the fundamental sources of students' behavior. He starts with the uncertain question, "Does psychiatry have anything useful to say about student unrest?" Three pages later, after an excellent review of the history of academies' turbulence, prolongation of adolescence, and social characteristics of student life, he states,

> But perhaps we have been addressing ourselves to the wrong question all along. Perhaps we should be asking, not why there is a student unrest, but why there is no *adult* unrest. . . . Why are we content to tolerate an immoral and futile war? Why do we as physicians permit health services to be cut back while $100 million each day is committed to the war in Vietnam? Is it perhaps because we have been complacent that the young are frantic? [p. 1691].

In an otherwise excellent review, Eisenberg becomes a doctor talking ethics, politics, and economics to other doctors through youth and the campus. It matters little that one may share his values as a man and even as a polemicist—one can't accept this as a scientific use of *psychiatry*. I shall speak more to this relevant moral, but not psychiatric explanation in a moment. If our stance is narrowly partisan, if our statements do not stem from factual analysis, if our attack is too personal and demeaning—we, too, shall forfeit our possibility of being responsible critics, let alone make our scientific observations useful to mankind.

As a result, we have been left with a wide assortment of speculations: theories based on what students *say;* theories based on what students *feel;* theories based on what students *mean,* regardless of what they say or feel; and on and on. What passes as empiric data is distorted not only by the eye of the beholder, but by our categorimania and our penchant for simplistic formulations. We seem to be seeking a single category of family structure or child-rearing pattern which will account for what we see. For Bettelheim, the villain is permissiveness and a failure of external control, which then doesn't become internalized. For Hendin at Columbia, it is a pseudopermissiveness, based on parental placation with the same results. For many observers, there are no villains or dangers—instead it is an exalted maturity based on an extended adolescence called youth, reared in close supportive families; for others, the same state of affairs is described as a confusion resulting from an extended adolescence and immature acting out. I fear that man is too complex an animal to yield to such simplistic explanations. Every attempt to do so shares the same fate, replete with all of the same sampling, conceptual, and theoretical errors which abound in any specificity hypothesis related to such a multivariate problem.

Yale

Perhaps I had best first speak of my own "sample" and my own view. First, I would not like to mislead you for one moment into thinking that I have either assimilated or understood all aspects of my experience as Master of one college at Yale. Second, it might be assumed that since the assignments to colleges are random, they are all similar. I do not know if that is true at all. There seem to me to be *some* differences which reflect the interests and personalities of the Masters, as well as the *small* degree of self-selection that occurs within the student body.

Like Medea, Yale's year started with the shriek of coeducation.

The tension increased throughout the year, spurting with the draft lottery, the Wright Hall incident, the Black Panther trial, and culminating in the May Day event with the subsequent Cambodia and Kent State aftermath. Although Yale undergraduates matriculate at Yale, the college is divided into 12 undergraduate residential colleges, each of which houses approximately 400 students. Each college has its own student housing, dining hall, recreational facilities, libraries, and classrooms. Each college has an academic function in that, by its own committees, it formulates a significant part of the curriculum which is taught for credit. It has a large number of internal committees which are responsible for its academic life, social life, and governance. Each college has a Master, a Dean, and a faculty fellowship. The Master's house is located within the physical confines of the college, and he is probably the man most intimately involved with students.

Each Master brought himself and his own expertise with him, and we all experienced different things as a result. Some seem to manage to avoid students by and large in any but a social setting; some minimize individual contact in favor of governance committees; all are approachable, but not all on an intense, personal, troubled level. In each college, a "following" seems to develop around the charisma, the interest, or the favorites of the Master. I should explain what happened to me.

I am a psychiatrist and a psychoanalyst, and this was well known from the beginning. Among other things, many students unburdened themselves to me on an exquisitely personal and sensitive level, revealing their joy, anguish, and torment. From my discussions with some of the other Masters, it did not seem that they usually elicited such a response. Accordingly, it may be asked if my professional background and personality did not superimpose something on the College in the sense that the students came to see me for things which represented what I was or what I presumably was most interested in. On the other hand, the converse may be true; i.e., they were afforded an easy opportunity to talk about things that concerned them. I have no definitive answer for this, although I did see many more students who had no major problems than those who did. Where I was confronted by neurotic or psychotic suffering, my clinical conviction was internally quite convincing. I would maintain that my professional skills were not invaded, compromised, or perverted. At the time, I was making no study, nor was I "researching" radical, conservative, or moderate students. I have only made an attempt to understand my experience in retrospect, and primarily in response to the existing literature.

I would like to state that being a Master of a college is a little like living in a goldfish bowl—where frequently one feels that the major function of the Master and his wife is to provide a fantasy life for students. There are precious few private things that happen in so intimate a living, working, eating, interacting situation such as this. This is not always very comfortable, but for our purposes, it is astonishing how well the Master knows the students in the college and vice versa. All are seen in numerous settings and conditions—and a core emerges. Long hours are spent in committee work, social life, and one to two meals are eaten with students every day. With individual contacts, I think the degree of reliability about impressions of students is high. And yet these are *impressions,* and they may allow more freedom than reason should allow.

I was immersed in all committees, ranging from curriculum through the social life of the college, and, in addition, as the year progressed, found that my office was increasingly besieged by all manner of students wanting to talk alone. I became quite intimately acquainted with a very large number of students—particularly the activist students, many of whom subsequently moved in the radical direction. Since I was used as an administrator, as a psychiatrist, or as a benevolent friend, which sometimes disguised a consultation function, or as a friend and colleague, I feel that the students I know, I know very well—I would say, far better than is possible with the interview-questionnaire techniques which have appeared in the literature. Of particular relevance are the astonishing differences, as well as similarities, of individual students in different settings, i.e., their behavior as related to their "reasons" for that behavior. My "method," if it was a method, is obviously that of most clinical research, an expert witness. I trust that some self-awareness as a psychoanalyst helped me through this morass.

In addition to the individual, social, and committee contacts with students, there were two other sources of involvement in the College. One was a program involving the entire college student body, which called for about 15 guest speakers, most of whom were concerned with the function and structure of universities. In the course of this, many general attitudes were expressed, as well as identifiable individual attitudes. The second, more important and intensive experience, was that Anna Freud accepted my invitation to live in the College as a Fellow in residence and to participate with me in the co-teaching of a course to undergraduate students, entitled "Normal and Abnormal Development in Childhood and Adolescence." Because of the interest in Anna Freud, this had to be limited to students in Davenport College, and we had to form two sections of 20 students each.

Of course, the original course plan around reading, demonstration, seminar discussion, and a required paper, was scrapped in favor of "rap" sessions about the events of the day, ranging from fem-lib to radicalism to revolution, etc. It was extremely fortunate for me that Anna Freud's visit coincided with May Day, and it was only with great resistance and reluctance that she accepted my insistence that she leave the College the night before the May Day event. However, her presence had an enormous impact on the College which I shall describe. In addition, it gave me an unusually sensitive, gifted, and experienced additional check to the events and the quality of adolescence.

About my personal attitude—I obviously like young people or would not have drifted into child and adolescent psychiatry and psychoanalysis, nor would I ever have accepted such a post. However, to me youth is not a virtue—but is a beguiling, perishable, confusing, enticing *developmental phase,* of crucial import and transient in nature. Although I enjoyed the year and like being with young people, I would not for a moment try to imply that I did not experience pain, anguish, and anger, in addition to fatigue. Nevertheless, pleasure was the dominant tone, and I remain most appreciative of the year I shared with them.

At the outset of the year, my major interest was in the question: has adolescence as a developmental process and phase changed? This is obviously too simply stated. For many of the students in the College, adolescence has not changed at all—I would say for most.

As a matter of fact, one's anticipation of change is so great that most students look like artifacts from a bygone day. Although their dress is "with it," they continue to cover the college with toilet paper, seek opportunities to sew and cook, ask for courses in home economics, and vacillate between euphoria and depression, passionate love and loneliness, in the age-old adolescent rhythm. I must admit there was something reassuring for Anna Freud and myself in rediscovering the normal student body. Adolescence as a developmental phase still exists.

The Students

Prior to this academic year, Yale College had experienced little disruption and few, if any, anticipated the degree to which political events would pre-empt the campus. I had no particular scientific interest in student radicals or activists. My basic interest in adolescence was accentuated by the presence of Anna Freud who wrote the classic developmental description of this phenomenon in 1936. We reasoned that it would be useful to compare what we could glean of intrapsychic processes and interpersonal relations in 1970 as contrasted with those of 1936.

Time and discretion will force me to speak of a composite and will prevent me from speaking in any detail about individual students. However, this accepts a biological developmental postulate, i.e., although developmental phases are distinguishable, individual variations and differences within a phase are the essence of development. Accordingly, individual modes of coping with typical adolescent crises, conflicts, and achievements are idiosyncratic and may be quite variable within individuals over a period of time.

Although I consider the *stance* of a general systems theory approach ideal to such a multidisciplinary problem, no such multidisciplinary approach has yet emerged which yields any fruitful *substance*. I shall leave to far wiser synthesizers the ultimate task of integrating and blending the multiplicity of forces which logic dictates are so contradictory. I refer to the inconsistency of a presumed earlier and more diverse choice of roles in the face of increased segmentation and specialization with increasing time needed for preparation; the increasing needs for individuality and individual expression in the face of the increasing needs of sociality; increasing societal restrictions due to continued industrialization, urbanization, and population increase—all of never-dreamed proportions and with profound ecological implications; the political, economic, and moral repercussions of war in a technological culture such as ours; and particularly relevant to the student—the problems of anonymity in ever-larger computerized educational establishments.

My clinical dimension relates to such factors as the demonstrably earlier physical maturity of puberty; changes in sexual mores, cultural ethics, and values, and their transmission; the use of drugs; and the prolongation of adolescence and what this does to ultimate conflict resolution, as well as internal and external commitments.

For the moment, I would like to focus on whether adolescent college students—whatever is changed in their lives—look different from those described by Anna Freud in 1936.

Let me at the outset say that I saw nothing which would lead me to suggest an increase in the incidence of those transient symptoms and states more usually called adolescent turmoils. Neurotic and psychotic breakdowns were present, but no more than I anticipated. More students *spoke* of "identity crises," but I think this is more apparent than real due to the popularization of this normal adolescent conflict through the work of Erikson. Contrary to my expectations, the students were not any more mature on an intrapersonal or interpersonal level than their predecessor generation. This is in spite of the fact that Yale undergraduates are brighter, better informed, better read, and more traveled than ever before. By and large, they have no more successfully resolved their dependency-independency conflicts than one would expect of adolescents of other decades. Parents still accompany their children to college, homesickness of the same proportions exists, and evidence of the struggle to emancipate oneself from the home abounds.

Although facets of adolescence have been given new names and more alternatives exist, Anna Freud and I came to the conclusion that the underlying process, geared to biological, epigenetic alterations as it is, remains strikingly similar and does not appear to be a process which in its most fundamental aspects can be anticipated, hurried, or resolved at a different pace—it has an inner momentum of its own. How this relates to political activism is a matter to which I shall return. Time does not permit me to speak of the one truly revolutionary change, i.e., the confusion for women adolescents with their new challenging and perplexing freedom.

The familiar upsurge in sexual urges was abundantly clear. Intense friendships, crushes, and love relationships produced the same "mating ceremonials" in a formal sense, although specific content yielded to fad and style. Identical degrees of painful shyness and exuberant lack of inhibition with attending "discovery" and growth spurts were omnipresent. The use of alcohol to dissolve that portion of the personality called superego was clearly diminished through drug use. The extent to which these different classes of intoxicants turn people inward or outward is also beyond the scope of this paper. I will just say that those who voluntarily left the college because of drug abuse demonstrated no greater licentiousness, peace, or social comfort than any other dropout group —actually they were sorely troubled.

The strikingly rapid mood shifts; the depression and euphoria; the sometimes happy, more often voluptuously melancholic "soul scrapes"; the provocative aggressive outbursts of fighting, antisocial and even delinquent acts—all were evanescently present.

The oft-described coping through asceticism was clearly present in the number of spartans who became long-distance, lonely runners, dieters, etc. "Bookworms" have been replaced by "book freaks," and share their coping effectiveness with "TV freaks," "bridge freaks," and "poker freaks." The changeableness, the passion, the futility of a fine intellect in the face of driven behavior, the idealism and empathy about love and fidelity—which do not prevent callousness and outrageous lack of consideration—the endless insatiable desire to think and talk on the highest level of abstraction have been better described in Anna Freud's 1936 book than ever since.

A more sophisticated approach to the problem of change within the framework described above is to wonder in what ways the present social, cultural, political, and economic forces have combined with and exaggerated the ordinary problems of adolescence to the extent of radical activism. To approach this I would like to contrast two groups of activist students. One was politically radical and the other was relatively apolitical, almost religious in its activism.

The major divergence in these two groups became apparent in mid-year with the "Wright Hall incident." The incident resulted from the firing of a young black woman from one of the dining rooms. She was a mother who was trying to get off welfare, work, and take care of her children. The aftermath of the firing was dominated by S.D.S., which took this as an opportunity to confront the university on its hiring, firing, and other personnel practices. After increasingly heated and acrimonious debates, the black students repudiated the S.D.S. efforts as opportunistic and exploitative. Continuing on their course, the white radical students engineered the seizure of a building and the holding of University officials.

In Davenport College, two young people decided that one way to help mothers work would be to construct and staff a day care center which would take care of their children, freeing the mothers to work. From the beginning, this was not to be a baby-sitting service, but a professionally run center which would enrich the lives of children. This nucleus of leadership represented the confluence of a wish to help and the presence of women at Yale. One of the leaders was a white young woman in her sophomore year, and the other was a black young man in his junior year. I was struck by the fact that both had a kind of religious background which made it possible for them to maintain a formal church affiliation in College. The young man was a prominent athlete, who by May Day emerged as one of the most respected, responsible, and persuasive student leaders (of white and black students) on campus.

These two students formed a group of concerned and dedicated students around them; and although they sought and used professional consultation, they never relinquished the responsible leadership of the project. They actively had to seek help from all sources and yet resist the numerous attempts at political "incursions" and opportunistic "takeover." They informed themselves of all aspects of children's care; they obtained a "home" for the center, obtained the appropriate licensure and health permits, wrote proposals, visited foundations, and mounted a successful fund-raising drive to which the entire University responded.

They convinced President Brewster to endorse Yale's participation in the venture; interviewed and hired a professional staff; surveyed the need, and recruited children. The Calvin Hill Day Care Center is now a going enterprise, taking care of 25 children with the highest professional standards. It is, in fact, a model center. It would be difficult for me to overestimate the determination, the degree of self-sacrifice in time and energy, the resilience in the face of disappointment; or the ingenuity it took to make this a success. The students continue to run the center actively via a board and participate in the teaching on a volunteer basis.

The characteristics of this activism were also noted around the May Day weekend. After weeks of tormented, fearful, challenging, and perplexing debate, the students voted an open college to welcome an undetermined number of visitors to the city. The days and nights of rhetoric had taken their toll, and a moderate degree of paralysis intervened. From this, the same spirit emerged in the decision to make the college a family center. They registered visitors, set up a communication system, housed and fed families and individuals, as did all other colleges. A protective marshall system protected the young charges, standing all-night watches, etc. In addition, they set up a day care center which took care of 50 children a day for the three days and nights while their parents attended the meetings. With characteristic determination, they obtained playground equipment, special foods, pediatric consultation, and supervisory help from the Yale University Child Study Center Nursery School. The 24-hour a day responsibility for 50 children ranging from infancy to preadolescence was impressive.

The caretaking of adults and children was done by students who were relatively apolitical. The leader and organizer of the Yale Marshalls was an incredibly gifted former Green Beret. He was called a "peace freak" by the other students and simply did not want people to hurt other people. He categorically stated that he had no interest in the Panthers and was in no way radical. The leader of the Davenport Marshalls was a prominent athlete and a gifted musician with no commitment to radical politics.

The radical group—approximately 16 in number—was passionately involved in the events. They were immersed in planning, persuading, arguing for strikes, confrontation, and support of the Panther cause. I would not consider any of them the leaders of the antiwar movements within the college, although their interests were in this area. They were unsuccessful in seizing leadership, although they did "seize" and operate the communication center. They did not participate in any of the above-mentioned care for people. They were more excited, more involved in the political rallies—of day and night duration—and more frequently teargassed than any of the others. Their intellectual preparation, political reasoning, and impassioned commitment were impressive.

Both groups of students were passionate in their activism. Even though their "demands" intersected around day care, one was theoretical—an item for confrontation and rhetoric—the other was practical with a different theoretical base and a matter to be accomplished, not used. The two groups never merged, nor did they ever work in concert—they sought no help from each other.

BIBLIOGRAPHY

BOULDING, K. E. (1956), General Systems Theory: The Skeleton of Science. *Management Science,* 2:197–208.

EISENBERG, L. (1970), Student Unrest: Sources and Consequences. *Science,* 167:1688–1692.

ERIKSON, E. H. (1959), *Identity and the Life Cycle* [*Psychological Issues,* Monogr. 1]. New York: International Universities Press.

FREUD, A. (1936), *The Ego and the Mechanisms of Defense.* New York: International Universities Press, rev. ed., 1966.

HIRSCH, E. D., JR. (1970), Value and Knowledge in the Humanities. *Daedalus,* 99:343–354.

KENISTON, K. (1968), *Young Radicals.* New York: Harcourt, Brace, & World.

LIFTON, R. J. (1970), On Psychohistory. In: *The State of American History,* ed. H. Bass. New York/Chicago: Quadrangle Books, pp. 276–297.

Cultural Values and the Superego in Late Adolescence

CALVIN F. SETTLAGE, M.D.

IN HIS FORMULATION OF THE AIMS OF THE PANEL ON "YOUTH ON THE Campus," Seymour Lustman invited us to apply our psychoanalytic knowledge to the understanding of youth not in the familiar context of the analytic situation, but in the context of the campus situation. Addressing himself to the phenomenon of student activism, Lustman (1971) wondered whether this behavior reflected a change in adolescence. His own answer was derived from the unique vantage point of his experience as Master of one of the res-

---

Training and Supervising Analyst in Adult and Child Analysis, San Francisco Psychoanalytic Society and Institute; Director, Child Psychiatry and Associate Chief of Psychiatry, Mt. Zion Hospital and Medical Center, San Francisco.

Paper presented at the Seymour Lustman Memorial Panel, held at the Annual Meeting of the Association for Child Psychoanalysis, Palm Springs, Calif., on March 25, 1972.

idential colleges at Yale. He and Anna Freud, who for a time also lived in the college and shared in Lustman's daily relationships and discussions with the students, came to the conclusion that the underlying process in adolescence, geared as it is to biological and epigenetic alterations, has not changed. Having so concluded, Lustman then sought to understand the ways in which changing social and cultural forces combine with and exaggerate the ordinary problems of adolescence so as to involve some adolescents in radical activism. Stating that there can be no doubt that the transmission and internalization of moral and cultural values is directly involved in this problem of change, he suggested that superego theory would be the most profitable area to which one must look for understanding. It is to this suggestion by Lustman that I am responding.

My interest, then, is in the question of the nature of the superego and its role in the interplay between the adolescent and the surrounding culture. In attempting to answer this question, I shall employ a developmental or genetic approach in regard to the theory of culture and the theory of the superego and ego ideal, and attempt to demonstrate the following: that the relationship between the individual and his culture takes its origins from the earliest experiences of play in the relationship with the mother; that the qualitative aspects of the ego ideal as a part of the superego are shaped by the process of separation-individuation and the attainment of object constancy; and that the nature of the relationship between the late adolescent and his society, between his superego and the values and traditions of his culture, and whether this relationship is mutually constructive, hinges in large measure on the adequacy of these developmental beginnings. It is my hope that the delineation of these concepts will add to the understanding of the developmental problems and the behavior of today's youth.

Culture and the Transmission of Values

Observing that Freud did not have a place in his topography of the mind for the experience of things cultural, Winnicott (1967) offered the thesis that cultural experience is located in the potential space between the individual and the environment, originally between the infant and his mother.[1] In advancing this idea, he builds upon his concept of the transitional object, which he views as a symbol of the union, in the baby's mind, of the baby and the mother, of two now separate things, at the point of initiation of their separateness. He further views that infant's use of this symbol, the first not-me possession, as the first experience of play. What Winnicott proposes is that the developmental prototype for the experiencing of things cultural is the infant's play with the transitional object in a location or space which is neither exclusively a part of the infant nor of the love object but shared by both.

Adding to Winnicott's formulation, I would emphasize that the thus-defined, first symbolic play experience also serves the purposes of internalization of experiences of relatedness, at first of those between infant and mother and later of those between individual and culture. One can conceptualize that the existing primitive memories of already past experiences are externalized into this in-between space where they are compared and correlated with the current and more consciously perceived experiences with the mother and the emerging self. The infant plays, as it were, with past and present images of self, object, and self-object relatedness as they are on their way toward stable intrapsychic representation. At the same time, and importantly, he is beginning to gain mastery over the sense of loss which comes with the dawning awareness of separateness. My addition to Winnicott's thesis also adds a further degree of abstraction, namely, that one can play with images or ideas in which we refer to as the mind's eye.

What has been formulated, then, is the process of internalization in its earliest form. According to this conceptualization, internalization also involves a re-externalization which permits the child to play with images of experience with the aim of discrimination and mastery, doing so in this intermediate area where they are, for the moment, held separate from both inner psychic reality and the larger world of outer reality. What I wish to suggest at this point is that internalization throughout human development, in-

[1] I am indebted to Philip M. Spielman, M. D. for his suggestions and formulations in clarification of Winnicott's theories of early development and his understanding of their relevance to late adolescence.

cluding the internalization of values and tradition, is based upon this prototype and has its features. A measure of support for this suggestion, which also anticipates the discussion of the superego and ego ideal, comes from Loewald (1962). He notes that the superego as the latest acquisition in ontogenetic and phylogenetic mental organization is peculiarly prone to regressive tendencies *in the direction of re-externalization* (my italics). I hasten to add that this kind of regression can be necessary, normal, and in the service of the ego, not only during adolescence, as has been clarified by Blos (1967) in particular, but during other developmental phases as well. While the superego represents the familial and cultural values and traditions taken in during the childhood years, it must also come to represent the values and ideals unique and appropriate to the experience of the individual in his own generation and his own particular sociocultural times.

Modification of the superego occurs primarily during late adolescence when values are reassessed, retained or discarded without discarding the basic attachment or union with the outside or what has been internalized from the outside. This modification of the superego can be thought of as a creative act in the in-between space, based upon the earlier mentioned prototype of play with the transitional object. It has elements of separation, union, and reunion characteristic of the process of separation-individuation (Mahler, 1971) and entails simultaneously, and often confusingly for the adolescent, a reliving of elements of the infantile separation-individuation and the new and different second individuation of adolescence (Blos, 1967).

Winnicott (1967) makes the further observation, made also by others, that the infant must have an adequate opportunity for play —play which must initially be fostered and participated in by the mother. The lack of opportunity for such early play is felt to impede or blunt the development not only of the capacity for play but for learning and creativity as well. Impairments in play ability tend to lead to impairments in the child's assimiliation of the cultural inheritance and in his later potential contribution to the cultural pool. An adolescent who has suffered such impairments may fear the loss of self to the culture or tradition (the old danger of fusion or re-engulfment in the symbiosis) or find himself unable to lend his unique and creative stamp to the culture, to make his mark on it without destroying it. In the case of severe psychopathology stemming from difficulties in early separation-individuation, there is the risk either of a total alienation from the culture or of a total rejection of it. A creative blending in the in-between, shared space of elements of what is in the self and what is outside the self in the culture is blocked.[2] All of this is of considerable importance on the philosophical level, since cultural experiences provide, as Winnicott notes, the continuity in the human race which transcends personal existence.

Although Winnicott's thoughts about play and the location of culture as derived from the concept of the transitional object have not been a part of Erikson's (1940) thinking, I perceive considerable similarity in their formulations. Winnicott's intermediate area sounds very much like Erikson's play space, the macrosphere and the microsphere. In the macrosphere the child plays out and potentially rearranges both his distant and immediately past experiences with his parents, using the parents or other human figures and himself as the symbolic participants in the fantasy. In the microsphere, the fantasy is played out in a spatially more limited way, with the child using dolls or other toys as the symbolic representations. From the developmental viewpoint, it seems tenable that there is a progression from play with one's own body and that of the mother in earliest infancy (Erikson's autosphere play), to the playing of roles wherein oneself and others are the symbolic representations, to play wherein self and others are represented by inanimate objects, to fantasy without play, and ultimately to thinking in the mind's eye. If this is the case, the type of play used would be diagnostic of the level of ego function, either as attained developmentally or as expressed regressively. And this may have some value in understanding the behavior of adolescents, even though their play, in many instances, has lost the qualities of make-believe

---

2 Here one is reminded of Winnicott's (1967) analysis of Tagore's statement that "On the seashore of endless worlds, children play." In addition to representation of sexual union, birth of the child, and the child and mother getting to know each other, the metaphor expresses the endless repetition of union, separation, and reunion, with the sea bathing the shore without submerging it and the sea and shore being enriched by each other.

and playfulness. Again, in keeping with the aim of mastery, the child's "playing it out" can be viewed as the most natural auto-therapeutic coping measure which childhood affords, as was noted by Erikson. In regard to the proposed prototype of internalization, play can also be thought of as an important delaying action which permits intended elements of future psychic structure to be worked over outside the self. This amounts to a kind of re-externalization and ego modulation, hopefully of ego-alien as well as ego-syntonic internalizations, prior to their becoming more fixed in psychic structure.

In Erikson's recent thinking, play space, whether external or in the mind's eye, provides a *Spielraum* or leeway vital to human functioning and adaptation in both childhood and adulthood. As was also noted by Winnicott (1953), such leeway offers both a needed relief from the otherwise unremitting strain of moderating between the demands of inner and outer reality, and an area for creative thought and problem solving.

Erikson (1968) has, of course, devoted much of his effort to understanding the relationship between culture and individual development within the broad framework of psychoanalytic theory as a general psychology. In connection with the process of identity formation, he noted that psychoanalysis had not developed terms to conceptualize the environment and that designating it as the world of outer reality has made for difficulty in taking account of the environment as a pervasive actuality (p. 24). He underscores this point by citing the fact that the German ethologists introduced the term *Umwelt* to denote not merely an environment which surrounds you but one which is also in you and you in it.

One might object that the analytic concept of internalization does, in fact, place the environment inside the individual. Erikson sought, however, to stress the relationship between environment and identity in its ongoing aspect, as an always changing process. Thus he conceptualizes identity formation as a process of mutual influence "located" in the core of the individual and yet also in the core of his communal culture. In the light of the preceding discussion, I wonder whether the *process* of identity formation, as opposed to the achieved identity on the one side and the characteristics of the communal culture on the other, might logically be thought of as taking place in the in-between area of play and cultural experience.

Erikson (1970) has observed that the line of development concerned with moral and ethical orientation has three stages: moral learning as an aspect of childhood; ideological experimentation as a part of adolescence; and ethical consolidation as an adult task. In my discussion, I have suggested that those processes which lead to earliest self-object differentiation and the earliest internalizations toward psychic structure and identity are prototypical for all internalizations, including the internalization of cultural values. The concept of internalization as a process which includes externalization and the "playing with" or working over, in an intermediate space, of that which has been a part of the self and that which may become a part of the self has a particular bearing on our understanding of youth. It is during late adolescence that one's moral and ideological acquisitions are assessed and shaped into the values which are to govern one's immediate future as an adult.

Superego and Ego Ideal

In my use of the terms superego and ego ideal, I am following the view of Hartmann and Loewenstein (1962) who formulate that the ego ideal becomes a function of the superego during and after the passing of the oedipal phase. At the same time, the theory that the anlage of the ego ideal develops during infancy is important to my understanding of the dynamics of late adolescent behavior. In my view (Settlage, 1971), a crucial step in early development derives from the infant's realization, toward the end of the first year of life, that what was felt from the beginning to belong to the self is in actuality a part of the nonself. This awareness that the all-important mother is separate from oneself and not under one's control evokes a sense of helplessness and presents the first threat of libidinal loss. The manifestation of this experience is the regularly observed phenomenon of anxiety appearing *de novo,* at about 8 months of age, in reaction to temporary separations from the mother. This early threatening experience can be thought of as a universal, and therefore normal, developmental "trauma."

Mahler's (1971) observation and formulation of the phenome-

non of "low-keyedness" or withdrawal into the self upon temporary separation from the mother suggest the nature of the infant's
defensive response to this normal, developmental trauma. She sees
the infant as attempting to hold onto a state of mind which has
been termed the ideal state of self (Sandler et al., 1963), doing so
by seeking to reunite with the symbiotic partner through an intrapsychic communion with her mental representations and with
those of the self in relation to the mother. Freud (1914, p. 94) and
later Jacobson (1964, p. 96) formulated the long-range developmental consequence of libidinal loss experience during infancy.
They proposed that what one projects ahead of him as his ideal is
merely a substitute for the lost narcissism of childhood, the time
when he was his own ideal. In their view, the thus-derived ego ideal
is forged from ideal concepts of the self, from idealized features of
love objects, and from these in relation to each other, and it has
the aim of gratifying the infantile longing to be one with the love
object. This conceptualization of the ego ideal as arising in infancy
and representing what one projects ahead of himself in a lifelong
striving for unity or perfection has important implications for
later development.

The anlage of the ego ideal would seem to originate in response
to the postulated normal, developmental trauma. Its valence and
aspirational power would appear, however, to be determined by
the extent of libidinal or narcissistic loss experienced thereafter,
mainly during the second and third years of life before the attainment of libidinal object constancy. Loss experience occurring after
this attainment, while also resulting in a wish for restitution of the
loss, would have a lesser impact. This is because of the reduced
vulnerability which results from the establishment of images of a
separate self and a separate object in a reasonably stable relationship to each other. What I am suggesting is that the greater the infantile narcissistic loss, the greater or more elevated and compensatory will be the ego ideal. Because the level of aspiration which
the ego ideal holds up to the ego is set so early, it influences the
later accumulated content of the ego ideal, as well as that of the
rest of the superego, in its qualitative aspects—i.e., how stringent
it is. This would be true regardless of the variations due to the specific familial and cultural environment.

I return now to the theory that the ego ideal becomes a function of the ego during and after the oedipal phase. In his outline of the successive stages in superego development, Loewald (1962) suggests that the "ideal ego" or ideal state of infancy, which is oriented toward the past and re-establishment of unity with the environment, gradually becomes something to be wished for in the future. For a time this wish is to be fulfilled through participation in the omnipotence and perfection of the parental figures of the preoedipal and oedipal phases. Later on, when the oedipal figures are relinquished as external objects and a more definitive superego is formed, the wished-for future is internalized as a part of the superego. The superego is thus the agency of *inner* demands, ideals, hopes, and concerns in regard to the ego, as well as the agency of inner rewards and punishments in respect to which the ego experiences contentment or guilt. The superego is the inner representative of the ego's future. Putting it succinctly, Loewald states that, in the structure of the superego, the ego confronts itself in the light of its own future.

Using Loewald's concept, one can postulate that the extent of the gap between where ego is and where it is felt that it ought to be is a crucial factor in the adolescent's difficulties with himself and with society, the latter because of the confrontation between the adolescent's ideals and the imperfections of the culture. Depending upon the defensive modes used to deal with the consequences of an elevated ego ideal, the resulting overt behavior can vary tremendously, ranging from extremely aggressive striving to extremely passive resignation and withdrawal. It is during late adolescence in particular that high ideals and a wish for perfection in oneself are likely to be confronted by a strong and dismaying sense of inadequacy and imperfection. As Blos (1954) has explained, this is due to the glaring incompatibility of the projected self image and reality achievement. The wish to escape from the pain of this self confrontation may of course lead to an intense preoccupation with the imperfections of the society. These formulations of the ego ideal may help to account for the difference between Lustman's two types of activist students, the politically radical, "revolutionary" and the relatively apolitical "caretaker" who seeks to meet people's immediate needs.

In keeping with his stated intent, Loewald (1962) stresses the role of time in the relationship of superego to ego, particularly psychic time in the sense of past, present, and future. Taking off from Loewald's ideas, Seton (1971) proposed that, if one conceives of guilt as being the measure of the discrepancy between inner present and inner future, then to make away with time is to effect relief from such guilt. In his view, the suspension of psychic time with the resulting relief from the coercion of the superego is a maneuver which may be resorted to by the late adolescent. In so doing the adolescent defers both the issue and the consequences of attempting to measure up to his ego ideal. While the suspension of psychic time may serve the same developmental purposes as Erikson's (1968) psychosocial moratorium, which also removes the pressure of time, the two are not the same. The suspension of psychic time is a self-granted delay, a defensive maneuver, which is not sanctioned by the society, even though it may be in part culturally determined, whereas the psychosocial moratorium is an institutionalized delay which grants time for development through an extension of the adolescent phase, a sanctioned deferring of adult commitments.

Ideally, these delays during late adolescence serve constructive purposes for both the individual and his society, providing time to play, to test out ideas, and to try out roles. In regard to the transmission of cultural values, they allow for the possibility of modification of the superego. Because the psychological forces initiated by puberty result in a general loosening of psychic structure and a high degree of perceptiveness about self and others, change is feasible. In some adolescents, the troublesome gap between high personal standards and the level of ego achievement can be narrowed by dint of persistent and strenuous efforts on the part of the ego. In others, it can be narrowed by a lowering or reformulation of the standards on the basis of a realistic appraisal and comparison of one's values with one's abilities and future opportunities. This latter change may be facilitated by the realization that certain values taken in during the childhood years as being representative of the culture are in fact more mythical than real.

In regard to the possible benefit for society and culture, I cite Freud's (1933) observation that the content of the superego tends to perpetuate the past, the tradition of the race and the people, which yields but slowly to the influence of the present and to new developments (p. 67). This suggests that change in cultural values requires change in individuals. Youth has a unique role in society and culture, not only because constructive change in the superego has its greatest feasibility during late adolescence, but because the concurrent major psychological separation from and relinquishment of the parents pushes the creative forces to the extreme. Speaking to these points, Erikson (1968) observed that "Adolescence is thus the vital regenerator in the process of social evolution; for youth can offer its loyalties and energies to that which continues to feel true and to the revolutionary correction of that which has lost its regenerative significance" (p. 134).

Conflict Solutions in Late Adolescence

Against the background of the preceding theoretical discussion of culture and superego, I wish to consider the predicament of today's youth and the kinds of defensive and adaptive options to which they may resort.

As was stated earlier, the developmental task of late adolescence in regard to values is to realign the internal value system—the superego and ego ideal—prior to taking on those adult commitments and responsibilities which, in Lustman's words, "seal" the resolution of adolescence. One can think of this as a process of evolving a more mature superego, an important aspect of which entails the lowering of an unrealistically high ego ideal. (See also Seton, 1971.)

The goals held up by the ego ideal may be excessively high in today's youth for reasons other than the high valence postulated as stemming from deficiencies in the infantile relationships with love objects. Largely because of television, today's adolescent has been exposed to societal and cultural problems on local, national, and international levels throughout his childhood years. As he moves toward independence and adulthood, these problems begin to weigh upon him. They can no longer be ignored, denied, or simply assigned to others, as one's prerogative as a child.

In past eras, a person could demarcate a limited segment of the world of reality and prepare himself to deal with a limited number of problems. Living in our age of instant communication at a time when the survival of mankind would appear to depend upon our ability to effect radical social change, today's generation feels its reality includes the entire world with all of its problems. As Erikson (1968) has put it, we live in an era when glorification of the pseudospecies—of national or cultural groups potentially in mortal conflict with each other—can now spell the end of the species.

Probably as a result of these same circumstances, today's adult generation is much less sure of its values than were past generations. Contradictions, duplicities, and uncertainties abound. As a result, youth are deprived of the sense of security which stems from the convictions of the older generation, even as they decry and rebel against its values in shaping their own.

In these times, the normal idealism of youth is confronted by an overwhelming array of challenges and responsibilities; it is considerably shaken and must be tempered *en route* to its role in adult functioning. But the tempering process involves a struggle, for both youth and adults. According to Erikson (1970), there exists in every individual and every generation a potential for an intensified adolescence, that is, a critical phase marked by the reciprocal aggravation of inner conflict and societal disorganization. Certainly in our era, this potentiality would appear to have become an actuality.

Under the circumstances of such an intensified adolescence, as well as under more usual circumstances, what kinds of defensive and adaptive "solutions" can young people employ? For many adolescents, the solution is to join as quickly as possible the older generation, the establishment. This would tend to be true mostly of those young people who, for whatever reasons, do not participate in the extended psychosocial moratorium of the college student. For them, the superego and ego ideal of the childhood years —essentially those of the parents—persist relatively unchanged, due to the early assumption of adult responsibilities such as are entailed in earning a living or being married.

All of the other kinds of solutions, or attempts at solution, appear to involve a prolongation of adolescence and a suspension of time, either through the institutionalized moratorium or by means of individual defensive maneuvers. And while time is suspended and the full attainment of adulthood is deferred, the cultural values, both as re-externalized from within the self and as represented in the external environment, are played out, tested, challenged, and accepted or rejected prior to the hoped-for eventual consolidation of the superego. Sometimes this is carried out primarily in the mind's eye, but more often it involves discussion, action, confrontation, and other experiences with people in current reality.

An illustration of the suspension of psychic time is provided by the case of a 17-year-old girl whose major symptom was an obsessively dealt-with fear that whatever she was in the process of learning would be lost to others, and could be regained only through great mental effort. She had experienced what I believed to have been excessive narcissistic loss during infancy because of repeated libidinal separations from her intensely anxious and phobic mother. She had set the extremely high self-expectation of becoming the world's most renowned expert in Egyptian culture. In order to achieve this goal she had to take advantage of every minute, and she felt constantly harassed by lack of time. During her latency years, she was equally preoccupied with the idea of a time machine and with death.

In recounting her experience on the just-past New Year's Eve, she was bothered because she had miscalculated and thought it was on the following day. Thus, she did not have time to prepare for it. The desired preparation was to have been a period of meditation so that she could become serious and solemn and properly sanctify the occasion. The transition from the old to the new year was more important than the anniversary of her birthday because the former is the occasion of a societal ceremony.

As she felt was true in the sun worship of the Stonehenge people, sanctification required acknowledgment of a precise moment in time. With the approach of midnight, she was thinking of the continuity of time, and she found herself concentrating on the flowing of the stream which ran beside her home. She guessed that it had been flowing for at least 20,000 years; it defied time. During the course of treatment, it became clear that fulfillment of her archaeological ambition would, in her mind, erase time altogether and, with it, her fear of aging and death. She would thereby merge with the peoples of the past and with their relics which deny time by continuing to withstand its ravages. In regard to her adolescence, the suspension of time deferred confrontation with her inflated self-expectations, and postponed an anxiety-laden acceptance of herself as a sexually mature female.

In addition to the temporary suspension of time, the various defensive and adaptive solutions can be understood as having the aims of changing the culture, of escaping the culture by changing the immediate environment, or of changing oneself. It is apparent that the garnering of time is valuable only if it is put to good use, a fact which underscores once again the importance of favorable early development. During infancy there needs to be not only the opportunity but the time for play, play which is not rushed and has leeway so that it can come to serve the purposes of creativity. Good mothering provides for such play moratoriums throughout separation-individuation and during later childhood as well.

One attempt at escaping the culture, and thus the pressure of the superego that is so closely linked to it, is that of running away from home and parents, and living in the subculture of one's peers, whether this be as a transient or as a member of some type of commune. A solution which seems to combine escape and an attempt at self-modification is the resort to consciousness-altering drugs. Here the hoped-for outcome is for freedom from conscience and societal mores at the same time as the urgency of the drives is either sedated or indulged and the self is felt to be all-encompassing and omnipotent, in a kind of symbiotic regression. Another attempted solution, which bears resemblance to the drug solution, is the escape into psychosis. Still another extreme kind of escape from the pressure of both internal and external expectations, as well as from the coercion of time, is that of suicide.

Suicide as a fantasied wish for such escape rather than a wish for death itself is illustrated by the case of a 19-year-old boy who survived his suicide attempt. During his childhood years, this boy seemed to be driven by a need to excel. As one example, and there were many others, at age 4 and entirely on his own initiative, he insisted on diving off the high diving board at the local swimming pool, doing so repeatedly in spite of admonitions to the contrary. Since this patient was seen in treatment at a time when the importance of a detailed exploration of the first 3 years of life was not so well recognized, the question of early libidinal loss remains conjectural.

Although this young man had equally high aspirations in his school work, his educational progress had been arduous. He managed to be admitted to college on two separate trys one year apart, but dropped out each time when he saw he was not making it. After the second failure, he went to a place where he had felt accepted during his teen-age vacations, an island which was a good distance from the mainland.

In a state of despondency, he walked to a remote beach and swallowed a handful of sleeping pills. Immediately after taking the pills, he felt a sense of ease and relaxation and of being at peace with himself and the world, something he had never before experienced. Time no longer mattered and there was no pressure to act or achieve. After a few minutes of contentment, he suddenly thought, "But I'm going to die!" With that he ran to the nearest inhabited cottage, which was over a mile away, and told the housewife what he had done. She called for help to take him to the nearest physician and hospital, which were on the mainland, and plied him with strong coffee until it arrived. He lapsed into a coma while being ferried to the mainland, but was eventually revived.

Because of the perspective which he gained from this experience and the insight which came through treatment, the patient was able to lower his self-expectations and proceed in his life with success and self-esteem instead of failure and self-derogation.

The aim of changing the culture is exemplified most vividly by Lustman's activist students. As stated earlier, Lustman sorted them into two types: the politically radical, revolutionary students who, for example, sought confrontation with the University and engineered the seizure of a building and the holding of University officials; and the relatively apolitical, caretaking students who set about meeting the needs of the involved people and their children in a manner which he noted was almost religious in its tone. While both groups of students were committed in their activism, the revolutionaries dedicated themselves to political goals and the caretakers to the practical goal of helping people.

Lustman noted that less than 20 of the students known to him would fit the radical, revolutionary category. While acknowledging the limitations of his observational position, he nevertheless ventured his impression that three fourths of the students in the radical group fell outside the range of the usual turbulence of adolescence, and that better than half of these were seriously, and more than neurotically disturbed.

In my view, this assessment suggests a high incidence of psychopathology stemming from difficulties in earliest object relationships. In keeping with my theoretical discussion of the origin and valence of the ego ideal, one can speculate that the revolutionary student is likely to be burdened by a hypertrophied, compensatory ego ideal. Because of his need to achieve perfection and his wish to escape guilt and feelings of worthlessness, he is likely to be particularly driven in his activist behavior. Psychologically speaking, he seeks to close a wide gap between ego and ego ideal, both by achievement of his high objectives and by exposure of the imperfections in the cultural institutions. It is my guess that this formulation either would not apply in the case of the healthy revolutionary and of the apolitical, activist caretaker, or it would embody a lesser degree of difficulty in early object relationships.

According to my observation, the solution for the great majority of students and late adolescents involves primarily a struggle to change oneself, but along with it there is an effort to change outmoded cultural institutions through other than revolutionary means, that is, by working with and within the framework of the adult society. I have felt that this is true of that familiar late, late adolescent group which includes residents in psychiatry and students in psychology and social work.

Many of these trainees are essentially independent and have assumed the adult responsibility of marriage and family. All of them are engaged, however, in a task important to their professional future. Each of them must assess himself and the abilities, values, and aspirations which he brings to his training; each must attempt to assess the needs of society and evaluate the plethora of treatment modalities and mental health delivery systems; and each must evaluate the training and its suitability for society and for him as a unique individual. This is not an easy process for most trainees, particularly those in an analytically oriented training program which is also attempting to respond to the concept of community mental health. Trainees, too, may suspend time, keeping open the question of whether they should strive to meet the staggering mandate held up to them by our society, and deferring difficult choices which would seal the end of their professional adolescence.

Some psychiatric trainees solve the problem by opting for psychoanalytic training where the mandate is much clearer and less complex. Other trainees evidence a seemingly excessive preoccupation with the here and now which denigrates time and the importance of experiences over time. This preoccupation is reflected in a treatment approach which tends to ignore both the past and the future, eschewing history taking, careful diagnostic formulation, the question of appropriate technique, and the planning of short-term and long-range therapeutic goals. The training staff, being of another generation, may perceive a seeming lack of diligence in the pursuit of knowledge as evidenced in a casual attitude about attending seminars and an apparent lack of interest in reading the scientific literature. The trainee may solve the problem of coercion by his superego by externalizing it onto the staff who are seen as holding up impossible expectations while offering outdated and inadequate information and techniques.

This process of measuring oneself and one's culture and modifying one's ideals and aspirations requires relinquishments which may engender a sense of loss, feelings of depression, and a kind of mourning. In relation to the self, one may have to give up a long-held wish for perfection. Such a relinquishment during adolescence is comparable to a similar relinquishment which occurs during a successful analysis, frequently as a part of termination. In both instances, the acceptance of one's personal limitations, along with the reality that time is finite for everyone, causes a painful sense of loss. But this acceptance also has its rewards, since, after the sense of loss is worked through, the individual finds that he sets more reasonable goals which can be more readily met, and he enjoys a new-found sense of achievement and self-esteem. In relation to culture and society, one may have to give up some cherished ideals and learn to live with uncertainty, ambiguity, and only partially attainable goals. In this connection, I offer the recently made statement of a well-known public servant:

Throughout our history we believed that effort was its own reward. Partly because so much has been achieved here in America, we have tended to suppose that every problem must have a solution and that good intentions should somehow guarantee good results. Utopia was seen not as a dream, but as our logical destination if we only traveled the right road. Our generation is the first to find that the road is endless, that in traveling it we will find not utopia but ourselves. The realization of our essential loneliness accounts for so much of the frustration and rage of our time [Henry Kissinger, 1972].

Conclusion

In keeping with my stated intent, I have taken a developmental approach to the subject of transmission of cultural values and the revision of the superego and ego ideal in late adolescence. In drawing this paper to a close, it occurs to me that the developmental approach has another kind of relevance to this general topic, namely, the fact that a detailed knowledge and understanding of childhood development, particularly of the first months and years of life, offers the best basis for accomplishing the urgently needed change in our species and culture. The need for this change was posed by Freud (1930) more than 40 years ago in the closing paragraph of his essay on *Civilization and Its Discontents:*

> The fateful question for the human species seems to me to be whether and to what extent their cultural development will succeed in mastering the disturbance of their communal life by the human instinct of aggression and self-destruction. It may be that in this respect precisely the present time deserves a special interest. Men have gained control over the forces of nature to such an extent that with their help they would have no difficulty in exterminating one another to the last man. They know this, and hence comes a large part of their current unrest, their unhappiness and their mood of anxiety. And now it is to be expected that the other of the two 'Heavenly Powers,' [3] eternal *Eros,* will make an effort to assert himself in the struggle with his equally immortal adversary. But who can foresee with what success and with what result?

[3] In speaking of the eternal struggle between the trends of love and death, Freud was reminded of Goethe's moving arraignment of the "Heavenly Powers."

BIBLIOGRAPHY

BLOS, P. (1954), Prolonged Adolescence: The Formulation of a Syndrome and Its Therapeutic Implications. *Amer. J. Orthopsychiat.*, 24:733–742.
— (1967), The Second Individuation Process of Adolescence. *This Annual*, 22:162–186.
ERIKSON, E. H. (1940), Studies in the Interpretation of Play: I. Clinical Observation of Play Disruption. *Genet. Psychol. Monogr.*, 22:557–671.
— (1968), *Identity, Youth and Crisis*. New York: Norton.
— (1970), Reflections on the Dissent of Contemporary Youth. *Int. J. Psycho-Anal.*, 51:11–22.
FREUD, S. (1914), On Narcissism: An Introduction. *Standard Edition*, 14:69–102. London: Hogarth Press, 1961.
— (1930), Civilization and Its Discontents. *Standard Edition*, 21:64–145. London: Hogarth Press, 1961.
— (1933), New Introductory Lectures on Psycho-Analysis. *Standard Edition*, 22:3–182. London: Hogarth Press, 1964.
HARTMANN, H. & LOEWENSTEIN, R. M. (1962), Notes on the Superego. *This Annual*, 17:42–81.
JACOBSON, E. (1964), *The Self and the Object World*. New York: International Universities Press.
KISSINGER, H. (1972), *Time Magazine*, Feb. 7, p. 19.
LOEWALD, H. W. (1962), The Superego and the Ego-Ideal: Superego and Time. *Int. J. Psycho-Anal.*, 43:264–268.
LUSTMAN, S. L. (1971), Yale's Year of Confrontation: A View from the Master's House. *This Annual*, 27:57–73.
MAHLER, M. S. (1971), On the First Three Subphases of the Separation-Individuation Process. Read at the Plenary Session Panel, The Experience of Separation-Individuation and Its Reverberations Throughout the Course of Life, at the meetings of the American Psychoanalytic Association, New York.
SANDLER, J., HOLDER, A., & MEERS, D. (1963), The Ego Ideal and the Ideal Self. *This Annual*, 18:139–158.
SETON, P. H. (1971), Time and the Sense of History in Late Adolescence. Read at the meetings of the American Psychoanalytic Association, Washington.
SETTLAGE, C. F. (1971), On the Libidinal Aspect of Early Psychic Development and the Genesis of the Infantile Neurosis. In: *Separation-Individuation: Essays in Honor of Margaret S. Mahler*, ed. J. B. McDevitt & C. F. Settlage. New York: International Universities Press, pp. 131–154.
WINNICOTT, D. W. (1953), Transitional Objects and Transitional Phenomena. *Int. J. Psycho-Anal.*, 34:89–97.
— (1967), The Location of Cultural Experience. *Int. J. Psycho-Anal.*, 48:368–372.

The Function of the Ego Ideal in Adolescence

PETER BLOS, PH.D.

.

THE PSYCHOANALYTIC LITERATURE OVERFLOWS WITH STUDIES OF THE superego. In contrast, the ego-ideal investigations are rather sparse, yet cursory references to the ego ideal are ubiquitous. The result is that the imprecision of the term plagues us to this day. The distinction between superego and ego ideal has been discussed again and again, and so has the place of the ego ideal in mental organization been argued for a long time. Is the ego ideal a substructure of the ego or the superego? Does it acquire an affiliation with both in the course of development? No doubt superego and ego ideal have congruities and differences; emphasizing one or the other

Presented at the Seymour Lustman Memorial Panel on "Youth: One Year Later," held by the Association for Child Psychoanalysis, Inc., in Palm Springs, Calif., on March 26, 1972.

leads to different conclusions. Perhaps it is the stage of late adolescence where this issue can best be studied, clarified, and decided. Permit me a small introductory detour before I return to the topic of ego ideal.

The reciprocal influence of culture (environment) and internal structure formation is a familiar concept, as both shape and support each other throughout life. This is particularly true for the formative stages of childhood, of which late adolescence is the last one. Perhaps the most important psychic acquisition—important for the survival of the psychic organism—is the automatization of the stimulus barrier and the screening of stimuli in accordance with their particular usefulness for keeping developmental progression in flux. The interaction between the child and his human environment leads to internalization in consonance with maturational advances and thus promotes the formation of internal control agencies. However, the child's symbiotic oneness with the mother is only partially succeeded by internalization; a remaining residue can be traced in what Winnicott (1967) calls the space that lies between individual and environment, the prototype for the "location of culture."

This in-between space lends itself to many uses and abuses; one of its abuses lies in self-aggrandizement and in the search for concrete perfection, both of which are characteristics of late adolescence. My clinical impression of some of the angry or activist adolescents who seek the creation of a perfect society has led me to assume that their belief in a perfect world is rooted in an archaic belief in parental perfection. The "idealized parent imago" (Kohut, 1971), when externalized, lends a fanatical vision to the striving for a perfect world, while the narcissistic rage in the face of parental disillusionment finds a belated expression in the irrationality of violence. An imperfect world either must yield to correction or must be destroyed. The so-called faults of the parents reappear magnified to the size of unforgivable insults of debasement or evil. In some (I say: some) youthful revolutionaries we find the sense of political or historical logic either distorted by "absolutes" or rendered nonexistent by the overriding belief in perfection. Far from being delusional, this behavior and thinking reflect the externalization of the lost parental perfection; or, in other words, it is a sign of the painful effort to transcend the loss or to demand restitution in every possible way human imagination can conjure up.

The sense of perfection, especially self-perfection or its externalization, belongs in the realm of narcissism. It finds its everlasting reverberations in the formation of the ego ideal. Both ego ideal and superego begin to develop early in life, long before they assume the structure of a psychic agency. They originate in response to the external world and remain prone to re-externalization. What I want to emphasize here is the fact that the ego ideal is subject to qualitative and quantitative changes during the course of development. This is to say, the ego ideal becomes enmeshed with new drive modalities as well as with new ego competencies as both emerge at different developmental stages. By virtue of this fact, we can expect the ego ideal to become drawn into the turmoil in which the libidinal and aggressive drives partake during late adolescence.

Psychoanalytic theory has always emphasized the connection between ego ideal and narcissistic (libidinal) loss in infancy. The ego ideal is, no doubt, a narcissistic formation. In accordance with its origin (which also influences its function), the ego ideal is averse to object-libido involvement: its roots lie in primary narcissism. It perpetuates an eternal approximation to the narcissistic perfection of infancy. If we follow the course which the ego ideal follows from infancy to adulthood, we can trace a continuous adaptation of its basic function to the increasingly complex value system as it accrues along developmental lines. Thus, the ego ideal gets further and further removed from those primitive efforts which aim at narcissistic restitution. In fact, the ego ideal remains an ideal only as long as its goal cannot be attained. Whatever man accomplishes, imperfection remains an everlasting ingredient of his endeavors; yet this has never held man back from renewing his efforts. In contrast, superego demands can be met and can be satisfied. The superego is an agency of prohibition, while the ego ideal is an agency of aspiration.

During the oedipal conflict, the ego ideal becomes drawn into the triadic struggle of a sexualized love of both parents. I refer to the positive and the negative oedipus complex. The ego ideal does not remain unaffected by the passions of this period. In fact, the ego ideal acquires a new quality by being drawn into the narcissistic object relation of the negative oedipus complex. This development I have found rather typical for the boy. The ego ideal contains from here on neutralized object libido of a narcissistic kind or, in other words, homosexual libido.

We are familiar with the thought that during adolescence the superego reacquires a visual and especially auditory cathexis, as well as a reinstinctualization. It is my opinion that the ego ideal becomes drawn into a reinstinctualization with the reawakening of the positive and negative oedipus complex. Both oedipal positions press toward a definitive resolution at the time when sexual maturity requires a firm and definitive sexual identity. Gender identity is established early in life. Superego and ego ideal both become repersonified and drawn into the final resolution of the oedipus complex at the end of the second decade of life, or at the end of childhood.

A great deal has been written about superego pathology at adolescence, but very little about ego-ideal pathology. I have made the observation in the analysis of late adolescent male patients that the ego ideal remained an immature, self-idealizing, wish-fulfilling agency, resisting any transformation into a more mature, namely, abstracted, goal-intentional, and action-motivating force, as long as the young man's negative oedipus complex could not be drawn into the analytic work. I am certain analysts know from experience how laborious this aspect of analytic work is and, often, how impenetrable this aspect of the defensive organization remains in the analysis of the male adolescent. Some of the obstructions in the way toward adult personality formation can be relegated to ego-ideal pathology. Only after the analysis of the fixation of the negative oedipus complex can the formation of a workable, i.e., a mature, ego ideal take its normal course. This leads me to say that the ego ideal which emerges at the termination of adolescence is the heir to the negative oedipus complex. I assume that the adolescent psychic restructuring which progresses unaided by therapeutic help follows a similar course.

I started out with the description of the origin of the ego ideal in the stage of narcissistic perfection. I have carried the ensuing psychic trend into the triadic stage of narcissistic object choice and its cathexis with homosexual libido. The component instincts of scoptophilia and exhibitionism tend to present tenacious and pleasure-enhancing fixations which lie at the root of ego-ideal pathology. This condition is comparable to the well-known fact that a sexualized superego fails to perform its function and, instead, bogs down in moral sadism or moral masochism. It is the momentous task of adolescence to accomplish the deinstinctualization of the oedipal ego ideal and to restore its original function on a higher level of mental life. Only after this alteration in the nature of the ego ideal has been achieved during late adolscence can this agency become a firm guide to action and serve as the guardian of the sense of integrity, self-esteem, and love of the self. The study of ego-ideal pathology has emerged as a proper subject for investigation which promises to advance our understanding of late adolescence as a developmental stage.

As a behavioral parallel, I might mention the fact that the ego ideal of the latency child remains predominantly within the realm of concrete realization, while the late adolescent ego ideal tends to become abstracted, value- and idea-oriented. In the successful formation of the adolescent ego ideal, homosexual libido becomes bound, absorbed, i.e., neutralized. There lies the source of the forcefulness with which the ego ideal works. The ego ideal is perhaps the most uncompromising influence on the conduct of the mature individual: its position always remains unequivocal.

BIBLIOGRAPHY

Kohut, H. (1971), *The Analysis of the Self*. New York: International Universities Press.
Winnicott, D. W. (1967), The Location of Cultural Experience. *Int. J. Psycho-Anal.* 48:368–373.

Youth and the Campus

The Search for Social Conscience

ALBERT J. SOLNIT, M.D.

IN THIS REPORT I SHALL CONCENTRATE ON THE ADOLESCENT'S RE-
search, quest, or longing for assistance in developing a social conscience. I believe this represents a universal need, which also reflects the unfolding of biological and psychological forces within
each adolescent. As a backdrop to a developing social conscience
in adolescents, we can be dimly aware of how each adult and adult
group is tempted to recapture his or her own youth or to ward off
its impact by championing the causes of youth groups or, at the
opposite extreme, by opposing them. In a sense, the adults do no

Sterling Professor of Pediatrics and Psychiatry; Director, Child Study Center, Yale
University, New Haven.

Presented in part at the Seymour Lustman Memorial Panel on "Youth: One Year
Later," held by the Association for Child Psychoanalysis, Inc., in Palm Springs,
Calif., on March 26, 1972.

favor to an individual adolescent or to youth groups by adopting either of these extreme postures.

In an incisive paper, "Adolescent Process and the Need for Personal Confrontation" (1969), Winnicott points out that adults abdicate their responsibility to adolescents if they ignore them or submit to their point of view or challenges. Winnicott emphasizes our understanding that adolescents, in giving up their infantile ties to their parents, undergo a developmental crisis of great intensity. In 1958 Anna Freud compared this developmental task to the process of mourning. As we know, the relinquishment of the dormant oedipal longings that are reawakened for this formative developmental separation is perceived as a painful, haunting loss —one not easily compensated for by the acceptance of the certainties of one's sex role and mortality.

Residues of infantile omnipotent longings are also further relinquished. The safety of certain regressive relationships and expectations is no longer acceptable. This process occurs at a time when biological and psychological forces combine to render the adolescent a rapidly changing, unstable, reforming individual.

Winnicott believes that the confrontation between adolescent and adult is a particularly compelling one because both realize that the adolescent will replace the adult. He suggests that the boundaries of mortality and immortality are set forth in this confrontation. He further gives evidence that the anguish of this psychological separation and confrontation is intolerably heightened during those periods when the adolescent has characteristic murderous feelings toward the parent.

The need for institutionalized social alternatives to meet the adolescent's quest for independence is universal. This need has been intensified by the conflicts and convergences created by two diametrically opposed forces: on the one hand, biological maturation now occurs at a much earlier time; on the other, the period of enforced dependency has been further prolonged by our educational, social, and political requirements (all institutionalized).[1] In another paper (1971) I have raised questions about the ways in which the changes in biological timetables, the changes in the so-

---

[1] This is also changing; e.g., the voting age has recently been lowered to 18 years.

cial-cultural-psychological expectations, and the rapidly increasing technological changes wrought on our physical and psychological environment have influenced adolescent experiences and development. The lack of viable, institutionalized, social alternatives for adolescents to express their independent and rebellious stirrings thwarts a tendency of adolescents to find altruistic solutions to their conflicts. Altruistic solutions are sought because adolescents tend to feel unworthy and in need of evidence that they are worthy. Self-esteem is a sensitive barometer of the direction and outcome of developmental storms during adolescence.

There is another view of that part of superego development that deals with social conscience. By social conscience I refer to the individual's capacity to feel self-approval or self-disapproval of his motives and behavior as they relate to his social group, neighborhood, and larger community. Of course, the primary social group, the family, which is the context of and the target of this behavior, is a primary determinant of social conscience.

> Youth has made it clear that it is far more mature and potentially responsible than the older generation has been prepared to admit [is one of the conclusions reached by a recent conference on the "Mental Health of Adolescents and Young Persons" conducted under the auspices of The World Health Organization at a 5-day conference of more than 50 behavioral and social scientists from 27 European, African and Mediterranean countries. This conference also concluded:] There is no doubt that today's youth is troubled, but previous generations had similar problems. The difference today lies in the fact that this is a more condensed world, a world that is every day becoming more and more depersonalized, a world that quite a few young people cannot identify with, for reasons that are intrinsic in the rapid technological society in which they grow up [WHO Public Health Paper #41].

Thus, the search for social alternatives to those offered by the family is motivated by the urgent needs to leave the family and to resolve the discrepancies between the ego ideal and the individual's capacities; to manage the rebellious, angry feelings toward the parents and the invitations to unacceptable regressive behavior toward and relationships with the parents. As Blos (1972) has indicated, the ego ideal serves narcissistic needs as well as the disguised attachment to the idealized parents.

In adolescence, particularly in mid- and late adolescence, the longing for experiences which will bolster the loosened superego's functions and which will form a bulwark against regressive tendencies is often felt as a need, as a yearning to serve tenuously held ideals in a concrete manner. Since the individual's yearning often cannot compete with regressive tendencies without outside or group support, there is an added interest in joining a group in order to borrow strength from the group's cohesiveness and the group identifications. If there is a conflict in choice between a rebellious or altruistic group, it signifies that neither group sufficiently fulfills simultaneously the individual adolescent's needs to rebel and bolster a shaky self-esteem.

For this reason altruistic aims must be coupled with a rebellion against parental values and finding a "better than thou" identity. In psychoanalytic treatment it often becomes clear that the identification with the parental values is disguised in order to be acceptable to the adolescent as he resists the regressive pull to avoid growing up. In fact, there is often a technical problem in the analysis of the 16- to 20-year-old adolescent as to when and how to interpret the hidden identifications with their parents that are contained in the rebellious, assertive, independent strivings represented by their values, activities, and fantasies. Probably, youth has always searched for a way in which to express a sense of personal worth through social participation in laudable group activities.

These adolescent longings can be characterized as the need to exercise a social conscience [2] in concert with others. In fact, when viewed from the perspective of individual development and psychopathology in adolescence, this patterned tendency is subjectively experienced with ebbing and flowing intensities in an appetitive way. For example, students who have arduously and long fought for representation on certain committees will then attend meetings quite erratically. Yet this longing or wish can be sustained by a receptive and nourishing group setting; or the wish

[2] My interest in the search and need for a social conscience in adolescents has developed in part as a result of discussions with Anna Freud, Joseph Goldstein, Seymour L. Lustman, and Lottie M. Newman.

can be blurred and diminished by the lack of such a setting. In other words, the adolescent's ability to work through toward mastery of the urge to express a social conscience as a member of a group can be encouraged and sustained, or it can be discouraged and diminished by the human setting in which the individual adolescent or group of adolescents are living and working. The social-political environment and the intuitive or deliberate understanding and value of such youth proclivities held by the adult leaders of a given community, culture, or nation are crucial influences in the options offered to and felt by adolescents.

These options provide psychoanalysts with an opportunity systematically to apply their knowledge about adolescents' vital needs, including the need to maintain attachments to important adults while changing their relationships to these adults. In this connection I am also referring to the needs of parents, grandparents, and other adults who remain engaged with adolescents.

Although we have given a good deal of attention to how the mother in early childhood facilitates, or interferes with, the infant's development, psychoanalysts have not been as systematic in relating the planning and behavior of adults to the vital needs of adolescents. Here I can give only the barest outline and emphasize some of the specific difficulties or requirements of adult behavior in facilitating adolescent development.

Unlike the infant whose needs are more clear-cut, the adolescent is pulled by regressive forces and pushed by maturational thrusts. Almost all of the adolescent's felt needs are in this way conflicted:

1. The need to relinquish his ties with the primary love objects is painfully opposed by the regressive attraction exerted by the revival of oedipal longings.

2. The need to find and become himself as an increasingly independent person is complicated by his real dependence on the persons against whom he has to rebel and on his old "crowd" of friends and peers who commonly drift apart.

3. The need to seek lofty, respectable ideals and values that are his own is, to a considerable extent, fueled by (less lofty) sexual and aggressive appetitive impulses.

4. The need to reintegrate or reorganize the personality struc-

ture requires more time than the tensions created by such a restructuring permit, frequently leading the adolescent to adopt a restricted or premature solution in order to gain relief from the intolerable tensions.

How can the psychoanalytic understanding of these crucial adolescent needs and conflicts, in the context of sound relationships with adults, lead to constructive social planning and expectations? It is essential for the adults, in guiding themselves, to be aware of their needs as well as those of the adolescents. In this connection, there may be many detours, but the alternatives of either submitting to a tyranny of adolescent demands and views or of defeating adolescent aspirations with an adult tyranny do not offer a healthy or constructive solution to a desirable and inevitable dilemma.

In fact, these unfruitful alternatives remind us of the technical error made by a psychoanalyst who sides with or rejects either one or the other side of the conflict in an ambivalent patient.

Guidelines for the parent or the leaders of the community should include the following:

1. Respect the rebellious criticisms and assertions, but on the merits of the situation express tactfully and firmly the disagreement that is a respectful expression of the adult's or community's point of view and values.

2. Do not assume that the adolescent criticism or assertion is the request for the authority and responsibility to deal with the socioeconomic, political, or educational dilemma.

3. Avoid the temptation to react with indifference because the adolescent has neither the power, nor the authority, nor the experience to take on sustained leadership or responsibilities in a peaceful, nontroubled situation. This guideline can be stated positively by formulating it as an opportunity to enable the adolescent to prepare for adult activities through "working-through" encounters with those whose place he or she will be taking.

4. Provide a reasonable range of viable alternative social and work opportunities for adolescents to express their interest in changing or improving the community according to the altruistic values that are selected by them as their own values for the community or world they hope to create. This includes a wide range of educational, work, and political channels which adolescents can

select because they are an institutionalized expression of their criticisms and aspirations.

One could say that an adult who wishes to function as a youth leader with these guidelines must, like the analyst, have a clear understanding of his own social conscience. He would exercise his social conscience in response to what Heinz Hartmann referred to as the "value testing function" (1960) . Moreover, since my emphasis is on "social conscience," an effective group leader would need more than an awareness of the development of his own individual conscience and the history of the social values he holds. He also should have a sophisticated view and understanding of the highly complex forces at work in society.

This, to my mind, is an important area for psychoanalysts to collaborate with others in developing a profession and the career of youth leaders. It follows in part the model of August Aichhorn who trained a number of young men and women to be such youth leaders. For the most part they were originally trained as educators and social workers who were analyzed and had analytic training. However, this model did not become systematically elaborated into a new profession, perhaps for the same reason that psychoanalytic contributions to current youth problems have failed to be as useful as they could be. That is, the psychoanalyst's view of individual adolescent pathology is valuable for these purposes only when it is combined with knowledge about group phenomena, education, and certain aspects of social science theory and its applications.

When we view the challenge and potential of those, the adolescents, who will become the next wave of adults, we should realize that we are also confronting the needs of our older adults. Will we make way gracefully and responsibly, not as acts of submission and not as acts of conquest, but as an ongoing dynamic process of collaboration in which each needs the other? For the older adult it represents a search for immortality and passing on in a responsible fashion the resources and issues of the next epoch. In this way the adults help to identify the pathways into which the social conscience of the individual adolescent and the collective conscience of adolescent social groups can be directed or channeled.

For adolescents the search for a social conscience is one of the major processes that enables each individual adolescent to relinquish childhood ties with the primary love objects, to rebel and somewhat independently to experiment and explore socially, sexually, and aggressively, forging individual values and self-esteem as the individual moves toward the integration of his or her adult personality.

It is my thesis that the search for social conscience has a changing, unstable expression unless the adult community and society provide viable, alternative, institutionalized opportunities for youth to express this interest and need. Where the adolescent's developmental needs and the adult's constructive involvement are joined through institutionalized forms of expression, each generation can maintain its integrity at the same time as they can cooperate. Youth's search for a social conscience that is an expression of their active choice, creation, and elaboration, and the adult's search for continuity which does not blur the distinctions of generational differences, can be seen in religious, ethnic, political, social, educational, athletic, and conquest-of-nature organizations and institutions. These junctures can be constructive or destructive of the relationships of adolescents and adults; they can heighten or they can reduce conflict; they can facilitate conflict resolution and continuity; or they can increase the resistance to conflict resolution.

BIBLIOGRAPHY

Blos, P. (1972), The Function of the Ego Ideal in Late Adolescence. *This Annual,* 27:93–97.

Freud, A. (1958), Adolescence. *This Annual,* 13:255–278.

Hartmann, H. (1960), *Psychoanalysis and Moral Values.* New York: International Universities Press.

Solnit, A. J. (1971), Adolescence and the Changing Reality. In: *Currents in Psychoanalysis,* ed. I. Marcus. New York: International Universities Press, pp. 98–110.

Winnicott, D. W. (1969), Adolescent Process and the Need for Personal Confrontation. *Pediatrics,* 44:752–756.

WHO *Public Health Paper* #41, "Mental Health of Adolescents and Young Persons."

The Epigenesis of the Adult Neurosis

PETER BLOS, PH.D.

IT IS THE INTENT OF THIS PAPER TO DELINEATE THE SPECIFIC CONTRI-
bution of adolescence to the formation of the adult neurosis. Even
though only one aspect of this issue will be explored here, its precise conceptualization should sharpen the clinical eye and lead to
the investigation of other, related problems, such as, for example,
the shift from a particular childhood neurosis to the somewhat different neurosis that might emerge during the postadolescent period. It is not a daring assertion to state that the psychic restructuring that takes place in adolescence exerts, in some fashion, a
decisive influence on the adult personality, regardless of whether
the outcome of this process is a normal or a pathological one.

My presentation will start by discussing, first, the concept of the

Faculty, New York Psychoanalytic Institute.

infantile neurosis from a developmental point of view. In the course of that discussion, I shall have to take another look at some well-known facts pertaining to the distinction between child and adult neurosis as well as to transference and transference neurosis. I do this in order to indicate the links which connect my proposition with the body of psychoanalytic theory. In tracing the formation of the adult neurosis, I shall be paying special attention to adolescence, particularly late adolescence. Finally, I shall support my thesis with clinical material. The way in which my proposition affects both theory and technique will be dealt with throughout the entire paper.

A Developmental View of the Infantile Neurosis

The psychoanalytic tenet that an infantile emotional disturbance lies at the core of every adult neurosis has survived the many years of discussion that the concept of the infantile neurosis has evoked. This clinical fact has become so closely linked with the definition of the adult neurosis that the latter has often been construed as the mere repetition or continuation of an illness that originated in prelatency. This simplistic formulation, however, has been challenged by child observation, longitudinal studies, and child analysis, which have pointed out the diffuse and transitory nature of most infantile disturbances, as well as the fact that these are, more or less, a ubiquitous part of normal child development. It has been generally accepted, moreover, that prelatency disturbances are unreliable predictive indicators of the nature and severity of an adult illness. No uniquely delineated clinical entity constituting the infantile neurosis has been found by the observer of early childhood, nor, conversely, are neurotic compromise solutions of an internalized conflict ever absent from early childhood; yet, in every analysis of an adult neurosis—every analysis, that is, of the transference neurosis type—the infantile neurosis makes its never-failing appearance.

From longitudinal studies, says Anna Freud (1965), "there emerged first a disappointing discovery concerning a discrepancy between infantile and adult neurotics . . . there is no certainty that a particular type of infantile neurosis will prove to be the forerunner of the same type of adult neurosis. On the contrary, there is much clinical evidence which points in the opposite direction" (p. 151f.). Once we acknowledge the prognostic fallibility of the so-called infantile neurosis, we are forced to discard the idea of any direct monocausal connection between the specific nature of an infantile disturbance and the specific nature of an adult neurosis. For example, a phobic neurosis of childhood may well change, in adulthood, into a compulsive-obsessional neurosis.[1]

A further dissimilarity appears in the degree to which symptoms or personality traits are integrated into the personality structure. In children, these can exist in a rather insular separateness, while the neurosis in the adult has permeated the entire personality structure, so that what we encounter is a highly structured and stable organization. As early as 1935, Waelder-Hall observed, in the classical child analysis of a pavor nocturnus case (Anton, age 7) : "What is really missing in this conflict is a picture of genuine compromise formation; instead we still have the conflict itself, instinctual drive and anxiety coexisting directly side by side. . . . The adult neurosis always presents a solution of the conflict, even if it be an unsuccessful, neurotic resolution" (p. 273).

The fact that such analytic observations have failed to be investigated in extenso may be attributed to the unqualified acceptance of Freud's belief in the universality of the infantile neurosis,[2] as well as to a literal adherence to Freud's statement that the neurosis of childhood represents "a type and model" of the adult neurosis (1909, p. 147). Genetic connections along these lines are borne out in every adult analysis, despite the fact that an infantile neurosis has not been demonstrable as a clinical entity in early childhood. No analyst would question that in "every case the later neurotic illness links up with the prelude in childhood" (Freud,

---

[1] I am not referring here to Frankie, who was presented by Ritvo (1966) as an example of the change of a neurosis from childhood (phobia) to adulthood (obsessional neurosis). It is my opinion that Frankie's illness belongs to the "borderline" disturbances and therefore lies outside the scope of the present study, which is restricted to the transference neurosis.

[2] "We know that a human child cannot successfully complete its development to the civilized stage without passing through a phase of neurosis sometimes of greater and sometimes of less distinctness. . . . Most of these infantile neuroses are overcome spontaneously in the course of growing up, and this is especially true of the obsessional neuroses of childhood" (Freud, 1927, p. 42).

1940, p. 184) . It is, however, a by now generally accepted opinion that the neurotic illness of the adult did not pre-exist in an immutable form from the prelatency years up to the time when it irrupts in the form of the adult neurosis. The maturation of the ego during latency and adolescence has effected distinctive psychological alterations, even though the original trauma or nuclear conflict remains preserved under the many layers of cumulative revisions.

We shall now turn from viewing the infantile neurosis retrospectively, and, in contrast, take a forward look at the possible sequels to a childhood disturbance. We stand on the firm ground of clinical observation when we say that certain aspects or components of a childhood disturbance can undergo changes with time, lose their neurotic valence, and arrive at a nonconflictual adaptive solution. On the other hand, they may become amalgamated with neurotic trends that have acquired a hegemonic position during the course of growing up. In this regard, the impact of accidental factors always remains unpredictable. It is by no means a novel idea that the irruption of a neurotic illness can be averted, despite the existence of a neurotic potential, whenever the growing individual is able to draw on constitutional resources, object relations, and environmental conditions so as to work out a serviceable adaptation to life.[3]

Such a favorable outcome is often helped along by the fact that possession of a special propensity—called gift, talent, "knack" or "bent"—facilitates the resolution of internal disharmonies. The individual's neurotic potential, however, continues to exist throughout his life; indeed, it may serve as both incentive and activator or, on the other hand, constitute a unique vulnerability. Both conditions, however, lend direction to the individual's adaptive tendencies and evoke his adaptive inventiveness: the mastery of early trauma, which is generally cumulative in nature, has become, under these conditions, a "life task" (Blos, 1962, pp. 132–136) . Freud wrote in a letter to Ferenczi: "One should not try to

---

[3] "There is no yardstick for the pathogenic potential of infantile neurosis except for the long-run developmental consideration. We have to bear in mind that every new phase of maturation creates new potential conflict situations and new ways to deal with these conflicts; but, on principle, it also carries with it, to a certain degree, the possibility of modifying the impact of earlier conflict solutions" (Hartmann, in Kris et al., 1954, p. 35) . See also Freud (1927, p. 42f.) .

eradicate one's complexes, but to come to terms with them; they are legitimate guiding forces of one's behavior in the world" (Jones, 1955, p. 452). Loewald pursues a related thought when he speaks of "repetition as re-creation," in contrast to "repetition as reproduction" (1971b, p. 60).

The foregoing considerations lead to the conclusion that there is no rigid causal chain between an infantile trauma and a later neurotic illness. The causality always remains one of *retrospective* determination and verification, both of these being exemplified in the work of reconstruction. From the study of creative persons, artists and charismatic personalities, we have come to comprehend, on a grand scale, the complex vicissitudes of the neurotic potential. Perhaps on a smaller scale a similar adaptive inventiveness is operative and, under favorable circumstances, this serves to keep the neurotic potential from consolidating into a neurotic illness.

Neurosogenesis appears, in this perspective, as an uninterrupted process of elaborating the neurosis. This process starts with an incipient injury to the psychic organism and then establishes a neurotic potential. This potential is laid down early in life, yet reaches its terminal stage only later when, in the form of the adult neurosis, an illness has irrupted that remains unalterable and irreversible by ordinary life circumstances. We have come to view the infantile neurosis as a specific potential, which may or may not lead to a neurotic illness in adult life. One could, indeed, question the usefulness and the correctness of postulating the existence of an infantile neurosis, if no adult neurosis, so to speak, ever materializes. Of one fact, however, we are sure: namely, that the infantile neurosis takes on its definitive structure and content only during the formative stage of the adult neurosis, when we acquire full knowledge of its existence through the transference neurosis—that is to say, only during analytic treatment (Tolpin, 1970, p. 277).

The formative stage of the adult neurosis often coincides with the period of adolescence—specifically, with late adolescence. After that point, the adult neurosis can make its appearance as the organized assemblage of selective and crucial experiences, impressions, and affects of an injurious nature, experienced during early childhood; together, these mark the fixation points—the characteristic etiological feature of every neurosis—and they are summarized under the concept of "infantile trauma." Greenacre speaks of "fixation to a pattern, rather than only to a phase" (Kris et al., 1954, p. 22). If these earliest interferences with normal development have then been carried forward to the phallic-oedipal level, they thereby come into a position to determine, to a great extent, the particular constellation of the triadic conflict that emerges (p. 18). However, should they fail to have thus been carried forward in sufficient strength, then the neurosis in later life is likely to show features that are characteristic of the preverbal, the dyadic, stage of development, or else the emotional illness will probably belong in the category of the borderline disturbances. In order to protect the clarity of my exposition, I have restricted myself to a discussion of the transference neuroses. Excluded from consideration are, therefore, those disturbances of child and adult that are, exclusively or predominantly, due to developmental deficits—i.e., faulty psychic structure—rather than to internal conflict, its neurotic solutions, and their debilitating consequences.

Since the structuralization of the neurosis is the outcome of a disequilibrium or conflict between the psychic agencies, it is necessarily contingent on both the intrinsic and the relative maturational strength of those agencies. This assumption is basic to the understanding of the neurosis, whether child or adult neurosis. If we contemplate for a moment the enormous difference between the prelatency and the late adolescent ego, we should not be surprised to discover different solutions of a basic neurotic conflict at each of these two stages. Whatever the outcome, we shall recognize in the respective conflict solutions, at different developmental levels, the history of the ego, which leaves its distinctive marks on the structuralization of any resolution of a disequilibrizing condition. The adaptive outcome, whether neurotic or healthy, if it is traced along a developmental continuum, cannot remain identical throughout and therefore cannot be regarded as unchanging or unchangeable.

Attempts have been made to distinguish between a child neurosis and an adult neurosis in terms of the nature, in each, of transference, resistance, and working through. The child's emotional dependence, together with the incompleteness of his physical maturation, necessarily sets limits to the analyzability of the pathogenetic potential. The aim of child analysis can be defined as helping the child to regain the developmental momentum commensurate with his age. Such an achievement, however, will not necessarily protect the child from the emotional hazards that are inherent in the process of growing up. We are never certain, in child analysis, how comprehensively the therapeutic process has eliminated the pathogenetic potential. The well-known fact that a relatively large number of analyzed children take up their analyses once again in later life—during adolescence or young adulthood—may find its explanation in the ideas outlined above.

Late adolescence signals the termination of childhood. As an integrative process it recapitulates, on a higher level of psychic functioning, an advance toward independence and autonomy that I have elsewhere conceptualized as the "second individuation process" in adolescence (Blos, 1967). Not until biological maturation has been attained, and not until sexual maturity compels a definitive break with infantile positions, will the neurotic potential—assuming it still possesses sufficient pathogenetic valence—become reorganized on a higher level of integration as the adult neurosis. This view of the adult neurosis gives the term "epigenesis" a special fitness in the title of this paper, in that it reminds us of the Harveian theory, according to which the embryo is built up gradually by the addition of one part after another in an orderly sequence and rising complexity. To this should be added that in the process some parts may atrophy, lose their function, and become atavistic relics of the past. The opposing theory is, of course, the one of "preformation" or of "encasement," which is as obsolete to the biologist as its implication runs contrary to the nature of neurosogenesis.

Distinguishing between the latent and the manifest state of the neurosis is a time-honored aspect of psychoanalytic theory. It is the latent state that has been conceptualized as the infantile neurosis. Freud (1939) has related the two in the following passage: "Not until later [after latency] does the change take place with which the definitive neurosis becomes manifest as a belated effect of the trauma. This occurs either at the irruption of puberty or some while later" [4] (p. 77). There are indeed many references in

---

[4] A German-language equivalent of the word "adolescent" was not yet in existence when Freud wrote this passage in 1939. *Adoleszenz* has entered the German language only lately. Until then, the German word for adolescence was puberty (*Pubertät*);

Freud's writing to the biphasic nature of neurosogenesis, to which the traumatic neuroses present an exception. When the neurotic disposition becomes manifest in adolescence—namely, when the infantile trauma impedes, distorts, or catastrophically disrupts the age-appropriate conduct of life, by way of symptom formation—then that illness constitutes the "definitive neurosis." My implication here is that the "definitive neurosis" is identical with the adult neurosis and, furthermore, that concomitantly with the formation of the adult neurosis, the infantile neurosis springs to life, as it were, acquiring delineation and structure. The two are complementary formations: both depend on an advanced stage of ego development for their structuralization, and they are forced into existence simultaneously by the adaptive demands that physical maturation, instinctual development, and social fitting-in exert on the growing personality. The normative regression in the service of development promotes adolescent psychic restructuring (Blos, 1962). Adolescent regression facilitates the overhauling of earlier faulty development at the terminal stage of childhood— namely, at late adolescence—and brings about (if all goes well) a settlement of those early conflictual residues or surviving inner disharmonies that would otherwise obstruct the formation of the post-adolescent personality. To this process we have assigned the term of consolidation.[5]

The structuralization of the adult neurosis is linked inherently with the developmental stage of late adolescence. This is the stage of life, as noted above, at which physical growth is completed and sexual maturity attained. In terms of psychosexual development, the major step forward to maturity consists in the relegation of pregenital drive modalities to the realm of forepleasure, thus rendering them subordinate and at the same time establishing a hier-

---

this one term was used to refer to both the stage of physical maturation and the concurrent psychological characteristics.

[5] Erikson (1968) had something similar in mind when he proposed the concept of the "psychosocial moratorium" and of the "identity crisis." The "Who am I?" query of the late adolescent arises, so it seems to me, out of the confrontations between the almost-adult and the still-childhood positions, during the alternating movements of regression and progression, as typical of the late adolescent period. Subjectively, this is felt as a transient diffusion of the self—which can also be said with reference to the process of consolidation.

archical drive constellation called genitality. The attainment of genital primacy (not to be confused with heterosexual activity) is gradual and usually remains incomplete. It is a rare instance that does not fall short of the ideal model.

Psychoanalytic theory and practice have left no doubt that the oedipus complex is reactivated in adolescence and that the individual lives through it once again. Far from this being a replication of its earlier edition, it would be more correct to say that the revived oedipus complex is this time carried toward its final resolution on a higher level of integration, while the individual moves toward a more definitive mastery of the attendant conflicts. The relatively advanced stage of the ego leads to the first "decline" of the oedipus complex, inaugurating the latency period; the second "decline," which takes place during adolescence, inaugurates adulthood. The respective resolutions will therefore be dissimilar, regardless of whether they are normal or pathological in nature. When we compare the outcomes of the two stages, one crucial point of difference appears: the coexistence of the positive and negative oedipus complex can be tolerated in childhood with far greater equanimity than it can in adolescence; at the latter stage, a decisive intolerance has developed, because of the social and maturational pressure toward the formation of a definitive and irreversible sexual identity (Blos, 1965, p. 162). The fact that the valence of the negative oedipus complex cannot be gauged with certainty during child analysis—especially not in terms of the potentiality of its resurgence at puberty—invites the assumption that, at the threshold of the latency period, the oedipal conflict has been brought only to a partial resolution and a correspondingly relative quietude. Neither the issues nor their forms of settlement are identical at the two stages of oedipal conflict. It was physical immaturity that brought the original oedipus complex to its first decline, and it is physical maturity that must bring it to its later definitive and irreversible resolution. The phase of late adolescence becomes, then, the Armageddon of the adult neurosis.

The personality changes that mark the termination of adolescence are those of integration and differentiation. On a complex level, this process is demonstrated in character formation (Blos, 1968). In their totality, psychological changes in the late adolescent personality are subsumed under the concept of consolidation. The "definitive neurosis," i.e., the adult neurosis, is the product of the consolidation process, which encompasses the entire pre-adult personality, and at the close of which an irreversible demarcation line has been drawn between childhood and adulthood. The synthetic function of the ego is relentlessly at work all through this stage, for better or for worse, in that the consolidation process effects normal as well as pathological personality organization.

The late adolescent patient thus confronts the analyst with a paradoxical situation. Developmentally, the patient is involved in the consolidation of the adult neurosis; on the other hand, the fact that this integrative process is still an ongoing one works against his involvement in the analytic process—except, by and large, on the level of acute, here-and-now discomforts and their relief. The attainment of the adult neurosis would, no doubt, facilitate genuine analyzability, a situation that poses a real dilemma for the analyst: he either forestalls the formation of the adult neurosis by interpretative pre-emption, or he hastens its formation so as to get the definitive analytic work under way. In many cases it becomes perfectly clear that the adolescent is not actually resisting analysis; yet, because of his limited involvement, his analyzability is, often unfairly, doubted. The burden of this "impasse" rests heavily on the analyst if he loses sight of the developmental process of late adolescence and attempts to proceed as if the adult neurosis already existed. The resultant ineffectiveness of his interpretations readily mobilizes narcissistic defenses in the analyst himself; these have the effect of beclouding, slowing down, or foreclosing the analysis of the adolescent patient. The difficulties, indeed, the inadvisability of adolescent analysis, have been debated for many years. A good portion of these difficulties, however, stems from a misapprehension of the adolescent process, one reflection of which appears in the technical dilemma I have alluded to.

Clinical Illustration

An 18-year-old male college student started analysis following an inexplicable yet total academic failure: his inability to study had, in fact, acquired the nature of a symptom. The onset of the difficulty had been so precipitous, and its severity so massive, that analytic treatment was indicated: a neurotic inhibition of intellectual functioning was threatening to wreck the life of an intelligent young man. Obviously, the presenting symptom only masked the many inroads through which the pathology had been extending its debilitating influence over the total personality. The emotional immaturity had become manifest in the one area that represented to the patient, more than any other, the symbolic attainment of maturity and independence—in short, of oedipal rivalry.

When the patient entered analysis, he was quite well aware of the fact that he could not deal with the problem of academic failure by himself. He realized the utter irrationality of his procrastinations, his continual hoping against hope to succeed, his compulsive disregard of the passage of time until no time was left to make up for time lost. Unwittingly, he had been inviting defeat, in spite of his unshakable intention to study, and in spite of the painful humiliation that his dismissal from college entailed. In brief, when the patient entered analysis, it was with a positive attitude and a genuine desire to resolve an acute problem: he readily acknowledged the irrationality of his behavior, being already aware of his emotional discomfort and loss of direction.

The patient was sophisticated enough to accept and follow the basic rule. He never missed any of his 5 weekly hours: he talked easily, reporting current events, fantasies, dreams, and childhood memories. In short, he behaved like a good patient. Nevertheless, something was missing that made the analytic work drag and stumble. While it is true that recollections, memories, reports on the day's happenings, fantasies, and life-history data had been piling up voluminously during the course of the first year of analysis, no "grand design" had yet emerged that would lend organization and continuity—in essence, meaning—to the patient's stream of communications.

The area of neurotic conflict, as well as the defensive organization, had already become evident within the first week of treatment. A dream and a transient obsessional thought will serve as illustrations. The patient brought the following dream to the first hour:

> I am in a restaurant with a friend. President Johnson drives
> up in a black car with his entourage. The car is about 15 years

old. It is a convertible. I was supposed to follow him and I drive a car after him. I didn't know which pedal to push, which one was the brake. Then my father was there. I got afraid and drove away [silence]. There was one more thing: there was a girl in the path of my car. I couldn't stop the car. Then the car stopped by itself, just touching her.

After he had finished telling the dream, the patient's mind went "blank." He was obviously blocked when he was "supposed to follow" the analyst's directions—namely, to let his mind "drive along." Instead, he put the brakes on, for fear of "losing control" of his mind. He "got afraid and drove away." Loss of emotional control and fear of the father seemed intrinsically interrelated here; flight was the only escape from both of them. Inhibitions and avoidances had become his "safety measures"; they represented the defensive organization that governed his life.

The historical dating of the President's car, which he is "supposed to follow" in his dream, places the height, if not the onset, of the neurotic anxiety at the age of about 3—namely, at the phallic-oedipal phase. The beginning of the dream ("in a restaurant with a friend") and its end ("there was a girl in the path of my car") tie the dream to the actuality of the patient's present life (day residue)—namely, to his fervent wish for friendship with boys and for emotional closeness to a girl. The unattainability of both was painfully felt by him like a strangled spontaneity, which had been impairing and bruising his social relationships for some time, especially since his expulsion from college.

The second indication of a central source of anxiety I found in a transient obsessional thought to which he gave expression during the third and fourth session. After he had assured me that he had to control his mind, since he wished to speak only of "relevant things," he suddenly became fascinated by a minute crack in the ceiling of my office. His mind remained "riveted" to the crack; all he could manage to say was, "It makes me think of nothing." Lewin's (1948, p. 525) comment on the thought of "nothing" led me to guess that both the female genital and a preoccupation with castration lay embedded in this patient's passivity and inhibition. No interpretation was given to him.

It is a common experience in analysis that a patient's first-reported dream or fantasy contains—in a nutshell, as it were—the

central conflict of his neurosis. Any conclusion that is drawn from
the opening stage of analysis, however, remains nothing more than
an educated guess: its verification, modification, or refutation has
to come during the course of treatment. Verification did come, indeed—but only after a waiting time of a year and a half.

The first phase of this patient's analysis (18 months) was given
over, as has been mentioned, to the obedient reporting of events,
past and present; but the associative inconclusiveness prevented
any genetic continuity from emerging. Much of the analytic time
was devoted to the accumulation of a thorough inventory of his life
history, including his secret memories and fantasies, as well as
those fears and wishes that had remained part of his conscious
memory. This does not mean to say that the analyst did not make
any use of the given material to help the patient recognize the psychological wellsprings of his affects and actions. However, such interpretations, while accepted by the patient, were kept by him
within the confines of the particular problem defined by him; as a
result, insights could not branch out, beyond a limited range of
actuality, into a deepening analytic collaboration.

The patient's hunger for understanding and insight was clearly
considerable and compelling; the analyst's attitude, of course, com-
plemented the patient's wish. Yet, instead of a genuine therapeutic
alliance, what the patient had contrived was an illusory empathic
liaison: "the two of us both want to understand." The patient was
obviously trying to please the analyst, whom he had put into the
role of an idealized father who would "understand," rather than
judge by achievement.

This spontaneous transference accounted for the good rapport;
but it also made the patient scan his mind in search of mental content that would please the analyst and afford the patient a favored
position in his affection and respect. Throughout this time, he remained cooperative, rather jovial, and pal-like.

There were many indications that he was imitating admired
persons, friends and family members, by using their idioms, gestures, and intonations. These imitations he employed as enhance-
ments of his own lovability and unique worth. Every communication had to be of special meaningfulness and extraordinary interest
and relevance; otherwise, it was not worth his talking about it.

The transference aspect of this selectivity was apparent enough; [6] yet neither transference nor resistance interpretations were of any noticeable consequence. I decided, finally, to refrain from such interpretations, after they had started to become repetitious, even though the material clamored for such comment. The analyst's persistence in repeating, driving home the psychologically obvious, was here rendered decisively more moderate by my theoretical propositions and by my engagement in their clinical investigation.

The first 18 months of analysis were thus taken up with an effort to bring the patient's own affects, moods, and fantasies to his awareness. Most helpful in this process, incidentally, was the patient's verbal expression of his inner stirrings in the presence of an attentive listener and, conversely, his listening to the analyst's comments. Spoken words and their responsive echoes render the elusive self-perceptions of the patient's inner life more real and observable (conscious) than they were before, when they existed in the caverns of contemplative silence (preconscious). By this laborious process, data belonging to the conscious layer of the mind were dynamically altered as well. In that way, these same data, having changed their quality through a new cathectic investment, were rendered more useful for the subsequent analytic work.

Dynamic, but not genetic, interpretations were given; yet even these were limited, because they were given outside the orbit of the transference and before the therapeutic alliance—in contradistinction to rapport and cooperation—was established. The analyst as a person was erased by the patient's relating himself instead to an ideal father figure, who would accept lovingly the verbal gifts of an obedient son. Those longings were gratified whenever I gave proof of the fact that I remembered some detail of what he had told me some time before.[7] The belief in the omnipotence of the

6 The fact that these transference aspects are part of a regressive activation of the "grandiose self" as well as of the "idealized parent image" (Kohut, 1971) will not occupy us here, because the case under discussion does not belong among the narcissistic disorders described by Kohut. However, it is of interest to note that Kohut's formulations have an additional and special relevance for those patients who are analyzed during the closing stage of childhood—namely, during late adolescence, or, to put it metapsychologically, during the "second individuation process" of adolescence (Blos, 1967).

7 I am reminded here of a little boy who was introduced by his mother to an outhouse when visiting a farm at the age of 20 months. The child looked with interest

loving father and, conversely, the belief in the certainty of a great reward waiting for a submissive and obedient son—these were the impenetrable convictions of a child who, by this very trust, had immobilized himself on the road to maturity. Such trust is akin to denial; frequently, it appears in the form of an irrational self-confidence, which stands on clay feet, because it lacks the support of any accomplishment in the real world.

It is the regressive aspect of adolescence—normally, a regression in the service of development (Blos, 1967)—that endows adolescent behavior with a childlike countenance. The trend toward idealization is perhaps the characteristic *par excellence* of youth. It was my impression that the patient's regression to the idealized father image represented his effort to reach the consolidation stage of late adolescence. The transference was thus not a regression in the customary sense—that of the reliving of a pathogenetic conflict; as a result, there was nothing in it that was akin to a transference neurosis. The childlike quality was derived from the fixation on his still family-centered emotional life, which the patient was laboring in vain to transcend by replacement.

Knowing that the transference neurosis—and the patient's illness belonged in this category—is the only means of reliving, and therefore of coming to terms with, the infantile roots of a neurotic symptom, I waited patiently for any signs of its appearance. The transference neurosis is, after all, an emotional involvement from which there is not a single moment's escape, while transference manifestations come and go. The two are of an essentially different order (Loewald, 1971a), even though both play a crucial (albeit different) role in the resolution of a neurotic conflict in the analysis of child and adult. The distinction between both is in reality not as precise as our terminology would indicate. It is, however, not an artificial one. Transference manifestations bear an *ad hoc* character, while the transference neurosis reflects a continuous and coherent reliving of the pathogenetic past in relation to the analyst and to the analytic situation; as such, it is a reflection of life *par excellence* insofar as it selects from among all available stimuli those that will sustain it. In order to avoid the narrow and perhaps stifling concept of the term "transference neurosis," Greenacre

into the hole, and after a while turned his shining eyes up to his mother with these words: "Mommie, so that's where you keep it!"

(1959) has suggested a less tight terminology. She wrote: "I have myself been a little questioning of the blanket term 'transference neurosis,' which may be misleading. I would prefer to speak of *active transference neurotic manifestations*" (p. 652f.). Keeping this proviso in mind, I continue to use the term "transference neurosis" as a useful term, being cognizant of the fact that it is an inclusive rather than an exclusive definition.

No signs of a transference neurosis made their appearance in my patient. When I decided to wait, I had also made the implicit decision neither to alleviate unduly his current suffering nor to offer such insights as would only play into the hands of his intellectual defenses and gratify his narcissism, thereby supporting the grandiose fantasies with which he was trying to obliterate his devastating sense of incompetence and helplessness.

I shall now turn to a shift in the analysis. This shift was not wholly attributable—if indeed it was attributable at all—to the analytic work done thus far. It was precisely that aspect of the analysis—namely, the unaccountability of the change—that gave me pause. Before speculating on this point, however, I shall present the clinical material of the second stage of the analysis.

After $1\frac{1}{2}$ years of analysis, the patient began to verbalize his inhibition against talking freely with me: his overriding desire had so far been to be "a good patient." The roving reporting now took on the character of a personalized message. He began, rather suddenly, to complain about the restrictions that the analytic schedule was forcing on him and about the dependency he had to endure. He felt that his prior commitment to the analysis had begun to wane, and that this was due to the coercion implicit in the analytic contract. These complaints seemed "natural" to him, and therefore required no further "explanation": it was self-evident that in a state of coercion and imposition one cannot "talk freely" or "open up."

One day, this new "theme song" of apparent resistance and negative transference was played in a different key. I had noticed that the tirades of provocation and accusing negativism had begun to give way to spontaneous associations. These were all memories, and what they had in common was the element of danger, fear, and disaster: at the age of 6, a pet animal had died on the living room couch; one night his bed had collapsed; wild animals in the zoo had frightened him, he had broken a chair, and he was paralyzed by fear of his father.

When I interpreted these associations by pointing out his fear of the analyst ("talk freely," "opening up"), the patient suddenly got excited. Instead of simply rejecting my comments as irrelevant, or pretending to accept them as he had previously done, he now responded with genuine affect. This gentle-voiced young man raised his voice to a shout: "That's it. I didn't know what I was saying, but *you* knew. That makes us unequal. *That* I cannot allow to happen." Nevertheless, he considered my comment and recognized some truth in my interpretation, which dealt with his fear of regression, his terror of becoming once again unequal, little and weak, at the mercy of the analyst-father's power. In short, what I had conveyed to him was the thought that his fear of being overwhelmed, punished, and subdued was being relived in the analytic situation, where it had become attached to the analytic rule and contract, both imposed on him by the analyst.

This interpretation was followed in the next session by the patient's recollection of a child's story in which a "man who never talks" is hit by his exasperated companion, who has all along been wanting to have a nice conversation with him. The allusion to the analyst was once again not obvious to the patient, and it had to be pointed out to him. Instead of becoming excited and argumentative, however, this time the patient recalled that his father had *never* talked to him—except to encourage him to be good and successful in school. What he had meant to convey by the tale was simply that all his life *he* had never had a "nice conversation" with his father, about matters that were of importance to the child. How could he dare talk to *me?* He had learned to give the appearance of an obedient child and to live with his rage and his desire for vengeance in a self-enforced solitary confinement.

After these transference experiences and their interpretations, the patient became pensive and introspective. He made the following self-observation: "Memories have taken on a different flavor. Up till now I enjoyed talking about my memories. I enjoyed reminiscing—about anything. It made me feel good. This seems to have changed. My memories have become—sort of threatening.

You have become part of them. You see something in them I don't. That makes all the difference, I suppose."

The patient opened one of the succeeding sessions with the remark: "The last few days I have been able to visualize the vagina. This has been totally impossible for me before this." He spoke of it as of a sudden illumination. This brought to mind the persevering thought of "Nothing" during the first week of the analysis. This sudden clarity of thought and imagery was sufficient to establish the etiological link between castration anxiety, repressed oedipal aggression, and the inhibition of thinking. Thinking had acquired, especially during adolescence, a defensive function: it had become a cold exercise in sophistry, designed to keep emotions strangulated by thought mastery. Since he had been using the weapons of intelligence, no accusation of hostile intent could be leveled against the victor. Yet the unconscious intent had aborted, more often than not, the effective use of those very weapons.

There was no question that the analytic work had now moved onto a different level. The transference neurosis was in formation, and an effective, object-directed quality had become attached to verbalizations. The emergence of this new affective quality was attributable to the fact that the transference had become an integral part of the patient's mental life. The reliving of the pathogenetic past is the transference neurosis; it gives "all the symptoms of the illness a new transference meaning" and replaces the patient's "ordinary neurosis by a 'transference neurosis' of which he can be cured by the therapeutic work. The transference thus creates an intermediate region between illness and real life through which the transition from one to the other is made" (Freud, 1914, p. 154; Loewald, 1971a, p. 62). Simultaneously with the emergence of the transference neurosis, the infantile neurosis acquires the structuralization and the clarity it had lacked until then. "The infantile neurosis is the leading pathology in the transference neuroses" (Tolpin, 1970, p. 277), or, in the light of my proposition: the infantile neurosis is the leading pathology in the adult neurosis of the transference neurosis type; only during psychoanalytic treatment are we enabled to investigate the realm of the infantile neurosis, and only so far as it is reflected in the transference neurosis.

A new dimension had clearly been added to my patient's analytic involvement: what had previously become a waning interest in the analysis was now replaced by an emerging therapeutic alliance. The analytic material, which was for the first time derived from *all* layers of the mind and from *all* periods of his life, acquired psychological cohesion and continuity. This condition rendered interpretations meaningful—that is, they were no longer an end in themselves, but instead the beginning of some new, but related, self-investigative move.

To employ an analogy, I might say that the first phase of the analysis had corresponded to the close observation and inspection of the myriad small pieces of colored glass or stone (isolated memories, problems, and conflicts), which were one day to be assembled into a large mosaic picture (adult neurosis). During the second phase (transference neurosis), the grand design of the mosaic becomes completed (infantile neurosis); now, every observation and every inspection of detail is necessarily carried out in relation to the overall picture, which has acquired a coherent design (the total or the historical personality).

In order to correct a misunderstanding I may have created—that it is only with the advent of the transference neurosis that any meaningful analytic work is possible—I must point out that the analytic work of the first period was, in its own way, unquestionably useful. I am inclined to speculate that roaming and wandering through a lifetime of memories—including fantasies, affects, and experiences, in conjunction with the current life of work, moods, relationships, family, etc.—were necessary in order to facilitate the consolidation of late adolescence, including the neurotic trends. It was the first phase that brought the patient into contact with his inner life; at the same time as it was dealing with acute conflicts as isolated events, it was also throwing light on the pervasiveness of his inhibitions, avoidances, and fears. In their totality, these gave the process of consolidation its scope and immediacy.

This in itself was no minor achievement. And yet, if the analytic work had been abandoned at that point, no durable reorganization of the personality would have been effected. Certain reality achievements, made possible by the analytic work during the first phase—such as financial independence and responsible, satisfactory performance on a job—were important in that they gave the patient a sense of success and of pride and, in general, made him feel better. Yet, just that sense of accomplishment might well have served the patient as his reason for wanting to terminate the analysis. In fact, just before the second phase of the analysis set in, that very step was near realization by the patient. It was averted by my making a transference interpretation that happened to be the first one to "hit home."

It has been my impression for many years that adolescence cannot remain indefinitely an open-ended process; it has to come to some closure, even if that be a pathological one, during late adolescence. By definition, late adolescence, as a period of personality consolidation, has its biological as well as its emotional and social timing. Having had a number of analytic patients who were in the stage of late adolescence, I have found that my theoretical propositions could be confirmed in other cases as well, so long as those cases also belonged among the transference neuroses. Naturally, where the pathology is overburdened by preoedipal ego aberrations and ego deficiencies, the analytic treatment will follow a different course, which lies outside the scope of this investigation. The diagnostic assessment of these latter cases often remains inconclusive at the start of analysis, but will gain in clarity during the first phase, the phase of consolidation.

A Comparison of Clinical Observations and Theoretical Propositions

I have been fortunate to find in the psychoanalytic literature several reports on the treatment of late adolescents and, thus, I have been in a position to compare my own clinical observations and theoretical assumptions with those of others. While these other writers had used their particular cases to demonstrate ideas that were quite different from those I am setting forth in this paper, they were nevertheless cognizant of the specific difficulties that this age group of patients presents. There are two writers in particular who have published clinical material to which I now turn my attention.

Hans Loewald opens his paper on "The Transference Neurosis" (1971a) with the case illustration of "an unusually gifted and inhibited young man of 19." There is no need here to go into this late adolescent's psychopathology, aside from pointing out that his clinical picture resembles my patient's to a remarkable degree. Both represent a rather typical maladaptive constellation, which brings a number of such young men of college age to the analyst's office. Loewald made the observation early in treatment "that his [the patient's] relationship to me [the analyst], from the very beginning, tended to be a duplicate of his relationship to his father, which seemed to be a kind of slavish adoration, imitation, and submissive love, with some evidence of rebellion against that position, deep resentment, and of attempts to extricate himself from it." At first sight, says Loewald, the patient seemed to be offering "an example of a very rapidly-developing transference neurosis" (p. 54). He then goes on to pose the question "whether one should speak here of a transference *neurosis* [sic], inasmuch as the transference was so immediate and massive. . . . [It] clearly had a primitive quality, perhaps not unlike that of children . . . , while desirable in the interest of maintaining rapport with this isolated patient . . . [it] worked as a powerful resistance" (p. 55f.). In view of the massive transference manifestations, the analyst decided that a "resistance analysis . . . was not called for at this time" (p. 56). Since the character of the transference "would tend in the direction of a mere transference repetition," the analyst's "concern in this case was the danger of an early stalemate or disruption of the analysis" (p. 57).

Loewald then proceeds to ask the pertinent question: does the concept of the transference neurosis imply the repetition of the infantile neurosis? If not, then what is it that distinguishes the massive transference manifestations at the opening phase of this patient's analysis from a transference neurosis? The analyst, if I may say so, felt it "in his bones" that the two were not the same; I might be so bold as to assume that it was the unworkable quality of the transference—or, simply, the patient's unresponsiveness to transference interpretations—that gave the distinction its plausibility. In addition, the apparent resistance remained equally unassailable by interpretations—or, at least, their repetition had such minor consequences that a possible miscomprehension of the pathology had to be considered. Loewald thus came to the apodictic conclusion: "No well-defined symptomatology, no well-defined in-

fantile neurosis and thus no transference neurosis" (p. 58) . Parenthetically, I might suggest that the rapidity of the patient's transference—indeed, his transference hunger or transference compulsion—is a reflection, in and of itself, of a symptom in formation
within the benign context of the analytic situation.

A further source of clinical material pertaining to the analytic
treatment of the late adolescent is to be found in two papers by
Adatto (1958, 1966) , who describes the analysis of five late adolescent patients. "Following an intensive working through of their
conflictual material, there was a period of psychic equilibrium and
absence of analytic motivation" (1966, p. 485) . The analytic treatment was therefore terminated at this point. But three of these
five patients returned for analysis when they had become young
adults. The striking difference between their first and second analyses lay in "the transference and the emotional investment in me
[the analyst], which had been sketchy or incomplete in the first
analysis" (1966, p. 486) . Analyzable transference dreams in the second analysis opened the way to new analytic depth, by moving "towards a situation in which finally every conflict has to be fought
out in the sphere of transference" (Freud, 1912, p. 104) .

I shall now turn to a comparative evaluation of Loewald's and
Adatto's cases, in the light of the thesis that I have advanced.
There are several aspects in all these cases that permit a comparative view. First, there is the fact that all the patients were in their
late adolescence—namely, at that developmental stage in which
adolescent psychic restructuring has reached its final stage in the
consolidation of the personality. The fact that all cases are male
seems, at first sight, coincidental; however, clinical observation
might indicate that female adolescent consolidation follows a pattern of its own. Loewald concluded that the absence of a well-
defined symptomatology—in other words, the absence of structuralization of the total scope of internal disharmonies, in terms of
compromise formations—rules out the appearance of a "well-defined infantile neurosis." This conclusion is borne out by my own
observation—namely, that the personality consolidation of late
adolescence is a precondition for the structuralization of the transference neurosis *and* of the infantile neurosis. If the consolidation
process of late adolescence has not yet taken place, we will look in
vain for the adult neurosis that constitutes the matrix out of which

the transference neurosis and, concomitantly, the infantile neurosis emerge. Loewald made the same observation as had aroused my own curiosity—namely, that a patient's excellent rapport can easily be taken as betokening the emergence of the transference neurosis and yet that can prove to be erroneous. Furthermore, the same patient's unresponsiveness to transference interpretations is then given the blanket designation of "resistance." Misjudgments of this kind lead frequently to a disruption of the analysis, or to its incompleteness.

Adatto's cases are extremely instructive in that they permit one to make a comparative study of the two analytic phases, by focusing on their points of difference. In the first phase, the patients had remained rather unresponsive to the analysis of transference and resistance; yet they had gained considerable relief from anxiety, through the resolution of some of the acute problems that had initially brought them to treatment. This first gain in treatment represents the typical danger point—as we have seen in Loewald's and my own case—threatening a premature termination of the analysis. Adatto (1958) postulated that, in the course of the analysis of the late adolescent, there takes place an ego reintegration that does constitute, in and of itself, a progression toward maturity. Concomitantly, however, the patient's need for the analysis wanes and the analysis is terminated. The "ego reintegration" proved, after all, to be less durable than was expected (Adatto, 1966).

By virtue of Adatto's concentrating—perhaps too exclusively— on the amelioration of his patients' acute life problems, these late adolescent patients were sufficiently relieved from anxiety to become able to stabilize their defensive organization. It was this that enabled them to go through the consolidation phase well defended, and thereby to gain a temporary postponement of the irruption of the adult neurosis. Here the first, even if incomplete, analysis stood them in good stead. Nevertheless, three of Adatto's patients later recognized the need to complete their prematurely disrupted analysis; this occurred after such accommodations as career, marriage, and children had proved to be of no avail for the attainment of a normal adult life.[8]

---

[8] Spiegel (1961) presented two late adolescent cases that show certain features in treatment similar to those discussed here.

Both Adatto and Loewald observed that the analyzability of resistance remains limited at the stage of static transference repetitions. It has been my experience that the developmental forces, which are at this point working against analytic involvement, can be kept within reasonable bounds if the analyst offers insight—even if such insights are limited to, or more or less remain on, the experiential level of comprehending the realities of psychic determinism. Be that as it may, a point of agreement with Loewald and Adatto emerges—namely, that at this preliminary stage of analysis in late adolescence, both the transference neurosis and the infantile neurosis are still to develop. In that regard, they constitute two sides of the same coin. Of course, formation of the transference neurosis takes its time in any adult analysis as well, and there too an introductory phase is common enough. The difference has to do, among other things, with the different function of the introductory phase and the different use to which the late adolescent patient generally puts the initial analytic situation. The basic point of difference, however, lies in the fact that the late adolescent patient is fulfilling a developmental requirement that affects the analytic work adversely, by contrast with the adult, whose initial reticence or effusiveness in analysis can be attributed entirely to resistance and defense.

We are now ready to say that the initial phase of late adolescent analysis confronts the analyst with a clinical phenomenon that belongs to the developmental process of personality consolidation. This process occurs in relative silence, outside the analytic work. The achievement of this silent work is the adult neurosis. This process is inherently helped along by the analytic situation, because that situation confronts the patient's ego with an avalanche of experiences on all levels of mental functioning, which the patient is reproducing, either silently or verbally. It is in order to prevent the flooding of the mental apparatus with disorganizing stimuli (thoughts, images, and affects) that the ego erects a "stimulus barrier" in the form of organizing principles; we refer to the implementation of these principles, in their totality, as "the consolidation process of late adolescence."

Contemplating, in retrospect, the disruption of the first analysis, Adatto reminds us of Freud's treatment of the late adolescent patient, Dora, and of his statement in the Postscript to that case history: "I did not succeed in mastering the transference in good time." As we consider Dora's disruption of her analysis in developmental terms, we could say, today, that the consolidation of her neurotic condition had been short-circuited by the fact that her analysis was being conducted as if an adult neurosis already existed. As a consequence, the adolescent ego became overwhelmed by interpretations it was unable to integrate, and it simply took to flight. If there is one thing adolescent analysis has taught us, it is that ill-timed id interpretations are unconsciously experienced by the adolescent as a parental—that is, incestuous—seduction.

Personality Consolidation and the Formation of the Adult Neurosis

From what I have said up to this point, it must have become obvious that I ascribe to the stage of late adolescence a specific and decisive role in the formation of the adult neurosis. The integrative process of consolidation which brings childhood to a close is the outstanding characteristic of late adolescence. This consolidation process entails a progression from partial adaptations and less than final conflict resolutions, as well as from reactive, transient, even disjointed emotional and social accommodations, to their unification in terms of a patterned interlacing of psychic functioning, under the aegis of an advanced ego. This is what we refer to in summary fashion as "personality consolidation." In the realm of character formation, it is reflected in the automatization of reaction patterns (Blos, 1968). The formative process of the adult neurosis draws on these developmental advances toward a definitive, integrated, and autonomous psychic organization.

This formulation stands in contradiction to a widely held opinion—namely, that the existence of a neurotic condition makes it impossible for the personality consolidation of late adolescence to take place; that consolidation *can* take place, so the argument goes, only by way of the analysis of the neurosis. This point of view restricts the consolidation process to normal development, regarding its completion as the true sign of maturity attained. It is my opinion, to the contrary, that it is only *after* the consolidation of late adolescence that an analysis can include in its scope the rectification or normalization of the total personality, including those enclaves of the neurotic potential to which child analytic work had often been unable to penetrate. Herein lies the limitations placed on the working-through process in the analytic endeavor, prior to the analysis of the adult neurosis (Blos, 1970, pp. 100–109). The consolidation process of late adolescence always proceeds turbulently—whether in a manifest or latent fashion—and even more so whenever a neurotic potential has survived the intervening years of childhood and adolescence.

Regardless of stalemates and retardations in the realms of ego and drive progression—or, what is more frequent, their lack of synchronization and their disharmony—late adolescence will nevertheless bring the process of psychic patterning and organization into a decisive ascendancy. This step forward, I repeat, takes place in relation to pathology as well as to normality. *It is the consolidation process itself that structures the adult neurosis.* The consolidation stage of late adolescence is therefore the incubation time of the adult neurosis, and the patient uses the analytic situation as part of that process. Consequently, patient and analyst often find themselves working at cross-purposes. The analyst's aim is to restructure a faulty *development,* while the patient is occupied with a comprehensive, yet faulty, *structure formation*—that is, with the formation of the adult neurosis.

The consolidation of the adult neurosis takes time, and during that time the patient remains, more or less, unresponsive to the standard technique. There is no lack of cooperation, nor is there any dearth of analytic material; yet what prevails is an ineffectualness or, rather, a significantly limited usefulness of resistance and transference interpretations. This looks like the outcome of either a negative therapeutic reaction or a massive resistance, but in my opinion it is neither; it rather constitutes a "holding operation," while the silent work of consolidation goes on. No doubt, defenses do play their role in this typical picture, and they can be drawn successfully into the analytic work. The technical problem at this developmental stage of adult psychic structure formation, however, consists in the analyst's carefully determining just how much relief from anxiety he should offer the patient vis-à-vis his current

acute distress and tension. Gauging the optimal level of abstinence thus becomes the delicate task of the analyst.[9]

Dynamic considerations permit one to speculate that too great
relief from anxiety will serve to foster a "consolidation" marked
by the defensive conviction that "all is well." A growing lack of
interest in the analytic work will then emerge and a premature
termination of the analysis may follow. Too little relief from anxiety, on the other, can lead to disappointment in the analytic work,
or to disillusionment with the analyst's ability or willingness to
help. It all comes down, then, to "too much" or "too little" responsiveness and stimulation from the side of the analyst.

It must be remembered that the consolidation process, while developmentally timed, requires sources of tension and conflict, as
well as trust and confidence, in order for its integrative work to
proceed. The aim of analytic work in late adolescence is, first of
all, a successful transition from the turmoil of the consolidation
stage to the analysis of the adult neurosis. Analytic interventions
during the *status nascendi* of the adult neurosis call for technical
inventiveness and tact, both of them firmly rooted in developmental and theoretical conceptualizations. Adaptation of the analytic
technique to the stage of psychic consolidation should be thought
of as being a no less appropriate analytic procedure than the one,
for example, that accepts, rather than rejects, the alternating existence of the analyst as a transference object and a real person, in
child analysis. The adaptation of analytic technique to developmental conditions does not, in and of itself, negate the analytic
process, but rather enhances it.

The idea that the irruption of the definitive neurosis, or the
adult neurosis, coincides with the termination of adolescence becomes plausible, once we realize that the oedipus complex is
brought to its definitive decline or definitive resolution only with
the attainment of somatic maturity at puberty.[10] What was an emo-

[9] The problem of abstinence plays a role, of course, in every analysis, and at any
age. In the present context, it has to do with the analyst's promoting the consolidation of the adult neurosis and thus preventing the disruption of the analysis.

[10] The origin, latent state, and irruption of the neurosis were summarized by
Freud (1940) as follows: "It seems that neuroses are acquired only in early childhood (up to the age of six), even though their symptoms may not make their appearance till much later" (p. 184). ". . . all the mutually contending emotional im-

tional reality in the form of a wish, during the phallic-oedipal phase, became thwarted at that time by the reality principle— namely, by physical immaturity; these same wishes, upon being brought to life again during puberty, have since become realizable by physical maturity, but now they are thwarted by emotional conflict. The mythical figure of Oedipus, we sometimes forget, was an adult man.

What we refer to, before adolescence, as "childhood neurosis" is attributable to specific conflicts and their maladaptive resolutions, which preclude normal progression along developmental lines.[11] The childhood neurosis lacks the involvement of the total personality; in terms of an all-inclusive and comprehensive organization, this does not exist before adulthood. The term adulthood is here used not as identical with emotional maturity, but as relative to physical status and psychic structure. It is this fact that makes the childhood neurosis different from the adult neurosis. What the two have in common, of course, is the internalization of conflict. With regard to their difference, Hartmann commented as follows: "many of the very early neuroses are really different from what we are used to calling neurosis in the adult. Many problems in children which we call neurotic are actually limited to a single functional disturbance; and the way from conflict to symptom seems often to be shorter than in adult neurosis" (in Kris et al., 1954, p. 33).

Psychoanalytic theory has always maintained that the infantile neurosis is relived in the form of the transference neurosis. But the fact is that the formation of the infantile neurosis is concomitant with the structuralization of the transference neurosis. The infantile neurosis never did exist as a "clinically manifest entity," but

---

pulses and reactions which are set going at that time [in early childhood] are preserved in the unconscious and ready to disturb the later development of the ego *after puberty*. When the somatic process of sexual maturation puts fresh life into the old libidinal fixations which had apparently been surmounted, sexual life will turn out to be inhibited, without homogeneity and fallen apart into mutually conflicting urges" (p. 191; my italics).

11 Freud used the terms infantile neurosis, childhood neurosis, neurosis of infancy, etc., as interchangeable designations of the "infantile neurosis," which is the term used in the literature today. Childhood neurosis refers to manifest neurotic illness before adolescence.

rather as "an unconscious configuration" (Tolpin, 1970, p. 278), a neurotic disposition or potential, the existence of which becomes manifest—that is, symptomatic—during adolescence or, certainly, during the terminal stage of adolescence (Freud, 1940, p. 191; 1939, pp. 77–80). I am in agreement with Tolpin's statement that the "term infantile neurosis should be reserved for the metapsychological concept that designates the repressed potentially pathogenic oedipal conflict . . . which is central in the pathology of the transference neuroses" (1970, p. 278).

Conclusion

Starting from analytic observations of late adolescent patients, I have come to the conclusion that the consolidation phase of late adolescence is the formative stage of the adult neurosis. Only after the formation of the adult neurosis can the transference neurosis, as the manifest form of the infantile neurosis, develop within the analytic situation. These considerations have therefore attributed a new and special importance to the consolidation stage of late adolescence. Explorations of the terminal stage of childhood—that is to say, of the formative stage of the adult personality, normal or pathological—has brought to the fore specific questions of analytic technique and theory. I have endeavored to open up to examination this particular area of clinical, developmental, and theoretical investigation, by offering a conceptualization of the unique role that late adolescence plays in the epigenesis of the adult neurosis.

BIBLIOGRAPHY

ADATTO, C. P. (1958), Ego Reintegration Observed in Analysis of Late Adolescents. *Int. J. Psycho Anal.,* 39:172–177.
— (1966), On the Metamorphosis from Adolescence into Adulthood. *J. Amer. Psychoanal. Assn.,* 14:485–509.
BLOS, P. (1962), *On Adolescence.* New York: Free Press of Glencoe.
— (1965), The Initial Stage of Male Adolescence. *This Annual,* 20:145–164.
— (1967), The Second Individuation Process of Adolescence. *This Annual,* 22:162–186.

— (1968), Character Formation in Adolescence. *This Annual,* 23:245–263.

— (1970), *The Young Adolescent: Clinical Studies.* New York: Free Press.

ERIKSON, E. H. (1968), *Identity, Youth and Crisis.* New York: Norton.

FREUD, A. (1965) *Normality and Pathology in Childhood.* New York: International Universities Press.

— (1971), The Infantile Neurosis: Genetic and Dynamic Considerations. *This Annual,* 26:79–90.

FREUD, S. (1909), Analysis of a Phobia in a Five-Year-Old Boy. *Standard Edition,* 10:3–149. London: Hogarth Press, 1955.

— (1912), The Dynamics of Transference. *Standard Edition,* 12:97–108. London: Hogarth Press, 1958.

— (1914), Remembering, Repeating and Working-Through. *Standard Edition,* 12:145–156. London: Hogarth Press, 1958.

— (1927), The Future of an Illusion. *Standard Edition,* 21:3–56. London: Hogarth Press, 1961.

— (1939), Moses and Monotheism. *Standard Edition,* 23:3–137. London: Hogarth Press, 1964.

— (1940) An Outline of Psycho-Analysis. *Standard Edition,* 23:141–207. London: Hogarth Press, 1964.

GREENACRE, P. (1959), Certain Technical Problems in the Transference Relationship. *Emotional Growth,* 2:651–669. New York: International Universities Press, 1971.

JONES, E. (1955), *The Life and Work of Sigmund Freud,* Vol. 2. New York: Basic Books.

KOHUT, H. (1971), *The Analysis of the Self.* New York: International Universities Press.

KRIS, E. ET AL. (1954), Problems of Infantile Neurosis: A Discussion. *This Annual,* 9:16–71.

LEWIN, B. D. (1948), The Nature of Reality, the Meaning of Nothing: With an Addendum on Concentration. *Psychoanal. Quart.,* 17:524–526.

LOEWALD, H. W. (1971a), The Transference Neurosis: Comments on the Concept and the Phenomenon. *J. Amer. Psychoanal. Assn.,* 19:54–66.

— (1971b), Some Considerations on Repetition and Repetition Compulsion. *Int. J. Psycho-Anal.,* 52:59–66.

RITVO, S. (1966), Correlation of a Childhood and Adult Neurosis. *Int. J. Psycho-Anal.,* 47:130–131.

SPIEGEL, L. A. (1961), Disorder and Consolidation in Adolescence. *J. Amer. Psychoanal. Assn.,* 9:406–416.

TOLPIN, M. (1970), The Infantile Neurosis: A Metapsychological Concept and a Paradigmatic Case History. *This Annual,* 25:273–305.

WAELDER-HALL, J. (1935), Structure of a Case of Pavor Nocturnus. *Bull. Phila. Assn. Psychoanal.,* 20:267–274.

Crowds and Crisis

Psychoanalytic Considerations

PHYLLIS GREENACRE, M.D.

THIS PAPER IS AN INQUIRY INTO THE PSYCHOLOGY OF CROWDS, ESPE-
cially in relation to states of stress and crisis. The basic considerations are common to almost all crowds, whether these have assembled for religious purposes, for sports events, for circus perform-
ances, or in the interest of political or patriotic aims. But once
there is a sense of stress, danger or potential crisis, new elements in
the crowd situation arise, which complicate and exacerbate conditions within the crowd, and may be followed by lasting and seemingly abrupt changes in crowd members.

This is a subject which naturally focuses on the present times, especially the last decade, with its overt beginning marked in this

This is a slightly revised edition of the Nunberg Lecture, delivered at the New
York Academy of Medicine, November 9, 1971, under the auspices of the Psychoanalytic Development and Research Foundation of New York.

country by resurgent interest in the Civil Rights Movement and legislation culminating in the 1960s exactly one century after the beginning of the American Civil War. The 20 years since the Second World War have been a period of fruition of phenomenal technological achievements with the outmoding of many facilities and the substitution of new ones even more awesome, promising simplification and enrichment of our lives through processes far beyond the comprehension of most of us. Somewhat similar series of events, with the times getting entirely out of joint, have recurred in the past centuries. But each time, after a preliminary period of strain, when the eruption comes it seems surprisingly sudden and appears unique.

The Second World War left us with high ideals sharpened by the shadow of the Atom Bomb and the question whether it would frighten us into global cooperation or into global destructiveness. In spite of the many high-minded and energetic efforts toward peace, wars—half a world away—have continued to be waged and made inroads into the lives of a whole generation of young people. It was a time of heightened affluence for many, but no spectacular relief for the abysmal poverty of many more. And there has been an ever-increasing population. This is a situation which, as it breeds unrest, arouses limitless ambitions in many directions as well as the opposite feelings of fear of utter helplessness and longings for a simple "good life." Yet, time and again, recently as in many past periods, the initial idealistic efforts in this peaceful direction have turned to violence in the hope of quickly and fundamentally changing the social organization of Church or State. Against this general background, I wish now to examine the nature of crowds, their formation, the process that goes on in them and their functioning in relation to concurrent activist movements. I hope that such an examination with a psychoanalytically trained eye may add something to our understanding not only of the phenomenon of crowds but, in turn, of some problems in psychoanalysis.

I

It has long been recognized that man in crowds may behave quite differently than when he acts as an individual. His behavior in a crowd presents startling and even alarming paradoxes. Toward the end of the last century, and later during a period associated with the First World War, several essays on the subject emphasized that unconscious forces were at work, but did not adequately specify how these took place in the individual. I refer here especially to Le Bon's *The Crowd* (1895), Trotter's *Instincts of the Herd in Peace and War* (1916), and Freud's *Group Psychology and the Analysis of the Ego* (1921).

It was particularly emphasized that an intensification of emotion occurred and passed through the crowd as though by contagion; that individuals lost their sense of separate personality, and showed increasing irritability and restlessness, leading to impulsive un-reasoning acts; that they gained a sense of power through merging with the crowd and that rational thinking was diminished or abrogated, while there was a further tendency for all members of the crowd to adopt the same attitude. Logic seemed to give way to a childish form of thought dominated by sensually determined imagery; what we would think of as the partial replacement of secondary process by primary process thinking. There was some tendency to explain this state of affairs in terms of a "collective" or racially determined mind, originating through the creation of a new "organism," the crowd, in which each individual is submerged, much as individual cells were thought of as losing the capacity for varied activity in the formation of a new biological organism. This conceptualization disregarded the gap between subhuman and human organisms, and bypassed the influence of the individual life and the role of the individual unconscious in determining who becomes part of a human crowd and the varying degrees to which participation in the crowd may or may not have a lasting effect upon its individual members.

It may be well at this point to clarify the difference between crowds and groups. The two terms are often used synonymously with the frequent implication that a crowd is simply a big group. Crowds and groups are interrelated; crowds may break down into groups and, in situations of crisis or danger, groups not infrequently flow together into a crowd. Both terms may be used of inanimate objects as well as animate ones.

The term *crowd*, derived from the Anglo-Saxon word (*crudan*) meaning press, shove or push, originally had the meaning of pressure with body contact between members.[1] It is closely related to the idea of cramming or crushing, putting too much into too small a space. The French word (*foule*), as in Le Bon's treatise, also signifies pressure and its verb form means to trample, to press or to crush; [2] and the German word (*das Gedränge*) means not only throng, but has the connotation of pressure, crowding with impetus or violence. *Group*, on the other hand, is a quieter word referring to a number of things or persons gathered together to form a unit or cluster because of some common special quality or characteristic of concern to themselves or others. In a group some elements of similarity of interest form a natural basis of the collection and so from the outset imply a tendency to organization. Crowds generally have a lesser degree of internal organization than is true in groups. They are amalgamated rather than structured. A crowd may gather, however, around an already established leader or in response to some unexpected event.

II

The behavior described in earlier articles, as especially characteristic of crowds, was generally considered as belonging only to "psychological crowds," those gathered for some special purpose, cause or movement, as distinct from spontaneous crowds assembled by chance. I believe that this distinction, though useful, cannot be a clear-cut one. The very fact of people being massed together brings a susceptibility to and at least a minimum amount of disturbed behavior, which may increase in any crowd situation where pressure is prolonged and fear of any kind becomes aroused.

The most powerful presentiments which attract persons into activistically oriented crowds seem to arise from feelings of grievance and apprehensions of danger. Whatever the basis of these individual feelings may be, resentments and anxieties from one source blend readily with those of other persons and increase as they are shared. The precipitants in individual personal situations may be

[1] See *Concise Oxford English Dictionary*, Oxford University Press, 1933.

[2] The crush, an overwhelming adolescent infatuation, and its relation to the crowd phenomenon cannot be discussed in this paper.

lost sight of in a mounting general feeling of indignation. It is often the mood of a crowd rather than its alleged specific purpose which first attracts the bystander. But in any case a sense of danger is in itself exciting and this, with the stimulation of scoptophilic impulses, may be enough to bring new additions to any crowd which has already formed. Thus, there is apt to be a fringe of members of the crowd, not primarily and deeply involved, who may subsequently drop away, *or* be caught up in the contagion of the crowd spirit and situation, according to the latent preconscious and unconscious disturbances in themselves and in their special foci of resentment.

Under any circumstances adolescence is likely to be a time of urgency for a new deal—due to the marked and rather abrupt changes, physical, emotional, and social, with which youth is then confronted. Young people have always been in the forefront of revolutionary activities. But the participation of youth in the present-day crowd and group demonstrations has been particularly strong. The amassments of present-day crowds have drawn from much wider geographical areas and been accomplished more rapidly than could even have been dreamed of in the past. These two influences, the increased participation of adolescents and the global nature of revolutionary activism, have increased the size, intensity, and probably the prolongation of recent crowd formations. Through the increase in the rapidity of communication and transportation, the periphery of a crowd may be so enlarged as to be indeterminable. The rapid dissemination of news by television and radio adds an immediate and unseen audience and at times forms an outer ring to the crowd itself.

Crowds may also gather more readily at present than in times past because of the enormous increase in urban populations. In ordinary times, large numbers of people may gather without their being any marked anxiety, for example, for some exciting pleasurable event of widespread interest or appeal, a colorful celebration, the arrival of a celebrity, or some special sports event; or they may accumulate more or less by chance. For many, there is a feeling of quickening or animation through being part of any group. But the prolonged massing of people together is only tolerable if there is the opportunity for some concurrent random activity. Restlessness is increased if there is genuine crowding and is accelerated if the cause of the crowding is an unpleasant one. Emotional volatility and irritability follow, especially if there is frustration without definite expectation of relief, even though the situation may not be a critical one.[3] For example, this is evident in crowds of commuters when homeward trips are delayed by some break in transportation. Animation turns to comradery, but with potential irritability, and may break out into anger or panic through some incidental misapprehension. The conditions inherent in a crowd not only arouse scoptophilic alertness but increase exhibitionistic pressures in many. Whenever leadership, whether by a sense of purpose or by the emergence of an organizer, is at a minimum, there is danger of deterioration into intracrowd fighting and of slight issues suddenly becoming magnified. My point here is that in all crowds, even in those which have assembled mainly by chance rather than plan, the phenomena of increasing tension, tendencies to irritability, and emotional contagion may make themselves felt.

III

I now turn to the conditions within the crowd which may be used to promote activism. While there is a close interrelation between groups and crowds, they differ in stability, in size, in degree of organization, and very importantly in the closeness of the physical contact of their members at the time of their assemblage. If either leadership or central interest is weak or unsustained, groups tend to disintegrate. In contrast to this, there is much less organization in a crowd and the appearance of a more diffuse spontaneity than in a group. While crowds may generally be assembled by plan or by chance, or by a combination of the two, they are often planned and exploited as a way of winning immediate or rapid support from the greatest possible number of people for issues of human interest. They lend themselves especially to the agitation of politi-

---

[3] Here we are reminded of Schopenhauer's story quoted by Freud (1921) of the freezing porcupine who sought to warm himself by crowding close to his fellow porcupines but was soon driven back by the discomfort from their quills. Hastily retreating, he was soon so out in the cold that he was again impelled to seek warmth with his fellows. This oscillation continued until he found a compromise position half way between freezing and being pierced to death by his companions.

cal and religious movements. In essence, they work through a process of conversion rather than one of deliberative and reasoned consideration. This can occur only in an atmosphere of excitement and high emotional pitch, conditions which preclude the opportunity for contemplation or even thoughtful discussions.

By its very nature a crowd has a self-limited duration which cannot be readily anticipated or foretold, since tolerance for the excitement and emotionality on which it depends for effectiveness is determined by many different and variable factors, including the weather. High-keyed emotionalism may progress with tension, mounting to frenzy or explosiveness, or to a withdrawal by a reversal of feeling with fatigue and saturation. Further, crowds cannot be subject to a regular program of reconvening since part of their access to and utilization of power depends on their seeming spontaneity. Activistically oriented crowds are necessarily not as spontaneous as they might appear. They grow against a background of rumbling unrest and already established propaganda and are dependent on genuine leadership often with the aid of provocateurs.

It is obvious that the very functioning of crowds and the utilization of their power must vary according to the condition of different historical settings as well as fluctuating according to unpredictable events in any given period of time. In its basic foundation with minimal organization together with high emotion, a crowd is capable of massive overresponsiveness and volatility sometimes leading to quite paradoxical results. Crowds are of particular significance in revolutionary times as they may serve as periodic launching platforms.

But what process actually goes on in a crowd as it is assembled at a time of social crisis? The very nature of the situation with many people in close bodily contact brings a considerable sensual stimulation through channels of touch, vision, hearing, and smell. There is also a communication of body heat, muscle tensions, and sometimes of body rhythms. The sensual stimulations come simultaneously and are intensified by the multiplicity of their sources. The individual is practically wrapped up in the crowd and gets a continuous sensual pounding through all the avenues that his body affords.

This state of affairs progressively strengthens moods and creates body tensions with an increasing pitch for activity, especially as the freedom of action and even sometimes of motion is hampered. With the lessened opportunity for direct and sustained conversation, speech tends to be dramatic, staccato, repetitive, and after a time develops an argot of its own. Through this very process of multiple reflection of and by the individual in relation to the many others surrounding him, there is a loss of sense of boundaries to the self and a feeling of primary, narcissistic, omnipotent expansion such as we ordinarily see only in certain psychoses or in states of religious fanaticism. I would quote here from Bakunin who described his state of mind while participating in the revolutionary upheaval in Paris in 1848, where he was in a fever of excitement and exaltation which fed on action. "I breathed through all my senses and through all my pores the intoxication of the revolutionary atmosphere. It was a holiday without beginning and without end. I saw everyone and I saw no one, for each individual was lost in the same innumerable and wandering crowd. I spoke to all I met without remembering either my own words or those of others, for my attention was absorbed at every step by new events and objects and by unexpected news" (Woodcock, 1962, p. 142).

The psychotic individual tends to feel set apart and alienated from society. In the crowd, however, this disturbance is accepted and authorized since it is shared through reflection to and from the surrounding crowd members. It is thus augmented and may reach a state combining fear and exhilarated expectation, somewhat similar to a religious rapture. The alienation is felt toward those outside "the movement" who do not share in its experience. Further, the crowd is paradoxically accepted as though it represented the populace if only the latter could be awakened. The very size of a crowd may give a temporary illusion of being a majority even while it is contending for the rights of a minority. Certainly, the loss of sense of individuality and even of identity, with its specific demands and obligations and the substitution of a higher or larger aim, indicates the closeness of the revolutionary crowd to religious revivalism. This extensive but partial regression resembles the state in infancy when individuation is still somewhat insecure.

In understanding this process, we must realize that the introjective-projective reaction leading ultimately to individuation, characteristic of the early stages of life, is never lost and may be revived with special strength in any situation of stress sufficient to cause a feeling of helplessness.[4] As the young child seemingly gets rest and renewal of initiative to push ahead on his own, through the primary identification with the mother in his repeated return to one kind or another of contact with her, so the individual in a crowd uses the multiple contacts with those around him as a collective mother of many faces which are often far from restful. Under reasonably good conditions in infancy, the predominantly one-to-one relationship with the mother promotes the infant's progress in the development of individuation. In contrast and working in the opposite direction, the potential revolutionist's contact with the multiple intense faces of the crowd has an overwhelming effect until he refinds his sense of power through merging with them. This state results in an increase in tension, seeking outlet in activity which cannot be expressed except at regressive levels.

Only in appreciating the degree and nature of the regression can we understand how the behavior in these crowds goes on to include the whole gamut of pregenital activity mobilized to express hostility. In recent years such behavior appeared occasionally in student crowds, some of whose members spat or used their body excretions to show contempt or rage. A similar deterioration took place in speech, which became increasingly vulgar, angry, and frequently lewd, characterized by cliché phrases which, originally significant, often lost their meaning through repetition and overapplication, and became a kind of name calling. Precise meaning might be blurred and speech become the channel of hostile aggressive excretion, comparable to an infantile mudslinging. To be sure, subsequently among the new slang phrases and idioms which appeared, some which were graphic, vigorous, and economical took hold and may become permanent parts of the working vocabulary. Some of these pay homage to the technological age and take over

---

[4] Freud has discussed this problem of identification and ambivalence in somewhat different terms and emphasis in his Chapter on Identification in *Group Psychology and the Analysis of the Ego* (1921). He refers to identification as the earliest expression of an emotional tie to another and, describing the ambivalence as it develops in the oedipal period, he remarks that identification behaves like a derivative of the first, *oral* phase of the organization of the libido. I would think that body contact is an important ingredient of the oral phase, and that the reaction to alternate body warmth and cooling is the forerunner of later ambivalence, which has other forms in the succeeding phases.

this vocabulary from "the enemy"—such as being "turned on or off," being "programmed," getting a "feedback," etc.

The successful exploitation of crowds to augment revolutionary movements depends not only on their use as a dramatic demonstration of power, both to the outer world and to crowd members, but on the degree to which lasting changes are effected in individual members following the initial conversion. Started in the mass meetings, these must be sustained by a repetition of such meetings and by the individual's participation in various other activities in order to intensify, perpetuate, and implement revolutionary tenets.

Lasting change in the individual convert to the cause may depend on how much a genuine and intellectual conviction grows or is built up, but perhaps even more on how the mass-induced regressions are related to earlier, even infantile disturbances which are rearoused, augmented, and displaced from the original family to society at large. Such a displacement is part of an ordinary course of affairs in adolescence under any circumstances but becomes important in times of revolutionary crisis, where it is more sweepingly intense, and may be associated with an increasing alienation from the original family as well as from nonrevolutionary members of society [5]—the "pigs" in current parlance.

But the development of an actual technique of alienation inculcated into young probationary revolutionists is described in Kropotkin's *Memoirs* (1899) as part of the establishment of the nihilist movement which preceded anarchism in pre-Marxist Russia. It consisted essentially of the development of a method based on ambivalence and the tendency to obsessional doubt.[6] The doubt could be relieved when the exaggerated ambivalence was polarized into

[5] *Diana: The Making of a Terrorist* (Powers, 1971) gives the account of a progressive but fluctuating course of development of a state of alienation occurring in the young woman, Diana Oughton, who lost her life in the accidental bomb explosion in the 11th Street house, the home of the father of one of her revolutionary colleagues.

[6] Freud (1921) mentions this situation briefly in a footnote in his discussion of Le Bon's treatise on *The Crowd*: "In young children, for instance, ambivalent emotional attitudes towards those who are nearest to them exist side by side for a long time, without either of them interfering with the expression of the other and opposite one. If eventually a conflict breaks out between the two, it is often settled by the child making a change of object [for one side of the ambivalence] and displacing one of the ambivalent emotions on to a substitute" (p. 79) .

an either-or attitude of absolutism of opposites. This would then be used in a dialectically argumentative fashion. The illustration given by Kropotkin was that of young nihilists, originally standing for peace as opposed to militarism, who then developed ideals of absolute sincerity, honesty, and mutual help. This was followed by the emergence of a righteous method of repetitively confronting their elders with the latter's hypocrisies and demanding absolute truth and sincerity—becoming as it were "holier than the pope" (my comment, not that of Kropotkin). This stance admits of no gradations of perception, judgment, or even ability. Furthermore, it takes scant account of the unconscious and when driven to an obsessional extreme, it becomes very provocative. There are no grays between black and white. Every action, but especially those having to do with social customs, values, and emotional relationships, may then be challenged—even such matters as ordinary courtesies. If these cannot be defended as absolutely honest, they may be condemned as utterly dishonest. It leads to the often declared attitude, "If you are not with us, then you are against us." It is the attitude of fanatics in many religious sects, where true believers are to be saved and all others will be lost.

Inevitably, however, the nihilists became committed to the use of violence. While violent activity clearly may arise in any situation in which mounting provocativeness is pushed to an extreme obsessional length, it may easily be rationalized as the only way in which a protesting group can make itself heard and felt. Unfortunately, a vigorously protesting group with demands for immediate and sweeping changes is rarely in a state to recognize when it *is* actually being heard and felt, except by counterviolence. Thus a vicious circle is established. When counterviolence or strong repressive forces are used, then violent destruction may be advocated and justified as necessary to clear the way for new growth—the creation of a new society out of the death of the old.[7] Although such

---

[7] The life of Kropotkin, "the noblest of the anarchists," is particularly significant in showing the cycle of this development, from extreme ideals of peace in young manhood, succeeded by acceptance of violence as a way of making the peace movement prominent, and further by advocacy of violent destruction in the interest of progress, to a final subsiding during his later years of semiretirement when he returned to developing his prerevolutionary interest in geography. See Kropotkin (1899) and Woodcock and Avakumoric (1950).

mounting destructive violence is most often planned and mediated through smaller (underground) groups, it gets its initial impetus in crowds and may be renewed there. While Kropotkin never officially relinquished the anarchist credo, in his last peaceful years he seemed to avoid even using the term "anarchist."

To return to considering further the nature of the psychological processes induced by crowd participation: I have already spoken of the body communication and intermittent primary identification which are inevitable in crowds. These may be strong enough to exert a pull of suggestion even on chance crowd members who are actually in opposition to the main doctrines which are being presented, whether these be religious or political. Such persons describe a fear of being "sucked in" to beliefs to which they are ordinarily antagonistic. This influence by suggestion, beginning in the introjective-projective mechanism, is furthered when the latter gives way to a process which may be described as "mirroring." In infancy it is an automatic reflective response which indicates the merest beginning of stabilization of the body-self image, containing incorporated ingredients from the mother or her substitute. Under ordinarily good conditions this mirrored response becomes modified by the natural individuation demands of growth; and out of it gradually emerges a self image which is quite different and yet always carries some trace of this early stage.

But when the mirroring takes place at a much later date, in a crowd with its concentrated multiplicity of forms, and there is simultaneously an appeal to the mind as well as to the sensual body responses, then it contributes largely to the loosening of the sense of individual boundaries, previously established, and weakens rather than promotes the sense of individual identity. At some point this kind of mass suggestion in a crowd prepares it for or even creates a demand for forceful leadership [8] (cf. Communist China and Mao's Little Red Book). By thus undermining the sense of individual differences, support is given to a feeling of equality and even of sameness: one-with-all-others. This in turn may be mistaken for democracy.

[8] In a rather strange way this need for the leader is related to the crush phenomenon of adolescence, one sample of which may be studied in the extraordinary career of Elvis Presley (Levy, 1960).

Whenever crowds or the special groups derived from them furnish more vividness and stimulation than is true in the ordinary environment, the sense of reality is susceptible to alteration. Such changes are influenced by the intensity of emotion which is aroused in crowds, as well as by the differences which crowd situations afford for reality testing. All strong emotional states, whether of mood or with specific content, affect the perceptions of outer reality and contribute to its interpretation. Among these, anger is most important (as it appears in its various forms), especially associated with a sense of grievance. At a pitch of emotional arousal, a person tends to see what he expects and wants to see. In an activistically oriented crowd, a propulsion to action occurs and readily spreads, while the amalgamation of individually determined resentments with socially determined ones channels the action in accordance with current issues. This may be looked upon as a sublimation or as a displacement according to the social point of view of the observer. In any case, the force of revolutionary activism arises from dual sources. Old intrafamily conflicts (complex oedipal jealousies together with sibling rivalries sometimes pregenital in origin) combine with those other grievances coming from social and economic inequities.

In a crowd at a time of crisis there is also a shift in the criteria of that part of reality testing which is based on the individual's comparing and checking his perception and observations with those of the majority of people around him who have shared his experience. Under ordinarily stable social conditions, this is a practical and dependable method of correcting subjective distortions of perception, which in turn affects observations and interpretations. But in states of crisis when the crowd itself becomes a small populace and the differences between individual reactions are diminished, the chance for correction is limited and conviction, one way or the other, is intensified. Further, if there has been alienation from the family and its standards, these are no longer accepted as a valuable part of the equipment for reality testing and tend rather to provoke negativistic disavowals. As the pressure for action rises, guidelines based on past experience may be abandoned as no longer suitable, not relevant, and too slow. The sense of crisis brooks no delay. Ambitions toward heroism and martyrdom are in the making.

This attempt to cut off the present from its attachment to the past in order to propel it into rapid realization of ideals for the future demands extreme changes in superego systems. There must be an obliteration of both the individually determined and the socially reinforced criteria for behavior, and the substitution of collective ones seen in accord with the aim of the movement. This radical change usually involves both aggressive and sexual behavior. Such changes appear spontaneously as part of the merging of the individual with the crowd, accompanying blurring of individual identities, the alteration in the sense of reality, and the ongoing process of alienation. They are favored by the inherent contagion of the crowd situation and by specific slogans and teachings of revolutionary leaders. The phrases "Property is theft," "God is dead," and the defense of violence as "Propaganda by the deed"—slogans voiced in the anarchist activities of the 19th century—are reproduced in slightly changed forms in the present period.

The one-for-all and all-for-one attitude in revolutionary crowds, transcending the limits of private property and justifying theft, extends itself as well to the sexual affiliation of members. Individual allegiances tend to be looked upon as too close to private ownerships and an ideal is promoted of group sharing of sex as of other matters of property. While this is rationalized and justified by idealistic principles—e.g., "Make love not war"—it seems to have its roots in the general process of regression to pregenital levels, which occurs under the stimulation of the multiple crowd contacts. Lasting loyalty between couples on occasion is regarded as dangerous to primary loyalty to the cause, in this respect resembling the strictures put on members in many religious communities. But it is probably true that there is actually a diminished ability to enter into or maintain personal emotional attachments between couples such as might be sustained under other circumstances; and revolutionary conditions are inherently incompatible with sustained family life.

Through personal communications from a few young people who have been involved in the most militant revolutionary crowd activities, I have had occasional glimpses into some of the sexual behavior which occurred during and after activistic assemblies. There seems, as one might expect, a great variety of responses to the mounting tension which may culminate in behavior which is both sexual and violent, but is often not really personal. It is probably impossible to determine how much this is due to so pervasive and suffusing a stimulation by a melange of emotions as to produce genital arousal anyway, and how much it is patterned by earlier, even childhood circumstances. Such sexual unions may be regarded as an incidental and almost automatic need, or at most as a temporary alliance, more of a bond in the movement than of lasting significance to the participants. In similar situations at other times with excitement of a less specifically activistic nature, it is probable that the response might have been one of masturbation with sadomasochistic fantasies. The sexual relationship seems not to be felt as part of a true object relationship with mutual appreciation of the individuality of the partners. Although in some of the smaller groups there may be more lasting alliances derived from or concurrent with the massive crowded rallies, marriage generally is looked upon as an unwarranted demand for private ownership and a disloyalty to the collective cause.

The ideal of complete equality (sameness) of all people carries with it the tendency to minimize or even deny differences between the sexes. This in turn is seen as eliminating problems of jealousy whether on a property or a sexual basis. It appears, however, that jealousy and envy, among the most ambivalent and basic of all emotions, cannot be completely repressed for long periods and may break out with particular virulence among members of the movement as well as between leaders. When such ambivalence is dealt with by an attempt at total repression and the projection of the hostile component onto the "enemy," it gives added motivation to the activist undertaking. But in the failing of this, it contributes to schisms and intramovement fighting. It also breeds temporary and fluctuating paranoid sensitivities.

The whole picture gives the impression of a general but inevitable regression to pregenital levels, in which genitality is used chiefly in the interest of narcissism and associated with polymorphous perverse impulses and activities. In some groups the practicing of perverse sexual acts is promoted or demanded as a sign of loyalty to the group and as evidence of genuine commitment. It is my impression that sexual activity, of whatever sort, is sometimes an effort to find the way to an as-if individual relationship to combat the feeling of lonely alienation if there is either a break in the continuum of excitement or a state of saturation with it.

Such dramatic sexual behavior is even more pronounced in crowds in which the special incisive rhythm of electronically produced rock music has played a part, as at Woodstock and Altamont. Here the special beat of the music so intensified the excitement that when disturbance occurred, a large portion of the crowd ran amok in a fantastic way showing wild sexual and aggressive behavior (Eisen, 1970).

Related to and perhaps derived from the fairly widespread change in sexual mores is a corresponding change in attitudes toward the care of infants. This is naturally seen more in the communes or other agglomerations of disaffected youth than in crowds as such. There has been some tendency to relegate the care of infants to collective rather than individual parents, rationalized as beneficial for the child not to be kept as private property but rather to be given the freedom of full and multiple experience with a variety of parents. This is sometimes carried to the extent that parents neglect young children scarcely able to walk and do not protect them even from situations of danger since they assert they have no right to inflict their standards or patterns of anxiety on the infant. While these situations may represent only a small minority, the idea of caring for children in groups even within the first 2 years of life, with minimal parent contact, seems to have taken hold rather generally. While it can be well defended as a compromise measure in situations of extreme economic deprivation, yet compromise seems on the way to being accepted as ideal. It is a situation worthy of careful study and consideration.

IV

Thus far I have attempted to describe the psychological situation in a crowd which produces changes in its members such as to permit the unleashing of primitive attitudes and behavior with increasing pressure for activity, all of which can be exploited for revolutionary aims. This implies certainly that there must already be a nucleus of activistically minded individuals, appearing either openly as leaders or scattered about through the crowd. There is always the question what force does the crowd actually lend: is this real or is it illusory? While the gathering of so great a number of people in a mass is an impressive sight, it is hard to estimate how many are deeply committed to a cause and how many are only excited drop-ins. It is obvious that the mounting pressure for activity in an aroused crowd threatens its very existence in its self-defeating excesses, unless there is leadership progressively developing along with some degree of organization. This leadership either may be implicit in the development of some central ideology which has already gained a considerable foothold, most often among smaller groups of intellectuals before it has become the subject of a movement; or leadership may be invested in a few individuals who have unusual charismatic qualities appealing to the crowd. But unless there is a unifying leadership and strong central cause, sufficient to absorb the diverse forms in which social grievances appear, disruptions and increasing violence between factions are bound to occur. At any rate, the crowd assemblages are to a certain extent showy demonstrations and must be supplemented by smaller, selected groups working underground.

The protest marches as demonstrations for peace and in support of the Black Civil Rights Movement were the forerunners of the crowds in the last decade. While the organizational structure of these marches was flexible and the number of participants far exceeded anticipation, a certain control existed by virtue of their being clearly oriented toward specific purposes and by the marching itself which offered an outlet of activity with a natural rhythm and progression. But these were soon succeeded by massive agglomerations of radical students. In these situations the preparatory organization was not usually publicly announced. This gave the semblance and atmosphere of spontaneous and vigorous force which soon turned to violence and vandalism, which then took on a distinctive turn toward anarchy. It is not clear, however, how much this is sustained in any central way, although violence seems to have infected smaller groups and possibly to have contributed to increased acts of violence in young delinquents. This situation is, however, further complicated by the concurrent drug problem.

In the studies of crowds during the last 100 years, two points of view emerge most clearly. One holds that although crowds show great irrationality, excessive emotion and volatility, with primitive behavior tending toward violence, still they represent a progressive force. According to this theory their very destructiveness is necessary to provide the dissolution of worn-out civilization and permit a new social order to grow up. This was expressed explicitly by Le Bon (1895). He further believed that in the loss of the individual by merging into the crowd, a new collective organism is formed which possesses strength and regenerative power. His comparison of the mass of the crowd to a new biological multicellular organism seems to me a misconceived analogy without evidence. Trotter (1916) and Freud (1921) have mentioned this same idea. It may rather be that the gathering crowds in times of trouble serve as warnings of danger and that the ultimate social rearrangement which occurs derives not so much from the inherent goodness and strength of the oppressed as from the awakening of the people and the efforts of the best members of the populace, not necessarily involved directly in the crowds. In his statement Le Bon seems possibly to confuse the crowd with the populace at large. His point of view is essentially an anarchistic one and was expressed earlier by Bakunin who in 1849 wrote of the necessity for destruction. "Let us put our trust in the external spirit which destroys and annihilates only because it is the unsearchable and eternally creative source of all life. The urge to destroy is also a creative urge. . . . There will be a qualitative transformation, a new living, life-giving revelation, a new heaven and a new earth, a young and mighty world in which all our present dissonances will be resolved into a harmonious whole" (Woodcock, 1962, p. 139). This has a religious ring to it. But it also resembles those suicidal ideas which seem to be based in part on a belief in rebirth. In individuals already psychotically predisposed, it may appear in the most gruesome expansions of ideas of persecution with world savior grandiosity. Belief in magic appears as part of a sweeping and severe regression and may give rise to fantastic cults.

Le Bon further felt that he was writing in a period of transformation; that there was a decline in the power of the church and of the state at the same time that the new conditions of existence accorded by new scientific and industrial developments were not yet securely established. He argued that in this period of transition, anarchy was inevitable and he predicted that mankind was entering an era of crowds. The repeated waves of revolution in France, accompanied by extreme amassment of crowds during the 19th century, undoubtedly colored Le Bon's conceptions. One senses also the influence of the teachings of Rousseau and the later writings and activities of men like Proudhon and Fourier, in Le Bon's confidence in the ultimate, regenerative, collective strength of man-in-crowds. It is not my intention here, however, to go into details of these developments. But I would contrast Le Bon's assumptions with Freud's views.

In his work *Group Psychology and the Analysis of the Ego,* Freud stressed particularly the role of the individual as seen in the leader in groups. Writing in 1921 soon after the end of the First World War, he believed that the era of crowds was past, having really belonged to the special conditions of the French revolutions. Consequently, he considered the "crowd" as described by Le Bon and others as no longer significant. He saw the crowds of the 20th century as large, organized groups and used as his illustrations the Army and the Church, both of which were highly organized with authoritative leadership. He discussed the relations of the leader to the individual members of a large group, essentially in terms of the libido theory, with the emphasis on the oedipal relationship involved. It was a period in which ego psychology in the terms in which we now know it had not yet been enunciated. A number of his footnotes, however, make suggestions regarding the processes going on in individual members of large groups in terms of early identifications essentially belonging to the period of separation and individuation, but then referred to simply as characteristic of the oral phase.

Neither Freud nor Le Bon nor any of the other writers (Trotter, McDougall, Moede, Sidis) of the period around the time of the First World War could anticipate how great would be the coming technological developments in communication and transportation which have caused the world to shrink in size and at the same time expand in space. Even the earlier stages of these developments meant a much greater ease in bringing together huge crowds, exploited, for example, in Germany before and during the Second World War as a means of spreading propaganda. Now crowds in any part of the world may communicate in some degree with crowds at any other part. It seems that it is, or soon will be, impossible for any revolutionary movement to remain sufficiently isolated and circumscribed to be rapidly successful. Ideological cross-fertilization between different areas of unrest may readily occur. This may have unexpected potentialities both of value and of risk, the full range of which it is impossible to predict.

BIBLIOGRAPHY

EISEN, J. (1970), *Altamont: Death of Innocence in the Woodstock Nation.* New York: Avon Books.

FREUD, S. (1921), Group Psychology and the Analysis of the Ego. *Standard Edition,* 18:67–143. London: Hogarth Press, 1955.

KROPOTKIN, P. (1899), *Memoirs of a Revolutionist.* Boston: Houghton Mifflin.

LE BON, G. (1895), *The Crowd: A Study of the Popular Mind.* London: Fisher Unwin, 1910.

LEVY, A. (1960), *Operation Elvis.* New York: Henry Holt.

MCDOUGALL, W. (1920), *The Group Mind.* New York & London: Putnam.

POWERS, T. (1971), *Diana: The Making of a Terrorist.* Boston: Houghton Mifflin.

TROTTER, W. (1916), *Instincts of the Herd in Peace and War.* London: Fisher Unwin, 1920.

WOODCOCK, G. (1962), *Anarchism: A History of Libertarian Ideas and Movements.* Cleveland & New York: Meridian Books.

— & AVAKUMORIC, I. (1950), *The Anarchist Prince.* New York: Shocken Books.

A Study of "Main-Line" Heroin Addiction

A Preliminary Report

PATRICIA RADFORD, M.A., STANLEY
WISEBERG, M.B., Ch.B., M.R.C. Psych.,
D.P.M., AND CLIFFORD YORKE, M.R.C.S.,
L.R.C.P., M.R.C. Psych., D.P.M.

IN A RECENT CRITICAL SURVEY OF PSYCHOANALYTIC WRITINGS ON drug addiction one of us (Yorke, 1970) drew attention to some of the anomalies that exist in the literature spanning a period of

Miss Radford is a child therapist of the Hampstead Training and Staff Member; Dr. Wiseberg is a psychiatrist; and Dr. Yorke is Psychiatrist-in-Charge, Hampstead Child-Therapy Course and Clinic.

The Hampstead Child-Therapy Course and Clinic is at present supported by the Field Foundation, Inc., New York; the Foundation for Research in Psychoanalysis, Beverly Hills, California; the Freud Centenary Fund, London; The Anna Freud Foundation, New York; the National Institute for Mental Health, Bethesda, Maryland; the New-Land Foundation, Inc., New York; and a number of private supporters.

We wish to express our warm appreciation to Dr. M. M. Glatt for his valuable help and advice. We are also indebted to Dr. Alan Edwards for the help he has given, and to the Staff of the Unit where our patients were treated, for their ready cooperation and helpful suggestions.

(156)

some 80 years and pointed to several possible sources of confusion and misunderstanding. The problem of definition was, and remains, one of the more obvious of these; but the difficulties in distinguishing between the psychological effects of a drug on the one hand and the pharmacological effects on the other, and the problem of whether addiction to different types of drugs could be distinguished on etiological grounds were, and remain, vexed questions. Although such difficulties were only to be expected, it was disappointing to conclude that "idiosyncratic viewpoints . . . can sometimes obscure otherwise useful clarifications of existing knowledge; that too many papers fail to supply convincing clinical evidence to support their assertions; [and] that, overall, there is a good deal of diagnostic disarray" (p. 156). In some instances, this was traced to an unfortunate tendency on the part of some writers to equate depressive affect and its relief with manic-depressive states; and in others, to mistake the impelling character of addictions for obsessive-compulsive states. Further grounds for criticism included the remarkable refusal of a number of writers to acknowledge the contributions of their colleagues and predecessors and even less to make use of them.

The diagnostic status of addictive states was the main focus of that review; and it was precisely in this respect that the literature appeared to be most uncertain or contradictory. A study group formed at the Hampstead Clinic as a result of these gloomy conclusions felt bound to re-emphasize that a psychoanalytic diagnosis was neither more nor less than a metapsychological diagnosis; and that it might therefore be profitable to devise a methodology by which Anna Freud's (1962) Diagnostic Profile could be used to clarify some of the nosological problems involved (see also A. Freud et al., 1965).

Methodology

The Profile has been used routinely for diagnostic assessment at the Clinic for the past ten years. It has been widely used elsewhere for a similar purpose. To quote Anna Freud (1965):

> Fact finding during the process of assessment produces a mass of information made up of data of different value and referring

to different areas and layers of the child's personality: organic and psychic, environmental, innate and historical elements; traumatic and beneficial events; past and present development, behavior, and achievements; successes and failures; defenses and symptomatology, etc. Although all the data that are elicited merit careful investigation, . . . it is basic to analytic thinking that the value of no single item should be judged independently, i.e., not without the item being seen within its setting [p. 138].

The information made available during the diagnostic procedure is therefore organized by the investigating psychoanalyst into a comprehensive picture of the patient in metapsychological terms —that is, in terms of dynamics, genetics, economics, structure, and adaptation. Such a profile is necessarily provisional, but it has the merit of attempting to assess the relevant contributions of a large number of variables to the personality and presenting clinical picture. In this way, it serves as a valuable pointer to diagnosis, management, and prognosis.

The use of the Profile as a research tool developed from this original application. It soon became evident that the Profile provided a standardized structure for the fullest possible assessment of the patient within the limits of the available data. Since this structure is known and reproducible by psychoanalytically trained clinical research workers anywhere, the Profile can be checked and rechecked wherever the original data are available. Furthermore, practiced users of the Profile should have a high standard of consistency from case to case; and there should, in addition, be reliable comparisons between the work of one group of investigators and another. Research workers are free to delineate points of comparison between one patient and another and between groups of patients.

The Profile thus becomes a systematic method for investigating problems of personality development and function. From the standpoint of the behavioral sciences, it affords a method that can be replicated and reviewed by outside observers. Within a standardized framework, it opens up the complexities of normative and deviant personality development to an investigative method which has a coherent theory—psychoanalysis—which is both its rationale and its organizing and defining basis.

It seems to us that it is precisely such considerations which make the Profile especially suited to the evaluation of groups of patients who, from a descriptive point of view, are commonly classified together but whose nosological status otherwise remains uncertain. In the present study we have taken as our focus of investigation a group of patients who would commonly be described as "main-line" heroin addicts, and have sought to apply to them, systematically, the method and technique of metapsychological assessment by Diagnostic Profile.

We decided to restrict our project to patients who had been admitted to an inpatient unit for the treatment of addiction; and to minimize the number of variables we confined our investigation to "main-line" heroin addicts, even though, in practice, such patients often used additional drugs. It was further decided to study only those cases where an independent family history that included the patient's early years was available—a requirement which limited the range of patients we assessed and caused a number of delays in the project. In every case the patient had been both psychologically and physiologically dependent on the drug; but no further criteria were adduced for the purposes of the study. These were therefore operational, but were made without prejudice as to whether or not other forms of "main-lining," or the use of other routes of ingestion, could be excluded from our findings.

Whatever its shortcomings, this pragmatic approach had the merit of making sure that the group of patients concerned were seriously addicted to their drug to a point at which the craving for it, and the need to procure it, were for each of them the major priorities. It excluded mere drug users, and it set aside, as a matter of policy, the varied applications and implications of such current terminology as "habituation" and "dependency" (a term favored by the World Health Organization) .

There were undoubted disadvantages in the method of selection employed. To begin with, we tied ourselves to the investigation of a group of patients who came to us from one type of source. They were all engaged in group treatment under a special inpatient regime, and had already been selected by the staff of the unit on a basis of their suitability for such a setting. Addicts who were unprepared for such measures were necessarily excluded, and many more of the seriously delinquent addicts would not be found in such a sample. If, for example, we had only investigated addicts who were sent to gaol, many more of this latter type would surely have been included.

Our criteria imposed further limitations. Few girls, for example, were to be found in the unit concerned. In effect, then, we appear to have chosen a type of addict in whom a serious addiction was both the leading complaint and the motivation for treatment. But it cannot be denied that this had important effects on our methodology and was restrictive in the type of patient coming under consideration. It seems possible that these limitations of selection may not be too serious as long as they are stated and kept in mind.

One point must be added. We were very skeptical of the possibility of deriving valid conclusions from diagnostic assessments alone. To begin with, therefore, we clung to the hope that a small number of the group we worked with would prove suitable for analysis—though albeit with modifications—in the expectation that additional data would come to light in a way which could hardly be expected from Profile applications alone. Yet, so far, only one patient was in thrice-weekly treatment as a preparation for full analysis, and she discontinued treatment after 18 months. It must, regretfully, be admitted that this aspect of our project remains so far unrealized.

We therefore embarked on a pilot series of Profiles, to include 10 in all, based on detailed interviews and detailed social histories by members of the diagnostic team. It was hoped that, by formulating the data in Profile form, we would lay a basis for certain conclusions, however tentative, about the diagnostic status of this group of patients.

Since our study is unfinished, we are not yet in a position to draw conclusions. But we are impressed by a lack of uniformity in the diagnostic status of the patients we have so far assessed, and it is this point we have chosen to illustrate in this interim report. We therefore present two cases of apparently disparate personalities and pathology, both of whom developed similar addictions. In the interests of readability, we have adopted a narrative style.

First, however, a word must be said in fairness to the existing literature which, for the most part, *preceded* the fashion for drugs —certainly in England, if not elsewhere. We do not know to what extent social trends and availability of drugs have altered the problem, and no one knows what clinical pictures our current cases would have presented had they lived in a different social environment and at earlier times. (In Scotland, where the incidence of drug addiction lags behind the English figures, the heavy use of alcohol has persisted in young people to a greater extent than it has in England.) Perhaps, then, some of these cases would have been alcoholics; others might simply have been delinquents or developed crippling neuroses. And perhaps some would have developed more acute depressions and a few committed suicide. Indeed, through their drug-taking, many still do.

Profiles

Sarah S.

This 20-year old girl was interviewed at the drug addiction unit following a conviction for attempting to smuggle drugs into the country. Treatment was a condition of probation imposed by the Court.

She had not taken drugs for 3 months. She was a pale, plump brunette with an overexpressive face and ungraceful gestures. She was a little euphoric, giggly, histrionic, and mildly flirtatious. She tended to be overfriendly and even ingratiating, and her manner was appropriate to a 15-year-old. She was careless and untidy in her everyday dress; but, while her stockings were laddered, her hair was beautifully kept. On one occasion when she was specially "got up," she looked quite smart, but her taste was uneven. She spoke very freely, and on the whole well, with a lot of fashionable incoherence. She was sometimes discursive and needed help to return to the point. She displayed an unvarying and humorous affect, with little appreciation of the importance of what she might be saying. She could not depict people *as people;* for the most part, only their actions emerged and even then only those that directly affected the patient.

She was the wanted first child in a respectable, upper-working-class family. The mother was timid, narrow, rigid, and so unadventurous that a short urban journey was regarded as a major expedition. She and the father had worked and known each other in the same office for about 10 years before they married. Both before and after marriage, Mrs. S. lived in her mother's house, largely shielded from the wider world. The pregnancy with Sarah was uneventful, though labor was protracted and led to a forceps delivery.

Sarah slept well, ate well, and was described as "the perfect baby." She was breast-fed for nearly a year and was weaned almost immediately to a cup. Although she sucked her thumb for many years, there were no food fads or feeding problems. An eiderdown functioned as a transitional object until the child was 10, when it fell to bits completely. She walked at 15 months, and talked in sentences almost from the time she first used words, at 2. She was clean about the same time and dry by 3, with an occasional wet bed until she was 5. Unhappily, at that time the grandmother, who had been a strong support to the mother and taken a kindly interest in the child, died.

Sarah was quiet, unadventurous, and never demanded affection, which, in any case, was rarely displayed to her. She met frustration with tears, and if these had no tangible effect, quickly complied with what the adults wanted. Although Sarah played, apparently happily, with one or two of the neighbor's children, the household remained quiet and was rarely visited. Her friends throughout latency were boys rather than girls. She preferred boys' games and toys, and never had a doll, though she did like a teddy bear. She was unable to show aggression, however; if one of her friends upset her, she cried and cried. In public, she bottled up her feelings; in private, she would give vent to them for hours.

From about the age of 3 or 4 Sarah was "Daddy's girl" and remained so until puberty. She showed little involvement with her mother. During latency she expressed some dissatisfaction with her family. She wanted a brother or sister "like other children," and, when she was 7 years old, her sister Jane was born— apparently in response to Sarah's wishes. But Sarah displayed little overt interest in the child.

At 9 she fell from her bicycle, suffered a concussion, and was taken to a hospital, where she remained for about a week, crying each time her parents left her.

Although she failed her 11+ examination (against all expectations), she was given a place in a grammar/secondary school. She failed to live up to her potential, though ultimately she passed 5 subjects at 0 (ordinary) levels and art at an A (advanced) level. By this time, however, her history was closely bound up with her drug taking, which will be described in detail. Meanwhile we can note that her menstruation began at $12\frac{1}{2}$ and that she apparently took it all in her stride. But her relationship with her father deteriorated. Rows easily developed, often provoked by Sarah, and would end in violence and mutual physical attack.

In her early teens she was openly contemptuous of her father; declined to go on any "boring" family holidays; began to stay out late; and turned her back on the Youth Club to which she had hitherto belonged. She started drinking nightly with a group of girls, and by the time she was 15 was managing 5 pints a night. She was already on hashish. She took dexedrine on odd occasions, increased the hashish, and soon gave up drink entirely. With the same group she moved on to heroin, and began to fix regularly with heroin *and* cocaine in substantial doses. It is not altogether clear where she obtained her money; but at 16 she was convicted of larceny. In spite of all this she passed art at the advanced level at 18, but when she was offered a deferred, and not an immediate, place at art school, she gave up art altogether. She drifted from job to job, and totally abandoned her parents' way of life for one of semivagrancy with a fellow addict (Tom) with whom she became inextricably entangled. The two of them ended up penniless in the Far East; the parents paid Sarah's fare home; and Sarah was arrested on arrival and charged with attempting to import cannabis into the country. While on remand in prison awaiting sentence, she heard that her boyfriend had died from an overdose of drugs. She was now quite friendless and utterly lonely; and her only interest was to get hold of and read every newspaper report on drugs and drug offenses.

Where the growth of an addictive syndrome is so difficult to separate from the life history, the isolation of significant environmental factors is wholly a matter of guesswork. We can merely note, *inter alia,* that the parental personalities were narrow, rigid, and unimaginative; that the mother's aggression was sufficiently inhibited to impoverish parental effectiveness; that she could rarely show Sarah affection; and that the father's potential warmth was never realized after the child's puberty. As for the early history, the death of the grandmother may have meant a significant loss of affectionate support. The importance of the birth of Jane and of the mother's confinement in the hospital is difficult to assess; but it *is* known that Sarah's accident, concussion, and hospitalization at the age of 9 occasioned her some distress. These and other possible factors remain matters of obscurity.

When we come to consider Sarah's instinctual life a number of points can be made with greater certainty. Although she claims to have reached orgasm in an adult, feminine, genital position, this occurred only in the drug-taking phase, and with one partner, Tom, whom she described as identical with herself. She had accepted, before this phase, penetration from a number of other males, with some excitement but without orgasm. But even Tom scarcely seems to have been a masculine object for her; and it is noteworthy that she had intense pleasure in watching him fix himself, in fixing herself, and in flushing. ("I got a kick out of giving myself injections, and didn't like it much if someone else injected me. I enjoyed the routine, finding a vein, filling a syringe, and flushing. . . . I would flush and flush and flush until I couldn't continue because it clotted. Having injected all the H, I would flush in and out the ordinary blood. I don't know why— it was a sort of compulsion to make the fix last longer. I couldn't bear to pull the needle out.") This description suggests not only the masturbatory significance of these acts, but also that the penis (and its substitutes) were more important than the sexual relationship itself.

The wish for the narcissistic possession of the penis seems important in the undoubtedly homosexual tendencies in her makeup: "I went through a lesbian phase from 11 to 14 . . . imitation lovemaking in bedrooms with a number of girlfriends, each pretending to be a boy and swapping roles." There was kissing and mutual masturbation between them. Although she mentioned fantasies of men in such situations, there was a continuous inclination toward homosexual practice beyond the age of 14 and, indeed, up to the present time. "I appreciate a woman's body. There was a girl at school I fancied when I was 16. . . . In prison Butch Lesbians fancied me, and if a woman had made advances, I just would have gone with her." This homosexuality was uninfluenced by the drug-taking; and it can therefore be said that she failed to resolve the re-emergence of the negative oedipal (phallic) position in adolescence.

These remarks anticipate the complexities of her self and object cathexes. Her libidinal investment in her body image, her psychic image of the self, and her superego is insufficient to insure adequate self-regard, self-esteem, or a continued sense of well-being. As a child she was not very confident and felt dominated by other people. As she recalled it, much later: "If they talked, they seemed to take all my vibrations and my life force. . . . When I met people with overbearing personalities, I just clammed up." At puberty, she had "an inferiority complex—like paranoia [*sic*]. I had no confidence in myself and I still have none when I'm not on drugs." Drugs bolstered her courage and made her feel bigger and better. She could not otherwise withstand minor disappointments; her deferment by the art school is a case in point. Disturbances of self-esteem may have contributed to depressive affect, feelings of unworthiness, and the suicidal thinking to which subsequent references will be made.

There were paradoxical tendencies in her bodily cathexis; and these were partly reflected in anomalies of dress and appearance. Furthermore, although she took menstruation in her stride, her ideal self image was far from wholly feminine.

Her choice of object, while need-fulfilling and relatively constant, was narcissistically determined to an unusual degree. Of her former girlfriend, Emily, she said: "I can't say much about her except we were the same sort of people; we were terribly alike; we used to think the same things were funny. She had black hair, the same color and length as mine. We always had it cut and grew it at the same time. She was the same height as me. We got into the same difficulties at school. . . . It was like knocking around with oneself." Of her boyfriend, Tom, she said: "We viewed the world in pretty much the same way; we were like just one person, not like two people courting; we adapted to each other immediately and have no other thoughts. It's the common bond in junk."

As for Sarah's family relationships, the sadistic wish to hurt the masochistic mother was coupled with denigration. Her contempt for her mother's timorous behavior was particularly striking. Nevertheless, she saw certain similarities between the mother and herself, while remaining well aware of the differences. She told the psychiatrist: "Mother is always so very long-suffering. I felt malicious trying to get her to show some hurt; she never did. If she wants something, she won't go out and get it. I think she's the opposite of myself." On the other hand, as a small child, when reproached by her mother, Sarah would dissolve into tears and, in the end, comply.

Although, from roughly the age of 3 years onward, she had a loving relationship with her father, this changed, around puberty, to a denigrating, sadomasochistic one, with hints of derogation of oedipal wishes. In describing her father's anger, she said: "I became terrified. I thought my father might kill me. He didn't bother where he hit me. This reached its peak when I began to control myself better when I was 14."

Her early friendship with Emily was lost after she took up with Tom. In spite of the latter, she emerged, during this phase of serious addiction, as a singularly lonely and pathetic figure. The continuing tie to the parents, which has survived the addiction to date, did nothing to mitigate this impression. On further specific points it can be said that:

1. For all her fantasies of herself and Tom as parents, she has nowhere achieved the attitude necessary for motherhood.

2. She has no group relationship of any kind; and, with the death of Tom, no close friendships remain.

3. Her narcissistic organization gives every sexual relationship, whether overtly heterosexual or covertly homosexual, a masturbatory quality.

4. This also holds true for her relationship to inanimate objects, such as drugs and their use in fixing.

At this point, some comment on Sarah's aggression seems called for. She was only too well aware of the defensive, if wavering, nature of her timidity. She said, for example: "I'm inclined to be aggressive, but when I was younger I didn't show it very much, but would burst into tears, crying hysterically for hours." But she added: "If someone else was spoiling for a fight, I'd lay into them, otherwise I'd bottle it up until my next outburst. After I was 8, when I got into a temper, I would yell and scream, attacking them with words but never physically." As already mentioned, however, she did have fights with her father in early puberty.

These quotations could be amplified, but illustrate, we believe, the uncertain nature of her ego control when drugs were not at her service. She *then* had particular reason to mistrust her aggressive inclinations. Indeed, after withdrawal from drugs in the hospital, she was afraid that her aggressive outbursts would be so catastrophic that she would be put in a locked ward. It is of some interest that, when superego functioning was mitigated in group activity, she took part in a combined attack on an elderly woman patient, who was knocked to the ground while Sarah and her accomplices danced round her, laughing.

On drugs, Sarah rarely experienced anger; but when drugs were withdrawn, she could be "very emotional" and easily aggressive. ("You want not to hurt people, like your parents, but you do.") Drugs appeared to reduce aggressive impulses and thus afford better control. Nevertheless, even in childhood, conscious control could at least delay discharge—for example, in crying; while, on occasion, hostility and associated affects could be dealt with by repression and denial. She showed no overt jealousy of Jane, but fainted at the sight of her sister's blood. Her aggression was not appreciably modified in the service of her personality, whether in sexual life, in work, or in sublimatory activities.

We have touched on the tenuous nature of Sarah's defense organization; and the fears of transfer to a locked ward imply some recognition of the need for auxiliary control. But the same example also suggests that she feared the aggression of others as much as she feared her own. Her fears of domination or derision may have had a similar basis; but her use of projection and externalization was modest compared with its severity in the drug psychoses to which we shall shortly refer. Nevertheless, externalization of the superego could be illustrated by numerous examples from childhood onward.

A fuller account of Sarah's defenses as they relate to libidinal as well as aggressive drives would emphasize the use of repression in dealing with some of the associated drive content; the use of displacement when the elderly victim of the group attack was seen as a "witch with a moustache" and thereby represented the phallic mother; and the partial use of denial in dealing, for example, with the *strength* of her homosexual drives: "There might be a slight persistence of lesbian feelings. I just appreciate a woman's body." But we would have to conclude that her defense organization was immature; that primitive mechanisms were prominent; that it was not well-balanced; and that its ineffectiveness reflected a more general lack of ego strength. And although defense organization *is* related to superego structure, this in itself had abnormal qualities. Lastly, the role of addiction in defense organization remains problematical, but its modification of realistic anxiety, instinctual anxiety, and superego anxiety must be born in mind.

In the early stages of drug-taking, Sarah's ego functions were relatively intact (she gained 5 O levels and one A level in spite of plentiful use of beer and hashish). Later, certain phases of amphetamine intoxication brought intermittent failure of reality testing. "I feared I might be regarded as psychotic. I'm thinking of the confused time; some people go on being mad after stopping the drug; my confusion was pretty terrible. People could read my thoughts, it was terrifying. They would laugh at me, and partly they'd be laughing at me thinking they could read my thoughts." She had visual illusions and possibly hallucinations. "I had paranoid things where people were walking around after me. It was always the police who were after us (Tom and me). We both got terrified of railway stations where we thought people were hiding and following us. When two people have the same horrors, it escalates." These features are entirely typical of an amphetamine psychosis and disappeared when that drug was discontinued. But although her reality testing has noticeably improved since withdrawal, it still showed impairment in certain directions. She still wondered "if some of these things really happened," and she still showed paranoid trends in her thinking. For example, she could be locked up, stopped from doing what she wanted, and her mind captured so that she would not be herself anymore.

When she was on drugs, but not psychotic, her appreciation of her relationships with other people was altered. To quote: "When on drugs you haven't noticed people. You wouldn't be aware of people as people who think or feel. You would talk to people only as someone to talk to, not as people."

The combination of an externalization of the superego with an impaired reality sense is of interest, since it operates inconsistently, to say the least. For example, when she described the attack on the old woman to the psychiatrist, she showed no expectation of disapproval from him and superego criticism was suspended, *not* externalized. Furthermore, her expectation that, as a representative of authority, he would identify with her illegal (as opposed to immoral) activity points to some defect, however temporary, in her reality testing.

Her superego, then, showed conflicting features. It was partly built on the introjection of strict and punitive paternal standards, while certain maternal introjects simultaneously provided the girl with more permissive standards and ideals. Matters were complicated by the introjection of the maternal narrowness and rigidity against which she had rebelled with delinquency, globe-trotting, and drug taking.

Perhaps it was the double-sidedness of her superego which accounted for its failure to provide consistently benign internal influences or to set adequate aims; and this may equally have had a bearing on the vacillating nature of her guilt. While she told the psychiatrist that she was very upset at Tom's death, she also expressed the conviction that she should have felt this more deeply, though the following quotation showed that this matter was complicated: "I should have cracked up. I think people felt I was very insensitive because of this. I wanted to have no personality so that people couldn't pin me down." Furthermore: "I don't blame myself consciously. I don't think I have done so *sub*consciously . . . at one time I didn't give a damn. . . ." Again: "If I tell a lie I feel very hung up about it. At the time I'm glad I put it over, but afterward I feel awful that they go around believing something that wasn't true." Again, on Tom's death: "If I had been strong-willed, I might have got Tom off drugs and he'd have been alive. Then again we might have broken off, but then perhaps I could have got him off."

While an apparent attitude of laissez-faire colored some of these assertions, the degree of self-punishment afforded by drug-taking may have reduced the severity of her guilt. We must also remember that Sarah's reflections were rooted in her preconscious experiences. We feel that a closer scrutiny of her history suggests that her unconscious relationship of superego to ego was deeply instinctualized, and that the battles of her early teens, fought out with external authority, reflected a personalized relationship between these internal structures of a strongly sadomasochistic kind. However this may be, it can be said, in fine, that her superego, while structuralized, was unstable, instinctualized, ineffective in providing adequate aims, and repeatedly worked against her own real interests. It is highly probable that, in one form or another,. this girl will succumb to her self-destructiveness.

At this point it will be convenient to summarize the evidence for fixation points at various instinctual levels. Different ones appeared to be prominent at different times. What follows is placed chronologically and not necessarily in order of importance.

As in all our assessments, evidence of oral fixation points will not be adduced from the addiction itself in spite of the importance of drinking and oral drugging in this patient's teens. However, there appeared to be significant oral components in Sarah's never-ending, unsatisfied, object hunger and her continuing search for an idealized and need-fulfilling (fantasied) object. (The phallic element in the search is mentioned below.) We have emphasized the strong narcissistic components in her object relations and that drugs too were important in this respect.

Anal-sadistic components were conspicuous in her relationships with her mother and in her teen-age fights with her father. The wish to hurt the mother was expressed in one of the interviews, and Sarah derived pleasure from tormenting her. Her anality also showed through in her appearance, and the interviewing psychiatrist also described Sarah as a "really messy personality." He felt that some of this was reflected in her fixing habits [1] and junkie surroundings.

Regressive shifts toward anality were linked with a concomitant degradation of oedipal relationships. The latter also showed evi-

---

[1] It is of interest that a common junkie name for heroin is "shit," although none of our patients to date has used this word in interviews.

dence of their phallic quality. Here the wish to hurt the mother was allied with the wish to play the man's role in intercourse; and although Sarah's discussion of this was largely in terms of her early adolescence, she left no doubt of the persistence and strength of these wishes, for example, in her account of imprisonment. The displacement of the wish for a penis to the syringe also was clear. Her homosexuality was almost overt, and included a denigration of the father in a wish for the sadistic possession of the mother.

As indicated, conclusions from Sarah's drug-taking symptomatology will not otherwise be drawn at this stage.

A few concluding words may be in order on the matter of Sarah's conflicts. Some of these have been mentioned; for example, the way in which the punishing and destructive aspects of the superego were at war with her bodily and psychic representations, and the manner in which her impoverished ego attempted to control her instinctual drives. Conflicts which at first sight appear *external* have generally proved to be re-externalizations of *internalized* struggles. The evidence for *internal* struggles was sometimes obscured, but conflicts between masculinity and femininity were nevertheless quite plain.

Richard R.

Richard, 20 years old, was a robust and athletic young man, of "open countenance," who was neatly dressed and polite. His manner was serious and "well-brought up"; and despite the mild depression he constantly showed, he could be humorous at times. He was anxious to be quite accurate and fair to all in the account he gave.

He was warm and forthright, and while he seemed to seek the good opinion of the interviewer, he was able to be comfortably assertive. If questioning annoyed him, he was able to acknowledge this without discomfort.

He expressed a deep and convincing concern for his relatives and perhaps his friends; and what he had to say of his mother, despite his marked ambivalence to her, reflected a protective attitude.

Richard was an illegitimate, only child, brought up by his

mother and her parents for his first 2 years. (The mother had refused to marry Richard's father.) She was ill throughout the pregnancy; although the baby presented abnormally, there was no physical abnormality at birth and developmental steps occurred normally. The mother and the maternal grandmother were bitterly disappointed that the patient was a boy, and from the start they apparently expected him to behave like a "good girl."

He was a contented and healthy baby, who was fed to a rigid timetable. He was habit-trained early, though he was enuretic until the age of 13. As a toddler, quietness was enforced "to avoid upsetting the neighbors," and even out of doors his mother expected him to stay clean and tidy. His passive behavior pleased his mother, and ensured him a central place in the family. The peace of the household, however, was disturbed by the drunken tempers of the maternal grandfather, to whom the patient was nevertheless attached.

When the patient was $2\frac{1}{2}$, his mother married, and the stepfather came to live in the household. The patient was displaced from his mother's bed by his stepfather, but continued to share the bedroom. Severe night terrors began and persisted until he was given his own room at the age of 7, when his family was rehoused.

When Richard started school, he was dressed prettily in a bow tie; he was bullied and was frightened by the rough boys. Soon there were some character changes; he became rebellious at home and at school; and nail biting, already present, increased in severity. A year later he started to put on weight, and would be embarrassed and blush when his school friends teased him about it. At the same time, both parents started affairs; and these were known to Richard. His rebelliousness increased; he began truanting; and he lost interest in schoolwork, though he continued to paint, swim, and play chess.

The stepfather, to whom Richard was quite attached, left home when the boy was 12 to live with another woman. A divorce followed and the father remarried. In his account of this, the patient spoke bitterly of this defection.

The mother's lover died, but she immediately found another, John, who came to live in the flat, although there was no question of marriage. John was more masculine than Richard's stepfather, but although he was generous and friendly toward the boy, Richard resented him and determined to join the Merchant Navy as soon as he was old enough. He enjoyed his training as a ship's cook, but he was less happy at sea, where he disliked the attentions of active homosexuals, though he felt at ease with passive, feminine ones. After 6 months he returned home and found work at a shop in a somewhat tough area. He did so well that he was soon put in charge, and continued this work successfully throughout the greater period of his addiction.

His drug-taking started in his middle teens.[2] After visiting a dying friend Richard was offered hashish, which he accepted. He then progressed rapidly via "skin popping" with physeptone to main-lining with methedrine and heroin. At first he allowed his friends to inject him, but later injected himself with meticulous care. He derived great pleasure from flushing for up to 5 or 10 minutes. He did this regularly for 2 years, during which time he had several attacks of methedrine psychosis.

Richard's sexual relations were limited, and he thought drugs replaced them. His most lasting relationship was with a girl who refused to have sexual intercourse with him. Furthermore, he was always attracted to girls who had some physical disability. He expressed a great deal of curiosity about what it would be like to experience homosexual relations, but said he always avoided them.

It is evident that several environmental factors may have adversely affected Richard's development: his mother's promiscuity and the consequent exposure to primal scene experiences; the lack of an adequate father figure; the mother's wish that Richard had been a girl and her tendency to treat him as such in early childhood; and the drunkenness and violence of the maternal grandfather.

Not surprisingly, Richard's close relationships, male and female, seemed strongly determined by his oedipus complex; in the positive form overtly, and more covertly in the negative form. His attachment to his mother, and his wish to possess her, dominated his life. He always showed marked rivalry with, and resentment

[2] All our cases proved to have started drug taking in their teens.

of, his mother's lovers. The wish to preserve the relationship by identifying with both male and female appeared throughout his account. This conflict may have underlain his night terrors between the age of $2\frac{1}{2}$ and 7 while he shared a bedroom with his mother and stepfather. His inability to cope with rivalry feelings was reflected in his decision to join the Merchant Navy when his mother took a new lover into the home when he was 14.

Latent wishes to be a passive feminine partner with men stemmed from competition with his mother for her partners, as well as from his relationships with father surrogates.

Conflicts in these spheres were reflected in his comment on his parents' separation: "My mother had another man friend, so you can't really blame him [the stepfather] for leaving. [But:] My father walked out . . . and didn't take me with him." He added, with a manner of feminine hurt: "I was old enough to know he didn't *want* to take me with him." Of his mother's lover, John, he merely said, "Another time we had a man living with us . . . he died when I was in the Navy."

His subsequent relationships with men had marked homosexual implications, and his fear of homosexuality made him leave the Merchant Navy. He told the psychiatrist: "I've never wanted it, but I thought about it, thought what it would be like, what it would be like with a man, any man."

He saw his fatness as embarrassingly feminine. He was pleased with himself when, under the influence of drugs, he became emaciated. But he did get *some* gratification from feminine identifications.

His friendships with girls stopped short of manifest sexuality. ("She wouldn't even let me touch her, that's why I went with her for so long—if she wouldn't let *me* touch her, she wouldn't let anyone else, so I was happy. She's married now.") On the very few occasions when he claimed to have had intercourse, he emphasized that he only went with girls for sex and that "she wasn't interested in me personally, only the sex I gave her."

Castration fears arising from his oedipal conflicts were shown in a need for damaged women and an excessive fear of hurting himself.

Under drugs his object cathexes did not change qualitatively, but apparently diminished in intensity in favor of drugs. In his own words: "I suppose drugs changed me in that I didn't always notice my family. I thought more about drugs, so I must have felt less about *them*. I was always preoccupied with the next fix."

A tattoo on his forearm displayed a dove with the word "meth" on a scroll underneath and not, as is customary, the name of a person.

While Richard's prominent pathology centered around the oedipal phase, there also was evidence of preoedipal fixations. Anal character traits were seen in the cleanliness and fastidiousness which had replaced previous pleasures in messiness; and anal phase fixations also were indicated by the ambivalent and sadomasochistic aspects of his object relations, particularly with regard to his mother.

He showed unusual pleasure in food, with consequent overeating and obesity at various times in his life. He longed for a secure, all-providing relationship with an ideal object.

Although Richard clearly manifested conflicts in his object relations, his cathexis of the self, while impaired, contributed less to his pathology. For example, he took great care of his appearance; he had reasonable expectations of regard from others; and he minimized the self-damaging effects of drug-taking by the great care with which he administered each fix: "I've never had jaundice. I've never wanted to mess my arms up. I always injected in the same place." He used a new needle and syringe for every injection. He took considerable pride in his achievements at work and in his boss's recognition of these.

On drugs, in particular methedrine, his sense of well-being and self-esteem was increased: "I don't like myself, but on 'meth' I liked my own company. On 'meth' I was the me I wanted to be." He thought he was too retiring and shy, but on methedrine "I was able to sell my goods with a great deal of confidence."

Narcissism, then, was in some respects adequate, and there was sufficient remaining libido with which to invest objects which, unlike Sarah's, were not chosen on a narcissistic basis. Nevertheless, his narcissism was largely regulated through object dependence on his mother and male peers.

We found that the aggressive drives were adequate in quantity (despite the notable passivity), and served the ego reasonably well. His aggression was under a normal degree of control, and a sufficient amount of it was available in the service of the personality for work and sublimatory activities. He was able to stand up for himself in the robust worlds of the Merchant Navy and in the rough area where he subsequently worked. He was a successful and skilled cardplayer. On occasion, he was able to be effectively forceful in the psychiatric interview. His aggressive attitude was epitomized in his statement: "I had normal quarrels and arguments, but I avoided fights. There'd be no sense in it. If anyone bashed me, I would bash them back, but if they only insulted me, I would walk away."

His passivity in his sexual relationships may not have stemmed from lack of aggression, but rather from his feminine attitude. He waited for girls to hang around his shop and was very pleased when they gave the impression that they would go out with him. Satisfied with this, he would make no active moves toward them.

Under drugs there were no marked qualitative differences, but his aggression toward his mother became more overt and direct. It is noteworthy that during the psychotic episodes projected hostility was focused on his mother. "I had thought my mother was plotting against me. She would kick me out and tell the police about my drugs. She seemed hostile." (Incidentally, it is of considerable interest that loving feelings toward his mother could be experienced only under drugs.)

Insofar as drug-taking is an attack on the body, he minimized the dangers of physical damage.

His ego functions usually were unimpaired, but in his drug-induced psychoses reality testing was defective in that he had paranoid delusions and tactile illusions; e.g., he then felt that his hair was like a mass of slimy, crawling creatures; but he recognized that these experiences were due to methedrine. He would then discontinue the drug and replace it with heroin for a few days. The effect of methedrine on his self-esteem did not appear to involve any direct effect upon self-perception. On the whole, drug-taking had surprisingly little effect on his ego functioning.

Brief mention must be made of this patient's defenses. They were employed chiefly against his libido and its affective expression, against fear of loss of love, and against castration anxiety. His defense organization was dependent on his own superego structure. His defensive measures included: identification with the physically damaged women with whom he repeatedly associated (for example, a girlfriend with a deformity of the arm) ; continual blame and reproach of his mother for all that went wrong in his development and his life; the use of reaction formation against dirtiness and untidiness; repression of childhood memories (for example, he had never, from childhood onward, remembered his fatherless early years) ; and denial of his awareness of his mother's sexual wishes toward various men who, he felt, had seduced her against her will. During his drug psychosis, his persecuting delusions relating to his mother appeared to be a projection of his own hostility toward her. In general, however, the mechanisms employed were not of an archaic order, and showed reasonable spread and variety. They were relatively effective in dealing with anxiety, but led to some disequilibrium and adaptive limitations.

Both heterosexual and homosexual drives were inhibited.

His relationships were generally impaired by these ways of dealing with his conflicts. Drug-taking may have alleviated his sexual anxieties: he said he regarded "meth" as a substitute for sex and that if he had had more sex, he might not have needed drugs. In this statement, however, he failed to acknowledge his fear of sexuality.

A few words on the superego. This was maturely structured, but its sources were not obvious. Parental influence in early life was one-sided, with guidance and discipline almost wholly maintained by his feminine relatives (mother and grandmother). The grandfather with whom Richard lived up to the age of 7 was a violent alcoholic and may have been a significant source of introjects.

The superego functioned mainly as a criticizing agency. To a limited extent it set aims, but offered little satisfaction. It was only under the influence of drugs that its strictness was relaxed, and that he could enjoy his achievement in work.

The superego was to some extent effective; and this effectiveness held up even in a drug-taking phase. It is problematical whether, in this case, the drug taking reflected a partial ineffectiveness of his superego or whether, indeed, the destructive aspect of addiction represented the sadistic side of that structure. Under internal and external pressure the superego remained stable. There was no evidence of any appreciable degree of secondary sexual or aggressive involvement, unless the drug-taking represented the latter.

In summarizing Richard's fixation points, brevity may minimize repetition. Oedipal fixation points, both positive and negative, have already been indicated in our discussion of object relationships and were regarded as dominant. The incest taboo was repeated with various girlfriends, and his fear of femininity was amply demonstrated in his account of his seafaring life. His anal fixations were clearly indicated in the way in which he used open and conspicuous drug-taking to promote a sadomasochistic relationship with his mother. His fastidiousness and cleanliness were character traits which had the status of reaction formations. Fixation in the oral phase was possibly suggested by his overeating and consequent obesity, but caution is necessary here in view of the strength of his feminine wishes.

Lastly, we venture a few observations about Richard's conflicts. External conflicts were not very evident. Internalized conflicts dominated his personality—in particular, unresolved oedipal conflicts aroused guilt and anxiety, and led to pathological solutions in terms of character formation, inhibitions, and neurotic compromises. It is possible that the drug-taking and subsequent addiction helped reduce the level of anxiety to a point at which such solutions could be maintained without recourse to further pathology. There were indications of internal, as opposed to internalized, conflicts between activity and passivity, and between masculinity and femininity.

Concluding Remarks

In the absence of conclusions drawn from the whole series of assessments, we must content ourselves with pointing to a few of the more striking comparisons these two cases present. Both had similar grave addictions, and both had episodes of amphetamine psychosis. Both experienced adverse circumstances in infancy and early childhood, though of a different nature; but their subsequent psychological growth and personality development were entirely different. This remains true, even though both came to grief over oedipal anxieties, and both showed homosexual inclinations; but these features are scarcely the prerogative of addicts.

Although Richard's oedipal conflicts were undoubtedly severe, and his defensive maneuvers largely related to these, their effects on his ego were in good measure secondary, and the resulting picture was not so very different from the neurotic or character disorders with which we are familiar in our daily analytic practice, though the addiction, of course, remains an important exception. It cannot be argued that the neuroses or character disorders in persons with an addiction have the same diagnostic status as those in persons who have no such addiction.

Nevertheless, in Richard, neither ego nor superego showed the degree of disturbance we found in Sarah; Richard's object relations, with some qualification, were more mature; he has shown some capacity for sustained and successful work even when gravely addicted; and he has maintained, throughout, relationships with peer groups.

There were other important differences, of which we select just a few. Richard's defenses, for example, were directed primarily against the libido; Sarah's, against aggression. But even the *effects* of drugs on these two people showed interesting differences. With Sarah, serious addiction diminished the force of her drives and their affective derivatives and perhaps enabled her relatively weakened ego to exert better control. In Richard's case, drugs had an opposite effect; under their influence he became aware of loving feelings as well as aggressive ones. Although the amphetamine psychosis in both cases demonstrated the characteristic features of that condition, with Richard, reality testing was never entirely lost and was quickly restored. With Sarah, however, some mild impairment persisted; a reminder, perhaps, of the more general weakness of her ego.

Indeed, Sarah's case showed an altogether more widespread and long-standing disorder. Her object relations were narcissistically determined, and her self-regard was largely achieved through narcissistic identification. Her narcissism stemmed from a fundamental lack of internal sources of self-esteem, and contrasted somewhat sharply with Richard's. Adequately modified drive expression was poor; and Sarah's superego seemed much more disturbed than Richard's, and afforded her some delinquency. All in all, Sarah's case showed a greater degree of personality impoverishment than almost any other case in our series.

Perhaps this last point, however, should lead to a word of caution. We have deliberately chosen for this publication two contrasting cases; and while we have the impression of considerable disparities between Profiles on other cases, it does not follow that closer examination will show these to be quite so wide as this selected presentation may suggest.

BIBLIOGRAPHY

FREUD, A. (1962), Assessment of Childhood Disturbances. *This Annual,* 17:149–158.
— (1965), *Normality and Pathology in Childhood.* New York: International Universities Press.
— NAGERA, H., & FREUD, W. E. (1965), Metapsychological Assessment of the Adult Personality: The Adult Profile. *This Annual,* 20:9–41.
GLOVER, E. (1956), *On the Early Development of Mind.* New York: International Universities Press.
YORKE, C. (1970), A Critical Review of Some Psychoanalytic Literature on Drug Addiction. *Brit. J. Med. Psychol.,* 43:141–159.

On the Writings
of Adolescents in a
General Hospital Ward

JOHN E. SCHOWALTER, M.D.
AND RUTH D. LORD, M.A.

PSYCHOANALYTIC LITERATURE CONCERNING THE IMPACT OF PHYSICAL illness on adolescents is relatively scanty; this is surprising because of the long accepted recognition of the importance and vulnerability of adolescence as a developmental phase. For instance, near the end of his life Freud (1939) emphasized three conditions which promote the return of the repressed: the weakening of the ego resulting in diminished anticathexis, the strengthening of the drives, and the awakening by current events of similar repressed impulses. Illness and puberty were Freud's illustrations of the

From the Department of Pediatrics, Child Study Center, Yale School of Medicine, and the Yale-New Haven Hospital.

Supported by The Children's Bureau, United States Department of Health, Education, and Welfare, The Connecticut Department of Health, and United States Public Health Service Grant No. 5T1 MH–5442–20.

(181)

first two conditions. The event of hospitalization frequently re-awakens in adolescents old conflicts about the fear of abandon-ment, the fear of body intactness or damage, and the bittersweet dilemma of forced dependency. Although to our knowledge there are no studies which conclusively show that neurotic illness reac-tions are more frequent following physical illness, surgery, or hospitalization—and there is some evidence that they are not (Vernon et al., 1966; Davenport and Werry, 1970) —such studies are fraught with enormous methodological difficulties. There is, however, no doubt that bodily illness has a significant and shap-ing influence on the mental life of children. In 1952 Anna Freud wrote a marvelously succinct article on this subject and after 20 years it remains the most seminal contribution to understanding the psychological burdens borne by sick children. Anna Freud's article, like most others in the field, deals primarily with the younger child rather than with the adolescent. This emphasis on younger children in the literature is understandable for both theoretical and practical reasons.

The insults of physical disability and of hospital separation are thought to be most damaging psychologically during the first years of life. Sylvester has pointed out that "earlier insults will have a profound and crippling effect on the development of the ego, whereas those traumata which occur after the consolidation of ego formation and of object relations will affect the ego func-tioning rather than its development" (Calef, 1959, p. 156). The Robertsons have well documented the risk which accompanies toddlers' hospitalization (1953, 1962). The adolescent, on the other hand, can communicate verbally far better than the younger child, but seldom is fully able to do so in the superficial contacts associated with the general hospital setting. There are a number of reasons for this.

The adolescent usually has a sufficient supply of defenses to mask at least partially his fears and conflicts. He is also more in-terested than the young child in doing so. Striving for final con-firmation of firm self boundaries and object stability, the ill and hospitalized adolescent often feels obliged to deny any incapacity in order to preserve a shaken belief in his own independence. De-spite his greater maturity and repertoire of ego capacities, the adolescent experiences rapid shifts and instability of identity as he is passing through a second individuation process (Blos, 1967). Only within the past decade have general hospitals begun developing separate wards for adolescent patients, thus responding to our own understanding of adolescence. The existence of these new wards in turn facilitates further study and understanding.

Setting

It was, in fact, the creation in 1966 of an adolescent ward by the Yale-New Haven Hospital's Department of Pediatrics which stimulated our interest in these patients' reactions to their plight. The ideal approach to gaining this information would be through the psychoanalysis of these patients before, during, and after their illness and hospitalization. Occasionally, individual cases such as this have been reported; but although many analysts have treated an adolescent through a serious illness, a fund of this information remains to be gathered and published.

On the Yale-New Haven Adolescent Ward, we have faced various problems in obtaining information about the patients. The average length of stay on the unit is only 5 days and since the patients come to the hospital primarily for relief of their physical malady, the study of their psychological reactions is highly condensed. Perforce, the data available to us lack the depth of unconscious meanings and associations possible to explore in psychoanalyzed patients, but they can provide a different kind of richness: namely, the attitudes of a large number of ill adolescents, the opportunity to identify concerns which seem common to many otherwise unexceptional patients, and the magnifying and uncovering effects of the study of adolescents in crisis.

Given the setting and in order to gain as much understanding as possible, we have used simultaneously a variety of approaches. First, in order to help the staff gain a better understanding of the psychological implications of their patients' disorders and to help us by supporting our various projects on the unit, we hold a weekly meeting for the entire ward staff and another for the nurses alone. During these meetings, cases are presented for discussion. Second, each year since the ward began, the staff pediatricians have referred for formal psychiatric consultation an increased number of patients who manifest obvious psychological symptoms of a primary nature or as secondary to their physical disorder. There are now between 70 and 90 such referrals annually. Third, a weekly educational meeting is held with interested patients where they may express concerns and ask questions about their hospital experience (Schowalter and Lord, 1970) Finally, over 4 years we have collected more than 250 contributions to a ward newspaper, *Hunter Highlights.* Patients are asked to volunteer their random thoughts about the ward and after several writings are available, they are mimeograped and distributed to patients, staff, and others interested in the ward. On the surface a few of the items appear philosophically profound, while many seem quite banal. When studied as a group, however, and coupled with personal knowledge about the writers, these 4 years of writings do reveal the prevailing concerns of physically ill and hospitalized adolescent patients.

Hunter Highlights

Of the first 250 contributions, 136 were by girls, 110 by boys, and 4 were unsigned. As mentioned earlier, writing for the paper is a voluntary exercise; so those who do so are usually the more outgoing and sociable adolescents. There were, however, notable exceptions when withdrawn patients agreed to contribute and by doing so gave the staff a unique glimpse of the psychological meanings their condition held for them.

In this paper we are going to present and discuss the adolescent patients' writings via a number of themes conspicuous by their presence or absence: Contradictory Attitudes, Food, Bowel Function, Sexual Differences and Concerns, Anger and Criticism, Basic Danger Situations, Staff, and Going Home. Since the patients know their contributions will be printed and read, it must be assumed that the writings serve not only as a catharsis but as an important source of communication to the staff.

Needless to say, there is much overlap of the themes as is noted in both individual writings and in the groups of contributions. However, for this presentation these headings provide a useful organization of our observations and inferences.

Contradictory Attitudes

The simultaneous existence of opposite attitudes toward the same object or situation is, of course, part of the human condition. It is because contradictory comments are present in most of the patient contributions that we call attention to this phenomenon at the outset.

Only very rarely do we see in our adolescent patients the immobilization typical of ambivalence of will in the Bleulerian sense (1911, p. 53). What is usual is for patients to dread and resent the hospital, its personnel and procedures, while still realizing their necessity and hinting at their fascination or fearful admiration. One is reminded of Little Hans first hitting his father on the hand and then affectionately kissing the same hand (Freud, 1909, p. 42). Over half of the contributions to *Hunter Highlights* contained a combination of positive and negative statements.

One patient described his hospital experience and came to what seems like an unexpected conclusion. "I came to Hunter 4 not two days ago, yet I have been shot with needles, have been stared at and have not been allowed to get out of my room. Everybody who comes in has masks on. But, I think Hunter 4 is the best division in the hospital."

Another example of how opposite feelings may be handled is reproduced below. The writer, a 13-year-old boy, splits his positive and negative feelings into separate paragraphs. Other dichotomies will be noted later in some of the other categories.

> I like Hunter 4. I enjoyed my visit here very much. The nurses are nice and treated me well and cheered me up.
> I can't stand the doctors who take the beautiful blood from my vein. I hate the food very much. It stinks.[1]

Usually we find in our patients an exaggeration of feelings of cheerfulness and satisfaction. The dread and resentment of the hospital situation tend to be suppressed or repressed. As will be

---

[1] Obviously, with this and many of the other contributions one is sorely tempted to jump in and plumb the multideterminants of the writer's motivation as well as his choice of style and content. We will resist this temptation for two reasons. First, in this communication our purpose is to set the stage, as it were, by highlighting the reactions of a large number of "normal" adolescents to illness and hospitalization. A more detailed study of individual patients awaits further investigation. Second, although in some cases we know quite a bit about the patient's background, in many others we do not and any comments would be mere speculation.

mentioned later, most of the negative comments concerning the ward are displaced onto the food. The typical contribution cloyingly praises everything about the ward except the food. We would like to believe that truth alone compels so many contributors to be complimentary. Through group interviews and individual consultations with some of those whose writings were the most saccharine, however, it became clear that many of these patients had abundant anger and resentment about their vulnerability and forced dependency, and that, specifically because of this, they were especially loath and fearful to criticize those from whom they feared retaliation and hoped for relief and health.

Food

Comments about food are ubiquitous on the adolescent unit, while much less frequently heard on the wards for younger children. There is little doubt that illness and hospitalization foster regression and that food represents the object of increased dependency needs, including oral expressions of them. Food is an acceptable target for the expression of feelings by adolescents. These feelings reveal the patients' acceptable "adult" sophistication as well as their unacceptable infantile reactions. More than two thirds of the contributors to *Hunter Highlights* mentioned food, by far the single most popular topic. More patients expressed dislike for the meals than approved of them, while some mentioned it both ways (i.e., "The food tastes terrible, but some dishes taste good" or "The food is good and sometimes horrible"). Satisfaction or dissatisfaction with the food was often coupled with satisfaction or dissatisfaction with the ward and the hospital experience: "I like the food when I'm in the mood." The truth is that hospital cooking is different from home cooking, but the fact that a substantial minority of patients commented that the food was good calls into question the validity of the intemperate abuse voiced by the majority (i.e., "I can't stand the food"; "The food is awful"; "The meals stink," etc.). Or, with more poetry and finesse:

> Potatoes are cold
> Roast beef is tough
> I'm finding the gravy
> Is not enough.

Carrots not cooked
(Untouched they seem)
Now what is melting
Is my ice cream.

Bread slice is stale,
Butter not there,
The salad is dry,
Dressing is where?

This meal makes
My stomach flutter,
Why can't they serve
Peanut Butter?!
　　P.S. This is my only complaint.

During the patient meetings not only the prepared foods, but milk, jello, and other relatively unalterable items are frequently denounced as poorly served and poor tasting. Discussions soon made it obvious that disappointment in bad food (whether it is really "bad" or not) allows meals to become a safe and acceptable symbol for all that is alien and justifiably resented about being discomforted, afraid, and away from home. Our impression is that those patients who complain less about the food seem also to have fewer complaints about their life at home. They also appear to be more trusting and better able to adjust to the hospital. Conversely, the most vocal complainers often seem to be those who have unsatisfactory relationships with their parents. A striking exception to this pattern, as we have observed, is shown by children who come from extremely deprived homes or from other institutions. Especially if hospitalized for more than a week or so, they may form an affectionate transference (Freud, 1912) —in essence, an unhealthy "overadjustment"—to the ward and sometimes go to great lengths, including that of making worse their physical condition, in order not to leave.

Although Anna Freud (1952, p. 73) comments that it is only ill children "with strong oral fixations for whom food and deprivation of food have heightened libidinal significance, who react to the situation with fantasies of being badly treated, unloved, rejected," we have found that the majority of our patients are at least preoccupied with food and that food represents care. Of course, characteristically, adolescents in this country have been recognized as notorious in their fads and erratic choice and quantity of food consumed. This consumption seems based not only on increased metabolic needs but also on the need for increased oral supplies at the time of breaking away from home and parents. Our patients' feelings may best be summarized by one boy's remarks as expressed in *Hunter Highlights:* "It's bad enough being in the hospital, but when our meals come and we lift the covers and lo and behold some strange meal stares back at us, then that homesick feeling comes right up at you. 'Food is where your home is.' "

Bowel Function

In contrast to the ubiquitous criticism of the food, we see relatively little direct expression of anal concerns. Fear of loss of autonomy and shame are to the anal stage what trust is to the oral (Erikson, 1950). As interviews with patients reveal, many adolescents are so ashamed of the possibility that they might be incontinent, need help with their bowels, or have to endure anal attack as represented by rectal thermometers or buttocks injection, that the subject is consciously avoided. As one 15-year-old boy in a body cast told us, "It's one thing to have your mother or a nurse feed you, but to have them wipe you, Ugh!" His shame was obvious, and it was clear that disgust had blotted out any old memories of anal gratification.

Those patients who did mention anal concerns in *Hunter Highlights* usually suffered from conditions which hypercathected the bowel or buttocks.

A 17-year-old boy with ulcerative colitis wrote: "My most pleasant surprise has been to find that temperatures are taken orally."

A 13-year-old diabetic girl wrote: "You wouldn't want to be crippled for life just because you refused a shot. Your life often *depends* on shots. All of these fit into *ONE BIG END* that we couldn't live without. Could we?"

A 13-year-old girl in a body cast:

> My bedpan is a splendid thing
> When I'm upon it I could sing
> It's smooth and hard and silv'ry gray
> It's always handy night or day.
>
> At first the pan is very cold
> It fits to you just like a mold.
> Although I'm very fond of it
> I dream of the day when I can sit.

Sexual Differences and Concerns

Before the ward's opening one of the biggest worries, especially for the senior members of the hospital's nursing department, concerned the anticipation of having all adolescents together on the same floor. Although sexes are mixed on the pediatric wards for younger children and on the adult services and although the boys and girls would occupy separate rooms, there were those who wanted our patients segregated sexually on different floors or, if on the same floor, at least separated by a partition placed down the middle of the hall. One could not help but be reminded of Pumpian-Mindlin's comment (1965) that one reason why adults react negatively to adolescents is that old frustrations are awakened and they fear that these youths will succeed where they failed.

Indeed, in view of the burgeoning quality of sexuality in the well adolescent, it is striking that there is almost total lack of genital sexual content in contributions to *Hunter Highlights* and that there has been no occurrence of a voluntary or a forced sexual incident since the ward was opened. Most of the patients hospitalized on the floor are quite sick, and we observe typically the regression of libidinal flow from object libido toward narcissism.

For example, a boy admitted because of testicular torsion wrote:

> Hunter 4 would be a bore,
> If a pretty nurse didn't stop by my door.
> As long as they call me "honey" and "sweety-pie"
> I do not think that I will ever die.

Needless to say, the possible meanings of such a piece are legion, but it appears the writer is expressing at least as much concern about being well cared for as he is concerned about his traumatized genitals. The two may, of course, be fused, i.e., if he can still attract pretty nurses' care and attention, his life is and will be spared.

Anna Freud (1952) has mentioned that for many male children undergoing surgery, it is the conflict over a feminine castration wish (a "seduction to passivity") rather than castration fear which later causes psychological problems. We also found this to be true for the hospitalized adolescent. This attraction to the socially permitted passive patient role is constantly pitted against a surge for the independence normative for his developmental phase. A 13-year-old boy, already sexually self-conscious because of having gynecomastia secondary to estrogen therapy, writes with a telling parapraxis of his indignation at being asked to sleep in the day (public) room and awakening to find his bedclothes had fallen off. He wants to warn the other patients of the possible sexual embarrassment involved with passively giving in to nurses' requests:

> The nurses managed to inform me I was to sleep in a *pubic* room because of an emergency. Don't let them do that to you. I was stupid enough to make a fool of myself. I awoke to find visitors around me.

Anger and Criticism

As we mentioned in the section on *Contradictory Attitudes*, most contributions to *Hunter Highlights* emphasize the excellence of the ward and staff, with vigorous dissatisfaction in food being the chief route of displacement for negative feelings. As noted in the last section, direct expression of genital sexuality is rare. However, about 10 percent of the contributions quite directly indicate aggressive feelings. This greater readiness on the part of some patients to show angry rather than affectionate impulses reminds one of Hartmann's comment: "Vis-à-vis an external danger an aggressive response is normal, while sexualization may lead to pathology" (1950, p. 89). There is little doubt that most adolescents view their disability as being an external danger, even though it is located in their own bodies. Those adolescent patients who do not evoke the germ theory or some other intellectualized explanation for their distress and view their unhappy state as retribution usually understand the malady as being imposed from an external source—such as parents, God or Fate. These findings are very reminiscent of Freud's comments about "the fear of death . . . which is a fear of the super-ego projected on to the powers of destiny" (1926, p. 140); but we will speak more about patients' fears of death in a later section. Missing in the writings is the blame, of self or parents, which one so commonly uncovers when talking with sick children. Perhaps such feelings are too strong or too intimate to put in the paper. There is a vulnerability in putting one's thoughts in the permanency of print.

Patients usually feel exploited and the adolescent is expressive about this reaction. Erikson (1970) has recently noted that adolescents commonly view their dependency as exploitation and a justification for revolt. The ill and hospitalized adolescent is all the more dependent. Also, because of the frequent difficulty of patients in fully distinguishing treatment from illness (Blom, 1958) and their common resentment about not being or not having been adequately protected (Beverly, 1936), the occasional outpouring of aggressive expression toward parents and hospital staff is not surprising. Finally, there is suggestive evidence that the experience of mental or physical pain can elicit aggression which is then directed against whoever is available or is felt to be the source of that pain (Ulrich, 1966).

As with the paucity of the direct expression of sexuality, at first it seems surprising that more aggression is not expressed. The patient's physical debilitation, the adolescent's efforts to control unacceptable or threatening emotional outflow (Jones, 1922), and the reluctance a patient feels about attacking those to whom his life is entrusted all tend to distort or redirect the suppression of aggressive feelings and fantasies. A few exceptions are noted below.

A 13-year-old boy wrote:

The food stinks, the nurses are trying to kill me and when the doctors come in my room, all they do is twist my cast and put the toes out of place. If you can't fall asleep at night and call a nurse, you wait an hour for them to come and say, "What do you expect, instant dreamland?" Then there's the nurse who tells you to wiggle your toes after you come out of surgery. Well, I told her she could go fly a kite.

A 16-year-old girl wrote:

Would you believe vampires? Yes, those gentle, harmless girls calling themselves technicians are none other than bad vamps. Would you also believe witches? I'm afraid those innocent nurses are not really so innocent. They attack any time and any place they find convenient (even if it means you can't sit down) and love to conjure up their brews to try them out on you. Oh, by the way let's not forget our Jekylls and Hydes, those doctors, really!

Entwined in this, of course, is Anna Freud's concept of identification with the aggressor and/or with his aggression (1936). Using a poetic version of splitting opposing thoughts into separate paragraphs, a 13-year-old girl expressed in separate stanzas her view of the staff's aggressiveness and the patients' revenge.

Hi, deedle, deedle, the Doc and the needle,
The patient jumped out of his bed.
The nurses all laughed to see such fear
But the poor patient just turned red.

Sing-a-song of doctors,
All on Hunter 4
4 and 20 interns
Kicked out the door.
When the door was open,
They all turned black and blue
Now wasn't that an awful thing
For all the kids to do?

Basic Danger Situations

The ill and hospitalized adolescent has many fears, of which helplessness is among the greatest. Others often mentioned to us are fear of loss of control or of self-esteem, fear of enforced passivity, fear of physical disability or disfigurement, fear of pain, and fear of death. Some of these are touched upon in other sections of this paper. But since the vast majority of adolescents are reluctant to admit these fears publicly, they are not for the most part represented in *Hunter Highlights*. The two exceptions are those of pain and of death; feelings publicized about these subjects are reported on as follows.

The subjective experience of discomfort or pain is undergone by most hospital patients, but the majority of those we see handle this with stoicism. Most concerns about pain, which appear in some 20 percent of these entries, are displaced onto "needles" in the form of complaints about injections or blood drawing. These procedures seem not too personal for public expression, although the majority of contributors who decry injections have undergone many more painful episodes than those suggested here (Bergmann & A. Freud, 1965). Be that as it may, few patients would contradict the view expressed by this 12-year-old girl: "I HATE NEEDLES. Every time you turn around someone is coming at you with the horrible things. In my opinion I hate them." Or this, from a 17-year-old boy: "Those pain-killing shots, oh yeah?" Certainly more study is indicated in further understanding this fear of needles by children of both sexes and all ages. This almost universal response suggests the presence of a powerful and primitive fear of penetration.

Many other vociferous examples on this subject could be cited. Exceptions, in the form of rationalizations, also appear and invariably come from diabetics. Typical for this group is what a 13-year-old boy wrote by way of rejoinder: "Everyone thinks that needles are terrible, but they aren't that bad. I even have to give myself needles, so stop complaining!" Another boy, a newly discovered diabetic, leads our discussion into death fears with this description of his feelings about injections coupled with his realization of their importance:

> In hospital, there's one thing on everyone's mind
> That's loads of shots in their behinds.
> One, two, three, away we go
> Just three more shots. Oh, no! Oh, no!
> No more shots for me you see,
> My backside's red as it can be.
> Oh well, since his backside is so red
> We'll have to let him just drop dead.

It is during adolescence that one first becomes capable of cogni-
tively and emotionally committing oneself to future possibilities
(Inhelder and Piaget, 1958). It is this fact which makes the possibility of death so overwhelming for adolescents and why pediatricians are often more distressed at a death during adolescence
than at any other age (Schowalter, 1970a). Adolescents are especially affected by what Solnit and Green (1963) have perceptively
pointed out as one of man's deepest fears—death before fulfillment. Also, the adolescent, to use Anthony's (1970) felicitous
phrase, "feels imprisoned, as it were, within a developmental
phase." He often seems abandoned because of his trouble communicating private pressures (Eissler, 1958; Deutsch, 1967; Spiegel, 1951). This developmental isolation tends painfully to accen-
tuate the feelings of separation anxiety inherent in dying (Freud,
1923, p. 58).

A total of 12 contributions to *Hunter Highlights* mention the
fact or the fear of death, and a number of these have already been
quoted. Almost half of these contributions are humorous and half
are in rhyme (rhymes make up only 10 percent of the total). Six-
teen other patients mention a variation of the theme that the ward
is "a nice place to visit but not to stay (or live)"—a comment that
is often a thinly veiled statement about the ward not being a nice
place in which to die. These techniques allow the writer some distance from his subject.

We would like to give three additional examples of writings
by dying children:

The first is from a 13-year-old boy with painful stomach cancer.
It is also our most direct written expression of a dying child's
agony and demonstrates the denial of all his death fears, here displaced onto his inability to eat and drink. Intravenous feedings
provided him with some calories and physiologically adequate
hydration.

> I really hate the hospital. I've been in for almost three weeks
> and didn't have anything to drink or eat, just nothing. No
> chocolate milk, orange juice, just nothing. I don't like some of
> the nurses. I'm always dying for something to drink. Please
> kids don't take water or any other liquid for granted. I love
> water. I'll never waste it. I just can't wait 'til I can drink golden
> water.

A 14-year-old boy following brain surgery muses:

> What would it be like
> To not have a nurse
> Who drives a hearse.
> Or a doctor who doesn't curse
> When you're feeling worse?

Finally, another child with cancer reveals her fears in arithmetical form:

$$
\begin{array}{r}
2 \text{ Nice} \\
2 \text{ Be} \\
\hline
4 \text{ Gotten}
\end{array}
$$

This 14-year-old girl, an exemplary patient whose mother withdrew from her during the terminal phase of her illness, here somehow seems to be trying to add up or put things together, in the succinct expression of a wish that she not be abandoned and that her good behavior somehow may still save her.

Staff

Parents are seldom mentioned in *Hunter Highlights,* in contrast to group or individual interviews in whch they are frequently and often critically discussed. One reason is that these writings are usually read by patients' families. By way of substitution, however, 188 *Hunter Highlights* contributions mention nurses and 136 mention doctors. Anna Freud has commented on the readiness of the adolescent libido to detach itself from the parents and cathect objects outside the family (1958) and, more specifically, how some adolescents put into the empty place of the parents a self-chosen leader (1969) . Since doctors and nurses are viewed as objects capable of helping them survive a threat against which parents seem powerless, our patients often treat the staff as parent substitutes or parent ideals.

Most of the *Hunter Highlights* contributions about staff were positive. In fact, the ratio of positive to negative comments was 8 to 1 in the case of nurses and 5 to 1 in the case of doctors, while 10 patients combined both positive and negative expressions in the same writing. For both nurses and doctors, boys tended to be more critical than girls. Perhaps this reflects a greater difficulty for adolescent males to accept a necessarily passive position. We recognize, naturally, that a patient's general ability to cope with hospitalization, and specifically the ways in which he relates to staff members, have multiple determinants: his own personality structure; the quality or extent of preparation received; the severity of his condition, etc. Another key factor, as noted earlier on the subject of food, is the patient's relationships with his parents. We observed that those who felt secure and who complimented the doctors and nurses were those who tended to get along well at home, while those who expressed dissatisfaction with the staff often also complained about their parents. It would appear that the quality of cathexis remained the same in spite of the shift in object. Exceptions to this tendency were seen in some adolescents who remained very tightly bound to their parents. They, along with their mothers, tended to resent staff as disruptors of their symbiotic relationship and had, as it were, no object libido to spare for the interlopers. The staff was either ignored or condemned as being too intrusive or demanding.

Patients from institutions or others who were relatively decathected from their parents would at times form extremely close bonds with staff members and, occasionally, literally treat a doctor or nurse as a leader (A. Freud, 1969). These patients would often express a wish to enter medical or nursing school and sometimes returned daily to visit the ward and staff members for weeks after discharge.

Although numerous examples of comments concerning staff could be given from *Hunter Highlights,* we have chosen three representative pieces. The first, from a boy with Hodgkin's disease, typifies the submissive praise most frequently given; the second, from a boy unhappy at home, condemns the staff in like manner; and the third, by a girl from another institution, expresses the presence of what Freud (1912) termed an overly affectionate transference to the hospital.

In every way the Nurses help you out whenever you need it. And we should listen to the Doctor. That is why I like Hunter 4.

I have learned: 1) Don't count on what a doctor tells you. For example, he may tell you one thing and do another. 2) Nurses are lazy, moody and always hungry.

I think Hunter 4 is real nice. In fact, I wouldn't mind staying here all the time. The nurses and doctors and everyone else are just great. There is only one thing wrong. They throw you out too fast after an operation and don't give you enough time to recover

For one type of reaction we lack a good example. Those patients who have a pathologically close relationship with their mothers experience as an intrusion a request to write for the paper and routinely refuse.

Roommates were commented upon in 29 of the contributions—always positively. The impact of roommates on each other, especially of patients suffering from similar illnesses or undergoing similar procedures, is a fascinating subject worthy of much more examination than it has received by us or any other investigators. For example, we have seen roommates, renal transplant co-recipients of the same cadaver donor, who formed a symbiotic relationship almost identical to the twinning phenomenon (Schowalter, 1970b). Further discussion of this complicated subject, however, cannot be included here.

Going Home
When young children are hospitalized for more than a few days, it has been noted that it is usual for their thoughts about going home to be wholly pleasurable, with the event often being endowed with unrealistic and magical expectations (Bergmann and A. Freud, 1965). With adolescents on a relatively short-stay unit, however, we have discovered that going home is marked by more ambivalence. Even with the suffering, pain, and uncertainty, many patients experience Hunter 4 as a sanctuary where they are sheltered from the conflicts which besieged them at home. Regression within limits is allowed, while physicians and nurses provide, as one boy put it, "super-parenting." On the other hand, since home represents health, security, and the opportunity to get on with their development, most patients do want to get well and go home.

The confusion some patients felt about leaving is expressed in the following two statements. One boy wrote: "Hunter 4 is all right and I like it, but when I go home I will miss all my friends and the comforts of the hospital." Another boy wrote: "I like it here, but I don't want to leave." Both of these patients were expressing more positive feelings for the ward than they seem to have intended.

Summary

Illness and hospitalization undoubtedly have much psychological impact on adolescents, although studies to date have primarily focused on younger children. The development of separate wards for adolescents has facilitated investigations of this age group.

On the Adolescent Unit of the Yale-New Haven Hospital various approaches have been adopted, which serve several purposes, including that of increasing our understanding of patients. One project is the publishing of a ward newspaper, whose writings over a 4-year period well reveal many of these adolescents' frequently expressed feelings and concerns. We have here attempted to outline and highlight them via the following themes: Contradictory Attitudes, Food, Bowel Function, Sexual Differences and Concerns, Anger and Criticism, Basic Danger Situations, Staff, and Going Home.

BIBLIOGRAPHY

ANTHONY, E. J. (1970), Two Contrasting Types of Adolescent Depression and Their Treatment. *J. Amer. Psychoanal. Assn.*, 18:841–859.

BERGMANN, T. & FREUD, A. (1965), *Children in the Hospital*. New York: International Universities Press.

BEVERLY, B. (1936), The Effect of Illness upon Emotional Development. *J. Pediat.*, 8:533–543.

BLEULER, E. (1911), *Dementia Praecox or The Group of Schizophrenias*. New York: International Universities Press, 1950.

BLOM, G. (1958), The Reactions of Hospitalized Children to Illness. *Pediatrics*, 22:590–600.

BLOS, P. (1967), The Second Individuation Process of Adolescence. *This Annual*, 22:162–186.

CALEF, V. (1959), Report on Panel: Psychological Consequences of Physical Illness in Childhood. *J. Amer. Psychoanal. Assn.*, 7:155–162.

DAVENPORT, H. & WERRY, J. (1970), The Effect of General Anesthesia, Surgery and Hospitalization upon the Behavior of Children. *Amer. J. Orthopsychiat.*, 40:806–824.

DEUTSCH, H. (1967), *Selected Problems of Adolescence*. New York: International Universities Press.

EISSLER, K. R. (1958), Notes on Problems of Technique in the Psychoanalytic Treatment of Adolescents: With Some Remarks on Perversions. *This Annual*, 13:223–254.

ERIKSON, E. H. (1950), *Childhood and Society*. New York: Norton.

— (1970), Reflections on the Dissent of Contemporary Youth. *Int. J. Psycho-Anal.*, 51:11–22.

FREUD, A. (1936), *The Ego and the Mechanisms of Defense*. New York: International Universities Press, rev. ed., 1966, pp. 109–121.

— (1952), The Role of Bodily Illness in the Mental Life of Children. *This Annual*, 7:69–81.

— (1958), Adolescence. *This Annual*, 13:255–278.

— (1969), Adolescence as a Developmental Disturbance. In: *Adolescence: Psychosocial Perspectives*, ed. G. Caplan & S. Lebovici. New York: Basic Books, pp. 5–10.

FREUD, S. (1909), Analysis of a Phobia in a Five-Year-Old Boy, *Standard Edition*, 10:5–149. London: Hogarth Press, 1955.

— (1912) The Dynamics of Transference. *Standard Edition*, 12:99–108. London: Hogarth Press, 1958.

— (1923), The Ego and the Id. *Standard Edition*, 19:12–66. London: Hogarth Press, 1961.

— (1926), Inhibitions, Symptoms and Anxiety. *Standard Edition*, 20:87–175. London: Hogarth Press, 1959.

— (1939), Moses and Monotheism. *Standard Edition*, 23:7–137. London: Hogarth Press, 1964.

HARTMANN, H. (1950), Comments on the Psychoanalytic Theory of the Ego. *This Annual*, 5:74–96.

INHELDER, B. & PIAGET, J. (1958), *The Growth of Logical Thinking from Childhood to Adolescence*. New York: Basic Books.

JONES, E. (1922), Some Problems of Adolescence. In: *Papers on Psycho-Analysis*. London: Ballière & Cox, 1948, pp. 389–406.

PUMPIAN-MINDLIN, E. (1965), Omnipotentiality, Youth and Commitment. *J. Amer. Acad. Child Psychiat.*, 4:1–18.

ROBERTSON, J. (1953), Some Responses of Young Children to the Loss of Maternal Care. *Nursing Times*, 49:382–386.

— (1962), *Hospitals and Children*. New York: International Universities Press.

SCHOWALTER, J. E. (1970a), Death and the Pediatric House Officer. *J. Pediat.*, 76:706–710.

— (1970b), Multiple Organ Transplantation and the Creation of Surgical Siblings. *Pediatrics*, 46:576–580.

— & LORD, R. D. (1969), Admission to an Adolescent Ward. *Pediatrics,* 44:1009–1011.

— — (1970), Utilization of Patient Meetings on an Adolescent Ward. *Psychiat. in Med.,* 1:197–206.

SOLNIT, A. J. & GREEN, M. (1963), The Pediatric Management of the Dying Child: Part II. The Child's Reaction to the Fear of Dying. In: *Modern Perspectives in Child Development,* ed. A. J. Solnit & S. Provence. New York: International Universities Press, pp. 217–228.

SPIEGEL, L. A. (1951), A Review of Contributions to a Psychoanalytic Theory of Adolescence. *This Annual,* 6:375–393.

ULRICH, R. (1966), Pain As a Cause of Aggression. *Amer. Zoologist,* 6:643–662.

VERNON, D., SCHULMAN, J., & FOLEY, J. (1966), Changes in Children's Behavior after Hospitalization. *Amer. J. Dis. Child.,* 3:581–593.

CONTRIBUTIONS TO

PSYCHOANALYTIC

THEORY

Language and Dreams
The Interpretation of Dreams Revisited

MARSHALL EDELSON, M.D., PH.D.

The Semiological Foundations of Psychoanalysis

ACCORDING TO FREUD'S GREAT CONCEPTION IN *The Interpretation of Dreams,* the dream is a symbolic entity. The dream is not intrinsically efficacious, as is the physical "cause" of a physical "effect." The dream derives its efficacy from its status as "signifier" of what is "signified." The manifest dream stands for or signifies meanings (latent thoughts); meaning, in this sense of the term, is that which is signified.

One may ask about the dream as a manifest representation of meaning: out of what materials is it made? by the use of what techniques are the materials treated, combined, or transformed to

Associate Professor of Psychiatry, Yale University School of Medicine; Western New England Psychoanalytic Society and Institute.

make a dream? The answers to such questions are especially germane to the interpretation of the manifest dream as a symbolic entity—to a consideration of the relation of the manifest dream to its meanings—rather than primarily to a consideration of the dream's causes or effects. Freud thus established psychoanalysis in the realm of semiotics or semiology, as a science of symbolic functioning, which studies symbolic systems (organizations of symbolic entities), their relations to each other, and their acquisition and use. Psychoanalysis inherently aspires, I believe, to a general theory of symbolic functioning (rather than to a general psychology or a general theory of behavior).[1]

The dream is a construction; it is actively constructed. The dreamer makes the dream—out of available materials (for example, somatic stimuli, and recent but indifferent impressions), and according to definite methods or techniques (the dreamwork). The dreamer chooses materials that will serve his aim or purpose, which is instigated by various disturbances of sleep. His aim (the intention of the dreamer as *"entrepreneur"*) is to compensate for these disturbances, to oppose certain virtual intrusions, by constructing in a state of sleep a virtual wish fulfillment—a dream. If suitable materials are unavailable, no dream can be constructed; intrusion during a state of sleep must then provide an occasion for some other act than dreaming. If no "capital" (unconscious wish) is available to support the work of obtaining the material and constructing a dream out of it, then the enterprise of the *entrepreneur* is impossible.

> A daytime thought may very well play the part of *entrepreneur* for a dream; but the *entrepreneur,* who, as people say, has the idea and the initiative to carry it out, can do nothing without capital; he needs a *capitalist* who can afford the outlay, and the capitalist who provides the psychical outlay for the dream is invariably and indisputably, whatever may be the thought of the previous day, *a wish from the unconscious.*
>
> Sometimes the capitalist is himself the *entrepreneur,* and indeed in the case of dreams this is the commoner event: an unconscious wish is stirred up by daytime activity and proceeds to construct a dream. So, too, the other possible variations in the economic situation that I have taken as an analogy have

[1] See Appendix A for a discussion of terminology in semiology.

their parallel in dream-processes. The *entrepreneur* may himself make a small contribution to the capital; several *entrepreneurs* may apply to the same capitalist; several capitalists may combine to put up what is necessary for the *entrepreneur*. In the same way, we come across dreams that are supported by more than one dream-wish; and so too with other similar variations, which could easily be run through, but which would be of no further interest to us [p. 561].

Freud was prescient in his choice of analogies. Money like the dream (and, implies Freud's analogy, like the wish, which is a psychic representation, not a physical force) is a symbolic entity. Money is efficacious only by virtue of what it symbolizes, the meanings it represents. Money is a symbolic resource that may be used in a social system to attain a wide variety of ends; the nature of these ends is not determined *a priori* by the resource used. By his analogy, Freud suggests that the wish is also a symbolic resource, representing a commitment to the attainment of ends; the wish may be used in a psychological system to attain a wide variety of ends, the exact nature of which is not predetermined by the resource used—thus, the well-known displaceability of so-called instinctual energy (Edelson, 1971, 1972).

The dream, then, is like an economic enterprise. Also, in the same sense, it is like a symbolic art form. Somatic sources of stimulation, as well as recent but indifferent impressions left over from the previous day, are

. . . brought in to help in the formation of a dream if they fit in appropriately with the ideational content derived from the dream's psychical sources, but otherwise not. They are treated like some cheap material always ready to hand, which is employed whenever it is needed, in contrast to a precious material which itself prescribes the way in which it shall be employed. If, to take a simile, a patron of the arts brings an artist some rare stone, such as a piece of onyx, and asks him to create a work of art from it, then the size of the stone, its colour and markings, help to decide what head or what scene shall be represented in it. Whereas in the case of a uniform and plentiful material such as marble or sandstone, the artist merely follows some idea that is present in his own mind [p. 237].

Analogies and similes like these begin to suggest to what an extent psychoanalysis rests upon semiological foundations.

This paper is part of a work in progress, in which I am attempting to discover the implications of regarding psychoanalysis as a science of semiology for understanding works of the mind of man as apparently disparate as poetry, music, metaphor, and the psychoanalyst's interpretation.

In this particular paper, I begin by bringing together the psychoanalyst Freud, represented by his greatest work, *The Interpretation of Dreams*, and the linguist Chomsky. Here I face the difficulties of any expositor who tries to relate the findings of two men in two fields who are separated not only by interests in what seem to be very different phenomena, and by different methods which are, for those untrained in their use, not easy to appreciate or evaluate, but also by markedly different technical vocabularies —an especially grievous obstacle to intercommunication. Given the limits of this presentation, I must assume that, with the assistance of my very brief discussion of Chomsky's work in the second section of the paper, the reader will be able to find his way through my exegetical revisit to *The Interpretation of Dreams* in the light of some current linguistic theory.[2] I must also assume a degree of familiarity with some of the literature on psychoanalysis and language.[3]

About that literature, I am constrained by the scope of my present purpose to make only a few comments in passing. Among psy-

[2] A supplement to the somewhat oversimplified discussion of Chomsky's theory of language in the second section of the paper may be found in Appendix B; the supplement contains more precise definitions—although, needless to say, not as precise as can be found in more technical works—as well as a discussion of the phonological and semantic components of language, which are not treated in the body of the paper. This theory might most easily be approached by the reader who is unfamiliar with it in the following order: Lyons (1970a, 1970b), Lenneberg (1967), Chomsky (1957, 1959), Fodor and Katz (1964), Katz and Postal (1964), Chomsky (1967, 1965, 1966a, 1966b, 1968).

[3] E.g., Atkin (1969), Balkányi (1964, 1968), Beres (1957, 1965), Edelheit (1969), Edelson (1971, 1972), Ekstein (1965), Ferenczi (1913), Fliess (1949), Freud (1891, 1900, 1901, 1905, 1910, 1911, 1913, 1915, 1925), Glauber (1944), Isakower (1939), Jones (1916), Katan (1961), Keiser (1962), Kolansky (1967), Kris (1951, 1952, 1956b), Kubie (1953), Lidz (1963), Loewenstein (1951, 1956, 1957, 1963), Peller (1966), Rosen (1961, 1966, 1967, 1969), Rycroft (1958), Shapiro (1970), Sharpe (1940), Sirota (1969), Stein (1958), Stone (1954, 1961), Voth (1970), Wolff (1967).

choanalysts who have written about psychoanalysis and language, Rosen mentions prominently and discusses in an informed way the work of the linguist Chomsky and, in addition, makes extensive and most apposite use of the work of the semiologist Jakobson (1941, 1955, 1956, 1964). The usefulness of some of the papers listed is perhaps attenuated—from the point of view of Chomsky's work on language, for example—by the following tendencies. Many psychoanalytic writers fail to distinguish consistently between language (a capacity) and speech (its realization in performance). Almost all psychoanalysts who write about language are preoccupied with words and naming rather than sentences and rules of grammar, and with semantic ambiguity rather than syntactic ambiguity. Most psychoanalysts emphasize the libidinal rather than the cognitive aspects of speech. In other words, they emphasize speech as expressive action rather than language as symbolic system. This emphasis on speech as expressive rather than symbolic tends to be accompanied by an inadequate differentiation of (1) speech as an index and means of discharge of presently aroused impulses from (2) various aspects of speech as motivated symbols representing unconscious conceptions.[4] Among such aspects of speech, which may become motivated symbols, are: the qualities of concrete speech acts (e.g., fluency, explosiveness, rate, pitch, dynamics); the physical concomitants of concrete speech acts (e.g., salivation, lip movements); and concrete speech entities (e.g., imitative sounds).

In this paper, following my discussion of Freud and Chomsky, I illustrate and examine the implications of Freud's semiological bent through a detailed examination of the first chapter of *The Interpretation of Dreams*. It may seem at first glance that I have written disproportionately much about this first chapter; what I have written is an appreciation of a scientifically beautiful and, unfortunately, on the whole neglected part of the whole. In the next part of the paper—its very center in more than one sense—I describe six dimensions of symbolic functioning, as these emerge from my reading of the remainder of *The Interpretation of*

---

[4] "Symbolic" in the specialized semiological (rather than usual psychoanalytic) sense; for a discussion of this and such terms as "index" and "motivated symbol," see Appendix A.

Dreams. These six dimensions appear to be equally salient to a consideration of dreams or language. In a penultimate section, I explore the exciting implications of Freud's description of the dream as a rebus. This section eventually comes to focus on two topics. The first topic concerns the determinacy of the meaning of dreams—what aspects of their mode of construction make their meaning determinable. The second topic concerns the value of using the linguistic distinction between deep and surface structures for appreciating the consequences of the operations of the dreamwork.

The paper concludes with a relatively brief statement of two hypotheses. One reconsiders the postulation of censorship as the primary motive for dream distortion. The other asserts the dependence of dreaming upon language.

Freud and Chomsky

Among semiological systems, Freud was especially interested in language. The most casual reading of *The Interpretation of Dreams* reaps ample evidence of this interest. "Indeed, dreams are so closely related to linguistic expression," he wrote, "that Ferenczi . . . has truly remarked that every tongue has its own dream-language" (p. 99). Again, in a paper (1913) in which he was considering the relation of philology and psychoanalysis, he declared: "psycho-analysts are entirely ignorant of the attitude and knowledge with which a philologist would approach such a problem as that presented by dreams" (p. 177). In many ways, as I hope this paper will demonstrate, in *The Interpretation of Dreams* Freud did approach dreams as a sophisticated linguist might have, albeit one who did not yet have access to the powerful conceptual tools of contemporary linguistic science—which may be considered to have begun with the work of Saussure (1916) and to have found its most compelling present-day exemplification in Noam Chomsky's transformational-generative theory of language.

No one who has read the following passage by Freud (1911), one among many of its kind, should be surprised by a characterization of him as a linguist or by the linkage of his thought to that of Chomsky. Freud represented the familiar principal forms of paranoia as contradictions or transformations of the proposition "*I* (a man) *love him* (a man)." Delusions of persecution assert: "I do not *love* him—I *hate* him, because HE PERSECUTES ME." Erotomania involves the transformation: "I do not love *him* —I love *her,* because SHE LOVES ME." Delusions of jealousy represent the contradiction: "It is not *I* who loves the man—*she* loves him" (p. 63f.). He concluded:

> Now it might be supposed that a proposition consisting of three terms, such as '*I love him,*' could only be contradicted in three different ways. Delusions of jealousy contradict the subject, delusions of persecution contradict the verb, and erotomania contradicts the object. But in fact a fourth kind of contradiction is possible—namely, one which rejects the proposition as a whole:
>
> '*I do not love at all—I do not love any one.*' And since, after all, one's libido must go somewhere, this proposition seems to be the psychological equivalent of the proposition: 'I love only myself.' So that this kind of contradiction would give us megalomania, which we may regard as a *sexual overvaluation of the ego* and may thus set beside the overvaluation of the love-object with which we are already familiar [p. 64f.].[5]

We can only speculate, as I have previously done (1971), about the form Freud's conceptualizations might have taken if he had had access to a body of scientific work to match his linguistic interests and intuitions; it is possible that, then, he might not have found it necessary to depend upon physicalistic models such as the "reflex arc" to the extent he did in some aspects of his theoretical formulations.

In any event, if in *The Interpretation of Dreams* we discover a theory of dreams in some way similar to that of Chomsky's theory of language, we may be led to formulate propositions about the relation between dreams and language,[6] and about the possible

---

[5] A further discussion of this passage in the light of linguistic theory may be found in Edelson (1972).

[6] There is no word for "dream" as a system to be distinguished from dreams as phenomena that is analogous to the word "language," which refers to a system to be distinguished from its phenomenal exemplifications in "speech." This unknown word for dream as a system might have some of the connotations of such a term as "id"; such a system would be characterized by "dream-work" and "primary process" as language as a system is characterized by "rules of grammar."

status of these two theories with respect to a more general theory of semiology or symbolic function that in combination they might suggest. The questions posed by the convergence and divergence of the theory of dreams and the theory of language may lead to an understanding of what each theory requires of the other if the formulations of both are to be most generally valid, and to the development of perhaps new, perhaps merely differently stated, hopefully clearer or more consistent propositions in each. Such perspectives by congruity and incongruity on symbolic functioning are, I believe, a minimal requirement for the foundation of a satisfactory psychoanalytic theory of art. More interesting, this comparison of the two theories may contribute to a general theory of symbolic function, which should embrace such disparate phenomena as dreams, psychopathological symptoms, the transference neurosis, myths, play, language, the many kinds of works of art, the many levels of communication and communion, the many varieties of social organization, social arrangements, or social institutions—to the extent that all of these phenomena may be understood as generated by semiological systems with comparable components and characteristics. Their differences and likenesses would to that extent be specifiable in terms of values assigned to each upon universal dimensions or variables—that is, dimensions or variables that are useful in the theoretical analysis of any semiological system. All of these phenomena could, then, indeed be usefully regarded from the viewpoint of the symbolic function, as (at least in part) symbolic entities—as representations or "forms of thought."

Freud's method for the study of dreams bears some striking similarities to Chomsky's method for the study of language.

Both seek and reason from the crucial example—e.g., a counterexample that seems to contradict a particular line of thought (such a line of thought is regarded by both as essentially a free invention of the scientist); or a heuristic example whose detailed analysis and the implications arising from that analysis suggest new directions of thought. Both find their examples primarily by sampling the constructions of their own minds—Freud his own dreams and Chomsky the sentences he himself devises. Both are confident in their own mental processes as exemplifications of the universal. Thus, Freud claims that, even though no one has ever dreamed or will ever dream a single one of his dreams, he shares with mankind the process by which these dreams are generated. Similarly, Chomsky claims that, even though each of the sentences he may devise is novel, he shares with mankind the process by which these sentences are generated. (Indeed, he boldly notices, most sentences are novel; this fact is not merely an inconvenience to the scientist seeking the repeatable event, but rather a crucial characteristic of language to be explained by him.) The explanation both seek does not rest with the enumeration of occurrences or surface regularities, but is intended to account for the characteristics of a class of events—speech, dreams—by explicating the nature of the operations by which such an event is brought into being.

Both Freud and Chomsky accept subjective report—the subject's intuitions concerning the grammaticalness of a linguistic form, for example, or the patient's description of his dream and what the elements of the dream evoke in him. Both see man as maker. Both seek to explain an entity by discovering how it is made—what materials are used, what rules or laws govern the treatment of these materials to generate the form being studied.

Yet, despite the admitted importance of access to the subjective realm, both are skeptical that introspection by the maker alone is sufficient to reveal these laws or rules, since the dreamer and the user of language alike are ordinarily, and especially in the act of making, unconscious of the processes, the rules or laws, governing the production of dreams and linguistic entities. Both Chomsky and Freud, perhaps for that reason, tend to see the rules or laws governing the production of symbolic entities as intrinsic characteristics of mind itself. If the capacity to act or create according to such rules or laws—and the realization of that capacity in action or creation—comprise what we essentially mean by "mind," mind as "act" cannot in the act apprehend that which has no separate existential status: mind itself reified as apprehendable "object."

In Chomsky's theory of language, language (a system) is distinguished from speech (empirical phenomena). Similarly, competence is distinguished from performance. Competence is an internalized capacity to acquire and use language; language is essentially a complex system of interrelated rules, which Chomsky—drawing upon the notions and to some extent the notations of various branches of mathematical or symbolic logic—strives to make explicit. Linguistic competence is the possession of a resource: knowledge of language as a system, i.e., knowledge of a system of linguistic elements and of categories of linguistic elements, and of the rules operating to construct ordered arrangements of such categories and thereby governing the interrelations of linguistic elements at a particular level of theoretical analysis—phonological, syntactic, or semantic. Performance (e.g., speech) represents a perceptible realization of competence constrained by a variety of extralinguistic factors, such as fatigue, levels of wakefulness, limitations of memory, and a variety of internal and external interruptions.

With only finite, fragmentary bits of speech as input, a complex, coherent, internalized system is constructed that can generate an infinite set of novel linguistic forms, i.e., sentences. This achievement is extraordinary, occurring as it does in so relatively short a period of time, apparently relatively independently of level of intelligence, and with exposure to only a very limited set of frequently debased fragments of speech (however necessary, without doubt, some such experience is). Chomsky believes, therefore, that the capacity to construct and make use of language must be an innate, species-specific, separate characteristic of the human mind. This capacity may be an aspect of a more general characteristic of the human mind called "the symbolic function," which I have been tempted to regard as that which constitutes mind (Edelson, 1971, 1972).

Chomsky's theory of language is intended to account for such empirically observable characteristics as the following:

1. Language is creative. With finite means (the system comprising language) an infinite set of novel, almost always never-before-experienced, improbable, appropriate, linguistic forms can be generated.[7]

---

[7] Improbable, since many sentences occur once or at most exceedingly infrequently given the vast corpus of possible sentences. A sentence can be *appropriate* to a situation or context without being *determined* by it; sentences that cannot be predicted either statistically from a knowledge of the frequency of their occurrence or from a knowledge of the situation in which they are uttered may nevertheless be appropriate.

2. Language is rule-governed.[8] Both well-formed sentences, i.e., those generated by the rules of the language, and unacceptable sentences, i.e., those violating such rules, may occur. Competence implies the observable usual ability to distinguish between well-formed and unacceptable sentences, even when as is often the case the possessor of the language is unable to make explicit the criteria, i.e., the rules of the language, according to which he makes such a distinction; he makes the distinction, we may say, "intuitively."

Since language is creative, some of the rules of the language must involve recursive operations (e.g., those rules embedding constituent sentences as clauses in matrix sentences). Recursive operations can be repeated an indefinite number of times (e.g., embedding another constituent sentence as a clause in a previously embedded sentence, and then again, and again, as in "The dog attacked the cat that ate the rat that ate the cheese"). Because language includes recursive operations, an endless number and variety of combinations of sentences forming new sentences are possible and no theoretical limit can be set upon the length or complexity of a well-formed sentence, i.e., a sentence generated by the rules of the language, although of course contraints upon performance set practical limits.

Chomsky makes an important distinction between rule-governed creativity of the kind I have just discussed and the creativity that results in changing the rules themselves.

3. Language is unconscious.[9] The processes involved in the production or recognition of an infinite set of novel linguistic forms occur outside awareness and are (frequently?) not accessible to introspection. Ordinarily, even one who is skilled and fluent is unable to explicate how—i.e., to make explicit the rules or the nature of the processes by which—he produces or recognizes meaningful, well-formed, context-appropriate sentences or knows their meaning or judges their form to be acceptable. Even if such op-

---

[8] For a discussion of the various senses of the term rule, see Black (1962, pp. 95–139) ; for a discussion of the importance of the notion of rules in social science, see Winch (1958) .

[9] "Unconscious" used in its descriptive sense; see footnote 10.

erations are partially explicable, one is not ordinarily aware of them at the same moment one is using them.

4. Language is ambiguous. Surface form and meaning do not bear an obvious one-to-one relationship. A word or sentence is capable of representing, without any change in its surface form, different meanings in different contexts or—in special contexts such as poetry—different meanings in the same context. (Chomsky and his colleagues, primarily concerned with problems of disambiguation, have not given much attention to this latter case—of great interest to psychoanalysis—in which ambiguity is intended and understood.)

Thus, a sentence that has a single surface structure—i.e., which as an arrangement of observable entities is susceptible to one and only one syntactic analysis—may nevertheless be capable of representing more than one meaning. For example, "The shooting of the hunters was terrible" might signify a judgment about someone's shooting hunters or it might signify a judgment about the way in which the hunters shot at something. In the structure underlying a proposition making the first judgment, "hunters" is, according to syntactic analysis, the object. In the structure underlying a proposition making the second judgment, "hunters" is the subject. These two inferred structures—called deep structures—are capable of being directly interpreted semantically to yield two syntactically unambiguous sentences. The surface structure, a final pattern which is capable of being phonologically interpreted so that it may be perceptibly realized in speech, is thought to result from the action of either one or the other of two different, so-called transformational rules operating upon one or the other of two different deep structures.

Similarly, two or more quite different surface structures may be capable of representing the same meaning. For example, "John gave Bill a book" and "A book was given to Bill by John" are ordinarily considered (almost?) exact paraphrases, although in the surface structure of the first sentence "John" has the function "subject" and "book" the function "object," while in the surface structure of the second sentence "book" has the function "subject" and "John" has become part of a prepositional phrase. (Subject and object can be defined solely in terms of syntactical order, as

Chomsky has demonstrated, and are not to be confused with the topic and comment of a sentence.)

Linguistic competence, then, ordinarily includes the ability to recognize the ambiguity of "the shooting of the hunters was terrible," at least if the ambiguity is pointed out, and certainly to recognize that the sentence has different meanings as it is encountered on different occasions, although its surface structure remains unchanged. In other words, competence includes the ability to recognize that, although "John is eager to please" and "John is easy to please" have identical surface structures—i.e., receive the same syntactic analysis—their deep structures must be quite different, since in one John is pleasing someone and in the other someone is pleasing John. Competence also ordinarily includes the ability to recognize a paraphrase.

The two meanings of "the shooting of the hunters was terrible" are derived from two different underlying or deep structures, the differences in which do in fact directly reflect the differences in meaning. Transformational processes or rules may generate the same surface structure from two different deep structures. Also, two paraphrases whose surface structures are different are derived through two different transformational processes or rules from the same underlying or deep structure that does in fact reflect the one meaning. The sentence—like the dream and symptom—yields its meanings only to one who knows its possible "histories" and actual "history": what structures could have been or have been transformed (through processes of combination, rearrangement, and deletion, for example) to give the structure of the manifest symbolic form.[10]

---

[10] Levi-Strauss (1964) has also shown that attention to the surface form of a symbolic entity does not result in understanding its deep structure, which is a consequence of the nature of the system of categories and logical operations that has generated it. So, analysis of the form and content of a single myth does not reveal that it is one manifestation—a single realized possibility—of an underlying mythic system of categories and the logical operations determining their possible combinations and permutations. Each myth in a set of myths realizes only one or some of these possibilities. Its deep structure is some combination or permutation of the categories of the mythic system. The set of myths must be studied if the basic abstract mythic system generating it is to be revealed. The mythic system is unconscious in the same sense that language as a system is unconscious; its user is not usually aware of the categories and logical operations he uses. (Of course, uncon-

It is possible that not only language but any exercise of the symbolic function—including dreaming—and therefore any semiological system involves in some way these four characteristics: creativity, rule-governedness, unconscious processes, and ambiguity.

What kind of theory of language can account for these four characteristics of language? [11]

1. Language is, according to Chomsky, tripartite. It has three autonomous components: syntactic, semantic, and phonological. The first component generates structures (ordered patterns), according to one set of rules. The second component interprets structures semantically, i.e., assigns them meanings, according to another set of rules. The third component realizes structures as perceptible forms (auditory, for example), according to still another set of rules.

2. Deep structures are those abstract, syntactic patterns that underlie the simplest, base, or kernel sentences of the language (exemplified, although this is an oversimplification, by simple—noncompound and noncomplex—sentences, which are active, declarative, and in the present tense [12]). The set of such patterns is finite. Such structures are the necessary and sufficient inputs to the semantic component, which according to its rules assigns them semantic interpretations. In other words, deep structures contain all the syntactic information necessary for the interpretation of meaning. (Are "wishes" similar "kernel" structures or rather perhaps analogues to that part of the syntactic component the rules of which generate such structures?)

3. A transformational set of rules—having special characteristics—constitutes another part of the syntactic component. These rules may alter deep structures in various ways (through additions, deletions, adjunctions, permutations, substitutions, etc.) to derive

---

scious is used by Chomsky and Levi-Strauss, and for the most part by Piaget as well, descriptively—as a quality—rather than systematically; that is, unconscious is used without the assumption of a motive that opposes ideas achieving consciousness.)

[11] What follows is a minimal statement of eight ideas that are probably essential to the discussion of *The Interpretation of Dreams* in the remainder of this paper. See Appendix B for a more detailed, systematic account of Chomsky's theory of language.

[12] Strikingly enough, just the form of those meanings Freud postulated as id contents.

surface structures. The set of such structures is infinite. Surface structures are those patterns underlying sentences that can be uttered. These structures are the necessary and sufficient inputs to the phonological component, which assigns them according to its rules phonological representations. In other words, surface structures contain all the syntactic information necessary for a realization of the sentence in perceptible (e.g., auditory) form. Chomsky has held that meaning—at least to the extent that meaning depends upon the nature of the interrelations among syntactic functions—remains invariant as the operations of the transformational part of the syntactic component transforms deep into surface structures. (Similarly, we may hold that meaning remains invariant as the latent thoughts are transformed into the manifest dream.) [13]

4. A lexicon, a kind of dictionary, categorizes lexical items as nouns, verbs, etc., and subcategorizes them according to (1) their features (abstract noun vs. concrete noun, animate noun vs. inanimate noun, human noun vs. animal noun, count noun vs. mass noun, etc.) or according to (2) the features or (3) the syntactic category (noun, verb, etc.) of some other lexical item(s) in the contexts in which they are by rule permitted to occur.[14]

Various degrees and kinds of deviant forms are possible, depending upon which kind of rule is violated. "John found sad" violates a rule specifying the syntactic category of the lexical item that may follow "found." In general, such a form is considered

[13] As previously discussed, abstract deep structures and the transformational processes which change them into surface structures are postulated to account for the fact that the syntactic analysis of the surface structure of some linguistic forms does not provide direct insight into the relations underlying the possible meanings of these forms. As in psychoanalysis (and any good theory), the postulation of such deep structures and transformational processes has led to the discovery of hitherto unsuspected systematic relations among different forms.

[14] The semantic component classifies words according to rules generating combinations of hierarchically organized, binary semantic markers—e.g., "animate" or 'inanimate" and, if animate, "human" or "animal" (Katz and Fodor, 1963). For a discussion of the differences between syntactic features and semantic markers, even when these bear the same or a similar name—e.g., "animate noun" and "animate"—see Katz and Fodor (1963): "semantic markers are introduced to specify something about the meaning of lexical items. . . . Grammatical markers have the function of marking the formal differences upon which the distribution between well-formed strings of morphemes rests" (p. 518).

more deviant than one such as "ideas sleep," which violates a rule specifying the features or kind of noun that may precede "sleep." Forms of this latter kind often suggest metaphor and may be interpreted metaphorically, according to Chomsky, by analogy to well-formed sentences (compare "misery loves company" with "John loves company").

Might any operations of the dreamwork produce such systematically deviant forms, particularly those we think of as metaphorical? There is one difficulty about thinking of the dreamwork this way. Subcategorization rules in the lexicon supposedly apply in the generation of deep structures, and the dreamwork seems to have its major role in the transformation of semantically interpreted deep structures—i.e., thoughts—to yield a structure susceptible to representation by dream images. However, I do not believe that Chomsky and his colleagues have given an adequate account of metaphor.[15] The presence of metaphor may be suggested by the violation of subcategorization rules, but the metaphor is not a metaphor simply because subcategorization rules have been violated. Rather, unusual transformations of syntactically acceptable deep structures are probably involved in generating a metaphor. The dreamwork might very well include such unusual transformations.

5. The relation between the syntactic component and semantic component is problematic, since the extent to which the hypothetical, abstract, deep structure generated by the syntactic component can be regarded as generated by rules independent of considerations of meaning—i.e., independent of the rules of a semantic component, is a matter still under investigation by linguists working with this theory. In any event, the form of the rules generating deep structures is governed, ultimately, by considerations of what is required for semantic interpretation—i.e., by considerations of meaningfulness. (Are latent thoughts, then, analogous to semantically interpreted deep structures?)

6. The transformational processes or rules of the syntactic component, which generate surface structures from deep structures, are ultimately governed by considerations of (phonological) repre-

---

15 There is a discussion of this point in the penultimate section of this paper.

sentability. (Similarly, the transformational operations of dreaming are governed by considerations of representability. Is the dreamwork the transformational part of the system dreaming?)

7. One part of the syntactic component generates an infinite set of structures underlying an infinite set of possible sentences. The transformational part of the syntax, through the form of its rules and the constraints upon them, acts as a filter that excludes some combinations of deep structures and permits others, by generating some surface structures and not others for phonological representation. (Are defense mechanisms and the proscriptions that motivate their use, operating to control access to conscious representation, the transformational processes of another semiological system?)

For example, the abstract structures underlying "the man went to the store" and "the man was short" can be combined into abstract structures underlying such sentences as "the short man went to the store" and "the man who was short went to the store." But the abstract structures underlying "the man went to the store" and "the girl was short" cannot be combined into an abstract structure underlying the unacceptable sentence "the short (girl) man went to the store," because there is a constraint upon deletion by transformational rules such that (as a rough approximation of an example) a deleted noun phrase must be identical with the noun phrase dominating the structure into which it is embedded. Another kind of constraint concerns the order in which transformational rules may apply. Such constraints are necessary if the rules of the syntactic component are to generate *all* and *only* the acceptable sentences of the language. The rules must be powerful enough to generate all the acceptable sentences of the language, but not so powerful that they generate unacceptable as well as acceptable sentences.

It should follow, then, that the form of and constraints upon the transformational processes of a semiological system are crucial in determining the nature of possible perceptible symbolic forms generated by that system. Further, a semiological system is conceivable that is "more powerful" (in the sense described in the previous paragraph) than a natural language such as English. In fact, such a semiological system can be constructed simply by relaxing one constraint or any number of constraints upon the rules generating the linguistic forms of a natural language. (A fascinating possibility that should be investigated: might it be possible to characterize the dreamwork in just these terms?) [16]

8. Since in a natural language the rules of the phonological component are independent of the rules of the semantic component, the relation between form and content or between signifier and signified is said to be arbitrary in the kind of semiological system constituted by natural language. (This may not be true of every kind of semiological system; it is not true of the systems generating works of art, dreams, or motivated symbols in general; see Appendix A

The First Chapter of *The Interpretation of Dreams*

Freud begins *The Interpretation of Dreams* with these words:

> . . . there is a *psychological technique* which makes it possible to *interpret* dreams . . . every dream reveals itself as a psychical *structure* which has a meaning. . . . I shall . . . elucidate the *processes* to which the *strangeness* and *obscurity* of dreams are due and . . . deduce from those processes the nature of the psychical forces by whose concurrent or mutually opposing action dreams are *generated* [p. 1; my italics].

Structure implies an organization of elements patterned according to some principle or principles. Psychical structure implies (if psychical does not merely redundantly signify meaningful) an organization of elements in the form of perceptible images (in this case, dream images). A structure which has a meaning implies a symbolic entity that relates a perceptible image or images to an idea or ideas as signifier to signified, in the same way that in language, according to Saussure (1916), signs relate sound images to concepts. A structure which has meaning but which is nevertheless

---

[16] Similarly, a semiological system that is "less powerful" than a natural language—that will not generate some of the forms generated by a natural language—can be constructed by adding constraints upon the rules generating the linguistic forms of a natural language. (If the syntactic component of a language contained no transformational rules combining "kernel" patterns, it would constitute a system "less powerful" than a natural language.)

strange and obscure implies that what is signified, then, is not transparently evident upon exposure to the signifying entity, whose perceptible form may be regarded as a realization (in the medium of imagery) of a surface structure or organization of elements giving little indication of, or access to, its meaning. However, it is possible to interpret such a structure realized in such a form. A meaning can be attributed to, assigned to, or imposed upon it, on the basis of a knowledge of the processes that have acted to obscure that meaning by transforming an underlying or deep structure in definable ways; the deep structure, unlike the surface structure, directly reflects or makes accessible that meaning. The need for interpretation suggests either that the system of processes generating such symbolic forms as dreams (unlike language perhaps) is not in any major way used in communication, and therefore is not primarily governed by or adapted to the exigencies and requirements of communicative interaction, or that the system of processes generating such symbolic forms as dreams is responsive to communicative requisites and so does operate, in fact, to obstruct the communication of meaning. Freud seems to have held both views (1900, Ch. IV, but also footnote 2 added in 1925, p. 506).

A psychological technique makes it possible to reconstruct the nature of the route traversed, as a deep structure revealing meaning is transformed in definable ways into a surface form obscuring—if not actually concealing—meaning.

Forces—the explication of which becomes the scientist's theory of the dream—act, combine, cancel each other, to generate dreams, to generate structures that have meaning, that can be interpreted, whose meaning can be made accessible. Does Freud's use of the term "forces" reflect some inattention on his part or vacillation with respect to the distinction between the question "what is the *meaning* of a symbolic form?" and the question "what is the *cause* of a physical phenomenon?" and to the differences between a system of processes, principles, or rules *generating* (therefore, "explaining") a symbolic form and a system of natural laws *causing* (therefore, "explaining") a physical phenomenon? Consider: "meaning" implies that an entity insofar as it has effects has symbolic efficacy by virtue of what it means or represents and "causation" that it has intrinsic efficacy by virtue of what it is. Also, one can violate the rules of a language, for example, but the laws of nature cannot be violated.

It is clear, in any event, that from Freud's opening statement we may in fact infer immediately that he is about to report an investigation of the symbolic function, that with him we are about to enter the realm of semiology.

The first chapter of *The Interpretation of Dreams* is a review of the scientific literature dealing with the problems of dreams. It contrasts—in its cogency, scientific sophistication, and the power of its organization and argument—with the obligatory, ritual "historical review" to which we so often succumb in our journals. The latter's usual echolalic string of quotations and citations descends, at its worst, to pedantry and appeal to authority; although occasionally a review does rise to an awareness of science as a corpus of interlocking propositions requiring an assessment of what has apparently been established by previous workers and of the consequences for the whole of the abandonment of old or the introduction of new "findings" and "usages."

Freud surpasses the scope of even such a superior view. No wonder he put off writing this chapter to the last and found writing it too exhausting to return to it in revising subsequent editions. For in this chapter, he re-creates the thought processes of a creative scientist: how he surveys a congeries of often contradictory assertions; how he seizes upon the theoretically significant fact; how he marshals his material according to the questions he asks and asking holds to with obstinate tenacity as to the thread that will lead out of the maze; how he proposes criteria for explanation, not the least of which is the power, transcending apparent contradictions, to answer his questions, even if these be not the questions of others; and, with the help of such criteria, how he trenchantly dismisses explanations that have satisfied others and begins to fashion in their stead those that will satisfy himself.[17]

Freud frames his account according to topics rather than authors, raising "each dream-problem in turn," because, despite the points of value of individual studies, no one "line of advance in

---

[17] Characteristically, in citing writers who present views compatible with his own, Freud chides one for putting himself "in the wrong by not giving any refutation of the material which contradicts his thesis" (p. 60) .

any particular direction can be traced," "no foundation has been laid of secure findings upon which a later investigator might build," but rather "each new writer examines the same problems afresh and begins again, as it were, from the beginning." He expresses his conviction "that in such obscure matters it will only be possible to arrive at explanations and agreed results by a series of detailed investigations" (p. 5f.).

In a casually noted but drastic step given the scientific milieu in which he worked—many of the assumptions of which he was to continue to accept even while he paved the way through his own work for their abandonment—he distinguishes his own "piece of detailed research," "predominantly psychological in character," from "a problem of physiology," such as the problem of sleep. He supposes, however, that "one of the characteristics of the state of sleep must be that it brings about modifications in the conditions of functioning of the mental apparatus" (p. 6).

The distinction Freud makes here is a subtle one, which he found difficult to adhere to, and which is by no means even today generally understood or accepted. As is apparent from the actual conceptual and investigative strategies he pursued in his own work, he regards the physiological and psychological realms as two different empirical and theoretical systems. The data of one system are not mere epiphenomena of the processes of the other, nor can the explanatory propositions accounting for data in one realm be used to account for data in the other. Nevertheless, there is a systematic relation between the two realms, neither a simple parallelism nor a metaphysical gap. Processes in the physiological realm set the conditions for—that is, provide resources or occasions for, or constrain or limit, but do not determine the direction of, control, cause, or explain—processes in the psychological realm.

> Dreaming has often been compared with 'the ten fingers of a man who knows nothing of music wandering over the keys of a piano' . . . ; and this simile shows as well as anything the sort of opinion that is usually held of dreaming by representatives of the exact sciences. On this view a dream is something wholly and completely incapable of interpretation; for how could the ten fingers of an unmusical player produce a piece of music? [p. 78.]

This passage is only one of many that makes clear that Freud is determined to follow an unusual interest for a scientist of his time: an interest in the phenomenon of the creative generation of the dream as a symbolic form. I emphasize "creative" because of his recurrent emphasis upon the problem of accounting for the "choice" of materials used in constructing the dream and especially upon the problem of the "choice" of the particular dream images that ultimately appear in the perceptible dream form. (The term "choice," if taken seriously, appears to imply rules that can be violated or an imagined end in terms of which choices are made. I prefer not to suppose that Freud has simply stumbled unwittingly into an anthropomorphic formulation of physical processes governed by causal laws of nature.)

Freud's emphasis, choice of words, and many examples suggest in fact that he considers the production of the dream as an analogue of the artist's activity or (perhaps more appropriately, since he thought there were significant differences between a dream and an artwork), as one of my students has suggested,[18] of the activity of the *bricoleur* [19] described by Levi-Strauss (1962) in his discussion of mythical thought as a kind of intellectual *bricolage*—the *bricoleur* "who works with his hands and uses devious means compared to those of a craftsman," who, while "adept at performing a large number of diverse tasks . . . does not subordinate each of them to the availability of raw materials and tools conceived and procured for the purpose of the project," but who makes do "with 'whatever is at hand,' that is to say with a set of tools and materials which is always finite and is also heterogeneous because what it contains bears no relation to the current project, or indeed to any particular project, but is the contingent result of all the occasions there have been to renew or enrich the stock or to maintain it with the remains of previous constructions or destructions," the elements having been "collected or retained on the principle that 'they may always come in handy' " (p. 17f.) .

18 Daniel Begel in a seminar "Organism, Personality, Society and Culture" that is part of the Behavioral Sciences Track program of Yale University School of Medicine. I am indebted to students in this seminar and in the seminar "Issues for Psychoanalysis" at Pierson College, Yale University, for opportunities to clarify my thinking in discussions with them.
19 Roughly translated: a jack-of-all-trades.

Since Freud's interest is in the "interpretation" and not the "causation" of dreams, he will not formulate propositions of the kind, "given this set of conditions (a specification of the characteristics of the situation in which the dream occurs), this dream will inevitably follow." In fact, since he is to demonstrate that the dream has meaning, is therefore a symbolic form, belongs to a semiological system, he is at the same time demonstrating that such propositions cannot be formulated or, if formulated, can have only minor import. He is rather interested in the interpretation of the meaning of a dream, that is, in the discovery of the conceptions or ideas it signifies or represents. That discovery is to be made by specifying with respect to a particular dream: (1) the circumstances that provide the occasion for the dream (not *determine* its meaning or form, any more than the characteristics of a situation, which provides the occasion for an act of speech appropriate to the situation, determine the choice of words or their particular arrangement into sentences); (2) the materials which the dreamer chooses as he begins the mental work of constructing the dream; (3) the nature of the system that is responsible for the ultimate transformation of these materials by processes that are universal—i.e., that are characteristic of all dreams and thus constitute a system underlying the generation of any dream—and the way in which these transformations act to create the final form of the dream, i.e., determine the choice of dream images.

I anticipate that there may be some objection to this focus on the symbolic function as scanting the status of motivational and conative elements in Freud's work in favor of cognitive elements. For the present, I merely draw attention to the perhaps too little-noticed passage in which Freud appears to identify "impulse" as at least a type of "idea," with particular characteristics or a structure that he was to attempt in later theoretical work to specify, but still in all perhaps an ideational element. In discussing in this first chapter moral consciousness in dreams, he says, "It will be seen that the emergence of impulses which are foreign to our moral consciousness is merely analogous to what we have already learnt—the fact that dreams have access to ideational material which is absent in our waking state or plays but a small part in it" (p. 71).

Affects in contrast to impulses, however—he mentions in passing—do not appear to be transformed by the processes that produce the dream images. Quoting Stricker as writing: " 'Dreams do not consist solely of illusions. If, for instance, one is afraid of robbers in a dream, the robbers, it is true, are imaginary—but the fear is real,' " Freud comments, "This calls our attention to the fact that *affects* in dreams cannot be judged in the same way as the remainder of their content" (p. 74). If this is true, impulses and feelings may be very different elements from the point of view of the symbolic function. Affects may best be regarded as an aspect of the attitude toward, or the state aroused by, the meaning of the dream. In this sense, then, the presence of the affect is an "index," as Piaget would term it (see Appendix A), rather than an exemplification of the symbolic function; that is, affect is an intrinsic part of an existing state of affairs—not abstract or conceptual in nature— for which it is then able to stand or which it is able to indicate. Impulses, on the other hand, may best be regarded as conceptions, oriented to the future, which can be represented by symbolic entities.

Embarking on another digression here, I should like to stress that Freud's interest in "meaning" is primarily in that sense of meaning that has to do with ideas or conceptions (which necessarily must involve some level of abstraction) signified by a symbolic form, i.e., with the connotative sense of "meaning," rather than with other senses of "meaning" I shall go on to enumerate. (Freud's work, therefore, contributes more to a cognitive psychology, to the extent such can be distinguished from a motivational psychology, than has been adequately recognized.) These other senses of "meaning" have to do with: (1) the intention inferred to underlie or dictate a particular suasive use or presentation in communicative processes of a symbolic form (motivational sense of "meaning"); (2) the concrete object or thing at which a symbolic form, which actually represents an abstraction, may sometimes mistakenly be said to point directly (the deictic or denotative sense of "meaning"); (3) the order or pattern discernible in a symbolic form, as in a work of art, which may be thought to constitute its "meaning" ("meaning" in the sense of "significant form" or "meaningfulness").

Significant form may be said to be meaningful, because like any exemplification of the symbolic function it is an outcome of a process involving choice among alternatives (choice among possible ordering or patterning of elements) and therefore is presumed to be significant or meaningful even when it may be difficult if not impossible—as in the musical composition performed by Freud's hypothetical musical player—to say that a significant form has *a* meaning in the same sense that an item that is part of a language with a semantic component may be said to have *a* meaning.

Without choice there cannot be meaning (in the sense of connotation) in language. For example, if a content dictates the presence of an element so that there is no choice but to include it, as in the frame calling for a single element "I want —— go to the store," where "to" is mandatory, it is therefore completely predictable, contains no new information, and is without meaning. "To" in this context may be considered an abstract operator, but it does not have semantic content. Similarly, if a situation actually coerces an utterance—that is, given the situation, the utterance is inevitable—then the utterance cannot be said to have meaning or to be a symbolic form. That is not to say that such an utterance—a scream, for example—would not communicate information; a "signal" or "index" both communicate information, although, in this rather uninteresting because so extended sense, almost anything may be said to communicate information, since from an observation of it a state of affairs may be inferred. Meaning (in the sense of connotation) implies a signified abstraction, a conception or idea. (Such considerations provide one basis for rejecting a strict stimulus-response account of "verbal behavior" or, indeed, of any behavior involving the symbolic function. See Chomsky, 1959.) All the more poignantly to our present purpose in this discussion is Freud's use of the word "choice" in "choice of dream image" as what he wishes to explain.

Freud's review of the literature follows four main lines of thought, concerning: (1) the materials used in the construction of dreams; (2) the occasions providing an opportunity for, or instigating, the construction of dreams; (3) the characteristics of the constructed dream; and (4) a theory of dreams. These are the problems that are to be investigated further throughout the remainder of *The Interpretation of Dreams*.

1. Dreams are a representation of thoughts and, in that sense, dreaming is a "form of thought"—"as a rule dream-pictures contain what the waking man already thinks" (p. 8).

We may say, then, that thoughts are represented by dream pictures or pictograms, rather than phonologically as in language. It follows that a major difference between language and dreams is the difference between the phonological component—which assigns a phonological representation to transformations of semantically interpreted deep structures through the operation of a set of rules specifying acceptable combinations among a finite set of discrete, differentiable, semantically meaningless sound selements—and that component in the system generating dreams whereby thoughts (semantically interpreted deep structures) are assigned a representation in dream images. The transformational processes in language and in the system generating dreams, whereby semantically interpreted deep structures become derived surface structures, must also differ, since the former transformational processes must generate a surface structure susceptible to phonological representation and the latter must generate a surface structure susceptible to representation in dream images.

"All the material making up the content of a dream is in some way derived from experience" (p. 11). So, "one of the sources from which dreams derive material for reproduction—material which is in part neither remembered nor used in the activities of waking thought—is childhood experience." But, also, "elements are to be found in most dreams, which are derived from the very last few days before they were dreamt." In addition, the "third, most striking and least comprehensible characteristic of memory in dreams is shown in the *choice* of material produced. For what is found worth remembering is not, as in waking life, only what is most important, but on the contrary what is most indifferent and insignificant as well" (pp. 15, 17, 18).

Freud, in contrast to others, does not choose any one of these as a foundation for the explanation of dreams. The three facts do not contradict each other; rather, all three must be encompassed by a theoretical account of dreams. The point of view that makes this possible involves seeing all three as exemplifications of the various types of materials chosen in creating the dream. That is, the material utilized in constructing the dream form is not a finite set of discrete, differentiable, semantically meaningless sound elements as in language, but is instead memory images—of past experiences, especially perhaps childhood experiences; of recent experiences; and, frequently, of apparently trivial, indifferent, insignificant experiences.

Freud, drawn to the paradoxical, unexpected fact, recognizes that the choice of indifferent, insignificant memory images has tended to lead to discounting or overlooking the connection between the dream and the experiences of waking life and even to abandoning a promising line of research. So, one writer, who was "unquestionably right in asserting that we should be able to explain the genesis of every dream-image if we devoted enough time and trouble to tracing its origin," allowed himself to be "deterred from following the path which has this inauspicious beginning" by the "exceedingly laborious and thankless" quality of the task involved, thus losing the opportunity to be led "to the very heart of the explanation of dreams" (p. 19f.). The gifted scientist, we may infer, confronted by the prospect of a possibly thankless labor among details of apparent triviality, does not shrink back; rather the reverse: he is moved to what appears to others as eccentrically persistent exertions.

Similarly, Freud seizes upon a fact that is not only odd but is of "remarkable . . . theoretical importance . . . that dreams have at their command memories which are inaccessible in waking life" (p. 12f.). "No one who occupies himself with dreams can, I believe, fail to discover that it is a very common event for a dream to give evidence of knowledge and memories which the waking subject is unaware of possessing" (p. 14). (Among the interesting examples of this fact, he mentions that "in dreams people speak foreign languages more fluently and correctly than in waking life" [p. 11].) "Certain theories" about dreams must be judged incorrect because they ignore this crucial fact in seeking "to account for their absurdity and incoherence by a partial forgetting of what we know during the day. When we bear in mind the extraordinary efficiency . . . exhibited by memory in dreams we shall have a lively sense of the contradiction which these theories involve" (p. 20).

One important contribution of psychoanalysis to those concerned with semiological theory, including the theory of language, may be this fact that memory images which are not available to waking consciousness are available for dream formation. This fact suggests that the availability or accessibility of some materials and not others to the component (such as the phonological component of language) assigning a perceptible realization to a derived surface structure determines the surface form of the symbol. In other words, then, transformational processes—by which semantically interpreted deep structures (thoughts) are rendered susceptible to imaged representation—are responsive to the availability or accessibility of some materials and not others for the representation of the manifest dream.

A transformational component may alter a semantically interpreted deep structure not because the structure itself is unacceptable (considered from the point of view of the meaning it is designed to reflect) but because some means—some images—for representing it in perceptible form are available while others are not. The nature of the transformational component may differ in some respects from language to language as well as from individual to individual (i.e., in the dreams of individuals and in individual ideolects or language variants in general, the ideolect being as rule-governed as—although the rules may be dfferent from—a standard language). Apparently, the nature of this component is shaped, however, in all cases by the availability and unavailability of various means, no matter what the mechanism (motivational or arbitrary) by which such materials are rendered inaccessible or made available.

Some materials (some memory images) are available for use in symbol construction in the sleeping state that are not available during the waking state. As I have noted, two factors, at least, seem to determine the nature of transformational processes in any symbolic system, i.e., how they will operate to alter and to filter or screen deep structures: (1) the availability of some materials and not others to the component assigning a perceptible representation to the derived surface structure supplied to this component by transformational processes; and (2) the particular constraints imposed in a particular symbolic system upon transformational processes. Both factors are apparently affected by the sleeping state, such that materials may be available for dream formation that are not available as memories during the waking state, and constraints imposed during the waking state upon transformational processes may be absent or relaxed during processes of symbol formation characteristic of the sleeping state.

I should like to emphasize again that the system by which dreams are generated creates a symbol by combining not meaningless but meaningful elements. Memory images are themselves symbolic entities. As Freud's later work was to make clear (see also Kris, 1956a), memories are the results of a creative, constructive process, which involves selecting, rejecting, combining, and altering certain details, so that the memory image represents an abstraction, a conception of experience, and not experience itself. We find one theory of art that is somewhat analogous in its formulation that meaningful elements are merely materials. Langer (1953, 1957, 1962) argues persuasively that meaningful images (a pictorial image of someone or something, an imitation of a particular sound) are but so much raw material pressed into service by the artist, not to indicate the meaning of a work of art but to create a significant form, an apparition, a virtual reality, an illusion of virtual powers (dance), virtual time (music), virtual space (plastic art), virtual events (poesis), virtual history (literature), or virtual present (drama), representing the real meaning of the work of art—a conception or idea of inner reality or the world of feeling. (Langer's theory of art also has some analogy, then, to a theory of the dream as the creation of an illusion—or, more strongly in the case of the dream, a hallucination—of an experience of wish fulfillment.)

Freud concludes that the dream cannot be simply a process by which memory images are reproduced as an end in itself; "views of this sort are inherently improbable owing to the manner in which dreams deal with the material that is remembered," deleting aspects of the memory image, substituting for part of it something else, altering some aspect of its form (p. 20f.).

Dreams, in other words, use only fragments of memory images and these are often altered in some way. By what processes are memory images transformed so that they may be used to construct the dream form? These processes do not appear to involve primarily rules that govern the combination of elements (i.e., memory-image fragments) with each other, as do the rules of the phonological component of language. Rather, the memory-image fragment is used to represent meaning either by virtue of the meaningfulness it already possesses as a part of a symbolic entity (i.e., a memory image) or because of other, apparently fortuitous features—certain formal or sensuous properties—which resemble in some way the idea or ideas it is to represent. In fact, the content of a memory image may not be crucial for its use at all but only "the fact of its being 'real' "—that is, the fact that it *is a memory image* and that it represents, therefore, a location in time—determines its being chosen to represent a thought such as: " 'I really *did* do all that yesterday' " (p. 21). In the system generating dreams, the component that realizes the dream in perceptible form is not independent of the semantic component (it is unlike language in this regard) ; the relation of form and content is not arbitrary or conventional; a dream is therefore a motivated or apparitional symbol, as previously defined (see Appendix A) .

2. One or another kind of stimuli has been taken by other investigators to be *the* cause of dreams. However, external stimuli cannot be accepted as explanations of dreams, for nothing about the stimulus accounts for one group of memories rather than another being aroused, or for one rather than another interpretation being made by the dreamer of any illusion called up in the state of sleep by an external stimulus. Subjective sensory excitations cannot constitute satisfactory explanations; they "are ready at hand, one might say, whenever they are needed as an explanation," and, furthermore, "the part they play . . . is scarcely or not at all open to confirmation . . . by observation and experiment" (p. 31). Medical men may prefer organic sensations or internal somatic stimuli as an "explanation" of dreams, because such stimuli provide a "single aetiology for dreams and mental diseases," but "one is often faced with the awkward fact that the only thing that reveals the existence of the organic stimulus is precisely the content of the dream itself," and again nothing about a somatic stimulus accounts for the choice of one particular dream image rather than another (p. 37) .

Therefore, external sensory excitations, internal sensory excitations, internal somatic stimuli, or purely psychical sources of stimulation are seen essentially by Freud as instigating dream construction but not explaining it. Such stimuli must therefore have the status of providing possible occasions for dream construction. They give us no clue in themselves as to the way in which particular dreams are constructed—the choice of dream images, for example —or what a particular dream means. The parallel, again, is to language. Situations requiring communication, calling for the expression of thoughts or feelings, demanding thought, may result in the use of language. These situations do not, on that account, explain the characteristics of language or determine the structure or meaning of the specific linguistic form generated in any particular situation.

3. The characteristics of the dream follow from the nature of what is finally constructed from these materials on these occasions.

First, some dreams are forgotten very quickly; some remembered with extraordinary persistence. Their lack of intelligibility and orderliness is especially important in accounting for their being so easily forgotten.

> If sensations, ideas, thoughts, and so on, are to attain a certain degree of susceptibility to being remembered, it is essential that they should not remain isolated but should be arranged in appropriate concatenations and groupings. If a short line of verse is divided up into its component words and these are mixed up, it becomes very hard to remember [p. 44].

Unlike the ordering of sound images in a linguistic form, the principles by which the dream images are ordered, if any order there be, are unknown. Whatever the principles, they are so different that to understand the dream, to know what thoughts the dream represents, to remember the dream, is difficult indeed in waking consciousness. The symbolic forms of waking consciousness, as phonological realizations of derived surface structures, are dominated by the rules of the transformational and phonological components of language. The persistent remembering of some dreams, on the other hand, is perhaps related in part to the unwitting contribution waking consciousness makes in the form of interpolations and filling in of gaps in the dream images in order to make causal connections between merely juxtaposed sequences, thereby rendering the dream more coherent.

Second, there are "modifications in the processes of the mind" that make the dream seem alien; "the strangeness cannot be due to the material that finds its way into their content, since that material is for the most part common to dreaming and waking life" (p. 48). In falling asleep, we notice that thoughts are represented by images, which rise involuntarily, in contrast to the voluntary flow of concepts while awake (presumably, Freud means here by *concepts* linguistic elements, which are capable of signifying abstract ideas). Dreams hallucinate; they represent an idea as actually happening; "we appear not to *think* but to *experience;* that is to say, we attach complete belief to the hallucinations," since in the state of sleep reality testing is not possible (p. 50ff.).

Furthermore, the value ordinarily attaching to such images seems detached from them; dreams "are disconnected, they accept the most violent contradictions without the least objection, they admit impossibilities, they disregard knowledge which carries great weight with us in the daytime, they reveal us as ethical and moral imbeciles" (p. 54). The judgment that the absurd, incoherent ideation of dreams is due to "lowered psychical efficiency," as Freud will show, is a judgment based on the surface form of the dream.[20] (The error here is the same as that of positivist, radically empiricist linguists, who limit themselves in attempting to account for language to a description and analysis of what is empirically given—the surface structure of actual utterances.)

Freud has already pointed out that the memory function in dreams is in some respects superior to that of waking life and he is to show in addition that the semantically interpreted deep structures underlying dreams are identical with those underlying linguistic forms generated in waking consciousness. In other words, the conceptions or ideas and the organization of these that are

[20] Freud, interestingly enough, offers a hypothesis concerning preferences for one theoretical approach over another: "Anyone who is inclined to take a low view of psychical functioning in dreams will naturally prefer to assign their source to somatic stimulation; whereas those who believe that the dreaming mind retains the greater part of its waking capacities have of course no reason for denying that the stimulus to dreaming can arise within the dreaming mind itself" (p. 64).

represented by dreams are the same as those represented by the symbolic forms generated in the state of waking consciousness. (It is still not generally understood that the view presented by Freud is that the thoughts—the semantically interpreted deep structures —underlying both dreams and psychopathological symptomatology are the same as the thoughts of normal, waking consciousness. Only the transformational processes operating upon these thoughts to produce derived surface structures susceptible to a particular mode of perceptible representation—e.g., a phonological representation in language or a memory-image representation in dreams— and the particular modes of perceptible representation of these derived surface structures are different.)

If Freud is to alter the judgment that the ideation of dreams is deficient, he must show: (1) that the difference between dreams and the linguistic forms of waking consciousness is not a difference in what is signified but a difference in the form and manner of construction of the signifier; and (2) that the incoherence of dreams does not involve a breakdown into lawlessness either of conception or of representation (as would be the case if symbolic forms were generated according to no discernible laws at all) ; rather it involves definable processes that depart from the rules generating symbolic forms in waking consciousness but that are theoretically as specifiable as those rules. (Even the rules of a language are enormously difficult to specify and have not been completely specified for any language.) That is, dreams are generated according to rules that are apparently to some extent differently formed and constrained than those dominating the symbolic function of the state of waking consciousness.

Not anything is possible in dreams. Dreams are a "form of thought," in which the representation of thought is by symbolic forms generated by definite, though special canons of symbolization. But the faculty of thought itself remains essentially intact. The state of sleep alters not the thought processes, but the processes by which symbolic forms are generated to represent these thought processes. (These formulations imply that "secondary process thought" and "primary process thought" signify differences in the symbolic representation of thought and not differences in thought itself.)

4. Freud proposes that a theory of dreams should seek "to explain as many as possible of their observed characteristics from a particular point of view," and, at the same time, should define "the position occupied by dreams in a wider sphere of phenomena" (p. 75). He also is inclined to formulate a theory from which it is possible to infer a function for dreaming (as, I would say, one ought to be able to infer from a theory of language what it is about language that makes it possible to use it in thinking and communication—but, I shall again repeat, that it is so used is not an explanation of it.)

Freud does not accept the idea that dreaming can be explained by theories assuming that psychic activity continues as usual during sleep but necessarily produces different results under such altered conditions. If the mind continues to function in all ways as usual, how derive the distinctions between dreams and waking thought? Moreover, such theories suggest no function for dreaming.

Freud does not accept theories attributing dreams to hypofunction of the psychic apparatus, which also leave "no room for assigning any function to dreaming," and which are based on an *a priori* devaluation of dreams as unworthy to rank with the psychic processes of waking life.

Freud does not accept theories attributing dreams to hyperfunction of the psychic apparatus, although these suggest a utilitarian —e.g., reviving, healing, creative—function for dreaming, primarily because of their vagueness and lack of universality (i.e., their inability to relate dreams to other phenomena). He is interested in Scherner's work, which stresses the role of the dream imagination that "makes use of recent waking memories for its building material" and "erects them into structures bearing not the remotest resemblance to those of waking life; it reveals itself in dreams as possessing not merely reproductive but *productive* powers." Since dream imagination is "without the power of conceptual speech," it is "obliged to paint what it has to say pictorially, and, since there are no concepts to exercise an attenuating influence, it makes full and powerful use of the pictorial form." However, Freud notes the arbitrary character of dream imagination and "its disobedience to all the rules of research seem only too obvious." Nevertheless, he urges that Scherner's ideas should not be rejected because they seem fantastic. "Ganglion cells can be fantastic too" (pp. 84–87).

The missing ingredients of function and universality are supplied by Freud in two propositions (which he does not separate, but which I think ought to be separated), suggested in a final section of the first chapter. The first has to do with the nature of the conception—the signified—of which the dream is the signifier. The second has to do with the function served by the particular kind of symbolic form—motivated or apparitional symbol—the dream is. The first proposition is that the ideas represented by dreams are uniquely and always concerned with the fulfillment of wishes. The second proposition is that the form of dreams (and psychoses), involving the use of memory images to create the illusion of a virtual reality (an apparently actual experience of a hallucinated event), ideally serves (as an apparitional or motivated symbol) the function of representing what are only ideas of wish fulfillment as actual experience of wish fulfillment.[21]

A central hypothesis in Freud's theory of dreams, already delineated in this first chapter, is that the thinking of the dreamer (or of some kinds of psychotic individuals) is not different from the thinking of the nonpsychotic individual in the waking state, where "thinking" refers to the most basic, probably universal categories and the most basic operations that relate these categories. What is different is the way in which identical thoughts of the dreamer (or of the psychotic individual), on the one hand, and of the nonpsychotic individual in the waking state, on the other, are represented in perceptible form.

In other words, transformational processes or rules and a component that represents thoughts in perceptible form are different in the symbolic functioning of the dreamer or psychotic individual —not the sets of rules generating and assigning semantic interpre-

[21] To say this function is the only function of the system generating dreams may seem similar to saying what is clearly not so—that language as a system can be put to only one use, such as communication. One must be clear here, however, about the distinction between "dreams" as phenomena and "the system generating dreams," which may generate other apparitional symbolic forms (e.g., psychopathological symptoms and even the transference neurosis) as well (Edelson, 1971).

tations to deep structures. The materials available to and used by that component and the operations by which these materials are used in constructing a perceptible form determine the nature of the transformational processes or rules providing inputs to the component. So, for example, linguistic representation is by a phonological component, which is made up of a finite stock of meaningless elements or phonemes (always a rather small subset of a possible range of such elements) combined according to the rules of the phonological component to form by concatenation meaningful elements or morphemes. The component realizing thoughts in perceptible "apparitional" form in dreams (and psychoses), however, appears to be made up of meaningful, allusive and imitative elements, which are gestaltlike or whole forms, i.e., not segmentable into meaningless elements taken from a small, finite stock of such elements. These materials are used to realize a perceptible representation of thought through processes of allusion.[22]

At least one implication of this formulation seems to be that where we have been preoccupied with differences in thought processes and with so-called functional "thought disorders," we might better be concerned with differences in the means by which thought is represented and therefore with differences in symbolic form, and with the dysfunctional consequences of such differences with respect to making obscure the relation of the subject's thoughts and feelings, creating obstacles to the subject's conscious recognition and understanding of his own thought, and interfering with the subject's communication of his thought to others.

---

[22] Manifest dream elements can be used to represent the dream thoughts, not because they can be combined like phonetic elements to form stable, semantically meaningful structures, but because of their allusiveness. "My recollection of the monograph on the genus Cyclamen would thus serve the purpose of being an *allusion* to the conversation with my friend, just as the 'smoked salmon' in the dream of the abandoned supper-party . . . served as an *allusion* to the dreamer's thought of her woman friend" (Freud, 1900, p. 175). The dream is a hallucinated wish fulfillment—a virtual reality, an *illusion*. Each of the elements of the manifest dream is an *allusion*. We may pause to note that both illusion and allusion are related to the Latin *ludus* (play), *ludere* (to play), *alludere* (to play on—e.g., a word), *illudere* (to mock or deceive) (Weekly, 1921, pp. 33, 746). Wallace Stevens (1949) wrote of Freud, "is it not possible that he might have said that in a civilization based on science there could be a science of illusions" (p. 139)? Freud in *The Interpretation of Dreams* is developing a science of illusions—illusions constructed of allusive entities—a science of the mind at play.

To what extent does the allusiveness of elements in the manifest dream (and the allusiveness of the "associations" to which these elements allude) reflect and depend upon linguistic competence? The manifest dream is, operationally, a linguistic entity. The verbal description of the dream is the object of study in the psychoanalytic situation, including casual, apparently extraneous comments about, or characterizations of, the dream as a whole, as well as emendations of its description. The process by which the dream is studied (free association) involves the relating of linguistic units to each other. That is, free associations may be analyzed as sentences, words, and phonemes, even when these constitute reports of memories or images. Linguistic elements that constitute the report of the manifest dream evoke or allude to "free associations," and various free associations in turn evoke or allude to other linguistic elements.

Freud repeatedly implies or explicitly states that language or, more specifically, knowledge about language is a resource that is used in constructing, as well as in interpreting, the dream.[23] It may even be that the canons according to which the dream is constructed are related in some regular way to the rules of language. We should ask to what extent the evocation of free associations to a dream not only makes use of language as material but is determined by principles of language. In other words, we want to know to what extent dreaming depends on, is a function of, is an expression of, or exemplifies a use of what Chomsky calls linguistic competence.

The Dimensions of Symbolic Functioning

It is possible that Freud adumbrated in *The Interpretation of Dreams* six dimensions of symbolic functioning, and therefore six dimensions by which different symbolic systems and their use may be compared and contrasted with each other.

---

[23] Freud even in this first chapter mentioned, for example, the number of interpretations of dream elements made by oriental dream books that depend on a play on words, "upon similarity of sounds and resemblances between words," as might be expected perhaps from a knowledge of the "extraordinarily important part played by punning and verbal quibbles in the ancient civilizations of the East" (p. 99) .

1. There is the symbolic form itself, a constructed image, which has some determinable relationship with abstraction, class or category, thought or idea, and which is significant not in and of itself but by virtue of its meaning—that which it signifies or represents. The symbolic form is constructed by means of a system of relatively discrete elements or materials; selection from among a limited range of all possible such elements and the relationships (classification, combination, transformation) among these elements are governed by the definable rules, methods, or techniques characteristic of the system. In dreaming, the symbolic form is the manifest dream, an organization of images that, according to Freud (p. 567), because of the very purposiveness of all psychic activity, must as the end of a process of psychic activity in the state of sleep take the form of a virtual or hallucinatory wish fulfillment. In language, the symbolic form is speech—language in performance.

Just as in dreaming, the manifest dream must be distinguished from the system (including the dreamwork, for example) that is logically prior to any use of it in constructing a manifest dream, so in language, speech or performance must be distinguished from the system comprising language competence or capacity (including the rules of phonology, syntax, and semantics) that is logically prior to any use of it in speech. Freud's considerable achievement was to go far in explicating the nature of one such system; Chomsky's contribution to linguistics, as we have seen, is of the same kind.

2. There are the materials used in constructing a symbolic form. In dreaming, these include representations of somatic stimuli of insufficient intensity to disturb sleep and representations of recent but indifferent impressions left over from the previous day. We may conclude that elements of language (partly by virtue of the situations or contexts in which they have appeared in experience, and to which they may therefore allude, and partly by virtue of the characteristics they possess as members of the symbolic system language) may also be classified as building materials, perhaps as common as or even commoner than those previously mentioned.

This conclusion follows from many of Freud's examples. He discusses the appearance in dreams of speech, which acts not as a representation of thought, but as an allusion to contexts. He demonstrates the use of syllables and words to form allusive links with other members of a class of sounds, a class of meanings, or a class of syllables or words by virtue of their membership in the same class. Syllables and words may also be used to form allusive links with members of other classes by virtue of their rule-determined connectedness or their capacity to combine to form a sequence or a sequential context. In other words, linguistic units may allude to or evoke each other because they belong to the same category or subcategory. These units—which, if they belong to the semantic component, may be completely synonymous, antonymous, partially synonymous, or contrasting—may be substituted for one another with respect to particular contexts because of their shared membership in a category or subcategory. Linguistic units also may allude to or evoke each other because they are connectable or combinable according to the rules of language. Such units may be said to join together to form contexts.[24] We are naturally interested with regard to the construction of dreams in the possibility of deviant substitutions—e.g., of one linguistic unit for another to which it is related not by shared membership in the same subcategory but rather by rules that connect or combine them. "Crown" may be substituted for "king" in "The crown issued a decree" by virtue of their contiguity in such (nondeviant) forms as "The king has a crown." "The crown issued a decree" is a mildly deviant sentence, because it violates a rule calling for a noun with certain features (which "crown" does not have) to precede "issued a decree."

Materials used in constructing a symbolic form may be considered from the point of view of their relative availability and the stringencies (a term used by Kris, 1952) they impose on the act of construction. As an earlier quoted passage from Freud suggests, some materials impose relatively little in the way of limitations upon what may be represented and how it may be represented; other materials—in particular, some used in art—may predetermine stringently what it is possible and what impossible to represent and how what is represented may be represented. In other

---

[24] For interesting discussions of these two different kinds of relations (described in terms of two dimensions, similarity and contiguity, and called paradigmatic and syntagmatic), see Saussure (1916), Jakobson (1941, 1955, 1956, 1964), Levi-Strauss (1958, 1962, 1964).

words, some materials demand, in the act of constructing a symbolic form, more accommodation to their intrinsic characteristics than others.

A principal advantage of recent impressions as materials in dream construction is that such impressions have not yet become committed or tied to certain meanings; in this sense, their recency enhances not only their availability but the relative lack of stringency their use imposes on dream construction. This relative lack of stringency is especially important because the dreamwork is governed by the necessity to represent a number of meanings simultaneously in the dream. A principal advantage of the use of indifferent impressions as materials in dream construction (in addition to its postulated service in censorship) is, similarly, that they are relatively empty of significance and therefore may more easily be used to evoke multiple meanings or make multiple allusions. "Both groups of impressions satisfy the demand of the repressed for material that is still clear of associations—the indifferent ones because they have given no occasion for the formation of many ties, and the recent ones because they have not yet had time to form them" (p. 564).

A crucial characteristic of these materials is that they have no claim to interest in and of themselves. Insofar as they are merely materials to be used in constructing the manifest dream, they do not act as disturbers of sleep and therefore in themselves do not instigate, or offer any incentive to, or provide any occasion for, dreaming. The limited range of sounds or phonemes, which are materials used in speech, are similar to materials used in dream construction—in their easy accessibility and the relative lack of stringency their use imposes on the representation of thought. Phonemes are not intrinsically significant sounds; to the extent a sound is intrinsically significant—a scream of pain, for example— it loses its value for use in the construction of a representation of an abstraction. (In this sense, the innate expressiveness of a sound and the use of the sound in the construction of a symbolic representation are inversely related; this raises some question concerning the postulation of the origins of language in emotional or interjectional utterance. As we have seen, Freud, interestingly enough, suggests that affect in a dream has a different status than that of other elements; an affect is likely to be an index of what the dreamer is actually feeling rather than a representation constructed by means of the dreamwork of what he is thinking.)

3. There are the instigators of dream construction which incite, or provide occasions for, symbolic functioning in the state of sleep. Dream instigators include external sensory stimuli, organic somatic stimuli, psychic stimuli—any intrusion sufficiently intense to threaten a disturbance or disruption of the state of sleep. Such dream instigators are not "causes" of dreams, any more than an incitement of, or occasion for, speech is its cause. There is no direct relation between a symbolic representation and the occasion for it. One cannot understand or predict the dream from an examination of the instigator, nor the speech from the most exact knowledge of the external situation that is its occasion. Many different dreams may be incited by the same instigator, and many—an indefinite number of—different utterances are possible in a given situation. The instigation or occasion does not necessarily even result in a dream or a symbolic representation of any kind, for such instigations or occasions may result in other kinds of acts or functioning. In themselves such instigations or occasions provide no commitment to construct a dream or symbolic representation of any kind, nor—if symbolic representation ensues—does an instigation or occasion determine what form the symbolic representation shall take. "Laws" in symbolic functioning govern the relations between members of the symbolic system and the construction of a symbolic form, rather than the relations between a stimulus and a response to it. These "laws" or rules permit choices among many alternatives, usually if not always involve normative considerations, and, for example, in the case of language in any particular instance of speech, may be violated to one degree or another, as is never true of "a law of nature." With regard to choices among alternatives in dreaming, it is important to note that when Freud discussed whether or not the associations to a dream necessarily involved the same elements that entered into its construction, he decided not. A set of associations available only from the day following the dream, for example, represents new connections "set up between thoughts which were already linked in some other way in the dream-thoughts"; these new elements may form links between

latent meanings and their manifest representation that are alternatives to those used in the construction of the dream, and are, "as it were, loop-lines or short-circuits, made possible by the existence of other and deeper-lying connecting paths" (p. 280) .

It is possible to argue that what is instigated by intrusions in the state of sleep is a process of thought, which may be given symbolic representation. In the conditions characteristic of the state of sleep, if thought is to be represented symbolically, it will be represented by the dream, as in the waking state, for example, thought is represented by inner or externalized speech; the first type of representation makes use of the techniques of the dreamwork, the second makes use of the phonological, syntactic, and semantic rules of language. There is a line of reasoning in Freud's later writing, especially concerning the two principles of mental functioning and the primary and secondary processes, which suggests that the dreamwork is to be considered one way of giving symbolic form or representation to thoughts, those techniques employed in the state of sleep. See, for example, the 1925 footnote added to *The Interpretation of Dreams:*

> At bottom, dreams are nothing other than a particular *form* of thinking, made possible by the conditions of the state of sleep. It is the *dream-work* which creates that form, and it alone is the essence of dreaming—the explanation of its particular nature. . . . The fact that dreams concern themselves with attempts at solving the problems by which our mental life is faced is no more strange than that our conscious waking life should do so [p. 506f.]

The phrase "form of thinking" here should not be taken to mean that the thoughts represented are different from those represented in waking life, but rather that the form given to the representations of thought in sleep is different from that given to representations of thought in waking life. The only "thinking" that is different in sleep is the dreamwork—the techniques employed for representing thoughts—if one wishes to regard this dreamwork as a kind of meta-thought-process. "[The dreamwork] does not think, calculate or judge in any way at all; it restricts itself to giving things a new form" (p. 507) .

This line of argument would suggest that censorship should not be given the status Freud attributes to it throughout *The Interpretation of Dreams*, that of a motive for using the techniques of the dreamwork. Rather, disguise or dream distortion may be one consequence of the use of the techniques of the dreamwork in the state of sleep, a functional consequence from the point of view of such requirements as the personality system may have for censorship. Similarly, the constraints upon transformational rules in syntax, which generate surface structures from deep structures, may be such that one consequence of using such rules is to maximize the possibility of recovering deep structures from surface structure. One need not postulate, on that account, a motive for communicative transparency or thought retrieval as the motive for the use of such transformational rules.

4. There is the capacity for, or commitment to, dream construction, what Freud called the required motive force, which he believed depended upon the activation or recruitment of an unconscious wish. The wish is necessary to commit the resources of the psychological system to a particular end: dream construction. In general, we may say that symbolic functioning requires a commitment to achieve ends by symbolic means, or, in other words, a commitment of the resources of the psychological system to actualize in performance a capacity. That capacity is best described by describing the characteristics of a symbolic system—for example, the dreamwork or the phonological, syntactic, and semantic rules (in Chomsky's sense, the grammar) of a language. The symbolic performance may become an end in itself or may be a means to the achievement of such ends as: (1) thinking, which broadly conceived might be regarded as involving the regulation of the relation of the personality system and reality; (2) communicating, which broadly conceived might be regarded as involving the regulation of systems of interaction; (3) the internal regulation of the psychological system (as exemplified by inner speech) ; (4) or the regulation of the relation of the personality system and the organism (as exemplified by dreaming insofar as dreaming is viewed as preserving sleep by the representation of a virtual wish fulfillment) .

In attempting to formulate a description of the nature of a wish,

Freud hypothesized that the psychological apparatus functions to eliminate stimuli; changes result that may achieve an "experience of satisfaction," which puts an end to disturbing stimuli.

> An essential component of this experience of satisfaction is a particular perception (that of nourishment, in our example) the mnemic image of which remains associated thenceforward with the memory trace of the excitation produced by the need. As a result of the link that has thus been established, next time this need arises a psychical impulse will at once emerge which will seek to re-cathect the mnemic image of the perception and to re-evoke the perception itself, that is to say, to re-establish the situation of the original satisfaction. An impulse of this kind is what we call a wish; the reappearance of the perception is the fulfillment of the wish; and the shortest path to the fulfilment of the wish is a path leading direct from the excitation produced by the need to a complete cathexis of the perception. Nothing prevents us from assuming that there was a primitive state of the psychical apparatus in which this path was actually traversed, that is, in which wishing ended in hallucinating. Thus, the aim of this first psychical activity was to produce a 'perceptual identity'—a repetition of the perception which was linked with the satisfaction of the need [p. 565f.].

If, later, after the development of thought and purposeful act, whose aim is to alter the world to re-evoke the perception, there are circumstances (for example, the state of sleep) in which the world cannot be altered, then, again, a wish may follow the short-cut to a hallucinatory wish fulfillment. The wish is necessary for dream construction not simply by virtue of its intensity but by its very nature as the representation, in the form of a mnemic image of a perception, of a commitment to re-evoke what is absent—that perception.

What is especially interesting in all this is that the mnemic image of the perception may be regarded as a representation of an absent state of affairs; the image guides or governs the personality system's efforts to re-evoke the perception. The mnemic image is a signifier. The image is not an exact imitation of the perception it represents, but represents rather the perception "as remembered." That is, the image represents an abstraction of the experienced perception—a conception of it. Insofar as an image of a perception of satisfaction is re-evoked for its own sake rather than the actual perception, the signifier and signified are relatively non-differentiated; the signifier is treated as if it were what it signifies. In addition, the mnemic image may eventually at one and the same time be regarded as representing a conception of a past state of affairs (projected into the future), therefore, also a conception of a future state of affairs and, as a wish, a commitment to its actualization.

The wish is clearly, then, not a blind, inchoate, unorganized, structureless, a-cognitive urge. (See on this point Schafer, 1968; Schur, 1966.) The wish represents (in the form of a mnemic image of a perception) a commitment (the unconscious wish, an especially intense commitment) to re-evoke (the term implies orientation to the future as well as the past) that perception; processes of actualization of this commitment are governed by the mnemic image, in a way that perhaps has some similarities to the way in which a representation such as a map governs a process of exploration or representations such as the verbal forms of inner speech regulate action. The logic of Freud's presentation implies that the wish, in this sense of the term, as a construct applicable to the psychological system, is the precursor of symbolic functioning.

5. There is the system of operations (techniques, rules, procedures) and the higher-order criteria (regulating principles) that act as constraints upon operations—determining what type of operations may be selected, and therefore what kind of aims these operations may achieve. This system is used in performance to construct out of available materials a symbolic entity such as a manifest dream. Operations, which determine in any construction of a symbolic entity the choice of elements used and the way these elements are combined, are connoted by such terms as "condensation," "displacement," and "representability." Principles, which determine the choice of operations used in constructing a symbolic entity, are connoted by such phrases as "pleasure principle" and "reality principle," and such a proposition as "the dream-work is under some kind of necessity to combine all the sources which have acted as stimuli for the dream into a single unity in the dream itself" (p. 179).

Operations in the system language are exemplified in the syntactic component of the system by the rules that generate deep structures; the rules that subcategorize lexical items; and the transformational rules, which generate surface structures. Language universals specify the criteria according to which some kinds of rules are "possible" in a language system and others are not.

The nature of the capacity or competence to construct a symbolic entity is best described by describing the operations and higher-order criteria characteristic of a particular symbolic system. It is this capacity or competence that is realized in the act of constructing a symbolic entity. An actual performance (speech, the manifest dream) is, of course, not solely determined by the nature of this competence; other, including extrasymbolic, factors influence performance. Neither, of course, is the end served by a symbolic performance, nor its actual effect, solely determined by the nature of capacity or competence.

Freud was explicit concerning the homology of the rules of language and the dreamwork: "the dream-content seems like a transcript of the dream-thoughts into another mode of expression, whose characters and syntactic laws it is our business to discover" (p. 277). In fact, I shall anticipate a line of thought about the relation of language and dreams by mentioning here that Freud in more than one place suggested that he thought the dreamwork operated, in part at least, through a linguistic transformation of one kind of linguistic structure (capable of bearing the meaning of the dream, the latent dream thought) into another kind of linguistic structure (capable of bearing the manifest form of the dream).

> . . . the dream-thought that was represented was in the optative: 'If only Otto were responsible for Irma's illness!' The dream repressed the optative and replaced it by a straightforward present: 'Yes, Otto is responsible for Irma's illness!' This, then, is the first of the transformations which is brought about in the dream-thoughts even by a distortionless dream. . . . Thus dreams make use of the present tense in the same manner and by the same right as day-dreams. The present tense is the one in which wishes are represented as fulfilled [p. 534f.].

Freud, as we have noted, considered the dreamwork the essence of dreaming. His penultimate chapter on the dreamwork is the climax of *The Interpretation of Dreams*—is in many ways the masterpiece of his masterpiece. He made explicit the operations by which a dream—a symptom, a joke, a myth, a work of art—is constructed, and this must rank as one of his greatest contributions to psychoanalysis as a science of semiology. His discovery of the dreamwork is the foundation of his theory of dreams and ultimately, involving his distinction between the primary and secondary processes, of his theory of the mind; upon this foundation these theories take their most secure position.

The explication of the operations by which a symbolic entity—the rules by which a meaningful symbolic form—is constructed is the most important step that can be taken toward an understanding of symbolic process. It is, as Chomsky has frequently argued, logically prior to the consideration and solution of other problems, which have to do, for example, with the acquisition and use of a symbolic system in performance and with their consequences and impairments. One must understand first the nature of that which is to be acquired, used, or impaired.

To understand a symbolic form is to be able to make it, see how it is made, or reconstruct it (see Kris, 1952). Freud declared that the easiest way of making the processes of the dreamwork clear and of defending his formulations about the dreamwork against criticism would be, if it were practical, to collect the dream thoughts he discovered through dream analysis and starting with them to reconstruct or synthesize the manifest dream (p. 310). When read from the point of view I have been developing here, many of his statements seem to me to cry out for reformulation as instructions specifying how to proceed—what is possible, what required, what impermissible—for an artisan who wanting to make a dream must make choices, among alternative available materials, for example. The dreamer as artisan is perhaps epitomized in that kind of dreamer of whom Freud said, when he "is dissatisfied with the turn taken by a dream, he can break it off without waking up and start it again in another direction—just as a popular dramatist may under pressure give his play a happier ending" (p. 571f.).

To understand a symbolic form is to know how it is made. To comprehend how it is made is to understand the mind that made it. To discover mind through an analysis of the modes of construction of the symbolic structures made by man—his poetry and his science, his mathematics and his history, his religion and his symptoms—is the strategy of an important group of scientists and philosophers: for example, Cassirer (1923–1929, 1944, 1946), who sought to know man through the study of his works of culture; Levi-Strauss (1958, 1962, 1964), who seeks to find the mind of man in the study of his myths and social institutions, and who has written that the mind of man is a mystery so long as music is a mystery; Chomsky, who reveals the mind of man through the study of his most unique possession, language. They all owe something, at least an acknowledgment of kinship, to this work of Freud's.

Throughout Freud's scientific life, he did his most creative work not when he tried to formulate a general psychology but in attempts to explain—by showing how constructed—relatively definite, discrete or bounded, isolatable symbolic structures: dreams, jokes, the psychopathology of everyday life, neurotic symptoms, works of art. He was what Piaget (1970) in his own terminology might now acknowledge him to have been: an ardent constructionist, the progenitor and prescient exemplar of constructive structuralism.

6. There is that which is signified by a signifier—abstractions or conceptions such as the latent thoughts, signified by a symbolic form such as the manifest dream. That which is signified is the meaning of a symbolic form.

We have previously distinguished those mental operations that comprise the dreamwork from the latent thoughts, which are represented by the manifest dream. These operations, of course, may arbitrarily be considered a kind of thinking, but they are only operations and do not involve thoughts in the sense of "thought as content." (I am here using "thought" to refer to some type of abstraction—configurative or conceptual—from the data, or organizing the data, of phenomenal experience.) Operations determine the nature of the form in which a thought as content is to be represented.

A man may be conscious of a thought, although, Freud suggests, representation of thought by verbal symbolic form—we may extend this to "some kind of symbolic form"—is probably necessary for consciousness of thought to occur. It is unlikely that a man can ever be conscious of an operation such as those that comprise the dreamwork in process. Rather, such an operation is inferred from an examination of its consequences—the effects on or transformations of the material upon which it acts.

Similarly, a grammar as defined by Chomsky does not involve "thoughts," whose content changes if the rules of the grammar are violated, but rather comprises operations or rules for representing thoughts symbolically. If these rules are violated, then the adequacy of the representation of thoughts—with respect to particular aims that such representations may serve—may be compromised. The nature of the thoughts themselves, however, is not necessarily thereby altered. We may become aware of, or formulate, a rule of language, of course; but when we are naming or designating such a rule, we are probably not aware of the rule as act in process. (These formulations do not imply that such operations and deviations from such operations do not function—that is, they probably do function—as constraints upon what thoughts and what kind of relations between thoughts are representable, and with what degree of adequacy with respect to given aims, by a particular symbolic system.)

In what form, if any, is the latent dream thought clothed? Is a thought—an abstraction or conception—without any manifest symbolic form to represent it, actuality or fiction? Do we suppose a naked thought waiting indifferently to be clothed in the form of one symbolic system or another, or do we suppose a thought to be always represented by the form of some symbolic system: that form, then, may be translated into the form of some other symbolic system? In the former case, we are interested in how a thought comes to be represented at all by a symbolic form; in the latter case, we are interested in the means, techniques, operations, or rules by which a symbolic form representing a thought in one symbolic system comes to be translated into a symbolic form representing (the same?) thought in another symbolic system. (In this discussion I am excluding, as not involving "thought," all problem solving that is unmediated by conceptual or configurative abstraction—for example, automatic reflex-arclike sequences, however complex an assembly of such sequences may become; or conditioned responses, when the relation between a nondifferentiated signifier and signified triggers behavior, and the signifier [a signal or index] is inseparably attached to and an aspect of that relatively immediate existent or concrete entity which it signifies. I am including, as a kind of symbolic form, a completely interiorized event such as an image, what Piaget calls an "interiorized imitation" of a reality that is not necessarily present, whether or not an exteriorization of such an image in an objective medium has taken place. See Appendix A.)

Freud, when he considers thought in the unconscious to have no verbal form and to require a verbal form to acquire consciousness, seems primarily interested in the first conception of the relation of thought and symbolic form discussed in the previous paragraph. When—in a passage to which Lacan (1957) at least has drawn our attention as crucial in understanding the work of Freud as semiologist—Freud describes the dream as a kind of rebus, he is clearly concerned, and perhaps the first semiologist to state the problem so explicitly, with the translation of the symbolic forms of one symbolic system into those of another symbolic system.

> We are thus presented with a new task which had no previous existence: the task, that is, of investigating the relations between the manifest content of dreams and the latent dream-thoughts, and of tracing out the processes by which the latter have been changed into the former.
>
> The dream-thoughts and the dream-content are presented to us like two versions of the same subject-matter in two different languages. Or, more properly, the dream-content seems like a transcript of the dream-thoughts into another mode of expression, whose characters and syntactic laws it is our business to discover by comparing the original and the translation. The dream-thoughts are immediately comprehensible, as soon as we have learnt them. The dream-content, on the other hand, is expressed as it were in a pictographic script, the characters of which have to be transposed individually into the language of the dream-thoughts. If we attempted to read these characters according to their pictorial value instead of according to their symbolic relation, we should clearly be led into error. Suppose I have a picture-puzzle, a rebus, in front of me. It depicts a house with a boat on its roof, a single letter of the alphabet, the figure of a running man whose head has been con-

jured away, and so on. Now I might be misled into raising objections and declaring that the picture as a whole and its component parts are nonsensical. A boat has no business to be on the roof of a house, and a headless man cannot run. Moreover, the man is bigger than the house; and if the whole picture is intended to represent a landscape, letters of the alphabet are out of place in it since such objects do not occur in nature. But obviously we can only form a proper judgment of the rebus if we put aside criticisms such as these of the whole composition and its parts and if, instead, we try to replace each separate element by a syllable or word that can be represented by that element in some way or other. The words which are put together in this way are no longer nonsensical but may form a poetical phrase of the greatest beauty and significance. A dream is a picture-puzzle of this sort and our predecessors in the field of dream-interpretation have made the mistake of treating the rebus as a pictorial composition: and as such it has seemed to them nonsensical and worthless [p. 277f.].

Language and Dreams

If it is true that "a dream is a picture-puzzle of this sort," then language and dreaming are, indeed, intimately related. Reflect upon how we come to understand a rebus. Suppose a picture of a building near a stream is followed by a picture of a road with trees on either side and that picture is followed by a picture of a key. We take each picture to signify—not a word or syllable, for that would mean a step in the process of our understanding has been skipped —we take each picture to signify an abstraction: a conception of a class of language elements. (This formulation is consistent with previous statements that the signified at the level of symbolic functioning is always an abstraction. See Appendix A.) The first picture may evoke, for example, the class of all syllables that sound like "mill," and will include, therefore, also, "Mil." The second picture may evoke the class of all syllables that sound like "walk," and will include, therefore, also, "wauk." The third picture may evoke the class of all syllables that sound like "key," and will include, therefore, also, "ky" and "kee." The next steps in the process of our interpretation of the rebus are to select a member of each class evoked, and to combine these to form a new entity—the word, phrase, or sentence (for example, Milwaukee) that is a symbolic representation in language of the same thought that was represented by the rebus but in another symbolic form. ("Milwaukee" does not signify a concrete thing or place, but—like all proper names—an abstraction: an identity class. See Edelson, 1971, p. 93.)

Freud has implied, then, at least one way in which one kind of symbolic representation may be translated into another. A twofold layer of relations between signifiers and signifieds is involved. In the first layer, the signifiers of one symbolic system, to be translated, are taken to have a double or ambiguous significance. They signify not only conceptions of physical reality, for example, but also (and most importantly for the translation) they signify conceptions of symbolic entities. These symbolic entities belong to a second symbolic system, into whose forms these first signifiers are to be translated. Then, in the second layer, from the signified classes of symbolic entities in the first layer, we choose the elements that will now serve as signifiers in the second layer, signifiers that belong to the second symbolic system. With these elements, we form a second symbolic representation (our translation of the first), which now represents the same thoughts represented in another form by the signifiers of the first layer. The translation essentially involves that one aspect of what was ambiguously signified in the first layer becomes transformed into a signifier (belonging to another symbolic system) in the second layer.

A rebus, like a dream, may evoke a class of words or syllables not only by means of the name of the object (including numbers, letters, or words) it pictures, but by formal characteristics of the picture—for example, the arrangement or placement, size, or sequence of such objects. A "stand" over an "eye" may evoke a class of words concerning position, which have similar or antonymous meanings, such as "under," "beneath," "below," "above," "over." This class ultimately yields the word "under" and the symbolic linguistic representation "I understand." The two letters "A L" may evoke, perhaps by such a verbal description as "A and L are together," a class of words concerning position, which have similar meanings, such as "close to," "next to," "together." This class ultimately yields the linguistic translation "altogether."

The manifest dream report—a verbal description of the dream —is essentially, then, a procedure for evoking the conceptions of language entities signified by the elements of the manifest dream. Hence, the emphasis Freud gives to the exact wording of the patient's description of any aspect of the dream.

Conceptions of the symbolic entities of language can be formed in a variety of ways, which either are determined by the rules of language or constitute systematic deviations from such rules.[25] (This statement is documented by many examples and discussions of them not only in *The Interpretation of Dreams*, but in *The Psychopathology of Everyday Life* and *Jokes and Their Relation to the Unconscious*—works to which we ought frequently to return to remind ourselves of and to examine the semiological foundations of psychoanalysis.) For example, a class may include all words or syllables having the same or similar sound (or, a somewhat deviant group, from which we form rhymes and half-rhymes, all words or syllables having one sound or combination of sounds in common). A class may include all words having the same or similar meaning, or the same or similar syntactic features or semantic markers. (Such a class may well include antonyms, accounting for Freud's observation about the apparent equivalence of antonyms or opposites in the construction of dreams, since antonyms usually differ from each other in only one semantic marker at the lowest level of generality.[26]) A class may include all words or syllables

[25] Chomsky's theory of language includes different kinds of rules for creating categories and subcategories of language units at each of three levels of analysis. It includes as well a way of formulating different kinds and degrees of deviance of symbolic forms (see Appendix B). What I am considering in this paper is the likelihood that linguistic competence, as described by that theory, plays a crucial role in the construction and interpretation of dreams.

[26] Freud (1910) has discussed the antithetical meanings apparently connoted by identical perceptible forms—certain primal words. He connected this phenomenon to the apparent absence of the negative in dreams and the way in which contradiction and contrariness are disregarded or combined into unities in dreams, which, as primal words do, "employ the same means of representation for expressing contraries" (p. 155). In regard to his discussion, it should be noted here that linguistic analysis at the semantic level reveals that antonyms are actually very close relatives, since each of a pair of antonyms has the same formal description as the other, that is, is described by exactly the same hierarchy of semantic markers except for only one "lower level" semantic marker whose sign is reversed—e.g., + polar, − polar. (See footnote 14 and Appendix B for a discussion of semantic markers.) Antonyms are reportedly the most common or frequent responses in experimental word asso-

that may occupy a particular context or all the words or syllables that may provide a context for a particular entity. In other words, membership in the class is determined by considerations of (1) substitutability or similarity or (2) combinability or contiguity. As an example of the first kind of class, homonyms; as an example of the second kind of class, synonyms; as an example of the third kind of class, to return to our rebus, a picture of a "mill" may evoke a class of words that includes "house," "building," and "factory," or a class of words that includes "stream," "race," and "miller."

In language, a linguistic entity may name a class without being a member of it. In the manifest dream, the name of the manifest element only stands for a class because the name is capable as a member of the class of evoking it.

It is the existence or formation of classes of language entities that makes condensation possible; we may speculate that abstraction is a precondition of the process of condensation. The dreamwork operates according to an imperative to synthesize, to represent simultaneously a multitude of thoughts by the same manifest symbolic form. Following Freud's examples, we see that a manifest dream element may be chosen because it evokes one class of language entities, which has a number of different members, each potentially capable of use in representing different thoughts linguistically. Therefore, these different thoughts may be simultaneously represented in the dream by the one manifest element.

If a manifest element is chosen because it evokes a class of language entities of which the name, for example, of the manifest element may be one member, but that name itself does not signify any of the different thoughts represented simultaneously in the manifest dream, then the dreamwork has made use of an "indifferent" or "intermediate" element. This indifferent or intermediate element may have been chosen both because of its representability in visual imagery, and because it is a member of—and therefore able to evoke—more than one class, each one of which contains members that are capable of signifying different latent dream

---

ciation procedures, supposedly because antonyms involve a change, but a change that is minimal (Clark, 1970). If antonyms, then, have common roots or even if opposite meanings are under certain circumstances represented by identical forms, that is perhaps not so surprising.

thoughts. Displacement, then, as Piaget (1945) has emphasized, is almost an inevitable result of a process of condensation (and not necessarily of a motive to censor or disguise).

What about the deviant allusions that are so much a part of the construction and interpretation of dreams? These allusions do not seem at first glance to be based on relations between linguistic units of class membership or combination governed by the rules of language. Many such allusions, however, do seem either metaphorical (the relation is one of resemblance) or metonymical (the relation is one of connectedness of some sort, e.g., part to whole). As psychoanalysts, we are continually responding to resemblances revealed in free association between objects or events in different realms or orders. For example, we become aware of similarities in patterns manifested in relations (1) between analysand as child and parent; (2) between various aspects of the analysand as "he" speaks to, loves, hates, bargains with, threatens, and struggles with "himself"; (3) between the analysand and various objects or events such as work, play, books, movies, music, and assassinations; and (4) between the analysand and psychoanalyst. All these relations are represented for the most part in language.

In a sense, the psychoanalyst's responsiveness to metaphor is an important part of his expertise. However, we are unable to explicate exactly what about that expertise depends upon linguistic competence, and what precisely is the nature of that competence. For such explication, an adequate linguistic theory of metaphor is required. When we have such a theory—and psychoanalysts might very well contribute to its formulation—we shall know a great deal more about how analysands construct and (with psychoanalysts) interpret dreams.

No one who has read Freud's detailed interpretation of the Irma dream will be left in much doubt about this assertion. Implicit resemblances and implicit comparisons between objects and events in different realms abound in his account. For example, mixed relationships with a patient (who is also an intimate) and with a junior and a senior colleague (who are also friends) are compared; mixed relationships are linked to the mixed results of treatment. The giving of interpretations (one kind of solution) is compared to the injection of drugs (another kind of solution). A patient's refusal to accept an interpretation is compared to a woman's refusal to yield to a man. Examination of the nose is likened to penetration into female sexual organs. Wives, widows, patients, and dreams all keep their secrets. Foul-smelling wastes are eliminated (diarrhea) ; offensive psychological symptoms are also eliminated. The connection of dirty injections and foul-smelling toxins with foul-smelling discharges is compared to the connection of words (e.g., interpretations), semen, food (e.g., strawberry) with "good" eliminations (discovery, birth, and the elimination of a diphtheritic membrane). This is a small sample of the possibilities in the material; to do it justice would require a paper in itself.

Clearly, metaphoric (and metonymic) allusions enter into both the construction and the interpretation (the reconstruction) of dreams. A tentative and only beginning analysis of the nature of metaphor and metonymy indicates that processes of metaphoric and metonymic allusion, far from being pre- or extralinguistic, assume, reflect, and are profoundly dependent upon linguistic competence. It is probable that the process by which one linguistic unit evokes another metaphorically or metonymically depends upon a nondeviant deep structure (including both units) undergoing transformation to yield a somewhat deviant surface structure from which units appearing in the deep structure have been deleted, substituted for one another, or recombined. (The degree of deviance is low; the deviance is motivated or systematic. See Appendix B.)

For example, suppose we have two "kernel" nondeviant propositions: "mind does not retain ideas," and "sieve does not retain water." These two kernel propositions may undergo a conjunctive transformation, which combines them to form: "mind does not retain ideas as sieve does not retain water." This nondeviant conjunctive transformation is possible because of the relation of similarity between "does not retain" in the two propositions. (In fact, that such a conjunctive transformation is possible is a test for or assertion of that relation of similarity.) In generating the deviant surface form through further transformations, linguistic units from the two, deep-structure, kernel propositions may be combined with each other (e.g., "his mind is a sieve," "ideas of water," "watery ideas") ; or one may be substituted for the other in a context in which the other would, according to the rules of the language, ordinarily appear (e.g., "all his ideas trickled away"). Because (as a part of linguistic competence) these processes can be reconstructed, it is possible for one linguistic unit to evoke or allude to another metaphorically.

While metaphor in a sense may be said to be governed by the combination at the level of surface structure of linguistic units from contexts formed at the level of deep structure which by the test of conjunctive transformation are similar to one another (i.e., the fundamental dimension of relation is similarity), metonymy may be said to be governed by the substitution at the level of surface structure of one linguistic unit for another when the two are at the level of deep structure connected or combined with one another (i.e., the fundamental dimension of relation is contiguity).

A metonymic relation exists between two linguistic units (e.g., "king," "crown") that have a nondeviant connection (as in, for example, the genitive constructions "the footgear of rubber," "the crown of the king," "the contents of the dish," "the plays of Shakespeare," "the mouths of children," "Minnesota's team," "the container of glass," "the ship's sails," "the workers' hands"), when one member of the relation may stand for the other in contexts in which the other might nondeviantly appear. (Genitive constructions result from genitive transformations: e.g., "I read Shakespeare" from "Shakespeare wrote the plays," "I read the plays Shakespeare wrote," and by genitive transformation "I read the plays of Shakespeare.") So, from such genitive constructions, one may through further transformations generate the metonymic forms: "he wore rubbers," "the crown ruled," "that was a tasty dish," "I read Shakespeare," "I had seven mouths to feed," "Minnesota won," "I drank from the glass," "they attacked with 7 sails," "the factory employed 100 hands." Such sequences are deviant, but the deviance is systematic. In these examples, it is the subject of a subjective genitive (Shakespeare), an attribute or substance (rubber, glass), what is inalienably possessed (mouth, hand), or an indication of location (dish, Minnesota) that substitutes for the other unit which is deleted.

It would appear that both metaphoric and metonymic constructions involve some deviant transformations (for example, the deletions in metonymy and the combinations of linguistic units from different deep structures in metaphor), and not simply violations of subcategorization rules as suggested by Chomsky (1965). Consider his example, "misery loves company." This construction cannot be understood simply as related to a set of nondeviant constructions such as "John loves company" (Katz, 1964). The deep structures underlying a number of propositions must be understood to have been transformed to generate the surface structure underlying "misery loves company": e.g., "one has misery," "others have misery," "others are company," "one loves company." ("Misery loves company," in our terminology, is a metonymic construction, which depends on the deep structure genitive "one has misery.")

From the point of view of syntax, the possibility of nondeviant conjunction or conjunctive transformation is a *sine qua non* of metaphor and the possibility of a nondeviant genitive construction or transformation a *sine qua non* of metonymy. I assume that this kind of knowledge (part of linguistic competence) makes it possible to recover relevant deep structures and therefore semantic meanings from surface forms whose structure or meaning is ambiguous or anomalous.[27]

Determinacy of Meaning

Given a system of representation governed by processes of allusion, can the meaning or meanings of a dream be determinate? Even supposing that multiple thoughts are represented by a particular dream, can the number of these thoughts be definite and their relation to one another discoverable?

Any manifest dream image evokes a class of linguistic entities. Each member of this class of linguistic entities may belong to, and therefore evoke, other (intermediate) classes of linguistic entities. It should be clear that different manifest dream images may evoke immediately or ultimately the same class of linguistic entities, and that any one manifest dream image may evoke immediately or ultimately different classes of linguistic entities. Therefore, as Freud proposed, different manifest dream images may represent

[27] For further discussion of metaphor and metonymy, see Jakobson (1941, 1955, 1956, 1964), Levi-Strauss (1958, 1962).

the same meaning; different meanings may be represented by the same manifest dream image.

Freud comments, "I had a feeling that the interpretation of this part of the dream was not carried far enough to make it possible to follow the whole of its concealed meaning. . . . There is at least one spot in every dream at which it is unplumbable—a navel, as it were, that is its point of contact with the unknown" (p. 111).

Nevertheless, this apparent indeterminacy of meaning is a matter of practical constraints and not theoretical limits; it is related to what allusions (associations) are practicably obtainable at a particular period of time. For there is a means by which the meaning or meanings of a dream can be determinately rendered. The allusions of the manifest dream images, though they may seem to radiate in all directions, will in fact be found ultimately to intersect—and, indeed, one can speculate that just those images are chosen that will in fact so intersect—at a common point, in allusion to a single class of linguistic entities, representing a single idea or group of ideas. This node of intersection points directly to a meaning of the dream. (The dream may be said to have multiple meanings—probably in some relation to each other—when there are multiple nodes of intersection.) [28]

> The dream represented a particular state of affairs as I should have wished it to be. *Thus its content was the fulfilment of a wish and its motive was a wish. . . .*
>
> Certain other themes played a part in the dream, which were not so obviously connected with my exculpation from Irma's illness. . . . But when I came to consider all of these, they could all be collected into a single group of ideas . . . this group of thoughts seemed to have put itself at my disposal, so that I could produce evidence of how highly conscientious I was, of how deeply I was concerned about the health of my relations, my friends and my patients . . . there was an unmistakable connection between this more extensive group of thoughts which underlay the dream and the narrower subject of the dream which gave rise to the wish to be innocent of Irma's illness [p. 118ff.].

[28] See Kris (1956a) for a somewhat related discussion of the nodes of intersection involved in the construction of personal histories considered as personal myths.

The criteria governing choice of a set of images for use in constructing a manifest dream will include the following: (1) each image will be capable (compared with possible alternatives) of allusion to a maximum number of the semantically interpreted deep structures—the latent thoughts—to be represented by the dream; (2) the set of images will contain (compared to possible alternative sets) a maximum density of nodes, where processes of allusion arising from each image intersect.

The first criterion is concerned with the economy of means for assigning a perceptible representation of meaning. The second criterion is concerned with providing a means for assuring the recovery (from the perceptible representation of a derived surface structure) of the theoretically determinate underlying meaning of the dream. The discovery of nodes of intersection through the technique of free association (which is designed to reduce the influence of processes that screen or suppress allusions) is the means by which a manifest dream may be disambiguated, despite the multiple, and apparently indefinite number of, allusions implied by its separate memory-image fragments. The "unplumbable navel" is a consequence of our practical inability to follow all lines of allusion to theoretically possible points of intersection. It is even *theoretically* possible that a hierarchy of meanings, in relations of supraordinacy and subordinacy to each other, might be indicated by the relation of nodes of intersection, as the transformational rules of clause formation are used to indicate such a hierarchy in language —that is, "possible" if we ignore for the moment the *practical* problems in obtaining for any particular dream at a particular point in time an adequate picture of these nodes.

Poetry and music, for example, also share with the system generating dreams this problem of providing for the recovery of determinate underlying meanings from the perceptible representations of derived surface structures when an apparitional symbolic form is constructed using resources that give rise to a large, indefinite number of allusions in order to realize with maximum economy the perceptible representation of underlying or deep complex structures (meanings). One is not necessarily forced by the demonstration of multiple ambiguities in an art form to accept the impossibility of discovering an intrinsic basis for preferring one meaning to another or for relating various meanings to each other —even granting that such ambiguities constitute a valuable resource in creating the effect, or carrying out the function, of the art form. (See Kris, 1952.) Also, in studying such art forms as poetry and music, as in studying language and the system generating dreams, one should distinguish between a symbolic system's theoretical potentialities for generating possible, conceivably comprehensible forms and the practical constraints that are imposed upon both the realization of form and its level of immediate comprehensibility by limitations in the capacities of either audience or performer or both.

Deep and Surface Structures

Freud postulated that a kind of censorship operates in the construction of manifest dreams, whose function is to disguise unacceptable latent thoughts. This formulation is suggested by the subjective experience of internal opposition in the waking state to the recovery of memory images, to free association, to the re-creation of processes of allusion (or the creation of processes parallel to those that were involved in constructing the dream, i.e., that lead to the same nodes of intersection) ; by the repugnance felt in the waking state toward the latent thought of wish fulfillment once it is discovered; and by the analogy of the distortions of this thought, as it is represented by the manifest dream, to conscious and often ingenious dissimulations, which operate in situations of communicative interaction to avert expected—imagined—negatively valued responses from others to a possible communication.

Freud suggested that the dream is a compromise formation of two agencies, one "defensive" and the other "creative" (p. 146). This is an especially interesting formulation, considered in the light of the distinction Chomsky makes between the infinitely generative part of the syntactic component of language, and the transformational part, which is merely interpretive, i.e., generates no new propositional content, and which like a "defense" serves as a filter; by its operations—and the constraints upon these operations—only acceptable combinations of deep structures are transformed into the derived surface structures that are accessible to perceptible representation (Chomsky, 1965, 1966b).

Before commenting further on Freud's proposal of a censorship to account for the existence of a difference between the manifest and latent content of a dream, I should like to examine a similar question: why are there deep and surface structures in language? (See, e.g., Chomsky, 1965, 1968; Langendoen, 1970.) Why is not the surface structure of a sentence—the manifest syntactic relations of its elements—a direct, explicit reflection of the meaning of the sentence? After all, one can certainly imagine a language in which the syntactic relations in observable sentences would be those required to reflect explicitly and directly all the meaning of any such sentence.

The most obvious contrast between deep structures and derived surface structures, as these are explicitly formulated in the writings of Chomsky (1957, 1965, 1966b) and his colleagues (Fodor and Katz, 1964; Jacobs and Rosenbaum, 1970; Katz and Postal, 1964), is the extraordinary amount of abbreviation or condensation that often occurs in the process of transforming deep into surface structures. Numbers of pages may be required to make explicit all the elements and their interrelations bearing meaning in the deep structure or structures from which the surface structure underlying a complex sentence has been derived. Even a relatively simple sentence such as "The short, happy boy, who wanted to go to the store, went with his mother" has a structure derived from a combination of the abstract structures underlying such sentences as "The boy was short," "The boy was happy," "The boy wanted to go to the store," "The boy went to the store," "The boy has a mother," "The mother went to the store" and includes as well—as only a brief sample of possible examples—indications that "the boy" is identical in all these propositions, indications that "who" refers to "boy" and not "mother," indications of tense and mood, and indications of gender and number concord. Similarly, Freud declares and his book demonstrates, "Dreams are brief, meagre and laconic in comparison with the range and wealth of the dream-thoughts. If a dream is written out it may perhaps fill half a page. The analysis setting out the dream-thoughts underlying it may occupy six, eight or a dozen times as much space" (p. 279).

One obvious function, then, served by the transformation of deep structures into derived surface structures is economy. As it is, we often have the experience that our thoughts race faster than our capacity to represent these thoughts using language resources. How much more difficult the representation of thought in language would become if one were required to reflect explicitly and directly all propositional content in the surface structure or arrangement of elements of a sentence.

The dreamer thinks and represents his thinking in the form of dreams. Even though the dream is not a vehicle promoting ease of communication, it may nevertheless from some points of view at least more or less adequately "keep up with" and at the same time embody thought in a perceptible medium, i.e., in manifest form, so that the process of thought may be sensually apprehended as object and contemplated as object by the thinking subject. We may speculate that any symbolic system provides means for the relatively economic representation of thought, and that the difference in deep and surface structures and the transformational processes changing one to the other constitute a minimum—perhaps, indeed, optimal—device of this sort.

Second, it is probably generally true that the intrinsic characteristics of any medium used to represent thoughts in perceptible symbolic forms dictate laws, require procedures, or give rise to processes governing its use that are relatively independent of considerations of meaning and relatively dominated by the properties, the intransigence, of the medium itself. (See Edelson [1971, Ch. 3] for further discussion of the properties of a medium used in constructing symbolic entities.) So, the phonological component of language has its own rules for ordering and combining sounds; these are determined by the properties of the system of sounds, relatively independently of the properties of a semantic system—e.g., the categories and the rules by which such a semantic system organizes meanings in one way rather than another (Saussure, 1916; Whorf, 1956).

The differentiation of deep and surface structure follows from the differentiation—intrinsic to or defined by the nature of a symbolic system—between the conceptual system of meanings (signified) and the sensuous system of perceptible representations (signifier) . Generation of deep structures is primarily governed by considerations of meaning. Transformation of deep structures into derived surface structures is primarily governed by considerations of perceptible representation.

Any deep structure may be represented in more than one medium. Systems or components for perceptible representation tend to be organized in terms of the intrinsic properties of the medium. It follows that a transformational component is required to alter deep structures in ways that render them, in the form of derived surface structures, optimally susceptible to representation using the special materials and following the rules, procedures, or laws of a particular kind of representational system or component.

The nature of transformations required by language is governed by the need to derive structures that will be susceptible to assignment of a perceptible representation by a phonological component —that component which includes the sound entities of a language and the rules for their organization. Similarly, considerations of representability in dream images govern the nature of the transformations (required in constructing a dream) of semantically interpreted deep structures (i.e., latent thoughts) . The range of permissible sounds and sound combinations is limited by the phonological component; deep structures must be transformed into surface structures amenable to permitted compositions of sound. Clearly, also, the range of resources available to the dreamer is limited—e.g., to his stock of images (the condition, extent, and nature of which may in part be determined by the effect of defense, inhibition, and constriction upon possibilities of experience) . In dreaming, the transformation of deep structures must operate to provide structures that are amenable to representation by dream images—the materials available.

Third, the pragmatics of symbolic process probably account for some alterations of deep structures (these deep structures reflecting primarily propositional content or meaning) into surface structures (propositional content remaining unchanged through such transformations) . These alterations may be motivated by, and yield a derived form especially appropriate to, a concrete situation for the use of a symbolic system. Certain nuances of word arrangement, for example, do not primarily affect propositional content or meaning but rather affect its presentation in an order that high-lights or suppresses, focuses attention upon or distracts attention from, one element rather than another—thereby affecting the attention, interest, and attitude of the other in a communicative interaction.

Forms suitable for complex thought are not necessarily suitable for different kinds of suasion in interactional communication, and vice versa. Forms may be created primarily, as Freud points out in discussing conscious dissimulation, with an expected response to a communication in mind, i.e., created to avert or encourage some response. Considerations of some displacements of value, and of some choices of one "subject" rather than another as "topic" and one predicate rather than another as "comment" (the grammatical "subject" defined by the rules of the linguistic system remaining invariant), probably also belong in the realm of pragmatics. In some of these cases at least, it is probable that meaning is conserved while only its manner of presentation varies.

The laws of pragmatics are, then, clearly to some extent "outside," and include variables other than, those of a symbolic system (such as language) itself. Factors belonging to the situation of use and having to do with the intended use or projected function of a symbolic entity may determine the choice of certain transformations and the construction of particular surface forms responsive to the features of such a situation and adapted to such a function or intended use. Such pragmatic factors may determine as well the choice of one medium rather than another, and of one symbolic system rather than another, for the representation of meaning— e.g., pictorial images rather than phonemes, discursive language rather than art.

Considerations of economy (the relation of thought and the representation of thought), of representability (the relation of conceptual signified and perceptible signifier), and of pragmatics all contribute to the existence of a difference between surface and deep structure in language. Given such a difference, along with the requirements of both thought and communication, a symbolic system must also provide means for recovering a deep structure or structures—and, therefore, the meaning directly and explicitly reflected by such a structure or structures—from which a surface structure has been derived. Such means are provided in language through constraints upon transformational operations and, as I have discussed, in dreaming through constraints upon the choice of allusive entities in constructing a dream such that the intersection of processes of allusion at circumscribed nodes is relatively maximized.

If the censorship Freud postulated in dreams may be considered to belong to the realm of pragmatics, then we may ask to what degree pragmatic considerations contribute to the construction of the dream in the dreaming of it (as distinct from the final form of the dream as remembered and reported) in comparison with considerations of economy and representability. There is after all no *a priori* reason to suppose that the tendencies to dissimulation and censorship that are responsive to the exigencies of communicative interaction must also operate in a major way in the sleeping state; although, of course, such tendencies may become active and even dominant in the final revision of the dream as it is remembered in the waking state and especially in anticipating the report of the dream in a situation of interaction. If the special characteristics of the dream can be explained by other considerations (necessary from the point of view of the nature of a symbolic system), such as economy and representability, without recourse to the postulation of a "censor" operating in the sleeping state, that is, without recourse to the postulation of a pragmatic factor, then it might be more parsimonious to attempt such an explanation.

The choice of allusive entities such as pictorial images as signifiers is probably a consequence of the conditions of the sleeping state and is required if the dream is to represent as an apparitional symbol the idea of a wish as a wish fulfilled. Given such images, the representational component of the system generating a dream necessarily involves processes of allusion. Economy dictates the choice of images that allude simultaneously to a maximum number of latent thoughts. Preservation of determinacy of meaning dictates the choice of a set of images whose allusions will intersect. Displacements of value are inevitable; such displacements are intrinsic consequences of processes of allusion and of the representation of meaning through the use of allusive entities whose allusions intersect "outside" the manifest dream. Distortions are inevitable, not only because of such displacements of value, but also because of the requirement that an image be chosen that will allude to a maximum number of latent thoughts and whose allusions will, at the same time, also intersect with the allusions of a set of images in such a way that their nodes of intersection involve representations of the latent thoughts. It is not clear what, if any, additional increment of contribution to such distortion must be attributed to a pragmatic factor such as censorship.

My reading of Freud's words is that he tended to give increasing priority as time went on to the intrinsic consequences of choosing a certain way of representing thoughts for determining the form of a dream, and felt less need to postulate the tendentious operation of censorship during a state of sleep as a major contribution to the construction of such a symbolic entity as a dream. The hypothesis of a primarily "defensive" agency (censor) interacting with a primarily "creative" agency (wish) is explicitly altered in a 1930 footnote (p. 146) with the reminder that, on the contrary, a dream may express a wish that belongs to the "defensive" agency (a reminder, also, that we should not separate too rigidly reified "impulses" and "defenses" as essentially different kinds of psychic entities) .

In my reading of him, Freud also enunciates in a footnote added in 1925 the perspective I have suggested he ultimately adopted— that "dreams are nothing other than a particular *form* of thinking, made possible by the conditions of the state of sleep. It is the *dream-work* which creates that form, and it alone is the essence of dreaming—the explanation of its peculiar nature" (p. 506f.) .

Two Hypotheses

Censorship and Dream Distortion

I should like to discuss, in conclusion, two empirical hypotheses that seem to follow from what has been presented so far. The first has to do with "censorship." What appears to be a consequence of a motive to censor may be primarily a consequence of such techniques of symbolic representation as: (1) condensation; (2) the choice of a member of a class-to-be-evoked for use in constructing the manifest dream according to its potential for pictorial representation; and (3) the necessity to represent a number of thoughts simultaneously rather than, for example, sequentially. This formulation implies the empirical hypothesis that there need be no difference in the nature of a manifest dream that is easily interpreted by a patient whose resistance to discovering and accepting the meaning of the dream is relatively low, from that of a manifest dream that cannot be interpreted by a patient whose resistance to discovering and accepting the meaning of the dream is relatively great. Both kinds of manifest dreams are constructed in the same way and as symbolic representations offer the same intrinsic difficulties to interpretation. One should not be able to tell from an inspection of manifest dreams which might be easy and which difficult to interpret. The same dream might be difficult to interpret at one time and much easier to interpret at another. Whatever differences in degree of difficulty of interpretation are observed are likely to be independent of the nature of the techniques by which the manifest dream has been constructed, which for all dreams is the same. This empirical hypothesis, of course, is consistent with what Freud recommended concerning the technique of dream interpretation in therapeutic situations. (A similar argument would hold that the difficulty of understanding a patient's symbolic representations, when the patient constructs these according to the primary process rather than the secondary process, may be a consequence of his use of techniques similar to those that comprise the dreamwork and also, insofar as the difficulty in understanding such representations varies from time to time, to the level of resistance in the interpreter; it does not follow that the difficulty arises from a motive to disguise or censor in the patient, who may be using such techniques of representation because no others are, for one reason or another, available to him at a particular level of functioning. See Edelson, 1971.)

The Dependence of Dreaming upon Language

The second empirical hypothesis that follows from what has been presented so far concerns the dependence of dreaming upon language. A principal implication of Freud's use of the rebus as a model of the dream is that the latent dream thoughts must be, to

begin with, represented linguistically or must come to be represented linguistically before a manifest dream can be constructed
according to the dreamwork. (Imagine the process in reverse—not
interpreting the rebus but constructing it.) Freud comments: "We
may suppose that a good part of the intermediate work done during the formation of a dream, which seeks to reduce the dispersed
dream-thoughts to the most succinct and unified expression possible, proceeds along the line of finding appropriate verbal transformations for the individual thoughts" (p. 340).

If this is the case, dreaming (perhaps any visual imagery to the
extent it is symbolic) cannot be regarded as a more primitive, or
as an example of an ontogenetically earlier, system of symbolization than language. Language as a symbolic system is, according
to the rebus model, logically prior and indispensable to dreaming
as a symbolic system. An empirical hypothesis might take the form
that dreaming will not appear before the development of language competence, or that impairments in language competence
should result in impairments in dreaming.[29]

In this connection, Piaget (1945) observes: "In the case of children, we have been unable to find evidence of authentic dreams
before the appearance of language" (p. 177).

Jakobson (1964), referring tantalizingly to two untranslated articles (apparently in Russian), comments in a discussion of aphasia: "The inhibition of visual dreams connected with encoding
disorders of language has been rightly interpreted as a break-down
of that code which provides the transition from verbal to visual
signals" (p. 32).

Sapir (1921) makes a related point, although he is describing
systems of voluntary communication: "We shall no doubt conclude that all voluntary communication of ideas, aside from normal speech, is either a transfer, direct or indirect, from the typical
symbolism of language as spoken and heard or, at least, involves
the intermediary of truly linguistic symbolism" (p. 21).

Similarly, Edelheit (1969) speculates about the priority of language (he appears to mean "speech" or not to differentiate sharply

---

[29] It is important in evaluating such a hypothesis to keep in mind the distinction
between dreaming as symbolic activity and the physiological conditions (e.g., the
REM sleep state, which has been observed in infants) that are necessary but not
sufficient for its occurrence. See Hartmann (1967, p. 22).

between the two) over the visual image, although the latter by "common sense" is supposed to characterize the concrete and the real.

> Visual consciousness and memory, which are comprised within the ego, are from earliest infancy conditioned by vocal utterance—by speech and the precursors of speech. Not only is consciousness mediated by speech and its derivatives; the ego itself is a language-determined apparatus. Visual and other sensory data are brought into consciousness through the instrumentality of language and through that instrumentality are structurally assimilated to the ego. . . . In the early stages of its development, the psyche has at its disposal no mechanism, such as exists for the development of speech, for the reproduction of visual images which can then, like sound images, be both self-reporting and capable of being brought into congruence with images emanating from the object (the mothering person). I assume, then, that visual elements are admitted to consciousness secondarily, via association with the reproducible auditory elements [p. 400].

Sapir, whom Edelheit quotes, attributes the priority of language not to its auditory representations as performed in speech but to the organization of language as a system, the rules or operations Chomsky would subsume under "language competence." "The ease with which speech symbolism can be transferred from one sense to another, from technique to technique, itself indicates that the mere sounds of speech are not the essential fact of language, which lies rather in the classification, in the formal patterning, and in the relating of concepts" (p. 21f.).

Finally, this hypothesis about the relation between language and dreams, which makes dreaming dependent upon language, is consistent with Chomsky's and others' emphasis on the probable innateness of language competence—given the species specificity of language competence, which is uniquely human; the early age of language development; the relative lack of correlation between language development and intelligence; and the rapidity with which the child constructs a language system with only a brief experience with what are at best debased and fragmentary speech utterances.

APPENDIX A: TERMINOLOGY
IN SEMIOLOGY

Terminology in semiology is not standardized and, therefore, usages in this paper may be perplexing to some readers. I shall always intend, when I write "symbolic functioning" or "symbol," to encompass three essential terms: abstraction, symbol, referent.

At the apex of a rather well-known triangle (see, for example, Langer, 1942, pp. 42–63; Ogden and Richards, 1923, p. 11; Shapiro, 1970, p. 402) is *abstraction*, the *sine qua non* of symbolic functioning. An abstraction is a conception or organization of experience, a class or category, an idea or thought (without any necessary implication of something either actual or proximate). An abstraction may be configurative or conceptual. Piaget (1945), similarly, distinguishes between imaged or preconceptual representations and concepts. (Both Piaget and Freud, in describing such mental events, often seem to use the terms representation or mental representation. I shall not use representation in this way, because a representation *represents* some sort of event or entity, which it evokes, and in symbolic functioning abstractions are what is *represented* and evoked.) I shall use the term conception, following Langer's similar usage, to encompass both configurative and conceptual abstractions. In many ways, I consider Freud's use of the term idea to be equivalent to my use of the term conception.

At the left corner of the base of the triangle is *symbol*. A symbol is any entity that represents and evokes an abstraction. It is the symbol that may best be termed a representation, whether that representation is interiorized (for example, a mental visual image, or inner speech) or exteriorized or objectified (for example, a work of art, or spoken speech). (Piaget describes the first symbols, symbolic images, as deferred interiorized imitations of reality.) I shall sometimes use the term symbolic form instead of symbol, especially when the symbol is both complex and perceptible.

Among symbols, we may distinguish, following Piaget, between motivated symbols and signs. For Piaget, the principal if not only example of a motivated symbol is a symbolic image that evokes in his terms an imaged or preconceptual representation. (Piaget's formulation seems to be that a motivated symbol does not evoke a class, but is rather a prototypical member of a class; it may refer to other members of the class, but it does not evoke an idea of the class as a class.) I shall use motivated symbol, as in previous works (1971, 1972) I have used symbol of resemblance or apparitional symbol, when a symbol and the conception it evokes are related by resemblance, that is, when symbol and conception belong with respect to some criterion, property, or properties, to the same class or set, when the symbol is a prototypical exemplar of the conception. Among motivated symbols are those that psychoanalysts discuss using the term symbol, essentially the same as the secondary symbols (unconscious motivated symbols) of Piaget, some symbols used in play, as well as works of art.

In this paper, I shall use sign when a symbol evokes an abstraction or conception to which its relation is arbitrary. That is, sign and conception are related by rule or convention. In the previous works mentioned I used the terms symbol of rule and rational symbol instead of sign in order to emphasize that both motivated symbols and signs are symbols, in the sense of the term symbol used here, to be distinguished from what Piaget terms signals and indices— signifiers that do not evoke or involve abstraction. For Piaget and commonly for linguists and semiologists, the principal example of a sign is to be found in discursive language; language involves an arbitrary or conventional relation between signs and concepts.

At the right corner of the base of the triangle is *referent*. The referent may be a thing or an object (as both Freud and Piaget use the term object). Symbolic functioning does not require the immediate presence of the object, nor does reference to the object in symbolic functioning require the presence of the relatively urgent pressure of an activated drive state.

A symbol may connote, symbolize, or represent a conception. A conception may be used to denote or refer to a referent.

A signifier is any entity that stands for another entity; the entity for which it stands is the signified. In symbolic functioning, a symbol is the signifier; a conception is the signified. At this level of functioning, I believe it is erroneous to term the referent the signified. At a level of functioning that is not symbolic, we lose the apex of the triangle or the term abstraction. The relation between signifier and signified is nonmediated by a mental event such as abstraction, and signifier and signified are nondifferentiated and inseparably attached. In this case, if the triangle is squashed down to two terms that we may represent as a line, we have at the left end of the line the signifier, an index or signal, and at the other end of the line, the signified, an immediate proximal object. (Indices and signals, according to Piaget, are aspects of sensorimotor schemata, which always involve an organization of the sensorimotor activity of the subject in relation to an object.) I shall use index when a signifier is intrinsically attached to what it signifies (e.g., the "footprint" that signifies or indicates "elephant is proximate"). (The reader should be aware that occasionally in the literature sign is used in the sense of index; it is not so used in this paper.) I shall use signal when a signifier is arbitrarily attached to what it automatically —that is, without mediation by abstraction—signifies (e.g., the "bell" that in conditioning signifies or signals "dinner is proximate").

Can an abstraction be conceived to exist independently of any form or signifier? I believe abstraction is always inferred from the translatability of one symbolic representation into another; these symbolic representations or symbolic forms may be, as in dreaming and language, members of different symbolic systems. This point is discussed further in the body of the paper.

APPENDIX B: LANGUAGE

There are three components of language, the phonological, the syntactic, and the semantic. Each component is a subsystem of language considered as a system. Each subsystem has a characteristic output or aim.

The parts of each subsystem are the distinctive linguistic units characteristic of language at the particular level of analysis represented by that subsystem. Linguistic units are related in two ways: through membership in classes of units and through combination. Thus, units are classified in each subsystem according to rules generating combinations of more or less abstract properties or features relevant for the level of analysis represented by that subsystem. The classes of units of each subsystem are themselves combined according to other rules of that subsystem.

The units of the syntactic component of language are primarily syntactic categories—as well as lexical units (which may be considered to be on the boundary between the syntactic component and the semantic component). Syntactic categories include such complex categories as "sentence," "noun phrase," and "verb phrase." Complex categories include (or may be rewritten as) combinations of simple categories such as "determiner," "noun," "verb," "past tense," "auxiliary," and other complex categories. Simple categories include (or may be rewritten as) only lexical units such as "the," "man," "run," or compound-lexical units such as "count up," or morphemes such as "ing," "be," or "en." Lexical units, compound-lexical units, and morphemes appear in the syntactic component because of their syntactic (and not their semantic) significance—that is, because of their role in the construction of a well-formed or grammatical, ordered arrangement or string or concatenation of syntactic categories. In other words, lexical units appear in the syntactic component to the extent it has been decided that the features by which such lexical units are classified must be specified to formulate rules that will generate grammatical strings.

Lexical units are subcategorized (i.e., classified into subcategories of syntactic categories) according to syntactic features. When the features are defined without regard to the context in which the lexical unit may appear, such syntactic features are called subcategorization features. These are typically hierarchical and binary in nature. Examples are "abstract noun" vs. "concrete noun"; "animate noun" vs. "inanimate noun"; "human noun" vs. "animal noun." Particular combinations of choices among such hierarchical, binary features define subcategories of nouns. When the syntactic features are defined with regard to the context in which the lexical unit may appear and the context is specified in terms of syntactic categories such as "noun phrase," then such syntactic features are called strict subcategorization features. If a "dash" represents a position for a lexical unit, then, "—— noun phrase" is a strict subcategorization feature, which is used to define or subcategorize a class of verbs called transitive verb, which may occupy the indicated position. Such verbs are characterized by the feature "followed by a noun phrase." When the syntactic features are defined with regard to the context in which the lexical unit may appear and the context is specified in terms of subcategorization features such as "human noun," "animate noun," "abstract noun," then such syntactic features are called selectional features. "Determiner plus —— plus animate noun" is a selectional feature, which is used to define or subcategorize a class of adjectives such as "frightened." Such a subcategory of adjectives is characterized by the feature "followed by an animate noun."

Subcategorization rules classify lexical units by generating combinations of subcategorization features to form a class. Strict subcategorization rules classify lexical units by generating combinations of strict subcategorization features to form a class. Selectional rules classify lexical units by generating combinations of selectional features to form a class.

Of the rules that generate combinations of the units of a syntactic system, we may distinguish between phrase-structure rules (unordered, structure-independent, context-free rules) and transformational rules (ordered, structure-dependent, context-sensitive rules). Phrase-structure rules, which are called "rewriting" rules for reasons that will be immediately apparent, generate a structural description of an initial element such as "sentence." The various steps in which "sentence" and the complex syntactic categories subsumed under "sentence" are rewritten according to various rules are included in the structural description. These rewriting procedures result in a final ordered arangement or string or concatenation of simple syntactic categories and such formatives as "past" (one possible rewriting of "verb tense") , and this final ordered arrangement is also part of the structural description generated by the phrase-structure rules. The entire structural description is called a phrase-structure marker. The initial element may be rewritten according to rules as a combination of complex categories such as "noun phrase plus verb phrase." Each complex category may be rewritten, according to rules indicating various possibilities, as a simple category such as "noun" or a combination of simple categories or of simple categories and complex categories such as "determiner plus noun," "verb plus noun phrase." The essential characteristics of the phrase-structure rules, which generate the structural descriptions of sentences called phrase-structure markers, are: (a) they are nonordered rather than ordered —that is, the sequence in which rewriting procedures occur does not matter; (b) they are structure-independent rather than structure-dependent—that is, they operate on a single category such as "noun phrase"; (c) they are context-free rather than context-sensitive—that is, a unit or category (e.g., noun phrase) may be rewritten as a combination of other units (e.g., determiner plus noun) without regard to the context in which the unit (i.e., noun phrase) appears (the other units with which it is combined, e.g., —— plus verb, or —— plus verb plus complement, or —— plus verb plus prepositional phrase, or —— plus verb plus noun phrase, where the dash represents the position occupied by "noun phrase") .

Transformational rules operate upon structures (a sequence of categories) not single categories; they reorder categories, delete or add categories, and most importantly adjoin final strings generated by phrase-structure rules to generate derived final strings, which may in turn be combined with other strings. That is, transformational rules are structure-dependent; they operate upon structures such as sequences of categories or final strings rather than single categories. Their operations are governed or limited by the particular phrase-structure rules that have generated the structures to be transformed. In addition, transformational rules are ordered; the sequence in which they are applied is specified.

The input to the syntactic component is the requirement for structures that will bear semantic interpretation, i.e., whose relations are such that the relations among semantic units are reflected in, or recoverable from, them. One kind of output of the syntactic component is a deep structure—a combination of units generated by phrase-structure rules—that will bear a semantic interpretation. The form of phrase-structure rules is therefore governed primarily by considerations of meaning. Another kind of output of the syntactic component is a surface structure—a combination of units generated by transformational rules operating upon deep structures—that will bear a phonological interpretation (i.e., that may be realized perceptively, or performed, according to phonological rules) . The form of transformational rules is therefore governed primarily by considerations of representability. The base component of the syntactic component includes: (a) the phrase-structure rules; and (b) the lexicon. The lexicon is a kind of dictionary of lexical items classified according to subcategorization, strict subcategorization, and selectional rules. The base component possesses recursive devices, i.e., rules permitting the repetition of certain operations *ad infinitum* and thereby generating an infinite set of deep structures. The transformational component, through the operation of transformational rules (deleting, substituting, adjoining) upon deep structures, transforms the deep structures generated by the base component to create an infinite set of surface structures. The output of the syntactic component is, then, an infinite set of structures that may bear semantic interpretation and that may be interpreted or realized phonologically.

Similarly, the units of the phonological component are phonemes, which are combined to form morphemes and words. Phonemes are classified according to rules generating combinations or matrices of distinctive phonetic features, such as "vocalic" vs. "nonvocalic"; "consonantal" vs. "nonconsonantal"; "interrupted" vs. "continuant"; "grave" vs. "acute"; "tense vs. "lax"; "nasal" vs. "oral" (Jakobson, et al., 1951; Jakobson and Halle, 1956) . The rules of the phonological component govern combination and performance (with regard, for example, to stress or accent) of phonemes to form perceptibly realizable morphemes and words. At least some rules of the phonological component are structure-dependent—those, for example, assigning an intonation pattern to the phonological realization of a surface structure according to the nature of the deep structures from which the surface structure was derived and the nature of the transformational rules operating upon these deep structures to generate that surface structure. The input to the phonological component consists of surface structures from the syntactic component. The output of the phonological component consists of perceptible realizations of these surface structures.

The units of the semantic component are semantically distinctive elements such as words (if one regards homonyms as identical phonological realizations of different "words"). Semantic units such as words are classified according to rules generating combinations of hierarchically organized, binary semantic markers, such as "animate" vs. "inanimate," and, if animate, either "human" or "animal" (Katz and Fodor, 1963). The input to the semantic component consists of deep structures from the syntactic component. The output of the semantic component consists of semantic interpretations of these deep structures.

In general, with respect to competence or the rules of language, any performance involving a use of language may be *rule-governed* or *deviant*. Deviance may be *random* or *nonmotivated*, or it may be *systematic* or *motivated*. That is, either there is no detectable order or pattern in the deviance, or an idiosyncratic new rule—consistently followed—has replaced an established rule of the language with respect to which performance is deviant.

Because language is hierarchically organized, we may speak of the degree of deviance. Deviance may be considered to be greater when a more strictly rule-governed component of language (such as the phonological component) rather than a less strictly rule-governed component (such as the semantic component) is involved. Deviance may be considered to be greater when rules affecting major categories such as "noun" and "verb" (e.g., phrase-structure rules) are involved than when rules forming subcategories such as "transitive verb" (e.g., strict subcategorization or selectional rules) are involved; and greater, too, when strict subcategorization rules (defining contexts in terms of syntactic categories) are involved than when selectional rules (defining contexts in terms of subcategorization features) are involved. Deviance may be considered to be greater when a rule affecting an entire set of rules (a constraint upon a set of transformations) is involved than when a single rule (a single transformation) is involved.

In considering different levels of analysis with regard to language as a system, then, I have discussed three components or subsystems of language and perhaps of any semiological system: one generates structures; one assigns meanings to structures; one realizes structures in perceptible representations. In other words, one component is concerned with the creation of structures, another with the interpretation of a structure in terms of "meaning" or "that which is signified," and a third with the interpretation or realizaton of a structure as "perceptible form" or "that which signifies."

BIBLIOGRAPHY

ATKIN, S. (1969), Psychoanalytic Considerations of Language and Thought. *Psychoanal. Quart.*, 38:549–582.

BALKÁNYI, C. (1964), On Verbalization. *Int. J. Psycho-Anal.*, 45:64–74.

— (1968), Verbalization and the Superego: Some Thoughts on the Development of the Sense of Rules. *Int. J. Psycho-Anal.*, 49:712–718.

BERES, D. (1957), Communication in Psychoanalysis and in the Creative Process: A Parallel. *J. Amer. Psychoanal. Assn.*, 5:408–423.

— (1965), Symbol and Object. *Bull. Menninger Clin.*, 29:3–23.

BLACK, M. (1962), *Models and Metaphors*. Ithaca: Cornell University Press.

CASSIRER, E. (1923–1929), *The Philosophy of Symbolic Forms*, Vol. 1: *Language;* Vol. 2: *Mythical Thought;* Vol. 3: *The Phenomenology of Knowledge*. New Haven: Yale University Press, 1953–1957.

— (1944), *An Essay on Man*. New Haven: Yale University Press.

— (1946), *Language and Myth*. New York: Dover, 1953.

CHOMSKY, N. (1957), *Syntactic Structures*. The Hague: Mouton.

— (1959), Review of B. F. Skinner's *Verbal Behavior*. In: Fodor & Katz (1964), pp. 547–578.

— (1965), Aspects of the Theory of Syntax. Cambridge, Mass.: M.I.T. Press.

— (1966a), *Cartesian Linguistics*. New York: Harper & Row.

— (1966b), *Topics in the Theory of Generative Grammar*. The Hague: Mouton.

— (1967), The Formal Nature of Language. In: Lenneberg (1967), pp. 397–442.

— (1968), *Language and Mind*. New York: Harcourt, Brace & World.

CLARK, H. (1970), Word Associations and Linguistic Theory. In: Lyons (1970b), pp. 271–286.

EDELHEIT, H. (1969), Speech and Psychic Structure. *J. Amer. Psychoanal. Assn.*, 17:381–412.

EDELSON, M. (1971), *The Idea of a Mental Illness*. New Haven: Yale University Press.

— (1972), Toward a Study of Interpretation in Psychoanalysis: An Essay on Symbolic Process in Psychoanalysis and the Theory of Action. In: *Explorations in General Theory in the Social Sciences*, ed. R. Baum, A. Effrat, V. Lidz, & J. Loubser. New York: Free Press (in press).

EKSTEIN, R. (1965), Historical Notes Concerning Psychoanalysis and Early Language Development. *J. Amer. Psychoanal. Assn.*, 13:707–731.

FERENCZI, S. (1913), Stages in the Development of the Sense of Reality. *Sex in Psychoanalysis*. New York: Basic Books, 1950, pp. 213–239.

FLIESS, R. (1949), Silence and Verbalization: A Supplement to the Theory of the Analytic Rule. *Int. J. Psycho-Anal.*, 30:21–30.

FODOR, J. & KATZ, J., eds. (1964), *The Structure of Language*. Englewood Cliffs, N.J.: Prentice-Hall.

FREUD, S. (1891), *On Aphasia*. New York: International Universities Press, 1953.

— (1900), The Interpretation of Dreams. *Standard Edition*, 4 & 5. London: Hogarth Press, 1953.

— (1901), The Psychopathology of Everyday Life. *Standard Edition*, 6. London: Hogarth Press, 1960.
— (1905), Jokes and Their Relation to the Unconscious. *Standard Edition*, 8. London: Hogarth Press, 1960.
— (1910), The Antithetical Meaning of Primal Words. *Standard Edition*, 11:153–161. London: Hogarth Press, 1957.
— (1911), Psycho-Analytic Notes on an Autobiographical Account of a Case of Paranoia (Dementia Paranoides). *Standard Edition*, 12:3–82. London: Hogarth Press, 1958.
— (1913), The Philological Interest of Psycho-Analysis. *Standard Edition*, 13:176–178. London: Hogarth Press, 1955.
— (1915), The Unconscious. *Standard Edition*, 14:159–215. London: Hogarth Press, 1957.
— (1925), Negation. *Standard Edition*, 19:235–239. London: Hogarth Press, 1961.
GLAUBER, I. (1944), Speech Characteristics of Psychoneurotic Patients. *J. Speech Disorders*, 9:18–30.
HARTMANN, E. (1967), *The Biology of Dreaming*. Springfield, Ill.: Thomas.
ISAKOWER, O. (1939), On the Exceptional Position of the Auditory Sphere. *Int. J. Psycho-Anal.*, 20:340–348.
JACOBS, R. & ROSENBAUM, P., eds. (1970), *Readings in English Transformational Grammar*. Waltham, Mass.: Ginn.
JAKOBSON, R. (1941), *Child Language, Aphasia and Phonological Universals*. The Hague: Mouton, 1968.
— (1955), Aphasia as a Linguistic Problem. In: *On Expressive Language*, ed. H. Werner. Worcester, Mass.: Clark University Press, pp. 69–81.
— (1956), Two Aspects of Language and Two Types of Aphasic Disturbances. In: Jakobson & Halle (1956), pp. 55–82.
— (1964), Towards a Linguistic Typology of Aphasic Impairment. In: *Disorders of Language*, ed. A. de Reuck & M. O'Connor. London: Churchill, pp. 21–46.
— FANT, C., & HALLE, M. (1951), *Preliminaries to Speech Analysis*. Cambridge, Mass.: M.I.T. Press, 1969.
— & HALLE, M. (1956), *Fundamentals of Language*. The Hague: Mouton.
JONES, E. (1916), The Theory of Symbolism. *Papers on Psycho-Analysis*. Baltimore: Williams & Wilkins, 1948, pp. 87–144.
KATAN, A. (1961), Some Thoughts about the Role of Verbalization in Early Childhood. *This Annual*, 16:184–188.
KATZ, J. (1964), Semi-sentences. In: Fodor & Katz (1964), pp. 400–416.
— & FODOR, J. (1963), The Structure of a Semantic Theory. In: Fodor & Katz (1964), pp. 479–518.
— & POSTAL, P. (1964), *An Integrated Theory of Linguistic Descriptions*. Cambridge, Mass.: M.I.T. Press.
KEISER, S. (1962), Disturbance of Ego Functions of Speech and Abstract Thinking. *J. Amer. Psychoanal. Assn.*, 10:50–73.

KOLANSKY, H. (1967), Some Psychoanalytic Considerations on Speech in Normal Development and Psychopathology. *This Annual*, 22:274–295.

KRIS, E. (1951), Ego Psychology and Interpretation in Psychoanalytic Therapy. *Psychoanal. Quart.*, 20:15–30.

— (1952), *Psychoanalytic Explorations in Art.* New York: Schocken Books, 1964.

— (1956a), The Recovery of Childhood Memories in Psychoanalysis. *This Annual*, 11:54–88.

— (1956b), On Some Vicissitudes of Insight in Psycho-Analysis. *Int. J. Psycho-Anal.*, 37: 445–455.

KUBIE, L. S. (1934), Body Symbolization and the Development of Language. *Psychoanal. Quart.*, 3:430–444.

LACAN, J. (1957), The Insistence of the Letter in the Unconscious. In: *Structuralism*, ed. J. Ehrmann. New York: Anchor Books, 1970, pp. 101–137.

LANGENDOEN, D. (1970), The Accessibility of Deep Structures. In: Jacobs & Rosenbaum (1970), pp. 99–104.

LANGER, S. (1942), *Philosophy in a New Key.* New York: Penguin Books, 1948.

— (1953), *Feeling and Form.* New York: Scribner's.

— (1957), *Problems of Art.* New York: Scribner's.

— (1962), *Philosophical Sketches.* New York: Mentor Book, 1964.

LENNEBERG, E. (1967), *Biological Foundations of Language.* New York: Wiley.

LEVI-STRAUSS, C. (1958), *Structural Anthropology.* New York: Anchor Books, 1967.

— (1962), *The Savage Mind.* Chicago: University of Chicago Press, 1966.

— (1964), *The Raw and the Cooked.* New York: Harper Torchbook, 1970.

LIDZ, T. (1963), *The Family and Human Adaptation.* New York: International Universities Press.

LOEWENSTEIN, R. M. (1951), The Problem of Interpretation. *Psychoanal. Quart.*, 20:1–14.

— (1956), Some Remarks on the Role of Speech in Psycho-Analytic Technique. *Int. J. Psycho-Anal.*, 37:460–468.

— (1957), Some Thoughts on Interpretation in the Theory and Practice of Psychoanalysis, *This Annual*, 12:127–150.

— (1963), Some Considerations on Free Association. *J. Amer. Psychoanal. Assn.*, 11:451–473.

LYONS, J. (1970a), *Noam Chomsky.* New York: Viking Press.

— ed. (1970b), *New Horizons in Linguistics.* Baltimore: Penguin Books.

OGDEN, C. & RICHARDS, I. (1923), *The Meaning of Meaning.* New York: Harvest Book, 1968.

PELLER, L. (1966), Freud's Contribution to Language Theory. *This Annual*, 21:448–467.

PIAGET, J. (1945), *Play, Dreams and Imitation in Childhood.* New York: Norton, 1962.

— (1970), *Structuralism.* New York: Basic Books.

ROSEN, V. H. (1961), On Style. *Int. J. Psycho-Anal.*, 42:446–457.
— (1966), Disturbances of Representation and Reference in Ego Deviations. In: *Psychoanalysis—A General Psychology*, ed. R. M. Loewenstein et al. New York: International Universities Press, pp. 634–654.
— (1967), Disorders of Communication in Psychoanalysis. *J. Amer. Psychoanal. Assn.*, 15:467–490.
— (1969), Introduction to Panel on Language and Psychoanalysis. *Int. J. Psycho-Anal.*, 50:113–116.
RYCROFT, C. (1958), An Enquiry into the Function of Words in the Psycho-Analytical Situation. *Int. J. Psycho-Anal.*, 39:408–415.
SAPIR, E. (1921), *Language*. New York: Harvest Book, 1970.
SAUSSURE, F. DE (1916), *Course in General Linguistics*. New York: Philosophic Library, 1959.
SCHAFER, R. (1968), *Aspects of Internalization*. New York: International Universities Press.
SCHUR, M. (1966), *The Id and the Regulatory Principles of Mental Functioning*. New York: International Universities Press.
SHAPIRO, T. (1970), Interpretation and Naming. *J. Amer. Psychoanal. Assn.*, 18:399–421.
SHARPE, E. F. (1940), Psycho-Physical Problems Revealed in Language: An Examination of Metaphor. *Int. J. Psycho-Anal.*, 21:201–213.
SIROTA, M. (1969), Urine or You're In: An Ambiguous Word and Its Relation to a Toilet Phobia in a Two-Year-Old. *This Annual*, 24:232–270.
STEIN, M. (1958), The Cliché. *J. Amer. Psychoanal. Assn.*, 6:263–277.
STEVENS, W. (1949), Imagination as Value. *The Necessary Angel*. New York: Vintage Books, 1951, pp. 131–156.
STONE, L. 1954), On the Principal Obscene Word of the English Language. *Int. J. Psycho-Anal.*, 35:30–56.
— (1961), *The Psychoanalytic Situation*. New York: International Universities Press.
VOTH, H. (1970), The Analysis of Metaphor. *J. Amer. Psychoanal. Assn.*, 18:599–621.
WEEKLY, E. (1921), *An Etymological Dictionary of Modern English*. New York: Dover, 1967.
WHORF, B. (1956), *Language, Thought, and Reality*. Cambridge, Mass.: M.I.T. Press, 1964.
WINCH, P. (1958), *The Idea of a Social Science*. New York: Humanities Press.
WOLFF, P. H. (1967), Cognitive Considerations for a Psychoanalytic Theory of Language Acquisition. In: *Motives and Thought*, ed. R. R. Holt [*Psychological Issues*, Monogr. 18/19]. New York: International Universities Press, pp. 300–343.

Some Problems in the Conceptualization of Early Object Relationships

Part I: The Concepts of Need Satisfaction and Need-Satisfying Relationships

ROSE EDGCUMBE, B.A., M.S.

AND MARION BURGNER, B.A.

CLOSE STUDY OF CLINICAL MATERIAL AND PSYCHOANALYTIC LITERA-ture reveals problems in regard to theoretical and clinical definitions of types and stages of relationships.[1] One of the main prob-

This paper forms part of a Research Project entitled "Childhood Pathology: Impact on Later Mental Health" which is conducted at the Hampstead Child-Therapy Course and Clinic, London. The project is financed by the National Institute of Mental Health, Washington, D.C., Grant No. MH–5683–09. The paper also forms part of the work carried out by the Index Committee, Chairman Dr. J. Sandler.

[1] These problems arose in the course of revision of the Object Relationships Manual of the Hampstead Clinic Index, which was set up as an instrument for the classification of clinical data from a large number of cases in analytic treatment. These data are categorized under both descriptive and metapsychological headings, and Manuals are provided to aid the therapist in assigning materials to appropriate headings. For a fuller account of the Index see Sandler (1962). The process of indexing analytic cases constantly necessitates clarification and finer discrimination of theoretical concepts, and hence leads to the revision of Manuals in order to permit a better understanding of clinical material.

lematic areas is the concept of need-satisfying relationships, which has been used to encompass such diverse phenomena as, for instance: the baby at the breast; the toddler's demand for mother's constant attention and immediate compliance with his wishes; the atypical, defective, or handicapped child's prolonged dependence on the object as an ego auxiliary; the insatiable demands for material supplies or prolonged dependence on objects found in certain types of neurotic disturbance.

In addition to distinguishing early stages in normal development, child analysts are frequently faced with the necessity of understanding regressive or arrested types of relationships in older children. A variety of concepts is used to describe both the early period of development and later manifestations of arrest or regression. Some terms are at times used descriptively, and at other times theoretically as explanatory concepts to define a specific stage in development or a particular type of object relationship.

We intend to demonstrate in this paper that a number of distinctions should be made between:

1. The primary biological and psychological aspects of need-satisfying relationships.

2. The development of the capacity to *perceive* the object and the development of the capacity to *cathect* the object.

3. Need satisfaction as a *stage* in the early development of object relationships and as an element in *all* relationships at every level.

4. Different types of needs: self-preservative needs, sexual and aggressive drive pressures, and ego requirements.

5. Expressions of actual needs and defensive exaggerations or minimizations of needs.

Basic Distinctions

1. The Primary Biological and Psychological Aspects of Need-Satisfying Relationships

From the *biological* point of view the infant has from birth a relationship to a need-satisfying object, usually the mother. For purposes of understanding psychological development, however, it is important to distinguish this *biological* relationship from its *psychological* counterpart, which cannot be discerned by the observer at birth and which takes many months to develop even to its early infantile form.

Some authors either do not make this distinction, or fail to distinguish clearly between earlier and later stages of psychological development in infants and children. M. Klein (1952), for example, writes of the existence of a psychological relationship in the first 3 months of life, and describes the infant's ego as integrating aspects of the first object, the breast.

M. Balint (1960) suggests that "the individual is born in a state of intense relatedness to his environment, both biologically and libidinally" (p. 37). He posits a very early, primitive form of object love, which has a biological basis in the instinctual interdependence of mother and child; he considers it to be a type of object relation distinguishable from autoerotism and narcissism, the remnants of which can be discerned in all later relationships (Balint, 1949).

Such formulations seem to us to take insufficient account of the infant's lack of structural development and to blur the distinction between biological and psychological functioning.

Greenacre (1962) speaks of an "emotional relationship" to the object which develops immediately after birth, depending at first largely on physical contact and bodily expression, and preceding the development of a psychological relationship. We find it difficult, however, to conceptualize the existence of an emotional relationship prior to a psychological one and prior to differentiation between self and object, unless what is referred to are the primitive affective (pleasure and unpleasure) responses which follow automatically on the biological interaction between infant and object; such responses do not, at this early stage, involve awareness of the object's existence, but may be considered the *bases* for later psychological differentiation and for an affective relationship to the object.

In understanding these very early stages of development we find more helpful the contributions of those authors who distinguish between biological and psychological relationships to the mother, and who attempt to clarify the *absence* of structural differentiation and psychic functioning at the beginning of life, and their subsequent gradual development.

Freud himself distinguishes between the primary biological and psychological relationships to the object. He was particularly concerned in his writings with the process of finding a *sexual* object rather than with early need-satisfying relationships in their own right. But his earlier (pre-1920) formulations on instinct theory contain pertinent comments on the way in which the self-preservative instincts pave the way for sexual object choice. He emphasizes the helplessness of the baby, whose pressing needs can be satisfied only by an external agency, a person upon whom the infant is, therefore, dependent (e.g., 1915). He makes an important distinction between the two affective states of loving and needing the object: "We do not say of objects which serve the interests of self-preservation that we *love* them; we emphasize the fact that we *need* them" (p. 137).

Anna Freud (1965) distinguishes between a first stage of "biological unity between the mother-infant couple'" and a second stage of "the part-object[2] . . . or . . . need-fulfilling relationship" (p. 65).

Hartmann (1939) says: "We should not assume, from the fact that the child and the environment interact from the outset, that the child is from the beginning psychologically directed toward the object as an object" (p. 52). He stresses the difference between the biological "state of adaptedness," which exists from birth, and the process of psychological adaptation to the object, which can occur only with the beginnings of structural differentiation and the ability to recognize the object as separate from the self: "The first signs of intentionality appear around the third month of life and mark a crucial phase of development, but true object comprehension makes a definite appearance only around the fifth or sixth month and is not complete even at the age of one year" (p. 54).

[2] Here, what is meant by "part-object" is really a *function* of the object, namely, that of satisfying needs. Some authors use the term "part-object" in a quite concrete way, with the assumption that the infant cathects a part of the mother's body: breast, face, hands, etc. Apart from the fact that it is doubtful whether the young infant has the perceptual capacity to recognize a part of the mother's body (see below), what is psychologically more important at this stage is the experience of satisfaction associated with the object's function of satisfying needs by feeding, holding, comforting, etc.

Mahler et al. (1959), emphasizing the state of biological unity but using different terminology, designate the first undifferentiated phase of life as "autistic" in that "there is no polarity between the self and any object."

> . . . the infant shows no sign of perceiving anything beyond his own body. He seems to live in a world of inner stimuli. . . . However, the functioning of the undifferentiated ego apparatuses of the infant, that is, the affecto-motor reactions, such as crying, enables him from the beginning of life to signal and summon the mother to minister to his needs [p. 811].

Spitz (1965) writes of the "preobjectal or objectless stage," which he sees as coinciding with the stage of primary narcissism and with Hartmann's undifferentiated phase; Spitz himself prefers the description: the "stage of undifferentiation."

Jacobson (1964), whose emphasis is on the experiential states of infancy, writes of the "primal psychophysiological self," which exists before structural differentiation and before self and object representations have been established. She says:

> . . . the infant, though gaining stimulation and gratification from an "object"—the mother—as well as from his own body, is as yet unaware of anything but pleasurable or unpleasureable sensations. . . . [She speaks of:] biologically predetermined, though limited, channels for discharge to the outside . . . [which are] the precursors of object-directed discharge [p. 9].

> [Concerning the organization of experiences, she writes:] there is no doubt that long before the infant becomes aware of the mother as a person and of his own self, engrams are laid down of experiences which reflect his responses to maternal care in the realm of his entire mental and body self [p. 34f.].

Winnicott (1948), emphasizing the paradox of the lack of a psychological relationship on the infant's part at the time of his greatest dependence on the object, says of the beginning of life: "initially there is a condition which could be described at one and the same time as one of *absolute independence* and *absolute dependence*. There is no feeling of dependence, and therefore that dependence must be absolute" (p. 163).

All these authors emphasize one aspect or another of the various distinctions between biological and psychological functioning and relationships. To the observer, the newborn infant appears dependent upon the mother, and may seem to have a relationship to her. But this relationship is, at first, a purely biological one, and the infant's functioning is of a reflex order, based on recurring needs, and serving self-preservative aims. Only with the beginning of ego development—that is, with the laying down of memory traces, the organization of experiential states, and the beginning ability perceptually to differentiate self and object—can the infant be said to recognize that something exists outside himself, and that this something satisfies his bodily needs; only then can he begin to relate in a psychological sense to this external something. Thus biological functioning and biological relationships may be said to form the basis on which later psychological functioning and psychological relationships are developed.

2. The Development of the Capacity to Perceive the Object and the Development of the Capacity to Cathect the Object

The gradual move from biological to psychological functioning and relationships involves on the one hand cognitive and perceptual organization, and on the other the organization of drives and affects in relation to the object.

Perceptual Development

We may conceptualize perception as a line of development beginning with the innate biological capacity to register gross stimuli (for example, the neonate can react to light and sound) ; upon this biological capacity is gradually built the psychological capacity to perceive the object in the external world and to structure an internal representation of this same object.

Freud (1930) suggests that the infant learns to distinguish his self from the external world through the discovery that some sources of excitation—later to be recognized as linked with his own bodily organs—are always available, whereas others—especially what will later be recognized as the mother's breast—disappear at times and reappear only as the result of his crying. A further incentive for differentiation is provided by sensations of pain and unpleasure which have to be removed or avoided in accordance with the pleasure principle. At first all sources of unpleasure are attributed to the external world, and a "pure pleasure ego" is created. But experience rectifies the boundaries of this primitive pleasure ego, as some unpleasurable experiences are gradually found to be of internal origin, some pleasurable experiences of external origin.

It is this perceptual awareness of the object which enables the infant gradually to recognize the object as separate from himself and to begin to build up a psychological relationship to it.

In examining the writings on perceptual development by authors other than Freud, we find that they fall into three broad categories, with some diversity of approach within each category.

The first approach, with which we are all familiar since it follows Freud's formulation and is basic to psychoanalytic theory, is that drive needs stimulate and elicit the development of perceptual discrimination.

Secondly, in their examination of ego development, psychoanalytic authors have more recently stressed the interaction between drive pressures and areas of autonomous ego development.

Thirdly, there are authors—mainly nonanalytic—who, discounting the contribution made by the pressures of drives and self-preservative needs to the development of perception, concentrate on behavioral mechanisms whose functioning is elicited by an external object.

In this third category belongs the work on attachment behavior by Bowlby (1969) who uses ethology and the theory of control systems. His theory of attachment behavior "postulates that the child's tie to his mother is a product of the activity of a number of behavioural systems that have proximity to mother as a predictable outcome" (p. 179). According to Bowlby, the onus for maintaining proximity between mother and infant falls, during the first 3 years of life, mainly on the mother, although the child is increasingly able to effect such proximity for himself. Various sorts of behavior serve to secure attachment, i.e., proximity to the mother: "crying and calling, babbling and smiling, clinging, nonnutritional sucking, and locomotion as used in approach, following, and seeking" (p. 244).

The infant orients himself to the attachment figure in various ways: "by the age of six months most infants are already adept at discriminating mother from other figures and at tracking her movements visually and aurally. By these means an infant is kept well informed of mother's whereabouts so that whatever form or forms of attachment behaviour become activated are directed towards her" (p. 244). Bowlby mentions other specific forms of behavior which make for attachment: signaling behavior (which brings mother to the child) and approach behavior (which brings the child to the mother).

This theory seems to take little account of the self-preservative needs and drive pressures which motivate the infant to become attached to the mother.

With regard to the second category of authors, who write of the interaction between drive pressures and autonomous ego development, we find that Hartmann and his co-workers, Sandler and his collaborators, Spitz, and Jacobson most specifically consider such interaction.

Hartmann et al. (1946) write about the gratification of needs in the context of the building up of self and object representations and of the development of psychic structures:

> . . . as long as all needs are gratified, i.e., under "total" indulgence, the infant tends to experience the source of satisfaction as part of the self; partial deprivation thus is probably an essential condition for the infant's ability to distinguish between the self and the object [p. 203]. [And:] The process of actually crystallizing objects . . . occurs in close connection to the needs of the instinctual drives on the one hand and to the development of the ego on the other. The recognition of the world of objects is partly based on the replacement (or modification) of the pleasure principle by the reality principle and is dependent upon the growing maturity and strength of the ego [Hartmann, 1944, p. 22].

Sandler and Rosenblatt (1962) assume:

> . . . that initially the child's representational world contains only the crudest representations of pleasure and unpleasure, of need-satisfying experiences and activities, and it is only gradually that the infant learns to distinguish self from not-self, and self from object in his representational world [p. 134]. Even with the differentiation of objects in the representational

world . . . object representations do not necessarily receive a libidinal cathexis except in so far as they serve a need-satisfying function [p. 142].

More recently, Sandler (1969) has elaborated the function of perceptual differentiation between self and object in the service of need satisfaction. He suggests that, first, there is a period of perceptual nondifferentiation. This is followed by a period during which perceptual structures are gradually created and used at moments of need to distinguish between self and object, and cease to be used once the need is gratified, although the capacity for such differentiation still remains. Eventually, a stage of functioning is reached in which these perceptual structures are kept in virtually constant use. This meets the new requirements of the developing ego which can no longer tolerate the chaos of nondifferentiation; hence, the function of differentiation becomes an autonomous one.

Spitz (1965) has carried out detailed work on the interaction between mother and baby in the first year of life, on the "closed system" between them and how this situation gradually changes; he traces development from the psychologically nondifferentiated neonate to the complex relationship existing between mother and baby at the end of this first year. Writing of perceptual development, he posits that between 3 and 6 months the *smiling response* is elicited by a sign Gestalt and not by the coordinated Gestalt of the mother's face; this recognition of the sign Gestalt is understood as denoting recognition of the "preobject" rather than recognition of the true object, i.e., the "libidinal object" in Spitz's terms.

Jacobson (1964) is particularly concerned with the formation of self and object representations:

> From the ever-increasing memory traces of pleasurable and unpleasurable instinctual, emotional, ideational, and functional experiences and of perceptions with which they become associated, images of the love objects as well as those of the bodily and psychic self emerge. Vague and variable at first, they gradually expand and develop into consistent and more or less realistic endopsychic representations of the object world and of the self [p. 19].

In summary, we may say that in normal psychological development the perceptual capacity for discrimination between self and object facilitates energic distribution and the gradual affective valuation of the object as opposed to the self, a valuation which eventually becomes relatively independent of the need-gratifying functions of the object. It has become theoretically and technically important, particularly for therapists working with borderline and psychotic children, to distinguish disturbances in perceptual differentiation (whether of organic or psychological origin) from disturbances in the capacity to form an emotional relationship with the object. It is mainly a relative failure in perceptual differentiation which precludes the formation of normal object relationships in some atypical children whose drives and affects are potentially available. In others, perceptual differentiation develops relatively normally, but the development of object relationships is arrested or distorted because of interference with their capacity to cathect the internal object representation, i.e., to relate to the object as separate from the self.

Cathexis

The concept of cathexis is a broad one, originally used by Freud in 1895 (see 1950) to denote a charge of energy in a neurological sense, and subsequently expanded by him to denote the investment of drive energy in an object. Other psychoanalytic authors have extended the concept to include the investment of various forms of energy in the object or, more correctly, in the object representation. The concept of cathexis on the psychological level refers to two elements in the process of relating which have to be differentiated. In common psychoanalytic usage these are: the direction of drive energy toward an object representation (the investment of the object with libido or aggression), which is the basis for forming a relationship; and the accompanying ego feelings and attitudes, the qualitative variations of which complement the drive manifestations.

Psychoanalytic thinking concerning the development of object cathexis takes into account both the move away from primary narcissism and the psychological relationship to the object during the oral phase of libidinal development. Elucidation of the development of the feeling of anxiety provides a further pointer to developments in the nature of the relationship to the object.

The Move Away from Primary Narcissism

Freud's earliest formulations (1911, 1914, 1915), stated largely in economic terms, relate to primary narcissism as a stage preceding the finding of a sexual object.

We cannot attempt to do justice to the vast literature on narcissism. In considering these early stages in the development of relationships, the conceptualization we have found most helpful is that which distinguishes between two aspects of narcissism; energic distribution between self and objects, and experiential states (e.g., Joffe and Sandler, 1967; Jacobson, 1964).

In distinguishing between primary narcissism and secondary narcissism, the following points are of relevance: primary narcissism may be conceptualized as an experiential state at times when the predominant feeling tone of the infant is one of pleasure. These primitive experiential states exist *prior* to the differentiation of self and object representations. Hence, it is theoretically incorrect to conceptualize primary narcissism in terms of cathexis of the self. In terms of energic distribution we may say that what is cathected at this early stage is the representation of an experiential state, not a representation of the self.

As the infant forms more reality-oriented representations of self and object, primary narcissism begins to recede and object relatedness and secondary narcissism appear. Thus, with this recession of primary narcissism, we see the beginning of the psychological relationship to the need-satisfying object (or part object).

The Oral Phase of Libidinal Development

Abraham (1924) delineates the main phases of libidinal development and of object love: he assigns the very beginning of an object relationship to the second, cannibalistic, half of the oral stage and stresses the oral physiological mode of incorporation which paves the way for the later psychological process of identification. Freud (1933) assigns the beginning of ambivalence to the second half of the oral stage; and he suggests that concern for the object makes its first appearance in the second half of the anal stage, when destructive trends of destroying and losing are replaced by trends of keeping and possessing.

Freud (1921, 1933) introduced the concept of an early form of identification based on the oral incorporative mode; he saw this as the earliest prototype of an emotional tie and one which had to be distinguished from later object choice. Although Freud does not specifically say so, this concept of an early identification seems to follow from the supposition that the infant cannot at first differentiate between self and object. He writes, for example: "At the very beginning, in the individual's primitive oral phase, object-cathexis and identification are no doubt indistinguishable from each other" (1923, p. 29).

Freud's comments on the early form of identification have been expanded by later writers into such concepts as primary identification, merging, and symbiosis—concepts which are designed to emphasize the lack of clear differentiation between self and object. In our terms, we would say that as long as there is neither clear perceptual differentiation of the object, nor differential energic distribution between self and object, there can be no emotional tie to a psychically recognized object.

There is no disagreement among psychoanalytic writers that the stage of the psychological need-satisfying relationship occurs during the oral phase of libidinal development. But the two are not synonymous, and only partially coincide chronologically. The concept of the oral phase is primarily concerned with the development of libido, and stresses the dominance of the mouth as the main erotogenic zone, with oral activity and gratification as the preferred sexual mode; the oral phase is generally considered to cover approximately the first 18 months of life. The concept of the stage of the need-satisfying relationship places less emphasis on drive development, and more on the development of object relationships. (We shall elaborate further on this point when we discuss the stage of the need-satisfying relationship.)

The Development of Anxiety

Freud's discussion of the nature of anxiety adds a further dimension to the understanding of the infant's and child's relationship to his mother. He links the child's anxiety in the absence of the object with the anxiety aroused by experiences of unsatisfied needs, which have led to growing, unpleasurable tension, and to a "disturbance in the economy of narcissistic libido." Once the infant has learned that the object can alleviate tension, anxiety is shifted, focusing first on loss of the object and later on loss of the object's love. Anxiety is described as a product of the infant's mental helplessness, the counterpart to its biological helplessness. He writes (1926) :

> When the infant has found out by experience that an external, perceptible object can put an end to the dangerous situation which is reminiscent of birth, the content of the danger it fears is displaced from the economic situation on to the condition which determined that situation, viz., the loss of object. It is the absence of the mother that is now the danger; and as soon as that danger arises the infant gives the signal of anxiety, before the dreaded economic situation has set in. This change constitutes a first great step forward in the provision made by the infant for its self-preservation, and at the same time represents a transition from the automatic and involuntary fresh appearance of anxiety to the intentional reproduction of anxiety as a signal of danger [p. 137f.].

While Spitz has used the criterion of how the child reacts to an overwhelming separation from the mother as a measurement of the development of object relations, he has also written about the loss of the love object within the context of the ordinary separations which occur in a normal day. For example, he writes as follows about the third quarter of the first year:

> The loss of the object is therefore a diminution of the Ego at this age and is as severe a narcissistic trauma as a loss of a large part of the body. The reaction to it is just as severe. Anxiety is the affect evoked by the threatening imminence of such a loss. This affect is produced in a constant flux during the daily contacts of the mother with the child. The child is assuaged when the mother is near it, when it sees her or hears her; it becomes anxious when she leaves it [1950, p. 141].

In Greenacre's work (1967) the early predisposition to anxiety is linked to severe narcissistic disturbances in adult life; the conditions which make for such predisposition are, she suggests, illness, injury, states involving pain and discomfort, severe birth experiences, as well as

> . . . various conditions in the mother which were reflected by
> and passed on to the infant in its almost wholly dependent
> state during the first months of life [p. 124f.]. The existence of
> any conditions which seriously impair the mother-infant re-
> lationship [in the first 18 months] interferes . . . with the very
> foundations of object relationship . . . and tends to dam-
> age the early ego in its very incipiency with special harm
> to the sense of reality and often to the beginning sense of
> identity, based as it is in the growing awareness of the body
> [p. 138].

Greenacre's formulations are of particular relevance to work with those borderline children in whom there is a gross disturbance in the capacity for object relationships and a marked emphasis on the need-satisfying aspects of these relationships.

These formulations on the anxiety evoked by disappearance of the object and, later, by withdrawal of the object's love highlight the continuing *need for the object* because of its multiple functions: protecting the infant from internal and external dangers as well as gratifying self-preservative needs and psychological requirements .

Summarizing this discussion of the development of object cathexis, we would suggest that primary narcissism may be conceptualized as referring to two aspects of psychological functioning: the early experiential states of the infant and the investment of energy in primitive representations of these experiential states. The formation of reality-oriented (though still primitive) representations of self and object, and recognition of the object as the source of satisfaction and tension relief, essential to the maintenance of pleasurable experiential states, facilitate the beginning of object relatedness, the recession of primary narcissism, and the shift to secondary narcissism. When the object begins to be recognized as the source of need satisfaction, the infant begins to experience anxiety in the absence of the object. This early form of relationship to the object develops during the oral phase of libidinal development, but is not synonymous with it.

3. Need Satisfaction as a Stage in the Early Development of Object Relationships and as an Element in All Relationships at Every Level

Though the importance of the infant's state of need and the gratification of such needs by the object is widely recognized, it is in fact only Anna Freud (1965) who specifically distinguishes the stage of the need-satisfying relationship to the object. She emphasizes that within this stage the relationship exists for the infant only at times of need and ceases to exist once these needs are gratified. Thus, she writes of "the part object . . . or need-fulfilling, anaclitic [3] relationship, which is based on the urgency of the child's body needs and drive derivatives and is intermittent and fluctuating, since object cathexis is sent out under the impact of imperative desires, and withdrawn again when satisfaction has been reached" (p. 65). She emphasizes the *egocentricity* of the infant's relations with the object world at this time, the mother being perceived only in terms of her role as a satisfier of needs.

Mahler's symbiotic phase (from 2 to 6 months) coincides with Anna Freud's stage of need satisfaction. Mahler (1965) states that "the period which Anna Freud designated as that of the 'need-satisfying object' . . . which begins when a person in the environment, under the specific condition of the infant's need hunger, is perceived . . . as being outside his orbit of the self" (p. 555).

Mahler et al. (1959) make explicit that during this phase the mother is not yet perceived "as a specific whole person" since "the 3- to 4-month-old baby is aware of the mother only as a need-satisfying quasi-extension of his own self" (p. 822). The boundaries between infant and mother become temporarily distinct only when the infant is in "a state of affect hunger" and disappear again as a consequence of gratification and satisfaction. On the basis of

---

[3] S. Freud (1914) used the term "anaclitic" (in German *Anlehnung* = "leaning on") to refer to the "attachment" of the sexual to the ego instincts. He distinguished two pathways toward mature *adult* object relationships: in *anaclitic* object choice the object is chosen for its similarity to the person who originally satisfied the ego instincts of self-preservation; in *narcissistic* object choice the object is chosen for its similarity to the subject's own self. A. Freud has extended the use of the term "anaclitic" to describe as well the early stage of the infant's need-satisfying relationship to the mother.

a gradual awareness that his homeostatic equilibrium is maintained and restored by his mother's ministrations, the infant begins to form more stable part images of the mother (breasts, face, hands) and a Gestalt of her ministrations as such (Mahler, 1958).

Like Mahler, Jacobson (1964) sees the need-gratifying relationship as one aspect of the symbiotic tie with the mother, and both recognize the ensuing struggle between "the child's need to retain the symbiotic situation, to depend and lean on the need-gratifying, protective, and supportive love objects, and opposing tendencies to loosen the symbiotic ties by way of aggressive, narcissistic expansion and independent ego functioning" (p. 50). While Mahler considers that the resolution of this conflict occurs around the end of the third year, Jacobson puts it somewhat later, toward the end of the oedipal period at the formation of the superego. Thus, for both Jacobson and Mahler, need gratification is not a specific stage, but is an ongoing factor in the infant's and child's developing object relationships.

Sandler and his co-workers (1969) have emphasized the persistence of earlier forms of relationships alongside developmentally later ones. They write:

> . . . we probably do not ever get a real replacement of one type of relationship by another. What we see is rather the addition of various new types of object relationship developing collaterally, being integrated with and dominating the old, but not necessarily replacing them. Thus even in the person who has attained the most mature type of object love, the infantile aspects, for example, the purely need-satisfying aspects, remain, although they may be subordinated to the higher-level developments [p. 643].

Bearing in mind the points made by these authors, we would conclude that the crucial distinguishing characteristic of the stage of need satisfaction (variously referred to also as the anaclitic or symbiotic phase) is that the object is recognized as separate from the self only at moments of need; once the need is satisfied, we assume that—from the infant's (subjective) point of view—the object then ceases to exist until a need arises again. In other terms, cathexis is withdrawn from the object. Moreover, from the infant's point of view, the relationship is not to a specific object (or part object) but rather to the *function* of having the need satisfied and to the accompanying pleasure afforded by the object in fulfilling that function.

Rapaport (1950) in the following excerpt (which forms part of a discussion of the role of the hallucinatory image in primary process ideation) pinpoints the nondifferentiation on the infant's part between the object and the function it performs. Writing from a genetic viewpoint, he states:

> From developmental psychology we know that the original experience of the need-satisfying object is a diffuse undifferentiated experience in which visual, accoustic, tactile, thermal, cutaneous, kinesthetic, and other stimulations are fused. Discrete objects do not as yet exist, and thus the need-satisfying object itself is not differentiated from the context in which it appears nor even from the experiences immediately preceding or following it. . . . It is this diffuse global image of the need-satisfying object which is pushed into consciousness when instinctual tension mounts. In the course of development this diffuse image differentiates into discrete objects and experiences, all of which are still related to instinctual drives in the same fashion as was the original and undifferentiated image of the need-satisfying object. Thus we find a multitude of instinct representations . . . any of which are mutually interchangeable since their essential meaning is that they are representations of the instinctual drive [p. 317].

At the point when the *specific* object becomes as important to the infant as the function it performs—namely, the gratification of bodily needs—we may assume that the stage of the need-satisfying relationship is being left behind for a higher level of psychological development, the attainment of object constancy.

As we have previously mentioned, the stage of the need-satisfying relationship occurs during the oral phase of libidinal development, but is not synonymous with it. The need-satisfying relationship revolves around the functions performed by the object, and is not *primarily* concerned with the sexual relationship to the object, even though it points the way for infantile sexual object choice. The stage of the need-satisfying relationship is of shorter duration than the oral phase, since it cannot begin until about the age of 2 to 3 months, when perceptual differentiation and psychological functioning have sufficiently advanced for the infant to recognize the intervention of something external to the self as essential to the satisfaction of needs; it is gradually superseded, toward the end of the oral phase, by the developing attachment to a specific object.[4]

Similarly, when speaking of regressive elements which may be present in relationships at later stages of development, the terms "oral" and "need-satisfying" should not be used synonymously. The term "need-satisfying" refers to a *mode* of relating, or to characteristics of the *relationship;* it is often used loosely and descriptively to refer to the predominance of demanding and greedy or passive and dependent attitudes toward the object. *Used in its strictest sense, the term should indicate a mode of relating in which only the object's need-satisfying functions are of prime importance to the subject.*

The term "oral" also is often used to indicate both the descriptive and the strictly defined "need-satisfying" type of relationship, again without distinguishing which is meant. This can lead to considerable confusion of thinking, since in addition to connoting either an arrested, or a severely regressed, or a descriptively immature *relationship,* the term "oral" is used loosely to refer to character traits and to other aspects of drive and ego functioning occurring during or persisting from the oral phase of drive development. *We think that the term "oral" should be strictly reserved for drive aspects pertaining to the oral phase of drive development.*[5]

4. Different Types of Needs: Self-Preservative Needs, Sexual and Aggressive Drive Pressures, and Ego Requirements

It goes without saying that all authors—implicitly or explicitly—include drive pressures and ego requirements in their conceptualization of the need-satisfying relationship. What possibly has to be spelled out further is the fact that within the child's developing

[4] See Burgner and Edgcumbe (*This Volume,* pp. 315–333).
[5] For a more detailed discussion and clarification of the many meanings of the term "oral" see Sandler and Dare (1970).

and expanding relationships, satisfaction of these *different* types of needs continues to play an important role. Anna Freud (1965), emphasizing the child's prolonged dependence on his parents, includes among the uses a child makes of them: "for leaning on their capacity to understand and manipulate external conditions so that body needs and drive derivatives can be satisfied; . . . to act as limiting agents to drive satisfaction, thereby initiating the child's own ego mastery of the id; to provide the patterns for identification which are needed for building up an independent structure" (p. 46).

These are requirements of the ego. We also have to take into account the continuing satisfaction by the object of bodily needs serving self-preservative aims; these needs and aims are, of course, biologically determined. Anna Freud notes that in contrast to autoerotic gratification, other body needs require the object's involvement: "the processes of feeding, sleeping, evacuation, body hygiene, and prevention of injury and illness have to undergo complex and lengthy developments before they become the growing individual's own concern" (p. 69).

With regard to the sources of needs, Freud himself does not restrict his use of the term to self-preservative needs. He uses the term "need" to refer to sexual drive tension (e.g., 1916/1917, 1923, 1940); and he also writes of ego needs and "new needs" which arise in the course of development (1916/1917, 1926). We would understand from his usage of the term that Freud concentrated more on the source of the need, rather than on the type of relationship within which such needs may be satisfied.

It seems to us desirable, in order to avoid both conceptual and clinical confusion, to differentiate between self-preservative, sexual and aggressive drive and ego needs by using different terms. We could, for example, speak of *self-preservative needs, sexual and aggressive drive pressures,* and *various requirements of the developing ego.* Different modes of behaving and relating to the object are used to express these different needs, pressures, and requirements, which in turn are satisfied via different sets of responses from the object. It also must be recognized that emotional requirements can, and do, become as imperative as instinctual needs and pressures.

Our study of clinical material in the Hampstead Index has suggested to us that it is particularly important to distinguish between clinical manifestations of developmental arrest at or regression to the *stage* of need-satisfying relationships (which, in fact, occurs only rarely even in severely disturbed psychotic or defective children) and relationships which are need-satisfying only in a descriptive sense. For example, many neurotic children who have firmly established constant relationships to specific objects, and who in many respects have retained oedipal relationships in spite of some regression, may because of conflict, guilt, and anxiety behave toward their objects in ways which are often loosely described as "need-satisfying": they are clinging, egocentric, demanding, greedy, selfish, babyish, etc.; they have to be cuddled, washed, dressed, hand-fed, etc. But closer inspection shows that the close bodily and emotional relationship to the object maintained by such children is being used to gratify sexual drive pressures and wishes from many levels of development, rather than the self-preservative bodily needs of the infant.

Children with physical handicaps, such as blindness, are forced into prolonged dependence upon objects for bodily care and support in ego development. But even children who have quite severe emotional disturbances, in addition to or partially resulting from their physical handicap, usually achieve object constancy and proceed, in some degree at least, to later stages of object relationships. This development may be obscured by their enforced continuing dependence upon objects because of their handicap, but they are by no means arrested at the *stage* of the need-satisfying relationship. Their objects are used for satisfaction of a variety of ego requirements and drive pressures as well as the bodily needs appropriate to the infant; the objects are valued for attributes other than the capacity to satisfy needs, and *specific* objects are preferred.

5. Expressions of Actual Needs and Defensive Exaggerations or Minimizations of Needs

In addition to distinguishing between different types of needs belonging to different areas and levels of development, it is also important, for the avoidance of conceptual confusion, to distinguish between direct expressions of genuine needs and the defensive exaggeration or minimization of needs. In order to make this distinction we must further distinguish between drive regression to the oral phase of libidinal development and regression in object relationships to the need-satisfying stage; and between the need-satisfying *mode* of relating to the object appropriate to the early infantile period, and later modes of relating appropriate to the satisfaction of needs, drive pressures, and ego requirements belonging to later levels of development.

Here again, the Hampstead Index provides many examples of cases in which these clinical and conceptual distinctions can be made. For example, a 5-year-old boy is loosely described as having an "oral" or "need-satisfying" relationship to his mother, but close inspection of the analytic material shows that he is clinging, greedy, and demanding, involves his mother in prolonged scenes over eating, becomes fearful when separated from her. There is also evidence that he has reached the phallic phase of drive development and the oedipal level of relationships, and much of his behavior is appropriate to these levels of development in drives and object relationships. Conflicts over phallic aggression are expressed in fears of harming his mother and thereby losing her love. He has reacted with a partial defensive drive regression, substituting oral sexual gratification for phallic sexuality, and involving his mother in this as a sexual object rather than as a satisfier of self-preservative needs. Regression to this level of drive expression is facilitated by his family's tendency to sexualize eating. His clinging and fear of separation, though partially defensive against fears of harming his mother by his phallic aggression, are also defensive against fears of loss of the need-satisfying object, a fear partly based on real experiences during his second year. But his clinging behavior and refusal to accept substitutes for his mother demonstrate his attachment to this *specific* object; i.e., in his relationship he has *not* regressed to the *stage* of the need-satisfying relationship, where the function is more important than the object. Thus, this boy's descriptively need-satisfying relationship to his mother proves to be composed of a phallic-oedipal type of relationship on a regressed oral drive level, and a defensive exaggeration of needs intended to bind the specific object to himself; it is in no sense a true regression to the need-satisfying stage of object relationships.

At the other extreme, we have children such as a 6-year-old girl who had become excessively independent and self-sufficient largely as a result of having to defend against her own drive demands which she had learned were intolerable to her seriously depressed mother. This defense had been extended to cover self-preservative and bodily needs, so that the child had taken over responsibility for physically caring for herself at a much earlier age than would normally be expected. Her behavior was not indicative of the absence of needs, only of their defensive minimization.

There is a group of patients whom it is particularly tempting to think of as relating on a need-satisfying level; these are children whose relationships have not matured to levels appropriate for their age, i.e., who demonstrate a partial failure in development rather than a regression. But these children too prove to have progressed at least to the attainment of object constancy. They are usually children in whom early distressing experiences of separation, and possibly collusion by the mother, have given rise to a tendency to retain certain characteristics of the mode of relating to the object belonging to the stage of the need-satisfying relationship: the expectation of immediate satisfaction, inability to tolerate frustration, a relative lack of concern for the rights and wishes of the object, and a lack of interest in aspects of the object other than its capacity to satisfy needs, etc. Such responses express anxiety about losing the specific love object, a defensive attempt to bind the object to them, and a fearful refusal to risk losing the close tie to the object by moving on to more mature modes of relating and greater independence. Very often in their drive and ego development these children proceed to relatively more mature levels of development; it is their relationships which lag behind. They may, however, give the impression of severe arrest or regression in other areas of development because the persistence of the early mode of relating distorts the expression of needs, drive pressures, and ego requirements belonging to later levels of development.

A young adolescent girl, for example, who had never resolved her conflict over early feelings of ambivalence to her mother, remained excessively demanding, unable to tolerate frustration, insisting that all her needs and wishes should be immediately satisfied. She had continued to use this way of demanding love, attention, and preferential treatment from her mother throughout her life; she also used it for drive demands on all levels, e.g., demanding innumerable gifts as penis equivalents when she reached the phallic phase of drive development, as well as for help with ego activities on all levels: her demandingness was also noted by her school teachers.

What such cases illustrate is a persistence of certain characteristics of the mode of relating appropriate to the need-satisfying stage, so that the development of object relationships fails to keep pace with drive and ego development; this delay leads to an overall distortion of personality development.

Discussion

1. A distinction between the primary biological and psychological aspects of need satisfaction has to include the following factors: that the purely biological state, which is a continuation of the homeostatic state *in utero,* lasts only for a very short time after birth. While this biological state continues, we may conceptualize that primitive psychological functioning is gradually superimposed upon it, in that memory traces are laid down of repetitive *experiences* of hunger (pain) and satiation (pleasure). These primitive memory traces are eventually made use of in the organization of perceptions relating to the external world, as the infant gradually perceives that homeostasis is capable of being restored by the actions of an object or part object [6] external to himself.

In addition to the physiological state of hunger, instinctual drive pressures pertaining to the oral phase soon begin to make themselves manifest in the additional pleasure derived from sucking; at this stage of development, however, such drive pressures

---

[6] While the perceived part object is understood by us, as we have stated earlier, in terms of the *functions* performed by the object, we have in more mature relationships to make a further distinction between a temporarily need-satisfying relationship to an otherwise "whole object," as compared with a restricted relationship to a "part object," as encountered in severely disturbed individuals incapable of even relatively mature relationships.

are virtually indistinguishable from the self-preservative needs and are satisfied via this same act of sucking. We could conceptualize two parallel lines of development: the biological tendencies—reflex actions, self-preservative needs, and instinctual drive pressures; and the developing psychological capacities, which in turn enable the individual to regulate, control, and direct the biological tendencies. While the satisfaction of needs would originally be subsumed under the biological tendencies in that—as far as the infant is concerned—homeostasis is regained without external intervention, satisfaction of these same needs moves over to the psychological sphere as soon as the infant becomes aware that his state of well-being is being restored by something external to himself.

While *psychological functioning* in the neonate begins shortly after birth, the beginning of *psychological relationships* has to be placed somewhat later. The infant has to be capable of forming a representation, primitive though it may be, of aspects of the environment external to himself before *any* type of relationship is possible. And it is probably not till the third month of life that the infant's psychological capacities and structures are adequate enough to allow him to form primitive representations of aspects of objects which subserve his needs. Even then this capacity is by no means firmly established, and weeks, or even months, of intermittent psychic confusion follow when representations of self and object and representations of various experiential states are superimposed one upon the other, or alternate in too rapid succession for the infant's immature mental apparatus to integrate them in meaningful and ordered terms. However, it may be said that once representations, albeit primitive ones, are capable of being formed, the *beginning* of a psychological relationship to the object, or rather at first to the functions performed by the object, has been established.

Therefore, while the early primary biological state and the concurrent primitive psychological state of functioning are undoubtedly states in which the satisfaction of self-preservative needs play a central role, such states cannot yet be characterized in terms of the psychological need-satisfying relationship, in that there is as yet neither self nor object representation. From the point of view of the development of object relationships, this stage of need satisfaction could be usefully subdivided: first, the primary biological state; then the primitive psychological state of functioning in which there is no psychological relationship to the need-satisfying object (in spite of the commencement of psychological functioning as such) ; and, finally, the *stage of the need-satisfying relationship* in which a representation of the object (or part object) is capable of being structured and is available to the infant whenever a need arises which can be satisfied only by an external object.

As we have said earlier, while the stage of need satisfaction develops during the oral phase of libidinal development, the two are by no means synonymous and should not be used interchangeably; a distinction has to be made between the *level of sexual drive activity* implied in the term "oral relationships" and the *quality* of the object relationship within the *stage of the need-satisfying relationship.*

2. In considering the development of the capacity to relate to objects, it is important to distinguish between the establishment of perceptual structures on the one hand, and drive investment and an affective relationship on the other. The emergence of certain perceptual capacities cannot be taken as evidence that other aspects of psychic functioning have also developed to the necessary degree. The capacity to organize primitive percepts begins to function shortly after birth and, as it develops, results in the formation of first primitive and then gradually more complex and sophisticated representations of part and whole objects. But the fact that these perceptual structures have come into being does not mean that they are immediately used by the infant to maintain a psychological relationship to the object. By the age of 2 to 3 months the infant is able to form some primitive kind of mental representation of those parts or functions of objects in the external world whose presence, it has learned, are essential for the satisfaction of needs; but drive energy is invested in these primitive representations only at moments of rising need, and no aspect other than the capacity to satisfy needs is affectively valued. Thus the fact that a hungry infant quietens and shows signs of recognizing sights and sounds associated with the preparation of food does not mean that he recognizes mother as a whole object, or that he can maintain any kind of relationship, either internal or external, with her

once his need is satisfied. Even the "stranger anxiety" of the 8-month-old must not be taken as indicating establishment of a constant relationship to the mother; what appears to happen at this age is that development of perceptual representations of objects reaches a point where the infant can distinguish different people in the external world, is beginning to invest energy in the representation of mother, and to anticipate and prefer the appearance of and handling by mother to others. It does not yet mean that the relationship to mother has become an entirely exclusive one, even for the purpose of satisfying needs; nor does it mean that mother is valued as a whole person, or for qualities and capacities other than her ability to satisfy needs.

3. We suggest that a distinction should be maintained between need satisfaction as a *stage* in the development of object relationships and as a *determinant* in all relationships at every level. The crucial point is not that needs cease to press for satisfaction after the end of this stage, but that *there is a change in the nature of the relationship,* as there also is, of course, a gradual shift in the nature of the needs. Since the satisfaction of various types of need continues to play a role at *all* levels of development of object relationships, the fact that needs are satisfied cannot, therefore, be used as the distinguishing characteristic of the *stage* of the need-satisfying relationship. To our understanding the crucial features of this stage are: there is no preference for a specific object until toward the end of this stage; the infant automatically employs his capacity to form a primitive representation of the object on the basis of memory traces of the object and of memory traces of previous experiences of satisfaction, and invests this representation with energy only at moments of need; once the need is satisfied, the representation of the object no longer serves a useful purpose and is therefore de-invested and not used again until a new need arises. In such a psychic process the object representation, though still a primitive one, is assigned a primitive affective value by the infant.

We may conceptualize this area of the satisfaction of needs in terms of the maturation of innate capacities and development, via interaction with the object, from primary biological and drive-related needs to object-related needs in the psychological sphere. Between these two stages falls the stage of need satisfaction in which primitive affective value is assigned to the part-object representation while the particular need is being satisfied. As objects become increasingly differentiated, their representations would be assigned value of increasing psychological complexity by the child's developing ego, so that an ego need for the object develops concurrently with his other needs; these values eventually acquire relative autonomy from the drive pressures and self-preservative needs. In these terms we may conceptualize one aspect of *object constancy* as the *constant relationship to a specific object,* a relationship which of course sometimes reflects the individual's wish for that object to satisfy his needs.

After the primary biological and the primitive psychological states and after the stage of the need-satisfying relationship, there follows a lengthy period during which the child, because of his physical and psychic immaturity, continues to be dependent on objects for satisfaction of his material needs. Due to cultural and socioeconomic factors, there is in our society an artificially prolonged period of dependence upon the parents for satisfaction of material needs, beyond the time when, physically and psychically, the individual is sufficiently mature to meet these needs himself. This period may last till the end of adolescence and beyond.

4. We consider next the *different types of needs*—primary biological needs, drive pressures, and ego requirements—all of which may legitimately be termed needs. Increasingly the infant himself initiates interaction with the object in order to repeat pleasurable experiences associated in the first instance with the gratification of such needs.

In relationships after the stage of the exclusively need-satisfying relationship, the child increasingly values attributes of the object other than its ability to satisfy primitive needs; among such necessary attributes of the object we include: its role as an object whom the child imitates and identifies with; its presence as an object onto whom the child directs his sexual and aggressive wishes and fantasies; as an auxiliary support in developing ego and superego functioning and in structuralization in general; and as the first provider of sources of safety, well-being, and self-esteem, which later form part of the internalized and autonomous structures. Since the satisfaction of all these needs depends to a greater or lesser extent on the object, a need for the presence of the specific object gradually develops; this need eventually becomes autonomous and contributes to the development of stable and constant relationships to specific objects.

It is probably only with the resolution of adolescent conflicts that concern for the object and reciprocity within relationships can become relatively stable and autonomous. However, transitory feelings of concern for the object and empathy with it may occur from the oedipal phase onward, or even earlier; and such feelings may sometimes serve to moderate the demand for need satisfaction; their existence is one indicator that the development of object relationships is progressing.

The basic and essential criterion for the move out of the stage of the need-satisfying relationship is simply the establishment of the autonomous and constant need for a *specific* object.

Pursuing our line of thought that needs of one kind or another continue to be satisfied within relationships throughout life, we could say that every relationship is to some extent a need-satisfying one, not only in its genetic derivation but also in its current functioning. In order, therefore, to distinguish between different developmental levels and types of relationship, we may differentiate them according to which bodily or material needs, drive pressures, or ego requirements predominate in demanding satisfaction. More important, however, is the *mode* of relating to the object. Although the child's needs continue to be satisfied, the child's *mode of seeking satisfaction* changes in those later relationships, as does the object's mode of response. We would suggest that, strictly speaking, later relationships should be characterized as need-satisfying only if the early *mode* of relating to the object belonging to the *stage* of the need-satisfying relationship *persists,* or is regressively revived, *entirely unchanged;* that is to say, if immediate satisfaction of a need is more important than the object which satisfies it, if the representation of the object is invested with drive energy only at moments of need, if the object (and it can be any object) is valued only at times of need and only for its function of satisfying needs, and if it ceases to be of any value or interest to the individual at times when needs are quiescent.

In passing, it is worth commenting that one can frequently

observe the persistence of other, earlier modes of relating to the object carried over to later developmental phases; for example, the sadomasochistic relationship appropriate to the toddler in the anal phase may persist through subsequent phases of libidinal development.

5. Direct expressions of needs of all kinds should be carefully distinguished from the defensive exaggeration of needs due to anxiety, which may occur in all later stages of object relationships; similarly, defensive minimization of needs should not be confused with the absence of needs. It is in many cases not the needs themselves which are important, but the relationship to the object, which the subject seeks to preserve in the face of threatening danger (of object loss, loss of love, danger to the object from the subject's own aggression, etc.) .

The attitudes of "demandingness," "dependence," "clinging," etc., so often noted in clinical descriptions of older individuals, are rarely indications of a complete regression to the stage of the need-satisfying relationship, though the relationships of such individuals are sometimes loosely described as need-satisfying; nor are they necessarily indications that drive regression has occurred. It seems to us most important to distinguish between cases where drive regression has actually taken place and cases where drives have remained mainly on higher levels while the regression has primarily taken place in the level of the object relationships.

While the development of object relationships is initially, at each new stage, dependent upon the development of the drives, as well as of the ego and affective states, it gradually gains a measure of autonomy. It is possible, then, for regression to take place in object relationships without a corresponding drive regression and without a corresponding regression to primitive bodily needs. Our clinical material demonstrates that in many cases the exaggeration of demands for satisfaction and the dependence upon the object refer neither to the material needs appropriate to the developmental stage of need satisfaction nor to the drive urges of the oral phase. The patient may continue to demand satisfaction of drive pressures and ego requirements appropriate to his higher level of development, and regress only with respect to his mode of interaction with the object; that is, he expects immediate satisfaction, does not appear to concern himself with the rights and wishes of the object, and may lose interest in the object once the need is satisfied. In fact, none of the cases in the Hampstead Index may be said to have *regressed* to the stage of the need-satisfying relationship as such, since among those who have attained higher levels of development and then regressed, none fulfills the criterion of indiscriminate use of objects. Even the most severely disturbed neurotic and borderline patients retain clear preferences for certain objects, which means that even they have not regressed in their relationships beyond the point of transition from the stage of the need-satisfying relationship to the stage of the constant relationship to a particular object. The patients who use this kind of defensive regression in object relationships are usually those whose disturbance centers around fears of destroying or losing the object or the object's love, so that the aim of the regression is to bind the object more firmly to them and *not* to replace it with various substitutes.

While total *arrest* at the stage of the need-satisfying relationship can occur, even this seems relatively rare, being found only in some severely defective autistic and psychotic children whose drive and ego development also remains wholly or partly arrested. Close examination of the material of our severely disturbed patients shows that most of them have made moves in some aspects of their relationships beyond the stage of need satisfaction, even though their mode of relating to and demanding satisfaction from their objects may appear to rest on that very early level.

Summary

In this study we elucidated some important aspects in the development of early object relationships. We subdivided the stage of need satisfaction and stressed the importance of the *stage of the need-satisfying relationship*. In concentrating particularly upon the stage of need satisfaction, we emphasized the distinction between primary biological and psychological functioning and the beginning of psychological relationships. We suggested further that the protraction of a descriptively need-satisfying relationship hardly ever represents a true arrest at or regression to that particular stage of development, but rather involves a persistence of an earlier mode of demanding satisfaction from, and of interaction with, the object.

BIBLIOGRAPHY

ABRAHAM, K. (1924), A Short Study of the Development of the Libido Viewed in the Light of Mental Disorders. In: *Selected Papers on Psycho-Analysis.* London: Hogarth Press, 1927, pp. 418–501.

BALINT, M.. (1949), Early Developmental States of the Ego: Primary Object Love. *Int. J. Psycho-Anal.,* 30:265–273

— (1960), Primary Narcissism and Primary Love. *Psychoanal. Quart.,* 29:6–43.

BOWLBY, J. (1969), *Attachment and Loss,* Vol. 1. New York: Basic Books.

FREUD, A. (1965), *Normality and Pathology in Childhood.* New York: International Universities Press.

FREUD, S. (1911), Psycho-Analytic Notes on an Autobiographical Account of a Case of Paranoia (Dementia Paranoides). *Standard Edition,* 12:3–82. London: Hogarth Press, 1958.

— (1914), On Narcissism: An Introduction. *Standard Edition,* 14:67–102. London: Hogarth Press, 1957.

— (1915), Instincts and Their Vicissitudes. *Standard Edition,* 14:111–140. London: Hogarth Press, 1957.

— (1916/1917), Introductory Lectures on Psycho-Analysis. *Standard Edition,* 15 & 16. London: Hogarth Press, 1963.

— (1921), Group Psychology and the Analysis of the Ego. *Standard Edition,* 18:67–143. London: Hogarth Press, 1955.

— (1923), The Ego and the Id. *Standard Edition,* 19:3–66. London: Hogarth Press, 1961.

— (1926), Inhibitions, Symptoms and Anxiety. *Standard Edition,* 20:77–175. London: Hogarth Press, 1959.

— (1930), Civilization and Its Discontents. *Standard Edition,* 21:59–145. London: Hogarth Press, 1961.

— (1933), New Introductory Lectures on Psycho-Analysis. *Standard Edition,* 22:3–182. London: Hogarth Press, 1964.

— (1940), An Outline of Psycho-Analysis. *Standard Edition,* 23:141–207. London: Hogarth Press, 1964.

— (1950 [1895]), Project for a Scientific Psychology. *Standard Edition,* 1:283–397). London: Hogarth Press, 1966.

GREENACRE, P. (1962), The Theory of the Parent-Infant Relationship: Further Remarks. *Int. J. Psycho-Anal.,* 43:235–237.

— (1967), The Influence of Infantile Trauma on Genetic Patterns. In: *Psychic Trauma,* ed. S. S. Furst. New York: Basic Books, pp. 108–153.

HARTMANN, H. (1939), *Ego Psychology and the Problem of Adaptation.* New York: International Universities Press, 1958.

— (1944), Psychoanalysis and Sociology. In: *Essays on Ego Psychology.* New York: International Universities Press, 1964, pp. 19–27.

— KRIS, E., & LOEWENSTEIN, R. M. (1946), Comments on the Formation of Psychic Structure. *This Annual,* 2:11–38.

JACOBSON, E. (1964), *The Self and the Object World.* New York: International Universities Press.

JOFFE, W. G. & SANDLER, J. (1967), On Some Conceptual Problems Involved in the Consideration of Disorders of Narcissism. *J. Child Psychother.,* 2:56–66.

KLEIN, M. (1952), *Developments in Psycho-Analysis.* London: Hogarth Press.

MAHLER, M. S. (1958), Autism and Symbiosis: Two Extreme Disturbances of Identity. *Int. J. Psycho-Anal.,* 39:77–83.

— (1965), On Early Infantile Psychosis: The Symbiotic and Autistic Syndromes. *J. Amer. Acad. Child Psychiat.,* 4:554–568.

— FURER, M., & SETTLAGE, C. F. (1959), Severe Emotional Disturbances in Childhood: Psychosis. In: *American Handbook of Psychiatry,* ed. S. Arieti. New York: Basic Books, pp. 816–839.

RAPAPORT, D. (1950), On the Psychoanalytic Theory of Thinking. In: *The Collected Papers of David Rapaport,* ed. M. M. Gill. New York: Basic Books, 1967, pp. 313–328.

SANDLER, J. (1962), Research in Psycho-Analysis: The Hampstead Index as an Instrument of Psycho-Analytic Research. *Int. J. Psycho-Anal.,* 43:287–292.

— (1969), Personal Communication.

— &.DARE, C. (1970), The Psychoanalytical Concept of Orality. *J. Psychosom. Res.,* 14:211–222.

— HOLDER, A., KAWENOKA, M., KENNEDY, H. E., & NEURATH, L. (1969), Notes on Some Theoretical and Clinical Aspects of Transference. *Int. J. Psycho-Anal.,* 50:633–645.

— & ROSENBLATT, B. (1962), The Concept of the Representational World. *This Annual,* 17:128–145.

SPITZ, R. A. (1950), Anxiety in Infancy: A Study of Its Manifestations in the First Year of Life. *Int. J. Psycho-Anal.,* 31:138–143.

— (1965), *The First Year of Life.* New York: International Universities Press.

WINNICOTT, D. W. (1948), Pediatrics and Psychiatry. In: *Collected Papers.* New York: Basic Books, 1958, pp. 157–173.

Some Problems in the Conceptualization of Early Object Relationships

Part II: The Concept of Object Constancy

MARION BURGNER, B.A.

AND ROSE EDGCUMBE, B.A., M.S.

THE CONCEPT OF OBJECT CONSTANCY AS USED IN PSYCHOANALYSIS IS an important one insofar as the establishment of object constancy is generally considered to mark the transition from the need-satisfying type of relationship to more mature psychological object relationships. Thus, it has been viewed as a concept of equal developmental and clinical importance: developmentally, the attainment of object constancy is understood as denoting the individual's capacity to differentiate between objects and to maintain a re-

---

This paper forms part of a Research Project entitled "Childhood Pathology: Impact on Later Mental Health" which is conducted at the Hampstead Child-Therapy Course and Clinic, London. The project is financed by the National Institute of Mental Health, Washington, D.C., Grant No. MH–5683–09. The paper also forms part of the work carried out by the Hampstead Index Committee, Chairman Dr. J. Sandler.

(315)

lationship to one specific object regardless of whether needs are being satisfied or not; and clinically, this concept is used as an indicator in differential diagnoses between psychotic, borderline, and neurotic disturbances. However, it has, in practice, often proved difficult to establish the presence or absence of object constancy in certain cases, as we have learned both from clinical material in the Hampstead Index,[1] and from the work of the Group for the Study of Borderline Children,[2] and this difficulty, we suggest, is due to lack of precise definition in the current usages of the concept.

In our view this concept would be far more useful, both theoretically and clinically, if we were able to clarify and differentiate between the contributions made, first, by drive investment in the object; second, by such aspects of ego functioning as perception, memory, and thought processes; and third, by feeling states.

Our main concern in this paper is with the psychoanalytic use of the concept *object constancy*. It is, however, appropriate briefly to examine nonpsychoanalytic usage of the term, and particularly the work of Piaget, since the term *constancy* (or permanence) originates in academic and experimental psychology. In academic psychology it refers specifically to the capacity to organize stimuli (usually visual) originating in the external world into stable and unvarying percepts, regardless of changes in the object's orientation, distance, color, shading, etc.; the object in question is usually an inanimate one. In these terms *constancy* refers only to perceptual organization, recognition, and generalization, and not to

[1] These difficulties arose in the course of revision of the Object Relationships Manual of the Hampstead Clinic Index, which was set up as an instrument for the classification of clinical data from a large number of cases in analytic treatment. These data are categorized under both descriptive and metapsychological headings, and Manuals are provided to aid the therapist in assigning material to appropriate headings. For a fuller account of the Index see Sandler (1962). The process of indexing analytic cases constantly necessitates clarification and finer discrimination of theoretical concepts, and hence leads to the revision of Manuals in order to permit a better understanding of clinical material.

[2] The Group for the Study of Borderline Children, Chairman, Mrs. Sara Rosenfeld, was originally formed to study technical, clinical, and theoretical problems in the treatment of borderline children at the Hampstead Clinic. By now the range of child and adolescent patients has been widened to include many forms of frankly psychotic, autistic, and atypical disturbances.

the ability to recall the representation of an object in its absence, nor to the capacity to cathect that object representation. Some of the existing confusion about the concept of object constancy in psychoanalyic usage seems to be attributable to the arbitrary widening of an originally precise concept to include instinctual and affective, in addition to the perceptual, elements.

Piaget's Work

The main contribution to the study of perceptual organization, and the one most useful for psychoanalytic conceptualization, was made by Piaget. His extensive examination of perceptual development in infants and children is primarily concerned with perception of inanimate objects, and his interest in this development is from the standpoint of sensorimotor development rather than the development of relationships to animate objects. Nonetheless, his data are of great value in elucidating the role of perception in the development of object relationships from a psychoanalytic viewpoint.[3]

Piaget's findings suggest that the infant's first primitive concept of the object does not differentiate between the object and the infant's own activity in regard to that object—for example, the breast is recognized only as part of the activity of sucking. Concomitant with the growing differentiation between self and nonself, the infant's own activity is gradually perceived as belonging to the self, while the object of the activity is perceived as external to the self. By 4 months visual recognition begins to supersede recognition within the context of activity: the infant opens his mouth at the sight of the breast, he smiles at a familiar face and frowns at an unfamiliar one. These early observations refer to the infant's interaction with the mother. The summary of Piaget's observations which follows refers mainly to inanimate objects—toys.

An important new advance occurs at about 5 months when the infant begins to search for objects after he has seen them disappear, an indication that perceptual organization has become sufficiently

[3] Attempts have been made to integrate Piaget's theories with those of psychoanalysis by Wolff (1960) and Décarie (1963), whose writings we have made use of in studying Piaget's work, without necessarily subscribing to their conclusions.

stable to allow the perceptual image of an object to be maintained in the absence of the object, at least for a short time. At first the infant searches only for objects with which he was playing at the moment they disappeared, indicating that the object representation is not yet fully separated from the context of the infant's own activity toward it. By 8 months, however, the infant searches for objects that have disappeared while he was merely looking at them and not playing with them, indicating that the perceptual representation of the object is becoming clearly differentiated from the representation of the infant's self acting upon the object. For a further period, however, the object continues to be perceived merely as part of a particular geographical context: the infant searches for an object that has disappeared only in places where he has previously found and played with it. At about 12 months, the infant begins to search for a missing object in places where he has not played with it, as long as he has seen it disappear from that place. And it is not until approximately 16 to 18 months that the child can recall a perceptual image and then purposively look for a missing object without the prior visual stimulus of watching the object disappear (Piaget, 1936, 1937).

Thus, as far as inanimate objects are concerned, it seems that object representations cannot be summoned up without the aid of external stimulation, until approximately the middle of the child's second year. Piaget's observations of the 5- to 18-month period, being based on the infant's interaction with inanimate objects, can perhaps not be directly applied to the interaction with the much more important animate object, the mother. The interaction between infant and mother in the service of his needs and their satisfaction could be assumed to facilitate the earlier perceptual organization of the representation of the mother.

What we may extrapolate from Piaget's findings as one factor in the development of animate object constancy is that in normal development the capacity to *recall* an organized perceptual representation [4] of the object makes its first tentative appearance at about 5 months, at which time an external stimulus (the disap-

---

[4] By this we mean the psychological capacity to perceive the object in the external world and to structure an internal representation of this same object. See Edgcumbe and Burgner (*This Volume,* pp. 283–314).

pearance of the object) is required to stimulate the memory function; it is finally established approximately one year later, by which time no external stimulus is required.

Hartmann (1953), writing about the subject of object constancy from a psychoanalytic point of view and enlarging upon the differentiation between self and object, a process which is an element in the constancy of the object, uses Piaget's formulations:

> First the infant does not distinguish between the objects and his activities vis à vis the objects. In the words of Piaget (1937), the object is still nothing but a prolongation of the child's activity. Later, in the course of those processes that lead to a distinction of object and self, the child also learns to make a distinction between his activity and the object toward which this activity is directed. The earlier stage may be correlated with magic action and probably represents a transitory step in ego (or, rather, pre-ego) development, interposed between simple discharge and true ego-directed and organized action. The later stage represents one aspect of "objectivation," which is an ego contribution to the development of object relations and an essential element in the institution of the reality principle. Piaget's finding agrees rather well with the findings of analysis, and it means, metapsychologically speaking, that from then on there is a difference between the cathexis of an object-directed ego function and the cathexis of an object representation [p. 187f.].

Psychoanalytic Literature

Our examination of some of the analytic literature on object constancy has reinforced the impression we formed when we studied earlier aspects of relationships: of the apparently uniform use of a term to denote a specific stage in the development of object relationships which, when scrutinized, reveals discrepancies, varying approaches, and even anomalies among the authors under review; often there is a blurring of the distinction between a theoretical construct and the observable clinical data.

In psychoanalytic writing the aspects which are mentioned as important in the development of object constancy include: perception (especially the ability to differentiate between self and object, to organize stable representations of self and object, and to maintain a perceptual image of the object in its absence) ; stability of cathexis (the capacity to invest drive energy, especially libidinal, in a particular preferred object representation) ; the capacity for neutralization and fusion of drives directed to a specific object; the capacity to maintain a positive (loving) emotional attachment to a particular object regardless of frustration or satisfaction of needs, drive pressures, and wishes; the capacity to tolerate ambivalent feelings toward the same object; the capacity to value the object for qualities not connected with its ability to satisfy needs and provide drive satisfactions. In other words, the establishment of object constancy is viewed as requiring the concomitant development of numerous, and disparate, aspects of id and ego functioning. Moreover, though most authors see the development of object constancy as a gradual process, estimates of the chronological age at which it is firmly established vary from the second half of the first year to the end of the third year of life.

Drive Cathexis

Various authors write about the libidinal cathexis of the object, a process which is generally understood to mature with the individual's developing ego, though the specific emphasis will vary with the individual author's preferred approach.

Anna Freud (1952) writes of the diminution of the intensity of drive pressure as the individual no longer requires such *immediate* satisfaction of his needs; she also stresses the maturation of the ego and the establishment of the reality principle, which facilitate "the ability to retain libidinal cathexis to absent love objects during separations of increasing lengths" (p. 45) .

Further, Anna Freud (1965) writes of object constancy as a developmental stage coming after the stages of biological unity with the mother and the need-satisfying relationship, but before the ambivalent stage. Frequently, she stresses the individual's capacity for positive libidinal cathexis of the object, regardless of the satisfactions involved: "The capacity to retain an inner image comes before object constancy. . . . But that is not the same as object constancy. Object constancy means, on top of that, to retain attachment even when the person is unsatisfactory" (1968, p. 507) .

Fraiberg (1969) too separates out the drive pressures and the states of need from the child's capacity to evoke an inner image of the libidinal object. Her distinction between "recognition" and "evocative" memory is an attempt to resolve the question of the stage in the development of the libidinal tie to the mother at which a mental representation of the mother becomes available to the child. Taking into account internal as well as external stimulation, she defines evocative memory (established at about 18 months) as "the production of a mental image that has relative autonomy from the stimuli of exteroceptive experience and the stimuli of drive and need states" (p. 45; italics omitted).

While Hoffer and Hartmann also write of object constancy in terms of cathectic processes, their points of emphasis differ from each other, as they also differ from Anna Freud's formulations.

In Hoffer's work (1952) stress is laid upon the *change* in the nature of the libidinal cathexis, from narcissistic libidinal cathexis to object cathexis. He suggests a first stage in which the external object is not differentiated from the infant's own body and in which both form part of the *milieu interne*. The relationship to the psychological object "irrespective of its physical presence or absence" is described in terms of this object being "desired," drawing "cathexis away from the body," capable of being "looked at," as well as an object which "progressively becomes separated from the exciting emotions (affects) inside, separated from the body-self experiences in the feeding and nursing situation" (p. 36f.).

In a slightly later work (1955), Hoffer's thoughts on object constancy move more in line with Hartmann's in his mention of the aggressive drives, as well as with Anna Freud's in his mention of the distancing from bodily needs. Object constancy is considered by him as:

> . . . the last and mature stage in the development of object relationships. It has a special bearing on the fate of the aggressive and hostile drives. In the state of "object constancy," the love object will not be rejected or exchanged for another if it cannot provide immediate and total satisfaction. It has ceased to be closely linked with the bodily needs, whose place in fact it has in part taken. In the state of "object constancy" the ab-

sent object is still longed for and not rejected (hated) as un-satisfactory [p. 90].

We assume that Hoffer did not mean to imply that the achievement of object constancy represented a mature relationship as such, but rather that it was a basic element in the developmental continuum toward mature object relationships.

The theory expounded by Hartman and his co-authors (1946) on the *neutralization of libidinal and aggressive energy* is seen by them to be important on two counts: first, to facilitate the shift from narcissistic to object cathexis (this is in accord with Hoffer's thinking) ; and, second, as a determinant in the formation of a permanent object relationship, which in turn depends upon the establishment of object constancy. "At the end of the first year, in the early phases of ego development, the child has formed lasting object relations; his attachment can outlast deprivation, and libidinal energy directed toward the love object has been partly transformed into aim-inhibited libidinal energy, transient into permanent cathexis" (p. 27) .

And in 1953 Hartmann said: "constant relations with the object, independent of the state of the needs, can be maintained because of a partial change of instinctual to neutralized cathexis of the object" (p. 187) .

Spitz (1965) uses the concept of fusion of libidinal and aggressive drives in his formulations about "true object relations." In fact, he nowhere seems to use the term *object constancy,* but we understand, from our perusal of his detailed observational studies on the formation of the "libidinal object," that the terms *constant object* and *libidinal object* could be synonymous in their meanings.

During the anaclitic stage (from 3 months) "the mother is the person who gratifies the infant's oral desires; she becomes the target of the infant's aggressive and libidinal drives" (p. 168) . However, she is not yet perceived as a "libidinal object." At about 6 months the representation of the "libidinal object" is capable of being formed, due to the ego's growing capacity to retain and to integrate memories, as well as its capacity to integrate percepts of objects and to divorce them from their functions; fusion of the libidinal and aggressive drives is seen as a further necessary element in the formation of the libidinal object.

After the sixth month the multiple percepts of the mother are fused due to the increasing retentiveness of the infant's memory function and his ego's integrative tendency. Underlying this achievement is an ideational process: successive memory traces of the preobject are recognized as identical with each other, independent of the situation, and the object is synthesized . . . the percept is recognized by virtue of its essential attributes. With this, the percept "mother" becomes a single one, will no longer be equated with any other person playing her role in identical situations. From now on she will focus on her person the infant's aggressive as well as his libidinal drives. The fusion of the two drives and the fusion of the good and the bad object into one, namely, into the libidinal object, are therefore the two facets of one and the same process. The "good" aspects of the mother immeasurably outweigh the "bad" aspects. And in the same way the child's libidinal drive outweighs the aggressive one, for his libidinal drive is proportionate to his need. Consequently the good object appears to predominate in this fusion, which is probably why the libidinal object was also called the love object. Now that the two drives are directed toward the one single, emotionally most strongly cathected, object we can speak of the establishment of the libidinal object *proper* and of the inception of true object relations [p. 169f.].

It becomes evident that though writing about the libidinal cathexis of the object, the specific emphasis will vary with the individual author's preferred approach: diminution of drive pressure so that the individual no longer requires *immediate* satisfaction of his needs and therefore develops the capacity to maintain a libidinal attachment to the object even when it proves unsatisfactory (Anna Freud) ; the change from narcissistic libidinal cathexis to object cathexis (Hoffer) ; the neutralization of libidinal and aggressive energy (Hartmann) ; fusion of libidinal and aggressive drives (Spitz) .

Separation Anxiety

In this area too, the emphasis depends upon the author's approach and encompasses anxiety about loss of the object and anxiety about loss of love.

Spitz (1950) describes the 8-month anxiety, seeming almost to

place together temporally perceptual differentiation of the libidinal object and the capacity for object love:

> In the third quarter [of the first year] the human object and
> also the inanimate object are recognized by virtue of their
> objectile attributes and perception has become truly objective.
> With this the period of the pre-objects has ended, and object
> libidinal relations have become possible. Trite as it may seem,
> love is not possible as long as objects are interchangeable. Be-
> tween the seventh and eighth months the libidinal object has
> become firmly established and the eighth-months anxiety is the
> sign of the infant's discrimination of its love object from all
> other humans [p. 70; italics omitted].

The distinction Kris (1950) makes between fear of loss of the
love object which has fulfilled primitive needs and fear of losing
the object's love once the object has become a personalized object
is relevant to the whole question of object constancy since both
anxieties continue to exist together during the first years of childhood. Kris writes of

> . . . the danger of losing the love object and the danger of
> losing the object's love. The first represents the anaclitic needs,
> the second the more integrated relationship to a permanent,
> personalized love object that can no longer easily be re-
> placed . . . there are not only fluctuations from one type of
> object relation to the other, older one, but the two types nor-
> mally overlap. The fear of object loss never quite disappears;
> the fear of loss of love has added a new dimension to a child's
> life and with it a new vulnerability [p. 33].

The fear of losing the love of the constant object is further
aligned by Hartmann, Kris, and Loewenstein (1949) with the
concept of neutralization of libidinal and aggressive strivings.
They say:

> When finally the constant object relationship has been estab-
> lished, and when the fear of losing the love object is replaced
> by the fear of losing love, then this conflict appears in a new
> form. The behavior of the child early in his second year of life
> toward his mother, to whom he clings tenaciously, whom he
> tortures by his demands, that appear concomitantly to rise

with his anxiety, may well be accounted for as a reflection of the battle between aggression and libido [p. 32].

Mahler (1965) understands the child's capacity to separate from the object as facilitating the separation-individuation process, and this process is seen by her as connected with the attainment of object constancy: *"The fourth subphase* of separation-individuation is the period during which an increasing degree of object constancy (in Hartmann's sense) is attained (twenty-five to thirty-six months) " (p. 167), when the child increasingly accepts and tolerates separation from the mother.

We would suggest that the behavioral manifestations denoting separation anxiety could also be understood in the following terms: that the gradual diminution and control of separation anxiety may be understood as a measure of the child's growing capacity to structure the object representation and maintain investment in it.

Affective Valuation of the Object

In the work of Sandler and Joffe (1966), object constancy is understood as reflecting id cathexis of, as well as ego needs for, a particular object. In distinguishing between drive, feeling, and "value" cathexis of the object, they suggest that "the component which differentiates constant object relationships from need-satisfying ones is a contribution of the ego, an additional affective ego value cathexis which we could describe in such terms as 'nonsensual love,' 'esteem for the object,' etc. This is not the same as the aim-inhibited instinctual components" (p. 343).

They emphasize elsewhere (1969) that this value cathexis remains related to the individual's own needs of one kind or another: "It is both theoretically and clinically important that from the point of view of psychic adaptation there is no such thing as an unselfish or altruistic love or concern [5] for an object. The ultimate

---

[5] We would add that this term *concern* is used in the psychoanalytic literature with more than one meaning; for instance, Winnicott (1954) is writing about a far more primitive feeling toward the mother when he states that, after the attainment of the depressive position, the infant moves from ruthless demandingness to "concern for the object," and particularly concern about the effects of his instinctual demands upon the mother.

criterion in determining whether or not a particular object relation is maintained or striven for is its effect on the central feeling state of the individual" (p. 89).

This point is elaborated in a paper on depression, in which Joffe and Sandler (1965) discuss the role of the object as the vehicle for the attainment of an ideal state of well-being, and conceptualize the importance of the object in terms of the maintenance of the state of well-being. They write: "the value which any object has is directly connected with its genetic and functional relation to the self. This would appear to be so even after the attainment of object constancy, when the object has developed 'uniqueness' and has become an indispensable key to states of well-being. . . . Object love, like the whole development of the ego, can be seen as a roundabout way of attempting to restore the ideal primary narcissistic state" (p. 398).

Clinical Descriptions of Object Constancy

When we examined the clinical material in the Hampstead Index, we had difficulty in finding precise clinical descriptions of object constancy, partly because of the age range of our patients, practically all of whom are well past the age at which object constancy, however it is defined, is considered to have been reached. Consequently, in most neurotic cases, it is taken for granted that object constancy has been achieved and that no statement need be made about it. The problem is touched upon in some severely disturbed neurotic patients whose demands for need satisfaction have remained unusually prominent in all relationships, even though object constancy has, according to most criteria, been attained. The fullest discussions of object constancy were to be found in cases with psychotic disturbances or organic defects. In these cases, perceptual constancy was, however, the only aspect of object constancy which could be considered unequivocally established. When we examined the child's capacity to differentiate between self and objects, it became clear that only the representations of physical body boundaries of both self and object and of the external appearance of the object had been firmly established; other, more developed, attributes of these representations, such as the self's constant affective attachment to a specific object, were far less clearly differentiated—that is, if they were described at all.

A further point to emerge from the clinical data on some of these children we studied was the unevenness of their ego development and the ego's inability both to control the drive pressures and to tolerate any frustration connected with the immediate satisfaction of needs. Thus, even with all the existing psychoanalytic definitions of object constancy to hand, we sometimes found it difficult to decide whether such children were in fact at all capable of a sustained and constant attachment to a specific object or whether the relationship was primarily based on the immediate satisfaction of their needs and on the added security offered by the perceptual unchangeability of the object. While some of these very disturbed children studied seemed to have surmounted the stage of the need-satisfying relationship, they had apparently remained at the beginnings of the establishment of object constancy, as evidenced in their capacity for perceptual differentiation and object representation. At this point in development, there comes into being the capacity for structuring a perceptual representation of the object as distinct from the self; recognition of primary objects as distinct from other objects; the recall of an object representation due to either external or internal stimuli; and, finally, the capacity to recall an object representation without such a stimulus. However, one does not in these particular children see much evidence of the capacity for a constant, affective relationship to one specific object.

Discussion

Our perusal of the relevant literature and of clinical material has shown us that the psychoanalytic conceptualizations of object constancy include several aspects of id and ego functioning. As we have seen, the term *object constancy* is a confusing one because of its links with the narrowly defined concept of perceptual constancy derived from academic psychology, whereas psychoanalysts are essentially interested in the establishment of a specific level of object relationships to animate objects and, in the first instance, to one specific and preferred object.

We suggest that a more appropriate term for this concept from the psychoanalytic viewpoint would be *the capacity for constant relationships*.

It is important to be clear about the status of this concept: it is a developmental one, insofar as the establishment of this capacity depends upon the normal development of several aspects of psychic functioning; but it is *not* a developmental phase which is reached and then superseded by a subsequent phase, as are the phases of libidinal development. The achievement of object constancy, or, as we prefer to call it, *the capacity for constant relationships*, is a crucial switch point in the development of object relationships. It requires the maturation and development of several capacities in the areas of drives, ego, and affects. These basic capacities are acquired gradually by the child over a long period of time; they enable him to move away from the purely need-satisfying type of relationship to more mature, constant types of relationship.

After this major shift in the quality of the child's relationships is achieved, it is not outgrown or left behind, but only extended, expanded, and built upon. Once the need-satisfying type of relationship has been superseded and the capacity for constant relationships has been established, all subsequent progress in object relationships may be viewed as developments of this constant type of relationship. Drive-based aspects of relationships acquire a different emphasis as the child moves through the libidinal phases; at the same time, other gradual changes occur concomitantly with ego maturation and affective development. However, if this capacity for constant relationships is not established, subsequent development in all areas—drives, ego, affects, and relationships—will be severely distorted.

This capacity may, as we have seen, be subdivided into several main elements: perceptual object constancy; the capacity to maintain drive investment in a specific object notwithstanding its presence or absence; the capacity to recognize and tolerate loving and hostile feelings toward the same object; the capacity to keep feelings centered on a specific object; and the capacity to value an object for attributes other than its function of satisfying needs.

Perceptual Object Constancy

Of the criteria mentioned in the literature as relevant to object constancy, the one most easy to determine (though by no means the most important in psychoanalytic thinking) is that of perceptual object constancy. We understand this to mean that a mental structure is established and an internal representation of the object can be maintained in the absence of the object, as well as in the absence of a primary need directed toward the object. In any conceptualization involving internal and external objects, we have to be clear as to what is understood by the terms *internal* and *external*. We assume that the individual forms *internal* representations of the self relating to the object and of the object relating to the self. Such representations evolve into increasingly complex *internal* interactions as the individual's drive pressures, ego requirements, defense structures, affects, fantasies, etc., develop. The relationship to the *external* object will, at any one time, only reflect aspects of the *internal* situation.

Perceptual object constancy is probably the factor most dependent upon maturation and least influenced by the environment, and it could be ranked with Hartmann's areas of "primary autonomy." The concept of perceptual object constancy would place due emphasis upon the subject's capacity to utilize these mental structures. The beginning of perceptual object constancy may be timed at approximately 8 months and the firm establishment of a stable perceptual structure at approximately 16 to 18 months, a timing which accords both with the work of Piaget and of psychoanalytic authors such as Spitz.

Drive Investment and Affect Relatedness

To our way of thinking, the most important aspect of drive development is the capacity of the individual to maintain a permanent investment of energy (be it libidinal or aggressive in its feeling tone) in the representation of a specific object, regardless of whether this object is present or absent.

Obviously, this specific object is initially the mother or mother substitute, and it is to this object representation that the primary libidinal relationship is made. At first this relationship is on a predominantly need-satisfying level, and it is the need-satisfying *functions* of the mothering figure which are of crucial importance to the infant. The representation of the mother which is associated with potential satisfaction of the infant's primary self-preservative and sexual needs is, essentially, the *libidinal object representation*. The beginning of the capacity to structure and invest this primary libidinal object representation coincides more or less temporally with the beginning capacity for perceptual object constancy. As the infant emerges from the *stage of the need-satisfying relationship*, opposing affects (for instance, love and hate) are very gradually experienced as directed toward this same object representation; and in the second half of the second year of life, psychic maturation is sufficiently advanced for the individual both to begin to recognize and to begin to tolerate such a conflictual feeling state toward the one object. Once these feelings can be reconciled by the individual as directed toward one and the same object representation, this representation can no longer be conceptualized as the simple *libidinal* object.

We would suggest therefore that the capacity for constant relationships denotes a progression from the constant investment of energy in the *libidinal* object and includes, over and above such energic investment, an *affective relationship to the love object*. Unlike the libidinal object which is solely the mother representation, love objects include mother and, as the child matures, father, siblings, and other valued objects in the close family environment. Subsequently, relationships are extended to objects in the wider social environment outside the family, such as friends and teachers. The assessment of the development of the capacity for constant relationships would need to include the child's developing capacity to make a gradually widening range of such relationships first within and then outside the family. This process of organization can begin as soon as the primary relationship to the mother develops beyond a purely need-satisfying one; and it involves the extension and elaboration of the earlier mode of relating to the libidinal object.

Obviously, the wider affective attachment develops out of the restricted libidinal relationship to the primary libidinal object.

But we consider it would be helpful, both clinically and theoretically, to distinguish between the *libidinal object* and the *love object*. The term *libidinal object* seems to be the more appropriate one for the primary object of the drives (thus including the need-fulfilling object), whereas the term *love object* would seem to have wider connotations and could more usefully be reserved for later stages of relationships when the object has also become the object of the ego. Both terms refer to the type of object representation available to the individual at successive stages in the development of object relationships. The representation of the libidinal object is a relatively simple one, primarily consisting of diverse images of the object satisfying various drive needs and with accompanying primitive states of pleasure or pain; whereas the representation of the love object contains, in addition, other, more organized attributes of the object, for which it becomes valued over and above its function of satisfying needs.

The growth of stable affective relationships to love objects includes the development of feelings of concern for the object and reciprocity within the relationship; such elements in relationships may make transitory appearances any time after the stage of the need-satisfying relationship, though they are probably not fully established until the adolescent reorganization of object relationships has taken place. Similarly, the valuing of the object for ego attributes (including attitudes, opinions, etc.) which accord with the subject's own follows a similar course, becoming increasingly important with ego maturation.

Summary

We have conceptualized the development of object relationships in terms of the gradual establishment of *perceptual object constancy* together with the gradual establishment of the *libidinal tie to the primary object*. These permit, in turn, the move away from the *stage of the need-satisfying relationship*, and form the foundation for the development of the *capacity for constant relationships*. Within such constant relationships drive investment in, and affect relatedness to, the object representation are of prime importance. We have further differentiated between the tie to the *primary libidinal object* and subsequent ties to *love objects*.

BIBLIOGRAPHY

DÉCARIE, T. G. (1963), *Intelligence and Affectivity in Early Childhood*. New York: International Universities Press, 1965.

FRAIBERG, S. (1969), Libidinal Object Constancy and Mental Representation. *This Annual*, 24:9–47.

FREUD, A. (1952), The Mutual Influences in the Development of Ego and Id. *This Annual*, 7:42–50.

— (1965), *Normality and Pathology in Childhool*. New York: International Universities Press.

— (1968), [Remarks in] Panel Discussion. *Int. J. Psycho-Anal.*, 49:506–507.

HARTMANN, H. (1953), Contribution to the Metapsychology of Schizophrenia. *Essays on Ego Psychology*. New York: International Universities Press, 1964, pp. 182–206.

— KRIS, E., & LOEWENSTEIN, R. M. (1946), Comments on the Formation of Psychic Structure. *This Annual*, 2:11–38.

— — — (1949), Notes on the Theory of Aggression, *This Annual*, 3/4:9–36.

HOFFER, W. (1952), The Mutual Influences in the Development of Ego and Id. *This Annual*, 7:31–41.

— (1955), *Psychoanalysis: Practical and Research Aspects*. Baltimore: Williams & Wilkins.

JOFFE, W. G. & SANDLER, J. (1965), Notes on Pain, Depression, and Individuation. *This Annual*, 20:394–424.

KRIS, E. (1950), Notes on the Development and on Some Current Problems of Psychoanalytic Child Psychology. *This Annual*, 5:24–46.

MAHLER, M. S. (1965), On the Significance of the Normal Separation-Individuation Phase. In: *Drives, Affects, Behavior*, Vol. 2, ed. M. Schur. New York: International Universities Press pp. 161–169.

PIAGET, J. (1936), *The Origins of Intelligence in Children*. New York: International Universities Press, 1952.

— (1937), *The Construction of Reality in the Child*. New York: Basic Books, 1954.

SANDLER, J. (1962), Research in Psycho-Analysis: The Hampstead Index as an Instrument of Psycho-Analytic Research. *Int. J. Psycho-Anal.*, 43:287–292.

— & JOFFE, W. G. (1966), On Skill and Sublimation. *J. Amer. Psychoanal. Assn.*, 14:335–355.

— — (1969), Towards a Basic Psychoanalytic Model. *Int. J. Psycho-Anal.*, 50:79–90.

SPITZ, R. A. (1950), Relevancy of Direct Infant Observation. *This Annual*, 5:66–73.

— (1965), *The First Year of Life*. New York: International Universities Press.

WINNICOTT, D. W. (1955), The Depressive Position in Normal Emotional Development. *Collected Papers.* New York: Basic Books, 1958, pp. 262–277.

WOLFF, P. H. (1960), *The Developmental Psychologies of Jean Piaget and Psychoanalysis* [*Psychological Issues*, Monogr. 5]. New York: International Universities Press.

Sublimation

The Study of an Instinctual Vicissitude

GEORGE E. GROSS, M.D. AND

ISAIAH A. RUBIN, M.D.

THE APPEARANCE OF SUBLIMATORY ACTIVITIES IN ANALYTIC PATIENTS is often thought to signal recovery from emotional illness. Anna O. suffered from a "hysterical psychosis," present at age 21, which was marked by paraphasia, diplopia, contractures, and paralyses of the extremities and neck, and a mood of anxiety and depression alternating with a state of altered consciousness in which she hallucinated, was paranoid, abusive, and destructive. These symptoms showed marked fluctuations during the course of the illness, which was still active at the age of 28, 5 years after the termination of her treatment by Professor Breuer in 1882. Within the succeeding 3 years a marked change in her must have taken place because at that time, in 1890, a book of fairy tales written by her was published.

Presented at the New York Psychoanalytic Society on February 29, 1972.

(334)

These stories, while written in the sentimental style of the period, were organized and exhibited the interest which occupied her for the rest of her life and which she pursued with remarkable intensity and dedication. She became a feminist leader, founding and heading a number of women's organizations. Her literary activities expanded, including both original works and translations. The consistent theme running through her social and political work and her writing was the rescue of women from their exploitation by men and society. The hysterical patient had become a pioneering professional woman and social activist whose intense productivity was broken only by her death at 77. Throughout her career she remained essentially free of symptoms (Karpe, 1961).

Sublimation appears to have replaced symptom. A dependent, inverse relationship seems to exist between sublimation on the one hand and symptom formation on the other. Conflict resolution has been brought about by means of a special vicissitude of the drives.

In contrast to Anna O., Little Hans does not exhibit this inverse relationship. In him, symptom, defense, and sublimation appear at the same time. Freud (1909) says:

> We have seen how our little patient was overtaken by a great wave of repression and that it caught precisely those of his sexual components that were dominant. He gave up masturbation, and turned away in disgust from everything that reminded him of excrement and of looking on at other people performing their natural functions. [He continues in a footnote:] Hans's father even observed that *simultaneously* with this repression a certain amount of sublimation set in. From the time of the beginning of his anxiety Hans began to show an increased interest in music and to develop his inherited musical gift [p. 138; our italics].

In the "little patient," the first appearance of anxiety is accompanied by two other changes in his behavior: the avoidance of certain previously pleasurable activities, and the emergence of a new interest. Three independent vicissitudes of drive activity can be inferred: sublimation, defense, and symptom formation. The relationship between these three psychic events is here a parallel one.

The two cases cited illustrate some of the many difficulties that arise when the explanation of sublimation is limited to its function as a drive vicissitude which solves conflict. For example, this explanation does not account for the configuration which appears in Little Hans—sublimation simultaneous with symptom and defense. To clarify the concept of sublimation this paper will deal with its genesis and function; its quality; its economic role; its relation to conflict, defense, and symptom; its relations to ego function as opposed to ego aim; its position regarding reality, interests, and pleasure; and the matter of "higher values"—a notion which appears at first glance to lie outside the purview of psychoanalysis.

Psychoanalytic assumptions are ordinarily viewed according to their level of abstraction. The level of observation refers to the communications of the patient plus the configurations in which they occur. The level of clinical theory utilizes those theoretical ideas which explain the relationships between the data of observation. Metapsychology utilizes more abstract conceptions, which, it is hoped, are capable of explaining, constructing, or revealing connections between the concepts of clinical theory.

It was on the level of metapsychology that Hartmann (1955) formulated the problem as follows: "Despite the broad and general use made by analysts of the concept of sublimation and despite many attempts to free it from ambiguities, there is no doubt that a certain amount of discontent with some of its facets is rather common among us" (p. 216). Hartmann deals with this problem almost entirely from the point of view of neutralization, stating in summary: "the most important single factor among several that at one time or another entered its definition is the process of deinstinctualization (neutralization)" (p. 239). He examined sublimation with regard to its origin, ontogenesis, and relation to the substructures of personality; its position in regard to ego functions as opposed to ego aims; its contrasting position with reference to defensive as opposed to nondefensive ego functions; its variations in regard to its differing functions; its connections with secondary ego autonomy; and its variation within and among individuals. In effect, then, Hartmann limited himself very much to metapsychology, devoting his paper to a detailed analysis of modes of energy deriving from both libidinal and aggressive drives. His proposition defining sublimation in terms of modes of energy and degrees of their neutralization, however, does not illuminate the clinical situation.

Freud's first published use of the term sublimation appears in the *Three Essays* (1905a) :

> Visual impressions remain the most frequent pathway along which libidinal excitation is aroused; indeed, natural selection counts upon the accessibility of this pathway—if such a teleological form of statement is permissible—when it encourages the development of beauty in the sexual object. The progressive concealment of the body which goes along with civilization keeps sexual curiosity awake. This curiosity seeks to complete the sexual object by revealing its hidden parts. It can, however, be diverted ('sublimated') in the direction of art, if its interest can be shifted away from the genitals on to the shape of the body as a whole [p. 156].
>
> What is it that goes to the making of these constructions [opposing mental forces] which are so important for the growth of a civilized and normal individual? They probably emerge at the cost of the infantile sexual impulses themselves. Thus the activity of those impulses does not cease even during this period of latency, though their energy is diverted, wholly or in great part, from their sexual use and directed to other ends. Historians of civilization seem to be at one in assuming that powerful components are acquired for every kind of cultural achievement by this diversion of sexual instinctual forces from sexual aims and their direction to new ones—a process which deserves the name of 'sublimation' [p. 178].

Although Freud uses the term freely in later papers (see especially 1914, 1915) , he does not deviate from the essential meaning he gave the term in the above quotations. While many authors have criticized his formulation and pointed up its various deficiencies when it is applied to clinical material, there seemed to be no successful revision of this definition of 1905. Hartmann (1955) puts the commonly accepted definition succinctly when he refers to sublimation as "a deflection of the sexual drives from instinctual aims to aims which are socially or culturally more acceptable or valued" (p. 216f.) . Although this definition is set on the level of clinical theory, it is afflicted with the narrowness of perspective which is the mark of its early origin. It would seem useful to develop the notion of sublimation to the point where it fulfills its initial promise as a vital concept in generating propositions that will enrich the body of psychoanalytic theory.

I

Deflection of instinctual aim is more widespread and appears much earlier in the child's development than is common supposed: a hungry infant shows signs of mounting drive tension—restless movements of arms and legs, a distressed facial expression, and an increasing crescendo of crying sounds. Before the mother can produce the infant's bottle, the observing stranger fixes the infant with his eyes and begins moving his extended arm in a wide vertical arc. The infant is distracted. As he begins to stare at the moving arm, his body relaxes and his crying ceases. We would advance the hypothesis that this change in behavior can be explained by the deflection of the drive from direct discharge into an auxiliary mode, one which in the course of development will come to be recognized as sublimation. Observing the two contrasting behaviors, we infer that they are manifestations of different drive qualities. This provides a basis for excluding the explanation that aim displacement, in contradistinction to drive deflection, has taken place. (We take aim displacement to refer to the shift of cathexis from one mental representation to another or from one instinctual mode to another.) If aim displacement were involved, we would not expect to observe a change in the infant's behavior. For in aim displacement—which exemplifies the primary process—the underlying drive quality would essentially be preserved: its urgency, immediacy, mobility, and pressure; and the infant's behavior would remain as before. It is precisely the dramatic alteration in the infant's state which so strongly suggests the hypothesis of a change in drive quality.

There are alternative possibilities of interpreting the change in the infant's behavior. An explanation could be formulated in terms of the two stimuli—hunger and external distraction—competing for attention cathexis, with the change of behavior resulting directly from one stimulus winning out over the other. In this formulation it would not be necessary to posit a change in drive quality. In our view, however, this is not a tenable position because it implies that the infant, with his primitive psychic apparatus and weak and rudimentary ego, is able to tolerate a state of unrelieved and mounting drive tension simply on the basis of shifts in atten-

⁺ion. Such a notion burdens the concept of attention cathexis with functions that go far beyond its role in accounting for the infant's interest in the external stimulus.

The quantitative dynamics of the discharge process in aim deflection deserve special attention. The cathexes bound to specific visual images and actions gain increasing stability, thereby making delay and consequent detour inevitable. In this way, when discharge occurs, it has been modified: while it accomplishes tension reduction in the organism, it no longer possesses the qualities of direct instinctual gratification. The transformation in the mode of gratification corresponds to a significant change in the pleasure conditions available to the organism. Direct instinctual discharge is no longer the organism's sole meaning of obtaining pleasure. Detour activities provide an alternate route; and an external distraction, which initially had an accidental component, becomes in the course of development internalized. The mental apparatus thereby obtains an increasing and varied assortment of pathways along which conditions of pleasure can be fulfilled. The infant is now able to manipulate images in his attempts to retrieve the pleasure associated with the original situation of distraction, and these images will at a later time become the material of play and fantasy. Because of the vastly increased range and sophistication of trial action available to the mental apparatus, the opportunities for sublimation are enhanced and its presence will be far easier to recognize.

The development of aim deflection and its corresponding detour activity cannot be studied in isolation. Ego development is an integral part of it. "Were it not for the intervention of the ego or of those external forces which the ego represents, every instinct would know only one fate—that of gratification" (A. Freud, 1936, p. 44). At birth there exist the precursors of those ego functions that are necessary for aim deflection. Hartmann (1956) says: "the postponement or control of discharge is one of the essential features of the human ego from its beginnings; it is probably an essential feature already of its forerunners. . . . I think, a necessary assumption [is] that the child is born with a certain degree of preadaptiveness" (p. 245f.). From the beginnings of its differentiation a major task of the ego is to accomplish the independence of the mental apparatus from drive pressure. This is achieved in different ways. The postponement of discharge and the toleration of mounting drive tension (unpleasure) directly manifest this ego activity. Subsequently the ego acquires the capacity to anticipate, allowing the consideration of future pleasure to play a role in the toleration of unpleasure. The capacity to anticipate must be accompanied by some degree of objectivation, that is, the conviction of the availability of specific external conditions that will permit identity of perception and thought to take place in a predictable fashion. The apparatuses of perception, memory, and motility (present at birth) have matured and developed to the point where trial action can be carried out and decisions made about the most pleasurable course of action. In its totality, this ensemble of functions—anticipation, objectivation, perception, thought, and the control of motility—provides the means for consistent and effective delay and control over drive pressure. They are detour activities. "In both [action and thought] is implied an element of inhibition, of delay of discharge. In this sense many aspects of the ego can be described as detour activities; they promote a more specific and safer form of adjustment by introducing a factor of growing independence from the immediate impact of present stimuli" (Hartmann, 1950, p. 115).

The developing ego makes a special contribution to the conditions for gratification of the aim-deflected drive. When the infant's need to suck is temporarily replaced by his staring at the moving arm with its attendant pleasure, a change in pleasure conditions can be said to have occurred. The activities of those functions (detour activities) by means of which the most pleasurable course of action was chosen become themselves a source of pleasure. The organized perception, thought, and action through which the aim deflection is accomplished participate in the pleasure which is the goal of the delayed or inhibited activity.

II

These considerations lead to the unsettled question of the genesis of the gratification experienced in such ego activity. The pleasure potentials offered by the ego fall into three overlapping categories: (1) direct gratification; (2) indirect gratification; and (3) "pleasure in functioning."

1. Direct gratification occurs when ego aims and drive aims are in harmony. The aim of the drives is to obtain satisfaction, to reduce tension. The aim of the ego refers to the goals of its actions. The ego anticipates its goals and organizes its activities (means/ends) accordingly. In direct drive gratification, then, ego function is placed in the service of unmodified drive discharge. Excluding other factors, the degree of collaboration between the two mental tendencies determines the organism's ensuing pleasure. A familiar instance of this collaboration occurs in sexual rape. In more usual circumstances, considerations of reality, inner and outer, exert a sufficient hold on the ego enabling it to enforce some degree of energic damming up in the course of the drive's unrelenting search for discharge. As a result the ego is less restricted in its pursuit of the drive's aims. The detouring of sexual impulses in seduction, as opposed to rape, can be laid to such considerations.[1]

2. Indirect gratification or sublimation (aim deflection) involves some modification of instinctual activity. Developmentally this must take place in accordance with the aims of the ego. Insofar as there has been a deflection, an alteration in drive quality, the pleasure premium is yielded by the ego activity through which the ego realizes its aims. The activities of gratification no longer have an instinctual quality. Hartmann (1947) touches on a number of these points:

> Now, the functions of the [partly autonomous] ego area . . . , including those underlying controlled and directed action, often have the character of inhibiting the immediate gratification of the instinctual drives; postponement or displacement

---

[1] È tutto amore.
Chi a una sola è fedele,
verso l'altre è crudele.
Io, che in me sento
si esteso sentimento,
vo' bene a tutte quante.
Le donne poi, che calcolar non sanno,
il mio buon natural chiamano inganno.

[It's all for love!
To be faithful to one
is to be faithless to the others.
I have so generous a heart
that I love every single one of them;
but women, who have no head for figures,
call my good nature deception.]

—*Don Giovanni* by Lorenzo Da Ponte
Act II, Scene 1

of gratification is frequently the consequence of their activity. On the other hand, the development of new ego functions, like, for instance, that of acting in the outer world, may open up new avenues for direct and indirect (sublimated) gratifications of instinctual tendencies [p. 40].

Ibsen's heroine Hedda Gabler illustrates the difficulty of distinguishing between aims of the ego and instinctual aims. She is a person preoccupied with beauty. She stresses aesthetic values in connection with her home, her marriage, the people she knows, her life style, and even in the death of Eilert Løvborg, who loves her.

> HEDDA. [prodding Eilert to shoot himself] (*coming a step closer*). Eilert Løvborg—listen to me. Couldn't you arrange that—that it's done beautifully?
> LØVBERG. Beautifully? (*smiles*). With vine-leaves in my hair, as you used to dream in the old days—
> HEDDA. No. I don't believe in vine-leaves anymore. But beautifully, all the same. For this once. . . .

Ibsen's protagonist appears to be expressing only ego aims in her preoccupation with beauty. Here, despite her overriding concern with suicide, aim deflection seems to predominate in Hedda's scrupulous insistence on its form. But listen to her after receiving word of Eilert's in fact sordid death:

> HEDDA (*in a low voice*). Oh what a sense of freedom it gives one, this act of Eilert Løvborg's.
> BRACK. Freedom, Mrs. Hedda? Well, of course, it is a release for him —
> HEDDA. I mean for me. It gives me a sense of freedom. . . .

Here we witness the emergence of drive quality. The release from drive tension has given Hedda her sense of freedom. What had appeared to be an ego aim was the mere expression of an ego interest and did not have sufficient claim on the drive to deflect it from its ordained course. Her ultimate suicide was the expression of its primacy.

Counterpoised to Hedda's instinct-driven behavior is that of Eilert Løvborg. Upon being congratulated for the praise lavished on his recent book, he disclaims its value and asserts that his only aim had been a pandering to popular taste. He then speaks of its successor:

> LØVBORG. But when this comes out—George Tesman—you'll have to read it. Because this is the real book—the one that speaks for my true self.

Løvborg subsequently describes his visionary work, and his manifest satisfaction with it, thereby providing additional testimony to the presence of a sublimation.

3. The third source of gratification, implicit in ego functioning, refers to the "pleasure inherent in activity whatever its goals and consequences" (pleasure in functioning) (Hartmann, 1939, p. 97). This is best understood when it is not limited to a narrow context of recently learned, or difficult to master, motor activities, but is instead seen in terms of Freud's (1905b) conception of pleasure in mental functioning: "If we do not require our mental apparatus at the moment for supplying one of our indispensable satisfactions, we allow it itself to work in the direction of pleasure and we seek to derive pleasure from its own activity" (p. 95f.). In a general sense, then, all psychic activity can yield pleasure. In this context Hartmann (1956) alludes to the pleasure in the activity of specific ego functions; e.g., "Organized thought or action, in which postponement is of the essence, can become a source of pleasure"; or: "the activities of the functions that constitute the reality principle can be pleasurable in themselves" (p. 244).

This last source of pleasure (pleasure in functioning) has the special importance of being ubiquitous. Thus, the pleasure yielded in drive discharge, whether direct or indirect, must to some degree draw on the pleasure in functioning afforded by the ego activity serving it.

III

Neutralization, referring to a change in the quality of drive energy—away from the instinctual and toward the noninstinctual—finds a particularly apt application in the attempt to understand the operation of ego functions, which, as is so frequently true in analysis, is best studied in cases in which there is an interference in functioning. Discussing the inhibitions of writing and walking, Freud (1926) explains that in these instances the activities have assumed an unconscious significance. Writing has become a symbolic substitute for copulation; walking for treading on the maternal corpus. These functions have taken on unconscious erotic meanings. On the level of clinical theory, Freud characterizes what has happened as an erotization of the apparatus. Fingers and legs have become too strongly sexualized. When the explanation is raised to the level of metapsychology, deneutralization is said to have occurred. The introduction of energy concepts pictures the process in a more succinct and elegant way. Sexualization of an activity then becomes a special instance of energy distribution. When the ego functions subserving an activity are sufficiently free of drive quality so that no conflict arises—when they are autonomous —the energy driving this activity is thought of as deinstinctualized or neutralized. When the functions take on an unconscious instinctual meaning, they have become instinctualized or deneutralized.

The elegance of the energy notion lies in its scope. All psychic processes can be understood in energic terms since ultimately they represent quantitative or qualitative energy changes. In particular, Hartmann used the energy concept to describe some aspects of the genesis and development of ego functions:

> Neutralization of energy is clearly to be postulated from the time at which the ego evolves as a more or less demarcated substructure of personality . . . it is not unlikely that the use of this form of energy starts much earlier and that already the primordial forms of postponement and inhibition of discharge are fed by energy that is partly neutralized [1952, p. 171].
> . . . we have to assume that neutralization starts very early. . . . It must start even before the ego as a definitive system is established and before constant objects are constituted—because it is likely that these achievements already presuppose some degree of neutralization [1955, p 238].

In Hartmann's view, the processing of instinctual energy into a continuum of neutralized energies is at the center of the functional development and structure of the ego. In this process the ego itself has a reciprocating role. As part of its neutralizing function the ego accumulates and maintains a reservoir of deinstinctualized energy, which is then available to the ego upon demand, thereby freeing it from the burden of impromptu acts of neutralization. As this reservoir serves impartially any and all of the ego's aims and functions, it can also meet the requirements for aim-deflected or sublimated energy. The ego nevertheless remains capable of meeting a particular energic requirement with specific (*ad hoc*) acts of neutralization.

In this framework, ego functions, whether serving the aims of the ego or being utilized in activities which carry out the aims of a sublimated drive, draw without distinction on the reservoir of neutralized energy. Whether a sublimation has occurred can be distinguished only in the case where the ego, requiring further support for an activity, must draw upon the id. For in those instances the appeal will be made to the id precursors of the ego activity in question—*a process which properly can be termed sublimation,* in contrast to the use of neutralized energy, the original source of which is indifferent. *It is apparent that the mode of energy used (degree of neutralization) does not specify whether an action is implementing an ego function or is expressing an aim, nor does it distinguish between the different types of aim (ego's own aim or drive aim, direct or indirect)*. To accomplish this, some specifying statement about the aim of the action is needed. Even the difficult notion that changes in aim and degrees of neutralization do not always coincide (see Hartmann, 1952, 1955) is of no assistance. The difficulty arises because of a global view of the position of neutralization. On the one hand, neutralization is closely tied to an energic view of ego functioning; on the other, it is associated with a view of sublimation which sets the process apart from specific contents and their origin, specific goals, interests in a particular material and so on. Hartmann, following Freud, defines sublimation as a change in mode of energy away from the instinctual and toward the noninstinctual. Yet, his equation of sublimation and neutralization has the difficulty of eliminating a specification of aim, an idea intrinsic to the concept of sublimation.

IV

Berta Bornstein (1935) tells of a little girl, 28 months old, whose phobic neurosis was based on the conflict between the "urge to soil herself and the fear of losing her mother's love." Her fear arose from "her early and strict training in cleanliness" which was the setting of an "early repression of the pleasure in soiling with feces." During the treatment the little girl was supplied with plasticine in an effort to encourage her to express a repressed wish to play with her feces. Surprisingly, she refused to do this, holding it to her nose and complaining that "bah smells." Bornstein explains that the patient was unable to differentiate between plasticine and feces. The plasticine must have been cathected by an anal drive which had not been deflected from its original aim. More usually, play with plasticine is welcomed by children in the anal phase. The child who is being educated away from direct drive gratification looks for a suitable substitute.

On the one hand, direct gratification with the anal object becomes associated with unpleasure as a result of both education and the "opposing mental forces" (Freud, 1905a, p. 178). On the other hand, plasticine, while a material readily adaptable to anal modes, is dissociated from anal sensations and feelings and can therefore be used in solving a conflict with opposing forces. This solution requires the relinquishment of direct drive discharge and the replacement of the anal product with an object that has its origin in the external world. When this takes place, aim deflection has occurred. This aim deflection has been underwritten by suitable impressions from the external world; at the same time, and in accordance with one of its primary functions, it organizes the representation of the external world into modalities that have a more secure and stable anchor in reality. Significantly, the external world is an essential part of this process. It must offer impressions suitable for the discharge of the aim-deflected drive. These impressions, organized by the drive activity, become one (more or less) stable aspect of reality. In this way sublimated drive activity (sublimation) comes to constitute an essential factor in the construction of reality.

Bornstein explains her patient's failure to sublimate by citing the early and strict suppression of pleasure in anal drive gratification. It is evident that the interference with these experiences of pleasure made it impossible for aim deflection to occur. The role of pleasure leads to certain important considerations which will be taken up later. Because of the premature repression of pleasure, the anal drive cathexis remained fixated on anal objects. Consequently, the child could not distinguish between plasticine and feces. As a result, not only was aim deflection delayed, but there was a parallel delay in the construction of reality and therefore of reality testing.

The consequences of the premature suppression of drive gratification in this case exemplify an important vicissitude of the drives. When a drive cannot be gratified in sublimation, defense and symptom make their inevitable appearance. Sublimation and defense/symptom are the two possible outcomes of opposition to the drives. In the case of sublimation the conflict is solved by aim deflection, which permits drive discharge. In Bornstein's case, had aim deflection been possible, the conflict over anal drives would have been solved because they could then have been gratified (discharged). Successful substitution of plasticine for feces would have constituted a conflict solution by sublimation.

The consideration of sublimation in the context of conflict solution is a fundamental one since aim deflection can occur only as a result of opposing forces (an essential proposition that cannot be derived from energic considerations alone). When this process is successful, the ensuing reduction in drive tension alters the equation of conflict. On the one hand, there is ongoing drive discharge; on the other, the aim of that drive is no longer offensive to the ego. Since sublimations provide the ego with a broad range of aims and activities which can be utilized in the service of its many interests and goals, they enormously enrich the ego. In the case of defense/ symptom the drive aim is unaltered and conflict solution can be attempted only by defensive measures. When these measures are successful, drive tension remains high; but, in contrast to sublimation, drive discharge continues to be opposed. Probably in the successful case, but certainly when defense measures fail, the effects on the ego will be restriction and impoverishment. Symptom formation will follow, allowing some (partial) gratification in drive discharge, and an enlarged defensive struggle will ensue. "A symptom is a sign of, and a substitute for, an instinctual satisfaction which has remained in abeyance" (Freud, 1926, p. 91).

The contrast between sublimation and defense/symptom makes it clear that sublimation cannot be thought of as a defense mechanism in the narrow sense. In the broader sense, however, since sublimation results in some independence from instinctual demands, it has a defensive function. On the side of the ego, then, sublimation is a process serving defense. (On the side of the drives, sublimation is a process serving gratification.)

V

In view of the fact that sublimation refers to a process of energy discharge, it occupies a central position in the psychic economy. The consequences of its success and failure are vividly illustrated in the life history of Yukio Mishima. Mishima, Japan's leading author and a renaissance man of undisputed genius, committed *seppuku* at the age of 45 on the day he completed his masterpiece, a tetralogy entitled *The Sea of Fertility*. An examination of his manifold artistic achievements permits a glimpse at the nature of the underlying drive impulses, the conflicts, and his sublimatory solutions.

This is revealed in his first important work, an autobiographical novel, *Confession of a Mask,* in which, according to Keene (1971), "he was attempting, as he later testified, to subdue the 'monsters in my heart.' . . . Mishima describes a young man who is not only incapable of sexual relations with a prostitute . . . but even of feeling desire for the girl he supposedly loves. He is drawn instead to an older classmate of unintellectual disposition and, at the end of the book, his sexual desire is aroused by a sweating workman he sees in a cafe." The pictures that had fascinated the autobiographical hero as a child helped to explain both his attraction to "coarse but superbly muscled men" and his "compulsion to wound and kill the objects of his desire": "Youthful European knights killed in battle, Samurai committing *seppuku* and, above all, St. Sebastian dying in the pride of his youthful beauty. St. Sebastian became an obsessive theme in Mishima's writings, from his schoolboy composition inspired by the Guido Reni painting that had brought on his first ejaculation to his later descriptions of the young god whose blood must be shed." Derivatives of the aggressive and libidinal components of his homosexuality can be found in the themes of all of Mishima's major writings (see Keene) as well as in his film acting, costume designing, preoccupation with physical culture and the martial arts (boxing and *Kendo*), and his organization of a small private army.

From all indications Mishima's sublimations were capable of successfully warding off the disruption of his psychic equilibrium; they enabled him to stabilize his homosexual defense against aggression. His writing was prolific and uninterrupted by fluctuations of mood or pathological mental processes. He was intolerant of depression and self-pity, stating, "A writer must be cheerful and proud of his profession." His writing was of such high quality that he had been considered a Nobel Prize candidate. Apart from his work, Keene describes Mishima as "happily married with two children . . . full of vitality and love of life . . . [a] marvelous man" and "incomparable friend." The success of Mishima's sublimations in solving conflicts is obvious. They even had the power to delay his suicide until the very day his tetralogy was completed. A few months earlier he had said that "once he had finished his new novel, into which he had poured all of his skill and experience, he would have nothing left to do but kill himself." That he did so represents the ultimate failure of his sublimations, which although intact could not prevent the fateful aggressive drive eruption.

Keene's view of Mishima testifies to the artist's dependence on sublimatory activities: "He died at his peak . . . he could only anticipate a diminution in the future: the steady weakening of his physical strength, the loss of interest in honors that once meant so much." The inference can be drawn that aging would erode the sublimatory achievement of his physical strength and mastery, his virility, and thus shift the balance of forces to the side of direct discharge of the drives. That Mishima anticipated this is revealed by the ubiquitous focus in his writings on heroes who die young but happy in a selfless cause.

Mishima's life demonstrates the important function that sublimation has as a regulator of intrapsychic equilibrium. Sublimation also plays a major part in maintaining a person's equilibrium with the external world. As Hartmann (1950) has pointed out, "for the acceptance of reality . . . the pleasure possibilities offered by the developing ego functions are essential" (p. 119). The acceptance of reality (and, in accordance with the development of the ego), knowledge of reality, insight into reality, and the ultimate attachment to reality have one essential root in the stable and predictable possibilities for pleasure that reality offers. The pleasure gained in sublimatory activities represents a considerable portion of those pleasure possibilities for the sake of which relations with reality were initiated and maintained. Genetically speaking, aim-deflected drives turn to the outer world in search of gratification and discharge, cathecting actions and trial actions until the pleasure situation is found. At first, the infant cannot clearly distinguish between the gratifying external situation and the activities through which it is perceived. In the course of growing objectivation, the child makes the crucial distinction between self and object, an essential element in the construction of reality. Aim deflection, through its increasing range of detour action, contributes to this differentiation. The pleasure-yielding images which are the goal of the aim-deflected strivings coalesce as they are organized by secondary process activities, building up stable internal representations of the external world. The most important of these is the constant object, to the formation of which aim-deflected strivings make an essential contribution. (Freud spoke of "tender" or "aim-deflected" strivings toward an object as a sublimatory process.) Offering increasingly reliable and predictable pleasures to the aim-deflected drives, the constant object will be especially sought out by discharge activity. As this takes place the gratifications which the object provides will result in the building up of those increasingly significant and stable representations which insure its constancy.

The establishment of reliable object relations not only is essential for the construction of reality but is also a necessary condition for the development of relations with the general object world. Aim-deflected drive activity (sublimatory) participates in the construction of the external world. It contributes to the building up of the constant object, and thus to the development of relations with the other objects. It can be said to play a major role in forming the attachment to reality.

VI

That sublimatory activity also plays an important and at times crucial role in the maintenance of relations with reality is illuminated in certain pathological states where the sublimation survives as the only bridge to reality and as the sole representative of the object world.

The life of Edvard Munch (1863–1944) reveals an intense and persistent struggle to maintain relations with the object world. He had a long and productive career unaltered by a psychotic break at the age of 46. His paintings during the years preceding the break were marked by the steady encroachment of the psychotic process and reflect his absorption with the malignant threat to his object relations. His fear of being engulfed and destroyed by the surrounding world was depicted in the themes and in the style of his paintings. Powerful urges to introject the object visually and to destroy it made it necessary for him to "freeze," so to speak, his first impression of an object by painting it. After the break, in contrast to his former active life, he became a recluse. His rare visitors were asked to say little and to look at the floor while he spoke. His painting continued at a prodigious pace, though somewhat altered in style and no longer reflecting his previous anguish at the threat of impending fusion. In addition, a dramatic change took place in Munch's relationship to his products. His paintings now were treated as objects. He marshaled them like sentries against the outside world, stacking them upright on the grounds surrounding his house and claiming that their exposure to every sort of weather was a "horse-doctor's cure" which would do them good. He was bored and restless when separated from them and could paint only in their presence. Despite the fact that his paintings were in great demand, he could hardly bear to part with one. He spoke of them as his children and on occasion would whip one, claiming the "horse treatment" would improve its character.

Munch's psychotic break resulted in a marked restructuring of his object world. Object relations appear to have been relinquished and his paintings to have taken on a new significance. From his treatment of them it is clear that after his break they constituted his object world. The graphic projections of his internal world replaced the external animate world, thereby permitting him to maintain diminished relations to external objects. By being fixed on canvas, objects were restituted and given stability. The paintings were even utilized as surrogates for attempted rapprochement with the world of external objects. Referring to a painting he had been persuaded to sell, Munch said to his biographer Stenersen, "Go in and fetch your lover. She has been strutting with pride all day because you like her" (Steinberg and Weiss, 1954, p. 421). Munch's approach to external objects was so tentative that after having been visited by a stranger whom Stenersen had brought, Munch said, "You should not have brought him here. Don't you know that I'll have to take him into my mind and then I'll have to paint him."

The unique relationship that Munch had to his reconstructed and externalized world provided him with a concrete and reliable world of objects and enabled him to achieve the tranquillity which characterized his postpsychotic life. The act of painting itself constituted his bridge to reality in the broader sense. It was a realistic activity performed with a broad consideration of the object world, its nature, demands, and requirements. He traveled to foreign countries, executed a number of commissions, and his style and skill were such that he was generally regarded as a master painter. The power of the sublimation is demonstrated by its capacity to maintain an attachment to reality despite the cathectic withdrawal of the psychotic process. In his 70s he told his physician: "The last part of my life has been an effort to stand up. My path has always been along an abyss" (Deknatel, 1950).

In view of the role that sublimatory activity plays in the maintenance and restitution of reality and the object world, one would anticipate that it will be sought out at times of threatened or actual psychic disorganization. The availability of such sublimations is determined by a multitude of factors which cannot be discussed here. Nevertheless, this hypothesis would seem to be supported by the common observation of frenzied (sublimatory) hyperactivity heralding (and at times continuing through) a disorganizing psychotic episode. The breakdown in sublimatory activity observed in certain psychotic patients is, in our view, related to a regressive interference with the sublimatory process itself (instinctualization of apparatus or aim) at the very time when it is most needed, its failure further facilitating the regressive movement.

Van Gogh shows in the increasing tempo of his creativity the way in which sublimation is called upon to maintain relations with reality. At the age of 30 he wrote his brother Theo, "My plan is not to spare myself; it is relatively indifferent to me whether I live longer or shorter" (Stone, 1946). His only concern in the last 8 years of his life was to create as he became increasingly haunted by the fear of his mental illness and a conviction of his impending death. Although hospitalizations became increasingly frequent, they "did not stem the creative flood, for his output increased enormously" (Hammacher, 1968), reaching its peak at Auvers in the last 2 months of his life.

Although Van Gogh, like Munch, sought to use his painting to preserve a relationship with the real world, in his case sublimation did not suffice to bridge over the break with reality. The act of painting did not seem to have sufficient meaning or value for him to make up for the threatened loss of his object relations: "Why am I so little an artist that I always regret that the statue and the picture are not alive? . . . People matter more than things, and the more trouble I take over pictures, the more pictures in themselves leave me cold" (Stone, 1946).

VII

The intrinsic connection that sublimation has with reality is the basis for its historic association with value and value judgment. Freud, characterizing the "higher aims" of sublimated activity, asserted that aim deflection had a particular cultural value. This has proved to be a difficult notion for psychoanalysts as it seemed to involve them with objective and socially determined criteria in the evaluation of an intrapsychic vicissitude of instinctual life. Thus, as a criterion of sublimation, "higher aim" has met with criticism from a number of authors, among them Glover (1931), Levey (1939), Brierley (1947), Jones (1941), and, implicitly, Hartmann. The soundness of Freud's notion can, however, be seen immediately when the ontogenesis of values is considered.

At the beginning of life, the infant has his first experience of "value" when he becomes aware of the lowering of instinctual tension in direct drive discharge. The pleasure of relief of tension is "good," the unpleasure of mounting tension is "bad" (purified pleasure ego). Thus, the primordial root of value lies in the polarization of pleasure and pain. Aim deflection brings about an alteration in drive quality and a consequent modification in discharge away from the directly instinctual. The change in mode is experienced as a kind of pleasure qualitatively different from that of direct gratification. Value becomes attached to the external pleasure situation, its internal representatives, and the detour activities through which the (aim-deflected) gratification is reached. Hartmann (1960) states, "every human being start[s] by attributing goodness, in a still undifferentiated way, to objects and actions in the measure they provide satisfaction" (p. 47f.). In terms of structural differentiation, value can be seen eventually to adhere to the aims of each of the mental systems.

Values arise in the course of the internalization of the pleasure situation. The quality of value becomes attached to the object representations and actions which bring about gratification at the same time as the objects in the external world take on that value. In this way, via pleasure, the values of the external world reflect the values of the inner world, what Jacobson (1964) refers to as "the values of eternal pleasure and gratification, of property and of physical or mental power and strength" (p. 109). (It is evident that the inner world must reflect the values of the outer world.) Although at first inner and outer values may be related in a one-to-one way, with maturation and development (e.g., structuralization), the relationship becomes increasingly complex. Of course, identification often plays a significant role in selecting the actions and trial actions of aim-deflected activity and in internalizing particular objects. However, in our view, identification along with other mental mechanisms which mediate the relationship between the inner and outer worlds must be thought of as subordinate to the process of internalizing values. The troublesome notion of value judgment, the objective social criterion, has taken on the dimension of value judgment, a regulator of drive discharge.

One of Lewin's (1939) patients, described in another connection, can be used to illustrate the formation of a sublimation under the supervision, so to speak, of "higher aims."

> The patient, a woman in her middle thirties, the only child of a Western ranch owner, spent her early childhood playing with the children of her father's labourers, learning a great many things about sexuality, adult and infantile. She was early aware of her father's anatomical make-up and was able to draw inferences as to coitus from certain impressions acquired on the sleeping porch she shared with her parents. For the first six years of her life her investigations into sex were unhampered and her conclusions on the whole correct. In this investigation she was naïve, natural, and unconcerned. One fact came to be shut off from her, and that through a traumatic event, the structure of her genitalia. Her *natural bent for research* suggested to her that she should find out for herself what her vulva was like and to that end she inserted a finger between her labia. At this point her father walked in on her and told her sternly that she must never 'do that' again. It is literally true that she obeyed him for over thirty years. She turned her curiosity into a field *approved of by her parents;* they had told her about the sex life of flowers and birds in the conventional way, and she seriously followed this cue, becoming unusually well informed as to wild life. She began botanical and zoological collections and took great pleasure in tramping through the woods [p. 26f.; our italics].

In this case a sublimation seems to have been instigated by the internalization of an external value—parental approval of the development of botanical and zoological interests. Nevertheless, this was possible only because the patient was able to gain pleasure from aim-inhibited discharge. Originally it was opposition to her sexual curiosity (in this case from external sources) that interfered with the pleasure of direct drive discharge. To insure discharge, aim deflection took place, the patient resorting to activities which were considerably removed from the directly instinctual. The gratification thus achieved held an inner value, the pleasure from indirect discharge of her sexual curiosity—represented in "her natural bent for research." Values from internal as well as external sources were thus present in the sublimation. The external value (parental approval) followed and combined with an inner pre-moral value (pleasure in research), the primacy of which constituted the essential precondition of the sublimation.

VIII

It may be well to remember that Freud (1915) lists sublimation and defense as the two possible vicissitudes which an instinct can undergo in the process of development and in the course of life. In *Inhibitions, Symptoms and Anxiety* (1926) he deals with the latter:

> In thus degrading a process of satisfaction [instinctual discharge] to a symptom, repression displays its power in a further respect. The substitutive process is prevented, if possible, from finding discharge through motility; and even if this cannot be done, the process is forced to expend itself in making alterations in the subject's own body and is not permitted to impinge upon the external world. It must not be transformed into action. For, as we know, in repression the ego is operating under the influence of external reality and therefore it debars the substitutive process from having any effect upon that reality [p. 95].

Sublimation, offering pleasure through aim-deflected discharge, unlocks the mental appartus from its dammed-up condition and releases it to action. Guided by values (pleasure) and interests, and inextricably linked to the external world of reality, the capacity to alter the intention of a drive offers a solution to conflict of particular elegance. Reaching out for reality in its search for pleasure, sublimation offers a special means for learning about the internal and external worlds and mastering them. Viewed from the side of the id, sublimation is discharge-seeking pleasure; from the side of the ego, it is a reaching out for reality and the object world.

The distinction between instinct and civilization in the broad sense is only between what is lower and what is higher in values. It is ironic that the "higher" activities in which civilized man takes his greatest pride are nothing more than the ultimate triumph of his essential instinctual nature.

To summarize: we find that sublimation has great value as a clinical theoretical concept. We have attempted to demonstrate some of its interrelationships with the body of clinical theory. In general, it is more fruitful for psychoanalysis to study sublimation in this context (clinical theory) than from the point of view of energy. While Hartmann's energy concept (neutralization) is elegant and powerful in explaining the maturation and development of ego function and structure, his emphasis on energy has certain weaknesses. It neglects essential aspects of sublimation which cannot be derived from energic considerations alone—i.e., aims, values, origin in conflict. The aim of sublimation is indirect gratification in which the aims of the drive become modified in accordance with the aims of the ego (particular values/interests, control over the drives). The necessary conditions for sublimation appear early in development when the functions of anticipation, objectivation, perception, thought, and control of motility have become sufficiently established to exert effective control over the drives via aim-deflected (detour) activity.

In addition to the nature and ontogenesis of the sublimation process, we have considered its defensive, economic, reality, and value functions. Sublimation is not a defense mechanism per se; it facilitates rather than opposes drive discharge. However, since it results in conflict solution by reducing direct drive pressure via aim deflection, it can be said to have a defensive function. On the basis of its economic and dynamic functions, sublimation plays a central role in regulating intrapsychic equilibrium. Sublimation is important and at times crucial for the maintenance and restitution of relations with reality. Moreover, pleasure in sublimated drive activity makes a major contribution to forming the attachment to reality. Finally, Freud's notion of the "higher aims" of a sublimation has had the difficulty of invoking criteria that are objective and socially determined for evaluating an intrapsychic vicissitude of instinctual life. These "higher aims"—external values—can, however, be shown to follow and combine with the primary inner value of pleasure in drive discharge. In this way value judgment takes on the dimension of a regulator of drive discharge.

BIBLIOGRAPHY

BREUER, J. & FREUD, S. (1893–1895), Studies on Hysteria. *Standard Edition,* 2. London: Hogarth Press, 1955.

BORNSTEIN, B. (1935), Phobia in a Two-and-a-Half-Year-Old Child. *Psychoanal. Quart.*, 4:93–119.

BRIERLEY, M. (1947), Notes on Psycho-Analysis and Integrative Living. *Int. J. Psycho-Anal.*, 28:57–105.

DEKNATEL, F. (1950), *Edvard Munch.* New York: Chanticleer Press.

FREUD, A. (1936), *The Ego and the Mechanisms of Defense.* New York: International Universities Press, rev. ed., 1966.

— (1965), *Normality and Pathology in Childhood.* New York: International Universities Press.

FREUD, S. (1905a), Three Essays on the Theory of Sexuality. *Standard Edition,* 5:125–243. London: Hogarth Press, 1953.

— (1905b), Jokes and Their Relation to the Unconscious. *Standard Edition,* 6. London: Hogarth Press, 1960.

— (1909), Analysis of a Phobia in a Five-Year-Old Boy. *Standard Edition,* 10:3–149. London: Hogarth Press, 1955.

— (1914), On Narcissism: An Introduction. *Standard Edition,* 14:67–102. London: Hogarth Press, 1957.

— (1915), Instincts and Their Vicissitudes. *Standard Edition,* 14:109–140. London: Hogarth Press, 1957.

— (1923), The Ego and the Id. *Standard Edition,* 19:3–66. London: Hogarth Press, 1961.

— (1926), Inhibitions, Symptoms and Anxiety. *Standard Edition,* 20:77–175. London: Hogarth Press, 1959.

GLOVER, E. (1931), Sublimation, Substitution and Social Anxiety. *On the Early Development of Mind.* New York: International Universities Press, 1956, pp. 130–160.

HAMMACHER, A. (1968), *Genius and Disaster.* New York: Harry N. Abrams.

HARTMANN, H. (1939), *Ego Psychology and the Problem of Adaptation.* New York: International Universities Press, 1958.

— (1947), On Rational and Irrational Action. *Essays on Ego Psychology.* New York: International Universities Press, 1964, pp. 37–68.

— (1948), Comments on the Psychoanalytic Theory of the Instinctual Drives. *Ibid.,* pp. 69–89.

— (1950), Comments on the Psychoanalytic Theory of the Ego. *Ibid.,* pp. 113–141.

— (1952), The Mutual Influences in the Development of Ego and Id. *Ibid.,* pp. 155–181.

— (1953), Contribution to the Metapsychology of Schizophrenia. *Ibid.,* pp. 182–206.

— (1955), Notes on the Theory of Sublimation. *Ibid.,* pp. 215–240.

— (1956), Notes on the Reality Principle. *Ibid.,* pp. 241–267.

— (1960), *Psychoanalysis and Moral Values.* New York: International Universities Press.

IBSEN, H. (1890), *Hedda Gabler.* New York: Dell, 1959.

JACOBSON, E. (1964), *The Self and the Object World.* New York: International Universities Press.

JONES, E. (1941), Evolution and Revolution. *Essays in Applied Psycho-Analysis,* 1:254–275. New York: International Universities Press.

KARPE, R. (1961), The Rescue Complex in Anna O's Final Identity. *Psychoanal. Quart.,* 30:1–27.

KEENE, D. (1971), Mishima. *New York Times Book Review,* January 3.

KRIS, E. (1955), Neutralization and Sublimation: Observations on Young Children. *This Annual,* 10:30–46.

LANGAARD, J. & RENOLD, R. (1964), *Masterpieces from the Artists' Collection in the Munch Museum in Oslo,* tr. M. Bullock. New York: McGraw-Hill.

LEVEY, H. (1939), A Critique of the Theory of Sublimation. *Psychiatry,* 2:239–270.

LEWIN, B. D. (1939), Some Observations on Knowledge, Belief and the Impulse to Know. *Int. J. Psycho-Anal.,* 20:426–431.

MISHIMA, Y. (1958), *Confessions of a Mask,* tr. M. Weatherby. New York: New Directions.

— (1970), *Sun and Steel,* tr. J. Bester. Tokyo: Kodansha International.

STEINBERG, S. & WEISS, J. (1954), The Art of Edvard Munch and Its Function in His Mental Life. *Psychoanal. Quart.,* 23:409–423.

STONE, I. (1946), *Dear Theo.* New York: Doubleday.

WAELDER, R. (1962), Psychoanalysis, Scientific Method, and Philosophy. *J. Amer. Psychoanal. Assn.,* 10:617–637.

Thoughts on Narcissism and Narcissistic Rage

HEINZ KOHUT, M.D.

ONE OF THE GEMS OF GERMAN LITERATURE IS AN ESSAY CALLED "ON
the Puppet Theater" by the dramatist Heinrich von Kleist (1777–
1810), written in 1811, not long before he ended his short life by

This essay was presented in an abbreviated version as the A. A. Brill Lecture of
the New York Psychoanalytic Society on November 30, 1971. Support by the Anne
Pollock Lederer Research Fund of the Institute for Psychoanalysis of the long-term
study of narcissism is gratefully acknowledged. Specifically, this essay sets forth the
principal lines of thought to be pursued in a detailed investigation of certain aspects of narcissism which is intended to be a continuation of the already published
work on the vicissitudes of the libidinal cathexis of the self (Kohut, 1971). The future work will deal with the following three topics: (1) the libidinal aspects of narcissism—retrospective and supplementary considerations; (2) narcissism and aggression; and (3) narcissism and group psychology. The present essay deals in a preliminary form with the first two of these three topics; the scope of the third topic is
briefly outlined at the end.

suicide. Kleist and his work are almost unknown outside the circle of the German language, but my fascination with his short essay—and with another one of his stories—has, as I can see in retrospect, a specific significance in my own intellectual development: it marks the first time that I felt drawn to the topic that has now absorbed my scientific interest for several years.

Ever since I read Kleist's story during my school days I had puzzled about the mysterious impact which the plain account has on the reader. A male ballet dancer, we are told, asserts in a fictitious conversation with the author that, by comparison with human dancing, the dance of puppets is near-perfect. The puppet's center of gravity is its soul; the puppeteer needs only to think himself into this point as he is moving the puppet, and the movements of its limbs will attain a degree of perfection that cannot be reached by the human dancer. Since puppets are not bound down by gravity, and since their physical center and soul are one, they are never artificial or pretentious. The human dancer, by comparison, is self-conscious, pretentious, artificial. The author responds to the dancer by recalling how, some years ago, he had admired the grace with which his nude male companion had set his foot upon a stool. Mischievously he had asked him to repeat the motion. He blushed and tried—but became self-conscious and clumsy. ". . . beginning at this moment," Kleist writes, "a puzzling change took hold of the young man. He began to stand in front of the mirror for days; . . . [An] incomprehensible force appeared to encage . . . the play of the motility which formerly had so freely expressed his emotions" (my tr.).

It is not my intention to bring our psychoanalytic knowledge to bear on this story. But the psychoanalytic reader will have no difficulty identifying the problems with which the writer of the story was preoccupied. Apprehensions about the aliveness of self and body, and the repudiation of these fears by the assertion that the inanimate can yet be graceful, even perfect. The topics of homosexuality (see Sadger, 1909); of poise and of exhibitionism; of blushing and self-consciousness are alluded to; and so is the theme of grandiosity in the fantasy of flying—the notion of "antigravity" —and that of merger with an omnipotent environment by which one is controlled—the puppeteer. Finally, there is the description of a profound change in a young man, ushered in by the ominous symptom of gazing at himself for days in the mirror.

Of all the facets of narcissism, only one is missing in Kleist's essay: aggression as it arises from the matrix of narcissistic imbalance. It is a striking manifestation of the unity of the creative forces in the depth of the personality of a great writer that Kleist had indeed dealt with this theme a year or two earlier, in the story of *Michael Kohlhaas* (1808), a gripping description of the insatiable search for revenge after a narcissistic injury—in its field, I believe, surpassed by one work only, Melville's great *Moby Dick*. Kleist's story relates the fate of a man who, like Captain Ahab, is in the grip of interminable narcissistic rage. It is the greatest rendition of the revenge motif in German literature, a theme which plays an important role in the national destiny of the German nation whose thirst for revenge after the defeat of 1918 came near to destroying all of Western civilization.

In recent years I have investigated some phenomena related to the self, its cohesion and its fragmentation (Kohut, 1966, 1968, 1970, 1971). Within my limits I have brought this work to a conclusion. The present essay gives me the opportunity to turn from the former topic to the relationship between narcissism and aggression. Still, I shall first deal once more with the work that lies behind, draw attention to topics which are in need of emphasis, and point up areas that will provide a basis for the subsequent formulations.

The Self and Its Libidinal Investment

The Influence of Parental Attitudes on the Formation of the Self

If I were asked what I consider to be the most important point to be stressed about narcissism I would answer: its independent line of development, from the primitive to the most mature, adaptive, and culturally valuable. This development has important innate determinants, but the specific interplay between the child and his environment which furthers, or hinders, the cohesion of the self and the formation of idealized psychic structures is well worth further detailed examination, especially with the aid of the study of the varieties of the narcissistic transferences. In this essay I shall add only one small point to the results which I have previously reported, namely, that the side-by-side existence of separate developmental lines in the narcissistic and in the object-instinctual realms in the child is intertwined with the parents' attitude toward the child, i.e., that they relate at times to the child in empathic narcissistic merger and look upon the psychic organization of the child as part of their own, while at other times they respond to the child as to an independent center of his own initiative, i.e., they invest him with object libido.

On the Acceptance of an Affirmative Attitude toward Narcissism in Theory and Practice

My second retrospective point refers to a broad question. In assuming an independent line of development in the narcissistic sector of the personality, a development that leads to the acquisition of mature, adaptive, and culturally valuable attributes in the narcissistic realm, I have, of course, taken an in essence affirmative attitude toward narcissism. But while I have become convinced of the appropriateness of this affirmative outlook on narcissism, I am also aware of the fact that it may be questioned, that indeed there exist a number of arguments which can be marshaled in opposition to a consideration of narcissism as an integral, self-contained set of psychic functions rather than as a regression product; that there exist a number of obstacles which stand in the way of its acceptance as potentially adaptive and valuable rather than as necessarily ill or evil.

One aspect of classical theory (see especially Freud, 1914b, 1915, 1917a)—and the in general appropriate conservatism of analysts concerning changes in theory—may, adventitiously, play a role in this regard. We are used to thinking of the relationship between narcissism and object love in a way which corresponds to the image of the fluid levels in a U-shaped tube. If the level of fluid in one end rises, it sinks in the other. There is no love where there is toothache; there is no pain where there is passionate love. Such thought models, however, should be replaced when they cannot accommodate the data of observation. The sense of heightened self-esteem, for example, which accompanies object love demonstrates a relationship between the two forms of libidinal cathexis which does not correspond to that of the oscillations in a U-tube system. And while the behavior of the fluid levels in the U-tube, and Freud's amoeba simile (1914b, p. 75), are models which adequately illustrate the total preoccupation of the sufferer with his aching tooth and the waiting lover's obliviousness to rain and cold, these phenomena can be readily explained in terms of the distribution of attention cathexes and do not *require* the U-tube theory.

Be that as it may, more formidable than the scientific context, in which the term narcissism may have acquired a slightly pejorative connotation as a product of regression or defense, is a specific emotional climate which is unfavorable to the acceptance of narcissism as a healthy and approvable psychological constellation. The deeply ingrained value system of the Occident (pervading the religion, the philosophy, the social utopias of Western man) extols altruism and concern for others and disparages egotism and concern for one's self. Yet, just as is true with man's sexual desires, so also with his narcissistic needs: neither a contemptuous attitude toward the powerful psychological forces which assert themselves in these two dimensions of human life nor the attempt at their total eradication will lead to genuine progress in man's self-control or social adaptation. Christianity, while leaving open narcissistic fulfillment in the realm of the merger with the omnipotent self-object, the divine figure of Christ, attempts to curb the manifestations of the grandiose self. The current materialistic rationalism in Western culture, on the other hand, while giving greater freedom to the enhancement of the self, tends to belittle, or (e.g., in the sphere where a militant atheism holds sway) to forbid, the traditional forms of institutionalized relatedness to the idealized object.

In response to ostracism and suppression the aspirations of the grandiose self may indeed seem to subside, and the yearning for a merger with the idealized self-object will be denied. The suppressed but unmodified narcissistic structures, however, become intensified as their expression is blocked; they will break through the brittle controls and will suddenly bring about, not only in individuals but also in whole groups, the unrestrained pursuit of grandiose aims and the resistanceless merger with omnipotent self-objects. I need only refer to the ruthlessly pursued ambitions of Nazi Germany, and of the German population's total surrender to the will of the *Führer,* to exemplify my meaning.

During quiescent historical periods the attitude in certain layers of society toward narcissism resembles Victorian hypocrisy toward sex. Officially the existence of the social manifestations emanating from the grandiose self and the omnipotent self-object are denied, yet their split-off dominance everywhere is obvious. I think that the overcoming of a hypocritical attitude toward narcissism is as much required today as was the overcoming of sexual hypocrisy a hundred years ago. We should not deny our ambitions, our wish to dominate, our wish to shine, and our yearning to merge into omnipotent figures, but should instead learn to acknowledge the legitimacy of these narcissistic forces as we have learned to acknowledge the legitimacy of our object-instinctual strivings. We shall then be able, as can be observed in the systematic therapeutic analysis of narcissistic personality disturbances, to transform our archaic grandiosity and exhibitionism into realistic self-esteem and into pleasure with ourselves, and our yearning to be at one with the omnipotent self-object into the socially useful, adaptive, and joyful capacity to be enthusiastic and to admire the great after whose lives, deeds, and personalities we can permit ourselves to model our own.

Ego Autonomy and Ego Dominance

It is in the context of assessing the value of the transformation (rather than of the suppression) of the archaic narcissistic structures for man as an active participant in human affairs—*l'homme engagé*—that I would like to mention a conceptual distinction which I have found useful, namely, the demarcation of *ego dominance* from *ego autonomy* (see Kohut, 1971, p. 187). There is a place for ego autonomy: the rider *off* the horse; man as he reflects, coolly and dispassionately, in particular as he scrutinizes the data of his observations. But there is also a place for ego dominance: the rider *on* the horse; man as he responds to the forces within himself;

as he shapes his goals and forms his major reactions to the environment; man as an effective participant on the stage of history. In the narcissistic realm, in particular, ego dominance increases our ability to react with the full spectrum of our emotions: with disappointment and rage, or with feelings of triumph; controlledly, but not necessarily restrainedly.

A Comparison of the Genetic and Dynamic Importance of Narcissistic and Object-Instinctual Factors

In my retrospective survey I shall now take up the question whether by focusing our attention on narcissism we may not run the risk of disregarding the object-instinctual forces in the psychic life of man. We must ask ourselves in particular whether our emphasis on the genetic and dynamic importance of the vicissitudes of the formation and cohesion of the self may not lead to a deemphasis of the crucial genetic and dynamic role played in normal and abnormal development by the specific object-instinctual investments of the oedipus complex.

A short while ago a younger colleague whom I might consider to be a pupil and who, at any rate, has followed my work on narcissism with interest, reviewed the relationship between the generations in our field and, speaking for the rising generation of analysts, suggested that the anxiety of the older group was not so much "that we become grownup, but that we become different" (Terman, 1972). I thought that the clear implication of this incisive statement was that the older generation was concerned less about being endangered by the oedipal killing wish than about being deprived in the narcissistic realm—and I felt strongly inclined to agree with this opinion. But then I began to worry. Am I the Pied Piper who leads the young away from the solid ground of the object-libidinal aspects of the oedipus complex? Are preoedipal and narcissistic factors perhaps no more than precursors and trimming? And will the preoccupation with them become a focus for the old resistances against the full acceptance of the emotional reality of the passions of the oedipal drama? Does not lie behind the preconscious fear that the younger generation will be "different" the deeper and more powerful fear of their killing wish for which the narcissistic concern is only cover and disguise?

I shall not attempt to pursue this question directly. I assume that it is not going to be answered in the form in which we see it now, but that it will some day be superseded by a reformulation of the nexus of causal factors in early life. (The work of Gedo and Goldberg [1972], for example, constitutes, I believe, a significant step in this direction.) In the meantime, however, we must, without prejudice, study all analytic data—oedipal and preoedipal, object-instinctual and narcissistic—and determine their developmental and genetic significance.

We shall therefore do well to refrain from setting up a choice between theoretical opposites concerning the question of the genetic importance of the young child's experiences in the narcissistic and in the object-instinctual realm. The examination of two topics will, however, illuminate the relative influence which these two sets of early experiences exert in later childhood and in adult life. The first topic concerns the significance of the pivotal developmental phase in which the nucleus of a cohesive self crystallizes; the second concerns the interplay between pathology of the self (narcissistic pathology) and pathology of structural conflict (oedipal pathology) .

The Prototypical Significance of the Period of the Formation of the Self

Concerning the first of these two topics it must be stressed that, similar to the persisting influence of the vicissitudes of the oedipus complex, the viscissitudes of the early formation of the self determine the form and the course of later psychological events which are analogous to the crucial early phase. Just as the period of pubertal drive increase, for example, or the time when a marriage partner is chosen, constitute emotional situations in which a dormant oedipus complex is prone to be reactivated, so do certain periods of transition which demand from us a reshuffling of the self, its change and its rebuilding, constitute emotional situations which reactivate the period of the formation of the self. The replacement of one long-term self representation by another endangers a self whose earlier, nuclear establishment was faulty; and the specific vicissitudes of the early pathology are experienced as specifically repeated by the new situation. Extensive changes of the self must, for example, be achieved in the transition from early childhood to latency, from latency to puberty, and from adolescence to young adulthood. But these sociobiologically prescheduled developmental processes are not the only ones which impose a drastic change of our self on us; we must also consider external shifts: such as moves from one culture to another; from private life into the army; from the small town to the big city; and the modification in the self which is necessitated when a person's social role is taking a turn—whether for better or worse, e.g., sudden financial success or sudden loss of fortune.

The psychopathological events of late adolescence described by Erikson (1956)—I would call them the vicissitudes of self-cohesion in the transitional period between adolescence and adulthood—should therefore neither be considered as occupying a uniquely significant developmental position, nor should they be explained primarily as due to the demands of this particular period. (These stresses constitute only the precipitating external circumstances.) But an adolescent's crumbling self experience should in each individual instance be investigated in depth—no less than in those equally frequent and important cases of self fragmentation which occur during other periods of transition which have overtaxed the solidity and resilience of the nucleus of the self. Why did the self break down in this specific adolescent? What is the specific mode of its fragmentation? In what specific form is the task of the construction of a new self—the self of young adulthood—experienced? How, specifically, does the present situation repeat the early one? What traumatic interplay between parent and child (when the child began to construct a grandiose-exhibitionistic self and an omnipotent self-object) is now being repeated for the patient, and—most importantly!—how is it revived in one of the specific forms of the narcissistic transference?

To repeat: just as the object-instinctual experiences of the oedipal period become the prototype of our later object-instinctual involvements and form the basis for our specific weaknesses and strengths in this area, so do the experiences during the period of the formation of the self [1] become the prototype of the specific

[1] To be exact one would have to call this point in development the *period of the formation of the nuclear self and self-object*. The archaic self-object is, of course, still (experienced as) part of the self.

forms of our later vulnerability and security in the narcissistic realm: of the ups and downs in our self-esteem; of our lesser or greater need for praise, for merger into idealized figures, and for other forms of narcissistic sustenance; and of the greater or lesser cohesion of our self during periods of transition, whether in the transition to latency, in early or late adolescence, in maturity, or in old age.

Pseudonarcissistic Disorders and Pseudotransference Neuroses

The relationship between the focus of the development of the object-instinctual strivings, the oedipus complex, and the focus of the development in the narcissistic realm, the phase of the formation of the self, will be further illuminated by comparing two paradigmatic forms of psychopathology: nuclear oedipal psychopathology which is hidden by a broad cover of narcissistic disturbance; and narcissistic disorders which are hidden by seemingly oedipal symptomatology.

Concerning the first a brief remark will suffice. Every analyst has seen the gradual emergence of the oedipal passions and anxieties from behind a broad cover of narcissistic vulnerabilities and complaints, and knows that the careful observation of the oedipal transference will also reveal how the narcissistic manifestations are related to the central oedipal experiences. How, for example, a sense of low self-esteem relates to phallic comparisons and a feeling of castration, how cycles of triumphant self-confidence and depression relate to fantasies of oedipal success and the discovery of being in fact excluded from the primal scene, and the like. Surely, I need not elaborate here.

Now to the second form of paradigmatic psychopathology. I have chosen to focus on a specific, somewhat complex type of narcissistic disorder despite its comparative infrequency because its examination is very instructive. (Cases, it may be added, in which the narcissistic blows suffered by the child in the oedipal phase lead to the first straight-forward breakdown of the self are much more common.) I believe that, among the in principle analyzable disorders, it confronts the analyst with one of his most trying and difficult therapeutic tasks. These patients initially create the impression of a classical neurosis. When their apparent psychopathology, however, is approached by interpretations, the immediate result is near-catastrophic: they act out wildly, overwhelm the analyst with oedipal love demands, threaten suicide—in short, although the content (of symptoms, fantasies, and manifest transference) is all triangular oedipal, the very openness of their infantile wishes, the lack of resistances to their being uncovered, is not in tune with the initial impression.

That the oedipal symptomatology in such cases (e.g., of "pseudohysteria") is not genuine is generally accepted. In contrast to what I believe to be the prevailing view, however, that we are dealing with hidden psychosis or with personalities whose psychic equilibrium is threatened by severe ego weakness, I have become convinced that many of these patients suffer from a narcissistic personality disturbance, will establish one of the forms of narcissistic transference, and are thus treatable by psychoanalysis.[2]

The nuclear psychopathology of these individuals concerns the self. Being threatened in the maintenance of a cohesive self because in early life they were lacking in adequate confirming responses ("mirroring") from the environment, they turned to self-stimulation in order to retain the precarious cohesion of their experiencing and acting self. The oedipal phase, including its conflicts and anxieties, became paradoxically a remedial stimulant, its very intensity being used by the psyche to counteract the tendency toward the breakup of the self—just as a small child may attempt to use self-inflicted pain (head banging, for example) in order to retain a sense of aliveness and cohesion. Patients whose manifest

[2] See in this context the differentiation between (a) *psychosis,* i.e., permanent or protracted fragmentation of the nuclear grandiose self and the nuclear omnipotent self-object, and (b) *narcissistic personality disturbance,* i.e., insecure cohesion of the nuclear self and self-object with only fleeting fragmentation of these configurations. See, furthermore, the classification of the disorders whose essential psychopathology consists in permanent or protracted fragmentation of the self or self-object, i.e., the psychoses. They fall into three groups, namely: (a) those cases, the frank *psychoses,* where the symptomatology openly reflects the breakup of the nuclear narcissistic structures; (b) those cases, the *latent psychoses* or *borderline cases,* where the symptomatology hides to a greater or lesser extent the fact that a breakup of the nuclear narcissistic structures has taken place; and (c) those cases, the *schizoid personalities,* where a breakup of the nuclear narcissistic structures (the development of an overt or latent psychosis) is the ever-present pathognomonic potentiality, which is however prevented by the patient's careful avoidance (through emotional distancing) of regression-provoking narcissistic injuries (Kohut, 1971, Ch. 1).

psychopathology serves this defensive function will react to the analyst's interpretations concerning the object-instinctual aspects of their behavior with the fear of losing the stimulation which prevents their fragmentation; and they will respond with an intensification of oedipal dramatizing so long as the analyst does not address himself to the defect of the self. It is only when a shift in the focus of the analyst's interpretations indicates that he is now in empathic closeness to the patient's fragmenting self, that the stimulation of the self through forced oedipal experiences (dramatizing in the analytic situation; acting out) begins to diminish.

It might bear repeating at this point what I have, of course, already said in earlier contributions: that the only reliable way by which the differential diagnosis between a narcissistic personality disturbance and a classical transference neurosis can be established clinically is the observation of the transference which emerges spontaneously in the analytic situation. In the classical transference neurosis the vicissitudes of the triangular oedipal situation will gradually unfold. If we are dealing with a narcissistic personality disturbance, however, then we will witness the emergence of one of the forms of narcissistic transference, i.e., of a transference in which the vicissitudes of the cohesion and (fleeting and reversible) fragmentation of the self are correlated to the vicissitudes of the patient's relationship to the analyst.

If we wish to state the differentiation between classical transference neurosis and narcissistic personality disturbance in metapsychological terms, then we must focus on the structure of the psychopathology. Concerning the two aforementioned contrasting paradigmatic disorders, for example, we can say the following. In the pseudohysterias, on the one hand, we are dealing with patients who are attempting to maintain the cohesion of an endangered self through the stimulation which they derive from the hypercathected oedipal strivings. An overt oedipal symptomatology is used to keep a hidden self pathology within bounds. In the pseudonarcissistic disorders, on the other hand, we are dealing with patients who are attempting to come to terms not only with the object-instinctual conflicts, wishes, and emotions of the oedipal period, but also—a point which deserves emphasis—with the narcissistic injuries to which their securely established self had been exposed within the context of the oedipal experience. The presence, in other words, of narcissistic features—and even their initial predominance within the total clinical picture—does not alter the fact that the essential psychopathology is a classical psychoneurosis.

Organ Inferiority and Shame

My comments up to this point may be regarded as my attempt to tidy up the house before going on a trip. The house is the work on the libidinal aspects of narcissism—work which is already done but where I wish to straighten out odds and ends before I can leave it. The trip should lead into the rugged terrain of narcissistic rage and, later, into the far-off region of group psychology. A final glance, however, at a topic which lies in the main within the familiar area of the libidinal cathexis of the self, yet which extends into the unfamiliar territory of narcissism and aggression, should, by virtue of its transitional position, provide confidence for the new undertaking. Let me refer to this topic by a nowadays somewhat discredited name [3] as "organ inferiority" (Adler, 1907).

In his *New Introductory Lectures* (1933, p. 66) Freud took the writer Emil Ludwig to task (without naming him, however) ; Ludwig had, in one of the biographical novels (1926) which were his specialty, interpreted the personality of Emperor Wilhelm II in accordance with the theories of Alfred Adler. In particular he had explained the Hohenzollern's readiness to take offense and to turn toward war as reactions to the sense of a specific organ inferiority. The Emperor had been born with a withered arm. The defective limb became the sore which remained sensitive throughout his life and brought about the specific character formation which, according to Ludwig, was one of the important factors which led to the outbreak of the First World War.

Not so!, said Freud. It was not the birth injury in itself which resulted in Emperor Wilhelm's sensitivity to narcissistic slights, but the rejection by his proud mother who could not tolerate an imperfect child.

It takes little effort to add the appropriate psychodynamic re-

---

[3] Freud (1914a), however, spoke of "the valuable work he [Adler] had done on 'organ-inferiority' " (p. 51).

finements to Freud's genetic formulation. A mother's lack of con-firming and approving "mirroring" responses to her child prevents the transformation of the archaic narcissistic cathexis of the child's body-self which normally is achieved with the aid of the increasing selectivity of the mother's admiration and approval. The crude and intense narcissistic cathexis of the grandiose body-self (in Emperor Wilhelm's case: the withered arm) remains thus unaltered and its archaic grandiosity and exhibitionism cannot be integrated with the remainder of the psychic organization which gradually reaches maturity. The archaic grandiosity and exhibitionism then become split off from the reality ego ("vertical split" in the psyche) or separated from it through repression ("horizontal split"). Deprived of the mediating function of the reality ego, they are, therefore, no longer modifiable by later external influences, be they ever so accepting or approving, i.e., there is no possibility for a "corrective emotional experience" (Alexander et al., 1946). On the other hand, the archaic grandiose-exhibitionistic (body-)self will from time to time assert its archaic claims, either by by-pass-ing the repression barrier via the vertically split-off sector of the psyche or by breaking through the brittle defenses of the central sector. It will suddenly flood the reality ego with unneutralized ex-hibitionistic cathexes and overwhelm the neutralizing powers of the ego, which becomes paralyzed and experiences intense shame and rage.

I do not know enough about the personality of Emperor Wil-helm to judge whether the foregoing formulation does indeed ap-ply to him. I believe, however, that I am on more solid ground when I suspect that Emil Ludwig did not take kindly to Freud's criticism. At any rate he later wrote a biography of Freud (Lud-wig, 1947) which was the undisguised expression of narcissistic rage—so coarse in fact [4] that even those inimical to psychoanalysis and Freud considered the crudity of Ludwig's attack an embarrass-ment and disassociated themselves from it.

Be this as it may with regard to Emperor Wilhelm and his biog-

[4] Lionel Trilling (1947), who reviewed Emil Ludwig's *Dr. Freud*, closed his re-marks about this biography with the following trenchant sentence: "We are not an age notable for fineness and precision of thought, but it is seldom indeed that we get a book as intellectually discreditable, as disingenuous and as vulgar as this."

rapher, I have no doubt that the ubiquitous sensitivity about bodily defects and shortcomings can be effortlessly explained within the metapsychological framework of the vicissitudes of the libidinal cathexes of the grandiose self and, in particular, of the grandiose-exhibitionistic body-self.

The specific topic of the sense of inferiority of children about the small size of their genitals (in the boy in comparison with the penis of the adult man; in the girl in comparison with the boy's organ) may, however, warrant a few special remarks. The sensitivity of children about their genitals is at its peak during the pivotal phallic phase of psychosexual development—later sensitivities concerning the genitals must be understood as residuals (e.g., during latency) or as revivals (e.g., during puberty) of the exhibitionism of the phallic phase. The significance of the genitals during the phallic phase is determined by the fact that at this period they temporarily constitute the *leading zone of the child's* (bodily) *narcissism*—they are not only the instruments of intense (fantasied) *object-libidinal* interactions, they also carry enormous *narcissistic* cathexes. (The narcissistic cathexis of feces during the anal phase of development and the narcissistic cathexis of certain autonomous ego functions during latency are examples of earlier and later leading zones of the child's narcissism during preceding and subsequent stages of his development.) The genitals are thus the focal point of the child's narcissistic aspirations and sensitivities during the phallic phase. If we keep these facts in mind and emphasize in addition that the exhibitionistic component of infantile narcissism is largely unneutralized, then we will also understand the much-disputed significance of infantile penis envy. This topic has aroused a great deal of unscientific and acrimonious discussion, leading even to the ludicrous spectacle of opposing scientific lineups of men who assign the phenomenon exclusively to women, and of women who either deny its existence or its importance.

Some of the difficulties may resolve themselves if the intensity of the exhibitionistic cathexes is taken into account, and if we, in particular, do not underestimate the importance of the *visible* genital in this context: in other words, if we keep in mind that the narcissistic demands of the phallic period are no more—but also no less!—than an important special instance in the developmental series of demands for immediate mirroring responses to concretely exhibited aspects of the child's body or of his physical or mental functions. That his penis will grow, is small consolation for the little boy; and that a complex but invisible apparatus will be maturing which will enable her to bear children, is small consolation for the little girl within the framework of the psychology of childhood exhibitionism—notwithstanding the simultaneous existence of other sources of direct narcissistic gratification and of acceptable substitutive mirroring which enhances the acquisition of sublimations in children of both sexes.

The shame of the adult, too, when a defective body part is looked at by others—indeed his conviction that others are staring at it! [5]—is due to the pressure of the unmodified, archaic, exhibitionistic libido with which the defective organ has remained cathected. And the self-consciousness concerning the defective organ and the tendency to blush when it is being scrutinized by others are the psychological and psychophysiological correlates of the breakthrough of the unmodified exhibitionistic cathexes. (I shall return to this topic in the context of the metapsychology of narcissistic rage.)

The Motivational Role of Disturbed Narcissism in Certain Types of Self-Mutilation and Suicide

Related to the preceding formulations about "organ inferiority" are those which concern the self-mutilation of the psychotic and certain types of suicide. With regard to both self-mutilations and suicide one must differentiate between the motive for these acts and the ability to perform them.

The motivation for the self-mutilations of psychotics emanates, I believe, in many instances not from specific conflicts—such as incest guilt leading to the self-punitive removal of an organ which symbolizes the evil penis. It is rather due to the fact that a breakup

---

[5] This quasi-delusion is, of course, a manifestation of the archaic exhibitionistic urge which (a) is isolated from the rest of the psychic organization and (b) projected (with reversed aim) upon the person who is the supposedly gloating onlooker. The relationship between this phenomenon and the paranoiac's delusion of being watched is obvious.

of the body-self has occurred and that the fragments of the body-self which cannot be retained within the total organization of the body-self become an unbearably painful burden and are therefore removed. The schizophrenic who (like the young man in Kleist's essay on the puppet theater) looks into the mirror for hours and days attempts to unite his fragmenting body-self with the aid of his gaze. If these and similar endeavors (e.g., stimulation of the total body-self through forced physical activity) to replace the cohesion-producing narcissistic cathexes fail, then the organ is removed.

The understanding, however, of the motivation for self-mutilation is not, by itself, sufficient to explain the actual performance of such acts. A person may sense in himself the analogue of the Biblical command, "If thine eye offend thee, pluck it out" (Matthew 18:9), but he would still be unable to obey this order. The ability to perform an act of gross self-mutilation depends, in some instances at least, on the fact that the organ which the psychotic removes has lost its narcissistic libidinal cathexis; i.e., it is not anymore part of the self and can therefore be discarded as if it were a foreign body. This explanation applies specifically in those instances in which the act of self-mutilation is performed calmly by the psychotic patient. Self-mutilations performed during stages of emotional frenzy may have different motivations, and the ability to carry them out rests on the near-total concentration of the psychotic's attention on some delusional aim. The ability to carry out the act then does not rest on the fragmentation of the body-self, but is based on a scotoma of the psychotic's perception—similar to those instances when soldiers during a frenzied attack on enemy lines may temporarily not be aware of the fact that they have suffered a severe physical injury.

Analogous considerations also apply to certain kinds of suicide with regard to both the motivation that leads to the act and the ability to carry it out. Such suicides are in the main based on the loss of the libidinal cathexis of the self. Analogous to certain self-mutilations, such a suicide does not emanate from specific structural conflicts—it does not constitute, for example, a step undertaken in order to expiate oedipal guilt. Characteristically, these suicides are preceded, not by guilt feelings, but by feelings of unbearable emptiness and deadness or by intense shame, i.e., by the signs of profound disturbance in the realm of the libidinal cathexis of the self.

Narcissism and Aggression

The hypothesis that a tendency to kill is deeply rooted in man's psychobiological makeup and stems from his animal past—the assumption, in other words, of man's inherent propensity toward aggression (and the correlated conceptualization of aggression as a drive) protects us against the lure of the comforting illusion that human pugnacity could be easily abolished if only our material needs were satisfied. But these broad formulations contribute little to the understanding of aggression as a psychological phenomenon. It is obviously not enough to say that such phenomena as warfare, intolerance, and persecution are due to man's regression toward the undisguised expression of a drive. And the often-heard complaint that it is the thinness of the civilized layer of the human personality which is responsible for the evils wrought by human aggression is appealing in its simplicity but misses the mark.

True, the protagonists of the most dreadful manifestation of aggression in the history of modern Western civilization proclaimed loudly that their destructive acts were performed in the service of a law of nature. The Nazis justified their warfare and the extermination of those whom they considered weak and inferior by seeing their misdeeds within the framework of a vulgarized Darwinism: the inherent right of the stronger; and the survival of the fittest race for the good of mankind. But despite their own theories, I do not believe that we can come closer to the understanding of the Nazi phenomenon by conceiving of it as a regression toward the biologically simple, toward animal behavior—whether such a regression be extolled, as it was by the Nazis themselves, or condemned and despised, as it was ultimately by the rest of the world.

It would on the whole be pleasant if we could do so; if we could state—in a simplistic application of a Civilization-and-Its-Discontents principle—that Hitler exploited the readiness of a civilized nation to shed the thin layer of its uncomfortably carried restraints, leading to the unspeakable events of the decade between 1935 and 1945. But the truth is—it must be admitted with sadness—that such events are not bestial, in the primary sense of the word, but that they are decidedly human. They are an intrinsic part of the human condition, a strand in the web of the complex pattern which makes up the human situation. So long as we turn away from these phenomena in terror and disgust and indignantly declare them to be a reversal to barbarism, a regression to the primitive and ani-mallike, so long do we deprive ourselves of the chance of increas-ing our understanding of human aggressivity and of our mastery over it. The psychoanalyst must, therefore, not shrink from the task of applying his knowledge about the individual to the field of history, in particular to the crucial role of human aggression as it has shaped the history of man. Specifically, it is my conviction that we will reach tangible results by focusing our attention on human aggression as it arises from the matrix of archaic narcissism, i.e., on the phenomenon of narcissistic rage.

Human aggression is most dangerous when it is attached to the two great absolutarian psychological constellations: the grandiose self and the archaic omnipotent object. And the most gruesome human destructiveness is encountered not in the form of wild, re-gressive, and primitive behavior, but in the form of orderly and organized activities in which the perpetrators' destructiveness is alloyed with absolutarian convictions about their greatness and with their devotion to archaic omnipotent figures. I could sup-port this thesis by quoting Himmler's self-pityingly boastful and idolatrous speeches to those cadres of the S.S. who were the execu-tors of the extermination policies of the Nazis (see Bracher, 1969; in particular p. 422f., i.e., the reference to Himmler's speech in Posen on October 4, 1943; see also Loewenberg, 1971, p. 639)—but I know that I shall be forgiven for not displaying this evidence here.

On Narcissistic Rage

In its undisguised form narcissistic rage is a familiar experience which is in general easily identified by the empathic observer of human behavior. But what is its dynamic essence? How should it be classified? How should we outline the concept and define the meaning of the term?

I shall first respond to the last of these interrelated questions. Strictly speaking, the term narcissistic rage refers to only one specific band in the wide spectrum of experiences that reaches from such trivial occurrences as a fleeting annoyance when someone fails to reciprocate our greeting or does not respond to our joke to such ominous derangements as the furor of the catatonic and the grudges of the paranoiac. Following Freud's example (1921, p. 91), however, I shall use the term *"a potiori"* and refer to all the points in the spectrum as narcissistic rage, since with this designation we are referring to the most characteristic or best known of a series of experiences which not only form a continuum but, with all their differences, are essentially related to each other.

But what is it that all these different experiences, which we designate by the same term, have in common? In what psychological category do they all belong? What are their common determinants? And what is their common metapsychological substance?

It is self-evident that narcissistic rage belongs to the large psychological field of aggression, anger, and destructiveness; and that it constitutes a specific, circumscribed phenomenon within this great area. From the point of view of social psychology, furthermore, it is clearly analogous to the fight component of the fight-flight reaction with which biological organisms respond to attack. Stated more specifically, it is easily observed that the narcissistically vulnerable individual responds to actual (or anticipated) narcissistic injury either with shamefaced withdrawal (flight) or with narcissistic rage (fight).

Since narcissistic rage is clearly a manifestation of the human propensity toward aggressive responses, some analysts believe that it requires no further explanation once the preconscious motivational context in which it is likely to occur has been established. Alexander, for example, dealt with this important psychological phenomenon by identifying its position in a typical sequence of preconscious and conscious attitudes. He attempted to clarify the psychological significance and the metapsychological position of shame and rage, these two principal experiential and behavioral manifestations of disturbed narcissistic equilibrium, in a paper

(1938) which has influenced the relevant work of a number of authors (e.g., Saul, 1947; Piers and Singer, 1953; and, with wider individual elaborations, Eidelberg, 1959; and Jacobson, 1964). In
this contribution he presented the schema of a self-perpetuating
cycle of psychological phenomena—an explanatory device which
is appealing in its pedagogical clarity and in its similarity to formulations which are cogently employed in other branches of science, e.g., in physics. Specifically he described the dynamic cycle of
hostility→guilt→submission→reactive aggression→guilt, etc. He
thus restricted himself to explaining narcissistic rage (in his terms:
reactive aggression which follows upon shameful submission) in
the context of the motivational dynamics of (pre)conscious experiences and overt behavior without investigating this phenomenon
in depth, i.e., without the attempt to uncover its unconscious dimensions and its developmental roots.

Narcissistic rage occurs in many forms; they all share, however, a
specific psychological flavor which gives them a distinct position
within the wide realm of human aggressions. The need for revenge, for righting a wrong, for undoing a hurt by whatever means,
and a deeply anchored, unrelenting compulsion in the pursuit of
all these aims which gives no rest to those who have suffered a narcissistic injury—these are features which are characteristic for the
phenomenon of narcissistic rage in all its forms and which set it
apart from other kinds of aggression.

And what is the specific significance of those psychological injuries (such as ridicule, contempt, and conspicuous defeat) which
tend to provoke narcissistic rage; and how do these specific external provocations interact with the sensitized aspects of the rage-
and revenge-prone personality?

The propensity toward narcissistic rage in the Japanese, for example, is attributed by Ruth Benedict (1946) to their methods of
child rearing through ridicule and the threat of ostracism, and to
the sociocultural importance which maintaining decorum has in
Japan. Small wonder, therefore, says Benedict, that "sometimes
people explode in the most aggressive acts. They are roused to
these aggressions not when their principles or their freedom is
challenged . . . but when they detect an insult or a detraction"
(p. 293).

The desire to turn a passive experience into an active one (Freud, 1920, p. 16), the mechanism of identification with the aggressor (A. Freud, 1936), the sadistic tensions retained in individuals who as children had been treated sadistically by their parents —all these factors help explain the readiness of the shame-prone individual to respond to a potentially shame-provoking situation by the employment of a simple remedy: the active (often anticipatory) inflicting on others of those narcissistic injuries which he is most afraid of suffering himself.

Mr. P., for example, who was exceedingly shame-prone and narcissistically vulnerable, was a master of a specific form of social sadism. Although he came from a conservative family, he had become very liberal in his political and social outlook. He was always eager, however, to inform himself about the national and religious background of acquaintances and, avowedly in the spirit of rationality and lack of prejudice, embarrassed them at social gatherings by introducing the topic of their minority status into the conversation. Although he defended himself against the recognition of the significance of his malicious maneuvers by well-thought-out rationalizations, he became in time aware of the fact that he experienced an erotically tinged excitement at these moments. There was, according to his description, a brief moment of silence in the conversation in which the victim struggled for composure after public attention had been directed to his social handicap and, although all acted as if they had not noticed the victim's embarrassment, the emotional significance of the situation was clear to everyone. Mr. P.'s increasing realization of the true nature of his sadistic attacks through the public exposure of a social defect, and his gradually deepening awareness of his own fear of exposure and ridicule, led to his recall of violent emotions of shame and rage in childhood. His mother, the daughter of a Fundamentalist minister, not only had embarrassed and shamed the boy in public, but had insisted on exposing and inspecting his genitals—as she claimed, to find out whether he had masturbated. As a child he had formed vengeful fantasies—the precursors of his current sadistic enactments—in which he would cruelly expose his mother to his own and to other peoples' gaze.

The existence of heightened sadism, the adoption of a policy of preventive attack, the need for revenge, and the desire to turn a passive experience into an active one,[6] do not, however, fully account for some of the most characteristic features of narcissistic rage. In its typical forms there is utter disregard for reasonable limitations and a boundless wish to redress an injury and to obtain revenge. The irrationality of the vengeful attitude becomes even more frightening in view of the fact that—in narcissistic personalities as in the paranoiac—the reasoning capacity, while totally under the domination and in the service of the overriding emotion, is often not only intact but even sharpened. (This dangerous feature of individual psychopathology is the parallel of an equally malignant social phenomenon: the subordination of the rational class of technicians to a paranoid leader and the efficiency—and even brilliance—of their amoral cooperation in carrying out his purposes.[7])

Two Phenomena Related to Narcissistic Rage

I shall now examine two forms of anger which are related to narcissistic rage: the anger of a person who, due to cerebral defect or brain injury, is unable to solve certain simple problems; and the anger of a child who has suffered a minor painful injury.

---

[6] Many psychotherapists, including psychoanalysts, traumatize their patients unnecessarily by sarcastic attacks on their archaic narcissism. Despite the analyst's increasing understanding of the significance of the reactivation of the patient's archaic narcissistic demands, such tendencies are hard to overcome and the analyst's inappropriate sarcasm intrudes again and again. The difficulty is, in some instances at least, due to the fact that the psychotherapist (or analyst) had himself been treated in similar fashion (by his parents and teachers, for example; and, specifically, by his training analyst). The fact that an analyst will persist, despite insight and effort, in his nontherapeutic sarcasm toward his narcissistic patients is evidence for the power of the need to turn a passive experience into an active one. In addition, we must not disregard the fact that the motivator of the deleterious attitude (i.e., the urge, which is deeply rooted in the unconscious, to inflict a narcissistic injury on others) can be easily rationalized. Specifically, the therapist's attacks can be justified as being undertaken for the good of the patient and in the service of a realism- or a maturity-morality.

[7] For a discussion of these events in National-Socialist Germany see Rauschning (1938). The relationship of Speer, Minister for Armaments and War Production—an organizational genius—to Hitler is especially revealing in this context (see Speer, 1969).

The "Catastrophic Reaction" and Similar Occurrences

If a person with a brain defect strives unsuccessfully to perform some task that should be easily accomplished—naming a familiar object, for example, or putting a round or square peg into the fitting hole—he may respond to his incapacity with the intense and frenzied anger that is known as "catastrophic reaction" (Goldstein, 1948) .[8] His rage is due to the fact that he is suddenly not in control of his own thought processes, of a function which people consider to be most intimately their own—i.e., as a part of the self. "It must not be! It cannot be!" the aphasic feels when he is unable to name a familiar object such as a pencil; and his furious refusal to accept the unpleasant truth that his incapacity is a reality is heightened by the fact that his spontaneous speech may be comparatively undisturbed and that his sensorium is clear.

Our thought processes are taken by us as belonging to the core of our self, and we refuse to admit that we may not be in control of them. To be deprived of the capacity to name a familiar object or to solve a simple problem is experienced as more incredible than even the loss of a limb. Our own body can be seen and, since perception is primarily directed toward the outside world, it is easier to think of our body in objective terms. The unseeable thought processes, however, are considered by us as inseparable from, or coinciding with, our very self. The loss of a limb can therefore be mourned, like the loss of a love object; [9] a defect in the realm of our mental functions, however, is experienced as a loss of self.

An attenuated variant of the catastrophic reaction is familiar to all: the annoyance when we cannot recall a word or name. And our patients, especially early in analysis, experience slips of the tongue and other manifestations of the unconscious as narcissistic blows. They are enraged about the sudden exposure of their lack of omnipotence in the area of their own mind—not about having dis-

---

[8] The organic defect itself undoubtedly contributes to the diminution of the capacity to control emotions and impulses. Yet, many patients who respond with the catastrophic reaction under comparatively bland conditions (e.g., in the harmless test situation) will not react with equal intensity under different circumstances which might arouse anger (e.g., when they are being teased or otherwise annoyed) .

[9] Tolstoy's description of Anatole Kurágin's farewell to his amputated leg is a deeply moving illustration of this process (1866, Book 10, Ch. 7, p. 907f.) .

closed a specific unconscious wish or fantasy. ". . . the trace of affect which follows the revelation of the slip," Freud said, "is clearly in the nature of shame" (1901, p. 83).

It is instructive to observe our own behavior after we have made a slip of the tongue, especially in a situation such as a lecture in which our exhibitionism is mobilized. The victim's reaction to the amusement of the audience is quite specific: he pretends either that the revelation had been intentional or he claims, at least, that he understands the meaning of the slip and can interpret it himself. Our immediate tendency is thus to deny our loss of control rather than to obliterate the unconscious content. Or, expressed differently: our defensive activity is primarily motivated by our shame concerning a defect in the realm of the omnipotent and omniscient grandiose self, not by guilt over the unconscious forbidden sexual or aggressive impulse which was revealed.

The excessive preoccupation with a situation in which one has suffered a shameful narcissistic injury (e.g., a social *faux pas*) must similarly be understood as an enraged attempt to eradicate the reality of the incident by magical means, even to the point of wishing to do away with oneself in order to wipe out the tormenting memory in this fashion.

The Child's Reaction to Painful Injuries

The other phenomenon that illuminates the significance of narcissistic rage is the emotional reaction of children to slight injuries. When a child has stubbed his toe or pinched his finger, his response expresses a number of feelings. We might say with Freud (1926) that in the child's feelings "certain things seem to be joined together . . . which will later on be separated out" (p. 169). The child gives voice not only to his physical pain and fear, but also to his wounded narcissism. "How can it be? How can it happen?" his outraged cries seem to ask. And it is instructive to observe how he may veer back and forth between enraged protests at the imperfection of his grandiose self and angry reproaches against the omnipotent self-object for having permitted the insult.[10]

___

[10] When the archaic self-object does not provide the needed narcissistic sustenance or does not prevent or dispel the child's discomfort, it is held to be sadistic by the child because it is experienced as all-powerful and all-knowing, and thus the conse-

The Experiential Content of Narcissistic Rage

The various forms of narcissistic rage, the catastrophic reaction of the brain-damaged, and the child's outrage at being suddenly exposed to a painful injury are experiences which are far apart in their psychological impact and social consequences. Yet underlying all these emotional states is the uncompromising insistence on the perfection of the idealized self-object and on the limitlessness of the power and knowledge of a grandiose self which must remain the equivalence of "purified pleasure" (Freud, 1915, p. 136). The fanaticism of the need for revenge and the unending compulsion of having to square the account after an offense are therefore not the attributes of an aggressivity which is integrated with the mature purposes of the ego—on the contrary, such bedevilment indicates that the aggression was mobilized in the service of an archaic grandiose self and that it is deployed within the framework of an archaic perception of reality. The shame-prone individual who is ready to experience setbacks as narcissistic injuries and to respond to them with insatiable rage does not recognize his opponent as a center of independent initiative with whom he happens to be at cross-purposes. Aggressions employed in the pursuit of maturely experienced causes are not limitless. However vigorously mobilized, their goal is definite: the defeat of the enemy who blocks the way to a cherished goal. The narcissistically injured, on the other hand, cannot rest until he has blotted out a vaguely experienced offender who dared to oppose him, to disagree with him, or to outshine him. "Mirror, mirror on the wall, who is the fairest of them all?" the grandiose-exhibitionistic self is asking. And when it is told that there is someone fairer, cleverer, or stronger, then, like the evil stepmother in Snow White, it cannot ever find rest anymore because it can never wipe out the evidence which has contradicted its conviction that it is unique and perfect.

The opponent who is the target of our mature aggressions is experienced as separate from ourselves, whether we attack him because he blocks us in reaching our object-libidinal goals or hate

---

quences of its actions and omissions are always viewed by the child as having been brought about intentionally.

him because he interferes with the fulfillment of our reality-integrated narcissistic wishes. The enemy, however, who calls forth the archaic rage of the narcissistically vulnerable is seen by him not as an autonomous source of impulsions, but as *a flaw in a narcissistically perceived reality.* He is a recalcitrant part of an expanded self over which he expects to exercise full control and whose mere independence or other-ness is an offense.

It has now become clear that narcissistic rage arises when self or object fail to live up to the absolutarian expectations which are directed at their function—whether by the child who, more or less phase-appropriately, insists on the grandiosity and omnipotence of the self and the self-object or by the narcissistically fixated adult whose archaic narcissistic structures have remained unmodified because they became isolated from the rest of the growing psyche after the phase-appropriate narcissistic demands of childhood had been traumatically frustrated. Or, describing the psychodynamic pattern in different words, we can say: although everybody tends to react to narcissistic injuries with embarrassment and anger, the most intense experiences of shame and the most violent forms of narcissistic rage arise in those individuals for whom a sense of absolute control over an archaic environment is indispensable because the maintenance of self-esteem—and indeed of the self—depends on the unconditional availability of the approving-mirroring functions of an admiring self-object, or on the ever-present opportunity for a merger with an idealized one.

Narcissistic rage occurs in a variety of forms which occupy a wide spectrum of diverse experiences and divergent behavioral manifestations: from the deepest and most inflexible grudge of the paranoiac to the apparently fleeting rage reaction of the narcissistically vulnerable after a minor slight. All instances of narcissistic rage have, nevertheless, certain features in common because they all arise from the matrix of a narcissistic or prenarcissistic view of the world. It is this archaic mode of experience which explains the fact that those who are in the grip of narcissistic rage show total lack of empathy toward the offender. It explains the unmodifiable wish to blot out the offense which was perpetrated against the grandiose self and the unforgiving fury which arises when the control over the mirroring self-object is lost or when the omnipotent self-object is unavailable. And the empathic observer will understand the deeper significance of the often seemingly minor irritant which has provoked an attack of narcissistic rage and will not be taken aback by the seemingly disproportionate severity of the reaction.

These considerations are, of course, also valid within the context of the psychoanalytic situation. Everybody tends to react to psychoanalysis as a narcissistic injury because it gives the lie to our conviction that we are in full control of our mind (see Freud, 1917b). The most severe narcissistic resistances against analysis, however, will arise in those patients whose archaic need to claim omniscience and total control had remained comparatively unaltered because they had been too rapidly or phase-inappropriately deprived of an omniscient self-object or had received inadequate confirmation of the phase-appropriate conviction of the perfection of the self.

Can Ego Dominance over Narcissistic Rage Be Achieved through Psychoanalysis?

Can narcissistic rage be tamed, i.e., can it come under the dominance of the ego? The answer to this question is affirmative—but the "yes" must be qualified and defined.

When during the analysis of a narcissistic personality disturbance a defensive wall of apparent tranquillity which had been maintained with the aid of social isolation, detachment, and fantasied superiority begins to give way, then one has the right to consider the emergence of narcissistic rage, of sudden attacks of fury at narcissistic injuries, as a sign of the loosening of a rigid personality structure and thus of analytic progress. These developments must therefore be neither censured by the analyst, nor hurriedly identified as a part of an archaic psychological world, but must for some time be accepted with implicit approval. Yet, whether present from the beginning of the analysis in the narcissistic analysand, or arising after a therapeutic loosening of his personality, such rage must not be confused with mature aggression. Narcissistic rage enslaves the ego and allows it to function only as its tool and rationalizer. Mature aggression, however, is under the control of the ego, and the degree of its neutralization is regulated by the ego in conformance with the purposes for which it is employed. The mobilization of narcissistic rage is therefore not an end point in analysis, but the beginning of a new phase—a phase of working through which is concluded when ego dominance in this sector of the personality has been established. The transformation of narcissistic rage, however, is not achieved directly—e.g., via appeals to the ego to increase its control over the angry impulses—but is brought about indirectly, secondary to the gradual transformation of the matrix of narcissism from which the rage arose. The analysand's archaic exhibitionism and grandiosity must be gradually transformed into aim-inhibited self-esteem and realistic ambitions; and his desire to merge into an archaic omnipotent self-object has to be replaced by attitudes which are under the control of the ego, e.g., by his enthusiasm for meaningful ideals and by his devotion to them. Concomitantly with these changes the narcissistic rage will gradually subside and the analysand's maturely modulated aggressions will be employed in the service of a securely established self and in the service of cherished values.

The relinquishment of narcissistic claims—the precondition for the subsidence of narcissistic rage—is, however, not absolute. (See in this context Tausk, 1913.) In accepting the existence of an unconscious psychic life, for example, we are not unconditionally renouncing a narcissistic position which had sustained the cohesion of the self, but we are shifting the focus of our narcissism on different ideational contents and are modulating the neutralization of the narcissistic cathexes. Instead of sustaining our sense of self-assurance through the belief in the all-encompassing scope of our consciousness, we now derive a new self-respect from such derivatives of qualities of the grandiose, omniscient self as the satisfaction of knowing about the existence of an unconscious; or from such derivatives of the relationship with the omniscient and omnipotent self-object as the joy about the superego's approval concerning our stamina in tolerating unpleasant aspects of reality or the joy about having lived up to the example of an admired teacher-figure, Freud.

My emphasis on the fact that narcissism need not be destroyed but that it can be transformed is in tune with my support of a nonhypocritical attitude toward narcissism as a psychological force *sui generis* which has its own line of development and which neither should—nor indeed could—be relinquished. In the psychoanalytic situation, too, the analyst's nonhypocritical attitude toward narcissism, his familiarity with the forms and transformations of this psychic constellation, and his uncensorious recognition of its biological and sociocultural value will diminish the analysand's narcissistic resistance and rage against the analytic procedure. The analyst's accepting objectivity toward the patient's narcissism can, of course, not do away with all narcissistic resistance and rage, but it will reduce the nonspecific initial resistance against a procedure in which another person may know something about one's thoughts and wishes before one knows them oneself. Through the diminution of the *nonspecific* narcissistic resistances, however, recognition of the significance of *specific* narcissistic resistances as repetition and transference is facilitated.

The analyst must therefore at first not ally himself unqualifiedly with the patient's reality ego when it rejects the claims of the unmodified grandiose self or when it tries to deny the persisting infantile need for full control over the narcissistically invested self-object.[11] On the contrary, he must even be understandingly tolerant of the rage which emerges in the patient when his narcissistic needs are not totally and immediately fulfilled. If the analyst maintains his empathic attitude toward the patient's needs and toward his anger, and if in response to the analyst's attitude the patient's reality ego, too, learns to be understandingly accepting of the demands of the grandiose self and of its propensity toward rage, then there will be a diminution of those nonspecific resistances in which the patient who feels treated like a naughty child begins indeed to act like a misunderstood naughty child. Only then will the specific resistances against the uncovering of specific repressed needs, wishes, and attitudes be brought into play. The nonspecific narcissistic resistances are in general accompanied by a great deal of rage;

---

11 This advice is valid not only where the grandiosity is on the whole in repression (horizontal split in the psyche) , but also where the archaic narcissistic claims are bypassing the reality ego (vertical split) , i.e., where the ego is disavowing the presence or significance of the narcissistic claims and enactments (see Kohut, 1971, pp. 183ff.) .

the specific resistances, however, are usually characterized by the presence of hypochondria and of other vague fears. The transference reactivation of the original need for approval through mirroring, and for the merger with an idealized archaic object, increases narcissistic tension and leads to hypochondria; and it creates the vague dread of having again to suffer the old traumatic rejection from the side of an environment which will not respond empathically to the rekindled narcissistic needs of childhood.

The Transformation of Narcissistic Rage into Mature Aggression

It is often more revealing to examine transitional phenomena than the extremes of a spectrum of contrasting manifestations; and it is often more instructive to study intermediate points in a developmental sequence than to compare its beginning with its end. This maxim also holds true for the study of the transformation of narcissistic rage into mature aggression: the way stations of this development and the remaining imperfections deserve our attention.

Patient A.'s insufficiently idealized superego could not provide him with an adequate internal supply of narcissistic sustenance (see the discussion of this case in Kohut, 1971, pp. 57–73) and he needed external approbation in order to maintain his narcissistic balance. He became, therefore, inordinately dependent on idealized figures in his environment whose praise he craved. Every time they remained unresponsive, because they failed to sense his need, he became enraged and criticized them with bitterness and sarcasm during the analytic sessions. When, however, as a result of the extensive working through of his idealizing transference, his structural defect became ameliorated, his rage changed. He continued to complain about the current stand-ins for the archaic idealized figure (his father who had disappointed him in his early life), but his attacks became less bitter and sarcastic, acquired an admixture of humor, and were more in tune with the real short-comings of those whom he criticized. And there was another remarkable change: while he had formerly nourished his grudges in isolation (even in the analytic sessions his complaints were predominantly soliloquy, not message), he now banded together with his fellow workers and was able to savor, in enjoyable comradeship with them, the pleasure of prolonged bull sessions in which the bosses were taken apart. In still later stages of his analysis when the patient had already mastered a large part of his psychological difficulties, and especially when certain homosexual fantasies of which he was very ashamed had disappeared, some anger at idealized figures for withholding their approval continued to be in evidence —but now there was not only benign humor instead of sarcasm, and companionship instead of isolation, but also the ability to see some positive features in those he criticized, side by side with their defects.

Now another clinical example: patient P., whose attitude toward his 8-year-old son was very revealing.[12] He was in general on excellent terms with the boy and spent a good deal of time with him in enjoyably shared activities. He could, however, become suddently outraged about minor transgressions, and would then punish the child severely. Slowly, as the analysis proceeded, he became aware of his narcissistic vulnerability and realized that he tended to respond with violent anger when he felt frustrated by narcissistically cathected objects. Yet, he was at first unable to recognize the often seemingly unmistakable fact that he reacted to the trauma of a narcissistic injury by becoming unduly harsh toward his son. He remained convinced that his severity was objectively justified, was adamant in the defense of his behavior, and claimed that consistency and unbending justice were better for his son than ill-placed kindness and unprincipled tolerance. His rationalizations seemed foolproof for a long time and no headway was made in the analysis. His moralistic punitiveness finally began to subside, and was replaced by his growing empathy for his son, after the memory of certain childhood scenes was recovered in the analysis and after their dynamic significance was understood. His mother had always reacted with severe, morally buttressed punishments

---

[12] I examined another, though not unrelated, aspect of this patient's behavior earlier in this presentation. (He is also referred to, but here in a clearly different context, in Kohut, 1971, pp. 321–324.) At a meeting of the Chicago Psychoanalytic Society (September 25, 1962), in discussing a presentation on psychosomatic disturbances (Bonnard, 1963), I described a transient speech disorder of the then 3½-year-old son of Mr. P. (see Kavka, 1962, esp. p. 176). I interpreted the child's stammer as a reaction to his father's narcissistic involvement with him and to his father's insistence on absolute control over him.

when he attempted to extricate himself from her narcissistic universe. He now did likewise when he felt that an alter ego tried to withdraw from him—either the analyst through activities (such as a temporary interruption of the treatment) which upset the balance of the narcissistic transference, or the son through activities which demonstrated his growing independence from him. It had usually been one of the latter moves—such as the son's stepping over to the neighbor's garden without having asked the father's permission; or his returning home behind time, even by one or two minutes—which the patient had considered a serious misdeed and had punished severely.

In both of the preceding examples I restricted myself to presenting a sequence of clinical events which demonstrates how narcissistic rage subsides (and is gradually replaced by aggressions which are under the control of the ego) in consequence of the analytically achieved transformation of the narcissistic matrix from which it arises. The first example (Mr. A.) illustrates how the patient's sarcastic rage gradually became tamed and how his empathy for the targets of his rage increased as the patient's neediness vis-à-vis the idealized object diminished. The second example (Mr. P.) illustrates how the patient's moralistic punitiveness became gradually tamed and how his empathy with the victim of his rage increased as the patient began to master his narcissistic involvement with alter-ego figures and grasped the fact that he was repeating a crucial situation from his own childhood.

Therapeutic Implications

I have here reached a point at which the convergence of clinical experience and theoretical reflection permits me to summarize, and to restate certain conclusions. Our therapeutic aim with regard to narcissistic rage is neither the direct transformation of the rage into constructive aggression nor the direct establishment of controls over the rage by the autonomous ego. Our principal goal is the gradual transformation of the narcissistic matrix from which the rage arises. If this objective is reached, then the aggressions in the narcissistic sector of the personality will be employed in the service of the realistic ambitions and purposes of a securely established self and in the service of the cherished ideals and goals of a superego which has taken over the function of the archaic omnipotent object and has become independent from it.

It must be admitted that in practice, e.g., at the end of a generally successful analysis of a narcissistic personality disturbance, it is at times not easy to assess to what extent the propensity toward narcissistic rage has been overcome; that it is at times not easy to know whether the aggressions are now the activities of a mature self and are under the dominance of the ego. But, as is true in general with regard to the completion of the analytic task in other sectors of the personality, so also here: we must make no excessive demands on our patients or on ourselves. On the contrary, the patient should face openly the fact that there exists in him a residual propensity to be temporarily under the sway of narcissistic rage when his archaic narcissistic expectations are frustrated and that he must be alert to the possibility that he might be overtaken by a tantrum. Such openly faced awareness of the existence of residual psychopathology will stand the patient in good stead when after the termination of the analysis he has to tend his psychological household without the aid of the analyst.[13]

The persistence of some subtle and seemingly peripheral manifestations of psychic malfunctioning is at times more dependable

[13] I am here advocating the taking of an attitude of tolerance vis-à-vis a relationship between ego and id which is neither one of ego autonomy nor of ego dominance —i.e., which is less than optimal. The comparative evaluation, however, which is implied in this context warrants a metapsychological elucidation. Ego autonomy is achieved when the ego can function without being disturbed by pressures from the depth. Ego dominance is achieved when the archaic forces have become integrated with the ego and when their power can be employed in accordance with the ego's purposes. When I speak acceptingly, however, of a former patient's postanalytic attitude of alertness with regard to the possibility that he might be overtaken by an attack of narcissistic rage, I am endorsing a condition which is, according to a strict definition of these terms, neither ego autonomy nor ego dominance (although it is closer to the former than to the latter state). I am here referring to the ego's surveillance of untamed archaic forces: of the ego's handling or manipulating them. Such a relationship between ego and id may be considered a tolerable imperfection if it concerns a narrow sector of the psyche, i.e., if, on the whole, a broad transformation in the area of the relevant psychopathology has taken place.

An analogy from another field may illustrate my meaning concerning the type of imperfection which I have in mind. I once knew a man who had so many muscular tics and spasms (probably on an organic basis) that his volitional motility was severely interfered with. He had, however, learned to wait for an appropriate tic movement that he could exploit for the action which he wanted to perform.

evidence of the incompleteness of the analytic work than the occasional recurrence of gross behavioral disturbance under stress. In the area of our scrutiny, in particular, we may be able to recognize one, often rather inconspicuous, residual of psychic malfunctioning which is, in my experience, an especially reliable indication that the work is still unfinished: the persistence of the patient's inability to mobilize even a modicum of empathy for the person who is the target of his anger. I consider this disturbance in empathy of much greater significance when I attempt to evaluate analytic progress than the patient's propensity to react occasionally—and under unusual stress—with the flare-up of the kind of rage which before the analysis had occurred frequently and in response to minor provocations. A patient's total and abiding lack of compassion for the offender and his arrogant and rigid refusal even to try to consider the other's position or motivations are, in other words, more reliable signs of the incompleteness of the analytic work in the narcissistic sector of the personality than the degree and the form of the residual rage attacks. Patient P.'s unfeeling moralism toward his son, and the immovable dogmatism of his conviction that he was acting appropriately when meting out the punishments, demonstrated more clearly that his behavior was in essence motivated by narcissistic rage than did the severity of the penalties which he imposed on the child. True enough, the penalties were disproportionate. (Unsurprisingly, they consisted mainly in the vindictive re-establishment of his narcissistic control in the form of the prolonged withdrawal from his son of such privileges as leaving the house; or in the boy's being banished to his room.) They were, however, never inflicted in an uncontrolled or in a sadistic manner.

A Metapsychological Formulation of Narcissistic Rage

The scrutiny of aggression as it is interrelated with the area of narcissism has, up to this point, been focused on the phenomenology of narcissistic rage and on the explanation of the matrix of archaic narcissism from which it arises. As my final task I shall now attempt to explain narcissistic rage in metapsychological terms—even though I know that metapsychology has fallen into disrepute and is considered by some to be hardly more than a sterile thought exercise.

In previous contributions (Kohut, 1966, 1968, 1971) I provided a metapsychological formulation of the emotion of shame. I said that it develops under the following conditions. Exhibitionistic libido is mobilized and deployed for discharge in expectation of mirroring and approving responses either from the environment or—I spoke in this context of "shame *signals*"—from the idealized superego, i.e., from the internal structure which took over the approving functions from the archaic environment. If the expected response is not forthcoming, however, then the flow of the exhibitionistic libido becomes disturbed. Instead of a smooth suffusion of self and body-self with a warm glow of approved and echoed exhibitionistic libido, the discharge and deployment processes disintegrate. The unexpected noncooperation of the mirroring object creates a psychoeconomic imbalance which disrupts the ego's capacity to regulate the outpouring of the exhibitionistic cathexes. In consequence of its temporary paralysis the ego yields, on the one hand, to the pressure of the exhibitionistic urge, while, on the other hand, it strives desperately to stop the flow. The exhibitionistic surface of the body-self, the skin, shows therefore not the pleasant warmth of successful exhibitionism, but heat and blushing side by side with pallor.[14] It is this disorganized mixture of massive discharge (tension decrease) and blockage (tension increase) in the area of exhibitionistic libido which is experienced as shame.

Similar considerations also apply to the experience of narcissistic rage. But while the essential disturbance which underlies the experience of shame concerns the boundless *exhibitionism* of the grandiose self, the essential disturbance underlying rage relates to

---

[14] I am grateful to Dr. Milton Malev for bringing to my attention the following passage from the Babylonian Talmud (Epstein, 1962, Tractate Baba Mezia, p. 58B) : "He who makes *pale* the face of his companion in public [i.e., embarrasses his companion], it is as if he had *spilled his blood*" (my italics) . This statement not only predicates the intense painfulness of narcissistic injuries, it also appears to take for granted that the physiological correlate of the painful experience is a derangement of the distribution of blood (pallor and blushing: "makes pale the face" and "spilled his blood") in the exhibitionistic surface of the body, especially in the skin of the face.

the *omnipotence* of this narcissistic structure. The grandiose self expects absolute control over a narcissistically experienced archaic environment. The appropriate mechanisms—they belong to the aggression-control-power sector of the personality—are set in motion, in expectation of total dominance over the self-object. When the environment fails to comply, however—be it the unempathic mother who does not respond to the child's wishes or the table leg which noncompliantly is in the way of the child's toe; or an analogous unempathic archaic object in the world of a narcissistically fixated adult—then the formerly smoothly deployed forces become deranged. Paralleling the processes described with regard to shame, we see discharge and inhibition side by side or in rapid succession, except that here, as stated before, the underlying force is not the grandiose self's boundless exhibitionism, i.e., its insistence on being admired, but its omnipotence, i.e., its insistence on the exercise of total control. It is the disorganized mixture of massive discharge (tension decrease) and blockage (tension increase) in the area of unneutralized aggression, arising after the noncompliance of the archaic self-object, which is the metapsychological substratum of the manifestations and of the experience of narcissistic rage.

Chronic Narcissistic Rage

If the rage does not subside, it may be added here, then the secondary processes tend to be pulled increasingly into the domain of the archaic aggressions which seek to re-establish control over a narcissistically experienced world. Conscious and preconscious ideation, in particular as it concerns the aims and goals of the personality, becomes more and more subservient to the pervasive rage. The ego, furthermore, increasingly surrenders its reasoning capacity to the task of rationalizing the persisting insistence on the limitlessness of the power of the grandiose self: it does not acknowledge the inherent limitations of the power of the self, but attributes its failures and weaknesses to the malevolence and corruption of the uncooperative archaic object. We are thus witnessing the gradual establishment of *chronic narcissistic rage,* one of the most pernicious afflictions of the human psyche—either, in its still endogenous and preliminary form, as grudge and spite; or, externalized and acted out, in disconnected vengeful acts or in a cunningly plotted vendetta.[15]

Concluding Remarks

A number of the topics discussed in this essay, especially those taken up in the retrospective survey of my earlier work (i.e., on the libidinal investment of the self), were of necessity only sketchily formulated and need elaboration. But what I regret even more than the shortcomings of this condensed presentation is the fact that I was unable to demonstrate the application of my older formulations about narcissism and of the preceding considerations about narcissistic rage to group psychology, to the behavior of man in history.

I hope very much that further efforts in this area will prove to be fruitful. But this is for the future, and only that much I would like to mention. I have begun work proceeding in two directions. First, regarding the contribution which the understanding of narcissism can make to the understanding of the formation and cohesion of groups: in particular the fact that group cohesion is brought about and maintained not only by an ego ideal held in common by the members of the group (Freud, 1921) but also by their shared subject-bound grandiosity, i.e., by a shared grandiose self. Indeed, there are groups which are characterized by the fact that they are held together by this latter bond—crudely stated, by their shared ambitions rather than by their shared ideals. Secondly, the psychic life of groups, like that of individuals, shows regressive transformations in the narcissistic realm. When the deployment of higher

---

[15] The relation between (a) acute and (b) chronic narcissistic rage in the area of the omnipotence of the grandiose self is paralleled by the relation between (a) acute shame and (b) chronic feelings of inferiority in the area of the exhibitionism of this narcissistic structure.

For completeness' sake it should also be mentioned here that narcissistic rage, especially in its chronic form, when it is blocked from being directed toward the self-object (which is experienced as being outside the self or body-self), may shift its focus and aim now at the self or at the body-self. The result in the first instance is self-destructive depression; the consequence in the second instance may be psychosomatic illness. It should be noted in this context that patient P. suffered not only from the manifestations of acute and chronic narcissistic rage (which were described earlier), but also from a rather severe degree of hypertension.

forms of narcissism is interfered with (such as, in the area of the grandiose self, through the blocking of acceptable outlets for national prestige; and in the area of the idealized parent imago, through the destruction of group values, e.g., religious values), then the narcissism of groups regresses, with deleterious consequences in the realm of group behavior. Such regressions become manifest in particular with regard to group aggression, which then takes on, overtly and covertly, the flavor of narcissistic rage in either its acute or, even more ominously, in its chronic form.

But this is work which still needs to be completed, even in its preliminary form, and I must resist the temptation of saying more about it at this point.

BIBLIOGRAPHY

ADLER, A. (1907), *Study of Organ Inferiority and Its Psychical Compensation.* New York: Nervous & Mental Disease Publishing Co., 1917.

ALEXANDER, F. (1938), Remarks about the Relation of Inferiority Feelings to Guilt Feelings. *Int. J. Psycho-Anal.*, 19:41–49.

— FRENCH, T. M., ET. AL. (1946), *Psychoanalytic Therapy: Principles and Application.* New York: Ronald Press.

BENEDICT, R. (1946), *The Chrysanthemum and the Sword.* Boston: Houghton Mifflin.

BONNARD, A. (1963), Impediments of Speech: A Special Psychosomatic Instance. *Int. J. Psycho-Anal.*, 44:151–162.

BRACHER, K. D. (1969), *The German Dictatorship: The Origins, Structure, and Effects of National Socialism,* tr. J. Steinberg; intro. P. Gay. New York & Washington: Praeger 1970.

EIDELBERG, L. (1959), A Second Contribution to the Study of the Narcissistic Mortification. *Psychiat. Quart.*, 33:634–646.

EPSTEIN, L., ed. (1962), *Hebrew and English Edition of the Babylonian Talmud.* London: Soncino Press.

ERIKSON, E. H. (1956), The Problem of Ego Identity. *J. Amer. Psychoanal. Assn.*, 4:56–121.

FREUD, A. (1936), *The Ego and the Mechanisms of Defense.* New York: International Universities Press, 2nd ed., 1966.

FREUD, S. (1901), The Psychopathology of Everyday Life. *Standard Edition*, 6. London: Hogarth Press, 1960.

— (1914a), On the History of the Psycho-Analytic Movement. *Standard Edition*, 14:7–66. London: Hogarth Press, 1957.

— (1914b), On Narcissism: An Introduction. *Standard Edition*, 14:73–102. London: Hogarth Press, 1957.
— (1915), Instincts and Their Vicissitudes. *Standard Edition*, 14:117–140. London: Hogarth Press, 1957.
— (1917a), Mourning and Melancholia. *Standard Edition*, 14:243–258. London: Hogarth Press, 1957.
— (1917b), A Difficulty in the Path of Psycho-Analysis. *Standard Edition*, 17:137–144. London: Hogarth Press, 1955.
— (1920), Beyond the Pleasure Principle. *Standard Edition*, 18:7–64. London: Hogarth Press, 1955.
— (1921), Group Psychology and the Analysis of the Ego. *Standard Edition*, 18:67–143. London: Hogarth Press, 1955.
— (1926), Inhibitions, Symptoms and Anxiety. *Standard Edition*, 20:87–174. London: Hogarth Press, 1959.
— (1933), New Introductory Lectures on Psycho-Analysis. *Standard Edition*, 22:3–182. London: Hogarth Press, 1964.
GEDO, J. & GOLDBERG, A. (1972), *Systems of Psychic Functions and Their Psychoanalytic Conceptualization*. Chicago: University of Chicago Press (in preparation).
GOLDSTEIN, K. (1948), *Language and Language Disturbances*. New York: Grune & Stratton.
JACOBSON, E. (1964), *The Self and the Object World*. New York: International Universities Press.
KAVKA, J. (1962), Meetings of the Chicago Psychoanalytic Society: A Report. *Bull. Phila. Assn. Psychoanal.*, 12:174–176.
KLEIST, H. VON (1808), *Michael Kohlhaas*. Clarendon German series, ed. J. Gearey. Oxford: Oxford University Press, 1967.
— (1810), Über das Marionettentheater. In: *Novellen und Aesthetische Schriften*, ed. R. E. Helbling. Oxford: Oxford University Press, 1967.
KOHUT, H. (1966), Forms and Transformations of Narcissism. *J. Amer. Psychoanal. Assn.*, 14:243–272.
— (1968), The Psychoanalytic Treatment of Narcissistic Personality Disorders. *This Annual*, 23:86–113.
— (1970), Opening [and] Closing Remarks of the Moderator. In: Discussion of "The Self: A Contribution to Its Place in Theory and Technique" by D. C. Levin. *Int. J. Psycho-Anal.*, 51:176–181.
— (1971), *The Analysis of the Self*. New York: International Universities Press.
LOEWENBERG, P. (1971), The Unsuccessful Adolescence of Heinrich Himmler. *Amer. Hist. Rev.*, 76:612–641.
LUDWIG, E. (1926), *Kaiser Wilhelm II*, tr. M. Colburn. London & New York: Putnam.
— (1947), *Dr. Freud: An Analysis and a Warning*. New York: Hellman, Williams, 1948.
PIERS, G. & SINGER, M. (1953), *Shame and Guilt*. Springfield, Ill.: Thomas.

RAUSCHNING, H. (1938), *Die Revolution des Nihilismus*. New edition with Introduction by G. Mann. Zurich: Europa Verlag, 1964.

SADGER, J. I. (1909), Heinrich von Kleist: Eine pathographisch-psychologische Studie. *Grenzfragen des Nerven- und Seelenlebens*, 70. Wiesbaden: Bergmann, 1910.

SAUL, L. (1947), *Emotional Maturity*. Philadelphia: Lippincott.

SPEER, A. (1969), *Inside the Third Reich: Memoirs of Albert Speer*. New York: Macmillan, 1970.

TAUSK, V. (1913), Compensation as a Means of Discounting the Motive of Repression. *Int. J. Psycho-Anal.*, 5:130–140, 1924.

TERMAN, D. (1972), Summary of the Candidates' Pre-Congress Conference, Vienna, 1971. *Int. J. Psycho-Anal.*, 53:47–48.

TOLSTOY, L. N. (1866), *War and Peace*. Inner Sanctum Edition. New York: Simon & Schuster, 1942.

TRILLING, L. (1947), Review of Emil Ludwig's Dr. Freud. *New York Times*, Dec. 14.

The Experience of Time

HANS W. LOEWALD, M.D.

> Transience is the backdrop for the play of human progress, for the improvement of man, the growth of his knowledge, the increase of his power, his corruption and his partial redemption. Our civilizations perish; the carved stone, the written word, the heroic act fade into a memory of memory and in the end are gone. The day will come when our race is gone; this house, this earth in which we live will one day be unfit for human habitation, as the sun ages and alters.
> Yet no man, be he agnostic or Buddhist or Christian, thinks wholly in these terms. His acts, his thoughts, what he sees of the world around him—the falling of a leaf or a child's joke or the rise of the moon—are part of history; but they are not only part of history; they are a part of becoming and of process but not only that: they also partake of the world outside of time; they partake of the light of eternity.
>
> J. ROBERT OPPENHEIMER (1954)

I

TIME AND THE EXPERIENCE OF TIME ARE OF CENTRAL IMPORTANCE IN mental life. Yet psychoanalytic contributions dealing with the subject in more than a tangential fashion are sparse, although there has been some increase in recent years. Despite our vast experience

Clinical Professor of Psychiatry, Yale University Medical School, New Haven, Conn.; Faculty, Western New England Institute for Psychoanalysis.
This paper consists of the Chairman's Introduction and contribution to the Panel on "The Experience of Time," held at the Fall Meeting of the American Psychoanalytic Association, New York, on December 18, 1971.

(401)

with time, despite our dealing with time in one way or another every day, and despite our common-sense knowledge of it, the phenomenon of time, and what is meant by the concept, have through the ages remained most elusive and may well be incomprehensible to the human mind. "It is impossible," Whitehead (1920) said, "to meditate on time and the mystery of the creative passage of nature without overwhelming emotion at the limitations of human intelligence" (p. 73). Freud (1933) has expressed similar feelings of frustration in regard to the problem of time (p. 74). Nevertheless, the experience of time, temporal phenomena, and the concept of time play an essential role in psychoanalysis, both as a method of treatment and research and as a body of theory.

Here are some of the temporal phenomena and concepts that most obviously are of importance in psychoanalysis: memory, forgetting, regression, repetition, anticipation, presentation, representation; the influence of the past on the present in thought, feeling, and behavior; delay of gratification and action; sleep-wakefulness and other rhythmicities in mental life; variations and abnormalities in the subjective sense of elapsed time; the so-called timelessness of the id; the role of imagination and fantasy in structuring the future; values, standards, ideals as future-oriented categories; concepts such as object constancy and self identity; not to mention the important factor of time in the psychoanalytic situation itself, in technical aspects, appointments, length of hour, etc.

More generally, psychoanalysis as a scientific discipline is unthinkable without the theory of evolution and of ontogenesis of mental development. In this regard psychoanalysis is in the mainstream of modern science and its "Discovery of Time" (see the book of that title by Toulmin and Goodfield, 1965) : time, the historical dimension, having gained equal importance in the natural sciences and in the social sciences.[1] In psychoanalysis, more than in any other form of psychological research and treatment, man is taken as a historical being, a being that as a race and as an individual has a history, has run and continues to run through a course

---

[1] For those who have more than a passing interest in the problems of time, I mention the book *The Voices of Time*, edited by J. T. Fraser (1966), being, in the words of the subtitle, "A cooperative survey of man's views of time as expressed by the sciences and the humanities." See also the review of this book by Blank (1967).

of development from something simple and primitive to something complex and "civilized." We are aware of the parallels, in certain respects, between archaeology and psychoanalysis. This time dimension, and the fact that human beings become, to a greater or less degree, aware of their history and their historicity, determine mental life. Furthermore, fixations, delays, detours, arrests, and developmental spurts are considered to be prime factors in shaping the course of mental life and its disturbances, all of them factors crucially involving the dimension of time. We hold that emotional-intellectual understanding and reworking of such developmental factors of the past in the present—in the psychoanalytic situation—may lead to a more harmonious, less disturbed integration of the personality. That man can own up to his past and thus gain some measure of mastery of his present life and the shape of his future, is part of his experience of time and implicit in the whole undertaking of psychoanalysis.

The "experience of time" may be understood as referring to the question: how is time, objectively measured by clocks as duration, subjectively experienced; what distortions of objective world time can we observe and how can we understand and explain such distortions? Further, phenomena such as *déjà vu* and other paramnesias, screen memories, amnesias, contraction of time in dreams and fantasy, fall under the rubric of time experience and its variations. We ask how time is experienced by children and in the various stages of life including old age; there is the problem of life cycles, the relationships between aging and its physical changes and time experience. What symbolic meanings of time play a role in mental life (Father Time, death, etc.)? There is the question how the sense and the concept of time as duration and succession of events in physical time-space develop; what determines the rise of this time concept in secondary process ideation?

In an earlier contribution (1962) I have attempted to outline a conception of time which is not based on the time concept of physical science and present-day common-sense experience, but which considers time in terms of the reciprocal relations between past, present, and future as active modes of psychic life. In this sense the experience of time, as a psychoanalytic topic, refers to the interactions and interrelations between these three temporal modes of psychic activity, as we discern them in our psychoanalytic work, for instance, in the play of transference, in the impact of unconscious and conscious remembering and anticipating on the present, in the interplay between primitive (stemming from the past) and higher-order ("present") motivations. In this conception time is understood neither as a dimension of objective external reality, nor merely as a form of our cognition or apprehension of this reality (Kant).

There is another aspect of the experience of time which deserves mention here. Is the course of our lives seen as propelled by forces of the past, by a *vis a tergo* (absolute determinism), or is it seen as pulled by the attraction or prospect of future possibilities or purposes (conscious or unconscious)? In the early stages of psychoanalysis, with its emphasis on id psychology, there was a decided tendency to understand psychic life as wholly determined by our unconscious past: unconscious forces from the past explained the development and vicissitudes of life; and future was nothing but a time when a past state would be attained again. With the ascendancy of the structural theory and ego psychology, with the growing importance of object relations in psychoanalytic theory, this time perspective shifted. The shift is perhaps most clearly exemplified by Freud's stipulation of a life or love instinct, which works in opposition to as well as in cooperation with a death instinct. The idea of a life instinct bespeaks an orientation toward a view in which life is not altogether motivated by forces of the past but is partially motivated by an attraction coming from something ahead of us. Our experience, I believe, tends to oscillate between these two time perspectives. It is the latter which makes it difficult to eliminate teleological considerations from biology and psychoanalysis.

Having taken this cursory glance at temporal phenomena and concepts relevant to the psychoanalyst, I now turn to the specific subject of my communication.

II

There are two experiences, at the opposite poles of time, which may throw some light on the problem of time. Both are exceptional in the sense that they rarely, for many people never, come to full awareness. In our present civilization they are apt to be seen as pathological, because they constitute extreme limits beyond which our accustomed, normal organization of the world no longer obtains.

At one extreme is the experience of eternity where the flux of time is stayed or suspended. Eternity is to be distinguished from sempiternity or everlasting time. Scholastic philosophers speak of the *nunc stans,* the abiding instant, where there is no division of past, present, and future, no remembering, no wish, no anticipation, merely the complete absorption in being, or in that which is. Insofar as that which seems to last forever, even in change such as the revolutions of the sun and stars, appears not to partake of a past and future different from the present, what lasts forever is confused with the eternity of the abiding instant. But the experience of eternity does not include everlastingness. Time as something which, in its modes of past, present, and future, articulates experience and conveys such concepts as succession, simultaneity, and duration is suspended in such a state. Inasmuch as this experience, however, can be remembered, it tends to be described retrospectively in temporal terms which seem to approximate or be similar to such a state.

States of this kind have been described by mystics and are in some respects akin to ecstatic states occurring under the influence of certain drugs or during emotional states of exceptional intensity. In conditions of extreme joy or sadness, sometimes during sexual intercourse and related orgastic experiences, at the height of manic and the depth of depressive conditions, in the depth of bliss or despair, the temporal attributes of experience fall away and only the now, as something outside of time, remains. In his discussion of the origins of religious feelings, Freud (1930) briefly considers the "oceanic" feeling and its relation to the concept of eternity, connects such "ego feelings" with the primal ego feeling of the infant, prior to the differentiation between subject and object, and alludes to relations between these issues and the "wisdom of mysticism" and "a number of obscure modifications of mental life, such as trances and ecstasies" (p. 72f.)

At the other pole of time is the experience of fragmentation, where one's world is in bits and pieces none of which have any meaning. The time continuum by which we hold our world together, the interrelatedness and the connections between a past, present, and future disintegrate, are broken in the most elementary sense, so that each instant loses its relation to any other instant and stands by itself, not embraced in a time continuum. While in the experience of eternity—which objectively may last only for a small fraction of time—temporal relations have vanished into a unity which abolishes time, in the experience of fragmentation time has been abolished in the annihilation of connectedness. To express this in a different way: in the experience of eternity, all meaning is condensed in the undifferentiated, global unity of the abiding instant, the *nunc stans,* and may flow out from there again to replenish the world of time with meaning; while in the experience of fragmentation, meaning, i.e., connectedness, has disappeared, each instant is only its empty self, a nothing. There are probably, here too, genetic affinities with early stages of psychic functioning in which the connectedness of experience—which is temporal—as yet is not, or not firmly, established. Experiences of estrangement, depersonalization, derealization may approximate such fragmentation.[2] The fact that experiences of eternity and fragmentation are often best understood as defenses against anxiety, as escapes from the world of temporal reality, does not invalidate their status as genuine representatives of transtemporal states.

I mentioned that the experience of eternity may itself last only for a fraction of time, and the same is true for fragmentation. When we say this, we speak of time as observed duration, of so-called objective time which can be clocked and measured. In that sense such experiences are of course not outside of time; in that sense they are moments or episodes in time, have a beginning and end and duration, may be located in the past and remembered, or feared or wished for in an anticipated future. By this standard of objective time we view such experiences as representatives of so-called subjective time. Subjective time here means a sense of time which conforms or does not conform to, or is a distortion of, observed time as duration which can be measured objectively.

---

[2] There are relations between the experience of fragmentation and Pious's (1961) concept of nadir.

I submit that this concept of time, as adequate as it may have been or still may be in the physical sciences, and as useful as it is for our orientation in what we have come to perceive as objective reality, is inadequate for a psychoanalytic investigation of time. If this is true, it follows that we have to abandon the concept of subjective time, insofar as the viewpoint from which we define subjective time is that of objective time as duration, as clock time. Even if one takes into account recent findings regarding biological time, internal clocks, circadian rhythms, etc., findings which raise fascinating questions about the relations between subjective and objective time and about a possible "objective" validity of "subjective" time—even then the time concept involved in such investigations remains essentially unchanged.

When we consider time as psychoanalysts, the concept of time as duration, objectively observed or subjectively experienced, loses much of its relevance. We encounter time in psychic life primarily as a linking activity in which what we call past, present, and future are woven into a nexus. The terms themselves, past, present, future, gain meaning only within the context of such a nexus. The nexus itself is not so much one of succession but of interaction. Past, present, and future present themselves in psychic life not primarily as one preceding or following the other, but as modes of time which determine and shape each other, which differentiate out of and articulate a pure now. There is no irreversibility on a linear continuum, as in the common concept of time as succession, but a reciprocal relationship whereby one time mode cannot be experienced or thought without the other and whereby they continually modify each other. As terms they are correlative, like the terms father and son; as experiential phenomena they interpenetrate.

The phenomenology of transference may serve as example: not only is the present relationship to the analyst partially determined by the patient's past (which is, as we say, still active in the present) and by a wished-for or feared future (itself codetermined by the past). It is also true that the present relationship, and the expectations it engenders, activate the past and influence how it is now experienced and remembered. This reintegration of the past, in its turn, modifies the present relationship with the analyst (and of course with other people as well) and has a bearing on the envisaged future. The modification of the past by the present does not change "what objectively happened in the past," but it changes that past which the patient carries within him as his living history.

Similar reciprocal relations between past, present, and future can be ascertained in the connections between day residue and infantile, unconscious wish in the construction of dreams (and I would add: in the construction of reality). Freud (1900) speaks of the need for attachment between one and the other. Without such mutual attachment, between the contemporary day residue and the past infantile wish, neither gains ascendancy in psychic life. The important and still poorly understood complex of problems subsumed under such titles as self or identity and object constancy (the latter being correlative to "ego identity") is directly related to the interactions between past, present, and future.

Such time phenomena, where the three temporal modes appear as active agents in mental life, are those which in my view are of primary concern to the psychoanalyst; the time concept of classical physical science and of everyday clock time is of little value or relevance here.

In the experience of fragmentation the reciprocal relationship between past, present, and future, taken as active agents, is broken, and the three words no longer carry meaning. What is experienced is a meaningless *now,* not a present as element in a temporal context. In the experience of eternity that context is not broken up but ceases to exist as a nexus by virtue of a fusion of its elements into a unitary *now.* This *now* does not lose but overflows its meaning, goes beyond meaning in the accepted sense in which meaning comes into being by connections, linkings between elements. We are familiar with momentary and isolated fragmentation, as when we focus on a word, perhaps by repeating it several times, and the very focusing may make the word into a meaningless sound; the same kind of thing may happen with visual objects if stared at long enough. There are hypnagogic and hypnopompic phenomena, especially regarding one's own mental processes, which are of a similar order. The connections between elements are broken or, to put it more correctly, are not re-created.

This leads to another aspect of time as active agent in psychic life. It concerns what I may call the microdynamics of memory. The examples just cited are not instances of all-including fragmentation of self and object world, but of minute fragmentations in the texture of mental processes, perceptions, etc. It is the memorial activity of the mind by which a before, now, and after in their meaningful connections, as well as the simultaneity of occurrences, are created. This memorial activity links what otherwise would be disparate bits into a nexus which has meaning and gives meaning to each element by virtue of the reciprocal relationship created between them. That this linking activity is automatic and unconscious in most of our daily life obscures the fact that it *is* an activity; in fragmentation this activity is interrupted. Related to such interruption of memorial processes is the compartmentalization engaged in by obsessive-compulsive characters. On the other hand, fragmentation in certain instances may be the starting point for novel linking processes which create new meanings.

When we consider time in mental life, time and memory are inseparable—memory here understood as mental activity (the words, mind and memory, are etymologically related), and not as a *fait accompli* which we find as one of the functions of the mental apparatus, perhaps ultimately based on so-called memory traces imprinted on a waxtablet brain. Memory, memorial activity, is understood here as a linking activity in which either a global event becomes articulated, a unity becoming a textured manifold ("analysis" in the literal sense of the word) which is held together by inner connections, or in which bits of events get linked together ("synthesis").

The microdynamics of memory is the microcosmic side of historicity, i.e., of the fact that the individual not only *has* a history which an observer may unravel and describe, but that he *is* history and makes his history by virtue of his memorial activity in which past-present-future are created as mutually interacting modes of time. Psychoanalysis is a method in which this memorial activity, shared by patient and analyst and more or less strongly defended against by the patient, is exercised, reactivated, and promoted. The personal myth, with the pathological aspects of which Ernst Kris (1956) has dealt, but in the creation of which every individual is unconsciously and sometimes consciously engaged, is a precipitate

of this history-making or time-weaving memorial activity. A patient, after considerable analytic work had been done on his relationship to his father, once put it this way: you have to create your
own history. Myth here is used not in the sense of a lie, or of an
ad hoc invented fable, although reconstructions in analysis, for example, may sometimes come dangerously close to the latter. Myth,
in other words, is not meant here as the opposite or as a distortion
of historical truth, of "how things actually were." Its use here emphasizes that any historical truth—whatever Freud might have
thought of the status of objective reality and of the truth of objectivity—is a reconstruction or construction which restructures in
novel ways what already at the time when it actually happened had
been a mental construction, a memorial structure unconsciously
built by the time agents of the mind.

BIBLIOGRAPHY

BLANK, H. R. (1967), Review of J. T. Fraser: *The Voices of Time. Psychoanal.
Quart.,* 36:297–300.

FRASER, J. T., ed. (1966), *The Voices of Time.* New York: George Braziller.

FREUD, S. (1900), The Interpretation of Dreams. *Standard Edition,* 4 & 5.
London: Hogarth Press, 1953, p. 564.

— (1930), Civilization and Its Discontents. *Standard Edition,* 21:59–145. London: Hogarth Press, 1961.

— (1933), New Introductory Lectures on Psycho-Analysis. *Standard Edition,*
22:3–182. London: Hogarth Press, 1964.

KRIS, E. (1956), The Personal Myth: A Problem in Psychoanalytic Technique.
J. Amer. Psychoanal. Assn., 5:653–681.

LOEWALD, H. W. (1962), Superego and Time. *Int. J. Psycho-Anal.,* 43:264–268.

OPPENHEIMER, J. R. (1954), Uncommon Sense. In: *Science and the Common
Understanding.* New York: Simon & Schuster, pp. 68–82.

PIOUS, W. L. (1961), A Hypothesis about the Nature of Schizophrenic Behavior. In: *Psychotherapy and the Psychoses,* ed. A. Burton. New York:
Basic Books, pp. 43–68.

TOULMIN, S. & GOODFIELD, J. (1965), *The Discovery of Time.* New York: Harper & Row, 1966.

WHITEHEAD, A. N. (1920), *Concept of Nature.* Cambridge: Cambridge University Press.

Internalization:
Process or Fantasy?

ROY SCHAFER, PH.D.

WHEN, SPEAKING AS PSYCHOANALYSTS, WE USE THE TERM "INCORPORA-
tion," we refer to a fantasy (ordinarily an unconscious fantasy) of
taking part or all of a person, creature, or other substance into
one's own body. When we use the term *internalization*, we refer
not to a fantasy but to a psychological process, and we are saying
that a shift of event, action, or situation in an inward direction or
to an inner locale has occurred. For example, a child imposes on
himself prohibitions hitherto imposed on him by his parents: we
think then of internality or inside-ness as having more or less replaced externality or outside-ness.

If, however, we ask, "Inside what?" we can provide no satisfactory answer. We do not mean inside the body or organism. Nor do

University Health Services, Yale University. This work has been supported by the
Old Dominion Fund and the Foundation for Research in Psychoanalysis.

(411)

we mean inside the brain, though we know the brain to be the necessary organ for all mental processes. Many of us would say we mean inside the mind or mental apparatus, or, more narrowly, inside the ego; in this usage, we are regarding mind, mental apparatus, and ego as places or locales. And yet this is not how we think of these terms when we define them formally. In our formal definitions we recognize them to be not places at all but concepts devised for descriptive and theoretical purposes; they refer to classes of events. (I shall return to this point.) At the same time, however, many analysts would be loath to agree that when they speak of internalization they intend merely to include an event within a class; they would feel that something essential in the way of empirical reference had been lost. And so they might then turn to the empirical-sounding "inside the self" as a way out of this difficulty. But "the self" refers only to mental content; in Freudian theory, at any rate, it is a descriptive or phenomenological concept and as such it cannot encompass the regulatory structures, functions, and relationships that are prime referents of the concept of internalization (Hartmann, 1939; Loewald, 1960, 1962; Schafer, 1968b) . "Inside the self" proves to be no more than a bloodless statement of an incorporation fantasy.[1]

It does not help matters to claim, finally, that the idea of the inside is a metaphor, and then to go on to claim that, since science or at least the science of psychoanalysis is necessarily metaphoric, the metaphor of the inside is legitimate and useful. Not only is this set of claims mostly false or in any case not demonstrably true; it also neglects to show that the metaphor of the inside is needed, is the best one for the purpose, and is being used in a proper and consistent fashion. For instance, as I have just indicated, this metaphor cannot be satisfactorily completed; we cannot specify in a systematically useful way what anything mental is inside of. That Freud used spatial analogies to help formulate his theoretical propositions carries no weight at all in this connection, for preparatory phases of thought and visual aids to explanation are not theory proper.

[1] Kohut (1971) has failed to provide a theoretical basis for his mixed structural-functional and phenomenological use of self concepts, and so has not helped resolve the difficulty with which we are here concerned (Schafer, 1973) .

As the notion of internality thus occupies an important but puzzling position in psychoanalytic inquiry, I shall devote this essay to an examination of the salient features of the language of internalization. First, I shall survey the *internalization words* we use.² In this connection I shall also have something to say about *structure words,* for these presuppose the legitimacy of internalization words and so both imply them and seem to contribute to their legitimacy. To round off this part of the argument I shall propose alternative conceptualizations of the ideas in question. Second, I shall discuss two topics—*introjects* and *affects*—with respect to which both psychoanalytic observation and conceptualization have followed common usage on internalization and in doing so have suffered significantly. Third, I shall discuss a number of reasons for the prevalence of internalization concepts in our everyday language and, through that language, in our psychological theory. Fourth and last, I shall offer some suggestions concerning the framing of interpretations; these suggestions follow from my conceptual analysis, and in my view they should serve to increase the clarity of analytic interventions and thereby to facilitate the orderly and effective development of the traditional psychoanalytic process.

Internalization Words

Setting aside *incorporation,* which we know we use to refer to fantasy only, the chief internalization words are *internalization, internal, inner world, intrapsychic, introjection, introject,* and less clearly, *identification* (both the process and the end result of that process) .³ I shall begin by concentrating on internalization itself.

I said before that by internalization we do not mean inside the body or organism. On this point I might be charged with neglecting Hartmann's (1939) discussion of the topic in which he emphasized the progressive interiorization of reaction and regulation as

---

² As it is a necessary extension of my argument to survey *externalization words,* but as I also wish not to add to the complexity of my exposition, I shall merely mention in footnotes some parallel considerations concerning externalization. I see no great problems in transposing this conceptual analysis of internalization to the conceptual analysis of externalization.

³ The chief externalization words are *externalization, external, external world* or *external reality, projection, reprojection,* and *interpersonal.*

the phylogenetic scale (and, by implication, the ontogenetic scale) is ascended. He said:

> In phylogenesis, evolution leads to an increased independence of the organism from its environment, so that reactions which originally occurred in relation to the external world are increasingly displaced into the interior of the organism. The development of thinking, of the superego, of the mastery of internal danger before it becomes external, and so forth, are examples of this process of internalization [p. 40].
>
> [He also said:] In the course of evolution, described here as a process of progressive "internalization," there arises a central regulating factor, usually called "the inner world" which is interpolated between the receptors and the effectors [p. 57].
>
> [And he said this, in a discussion of thinking:] It appears that in higher organisms, trial activity is increasingly displaced into the interior of the organism, and no longer appears in the form of motor action directed toward the external world [p. 59f.].

So far as the term internalization is concerned, Hartmann engaged in a certain amount of begging the question in these (and other such) formulations. He spoke of what is "central," "inner," and "between" as if these words were factual referents of and justifications for a concept like internalization. And yet "central" makes sense only as conceptually central and strategically central; "inner" makes sense only as a synonym for mental or psychological; and "between" refers to the increasing size and complexity of the central nervous system—the system which, though it does lie anatomically between receptors and effectors, has no bearing on the question of a spatial location for mental processes. The terms of brain theory cannot be the terms of psychological theory. Only by contaminating the location of the brain with the location of ideas can one create this misunderstanding. The contamination of the two ideas is evident in the notion that thinking is trial activity which has been displaced spatially into the "interior of the organism." The correct way to put it is that thinking is activity *of a different kind* rather than *in a different place.*

Thus, even as a biological, evolutionary conception, internalization is faulty. It expresses an illogical leap. The leap is from greater organismic complexity, especially of the central nervous system, and increasing organismic independence from environmental stimulation to some vague attribution of location to thought and subjective experience in general.

Conceptual difficulties are even greater when we turn from phylogenesis to ontogenesis. In this regard there is not even a fundamental change in physical makeup to point to, however erroneously, as the spatial referent of internalization. The unreflective subject may ascribe internality to his own thinking on the basis of all kinds of "physical" fantasies about mental processes. (Freud noted this factor particularly in his paper on negation [1925], where he described the subjective link between early thinking and oral activity.) The subject may also ascribe internality to the thinking of others, not only for this reason but also because he is likely to infer illogically and concretistically that anything he cannot perceive must be within, behind, or beneath something else. On his part, the psychological observer must not repeat these mistakes; he has no warrant to locate thinking anywhere. Moreover, it is of the utmost importance that he not confuse his viewpoint with that of the unreflective subject; he must maintain his own criteria for applying or rejecting notions concerning the designations inside and outside. With respect to mental processes, then, we are left with no answer at all to the question "Inside what?"

Actually, the evolutionary and especially the developmental propositions concerning internalization may be formulated in nonspatial ways that entail fewer assumptions and achieve more exactness than the spatial or pseudospatial. For example, with regard to phylogenesis, we may speak of increasing delay, selectivity, and modifiability of response; decreasing automaticity and stereotypy of behavior; less fixed dependence on specific environmental stimuli in the initiation or release, guidance, and stability of action; increasing self-stimulation; and so forth. Although Hartmann, like Freud before him, spoke in these very terms or terms like them, he thought it a scientific step forward to subsume these descriptions under some notion of increased interiorization; his theorizing was in this regard, as in so many others, predominantly biological rather than psychological (Schafer, 1968a, 1968b, 1971). I have already indicated that even *considered as a purely biological proposition,* this view of internalization is unsatisfactory.

Let us pursue the matter further. As I mentioned, Hartmann emphasized the evolution of thinking among the signs of increased interiorization. Although thinking is undoubtedly an advance in self-regulation and adaptational flexibility and accomplishment, what exactly is thinking inside of? Where is a thought? We can locate neural structures, glands, muscles, and chemicals in space, but where is a dream, a self-reproach, an introject? If one answers, "In the mind," he can be making a meaningful statement in only one sense of mind, namely, mind as an abstraction that includes thinking among its referents. In this sense, there is no question of spatial localization. To argue otherwise about "in the mind" is to be guilty of reification, that is, to be mistaking abstractions for things. For mind itself is not anywhere; logically, it is like liberty, truth, justice, and beauty in having no extension or habitation, requiring none and tolerating none. It is pure abstraction. The boundaries of mind are those of a concept, not of a place. Only certain referents of these abstractions may have place and substance.

Suppose that we have dispensed with the idea of the inside. Then, in describing human psychological development, we could, for example, say with greater parsimony and exactness that as one becomes an adult, he stops saying everything aloud; he thinks more often, more verbally, and with greater complexity and consistency of conceptualization than he did as a child; he uses words instead of motility far more often; more frequently than before he anticipates (e.g., danger) and engages in mental experimentation concerning possible physical and verbal action; his fantasies can be more detailed and organized; and so on and so forth. In all these ways he becomes both more private and more elaborately mental. The observer, on his part, has increasingly to depend on the developing subject's reports in words to know what his situation is, and often these reports are *of* words or *about* words, the words that make up unexpressed thoughts.

Additionally, dispensing with the idea of the inside enables us to recognize that a person is not keeping ideas or feelings *within* himself when he keeps them *to* himself, that is, remains silent about them. In the same way we recognize that a person does not have an *inner world* just because he has a *private world.* "Private" is a key concept here. It refers to what is not communicated, perhaps not yet formulated or even not directly or exactly communicable; it includes what is unconscious as well as what is consciously kept secret or passed over. "Private" is not just another word for "inner": it expresses an entirely different way of thinking about mental processes.

It follows from these considerations that *introjection* can only be a synonym of incorporation, which is to say that it must refer to the fantasy of taking something into one's body. In this light, it is redundant without appearing to be so, and if kept in use can only be confusing. *Introject* now becomes the thing that is fantasied as having been taken into one's body and as retaining in the fantasy some identity or some characteristic form of activity; it means the same as "the incorporated object," which is a more exact designation of the phenomenon in question. *Intrapsychic* now refers to what is private; in many instances, it pertains to the person's private and to a large extent unconscious regulation of his own desires, thoughts, feelings, etc.

Identification, finally, is a bit more difficult to reconceptualize inasmuch as in psychoanalytic usage it has not been used to imply internality directly. Traditionally, however, psychoanalysts have assumed that identification goes on "in the inner world," gets established there, and may transform its "internal" setting (e.g., in the case of superego identification). Once we dispense with the theoretical vocabulary of internality, however, we are able to speak about identification as a change in the way one conceives of himself and perhaps a corresponding change in the way he behaves publicly; as before, the change would be modeled on personal versions of significant figures in his real life or imaginative life (e.g., fictional or historical characters). I have discussed the full sense of identification at length elsewhere (Schafer, 1968b, esp. Ch. 6).[4]

[4] *Projection* can now be regarded as being simply synonymous with fantasied expulsion from the body; the "projected" content expelled and then localized within the boundaries of someone else is often a concretized (fecal, fetal, etc.) version of a trait, feeling, wish, or demand that one does not wish to recognize as one's own. *Reprojection* should refer to a second expulsion after an intermediate phase of reincorporation; usage is unsatisfactory in this instance, however, in that reprojection is often used to mean simply the expulsion of something that has been incorporated,

Having mentioned identification, I can pass right on to *structure words* or *structural concepts* since they are so closely intertwined with identification in psychoanalytic theory. Though it may not be apparent at first, the idea of psychic structure relies implicitly on a spatial metaphor—specifically, the metaphor of mind as a place, an entity characterized by extension. Thus, Freud positioned the superego (*"Überich"*) in some unspecified upper space—either directly (*"über"* as "over") or indirectly (*"über"* as "higher," as in "higher ideals"). And we all think of "levels" and "layers"; we all resort to "underlying" factors or causes; we all speak of "hierarchic" arrangements, "surfaces," and "depths." Indeed, who would object to the idea that psychoanalysis is a "depth" psychology or the idea that for Freudians, at any rate, interpretation must work from "the surface"? But, again, within what space?

Despite this spatialization of mind, when pressed for a strict definition of psychic *structure,* we do not resort to spatial metaphors. We refer instead to stability of modes of function, slow rates of change, resistiveness to regressive transformations, and the like. In another respect, we refer to certain similarities—of aims, of amenability to delay, of relative degree of desomatization, and so forth.

---

in which genital anesthesia and incapacity for erections provide a similar analogue *external* is quite unsatisfactory, too, in that in the psychological literature it has been used to mean three things—one biological, one psychological-observational, and one psychological-subjective. The biological meaning of external is outside the physical boundaries of the organism; for this purpose the word environmental is clearer than the word external. The psychological-observational meaning of external is all the mental functioning that can be perceived by an independent observer; here, external refers to what is public rather than private. The psychological-subjective meaning of external is everything the subject does not include in his idea of himself; in this respect even his entire body may be external to one subject, while possessions, love objects, home and nation may be internal to another subject. The psychological-subjective meaning of external is the one that corresponds to the restricted usage of internal being established in this paper; for other purposes, environmental and public should be the preferred words. *Interpersonal,* finally, refers to what the objective observer sees, that is to say, two or more people interacting. Insofar as the subject is realistic, he will be the objective observer of his interpersonal situation. We know, however, how often it is the case that when the subject is ostensibly dealing with another real person, he is found on analytic examination to be dealing more or less with a fantasied version of that person; and that version is likely to include details of significant figures from the subject's childhood. We encounter the limits of the "externality" of the interpersonal most clearly in the analysis of the transference.

This is how we speak of id, ego, and superego—as functions grouped together by the observer or theoretician on the basis of such criteria as I have just listed. They are classes of events, and to include an event "within" a class, rather than being inherently and inescapably a spatial designation, is merely to say, "I consider *this* event a member of *that* class." Hartmann, Kris, and Loewenstein (1946) (see also Hartmann, 1964) and Rapaport (1959, 1967) stand out among those who have established this mode of conceptualization of structure as the right one for traditional psychoanalytic theory.

What does it mean, then, that identification is assigned so important a role in the development of psychic structure by Freud (see, e.g., 1923) and others after him? It means that modeling change of ideas about oneself and change of one's behavior on aspects of important real or imaginary people plays a decisive part in the progressive stabilization and integration of one's specifically human activity. It means that to develop as a specific person one must have models; one cannot and does not have to create his idea of being fully human by himself. We know that the process of modeling oneself after another person is typically fantasied as an incorporation of that person and may even be undertaken for that very purpose (e.g., to preserve a sense of the presence of that person or of one of his qualities). But we realize too that when we say "incorporation," we are speaking of imagination or fantasy; we are not conceptualizing psychological processes for systematic purposes.

It comes then to this: identification is or may be "structure-building" in the sense that it may make possible a high degree of consistency in certain modes of subjective experience and behavior; on the basis of identification, specific modes of desiring, feeling, thinking, and doing things, along with specific ideas and feelings associated with these modes, may be in evidence much more regularly and readily than they would be otherwise. But we speak of structure in this instance because, thinking metaphorically, we are picturing mind as a matter of places, currents, quantities, interactions—in short, as a spatial entity containing other localizable entities and processes. This entire notion, once made explicit, can be seen to be the archaic invention it is.

Not only invention, but convention: the spatial notion is so well established in common usage, it has so many variations and so wide a range of application, that it seems the very stuff of thought. This usage is so powerful that if I were to say "John's internal standards," who, under ordinary circumstances, would think I was referring not to a fact but to a problematic metaphoric rendition of an observation? The observation itself, I suggest, would be stated more exactly in "John's standards" or "John's private standards," or perhaps "the standards John abides by unconsciously." And, if it was structure that was to be emphasized in this regard, the observation would not be rendered directly or exactly in "John's structuralized internal standards" but in "John is pretty consistent, even when under stress, in abiding by his unconscious standards" or "John may be counted on to abide by certain standards he maintains privately even when in intense conflict." It should be evident by now that the spatial metaphor comes between us and the potential fact. With which observation I shall go on to consider two sets of phenomena—usually subsumed under the headings *introjects* and *affects*—the observation and conceptualization of which have been seriously hampered by pseudospatial references to the inside and outside in mental functioning. But first I should clarify some of the context and implications of the general trend of my argument.

A Methodological Interlude

This conceptual critique and reformulation is strong stuff. It undermines our confidence in the utility of words like internalization, structure—and drive and energy, too. Moreover, in the next two sections, I shall discuss "introjects" and "affects" in some novel ways. The question, "What will be left to work with in psychoanalytic theory?" becomes inescapable. It will be well to pause, therefore, to reflect on where we have come from, where we are, and where we seem to be heading.

Freud used the conceptual tools he had at hand. He relied (as we have, in following him) on a mixture of two languages—one suitable for stating facts about neural organizations and chemical processes, and one suitable for the utterly unsystematic discourse of everyday life. But Freud had no warrant to expect the language of the laboratory or the home to be suitable for defining or expressing his data. He seems never to have considered that before it could be a system with a real claim to dignity and elegance, his psychoanalysis would have to have a language peculiarly its own. At least, it would need a set of rules about the usage of common words which could help achieve a consistent rendering and ordering of *the observations specific to his method.*

In this paper, as well as elsewhere, I have been re-examining psychoanalytic terms in the interest of eliminating from our theory confusing, unnecessary, and meaningless metaphors and the assumptions they both express and generate. Additionally, although I am not proposing a new theory, at least not in any traditional sense of the word theory, I am, one might say, attempting to develop a sublanguage within the English language that will make it possible to specify mental facts in an unambiguous, parsimonious, consistent, and meaningful fashion; I refer especially to facts of interest to psychoanalysts and analysands. Thus, according to this sublanguage and its rules, internalization refers to a fantasy, not a process; the fantasy is that of incorporation. Additionally, as mental processes do not occur in space, they neither have insides and outsides nor move from place to place—except in fantasy!

Clearly, the trend of my argument is that well-established habits of thought will have to be changed. But it is difficult to change such habits of thought. Change of that nature requires continuous conscious alertness and effort. In turn, that alertness and effort disrupt the ease and smoothness of thought and speech that we have laboriously achieved during our personal and professional developments—with an accompanying sense of loss and of being at a loss, especially for words. Inevitably, we fear, resent, and resist the demand for change; this is as true for psychoanalytic conceptualizing as it is for neurotic fantasizing.

Viewed most broadly, the habit of thought or the type of language I am calling into question is the one that relies on concretistic, substantial references to abstract or at least nonsubstantial ideas. The fact is that habitually we speak of thoughts, feelings, motives, and entire personalities as though they had the properties of things, such as extension, location, and momentum. This pervasive reliance on what ultimately are infantile or primary process modes of thought undoubtedly adds vividness, charm, and drama to our discourse in everyday life and to psychoanalytic work and theorizing. It is gratifying as well as reassuringly familiar. But in the end, we discover ourselves to be engaged in anthropomorphic thinking (Grossman and Simon, 1969; Schafer, 1973), which, in sound Freudian theorizing, at any rate, cannot be acceptable.

In this paper, which is part of a larger effort to resolve chronic problems in psychoanalytic conceptualization, I am limiting myself to dealing mainly with confusing, unproductive, and dispensable notions of location, especially of inside and outside, in the case of mental processes. Other aspects of the substantialization and personification of abstract terms pertaining to mental processes include references to their mass, energy, momentum, and intentionality; I shall, however, merely indicate these as I go along (see also Schafer, 1968b, 1971, esp. 1973).[5]

Introjects

There is no topic to which the preceding considerations may be applied with more emphasis than traditional discussions of introjects. First of all, the custom is to speak of introjects as if they were angels and demons with minds and powers of their own. One speaks of them not as an analysand's description of experience but as unqualified facts. This is the case, for example, when, without qualification, introjects are said to persecute, scold, comfort, etc., the person under consideration. In these instances we forget that an introject can only be a fantasy, that is, a special kind of daydream which, in a more or less clearly hallucinatory experience, the subject takes for a real-life event. We forget then that the introject can have no powers or motives of its own, and no perceptual and judgmental functions, except as, like a dream figure, it has these properties archaically ascribed to it by the imagining subject. The subject is, as it were, dreaming while ostensibly fully and consistently awake. His introject has the "reality" of a dream figure, and is a "hallucination" in the same sense as a dream is.

5 I am aware of how many conceptualizations will have to be reworked, and on how many levels of theoretical formulation, once one embarks on this course. And I am equally aware of how much remains to be done and how cumbersome revised formulations will be or seem for a long time to come.

In the second place, we have designated as introjects many dreamlike experiences of the nearness and influence of other persons or parts of persons when, according to the spontaneous reports of the analysand, he has either not localized them in subjective space at all or has indicated that they are "outside" himself (e.g., behind him). Why then "introject"? Is it not the result of reasoning that goes something like this: since the presence, as I call it, is objectively not outside the subject, and since thinking somehow goes on "in the head" because the mind is somehow "in the head," the presence must be inside the head, too, and so must be an introject? It is all quite crude, but there it is!

Thus, owing to the tenacity with which we hold on to our ideas about mind *in* space and mind *as* space, we do not always listen carefully to our analysands when they report these vivid imaginary experiences. We do not sort out the subject's experiential language and the observer's conceptual language. Consequently, the theory of introjects has always had the same spooky quality as the subjective experience it refers to; it has remained more a repetition or continuation of the problem than a clarification or explanation of it.

Obviously, this conceptual analysis may be applied to the related concept "internal objects" and all the pseudospatial words associated with it. And since, as I indicated earlier, incorporation is to be preferred to introjection, I think we would achieve the greatest clarity in our discussions of these matters by speaking of some presences as "incorporated objects" while remembering that not all presences have been incorporated; some presences remain unlocalized in subjective space and perhaps, owing to the elusiveness of many of these phenomena, are altogether unlocalizable. I have discussed the "power" and the "locale" of introjects and other "presences" in greater detail elsewhere (1968b, esp. Ch. 5).

Affects

Rather than take up affects in general, which course would require me to consider issues that extend far beyond the scope of this paper, I shall single out *anger* as an example of an affect the observation and conceptualization of which have been seriously hampered by our adhering to the notions of the inside and outside. In order to develop the implications and consequences of my critique, I shall go into some detail about spatial and nonspatial ways of talking about anger.

People speak of anger as being held in or suppressed, dammed up or pent up, exploding or erupting, consuming one or simmering. Similarly, they say that they express anger or let it out, that it spills out or spreads, and so on. It is as if anger were some kind of hot lava in a volcanic cone. In psychoanalytic parlance, we also speak of displacing anger, discharging it, and turning it around upon the self. All these words presuppose that anger has the properties not only of substance and quantity, but extension, place or locale as well (these properties go together, necessarily). The vocabulary of anger thus depends on the legitimacy of assuming or referring to an inside and an outside—but, I ask again, inside or outside of what? Where? Is anger anywhere? And where does anger go when it is discharged or expressed? And what is left in the place occupied by anger before its purgation? A vacuum? A clean inside?

The questions are unanswerable, of course, because they cannot be asked in a logical inquiry. Anger is not the kind of word about which such questions may be asked, and we shall soon see what kind of word it is. Meanwhile, it follows from what I have said that with respect to psychological theory the spatial metaphor and the spatial (and substance-quantity) implications of our affect words are to be treated as unreal or not serious. It should be noted that affect theory and psychic energy theory are not independent in this respect, in that, according to the latter theory, affects are quantities, and, being quantities, they must therefore (we suppose) be somewhere or be going somewhere, even if only within an ill-considered spatial metaphor.[6]

Much of the problem issues from the archaic notion, familiar to us from our studies of primary process thinking or unconscious fantasy, of affect as substance (see, e.g., Brierley, 1937; Schafer, 1964). Thus, when we speak of anger, we have the illusion that we are referring to something that may be designated by a concrete

6 In his final major formulation of the matter (as translated by Strachey), Freud said that the ego was the "seat" of anxiety, and, by implication, of the affects in general (1926, p. 93). Freud's word was *"Ångststätte"* which more literally would be translated "place (or locus) of anxiety." Being engrossed in establishing his implicitly spatial "structural theory," Freud understandably relied on the notion that affects have locales.

noun, that is, to a unit that can be pointed to, like a claw or a fang or a fecal mass. But that is not what anger is. The anger of common usage is really an abstract noun; it is a rubric for a set of referents, and it is the referents rather than anger that can be pointed to, at least in some instances. These referents include physiological arousal reactions and ideas of having been wronged and of doing something more or less violent about that. These ideas or fantasies may be repressed altogether or replaced by "tamed" ideas or fantasies of some sort of retaliation against someone or other. I need not spell out all the variations in this regard.

There is, of course, a quantitative or quantifiable aspect of physiological arousal or activity. Ordinarily, this quantity will correspond to the total situation as the subject defines it, especially unconsciously. But by itself this arousal is not "anger."

That anger is an abstract noun rather than an irreducible subjective experience, a pure feeling, is evident from the fact that it makes perfect sense to ask a person who says he is angry, "How do you know you are?" It makes sense because that person can then attempt to answer by surveying the referents of the term anger as he uses it, which is to say by pointing to the signs from which he draws the conclusion that he *is* angry. He might, of course, protest that the question as to how he knows he is angry makes no sense since this knowledge is given to him directly as experience; that is, he might claim to be experiencing what has been called "pure anger" as such. But this objection will not stand up to such further questions as "How can you tell that you are angry rather than anxious?" "How can you tell that you are angry rather than irked?" and "How did you ever learn that the term anger was the one to apply to that 'pure feeling' you are feeling now?" For even if he were to say in response merely that each emotion is a distinctive and immediately recognizable experience, he would be obliging himself to specify its distinguishing features—in which case he would have granted the legitimacy of the question to which he had initially objected. Additionally, the distinguishing features cited would prove to be equally applicable to others as well as himself; it would become clear then that there is no privileged access to anger.

For these reasons we can (and we do) on occasion say sensibly (and usefully) in the course of our analytic work that an analysand who claims to be angry is not angry, that he is only saying so, that he is in fact trying to obscure his feeling nothing or his feeling excited. Similarly, we can (and we do) on occasion say sensibly that an analysand is only pretending to be angry, that despite his sounding irate and belligerent he is only trying to convince himself or us that he is angry when he is not. On his part, the analysand whose anger we have called into question can ask us sensibly, "How do *you* know?" for we, too, base our judgments in this regard on criteria; that is to say, our labeling someone angry or not angry is stating a conclusion rather than a direct perception of a pure something which is anger and which someone "has" or "doesn't have." That we need not be conscious of our process of appraisal and that it may take place quickly, both contribute to the incorrect impression that anger is directly experienced or perceived as a "pure feeling."

Being an abstract noun, anger is, of course, undischargeable. Moreover, the force of the word anger is not nominative but adverbial; it refers to a way of acting, though perhaps only to an inhibited, fantasied or oblique way of acting—namely, *angrily*. In clinical work, when we analyze "angry" fantasy and behavior, this is how we understand them—as thinking and behaving angrily. We may obscure this fact by using spatial metaphors ourselves; we use them because we think (invalidly) that these metaphors (a) describe something tangible, and (b) help us to understand the angry fantasy and behavior. In fact, however, by using the spatial metaphor we introduce primary process modes of thought into systematic thinking, and so, as we do in the spooky theory of introjects, we contaminate the explanation with what is to be explained. In this light we can see that "catharsis" expresses an anal-expulsive fantasy! The anger that is pent up, simmers, explodes, or spills over expresses a volcanic anal fantasy; it is psychological content to be explained, not psychological explanation. "Catharsis," thus, is peculiarly well suited for expressing in an aseptic fashion archaic ideas about anger as a spatially localizable, destructive substance or quantity; it cannot be a useful theoretical term.

If we give up the illusion that anger is a concrete noun, and think instead that *angrily* denotes a way of acting, we may proceed quite logically. We will state our propositions somewhat as follows.

People act angrily. A number of ways of acting may be subsumed under *angrily*. Adjectival forms are easily transposed into adverbial ("an angry man" refers to a man acting angrily). A person may or may not be conscious that he is acting angrily. He may imagine himself to be filled with some sort of quantity of anger. He may try to avoid acting angrily or to avoid being aware that he is so acting, and he may succeed entirely or intermittently. He may act more angrily in certain situations than others. He may act angrily in different ways at different times. He may put on a show of behaving angrily.

Further, he is not likely to go on acting angrily if he has done something that signifies to him adequate revenge or retaliation, or adequate communication and effectiveness of action wih regard to his grievance, for then he will see his situation as having changed for the better, and he will no longer be provoked to think or behave angrily. Concurrently, his physiological arousal for vigorous action will subside, and he may begin to think of other, perhaps more pleasant matters. He will then be said to be "feeling better." This, in nonspatial, nonquantitative, nonsubstantial—and so, nonpurgative—terms is "anger" and diminution of "anger," possibly cessation of "anger" as well. Nothing has gotten into or out of anyone's system except in fantasy. Objectively, there has been no anal event.

To anticipate a possible objection to my argument at this point, I want to point out that I am not advocating or slipping into a psychology of consciousness. The entire process I have described may—and often does—take place unconsciously. It is quite possible, as Freud demonstrated, to say "think," "believe," "conclude," "put on a show," and so forth, without implying "consciously" or "superficially." There is no opening here for the facile charge of superficiality—a charge which has too often hampered exploratory psychoanalytic discussion.

This, then, is the kind of word that anger is. Whenever we tail to realize or remember that this is so, we make the mistake of thinking of anger as an entity to which notions of substance, quantity, and place (inside and outside) are applicable. This is the mistake involved in using notions of discharging or abreacting anger. Also in error on this account is the assumption that some pure feeling of anger exists apart from all its observable or communicable characteristics; in other words, that the subject has privileged access to this pure feeling of anger.

A few remarks regarding the so-called unconscious affects are in order here. According to the viewpoint I am developing, these "unconscious affects" must be understood always to be fully realized properties of action, that is, as unqualified adverbial characterizations; this is so provided that it is also understood that the subject is successfully resisting being aware that some or all of his actions have these properties. Thus, it is quite common for the analyst to point out to an analysand that he is speaking angrily (or tearfully, etc.) while remaining defensively oblivious of the fact. That this emotional property is likely to become more vivid following the analysand's becoming consciously aware of it, or following his restraining overt action with this emotional property despite continued (subjective) provocation, does not show that a potential affect has been actualized (which is one main sense of unconscious affect) ; nor does it show that a dammed-up and unacknowledged affect has been released (the other main sense of unconscious affect) : it does show that the analysand's attitude toward action with this emotional property has changed sufficiently for him to be able to tolerate being consciously aware of it or to be no longer willing to abstain from action of this sort, and, this being so, that he has defined a new situation for himself in which it is subjectively appropriate and possible for him to behave in a more emphatic or demonstrative fashion and with more varied ideas of grievance and retaliation available to him. "Discharge" and "abreaction" are now seen to be emotional actions appropriate to changed situations rather than movement of quantities of psychic energy.

It might be surmised—correctly!—that I am dispensing with the hypothesis of an instinctual drive of aggression whose psychic energy (also called "aggression") is accumulated and discharged in anger (among other responses) . I, along with many others (e.g., Holt, 1967; Applegarth, 1971) , have advanced at some length reasons for discarding "psychic energy" as a fundamental hypothesis in psychoanalytic theory (1968b, esp. Ch. 3) ; I shall not repeat these arguments here.

Although I could extend this discussion to other affect words, such as joy, sadness, anxiety, and guilt, I shall not do so at this time. My reason is that I planned only to make a methodological point in taking up anger (as well as introjects). The point is to expose a serious problem and suggest a possible solution. The problem is the confusion of observation and theory that results from our unwittingly employing the archaic notion of internality to mental processes. The solution is the elimination of words of the "inside" and "outside" variety from *theoretical* discourse. This change in our thinking will be one part of a general strategy for avoiding the concretistic error of ascribing substance (quantity, extension, momentum, etc.) to mental processes.

The Prevalence of the Idea of the Inside

Judging by its prevalence in our everyday language, the idea of the inside appears to have profound significance in human experience. So much is this so that without our realizing it we have used the idea extensively in fashioning psychoanalytic theory. From among the factors contributing to the pervasiveness of the idea of the inside, I single out the following as being especially important.[7]

1. Earliest subjective experience seems to get organized around bodily sensations with their varying pleasure-pain properties. This early subjective experience is the "body ego" that, according to Freud (1923), is the first ego. Thus, from its very beginnings, the organization of experience implies physical referents such as are later subjectively defined as being inside and outside (Schafer, 1968b, esp. Ch. 4).

2. Throughout subsequent experience, the notion of the interiority of one's own being is supported by the often prominent physiological changes that are part aspects of the emotional side of significant activities, such as the sexual, the angry, and the frightened. With regard to the makeup and boundaries of the physical body, these physiological changes are indeed mostly "beneath the surface" or "inside," and in some instances "deep."

[7] I am indebted to Dr. Ernst Prelinger for helping me to develop a number of the main propositions I shall set forth in this section—and also for his helpful suggestions regarding this paper as a whole.

3. Adding further to the idea of mental processes as occupying space and as moving in space are the crucial anatomical foci of psychosexual development—mouth, anus, genitalia—with their openings and closings, and the passage of substances in and out of them, all of which is associated with highly sensuous and emotional actions and events. So much of mental life concerns these places, spaces, substances, feelings, and sensations, that inevitably, when we begin to think about mind at all, we model it after the "body ego" and assume that it is somehow a substantial and sensitive entity with spatial characteristics.

4. Early notions of self are strongly influenced by these archaic, concretistic factors. Self, too, is then thought of as being a place as well as being in places, e.g., within the physical boundaries of the body, though not necessarily filling it. As *a* place, self is thought to be like a body in having boundaries which contain processes or contents that "belong" to it. Sometimes the boundaries of self are thought to include possessions and other people we love, hate, or fear. And sometimes, as when we engage in projecting, these boundaries exclude features of our own being that we have repudiated. Other ways in which we spatialize self are by thinking of it as having parts, splits, layers, and levels. These pseudospatial metaphors are repeatedly emphasized in social discourse, a matter about which I shall say more under point 7.

5. Our perceptions of others being, as we learn from experience, limited, fragmentary, and insufficient for predictive purposes, we think from early on that the "more" that eludes us must be "behind" or "within" what we do perceive.

6. Earlier in this paper, I mentioned how we have contaminated the idea of the brain, which mediates mental processes and is inside the head, with the idea of mental processes. The result of this conceptual contamination is that these processes, too, are thought to be somehow or other characterized by inside-ness.

7. Finally, there is the factor of well-learned metaphysical assumptions. These assumptions are conveyed and perpetuated in the basic language of "experience." The child learns them from people in his environment, and he relies on them as he learns to speak and to think in words. Moreover, and as one would expect from points 1–5 above, he finds these assumptions congenial. That

is to say, they match his own physical, sensuous, psychosexual matrix for comprehending and organizing ideas. I do not mean that children or even most adults realize that they entertain metaphysical assumptions, but, from the study of young children, dreams, and neurotic and psychotic symptoms, we know all too well the extent to which physical reference constitutes the core of understanding.[8]

Implications for the Language of Interpretation

In many instances analysts unwittingly encourage their analysands to use archaic (though also everyday) internalization language. They do so whenever they themselves use spatial metaphors to render mental processes and do so not in the service of empathically verbalizing how a process seems or "feels" to an analysand but in the service of objectively describing how mental events take place *in fact.* For example, the analyst might say "your internal standards," "your inner image," "your innermost conviction," "on another level," "the deepest meaning," and so on and so forth along the lines I laid down earlier. Of greater significance often is the analyst's use of internalization language in dealing with so-called introjects or internal objects and other presences, and also in dealing with affects and their disposition.[9] Every time the analyst speaks of "the mother inside you," "the values you took in," "the structure you set up," "the boundaries between you and others," "the feelings you let out," etc., he confirms the analysand's unconscious fantasy that being is a spatial, ultimately incorporative and expulsive affair rather than actions of various kinds by various people. Rendering these actions exclusively in the form of spatial

[8] Further consideration of this factor would require formulating fundamental doubts concerning the logical necessity and legitimacy of using *motivation words* to explain behavior. This is so because the term "motive," for example, refers to a mover of action that is prior to it in time and "interior" to it as an inner or behind-the-scenes entity that is personlike in its comprehension and activity. I cannot do justice to this problem in this paper. I refer the interested reader to Ryle's (1949) and Hampshire's (1958, 1962) discussions of mind, action, and dispositions. These discussions are an important part of the intellectual background of this paper.

[9] Externalization words are used by the analyst in the same way; for example, "your outer manner," "the outward manifestation," "an external danger," "you projected your feeling into him," etc.

metaphor can be done only at great expense to understanding. Objectively, "the mother inside you" is better said "the mother you think of whenever you thus and so," or "the mother you imagine inside you in order that you thus and so." I am here suggesting a nonspatial language as an alternative to our familiar one; actually, this alternative is one we all use at times, perhaps often or even regularly. And yet we do not altogether believe in it or appreciate it for we lapse so readily into unacknowledged and unqualified spatial metaphor.

Certainly, there are many analytic contexts where it seems right for the analyst to use language that has the same archaic (though also everyday) implications as the analysand's language. Particularly is this so when the analysand is beginning to say new, significant, and difficult things in the analysis. But the analysand must have some steadily available sense, though not necessarily a steady conscious awareness, that at least the analyst is being metaphoric in his effort to help find the best words for hitherto unverbalized fantasies. In other words, the analysand should increasingly appreciate that words are being used "as if" mind or being or ego were space and structure with objects moving into, out of, and through it all.

I want at least to mention here a matter I have discussed at greater length elsewhere (Schafer, 1973). By joining in saying that things come to mind, or slip the mind, or are brought to mind, the analyst tends to confirm the idea of mind as place rather than as an abstract rubric which has expanse only in the sense of conceptual inclusiveness. These locutions also confirm the archaic, anthropomorphic belief that ideas are like animate beings that can "come," "slip away," and "bring" more like them.

The ideal language for interpretation that is aimed at objectifying mental processes would, according to my argument, never refer to inside or outside, structure and its variants (barriers, limits, boundaries, etc.), introjection and introject, and affects as moving or movable quantities that are implicitly objectlike. References to inside and outside would be made, of course, in the many appropriate comments by the analyst that express empathy, recognition, and articulation of archaic and obscure experiences. *In the main, the analyst would be working in that manner.* But when speaking strictly objectively, the analyst would avoid treating abstractions as spatial and personal entities.

Here are a series of translations of the sort I mean. (Elsewhere in this paper I have indicated other translations—e.g., regarding introjects, affects, and mind.)

1a. It was an old anger you finally got out.

1b. You allowed yourself to act angrily after all this time.

2a. You broke through the internal barriers against your feelings of love.

2b. You finally did not stop yourself from acting lovingly.

3a. Your chronic deep sense of worthlessness comes from the condemning inner voice of your mother.

3b. You regularly imagine your mother's voice condemning you, and, agreeing with it, regard yourself as being essentially worthless.

4a. Your underlying reason for being superficial is avoiding the shame about your past that haunts you.

4b. There is an unacknowledged but crucial reason why you dwell on obvious or trivial matters: if you did not do so, you would be shaming yourself about your past over and over again; your contrived obviousness and triviality help you avoid that.

5a. You are afraid of your impulse to throw caution to the winds.

5b. You are afraid you might act extremely recklessly.

I offer these illustrative translations with the full realization that, like translations of the King James Bible into modern English, they seem to take the "body" and "soul" out of the language. But that is the point! A soulful language cannot help us understand all we wish to understand about "soul," "soulfulness," and, in Schreber's phrase, "soul-murder" (Freud, 1911). And a language that is not "disembodied" cannot help us understand all we wish to understand about the fantastic concreteness and "embodiment" of unconscious or primary process thinking (Freud, 1915,

1925). I mentioned earlier the actual disruption of habitual thought and speech and the sense of loss that accompany change in well-established modes of thought, and I argued then that these difficulties should not deter us from thinking through—and working through—chronic and crucial problems in psychoanalytic conceptualization. I must also mention again that the type of non-anthropomorphic, nonspatial locutions I am emphasizing are widely used anyway; my argument is to establish their value for systematic thinking in theory and practice.

Conclusion

The gist of my argument is that internalization is a spatial—actually, pseudospatial—metaphor that is so grossly incomplete and unworkable that we would do best to avoid it in psychoanalytic conceptualization.[10] Incorporation (and incorporated object or person) is the only term that has a real referent, namely, archaic fantasies of taking objects into the body. Logically, internalization cannot mean anything more than that: it refers to a fantasy, not to a process.

The unsatisfactoriness of "internalization" *for systematic purposes* is all the more apparent when, upon further reflection, we realize that a clear need for this metaphor has never been established in psychoanalytic theory. We realize, that is, that invalidly we have assumed a condition of conceptual need or impotence in this connection. After all, why do we have to add anything about localization once we have said that a child now reminds himself to do things when before it was his mother who did so; or that he imagines his father's commanding visage in his father's absence; or that he thinks of himself as looking after himself? Typically we have hastened to invoke internalization words to describe these phenomena. But why this haste or urgency? How were we in a primitive, obstructed, or incomplete conceptual condition in the

10 It is not so strange as it might seem at first that this sentence has been written by the author of a book on psychoanalytic theory entitled *Aspects of Internalization* (1968b). The reader of that book will find that to a great extent I was already redefining the central concepts in nonspatial terms. But, while writing that book, I did not yet realize the extent to which "internalization" itself was part of a major problem in psychoanalytic theorizing.

simple (though not naïve) descriptions? In no way at all. If we say that the child "internalized" his mother's reminders or his reminding mother, that he "introjected" his father's authority or his authoritarian father, etc., have we understood or conveyed anything more? If anything, we are working with less. I maintain this for these reasons: we have complicated our thinking unnecessarily; we are using a pseudospatial metaphor from which it is all too easy to slip into concreteness of thought; once embarked on metaphor, we tend to develop a sense of obligation to be metaphorically consistent, and involve ourselves in extravagant niceties of formulation; and perhaps we even introduce still another assumption into theory where none is needed. The history of the pseudoquantitative energy metaphor in Freudian metapsycho'ogy demonstrates what I mean.

I have also indicated how our observations, understanding, and conceptualization of introjects, affects, and what we call psychic structure may be improved by our dispensing with notions of the inside and the outside in our theorizing. The terms organism and environment suffice for biological discussion; the terms inside and outside (and their variations) are suitable for verbalizing fantasies about mental processes, self, and human relations. But mental processes themselves—the referents of our theoretical propositions —are not localizable in any kind of space for they are classes of nonsubstantial and therefore nonspatial psychological events. They do not exist anywhere and they do not move anywhere; we only—and fatefully!—think they do.

BIBLIOGRAPHY

APPLEGARTH, A. (1971), Comments on Aspects of the Theory of Psychic Energy. *J. Amer. Psychoanal. Assn.*, 19:379–416.

BRIERLEY, M. (1937), Affects in Theory and Practice. *Trends in Psycho-Analysis*. London: Hogarth Press, 1951, pp. 43–56.

FREUD, S. (1911), Psycho-Analytic Notes on an Autobiographical Account of a Case of Paranoia (Dementia Paranoides). *Standard Edition*, 12:3–82. London: Hogarth Press, 1958.

— (1915), The Unconscious. *Standard Edition*, 14:159–215. London: Hogarth Press, 1957.

— (1923), The Ego and the Id. *Standard Edition*, 19:3–66. London: Hogarth Press, 1961.

— (1925), Negation. *Standard Edition*, 19:233–239. London: Hogarth Press, 1961.

— (1926), Inhibitions, Symptoms and Anxiety. *Standard Edition*, 20:77–175. London: Hogarth Press, 1959.

GROSSMAN, W. I. & SIMON, B. (1969), Anthropomorphism: Motive, Meaning, and Causality in Psychoanalytic Theory. *This Annual*, 24:78–114.

HAMPSHIRE, S. (1958), *Thought and Action*. New York: Viking Press.

— (1962), Disposition and Memory. *Int. J. Psycho-Anal.*, 43:59–68.

HARTMANN, H. (1939), *Ego Psychology and the Problem of Adaptation*. New York: International Universities Press, 1958.

— (1964), *Essays on Ego Psychology*. New York: International Universities Press.

— KRIS, E., & LOEWENSTEIN, R. M. (1946), Comments on the Formation of Psychic Structure. *This Annual*, 2:11–38.

HOLT, R. R. (1967), Beyond Vitalism and Mechanism: Freud's Concept of Psychic Energy. *Science and Psychoanalysis*, 11:1–41. New York: Grune & Stratton.

KOHUT, H. (1971), *The Analysis of the Self*. New York: International Universities Press.

LOEWALD, H. W. (1960), On the Therapeutic Action of Psycho-Analysis. *Int. J. Psycho-Anal.*, 41:16–33.

— (1962), Internalization, Separation, Mourning, and the Superego. *Psychoanal. Quart.*, 31:483–504.

RAPAPORT, D. (1959), *The Structure of Psychoanalytic Theory: A Systematizing Attempt* [*Psychol. Issues*, Monogr. 6]. New York: International Universities Press, 1960.

— (1967), *The Collected Papers of David Rapaport*, ed. M. M. Gill. New York: Basic Books.

RYLE, G. (1949), *The Concept of Mind*. New York: Barnes & Noble, 1965.

SCHAFER, R. (1964), The Clinical Analysis of Affects. *J. Amer. Psychoanal. Assn.*, 12:275–299.

— (1968a), The Mechanisms of Defence. *Int. J. Psycho-Anal.*, 49:49–62.

— (1968b), *Aspects of Internalization*. New York: International Universities Press.

— (1971), An Overview of Heinz Hartmann's Contributions to Psycho-Analysis. *Int. J. Psycho-Anal.*, 51:425–446.

— (1973), Action: Its Place in Psychoanalytic Interpretation and Theory. *The Annual of Psychoanalysis*, 1 (in press).

CLINICAL

CONTRIBUTIONS

Some Characteristics of Genital Arousal and Discharge in Latency Girls

SELMA FRAIBERG

IN THIS PAPER I PROPOSE TO BRING TOGETHER ANALYTIC MATERIAL from three cases which made me consider possible links between genital anesthesia in the adult female and loss of genital sensation in early childhood and latency. One of the three patients was an adult, Mrs. M. The other two cases were girls in latency, Nancy, who had begun her analysis at the age of 7, and Suzanne, who had started analysis at 8 years of age.

The three patients came to analysis with illnesses that were clinically unrelated, yet they had a specific experience in common. In latency there had been a fateful turning away from the genital coinciding with total loss of erotic sensation. As if they had all chosen a common metaphor, the woman and the two girls dreamed of

Professor of Child Psychoanalysis and Director of the Child Development Project, University of Michigan, Ann Arbor, Michigan.

searches in attics or empty houses for something precious that had been lost (although this, in itself, is unremarkable as a castration symbol) and each of them had a repertoire of dreams in which a child took flight from a fire, an inferno, or an explosion which in the analysis represented an erotic conflagration. Their dissimilar neuroses had two other features in common: isolation of affect; and a characterological picture of stillness or deadness in mood, in voice, in their postures of lying or sitting.

In each case genital anesthesia was linked to a disaster which on one level was clearly castration, the loss of sensation representing a dreadful confirmation of castration fears. But the details of "an inferno," "an explosion," and the metaphoric burning out of the erotic fires led back in each case to an experience of insupportable erotic excitement at the height of the oedipal phase and a flight from the genitals.

The three patients overlapped in periods of treatment, although at one point Mrs. M. and Suzanne had analytic hours which followed each other. It was this coincidence, perhaps, that invited the questions that I raise in this paper. It was as if Mrs. M. at 35, then in the early stages of her analysis, was "asking the questions" and 8-year-old Suzanne was carrying on an uncanny dialogue with her. And if I reached back 3 years into the analysis of Nancy and my detailed analytic notes, the extraordinary parallels invited close study. In this paper I cannot do more than examine the questions raised by these three patients.

The Questions

Mrs. M. had entered analysis with me at the age of 35. She had been sexually unresponsive throughout the 10 years of her marriage. At the time she started analysis she was suffering from a severe depression which had come on during her second pregnancy. In the 2 years that followed the birth of her son, the depression had deepened and she herself was now alarmed by the growing constrictions in everyday functioning and phobic dreads in leaving her home for visiting, marketing, and the most ordinary excursions.

She was a shy, self-abasing woman, tender to her children and to her husband, not incapable of love, yet sexually anesthetic. She had had rare moments in her marriage when she experienced arousal, but this flickering excitement was quickly extinguished. In recent years, there had not been so much as a flicker of feelings, she told me.

During the early months of analysis I sometimes had the impression that there was an anesthetized patient on the couch. Whenever there should have been grief or pain or anger or pleasure, there was silence, or only her dead voice describing a state or feeling that was not there. All of her memories were somehow dead, too. She could not evoke her childhood and, in fact, told me that she had no memories of the period 6 to 10 years beyond "place memories" or cloudy pictures of the progression through grades in school.

In her dreams, too, she seemed interminably occupied with searching in attics and basements for something lost. She feared that she could never be analyzed because she had no memories of consequence. I told her, of course, that she did not need to concern herself at this point with her unremembered past, and centered the analysis in this period on the defenses against affect.

The first outbreak of feeling came about in this extraordinary way. In her hour she began to cry and at first she could not even name her sorrow. Something lost, dead, a long time ago. She was a little girl. Then it came to her. "My pussycat!" she said, and wept hopelessly. "Oh, how I loved her! I found her dead on the table. My father brought her in from the road." For nearly 10 minutes she sobbed on the couch. Then the incongruity of her 35-year-old self weeping for her dead "pussycat" hit her. She laughed a little and when she spoke of her grief again, the pussycat was called simply, "my cat."

In the following session she came in "shattered by a dream," she said. "There was an explosion in the basement—my childhood home—and the house was on fire—I was trying to save everyone— we were all going to die. I woke up in a sweat."

The "pussycat," we learned, was her genital that had "died" in childhood, and we now began to seek the links between the sexual anesthesia of her adult life and a disaster in early childhood that sealed off her infantile sexual life. There was reason to believe that anesthesia had followed the disaster and was sustained throughout latency, corresponding to her amnesia for this period of childhood.

The dream of the "explosion in the basement" occupied many months of analysis. The "explosion" was highly overdetermined, of course. It represented the uncontrollable excitement in the genitals, the "burning out" of the genital in an erotic conflagration, and the extinction of the erotic fire during the period of latency. But the detail, "an explosion," was further illuminated in the analysis after she began to recover genital sensations. It was clear that in intercourse she inhibited excitement; she was afraid of the orgastic "explosion."

Then, one hour, she recalled an experience in her marriage which she had never remembered to tell me. There had been one occasion prior to her second pregnancy and the emergence of her depression when she had experienced a flare-up of excitement in intercourse—an exceptional experience—and, as she felt mounting excitement, she was overwhelmed with panic and the erotic feelings dissolved. She could not recover sensation again, and she dated her depression to this experience.

Somewhere, I thought, we would find that the chapter on childhood sexuality would disclose a parallel here—that uncontrollable excitement had produced great anxiety and a motive for inhibition of erotic sensation. But we had no time to find the links. At the end of the second year of analysis, when my patient was much improved, now free of depression and recovering genital sensation, another disaster occurred. Her husband became critically ill and the analysis had to come to a stop.

Some Parallels in Child Analysis

During the analytic work with my adult patient I found my thoughts traveling back and forth between the older woman on the couch and girls whom I had analyzed in the latency years. When I could ascertain with certainty that a latency girl had abandoned masturbation, I could also be reasonably sure that a hysterical anesthesia existed. (I had learned from both boys and girls that there is no heroic conquest of masturbation, a very small capacity in childhood to say "no" to intense erotic urges. But when the erotic impulses have undergone repression, temptation is removed and, as a consequence, masturbation is relinquished.) Could the genital anesthesia sometimes encountered in latency provide us with vital links to sexual anesthesia in adult life?

The "explosion in the basement," the fear of overwhelming sexual excitement reported by my adult patient, also had prototypes in the sexual experience of girls whom I had analyzed. While nothing in these children's reports was equivalent to orgasm, I had a number of experiences described to me that showed anxiety at insupportable excitement. There were, in fact, "peaks of excitement" which were not orgastic and differed qualitatively from orgasm in ways which I shall describe later.

What, in fact, were the characteristics of erotic *sensation* in girls of latency age? We know much about the masturbatory *fantasies* of this age. We know that typically there is a decline in masturbatory activity at this age, but we do not expect either masturbation or the capacity for genital sensation to be extinguished in the healthy child in latency (Bornstein, 1953). If erotic feelings manifest themselves in the latency girl, where are they localized? The role of the clitoris has been well documented in psychoanalytic research. Does the clitoris play an exclusive role in erotic experience in latency? And, in the light of new information on the transmission of physiological response in the mature female (Masters and Johnson, 1966), can we exclude the possibility that the vaginal orifice and even an accessible intravaginal area are capable of arousal in a latency girl? In the mature female, the external genitalia and the vagina act in concert in the excitement phase and the orgasmic phase. If the capacity for orgasm has rarely been reported in latency girls, is it still conceivable that childhood excitement may follow the same route with qualitative and quantitative differences? Many little girls discover the vagina itself. What sensations, if any, accompany these explorations?

In the course of analytic treatment both Susan and Nancy helped me to a greater understanding of masturbatory experience. I learned of the vicissitudes of "good feelings" in latency, of their "comings and goings," and of transitory periods of anesthesia. As articulate children and as serious patients, strongly motivated to get well, they were able to link masturbatory fantasies with specific states of feeling and to localize those feelings—a rare feat for children. Both girls had discovered and explored the vagina, and one of them helped me understand this as a childhood experience.

In both cases masturbatory conflicts were at the center of the neurosis. Yet both children had entered analysis after masturbation had been given up and symptoms had been formed to maintain the masturbatory experiences in repression. The genital was "dead"—in terms that one child used with me. As analysis of the symptoms revived sensation in the genitals, the vicissitudes of the earlier masturbatory conflicts were re-experienced in the analysis.

We cannot generalize from these two cases to a normal population of latency girls. We do not know whether the characteristics of autoerotic experience described by these two children are to be found among all latency girls. We have no right, of course, to inquire into the sexual secrets of normal girls. The right is obtained only in the cases of patients in whom sexual conflict has taken a morbid turn. The child patient then grants the permission, explicitly or implicitly, for us to learn about his intimate experience. Since the analytic experience is the only condition under which such self-observation and intimate revelation can take place, we can value the reports of the child patient for the information we can obtain of the range of the autoerotic experience open to the child. Clinically, these reports may also prove to be of value in examining the links between childhood autoerotic conflicts and the sexual inhibitions of adults who have carried their unresolved masturbatory conflicts into the sexual partnership.

Under the most favorable conditions in child analysis, with serious and deeply committed child patients, we still encounter great obstacles to understanding the child's sexual experience through language. The child—even one who has received a candid sex education in his home—will not have a vocabulary to describe erotic sensation or grades of excitement. He will still be confused about anatomical terms and use global words for the genital apparatus that make it difficult for us to know to which organ he is referring. The child in latency has no handy word which corresponds to "erotic," or "sexual feeling," or "genital sensation"; and when we begin to work with his masturbatory conflicts, we find that we need to help him find a vocabulary. In the course of years I have found that some words will be understood exactly by the child patient.

"Good feelings" is understood in relation to excitement in the genitals. Some children, given the lead to talk about "good feelings," found their own vocabulary, all the way from "prickly feelings" to "hot feelings," but once we had a vocabulary children were astonishing in their ability to describe differentiated states. The anatomical confusions are so much part of the fabric of childhood and child analysis that they need no discussion here. However, if we need to know exactly which organ a child is referring to, the persistence of these confusions becomes a barrier to understanding. Little girls will use "vagina" in global terms, referring to the entire genital region and including the urethra. Several girls referred to the clitoris as the vagina. In each example, cited in the text that follows, I ascertained, either through clarifying questions or through the child's drawing or plasteline model, to which part she was referring. Where confusion persisted, I indicated this in the text.

Genital Anesthesia

Both Nancy and Suzanne gave me convincing evidence in the early months of analysis that masturbation was no longer in the picture and that, in fact, there was no awareness of erotic feeling in the genitals. In both cases analysis brought about recovery of genital sensation, but there were many occasions when anesthesia returned on a transitory basis.

Nancy entered analysis one year after the onset of petit mal seizures (see also Fraiberg, 1967). When I first met her, she was severely withdrawn; her voice and face seemed drained of affect. She spoke in a still small voice and recounted her complaints in a mechanical speech. Only once did her voice approach something like feeling. She blamed her mother for her unhappiness. At home, I had learned, she kept up a nagging complaint to her mother, "You are to blame"; and when the exhausted mother begged her to explain, she would say in an insistent voice, "You took something away from me!" She could not "remember" what it was that mother had taken from her. In her stories and plays in the analytic hours there was a witch who cast spells upon children and, in one variation or another, changed good children into bad children who went about robbing and killing or doing other wicked things. Nancy blamed her mother for her "forgetting spells" (her seizures), though she did not know why. But the witch who cast an evil spell was not only the mother who was blamed for the seizures. Later in the analysis we learned that the mother had played an accidental role in the suppression of masturbation and sex play.

As I have indicated, Nancy did not masturbate and had no awareness of erotic feelings in the genitals. Yet she had a bedtime ritual which was of considerable interest in this context. She could not fall asleep unless she had a rubber ball in her bed. She was quite candid in describing to me how the ball must always be between her legs, and there was an innocence in her manner of describing this that made me attentive. When I felt that our relationship was sufficiently secure, I began to ask Nancy about the feelings that accompanied this bedtime ritual. There was "no feeling," she said. On the chance that her child's vocabulary might be inadequate to describe feelings if she had them, I went a little further and asked if sometimes there were good feelings or tickly feelings when she put the ball between her legs. "No feelings," she said. "Not good feelings and not bad feelings. Just no feelings." It was in this way that I began to understand that she was truly anesthetic in the genital region, and I had the suspicion, later confirmed in all details, that masturbation and its attendant feelings had been lost, and that the ball was a souvenir from the old days —properly speaking, a fetish.

Was it possible that Nancy was concealing her masturbation from me? This was certainly something we must take into account in a child analysis, but all the later events of the analysis proved that she had been quite truthful. When analysis brought about recovery of genital sensation, she began to report "good feelings sometimes" when the ball was between her legs, and with the recovery of sensation there were dramatic changes in her symptom picture and in the general realm of affects. Her whole personality came alive. The "deadness" of affect, which had once concerned me greatly, now receded and she seemed to be in touch with her own feelings again. The persecutory feelings in relation to her mother disappeared, and the old repetitive accusations that "mother took something away from me" were translated as the analytic material illuminated the mother's accidental role in linking masturbation and danger when Nancy was 6.

Yet, throughout the analysis, there were transitory periods of genital anesthesia which Nancy reported to me. Fear of mother's anger was linked several times to the "loss of good feelings." Fantasies of damaging the genital were linked to the loss of sensation. On each of these occasions the anesthesia was clearly produced on a hysterical basis. With each recurrence, the same syndrome was reactivated: repression of all affects, with the consequent stillness of personality, increases in seizures, and a return of the persecutory feelings in relation to mother.

I now understood that the stillness in Nancy's personality, which had so troubled me when I first knew her, was the counterpart in the ego of the genital that was silent.

Suzanne, too, presented a picture of emotional deadness, when I first met her at the age of 7. Her presenting symptoms were enuresis and a severe paroxysmal coughing. She was joyless, constricted, unable to cry, incapable of expressing anger. Among other things, her parents told me, Suzanne in the past year seemed to be always losing things, and "losing things" would throw her into a panic. She was Queen of the Fairies in her fantasies, exiled from her fairy domain by witches who had seized her magic power. She still possessed her wand, but her wand was powerless. Her fairy subjects were trying to get messages through to her. At least once or twice in every analytic hour the exiled Queen excused herself to go to the toilet.

Suzanne would clutch herself so urgently between the legs before she fled to the toilet that I began to look for the right moment to raise some questions. When I finally found it, she discussed the urgency quite candidly. "I really don't have to go to the toilet. Only a little bit. A couple of drops." That happened to her a lot, she confided. If she only felt "a couple of drops," she felt as if she must get to the toilet. (Suzanne was also a bedwetter.) What were the feelings that made her feel as if she had to go to the toilet? She was puzzled. Well, it was kind of an "itchy" feeling. And after she got out the "one or two drops," she "got rid of the feeling."

For many weeks I remained unsure about whether Suzanne was alluding to erotic feelings per se or to tensions that were localized in the urethra. As more material emerged in the analysis it became increasingly clear that Suzanne had no "good feelings" localized by her in the genitals.

She was talking about bugs in the bathroom at home, how she hated them. If they got on you, they "tickle." "Ugh!" she looked as if she were gagging at the thought. Asked what this reminded her of, she mused: "Bugs . . . tickle . . . potty . . . Oh! I told you about the tickly feelings when I have to go to the potty. Maybe that's a connection, but if it is, I don't want to talk about it. It's icky." "What?" "The feeling. And sometimes it *hurts* until I go potty." I asked if the "icky" feeling was connected with anything else. Would it be there if she touched herself there? She made a face. "It's wet there!" she said with loathing, astonished that I would even ask. Why should she want to touch such a disgusting place—was implied in her voice. I commented on her reaction. Had anyone ever given her that feeling. "No, just myself. *I* don't like to [touch myself]."

I learned in the next months of analysis that she was being quite truthful. She did not masturbate. There were no erotic feelings localized in the genitals. What she experienced in urinary frequency and urgency was an unpleasant tension, sometimes reported as distinctly painful, which could be relieved only by urinating.

When analysis helped Suzanne to recover "good feelings," she was clearly able to identify them as "good" feelings, in contrast to the painful tension she described in urinary urgency. She was able to localize these "good feelings" in the genital area (diffusely experienced). Yet, throughout the first 3 years of analysis, the "good feelings" would disappear for days or weeks at a time (conscientiously reported by Suzanne) and symptoms would take their place. Most frequently urinary urgency or bed wetting would return. On several occasions a paroxysmal coughing appeared which began with "a tickly feeling in the throat." Each time, as we uncovered the motive for displacement into symptoms, the symptom disappeared and genital sensations were recovered.

With each transitory return of genital anesthesia, there occurred dramatic shifts of mood. Suzanne would become silent for long periods in her session. The silence represented resistance, of course, but, I also felt, the "silence" of the genital. There were affective transformations. Spontaneity was lost. The range of joy and anger became constricted again. Often, too, she would begin losing things—things that were precious or necessary to her, a ring, her watch, her dental braces, a purse. And she was always in a panic when she lost things. Typically, too, there was disorder in fairy land, in the long-continuing fantasy which occupied many hours during the first 3 years of analysis. The witches regained power, the Queen's magic was lost, the fairy subjects tried frantically to get messages to the Queen through the barrier that separated the fairy realm from the real world. Suzanne understood her fantasies very well and when she told me, "I lost my magic again," we both knew what she meant.

Where Do Girls Localize Genital Sensation?

Suzanne (age 9 years in this excerpt) was preoccupied in one hour with one of the elaborate mazes she sometimes drew. We had long understood that the maze represented the "roads" in her own body. She was creating "road blocks" in her drawing and I asked her about this. She said soberly: "Do you remember how we once figured out how the tickly feeling in my throat made me begin coughing? I used to feel like there were little men in there. That's a blocking of a road, too. And we figured out how the tickly feeling got moved from my pe-pe-jina to my throat?" (Note: "vagina," which she always stumbled over, and fused with penis as "pejina," did not necessarily represent the vagina; Suzanne, like other little girls I have known, still used the term vagina to designate the entire genital area, though occasionally she used it correctly for the vagina itself.) Since at that time I was not yet certain what she was referring to by "pejina," I asked her to help me understand this better. Could she draw it for me, or could she take some plasteline and make a model of a "front bottom" (her word for genitals)? Suzanne: "It'll be hard, but I'll try."

She hollowed out a lump of plasteline, made a very prominent clitoris, which she named. I: "And where is the tickly feeling?" Suzanne (pointing to the deepest part of the hollow) : "Back here." I asked where the vagina, the opening, was located in her model.

She was surprised, she had left it out. She did not hollow out a hole or passageway, but only pointed to the place. I: "And where are the tickly feelings?" She: "All around here and inside." (She demonstrated on the model the area around the clitoris, the hollow, she had created in clay.) Still wondering to myself about the meaning of the "roadblock" which had appeared many times in the analytic material, I asked, "And what stops the tickly feelings?" She: "I do. When my story doesn't go on. . . . You know how I never finish those stories. When the story doesn't go on, when it stops, then the tickly feeling stops. [And replying to my question:] Oh, the same story, you know. Usually the same. The girl tied up naked. Sometimes they [the "bad men"] take pictures of her. No, they don't do anything that hurts her, but they, uh, sometimes poke pins in her, all over her. That's all." I: "Does that hurt?" "Not much."

On another occasion Suzanne was describing to me how she got "good feelings." "I lie on my stomach and squirm." She picked up a doll to demonstrate, making a mark with a pencil which she said stood for the vagina. Then she placed the doll's hands there and put the doll on the stomach. "Then I think about having no clothes and a man there." (Note: Suzanne during this period always masturbated with a layer of clothing between her hand and the genitals.) I: "And where are the feelings?" She pointed to the spot on the doll she had named vagina and then circled the area around.

In these examples and others it was clear that Suzanne experienced excitement diffusely in the external genitalia, but there was also excitement specifically identified in the area that must correspond to the vaginal opening. Then it stopped. We note that she did not single out the clitoris as the locus of excitement, although it did, indeed, have a prominent place in her plasteline model. Here, there may be some limited correspondence with what Masters and Johnson describe in the "plateau phase" of sexual arousal in the woman, in that excitement suffuses the external genitalia. What we do not see in the child's report is the localization of any excitement in the vagina itself.

In another drawing which Suzanne made for me when she was trying to explain her ideas about intercourse (also at age 9), she designated the vaginal orifice, "the hole," as "the stop place." Impregnation, in her theory, took place when the father's penis touched the mother's clitoris. One of the most difficult tasks of analysis during the first 2 years was to help Suzanne understand the role of the vagina in intercourse and impregnation. The idea of vaginal penetration was loathsome and actually terrifying to her.

Yet, she had long ago discovered her own vagina! For as the mazes came into the analytic picture for detailed work, and fantasies of dark and terrible tunnels emerged in the analytic material, Suzanne began to speak of her own explorations.

I asked: "When did you first know you had a vagina?"

Suzanne: "As long as I can remember. Maybe I didn't know the name but I knew it."

I: "How do you think you discovered it?"

Suzanne: "Oh, I must have poked my finger into it."

During this phase of the analysis we were dealing with anxiety around "the hole," and I felt it was not the time to raise questions regarding the possibility of vaginal sensation. But I should mention that from this point on, whenever we spoke of vaginas, either hysterical coughing or urinary urgency appeared immediately.[1] The simplest explanation for the emergence of symptoms was anxiety in association with "the hole," and there was ample material to confirm this. But the urinary urgency was another matter. The urge to urinate under all other circumstances observed in the analysis was an erotic substitution, and even retained erotic quality in its displaced manifestations. Why would talk about "the hole," or even a displacement activity like drawing mazes, create the urge to urinate unless an erotic component in the experience of exploring the vagina had undergone a transformation into this symptom? I received no clues from Suzanne at this time.

Fully a year later, the tunnels and holes reappeared in the analytic material. Suzanne now spoke candidly about occasionally exploring her vagina, but still had many puzzled questions about this passageway. In this context, rushing off to the toilet also reappeared. I chose one of these occasions to make a neutral inquiry about exploring the vagina. Could she describe the feeling to me?

---

[1] See Greenacre (1950) for related clinical findings.

Suzanne: "Well, it's slippery and wet. I can only get my finger so far and it goes on quite a way I think. It feels—I guess you can say, like the inside of my mouth. Slippery and wet. That's all I can say."

I: "Any other feelings?"

Suzanne: "No."

I: "No good feelings or bad feelings?"

Suzanne (with an exasperated laugh) : "Mrs. Fraiberg, you don't do *that* to get good feelings. If you're exploring the vagina, that's one thing. But you don't do that to get good feelings. I've already told you a million times how I get good feelings. They are two different things."

She was very convincing. From this report and several others, it was clear that at this time she had no awareness of pleasurable sensations in her vagina and that the vagina was not included in her masturbation. Which left me with the same puzzle: how could we explain the urinary urgency when she was exploring the vagina? And how could we explain the hysterical coughing which began with "a tickly feeling in the throat" and appeared so frequently in connection with "exploring passageways" and related material? (I shall return to this problem.)

Peaks of Excitement

I have not myself encountered a girl in latency who experienced or described anything like an orgasm (although later I shall cite some reports in the literature) . However, both Suzanne and Nancy described something that I am calling here "peaks of excitement" or, in Nancy's words, "a very strong feeling." Yet these peaks of excitement differed markedly from the experience of orgasm.

Nancy (9 years in this excerpt) was explaining to me a rise in tensions in masturbation, yet had no vocabulary for this experience: "You know what it's like? It's like when you're playing the piano. Suppose you play *do, re, me,* and *fa.* Well, the *fa* is like just crying for *sol* to get finished. It's like a baby whining for its mother."

I: "And do the feelings get finished?"

Nancy: "Well, I'd say no."

I: "Tell me what it is like. Use a song to show me how your feelings went."

Nancy: "All right. It went like this. [She now sang in a queer atonal voice, using, of all things, the first phrase of "My country, 'tis of thee."] All right it goes like this. My country 'tis . . . my country 'tis . . . my country 'tis. . . ."

She seemed prepared to repeat this interminably. Finally, I asked: "And how does it get finished?"

Nancy: "Well, it ends when I go to sleep."

In other words, I understood, there is a rise in tension (*do* to *sol*) which is "unfinished," not discharged at the peak, but dissipated or exhausted in the course of repetition.

In the masturbatory fantasy there usually is a high point which corresponds to the high point of excitement. With both Nancy and Suzanne a sadistic fantasy was *required* to reach this point.

In one of Nancy's fantasies (age 10) a boy and a girl were captured by animals and forced to work as slaves. When they were too slow at work, they were tortured. One torture which Nancy appeared to regard as the most exquisite was this: "They [the slave owners] put a bit in their mouths and drive the girl and boy like horses. When they have to pull a heavy load, the bit cuts into their mouths." She was deeply ashamed as she told me this and her voice was close to a whisper. As we talked further, it became clear that she was ashamed because the torture was exciting to her, which she admitted in a strained voice. Returning to the fantasy on a later occasion, I reminded her that every piece of the puzzle made some sense somewhere. What associations did she have to this torture (the bit in the mouth)? Nancy (gesturing toward her genitals) : "When I tighten up there with my hands. And it gives a good feeling." Then I understood. The bit-in-mouth torture was an exact representation of her hands exerting pressure in the region of the genitals.

Why torture? The "torture daydreams" were so necessary to Nancy that we had a long period of resistance at this point in the analysis. She flatly told me that she was afraid that if she told me the torture fantasies, she would not be able to have them, "and if I can't have my torture daydreams, I can't get strong feeling!" I had to remind her many times that analysis did not "take away";

that her fantasies were, indeed, her private business; and that it was *she* who brought the torture daydreams to analysis because they frightened her, made her feel ashamed, and were associated with her symptoms. The analysis of the sadistic fantasies proceeded and eventually led the way to a primal scene memory.

As I described in the more detailed analytic case report (Fraiberg, 1967), the sadistic daydreams were linked with a number of sexual experiences in Nancy's past. But since the focus of this study is on genital sensation, it is worth pointing out that such sadistic fantasies reflect both the level of drive organization in latency and the incapacity to achieve anything like a consummatory experience and adequate discharge. Nancy's description of rising tension—the *so* calling for the *fa* to get finished, "but never finished"—is, in a sense, a metaphor for torment or torture, the condition of unsatisfied hunger or longing. Or, to put it more exactly, unsatisfied longing finds metaphors in self-torment and torture.

When we further consider that both the erotic and aggressive components of sexuality are to large measure centered upon the child's own body in the act of masturbation at this age, there is no possibility of dealing with the antagonistic drives in masturbation, except through fusing their aims and their characteristics and finding a common object (the genital) for a temporary alliance in latency. At a later stage of drive organization, in middle or late adolescence, the finding of the heterosexual love object will effectively bind and modify the sadistic components, the indispensable condition for a consummatory heterosexual experience. But for the years of childhood in which no sexual objects exist in the genital sense, both the erotic and the aggressive components of sexuality are fused in the masturbatory experience.

And why not a consummatory experience in the masturbation of this latency girl? Here, I am not speaking of orgasm which is organized on a physiological and psychological level of complexity that appears to be beyond latency. But why should there not be some kind of completion or resolution of tension in Nancy's masturbatory experience? On a simple tension-and-reduction-of-tension basis there should be no physiological impediment to completion or the experience of relief. I think the impediment lies in the admixture of sadism. Where the satisfaction of the erotic long-ing is united with aggression, as it is in Nancy's masturbation, the aims of neither drive can be achieved.

Suzanne, too, never "finished" her good feelings during mastur-bation and never finished the accompanying daydreams. In one of her early descriptions of a masturbatory daydream (age 9) she spoke of her "favorite daydream": the Damsel in Distress Story (her words) in which a girl is kidnapped by bad men and carried off to a tower. The bad men strip the girl of her clothes. Then they stand around and look at her. "You know," she said, "I never fin-ish that daydream. When the bad men carry her off, I don't finish it. Because the girl is going to be very famous one day for doing great things and I don't want to spoil her record. So I never know how the story ends."

I: "What happens to the feelings, then, that go along with the daydream?"

Suzanne: "Oh, they just die out."

I: "Is it a feeling that gets bigger and bigger as the daydream goes along?"

Suzanne: "No, I don't think so."

I: "Do the feelings stop when the daydream stops?"

Suzanne (very thoughtfully) : "Yes, I think so."

I: "And if the feelings went on and the daydream went on?"

Suzanne (quickly) : "You make me feel like a criminal."

I: "Do you really think I want you to feel that way?"

Suzanne: "No, I am just telling you what I thought."

We then proceeded to examine her feelings about "being a criminal." This was, in fact, the first time in the analysis that shame in connection with masturbation had appeared so strongly. For many months to come the "criminal" feelings were at the center of the analytic work and eventually they were linked with circumstances in which she felt "like a criminal" for mastur-bating.

Here, then, we have another example in another case of excite-ment that reaches no resolution. The feelings "just die out," Su-zanne said. Completion of the daydream (and the feelings) would bring shame. Two years later in the analysis, the "bad man" of her fantasies was unmasked and Suzanne began to understand that shame was linked with forbidden thoughts about her father—which, in itself, explained why neither the daydreams nor the feelings can be "finished."

Analysis of the oedipal wishes toward father had no effect upon either the "unfinished dream" or the "unfinished feelings." The Damsel in Distress daydream continued with variations for 3 years, simply reflecting the changing tastes of a Damsel in Distress at 9, 10, and 11 years. The bad man, or sometimes the gallery of bad men, who kidnapped the damsel was furnished with new masks, shortly after one of the men was unmasked as the Damsel's father. It was as if the Damsel said, "Very well, then, *that* man in the daydream turned out to be my father and I'll work on that in my analysis. But the *new* man that I invented has no connection with my father as anyone can see since I gave him red hair and brown eyes. And since he has nothing to do with my father, the kidnapping will go on as usual tonight. But I won't finish it."

What happens, then, to the "unfinished feelings" in masturbation? Suzanne told us earlier that "they must die out," which we can probably take to mean "dissipated" or "exhausted." But then we would have to assume a fairly low level of excitement in the act. There were other occasions, I learned as the analysis progressed, when excitement reached intolerable levels. The physiological and psychological mechanisms which Suzanne employed under these circumstances are of considerable interest to us.

Suzanne (11 years old) made a discovery one night. She was half asleep when she felt an urge to urinate. She allowed "a little trickle" to come out, "then I decided to stop it." Should she go to the toilet? she asked herself. She decided to stay in bed. "And then I finished it. I let it come out. It was such a relief!" This experience, in consciousness, made her see clearly what must take place in sleep when she wet her bed (still an occasional experience).

Since in the analysis there had been many transitions from clitoral excitement to urination, I now drew Suzanne's attention to the sense of *relief* which she had described to me. What about the "feeling of relief," then, I asked her. When she had "good feelings" around the clitoris, did she feel "relief." "No," she said, after a moment's reflection. How would she describe it? "Well, let's say I have a real good story and it gets to the best part. Then after the best part, it just dwindles away. I never finish the story, you know. But sometimes if I am interrupted in the middle, like mother saying, 'Suzanne, come down and set the table,' then I feel angry as if someone was an intruder, you know, and there is a feeling of like not finishing. The feelings—oh, I just thought of an example. Like you were climbing a mountain and you finally are getting to the top. And somebody stops you."

I: "And if you had gotten to the top, what would happen to the feelings? Afterward?"

Suzanne: "Well, like I said, they just dwindle down."

I then drew Suzanne's attention to the "feeling of relief" in urination and the absence of "relief" in masturbation. I said, "Is that a clue? That for some reason you can't let yourself have the feeling of relief there, and you have to have the feeling through urination?"

Suzanne was suddenly struck by this. She said, thoughtfully, "I wouldn't be surprised. Say, are we gettting some place on this?" Suddenly smiling, "I just thought of something funny. You know in my daydreams of the queen who is kidnapped to another country and stripped. Do you know when she is stripped that's all I care about. I never finish the story. I never get her back home." Now, laughing uproariously, "Isn't that terrible? I don't even get her back home. I just leave her there. Just forget the whole thing!"

And we were "getting some place." We had been there before, of course, but never with such clear-cut evidence that physiological release of tension was accomplished through a transfer of excitation to the urinary tract and discharge through expelling urine.

And what factors inhibited "relief" in the genitals themselves? The analytic material during this period showed the presence of the father, masked in the masturbatory daydreams, unmasked by day through her own associations in analysis, and masked by night in the interminable tale of the assaulted girl.

The Vagina

We already know that Suzanne had discovered her vagina "a long time ago, so long I can't remember when." She told us she had explored it with her finger (still did occasionally), that it was wet and slippery, and there were "no feelings" that she could ever remember. From everything I learned in Suzanne's analysis I regard this as a truthful account, certainly so far as conscious memory goes. Yet, side by side with this factual report of "exploring the vagina" was another story that emerged from dreams and symptomatic acts at many critical points in the analysis.

For much of the first 2 years of analysis the theme of "making holes" appeared in Suzanne's hours. Most frequently this would take the form of a repetitive game with a push-pin and the cork wall that lined one side of my office. During periods of resistance she would rhythmically push pins in and out of the corkboard. It was an obsessive game which sometimes excluded every other form of communication in the hour. Sometimes there was even a savage acceleration of tempo as she would literally gouge holes out of the cork. At this point, when I attempted to redirect her to some other material for "making holes," like plasteline, she would chant, "I *want* to make holes; *I'll be glad if I ruin the wall for you!*"

Apart from the obvious inference that Suzanne was using this hole-gouging activity to express her defiance of me, I needed to be attentive to the form of defiance. For in numerous other communications during this period, "holes," "tunnels," and "mazes" had become a recurrent theme with the same kind of driven and obsessional preoccupation I had seen with the push-pin game.

The preoccupation with holes and tunnels led, of course, to her anatomical concerns. In the early stage of analysis the concerns came out in the form of questions about where the baby came out of the mother, how the baby got in. Eventually she was able to tell me, as I have already reported, that she had long ago discovered her own "hole."

At one point when Suzanne was 9, the push-pin games were succeeded by a new preoccupation with map making. With great deliberation she drew roads—and always one that stopped short and led to nowhere. During the same period Suzanne had the first of a series of accidents. In this one she accidentally burned her hand with scalding water.

One day when she was drawing another map, she placed one road in the center of the map, stopped the road soon after its point of origin, and placed question marks along the road. Interpreting the question marks as a sign of her readiness to tell me something,

I asked for associations to this particular road. She said, "Me, *my* holes. The roads we talked about before." I waited a few moments and she went on. "Now I want you to give me something. I don't know what. No, that's really Mommy. I want something from her. . . ." Meanwhile she was fiddling with a stapler on my desk. Then, in a perfectly calm voice, she said, "I stapled my finger. Someone will have to get it out."

Incredibly she *had* stapled her finger. The staple was imbedded in her finger about a quarter of an inch. Still absolutely calm, almost trancelike, she pulled the staple out. There was no outcry. I said, "Suzanne, you must have been terribly frightened. How could you have been so calm?"

"I'm always like that when I'm scared," she said, and left the room to wash her hands with soap.

When she returned I asked her to discuss this. "It was an accident," she said lamely. I said, "Yes, but accidents are sometimes caused by thoughts we don't even know about." She said, immediately, "Yes, like burning my hands that day. You know, you're the only person I know who can make sense about how you can have an accident and yet cause it through thoughts." I asked her whether she remembered what we had been talking about just before she stapled her finger. Surprised, she said: "Holes!"

I: "Yes, and somehow you accidentally made a hole in your finger." She listened with deep attention, but she did not yet make the connection. I reminded her that she had been talking about her "hole," her vagina. To help her out I asked her when she first knew she had a vagina. She then related the material cited earlier, that she knew as long as she could remember. "Maybe I didn't know the name, but I knew it." How did she think she discovered it.

Suzanne (grinning shyly): "Oh, I must have poked my finger into it."

I: "Do you think you were surprised?"

Suzanne: "I might have been. I don't know."

I: "Do you think that if a child had just discovered her vagina for the first time, she might have thought she had made the hole somehow, accidentally hurt herself?"

Suzanne (catching on instantly): "Like I made the hole just then with the stapler!"

Following this hour Suzanne's symptoms returned. She tried like a conscientious patient to go back to the material on "holes." At one point in a session when there was a very clear connection between her concern with "holes" and an attack of coughing, I said, "Isn't it interesting that just when you are talking about holes you begin to cough?"

Suzanne: "Yes. My throat hurts. It hurts when I try not to cough and it hurts worse when I cough."

I: "So we were talking about holes and the throat hurts. There must be some connection."

Suzanne: "Yes. But I don't know what it is."

I: "Maybe it's like one opening is having a conversation with another opening, but they won't tell us what it is. [This delighted her.] Suzanne: "It's like they have a secret and don't want us to find out. But we will. Oh, we haven't done so good for a long time in figuring things out." She was really pleased.

At another point in this sequence of analytic sessions Suzanne made a drawing. She was very intent and silent as she drew. Then she told me its story:

"It's a volcano. Families are trying to get out of the crater. The mothers and fathers push the children out first, but some of the parents fall back into the volcano. This girl's father gets killed in the volcano. Both parents die, but the two sisters and the baby survive." The drawing showed an inferno with people struggling to climb out of the burning crater, and "sliding back on the lava." Suddenly, as she was describing her picture, Suzanne got up to leave the room. I asked her where she was going. She would not tell me. She returned a few minutes later from the bathroom, looking very ashamed. She was unable to explain why she was ashamed to tell me she had had to go to the bathroom. I suggested there might be some connection between drawing the picture of the great fire and her need to urinate. She admitted this very reluctantly. Two sessions later, when Suzanne revived the inferno drawing and began to talk again about the people burning, she suddenly burst into a hysterical giggle. When I asked her about the giggling, she said, "It makes me feel good. I don't know why." I suggested the links between fire and "good feelings."

The excitement manifest with the inferno drawing, the people struggling to get out of the burning crater, sliding back on the lava, must be seen against the background of Suzanne's preoccupation with "holes" during this period. We already have confirmation through her material that exploration of the hole had led her once to the fantasy of having damaged herself, of "making the hole," so to speak. The burning crater, "sliding back on the lava," is strongly suggestive of the vagina. But the fires represent not only destruction but also erotic fires, for the patient instantly left for the toilet. Two sessions later she admitted that the fantasy made her feel good.

The dangers and horrors of the vagina came in for considerable analytic work in the succeeding months.

Once again absorbed in maze drawings (age 11), she designed "a very tricky" path, "so tricky no one can solve it," in which two of the channels led to "blind alleys." This reminded her that once, in searching for the vagina, she could not find the opening. "As if it was lost."

I: "Was that scary?"

Suzanne: "I don't remember."

But the following day she brought in a dream. "My brother Billy was coming downstairs. He was a little boy, about 4. He smiled at me to say good morning, and when he opened his mouth I saw there were braces on his teeth. I was very surprised, because Billy doesn't have braces." (Suzanne did.)

One group of associations led to observations of a little boy's penis—"surprised" to see the unexpected. But another group of associations, which, she said, "I didn't tell you when they first came into my mind," were these: "I thought of exploring the vagina, *something there,* like a blocking, but I don't know how that came in, because it's not metal" (i.e., like the dental braces).

From this point on the significance of the dental braces in the dream was acted out in an extraordinary sequence of events. On the following day Susan burst into tears as soon as she arrived. "I lost my retainer [dental wires]. I've got to tell you about it. You know how I've been losing things for the past two weeks. Well, now I did it. I lost my retainer again. And this time I really lost it. I can't find it anywhere. I took it off yesterday when I had my snack. I went out to play and forgot it on the counter. Mother and

Daddy were angry. It's very expensive to buy new retainers and I just lost one a few months ago." I had no trouble convincing her that this losing of the retainer was a symptom and that by working on the problem we might get some clues that would help her find it. I reminded her of her dream in which Billy was wearing dental braces.

After pursuing a number of associations, Suzanne told me: "I think of what I told you, too, about how I couldn't sometimes find the opening of the vagina" (lost the way; lost the opening). She was silent for a while. Now, quite unconsciously, she began to play a hand game, the fingers opening and closing (like a jaw, I realized later when she gave further associations). I drew her attention to the hand game. Suzanne, in mock exasperation, "Does everything come into this analysis? All right." She flexed her fingers reflectively. "A mouth, gnawing, biting, the time I bit Andy. Boys. How disgusting and loathsome they are."

That evening Suzanne telephoned me. Her voice was choked with tears. "I found it. In the garbage disposal. All chewed up. Just pieces. And the wire band which wouldn't go down the disposal." How had it happened? Well, she had taken off the retainer when she sat down for her snack at the counter bar next to the sink. She left it on the counter with the odds and ends of her snack. Mother just swept it all into the sink. But it wasn't mother's fault, she said. She, Suzanne, shouldn't have left it there.

When she arrived for her hour the following day she was composed and very serious. "I just know that that retainer and losing things is all mixed up with what we've been talking about." She told me again how after her hour she went home and knew just where to look for the lost retainer: in the garbage disposal. "And there it was, all chewed up." I reminded her of her hand game the day before and she looked enlightened. "The same thing." I asked her if she thought that unconsciously she already knew yesterday where the band had gone. Then I reminded her of how she herself had made the connections "mouth and vagina." Did anything else come to mind? "Yes, the losing something. The first thing is not being able to find the opening. That's like losing something." Her associations were scattered for a few minutes, then she came back to yesterday's hour and made a slip. "When we talked about my pejina." (She had not used this hybrid word for a long time.) I drew her attention to her slip. She could not imagine why she said that. Then she remembered how this was her old word for vagina, i.e., penis-vagina, and how she used to think that the clitoris was a little penis. Then, with some help from me, she made a further connection with "something lost." The hole. Something lost. She supplied the words: "Like when I used to think maybe I had a penis and lost it."

The discovery of the vagina, then, was clearly linked with castration in Suzanne's case. The "hole" was not only the "proof" of castration, but the vagina itself was conceived as a devouring and destructive mouth, like the disposal which chewed up the valuable retainer.

Some time later when we were working on her fear of losing control, of being overwhelmed by strong feelings, Suzanne (then 12) reported the "Big Wave Dream." This dream, which occupied many months of analysis, provided the key to many elusive factors in her neurosis.

> I was playing at the beach at Aunt Dee's house [on the seashore]. There was rough sand in the yard and then the soft wet sand on the beach and then the water. And then for a long time I played in the rough sand because I forgot about the smooth wet sand. I forgot the smooth sand was there. Then I walked down the steps that connected the rough sand and the smooth sand and started playing in the smooth sand. By the way, I didn't feel like swimming.
>
> Then I looked up and saw this huge greenish blue wave about three stories high! It was going up the side of the beach and getting bigger and bigger. It was going to crash on me and I was trying to get out of the way, using every ounce of strength. I couldn't move at first and then I crawled toward the steps and got out of the way just as the wave hit. The feeling was . . . I can't describe it . . . well, tremendously overawed. Just looking and not being able to move. After I escaped I waited a little while and then I went back on the sand, the rough sand. Always keeping a close watch for waves. [To my question about how she felt at the end:] A feeling of being exhausted, too tired to move.
>
> [Asked whether there was a feeling of relief:] I can't remember.

Suzanne's own association led directly to masturbation. "Playing in the sand, playing with myself." "The rough sand," she said, "was the scrubby part of the beach. *That* makes me think of playing with myself through my panties or cloth." And the smooth wet sand, "If I played with myself without any panties or a cloth." (At this time Suzanne still did not masturbate with direct manual contact). From the details "playing in the smooth sand" and "the Big Wave" we understood that the dream represented an experience in which Suzanne, manually playing with her naked genitals, had experienced a great and overwhelming wave of feeling that made her feel in great danger and she therefore fled from the too-big feeling.

From this point on Suzanne was fully aware that her "unfinished feelings" in masturbation which usually resulted in an urge to urinate or actual bed wetting, and which were often associated with the paroxysmal coughing, were "unfinished" out of fear of being overwhelmed by "the big wave" of feeling.

She began to observe in masturbation how she would "cut off" the feeling and "cut off" the story before the feelings reached dangerous intensity. "Cut off" was her phrase and provided still another link with her castration fears.

As the analysis of the "cut-off feelings" progressed, the paroxysmal coughing returned and Suzanne discovered, with my help, that with the coughing there was "sometimes" a feeling in the genital region. "Sometimes," she said, "it actually hurts." She had the feeling of something "like a big bump inside that is trying to push out, like inside turning outside." From this I gathered that she was referring to sensations of congestion, a focused genital excitement without the means for discharge. And because the means for genital discharge were not available to her, the conflict found an oral vocabulary in which spasms were translated "oral spasms, coughing" and discharge was accomplished through exhaustion in coughing. Greenacre (1950) offers clinical examples of the same phenomena.

More and more as the analytic work centered on sensations which Suzanne localized uncertainly in the area of the vaginal orifice, an oral symptomatology provided the vocabulary for the genitals when Suzanne could not find words or representations. The mouth and an increasing tension in the month, biting her lips, biting and biting-off fantasies emerged in profusion. Finally, at one point, Suzanne herself became aware in masturbating of muscular contractions, and the image of "a mouth clamping down" came to her. It was then only a short route to another discovery. The episode of stapling her own finger, which had occurred when vaginal exploration had first emerged in the analytic material, now came back and we found another dimension of meaning. That once, in exploring her vagina, long ago, a spasm had occurred, and her own exploring finger was caught for a moment in the contracted orifice. This also led back to recurring fantasies of intercourse in which the penis is trapped in the vagina of the woman and can be freed only through "cutting off."

Discussion

The story of a frigid adult patient who wept for her "dead pussycat" and took flight from "an explosion in the basement" spoke for an erotic conflagration in childhood that had extinguished genital sensation. From the two child patients, Nancy and Suzanne, we have evidence that there are antecedents in latency or earlier for the condition of genital anesthesia in which overwhelming sensation caused flight from the genitals and a sealing off of erotic experience.

There is strong evidence from these cases and from others known to me that there may be a childhood prototype for frigidity in the genital anesthesias of latency.[2] These observations suggest that dread of penetration and the fear of the orgastic explosion encountered in many frigid adult women may have antecedents in infantile experience.

Latency does not mean that the genital is silent. As Berta Bornstein (1953) pointed out, we should expect some masturbation in latency with, perhaps, "some twinges of guilt." From my own experience with boys and girls, the child who reports "no feelings" is usually a child whose infantile sexual life has taken a grave turn.

---

[2] In a separate publication I propose to report on observations of boys in latency in which genital anesthesia and incapacity for erections provide a similar analogue for the potency problems of the adult male. One case is described in Fraiberg (1962).

The question of "peaks of excitement" or orgastic equivalents in childhood are examined in detail in the clinical reports I have presented, and a number of analytic reports which I shall cite from the literature describe excitement and discharge patterns in younger latency girls which require a reappraisal of the arousal potential of the juvenile genitalia and capacity for discharge.

Similarly, "the silent vagina" in girlhood has been questioned in a number of clinical studies in the psychoanalytic literature. Suzanne is not alone among little girls who experienced insupportable excitement and withdrawal in panic following vaginal exploration.

In 1950 Phyllis Greenacre published her clinical study of early vaginal sensations and conditions of vaginal dominance. On the basis of clinical experience, Greenacre found she differed slightly from Freud's idea that children of both sexes know nothing of the vagina. Greenacre says, "I am impressed in the course of analyses that in some female patients there has been some kind of vaginal awareness very early, hazy and unverified though it is" (p. 126).

On anatomical grounds Greenacre points out that distension of the bladder or bowel would produce mechanical pressure on the vagina more readily than on the clitoris. This "borrowing" of stimulation from adjacent organs could, theoretically, give rise to awareness of the vagina. Irritability of the urethra, Greenacre points out, may sometimes combine with clitorial sensations, but more often with sensations from the vaginal introitus. While it can be argued, of course, that the girl child may not be able to discriminate the source of stimulation, if mechanical pressure results from distension of an adjacent organ, there may still be a registration of sensation and even contractions in the vaginal introitus which produce some sense of organ awareness.

The spontaneous vaginal orgasms reported and observed among prepsychotic patients, the "genital orgastic explosions" of deeply regressed psychotic patients, which are clearly localized in the vagina, are cited by Greenacre for the occurrence of vaginal sensations under conditions of massive anxiety, in which case the vagina can serve as a channel for discharge of undifferentiated excitement. The close association of acts of sucking and swallowing with vaginal contractions is further cited by Greenacre for the occurrence of vaginal sensation in the absence of either mechanical pressure or external stimulation of the vagina itself. In this context Greenacre cites the case of a patient who suffered from a severe paroxysmal cough, who wakened in a coughing fit to find herself in a simultaneous vaginal orgasm, associated with a dream in which the mouth and vagina were fused. Greenacre also reported vaginal arousal in childhood in patients who had then suffered from severe whooping cough. (Suzanne's paroxysmal coughing offers an exact parallel.)

From the work of Masters and Johnson and a number of psychoanalytic writings which appeared in response to their published study, I shall excerpt material which has bearing on the subject of the function of the vagina in the psychosexual development of the girl.

The roles of the clitoris and the vagina in states of arousal in the mature female have been subjected to close scrutiny in the Masters and Johnson study. Speaking of the clitoris, Masters and Johnson say: "Its express purpose is to serve both as a receptor and transformer of sensual stimuli" (p. 45). Regarding the clitoris in the orgasmic phase they report: "No specific orgasmic-phase reaction of the clitoris has been established. In fact, due to the severity of the normal clitoral retraction beneath the minor labial hood, the clitoral glans has never been available to direct observation during an orgasmic experience" (p. 52).

According to the observations of Masters and Johnson, "The first physiologic evidence of the human female's response to any form of sexual stimulation is the production of vaginal lubrication." This is a "sweating" phenomenon described in some detail in their writings. It is important to note in this context that the authors say, "Neither the healthy cervix nor the Bartholin's glands make any essential contribution to the total of vaginal lubrication" (p. 69). With mounting tension in the excitement phase there is lengthening and distension of the inner two thirds of the vaginal barrel and some minimal distension of the outer third of the vagina.

However, in the plateau phase, the entire outer third of the vagina becomes grossly distended. "The base of vasocongestion which encompasses the entire outer third of the vagina, together with the engorged labia minora, provides the anatomic foundation for the vagina's physiologic expression of the orgasmic experience. This area of plateau-phase vasocongestion has been termed the *orgasmic platform"* (p. 76).

In the orgasmic phase, "The specific response of the vaginal barrel to the explosive physiologic entity of orgasm is confined to the orgasmic platform in the outer third of the vagina." In this phase strong contractions have their onset in the outer third of the vagina. The authors say: "These recurrent contractions in the outer third of the vagina are the only physiologic responses of the vaginal barrel that are confined entirely to the orgasmic phase of the sexual cycle" (p. 77f.).

The question of "clitoral orgasm" and "vaginal orgasm" is considered by Masters and Johnson. "Are clitoral and vaginal orgasms truly separate anatomic entities? From a biologic point of view, the answer to this question is an unequivocal No. . . . From an anatomic point of view, there is absolutely no difference in the responses of the pelvic viscera to effective sexual stimulation, regardless of whether the stimulation occurs as a result of clitoral-body or mons area manipulation, natural or artificial coition, or, for that matter, specific stimulation of any other erogenous area of the female body" (p. 66).

In summary, the authors say, "when any woman experiences orgasmic response to effective sexual stimulation, the vagina and clitoris react in consistent physiologic patterns. Thus, clitoral and vaginal orgasms are not separate biologic entities" (p. 67).

Even in cases (cited by Masters and Johnson) in which automanipulation was employed without vaginal penetration (employing breast stimulation alone, clitoral-body or mons area manipulation), identical vaginal response patterns were observed from each of these modes of stimulation (p. 67).

For the study of childhood sexuality among females these records of physiological response in the adult female raise very important questions.

1. If stimulation of the external genitalia alone gives rise to vaginal response in the adult female masturbatory experience, is there a prototype in childhood masturbatory experience among girls? Even granting qualitative and quantitative differences in the child-

hood capacity for experiencing and discharging erotic excitement, is there any reason to posit a difference in the systems for transmitting stimuli to the vagina? If clinical reports of vaginal *masturbation* in little girls are rare, can we for this reason dismiss the possibility of vaginal *response* to the forms of external manipulation commonly employed by girls?

2. Granted that the hormone level in childhood will restrict the capacity for vaginal responsiveness, and that lubrication of the vaginal barrel before puberty remains an unknown factor, we cannot close the issue of arousal potential in the juvenile vagina without attention to such facts as these.

(a) The senescent vagina, also "steroid starved" as Kestenberg (1968) points out, responds to stimulation through lubrication and retains orgastic capacity as well. While it is risky to assume parallels here with the young girl, since the senescent woman has had a functioning vagina and genital capability, there is at least the possibility that the vagina of the small girl can, under certain conditions, have some functional capacity even with the low hormonal levels present in the years before puberty. (Suzanne described her vagina as "slippery and wet.")

Barnett (1968) refers to the response to stimulation of adult women with juvenile pelvic condition, wherein hormonal levels and congestion are low. She says: "It would seem, then, that stimulation of the vagina in prepubertal girls, despite their poor genital vascularization and low hormonal level, could result in the same vaginal response as occurs in adults having a juvenile pelvic condition" (p. 589f.) .

(b) The psychoanalytic literature contains case presentations in which mature women reported vaginal masturbation in childhood with memories of erotic arousal and relief, and some rare cases of little girls who reported vaginal masturbation with accompanying excitement. (These cases will be summarized later.) While the cases are few in number, if *any* small girl is capable of experiencing vaginal sensation, this tells us that the vagina is not, under all circumstances, incapable of response in childhood.

The psychoanalytic case literature on vaginal awareness and vaginal sensation in childhood falls roughly into two groups. In the first group are fantasies reported in child analyses in which the representation of the vagina is implicit, but verbal confirmation by the child is not provided. In the second group are explicit statements by little girls or adult women in which vaginal response is described. While the fantasies in the first group tell us a great deal about the vagina as a place of mystery, and sensation is represented through familiar symbols, the absence of explicit verbal reports leaves many questions unanswered. I propose, then, to begin this summary with the verbal reports of little girls and adults available in the literature.

Paul Kramer (1954) reports three cases, adult women in analysis, who described vaginal masturbation to orgasm in childhood. The first patient reported her first experience at the age of 4 or 5 years, in which intensive masturbation involving both the clitoris and vagina led to her first orgastic experience. At that time the experience was frightening, but later she sought it repeatedly because it brought "relief and relaxation." The second patient recalled that shortly before her third birthday she was once masturbating by rubbing her genitalia with her fingers. She then inserted her finger into the vagina and experienced orgasm with strong contractions of the vagina. She was "scared to death," and tried by pressing her legs together to halt the frightening sensations. She was relieved when they came to an end. Following this experience "she suppressed all temptation to masturbate, but incidents of bed-wetting began to occur instead" (p. 136). A third patient reported a history of masturbation with orgasmlike experiences in which seduction by an adult had played an important role. Kramer felt that this case, in contrast to his other two cases, showed severe disturbances in reality testing. The first two women showed no severe pathology, Kramer suggests, because of the possibility of self-regulation of the orgastic experience. Kramer also reports that he had no examples among male patients of masturbation to the point of orgasm in childhood.

Marjorie Barnett (1968) reports findings which emerged from a survey she conducted on a nonpatient population of women who had never had difficulty experiencing coital orgasm. "Without exception, these women could recall being consciously aware of having a 'vagina'—an erotically stimulable cavity since early childhood. Many described their childhood masturbatory orgasms as experienced 'inside,' with spasms and throbbing, and several had masturbated vaginally using shower hoses, jets of water, etc." (p. 590).

In the child analytic literature there are a small number of cases in which little girls *reported* vaginal exploration with some form of sensation.

In 1952 I described the case of Sally whose obsession with "holes" was related to a vaginal examination by a pediatrician. In one session she addressed a doll, Barbara. " 'Barbara has a hole! [hesitantly] *I* have a hole [turning to Barbara]. Did you put something into your hole, Barbara?' To my direct question of *who,* Sally replied, 'I did. I put my finger in my hole and it makes me happy' " (p. 187).

Kestenberg (1968) reports the case of Gigi, aged 4, who masturbated externally and vaginally, but also anally. "At night the focus of her distress was clearly centered on genital irritations. She would wake up and complain: 'My vagina hurts' " (p. 473). Her mother would then bathe her or apply an ointment outside and in the vagina, to alleviate the irritation. Gigi had had an earlier fungus infection which involved the genitals and there were recurrent sources of irritation such as pinworms and very sensitive mucous membranes. Kestenberg, however, is uncertain about whether the reference to "vagina" was specifically the vagina or the vulva since Gigi, like many little girls, called both inner and outer genitals "vagina."

Uncontrollable excitement characterized Gigi's everyday behavior. There was very little interest in toys or dolls and Kestenberg demonstrates how the child's behavior represented an attempt to eject all the clashing stimuli from her body and transfer them outside. When the analyst was able to eliminate the current sources of genital excitement which prevented externalization, there were marked changes in the child's personality. In the analysis, Gigi's premature discovery of her introitus was recovered through a screen memory in which workmen in her home had made doors and windows where none had existed before. With the termination of the analysis Gigi had achieved "a successful denial of the introitus," which, Kestenberg feels, is essential for the drive organization of the girl in latency.

In the same paper, Kestenberg reports the case of Magda, who began her analysis at the age of 9. Magda, too, suffered with overwhelming excitement, "unrelieved by masturbation," which she discharged through "passing on her excitement to others, and by projecting all blame." In the analysis of masturbation, Magda discovered that her excitement was "inside" and named it "Sit." " 'Sit' was a cripple who tortured and pursued her relentlessly. He tried to entice her to enter the 'upstairs room'; he forced her to trap women to enter and be trapped there with him. . . . He enslaved Magda, swallowed people she liked, and made them do anything 'he' pleased." Magda denied to the analyst that her explorations of her vagina led to "good feelings" there, but said that she was playing "getting a baby and it's coming out." She complained that she could not penetrate very far and blamed this on "Sit." "He wants to stay there, he does not want the box in which he hides to be broken" (p. 475f.) .

Majorie Barnett (1966) reports the case of 8-year-old Peggy whose pleasure in masturbation was fraught with anxiety upon the discovery of her vagina. Barnett felt that excitement was evidenced in her fear of vacuum cleaners at an early age, "of something rushing along and sweeping me up," in the child's words. Peggy also reported a fairy tale which dealt with her discovery of her vagina while masturbating. Peggy's story was a variation of the Princess who had been playing with her golden ball and had dropped it in the pond. A frog retrieved it, slept with the princess in her bed for three nights and turned into a prince. Barnett feels that the discovery of the vagina, of an empty space that cannot be integrated into a body schema, creates a need to "fill the space" in the girl's fantasy. "There are no 'contents' . . . which in themselves, by passing into and out of the cavity, give some discharge of tension as the passage of food in, and the passage of feces out, allows discharge via these latter organs. The lack of these familiar, necessary attributes in relation to the vaginal cavity gives rise to anxiety, which in turn gives rise to the need to repress awareness of the organ" (p. 132f.) .

As we have seen, some writers, in describing vaginal sensations in girls, also reported orgastic experience by the children. The question of orgastic capability in prepubertal girls deserves further inquiry. (I, myself, was surprised at the number of reports in the literature. Even as "exceptional cases" they point to the fact that some form of orgasm can be achieved by girls.)

Bornstein (1953) cites several cases of girls who explicitly described fear of a climax and interrupted masturbation at a peak of excitement out of fear of the oncoming climax. She reports the following cases:

"A six-year-old girl regularly interrupted the following masturbatory fantasy: she saw herself as a queen living in the stump of a tree and putting a baby to her breast. Just at the point of the fulfillment of her deepest longings, the baby would suddenly fly into the air, screaming, 'Oh, oh, what is happening to me!' At the same time the child felt that the whole world was changing and perishing." Another patient, a 10-year-old girl, "confessed that it was not masturbation but specifically its climax which she feared. She compared the climactic sensations to those she had experienced in feverish states. The climax was dangerous: it might lead to sickness and death" (p. 70).

Bornstein felt that the orgastic sensations reported to her by children in latency were not, however, comparable to those of adults—"not even at the end of their analysis when they appear to be far less neurotic."

She says, "Only in three cases, all of them girls, did I learn about intense orgastic sensations connected with masturbation. These girls had experienced the orgasm with an acute sense of bodily changes; sensations of dizziness which left them with a feeling of confusion." All three of these girls refrained from manual masturbation, and "obtained their strong orgastic sensations only by thigh pressure, in which I assume that vaginal sensations were involved. The conscious fear and shame of these children was related to their orgastic sensations. One ten-year-old child, when giving descriptions of her experiences, was overcome by an outburst of tears and excitement, convinced that these orgastic experiences were a sign of craziness" (p. 71).

Conclusion

The clinical reports which I have cited, drawn from my own cases and the psychoanalytic literature, invite a re-examination of the problems of genital sensation in early childhood and latency. My own reports of genital anesthesias in latency girls must await confirmation from other clinicians. In other respects my cases add to a growing body of literature in which the vagina has not been "silent" for many small girls and where flight from an erotic conflagration points to an unsuspected capacity in some girls for an explosive discharge that has the characteristics of orgasm, even if it may not be identical with orgasm.

If, in fact, there are links between frigidity in the adult female and infantile erotic experience which has led to anesthesia and flight from the genitals, there should be valuable clinical applications. We would then have another dimension of meaning in the frigid woman's dread of penetration and her fear of orgastic discharge. The analysis of childhood masturbation might then include the original flight from the genitals as the results of insupportable, overwhelming excitement and an anesthesia in childhood which was the prototype for frigidity in later years.

BIBLIOGRAPHY

BARNETT, M. C. (1966), Vaginal Awareness in the Infancy and Childhood of Girls. J. Amer. Psychoanal. Assn., 14:129–141.
— (1968), "I Can't" versus "He Won't": Further Considerations of the Psychical Consequences of the Anatomic and Physiological Differences between the Sexes. J. Amer. Psychoanal. Assn., 16:588–600.
BORNSTEIN, B. (1953), Masturbation in the Latency Period. This Annual, 8:65–78.
FRAIBERG, S. (1952), A Critical Neurosis in a Two-and-a-Half-Year-Old Girl. This Annual, 7:173–215.
— (1962), Technical Aspects of the Analysis of a Child with a Severe Behavior Disorder. J. Amer. Psychoanal. Assn., 10:338–367.
— (1967), The Analysis of an Eight-Year-Old Girl with Epilepsy. In: The Child Analyst at Work, ed. E. R. Geleerd. New York: International Universities Press, pp. 229–287.
GREENACRE, P. (1950), Special Problems of Early Female Sexual Development. This Annual, 5:122–138.
KEISER, S. (1968), Discussion of Mary Jane Sherfey's "The Evolution and Nature of Female Sexuality in Relation to Psychoanalytic Theory." J. Amer. Psychoanal. Assn., 16:449–456.
KESTENBERG, J. S. (1968), Outside and Inside, Male and Female. J. Amer. Psychoanal Assn., 16:457–520.

KRAMER, P. (1954), Early Capacity for Orgastic Discharge and Character Formation. *This Annual*, 9:128–141.

LAMPL-DE GROOT, J. (1950), On Masturbation and Its Influence on General Development. *This Annual*, 5:153–174.

MASTERS, W. H. & JOHNSON, V. E. (1966), *Human Sexual Response*. Boston: Little, Brown.

NAGERA, H. (1966), *On the Oedipus Complex and Female Sexuality*. London: Allen & Unwin.

SHERFEY, M. J. (1966), The Evolution and Nature of Female Sexuality in Relation to Psychoanalytic Theory. *J. Amer. Psychoanal. Assn.*, 14:28–128.

Some Interferences with the Analysis of an Atypical Child

ANNE HAYMAN, M.B., B.Ch., M.R.C. Psych., D.P.M.

THIS PAPER TOUCHES ON TWO OF THE MANY POSSIBLE AREAS FOR psychoanalytic investigation of "atypical" children. This term is applied to children who fall neither into the category of "neurosis" (i.e., who have an adequate developmental history and structuralization), nor within the categories of childhood psychosis, autism,

This paper forms part of a research project entitled "Childhood Pathology: Impact on Later Mental Health," conducted at the Hampstead Child-Therapy Clinic, London. The project is financed by Grant No. MH–5683–09, the National Institute of Mental Health, Washington, D.C.

Acknowledgments are due particularly to Mrs. Dorothy Burlingham for wise, patient, and perceptive guidance over the clinical work; and to Miss Anna Freud for brilliantly illuminating the theoretical aspects.

This is a slightly modified version of a paper presented at a meeting of the Hampstead Child-Therapy Clinic in June, 1971; and a greatly enlarged version of a short communication presented to the 7th Congress of the International Congress of Child Psychiatry and Allied Professions, held in Jerusalem in August, 1970.

(476)

mental defect, or those described as "borderline." The "atypical" group is thus defined negatively in terms of what the children do not display, rather than positively in terms of what they do. There is room for much research to chart out some of the different types of atypical development, from the points of view of symptomatology and personality; and of psychoanalytic findings, ranging from metapsychological formulations of the underlying dynamics and structure, to problems in technique. An ultimate aim might be to see if it is possible to assign different types of aberration (seen clinically and understood metapsychologically) to different stages and facets of development, in this way formulating a "developmental line" (A. Freud, 1965) of the foci of unusual development, from which factors underlying or preceding different aberrations might be isolated.

What follows is the description of the treatment of a child whose pathology stemmed, to a considerate extent, from the effects that early and continuing environmental stresses had on development, with the result that conflicts were experienced mainly as "external," rather than the "internalized" conflicts of neurosis (A. Freud, 1965). The analysis that was attempted with such an unpromising case was additionally impeded by ongoing, grave environmental disturbances. I shall focus primarily on two areas: namely, the metapsychological problem of conceptualizing the factors inherent in those areas of maldevelopment that interfered with analysis; and the ways of dealing with the technical problems that inevitably arose.

Case Presentation

When Charlie C. started treatment shortly before his 8th birthday, he was a fat, nearly toothless little boy with a number of symptoms. He was anxious and often showed negativistic behavior. He walked in his sleep, had pavor nocturnus, and would not go to sleep alone. By day he clung demandingly to his mother, or had tantrums, except at school, where he was overcompliant or overhelpful in order to get attention. His scholastic progress was poor. He had no friends, being timid and fearful. He had food fads, and somehow managed to use his few teeth and bare gums for constantly nibbling sweets and biscuits, and even for nail biting. He was universally known as a liar and a cheat.

Two and a half years later he was still a fat, if larger, boy, who now had a good set of teeth. He still had food fads and still bit his nails and nibbled sweet things, though less constantly. He still bent the truth or behaved negatively if he could get away with it; but his other symptoms had greaty remitted. He was no longer anxious, timid, or clinging. He had friends with whom he enjoyed rough games. His schoolwork was progressing. An incapacity for play, recognized only during treatment, had lifted to allow the flowering of limited, but constructive sublimations. Nighttime disturbances were rare; and he had just begun to sleep alone in his own room.

This could sound like a summary of what happened in the analysis of a neurotic child; but if so, it is misleading. Although he came regularly 5 times a week, none of the changes really arose from Charlie's getting insight into unconscious conflicts. His pathology was only minimally due to neurotic compromise formations, and largely stemmed from widespread developmental delays, greatly fostered by lifelong and continuing environmental traumas, emanating in particular from his mother.

History

Charlie was the fourth child in a working-class family. His father was a thin little man, passive and obsessionally inhibited, and totally dominated by his wife, who described him as being "like another child." Mrs. C. was a large woman, who in good periods was quite capable and conscientious in holding her family together; but she had a long history of severe depression, for which she had had intermittent psychiatric outpatient treatment, starting before Charlie's birth. She may have been all right in Charlie's earliest days, but her depression certainly returned by the time she became pregnant again when he was 7 months old, and during this pregnancy she often thought of, and may have attempted, suicide. Nicholas, born when Charlie was 16 months old, was never brought home, but in the 4 months that he still remained in the hospital, the mother visited him regularly, taking Charlie with her; afterward she told us of Charlie's screaming. Thereafter, Mrs. C.

sought to alleviate her depression by going out to work, leaving Charlie in the care of two sets of neighbors until he was 3. The mother could give us no information about his early history. At 3, Charlie was diagnosed as having severe hypochromic anemia, probably due to dietary deficiency; his teeth were so carious that all of them had to be extracted. As soon as Charlie was strong enough, at less than 4, he was sent to nursery school. At 6 he had a tonsillectomy and reacted with much screaming; throughout the following year he had nightmares.

The mother's early attitudes could be inferred only from what was seen during Charlie's treatment. The kingpin of the family, she was highly contradictory and irrational, and extremely changeable, her moods swinging from sublime casualness or cheerful overgenerosity to vicious, punitive tempers or marked depression. She took sides with one family member against another, often favoring Charlie over his father. He shared their bedroom, often slept in their double bed, and Mrs. C. used to go to bed with him to settle him at night.

Two of Charlie's siblings also were disturbed. His brother, Richard, 11 years his senior, had a long history of mood disturbance, great irascibility, erratic work habits, and delinquencies. At 17, when Charlie was 6, he attempted suicide by gas at home. The mother insisted that Charlie knew nothing about it, but he described it in his first week of treatment. When Charlie started treatment, Richard was in some trouble with the police, and shortly afterward left home in a rage. With Jane, 9 years older than he, Charlie apparently had a mutually provocative, sexualized relationship. He would pinch her belongings, exhibit to her, and spy on her, which she did not prevent as she dressed with her door open. A year after Richard's attempt, she too attempted suicide, which Charlie also knew about. When Mrs. C. sought help for Charlie a few months later, her main aim was to prevent Charlie "going the same way as the others."

Personality

Charlie was a "nice" little boy, occasionally even helpful. In the time he attended, he changed from being a timid or impulsively disturbed 8-year-old, to showing the casual competence in ordinary affairs of any 10-year-old of his intelligence. He had an IQ of just about 100, and resembled his family in being essentially a doer rather than a thinker, with very little ability to conceptualize. To say he was no intellectual is an understatement; among the interests he has shown are: playing football, watching football on TV, looking at pictures of football teams, watching other things on TV, sewing, swimming, climbing on the apparatus at gym, eating sweets, and yet again football.

During the treatment, Charlie generally behaved as if he were in favor of coming, but only rarely did he show any understanding of what it was all about. Though sometimes grumbling, he developed considerable friendliness, but he seldom participated affectively. Warm smiles or chuckles were so rare that I remember every single occasion; and I saw him near tears only once. The impression of his being "shut in" was not confined to treatment, but seemed general. Whether due to affective denials, perceptual blocks, hostile rejections, or to his failures on the simplest levels of abstract or objective thought, most of Charlie's everyday talk seemed to be on the surface. A consequence of this massive barrier to communicativeness was that trying to work with him was mostly frustrating to the point of agonizing boredom. If no picture of a real, live, young person is conveyed, it is a reflection of what he was actually like. He presented an unusually impervious barrier to my feeling in contact with him. His enormous ability to make me feel "shut out" was reminiscent of the same feature in just one adult patient I have treated; perhaps it is not a mere coincidence that he, too, had a psychotically depressed mother.

There was a further difficulty. If opportunities were missed, it may partly have been because of my inexperience in analyzing children as compared with adults. Work with adults may perhaps not immediately equip the analyst for the technically more complicated task with children. But Charlie presented another and special complication, as items of unconscious concern would burst out of him in isolation. Even when they were caught and understood, there was no continuity, because he would immediately "seal up" again.

The Early Period of Treatment

In discussing the first year of treatment, I shall mention what seem to have been some atypical features and their probable connection with the disturbed early environment. I shall indicate how these interfered with analysis, and describe some unusual techniques which as a consequence I had to adopt.

Charlie's developmental abnormalities produced a number of ego distortions; first, a total inability to master anxiety. Initially very compliant, his behavior soon became wild and chaotic. He spoke fearfully of past accidents, of his fear of witches and horror of bad smells; but interpretations, instead of easing matters, nearly always enhanced or precipitated his terror, so he would run from the room. Secondly, he could not use meaningful words, for at least two reasons. One was an ego identification with his mother's muddled and contradictory use of them. He would parrot her words, or just use them as vehicles for discharge, as she did. For both of them, words could mean anything or nothing. Early in treatment he described a villain's death in a TV adventure, the death of a neighbor's cat, and his idea of killing the frightening neighbor he thought was a witch as if he equally believed or disbelieved in them all. As time passed, words did come to have more genuine meaning for Charlie; but this ego function may have remained too tenuous to withstand any further strain, in the sense that once a word was assigned an incontrovertible meaning, Charlie could not risk this link being challenged. To Charlie, fantasy was just such a challenge, and much later he showed a total inability to conceive of an imaginary story. The nearest he ever came to telling what in another child would have been a conscious daydream or hope was to tell it as a fact and then say it was a lie. Instead of regarding a daydream as permissible just because it was not real, its very unreality made it into a culpable falsehood to him. Thus, the many wish-fulfilling fantasies he produced to defend against painful disappointments were always judged by him only in terms of their veracity. He never seemed to grasp the idea of what a daydream is. I regard this inability to conceive of such a thing as fantasy as a serious delay in an aspect of ego development. I should stress that

I have never regarded Charlie as psychotic. It was what he had to identify with that was so very abnormal.

The other interference with his using words meaningfully was that he was unbearably overstimulated by his mother's frequent, gross, verbal enactments of her own distorted excitements. When the sexual excitement was his own, linked with his own phallic phase conflicts, Charlie could repress the accompanying fantasy and get some release following interpretation, though work at this structured level was very rare. For example, when his eldest brother's fiancée came to their home and slept in his brother's bed, Charlie was vague and uncertain as to where his brother had slept. While my eyes were shut during a game of hunt-the-pencil, he found a squeaky board on the floor and bounced up and down on it, wondering if I knew what he had discovered. When I interpreted the reversal of his own curiosity about bouncy noises in the night, when *he* could not see, he leapt onto the couch and bounced excitedly up and down on it; and subsequently he could talk a little about his uncertainties about adult sex. But when the excitement was the objects', he could be traumatized into grossly sexualized behavior; the best he could then do was to scotomize or block his perception of the behavior of others. He reacted in this way to interpretations, when he had managed to stay in the room with me.

I could observe his reaction to his mother's madly dramatic and contradictory behavior about 4 months after treatment had begun. His 16-year-old sister had stayed out late, probably on some adolescent adventure, for which she invented a glamorous alibi. Mrs. C. believed every word of it, and vicariously derived enormous gratification. She came red-eyed and weeping to the waiting room 45 minutes early, to pour out the whole story to the Clinic's receptionist, totally caught up in a lurid fantasy of kidnapping and near rape. When Charlie and I came down after the session, I got some of it too, which was my first view of Mrs. C.'s logorrhea. She could not stop herself talking. She knew Charlie was listening and had a vague feeling it was not a good idea. She dealt with this by telling me that Charlie knew nothing about it—then went on pouring it out in front of him. Charlie was walking around the waiting room, looking as if he had pulled something down over his ears. He had precisely the same blank expression with which he met interpretations.

Charlie's reaction to aggressiveness, e.g., his mother's open hostility, or to feared realities, e.g., someone's illness (a frequent occurrence), was a total denial of misery and fear. This precluded affective insight, and all he could do was to follow the lead of his objects. The day after the "kidnap" hullabaloo, the mother's feelings had turned to rage against Charlie. My guess was that the police had not taken her story seriously and she felt she had made a fool of herself at the Clinic. She angrily told Charlie that she would stop bringing him for treatment, and justified this by telling me how dreadfully naughty he had been over the past few days. His crime was that he had not slept, and, I suppose, had wanted attention. That he might have been upset by her weeping and wailing never occurred to her. Charlie's reaction to her threat was manic denial. He told me that he would soon stop coming with the almost mad-looking smile I had come to recognize as covering deep distress.

Charlie also showed delays in the development of narcissism and object relationships. His attempts to bolster his very low self-esteem were obvious in his constantly nibbling sweet things, his fantasies of grandiose achievement, and his continual use of objects only to raise narcissistic supplies. Much of his clinging demandingness, his lying and cheating, was an attempt to get reassuring gifts, or to triumph over his objects. He did not develop a transference neurosis, but similarly used me in a primitive way. The mother's early contributions were presumably her absences and her ambivalent cathexes of him. An additional early factor might have been the illness and weakness which denied him muscular pleasures when he was 3 to 4 years old; and his toothlessness from 3 to 6, which deprived him of normally gratifying oral-aggressive pleasure in chewing. Developmentally, he was of course arrested at a presuperego level. Like a young child, he relied on parental guidance; but his mother was so inconsistent that he got no clear rules from her. When in fury she sent him to bed early, then later let him get up to watch the moon-shot on TV, I had to show him that he was confused. I, too, could not understand what had angered her, nor why she had relented. He saw that he would almost have preferred her not to, because then he would at least have known where he stood; but with her he never knew. Hence the only rule he followed was to get away with whatever he could, for which he also had the model of Richard's delinquencies. From the point of view of technique, it was my setting some consistent standards that brought about his first change in treatment.

As stated earlier, Charlie's frequent anxiety attacks led to chaotic play and wilder and wilder behavior, which were not helped by interpretations. I *had* to stop his climbing onto the fire escape, or throwing things out of the window, and similar exploits. I did so, bit by bit, always explaining why. Charlie did his best to get around me. He tried trickery; getting me to shut my eyes in a game so he could creep past me, or pretending he was going to the lavatory. He would threaten. He tried to bargain with me or bribe me with promises of something he imagined I wanted. He would plead with the utter charm of the talented confidence trickster: "Just once"—obviously all measures he used at home. As he began to realize that, unlike his mother, I was not contradictory, angry, or placatory, but reliable and trustworthy, a change began to come over him. His anxiety dropped, he ran out of the room far less frequently, and he began to play. Only then did I become aware of what had been lacking. Previously he had obligingly joined me in any activity he thought I wanted, but his only motive, I could now see, had been to please or placate me. He himself had shown no pleasure in play. Now pleasure and with it a feeling of simple creativity came to life in him. At first it was nothing more startling than Charlie's suddenly deciding to go to the locker to get out his drawing book and crayons. Yet there was all the difference in the world between his earlier mechanical activities and the newly found pleasurable pursuit of them. The whole emotional atmosphere had changed. It was soon after this that the school also began to notice an opening up of the limited skills he had.

It took another 3 weeks until we were able to talk about what had been happening. We were playing with Meccano. Since the screws were the same color as the linoleum, we had gotten into the habit of immediately picking them up when we dropped them in order not to lose them. On this day Charlie dropped a screw. We could hear it, and I drew his attention to it automatically. He stared me in the face and said he had not dropped it. He obviously knew he had, and was behaving as if he had been accused of doing something wrong. I said this to him, adding that he never knew when things were, or were not, going to be taken as naughty. To my surprise—I was always surprised because it happened so rarely and I never knew when it was going to happen—he nodded and picked up the screw. I added that he felt that way because his mother was sometimes cross and sometimes pleased about the same thing; so he just did not know what was "right" or "wrong" and felt the safest thing was always to say "no." He nodded again. This removal of a barrier was not a response to an interpretation. He had *already partly achieved* the change by an identificatory response to my consistent attitude and knew that some things were always right and others were always wrong because I knew. Now he was signaling some (verbal) understanding of this.

All major developments in Charlie's treatment came gradually, sometimes obviously in response to what I (or his mother) was doing, sometimes mysteriously, but never clearly in response to content interpretations. Although I never stopped interpreting, a big part of my technique consisted in adapting my behavior to the level that best suited him at a particular moment. For example, at this stage he seemed to rely on me as the external object who, when present, safely controlled him; so I behaved accordingly. When he impulsively threw my keys out of the window and waited, aghast, for punishment, I told him sympathetically that I knew he could not stop himself and therefore, to help him, would close the window. Two years later he showed that he had internalized the controls. He asked to have the window open, and from the context (to which I shall refer later) it was clear that he was showing both of us that he no longer needed this external bar.

Charlie's acceptance of me as a reliable prop ushered in a period of about 6 months during which he seemed to experience with me various stages appropriate to an early mother-child relationship. A few times this hitherto frenetically overactive little boy surreptitiously snuggled close to me, quietly sucking his thumb, or resting his cheek on my hand. He began to treat me like a toddler treats his mother, as someone to learn from. Whenever we played games, he had *always* had to win (to bolster self-esteem) and had always

expected me to overlook his blatant cheating (as his father did).
But in line with his new capacity to play, he set about mastering
the games. When he skillfully beat me and I warmly praised him,
saying that he did not have to cheat to win, he gave me a heart-
warming smile and said, "But you learned me."

Although we talked a great deal, in a way this was a nonverbal
relationship in which my contribution was a replenishment of
what he had missed in his early years—praise, warmth, sympathy,
guidance; and even protection, as when I rang his dentist to prevent unnecessary surgery, and contacted his school to insure that
he would not be sent to a distant one too soon. (He had had several
operations and repeated separations in early childhood.) Then,
fragmentarily, he began listening to interpretative words. We had
a verbal game. He was the pilot coming in to land and I was the
control tower. Abruptly he said he was loaded with bombs and
was going to bomb me. I did not interpret, but just told the pilot
to fly out and drop the bombs over the sea. Charlie obeyed me! He
got up to dash to the lavatory. When I called after him that I
agreed that the toilet was the place for his "poofy" bombs, instead
of ignoring me he turned at the door to beam acknowledgingly.

During the following weeks Charlie brought up a lot of anal material. There was also a new, protracted hullabaloo at home, because Richard had made a young girl pregnant. I thought Charlie
was just showing anal pregnancy fantasies, and variously interpreted this; I never dreamed that he was actually encopretic because his mother was deliberately secretive in order "not to shame
him."

I insert a few words about the mother. Soon after starting Charlie's treatment, I realized that her enormous tensions were an intolerable burden to him. She wanted and needed help for herself,
but at the time no one was available or willing to take her on. I
could sympathize because I was aware of my own attempts to protect myself from being flooded and battered by her emotional out-
pourings. But toward the end of the first year, Mrs. C. became an-
grier, because no one was seeing her, and more anxious. Charlie,
though jealous, was actively trying to arrange my seeing her. Since
it had to be done, I began to see her regularly. It was only then
that the mother, angry with Charlie, reported his encopresis;

whereupon it stopped, according to her. I suspect she often spoke to him as if I were a threat, and I have wondered how much *his* "secrecy" with me was due to his inability to differ with her.

Nevertheless, by the end of the first treatment year, he slowly became able to communicate. My new technical contribution was an attempt to extend my "reliability" from showing him rules, to showing him real reality. First, I tried to approach his lying in a different way. In view of its multiple sources, I had previously tackled it in various ways: I had shown him where grandiose fantasies were a defense against his low self-esteem; or I had teasingly indicated that we both knew that what he had said was not true; or I had simply stated that we knew that when he lied and cheated so much, he was worried about something and asked him to tell me what it was, which had sometimes led to his reporting the latest upheaval at home. Now I said only that for some reason he was saying something that was not true. Being confronted with this simple fact, uncluttered by blame or interpretations, had a startling effect on Charlie. He stared at me, ostentatiously held something out and dropped it, and then said he had not dropped it. When I described this as "playing at lying," designed to show me that he understood and agreed with what I had said, he smiled very happily. I felt that from then on he began to believe that he might trust words.

My second piece of realistic behavior came through a game of cards. Of course, I had always taken care to match my standard with his, as one does with a child, but one day I found I was excruciatingly bored. I felt I was up against an intractable resistance that I must handle in some new way. I decided to stop appeasing him, as his parents always did, and allowed myself to beat him. I then explained that this was quite realistic because a grownup naturally could beat a child unless she handicapped herself; which I then openly proceeded to do. The atmosphere changed and the session became alive. At the end of it he called back gayly that he would see me tomorrow, which he had never done before. The next day I followed the same technique with a game of hunt-the-pencil; instead of pretending I could not hear him when my eyes were shut, I told him that I could, and suggested that since we could both hear each other, we stop giving the "warm" and "cold" clues that made the game too easy. He did not want to do this; so I spoke his sort of language: I offered him a bargain which was really a bribe. I said that I would play the game he wanted, if he would agree to play the "Charlie-puzzle" game, a term I had recently introduced when he became interested in jigsaw puzzles. He refused vehemently and, picking up a large piece of paper, waved it around, saying he had a sword. I said that I was *going* to play the "Charlie-puzzle" game by explaining that he *wished* he had a sword. He immediately said that he did once have a sword; so I promptly replied that it had not been a real one. He agreed. It had only been plastic—but it had a diamond in it! I again pulled him up, saying it could not have been a real diamond, but he wished it had been. This sort of exchange went on for some time, with Charlie enjoying it hugely. I believe he could accept it, partly because I had used his mode of "bargains," partly because he was very relieved that I was quite honest with him. But he also showed some readiness for real understanding. He was much less anxious, and had even started to play with his peers at school.

The next 7 sessions were delightful, but I shall not report them in detail because they were totally uncharacteristic of Charlie's treatment as a whole. Charlie really began to talk, to listen, and to understand. He brought masses of material. He recognized his conflict between trying to be honest and his craving to win. He learned something about defense, realizing that he had changed the subject because it worried him when the material led to his masturbation. Ideas about his dangerous aggressiveness emerged; he told first of a TV comedy where a boy dropped a brick on his father's head, and then of a real murder much publicized in the news media at that time. He grasped the essence of "unconscious," coining his own phrase: "My brain [touching the back of his head] knows it, but I don't." It was clear that some structuralization of his personality had taken place, which in the right circumstances should make analysis possible. At the end of the week he gave me the accolade. He was the baby calf and I was Dr. Dolittle, that film and storybook character who alone can understand and talk to animals. But, alas, I did not go on being Dr. Dolittle.

A Period of Family Chaos

The next week was half-term during which Charlie ordinarily did not come; but this time he seemed very eager to continue. His father had promised to bring Charlie, but he did not. When I saw Charlie in the waiting room the following week, he looked like a child who had been in an air raid: pale, exhausted, and withdrawn. During the session he told me of the new twin crises at home. Richard had come home, crying to mother because the pregnant girl had rejected him. Charlie, who had spied on them, had called Richard a "cry-baby," whereupon his mother threatened to slap him if he did that again. Of course he did, and of course so did she. When I saw Mrs. C. that week, I tried to help her understand Charlie's behavior. I suggested that perhaps Charlie was only saying to Richard what Richard had often said to him. She interrupted me to agree: Richard *had* often called Charlie a cry-baby, "but," she said triumphantly, like one child scoring off another, "Charlie *is* a cry-baby." *Ergo*—nothing more need to be said! Mrs. C. was always very ambivalent toward Richard, and this was now increased by his presence; but remembering his suicide attempt, she was frightened by his misery and tried to protect him by displacing her fury (presumably about Richard's careless sexuality) onto Charlie. This became even clearer in the second episode, which for Charlie was a major crisis, because it concerned his dog, Podgy.

In the previous months, Charlie had apparently been grossly overstimulated by all the talk and excitement about the girl's pregnancy. Not only was he encopretic, but he also engaged in open sexual play with Podgy. Now, Charlie told me, his parents were going to give Podgy "that operation." Mrs. C. later explained to me that they were embarrassed by the dog's masturbating against a visitor's leg; but she most viciously implicated Charlie in Podgy's behavior, while simultaneously fulminating against Charlie's "filthy ways." Her vengeful attitude made it quite clear that the intended castration of the dog was at the same time aimed at Charlie.

When Charlie sensed that I did not feel as his mother did, he actively sought my help in preventing the operation. In fact, it never happened, because it was too expensive; but the damage to Charlie was done. Whether he felt guilty, or was only complying with his mother's traumatizing behavior, within 3 days he agreed to the operation, saying resignedly (almost certainly in his mother's words) that "at least Podgy won't die." He still showed some of the constructive gains he had made during that hopeful week. He had invented a new informative game in which we made a cardboard house together, on the inside of which he painted his own name. A long red path led to the front door of the house. The day Charlie accepted Podgy's castration, he tore off the path and threw it away, saying he did not need it anymore.

I did attempt to interpret his identification with Podgy, but this was not just an internal matter to be made conscious. It was really happening all around him. He might have been able to cope with his own contribution; but I do not think it is possible for a child to re-repress the conflicts and fantasies that *his objects* continually enact and inundate him with. In the second treatment year, Charlie's progress was constantly interrupted by *ongoing* (as distinct from early) environmental impingements, of which this was the first. With his token abandonment of masculinity, he also abandoned his dawning achievements of meaningful communicativeness and conscious insight. Sadly, I believe that the exciting and promising "Dr. Dolittle" period contributed to this retreat. In those sessions Charlie had practically abandoned his old protective mechanisms of scotomization and avoidance. He obviously had not had time to adjust to the fact that it was not safe to do that at home; as a result, he might temporarily have been extra vulnerable to the awful things said to him. But he did retain his earlier gains. He never again showed panicky anxiety; and he never really lost his growing capacities for creative play and work, and peer relationships.

In fact, over the next few months, the issue of whether he would be able to pick up and carry on with the "Charlie-puzzle" hung in the balance. Quite often he seemed to be on the verge of communicating again; but there was always a new upheaval at home, where everyone was anxiously waiting to see what the girl would do when the baby was born, and where Richard continued to display his demanding and unhappy behavior. I am sure the parents persisted in making Charlie the scapegoat. Their intense preoccupation with the unwanted birth must have had a great deal to do with the wretchedly cold way they treated Charlie's 9th birthday. There was no celebration. The day before, he was told they would not be able to get the present he had joyfully been anticipating, and they gave him some money instead. He stoically insisted that he preferred money because he could then buy what he wanted; but the pathetic pleasure he took in joining me in a game I contrived with a birthday card I gave him, and his delight in having it, demonstrated how much he was missing the ordinary childhood pleasure of playing with a parental gift with the parents. Nine is a bit young for giving a child money, and was especially unsuitable for Charlie, who was constantly being bribed with money in any event.

Neither Richard nor any of his family ever saw the baby girl who was born in April. A week after the event Jane heard about it and announced it to the family by coming home and addressing Charlie as "uncle." This may have made the baby real to him, because the only genuine communication he made in this period was about the infant. The girl refused to share the baby with Richard, but as there was grave discord between her mother and stepfather, the baby's future remained uncertain. In the middle of a mechanical sort of game, Charlie suddenly burst out in anguish: "But who is going to look after her?"

The crowning catastrophe came during the summer half-term when the Clinic was closed. Early one morning Charlie walked into Richard's room to find him lying in bed in blood and vomit. He had cut his wrists and taken an overdose.

For several weeks after the suicide attempt Charlie was sad, pale, and withdrawn. When I first saw him 5 days later, he looked thinner because he had not been eating. He presented a shadow of his old mixture of affective denial and reports of what he had heard the family say. The family doctor had discovered that Charlie had hidden under the bed and cried for hours after finding Richard, and he had been crying ever since. He soon told me all about what had happened, except for the fact that he had cried, which he never acknowledged; though he did come near to acknowledging his mother's distress when he eventually responded to my attempts to prevent his repressing it all. I said that perhaps his mother cried at night, but he had never heard it. During the rest of the summer term Charlie spoke a great deal about his visits to Richard in a mental hospital. He showed concern when Richard would not speak or banged on the table, and was delighted when Richard seemed to be improving. The mother had done her muddled best to cope, telling Charlie the conflicting stories that Richard had cut himself accidentally with a bread knife, and that he had done so because he was so unhappy about losing his girlfriend. Charlie obviously knew what had happened, and why, but for weeks he warded off this knowledge by his usual defense of blocking or confusion. I could make some headway with him only after the day he brightly told me that his mother had said that Richard was in the hospital to get the same sort of treatment that he was having here. I said that it seemed to be true that Richard's illness, strange though it was, was really being very unhappy. "Yep," said Charlie, "must be." Soon afterward he began to put on weight and come to life. What made him really happy was telling me, shortly before the summer break, that Richard had a new girl, Doris. He knew that this meant relief for Richard's misery.

New Developments

In presenting this paper, I have tried to distinguish between the stultifying effects of external traumatizations on Charlie and the few signs pointing to an internalized conflict. Richard's second suicide attempt was immediately experienced as an external trauma. Charlie seemed physically shocked: pale, withdrawn, and frozen. At the same time, though, and in the long run, Charlie seemed to react to it not only in terms of important unconscious oedipal conflicts, but also—and this is one of the unusual features—almost as if the real event were his own creation arising from his displaced, hostile, positive oedipal feelings. I say this because, after the weeks which I have just described, Charlie seemed to pass into something resembling latency; as if he had partly resolved (displaced) oedipal conflicts, and was feeling guilty about Richard. That he felt responsible for the catastrophe was quite obvious. He told me he had gone into Richard's room that morning to borrow money, which I am sure really meant that he hoping to pinch some. The first time I saw him afterward, the only thing that helped him at all was my saying repeatedly that it was "not his fault." Thereafter, while there were many occasions when he would have had reason to resent or hate Richard, whom he had always criticized and disliked, Charlie's infrequent references to him were only protective, concerned, and friendly.

Richard had met Doris in the hospital, and she was an extremely disturbed young woman. He soon began to dislike her because of her rages, laziness, and dependency; but he would not drop her for fear that she would commit suicide. During August, the two of them moved into the family flat, where they made Mrs. C. desperate by their demands, unhelpfulness, and bad behavior. But Charlie rode the storm. His latencylike change had developed over the summer break. His mother also noticed it, mainly in terms of how well Charlie was standing the latest troubles at home, but perhaps she was most relieved that he did not bother her. She illustrated how much more grown up he seemed by saying that he was no longer frightened of Richard, adding that he would not come up to the flat when Richard was there, but would call up to her that he was going to be out playing all day. That there was a change was certain, and from the point of view of analysis, it was not a useful one since he was even more resistant than before; but at the same time he gave an air of greater maturity, and attempted independence and mastery. He continued to do well at his lowish level at school, and his good relationships with peers continued and flourished.

The next big change was due largely to my work with the mother, whose attitudes were of paramount importance to Charlie. I have already spoken of his vast areas of ego identification with her pathology. Now I must mention his ambivalence to her. From the start the difference in his behavior at school and at home had suggested a defensive splitting of ambivalence; the early discovery of his terror of witches pointed to where negative feelings were lodged. When he and another 9-year-old were bothered by an overactive 4-year-old who stayed with them all day and involved them in his misdemeanors, Charlie could not ask the child's mother for help. He was sure the little boy would be (unreasonably) punished, as he had so often been. He was even afraid to say anything to me about that mother: he could talk only of his old fear of witches. This sort of splitting made his conscious view of his own mother unassailable. Only twice did I hear him go so far as to mutter half-critically that she "does talk a lot." Usually, he quoted her declamations as gospel, often in the teeth of blatantly obvious evidence to the contrary. Although he had earlier been able to *use* my behavior, which differed so much from mother's, he could never let me *talk* about his feelings for her, perhaps out of loyalty. The reality of mother and I differing in so many ways presumably supported the defensive splitting. If Charlie could not resolve it, then perhaps the only thing left was for one of us to change! This is what actually did happen, in connection with a theme that had constantly arisen.

At various times when the subject of babies and young ones had come up, Charlie had shown marked concern about their being in need, abandoned, or dying. A year earlier he had been desperately upset when his mother threatened to abandon Podgy in the park. In that fabulous "Dr. Dolittle" week, the "neglected baby" theme also had come up. Speaking of a big and small magnet he had brought to the hour, he suddenly said that magnets were better than people, because "the one can't drop the other"; and he agreed that a mummy could drop a baby. In defended anxiety, he had remembered being told that he had gone "blue as a baby" when he had been seriously ill from dietary deficiency; and the game of being a baby calf was connected with a sudden question about what remained for the calves if humans took the milk. In the wealth of material of that week, I had left this aside; and it had been lost with everything else. Four months later, after the birth of Richard's daughter, his anguished cry of "but who will look after her?" showed his deep concern, as did his worry, when Doris became pregnant, how such a bad-tempered girl would treat a baby. From time to time Charlie told tales of dead goldfish or dead baby birds. There was no doubt that the topic of babies at risk recurred frequently and was often in the foreground. Whenever it came up, I remembered Nicholas, who was born when Charlie was 16 months old, and who did not survive to come home.

But, try as I would, I could never get through to Charlie about Nicholas. Officially he "knew nothing about him." When Mrs. C. was pregnant with Nicholas, her depression had made her want to kill herself and all the children, rather than let another one be born. I am sure she felt guilty about the lost baby, but she "managed" by consciously deciding never to think of those dreadful times again, let alone talk about them. Consequently, Nicholas was a "family secret" of considerable proportions, fostering, as such secrets so often do, secretiveness in the child. I had received a hint of the degree to which such an attitude burdens a child when, nearly a year earlier, Charlie had actually seemed *relieved* when his mother told me the "secret" of his encopresis. While I continued to make interpretations linking Charlie's concern about babies at risk with Nicholas (as well as himself), I found that they had little effect. I therefore decided to ask Mrs. C. to tell Charlie about his baby brother. She derided my idea that the early events had affected Charlie; but about a month later she did tell him.

The effect on Charlie was pronounced. Being told the old secret produced in him a new happiness and a release from having to pretend; for the first time ever, he acknowledged a "lie"; after one of his perennial boasts, he laughingly said, "I didn't really."

My words had apparently had a therapeutic effect on the mother herself, somehow lessening her own long-standing conflicts and miseries over babies. Initially, she had been furious and derisive about Doris's claim to be pregnant, but by the New Year, she had swung around to some grandmotherly warmth about the expected baby and went out of her way to help Doris. Charlie was also affected when he observed this and when his mother began to discuss his future contact with his expected niece or nephew in a charmingly positive way, telling little stories of how the child would come to Charlie and ask him for ice cream. Charlie was overjoyed when his mother said that whatever happened, even if the new baby were fostered, she and he could continue to see this new family member.

I do not have the material even to guess what his mother's new attitudes meant to Charlie; there are so many possibilities. But I know that something that happened at that time somehow lessened his pathological tie. He began experimenting with independence,

He had been terrified of swimming lessons, but during the Christmas holiday, this formerly clinging, timid little boy went off to the baths and tried it out on his own, telling his mother about it only afterward.

Charlie was by now doing adequately at school, and playing happily with friends. His nights were generally undisturbed, but he was still unable to sleep alone.

Early in the third treatment year, I decided to handle this situation on the lines I had handled the issue of the babies. However the symptom might have arisen, it certainly seemed to be one of those that cannot be changed until parental collusion with it is lessened. Mrs. C. clearly supported Charlie's staying in their bedroom. Covertly, she relied on his presence to keep her husband away sexually, and she wanted Charlie for company when his father was on night duty. I raised the problem by asking her to think of how it would be when Charlie reached adolescence. She thought it over and then tackled the problem very sensibly, talking reasonably to Charlie and giving him time, by first redecorating the room vacated by Jane, who had recently married. Facing this step, Charlie showed me how he was testing out his own strengths. This was when he asked for the long-closed window to be opened. We played patience together, and for the first time he insisted that I should not help him, because he wanted to do it on his own. After $2\frac{1}{2}$ years of treatment, for the first time in his life, he slept alone.

The food fads were not materially changed, but Charlie did try to cut down on sweets. The week he tested his ability to manage on his own with the open window and with card play, he also left his bag of sweets in his treatment room locker every night, restricting himself to a few each day. This was an astonishing change from his earlier incessant nibbling for comfort. He was exerting his own controls, with me as a background prop. He may even have been planning to stop nail biting, if his comments about my "long nails" are anything to go by!

What impressed me most during the last year was Charlie's stoical courage in quietly going forward on his own. While his negativism, which was still present, was obviously aggressive, it often seemed to be in the service of a desperate attempt to resist his parents' unrealistic and often shocking attitudes and expectations. Although it frequently provoked arguments, the attempt to assert his independence was becoming less self-defeating.

Discussion

In the introduction to this paper, I noted that the diagnosis of "atypical" development is usually reached, not on the basis of any positive findings, but negatively, because these children do not display the characteristics typical of the well-established nosological groups of childhood disturbance. While it is our hope that, ultimately, different types of atypical development might be charted, Charlie's treatment did not provide anything approaching a clear sequential outline of his unusual development. Having described some aberrations in his ego development in the body of the paper, I can only offer some comments on a few significant theoretical and technical problems as a step toward describing the features specific to this one case.

Clinically, the outstandingly unusual feature was Charlie's impregnability to psychoanalytic interpretations. I suggested that the reason for this was that his problems did not stem primarily from unconscious internalized conflicts. A more specific reason will be mentioned later, in the discussion of the transference, but I must first deal with certain aspects of Charlie's object relationships.

Object Relations

Charlie's overall immaturity in object relatedness seemed to leave him primitively overresponsive to the inconsistent attitudes and behavior of the people around him. As a result his responses were relatively unstructured, holistic, and impervious to immediate modification. During treatment it was seen that their effect could be anything from disastrous to helpful. The first big change—a diminution of anxiety and a freeing of some sublimations—appeared to derive from my providing some vital aids to primitive development by filling an early maternal role. In this child it appeared that the replenishment of something that had been missed in his earliest years could be effective as late as mid-latency. Its continuance at an increasingly sophisticated level seemed to foster his development to the point where he could "use" words so that he almost got into analysis. While his retreat from analysis seemed to be caused by an intensification of castration fears, this was not caused in the usual way of the analysis uncovering the early anxieties: rather they were aroused by the genuinely castrating attitudes of his family. This susceptibility to external influences, rather than to superego rulings, underlines the paucity of firmly internalized conflicts. This faulty internalization seems confirmed by his otherwise inexplicable advance toward a quasi-latency 7 months later, when Charlie reacted to the reality of his hated brother's suicide attempt as if it had been an inner matter, arising from his positive oedipal hatred for a father figure. This event presumably rearoused his earlier and hitherto unresolved oedipal conflicts; but once again their rearousal (if it occurred) was achieved not by the analytic means of unraveling repressed conflicts, but under the influence of ongoing external events. (This advance may also have revealed the presence of quite a strong innate propulsion toward developmental progress—but one that, paradoxically, militated against progress in treatment, because it propelled him into the next libidinal phase, in his case, latency during which resistances are always intensified.) The importance of the ongoing external events was also shown in Charlie's later advances, which were largely promulgated by changes in his mother's attitudes.

It is, of course, not impossible that the interpretative work, which never ceased, played a silent part in facilitating the progressive changes; and it is certainly true that at various points interpretative words helped Charlie see, understand, and resolve his confusion (for example, when I showed Charlie how muddled he was because of his mother's contradictory rulings) . Nevertheless, it seems clear to me that the essential work of this therapy was not psychoanalytic. This raises the *technical* question as to whether other, rather unusual (nonanalytic) procedures, may not have been advisable in this unusual case.

In view of the helpful effects that my interventions had on the mother during the last treatment year, it must be queried whether more intensive work with her, perhaps starting earlier, might not have been indicated. The mother-son ambivalent possessiveness was mutual, and lessening of the mother's needs would seem an obviously necessary prelude to remission of the son's, even if his had theoretically been analyzable. The problem here lay in the extent and depth of the mother's pathology, and our grave doubts about the possibility of helping her, which in retrospect seemed justified. It is certainly true that at two points she was able to modify her behavior to Charlie in helpful ways; but this was the result not of any understanding, but of a sort of blind obedience which, lacking any insight, also was often responsible for ludicrous misunderstandings and very unhelpful behavior on her part. This "stupidity" seemed part of her extremely rigid pathological character distortion which, probably being part of a long-standing defense against psychotic depression, really did appear to be immutable.

Although Mrs. C. was frequently angry with me, she continued to bring Charlie for treatment. It was my impression, however, that a significant motive for this derived from her partial inability to distinguish between herself and Charlie: she sent him as her proxy, to get help for herself; and insofar as she cathected him as a separate person, she saw his problems only as they affected her, and generally came to see me only to talk about her own miseries. Her part identification with him, her affective inability fully to regard him as a separate being, meant, I think, that any transient good that arose from my seeing her strengthened her primitive dependent cathexis of me as if she were the patient. As a consequence her side of the identificatory ties between the two was strengthened rather than minimized. Thus there apparently arose an unusual situation: what helped the mother interfered with, rather than helped, the child's vital need to dissolve the pathological tie to her and begin to function as an individual in his own right.

Identification

Identification, which plays a part in all therapeutic relationships, may have particular significance in the treatment of very disturbed children. Any young child who has had a traumatizing and depriving environment (indeed, such a person of any age) may well require a period of treatment in which the mutative elements consist of affective replenishment and something more or less "educational" in the sense of clarifying confusions caused by the confusing environment. If such a child then achieves some remission of affective and intellectual confusions, and also becomes analyzable, one would assume that this has come about to a large extent by his substituting some identifications with a calm, positive, and unmuddled analyst for identifications with highly ambivalent and confused parents. Presumably such identifications would be at preverbal or, at any rate, nonverbal levels. With Charlie, they might have occurred significantly during the months when he clearly related to me as the safely controlling authority, or as an "early mother." But, since some aspects of identification with the analyst must play a part in every analysis, important theoretical questions might arise concerning the distinctions between these ubiquitous phenomena and the special situations in the treatment of such atypical children as Charlie.

This is too vast a subject to deal with properly in this paper, but one or two points might be mentioned. The term "identification" most likely encompasses a wide span of phenomena. The $3\frac{1}{2}$-year-old boy who holds the newspaper as daddy does (even if upsidedown), and who is carefully checking to see whether he is crossing his legs as daddy does, is emulating his father because of admiration and dawning oedipal rivalry; here the conscious and intentional identification promulgates advance in skills. In this it resembles the learning of speech; but while similar processes may operate at later ages, the beginnings of speech must involve less conscious intention and identification at a far more primitive level, which is probably far more holistic and affect-laden, with sound and object-making-the-sound not being fully discriminated. An even more primitive and less discriminating form of identification beginning in the first year of life may, for example, result in an entrenched hostile secondary narcissistic identification with a rejecting mother. I have seen a variant of this very early response, which involved muscular action, in the case of a 1-year-old who made a facial grimace identical with the very individual scowl made by his mother when she was feeding him. Such transactions involve the mysterious capacity for responding meaningfully to other people's affects; it is questionable whether anything like the conscious recognition and intent of the $3\frac{1}{2}$-year-old can be involved. In the later situations identification serves, *inter alia,* the development of ego activities and also plays a part in libidinal development; while in the earlier stages, identification serves, *inter alia,* in the realm of the prestages of the development of the "self," the sense of self, and the feelings about this self. Much later in the more ordinary analytic situation, we are not surprised when analysands acquire some relatively permanent ego identifications with some of their analyst's skills, quite aside from the (possibly more transient) identifications with what they perceive of the analyst as superego or ego-ideal model. The functions, the sources (structurally speaking), the aims (dynamically speaking), the permanence, the degree of ego maturation and of consciousness involved, must differ in complex ways in the various types of situation.

Charlie may illustrate yet another sort of complexity. If during his first year of treatment, he did achieve a significant partial identification with me, it might have seemed to be largely undeveloped, undiscriminating, and holistic, so that he "imbibed" my reliance on words together with my unanxious cohesion. The period in which he began to listen and react to my words, his silent responses gradually leading to his dawning participation in affectively meaningful verbal interchange, resembled the situations in those very disturbed children with whom the analyst's nonverbal communications are preparatory steps toward enabling the child to use verbal interpretations. In such situations, the child's partial identification with the analyst may serve as an essential source of strength, perhaps protecting him against impingements of a home environment. This did not happen with Charlie, because after the signal progress seen in the "Dr. Dolittle" week, he abandoned his awakening trust in my use of words and fell back unremittingly to reacting to his parents' castrating words. At the same time, however, he maintained the level of diminished anxiety and never lost his new interest in using his limited skills. Insofar as these three big advances (lessened anxiety, flowering of sublimations, and trust in words) derived from partial identification with facets of how he perceived me, it would seem that two very different types or levels of identification were involved; but why the more primitive affective elements survived, while those involving more mature, secondary process functioning did not, cannot be understood. At this stage it is only possible to speak very generally, perhaps in terms of biological principles which state that more mature and more recently developed functions always suffer first in any injury, and take the longest to repair. This casts little light on the wide and very complicated subject of identification per se, which requires much further investigation.

It has already been stressed that, metapsychologically speaking, the paucity of internalized conflicts was a central reason for Charlie's inability to gain insight from interpretations. At the level of clinical theorizing, probably the single most important factor responsible for his inability to use analysis was his incapacity for listening to and understanding affect-laden words. From the point of view of development, this incapacity must have interfered massively with all those areas of ego integration and synthesis (some already partly referred to) that flower in the more normal child from the time he begins to speak, and which subsequently must play a vital part in all areas of development. With Charlie, areas particularly implicated include the development of abstract thinking and the evolution of sophisticated ego defenses; and, indirectly, to some extent, his disturbed superego and ego-ideal development, largely deriving from his lifelong lacks and abnormalities in object relationships.

Transference

Abnormalities in object relationships obviously play a big part in shaping the nature of the transference in treatment. Since affective and verbal interchanges were so very limited with Charlie, attempts to evaluate his transference rest, unsatisfactorily, on a few impressions and assumptions. Insofar as he was "blocking" my words as if they were mother's logorrhea, this might seem to have been an example of transference neurosis; and since its very existence precluded an understanding of the symptom, it cannot be stated definitely that this was not the case. However, there are features pointing in another direction. As indicated in the body of the paper, it appeared that this "deafness" was not the result of a neurotic internalized conflict, in which the defense would be directed against the drives or the superego; rather, it derived from an external conflict induced by parental overstimulation and traumatization, which did not involve the usual ego defenses, but grossly distorted and impaired ego functioning. Thus, what was "transferred" to me was very far removed from being part of a "neurosis."

Then there was the matter of his responding so positively to my "extra" nonanalytic behavior. From a technical point of view, my going out of my way to treat him differently from the way his parents treated him, with constant and reliable warmth, guidance, and protection, clearly had positive results; but at the same time it must have interfered with whatever possibilities may have existed of his developing an analyzable transference neurosis, particularly with regard to the negative transference.

From a theoretical point of view, his mode of relating shows, not the presence of *transference neurosis,* but the *transference of his earliest dependent expectancy*—an expectancy which, unlike that of his babyhood, was mainly appropriately responded to. (When this dependence was marginally satisfied by his mother late in treatment, the readiness of his response speaks in a parallel way for his showing a very primitive dependent relationship with her.) Other examples of his behavior in treatment, such as his initial obedience followed by attempts to get his way by wheedling, also resemble transference manifestations, because he behaved similarly at home and at school. But the fact that they came so early in treatment, and in response to my "extra" behavior and not to my words, tends to support the assumption that these were *characteristic modes of behavior in all relationships,* rather than evidence of a transference neurosis specific to the psychoanalytic relationship. Ultimately, this question as to which of the two they were must be left open; and the same uncertainty applies to Charlie's being as little able to criticize me as his mother. Whatever the reasons, I must conclude that most of the significant work was done without the meaningful interpretations of unconscious transference manifestations that are basic to psychoanalysis.

Perhaps it was this last feature that elicited the following comment when a short description of the case was presented to a mainly nonanalytic professional audience in Jerusalem in 1970: one of the discussants suggested that, without realizing it, what I had been doing was *very good behavior therapy!* If this were true, it might imply that psychoanalytic skills were wasted on this child. But two points speak against this.

First, however much Charlie may have worked without gaining conscious psychoanalytic insight, I could certainly have done nothing without it. Whatever I may have done toward lessening the grimness of his future, I could not have managed without arriving at some psychoanalytic conceptualization of how he was functioning. This leads to the second point, which is that it is only by such means that we can hope to arrive at sufficient theoretical and clinical understanding of these atypical cases to be able to work out the appropriate modes of treatment for them.

BIBLIOGRAPHY

FREUD, A. (1965), *Normality and Pathology in Childhood: Assessments of Development.* New York: International Universities Press.

Self-Pity, Self-Comforting, and the Superego

DAVID MILROD, M.D.

SELF-PITY AND SELF-COMFORTING ARE RELATED AFFECTIVE STATES which play some role in every person's experience. There are, however, wide individual variations in the degree to which they dominate a person's character as well as in the dynamic factors at work. The self-pitying behavior may involve no more than an occasional transitory reaction to a real injury, such as a child gorging himself on cookies after feeling defeated and humiliated in a fight. At the other extreme self-pity may constitute a persistent major characteristic of a person who uses a grievance, even if imagined or provoked, as the stimulus to withdraw for a prolonged spell of feeling sorry for himself. In the first example the entire reaction is brief and involves only relatively little cathectic diminution of the object world. By contrast, cases of pervasive self-pity and self-com-

Presented at the New York Psychoanalytic Society June 8, 1971.

forting are characterized by withdrawal and isolation which severely interfere with object relationships, often to the point of a major decathexis of object representations. This paper deals with the latter group that shows more severe psychopathology. My purpose is to draw attention to a form of resistance, often quite formidable, which has not received much attention in the literature and which may account for some analyses reaching a stalemate or even failing.

Self-pity may be described as an affective state involving a special combination of pain and pleasure in which, in economic terms, the self representation is hypercathected with libidinal energy. It can be observed in the preoedipal period, but once the superego has been formed as the heir to the oedipus complex, self-pity may draw heavily on the functions and energies of the superego. In exercising its punitive and rewarding function, the superego not only metes out punishment for wrongdoing, thereby investing the self representation with aggressive energy, as in those depressions which are based on an intersystemic conflict; but it may also instigate the investment of the self representation with libidinal energy in the form of self-pity or self-comforting.

Self-pity is not the only form in which the self representation can be invested with libido. Whenever a child in the preoedipal period behaves according to his parents' wishes, he experiences a rise in his self-esteem, which results from both the approval showered on him by the parent and his own self-praise built on an identification with the praising love object.

As maturation goes forward and a wished-for self image is formed, it becomes less important that there be parental approval to produce this rising self-esteem. Approximating one's wished-for self image is a sufficient stimulus to produce it. After the superego is formed and moral and ethical issues have become most valued, a person experiences high self-esteem whenever he lives up to his own moral standards, the rewarding function of the superego instigating the investment of the self representation with libido. Freud first referred to this in 1921 when he pointed to the feeling of triumph and release which results when some thought or activity in the ego coincides with the standards of the ego ideal.

In its exaggerated form we recognize the superego's investment of the self representation with libido as a swelling sense of moral pride, a quality which, as Hartmann and Loewenstein (1962) were careful to point out, sometimes has a pejorative connotation, depending on the prevailing circumstances. One does not always like an overly proud person anymore than one likes a very smug person. In this sense, self-pity has the advantage of *initially* evoking empathy in the observer and for this reason is morally less unacceptable than pride. In order to understand this important difference between pride and self-pity we must keep in mind that the peculiar blend of pain and pleasure found in self-pity owes its origin to the *obligatory* requirement of a narcissistic wound or injury that precipitates the reaction, whether that wound is real, imagined, or self-provoked. Freud (1927) also referred to humor as a form of self-comforting. Since it results from an avoidance of painful reality rather than from a libidinal investment of the self representation, however, that form of self-comforting comes closer to a generalized ego-adaptive process. Freud stated that in humor the ego asserts its invulnerability and refuses to be compelled to suffer. It is not resigned but is rebellious. In these respects the ego in humor is the very opposite of the ego in self-pity where suffering or injury is sought out or savored, and where there is a readiness to accept vulnerability.

Descriptively, patients with prominent patterns of self-pity tend to withdraw following a narcissistic wound, often into a darkened room, where in their solitude they can mull over their pain and savor the gratifications of comforting and consolation that they lavish on themselves. It is a narcissistic orgy, tinged with masochism. The gratification derived from self-comforting surpasses in importance the experience of pain associated with the hurt or wound. This unique bittersweet gratification can become so important, and can be made so readily available by the individual himself, that it may appear as a rigid pattern of behavior not unlike an addiction. The narcissistic wound is of central importance to these people, who are collectors of grievances, inviting, provoking, misinterpreting external reality, or unconsciously inflicting the wound on themselves in order to initiate the self-pity. The role of the victim, with special emphasis on his innocence, is their characteristic self image. They complain of the injustice done to them and feel unfairly treated or misjudged. Their treatment at the hands of others is characterized as immoral or unethical, and from this we would expect to find a relationship to superego functioning. It is also true that many of these patients share the psychology of the exception (Freud, 1916; Jacobson, 1959), which should not be surprising when we consider the prominence of their conviction that an injustice has been done them.

During periods of self-pity the essentially maternal function of comforting is performed by these patients for themselves. They are both the injured child and the loving, comforting mother. Related to this is a characteristic trait these patients display while on the couch. They gently caress part of their face, usually the cheek, nose, lips or forehead, with the convex dorsum of their hand or with their fingertips. One of my patients gradually intruded his fingers into his mouth and was unaware until told so that his speech was no longer intelligible. These patients also have a tendency toward eating disturbances during periods of self-pity. There is a split in the ego which leads to the setting up of a comforting self and a comforted self. In this connection it is of interest that a number of patients have associated the comforting and caressing hand to the breast.

Self-Pity and Narcissism

In his paper on pity (*Mitleid*), Jekels (1930) cites a case of self-pity, a man who at the peak of his emotional distress would stand before a mirror and tenderly caress his face, saying, "You poor, poor thing." Similarly, Kris (1951) refers to Maloney (1949), who stressed the traumatic impact of prolonged physical contact with one's mother throughout childhood. Kris says that if a child cannot reinstitute the positive relationship between himself and his mother, he enlists some other means of allaying anxiety, often retreating into fantasy where he replaces the mother and sucks himself, fondles his ear, nose, or any body part, tickles himself with a feather or fuzz. Kris adds that, once started, it is not easy to rob him of the substitute for the delinquent parent.[1]

[1] One of my patients (Illustration I) had such a history.

More recently Furer (1967) explored the toddler's identification with the mother as comforter. He points out that the child's affective statement, "I am sorry," made to his mother when she is experiencing some form of emotional pain, shows his capacity for empathy or partial identification with the mother, not as the frustrating aggressor, but as the comforter. This identification with the mother as comforter is, in Furer's opinion, one of the sources of libinal energies later made available to the superego. A more primitive reaction would be a refusion with the primary love object, the child becoming sad like the mother. The "I am sorry" reaction indicates a partial refusion with the mother, consistent with feeling some of her pain, but the child retains some ability to see the object as separate from the self. Further, every experience of separation from the mother which the young toddler has, leads both to an aggressive response and to a wish for reunion with her. In order to be able to comfort the mother, the child must have the capacity to neutralize that aggression. Furer calls this forerunner of the superego "identification with the comforter." Furer was dealing with developmental, progressive, maturational aspects of object-directed libidinal processes. In self-pity, the individual treats the self as the suffering object and turns the comforting activity toward the self. Furer points out that the "I am sorry" reaction in the toddler represents an advance from the stage of need-satisfying object toward that of object constancy. Self-pity is, however, no longer object-directed; it represents a return to a need-satisfying relationship in which both object and subject are within the self. Self-pity is, in other words, a narcissistic regression involving object relationships and the drives.

Narcissism is one of the most prominent features of this behavior pattern. Such a patient declares he is sufficient unto himself, being both the comforter and comforted. Clinically, the severe interference with object relationships can be seen when love objects are subtly invited to join that part of the ego which is engaged in self-comforting. Little mutuality exists; in fact, these people often complain that they cannot comfort anyone else even at times of grief or bereavement, although they themselves demand a great deal of comforting and attention. The narcissism and disturbed object relationships are especially noticeable in the transference,

where the analyst will often find himself feeling unnecessary or
superfluous. Being a witness to a grand display of self-pity, he may
experience some degree of pressure to comfort the patient. He will
also note that transference phenomena do not unfold in the characteristic way and the therapeutic alliance tends to be thin. These
were the qualities that first attracted my attention to the syndrome
and, in my experience, they are important areas for analytic work
in order to overcome the powerful resistance that self-pity can become. Some clinical examples will illustrate these features.

Illustration 1

Mrs. A. was a 23-year-old advertising executive. An attractive seductive woman, she nevertheless remained unpopular with men
because of her severe sexual conflicts and inhibitions and her intense difficulties in separating from her mother. For years her emotional life was dominated by a prevailing mood of sadness and depression, but she consciously experienced the sad states as pleasurable, frequently sought after this mood, and tried to reproduce it
at will. Often a happy event would be unwelcome because she
hated to give up the sadness. In her sad state she felt misunderstood, unappreciated, or unfairly treated, and she would lie down
motionless and alone, full of self-pity and self-comforting, with her
left hand to her face as described above. After several years of
analysis she married and had much less reason or occasion to feel
so lonely or unappreciated. But she regretted losing the sad periods of self-pity and missed them. In her case self-pity had become
solidified into a structured identity with a proper name. She
thought of herself in that state as "Poor Pitiful Pauline."

In this woman narcissism was prominent in ways other than
self-pity. She constantly felt herself to be on display, like an actress
on stage. Even when nobody was present, she was both audience
and performer. Sometimes she posed in the nude in front of a mirror. All behavior had a stilted, unspontaneous, calculated, and
usually seductive quality, announcing, as it were, "Don't you think
I'm special?" She behaved this way with men socially. She toyed
with those who were enchanted, raising their hopes only to crush
them at the end of the evening, and for this purpose she even went

out with men she actively disliked. They were of no importance to her as people. They were her audience, and often she did not recall their names, their appearance, or even *hear* what they were saying to her. By contrast, she became overly attached to those men who were more or less immune to her charms, and fantasied endlessly about winning them over. They became idealized superhuman figures not at all related to the real person. With either type of man, however, the result was the same. She would come home and feel desperately alone, sad, and then go into an episode of self-pity and self-comforting with the emphasis on how unfair life was to her.

Illustration 2

Miss B., a mature, lonely, and severely depressed woman, filled many analytic sessions bemoaning her sad fate in life and the terrible burdens which were unjustly placed upon her. She longed for a good and lasting relationship with a man, but could never establish one because she either subtly discouraged their interest in her or, if interest was present, suddenly disappointed or frustrated the man with her cold and aloof manner. Although she had good psychological aptitude, she could not see her own role in her disappointment, but experienced it as cruel fate or even as a spell that was cast upon her. As a child she had been uprooted from her home by the war and had felt a stranger in her new country, England, a feeling enhanced by a neglectful, rejecting attitude on the part of her narcissistic, hypochrondriacal mother. All these circumstances were experienced as unfair injuries to herself and set up a strong tendency to self-pity.

At an early point in her analysis she complained at length about one of her hours being inconvenient. The complaint had the quality of subtly accusing me of hurting her deliberately, and she felt very sorry for herself having to suffer such an injustice. Eventually I was able to change the hour to a time more convenient for her. The first time she kept the new hour she complained that she no longer wanted to come for analysis, she was not being helped, and she was angry with me because I knew nothing about her. After some brief exploration I pointed out that where we would expect to find relief with the new, more convenient hour, even a sense of gratitude, we found instead anger, a wish no longer to come, accompanied by a morbid depression. I then suggested that having felt grateful and more friendly to me, she became very anxious and warded off the cause of her anxiety, namely, the friendly feelings, by becoming angry. She agreed with obvious relief, but went on to express guilt about having things made easier for her than other people she knew. She was afraid, she said, that she would be punished. I suggested that her morbid mood already was her punishment, prompted by her bad conscience. After a pause she said, "You know, I always have to feel sorry for myself." After a silence she went on, "You are right most of the time and I resent it." She did not know why she felt this way and knew it was silly, but still she wished I would make a few blunders.

Further exploration led her to differentiate two kinds of anger, one which would result if I made blunders and one which was present that day. If I made blunders, she could feel angry with me and sorry for herself for being mistreated, whereas that day she could not feel sorry for herself. I pointed out to her that if only she could feel an injustice was done to her and that she had a grievance, she could then withdraw into self-pity and be occupied with comforting herself. She could lose touch with me. Without the grievance or, in her terms, if I was right, she had to stay involved with me and could not so readily withdraw. It was the closer relationship which made her anxious and which therefore led her to want to end treatment. After pondering this she said she felt it was so, but she bitterly resented my having said it. Two sessions later we had a clue to her fear of closeness when a memory emerged from early puberty involving a sexual advance from her father, but in relation to which she felt very guilty because of her interest and pleasure in the experience.

Superego Development and Self-Pity

Hartmann and Loewenstein (1962) point out that the superego does not mature, it forms. By this they want to stress that, unlike the gradual and steady unfolding of increasingly complex structure and function, as in the development of the ego, an epochal event occurs in the formation of the superego with the passing of the oedipus complex. There are precursors, to be sure, but there is an important difference between psychic functioning after superego formation and that which existed earlier. Superego precursors require the presence and support of the external object and concern themselves with a broader range of values, whereas once the superego is formed, superego functions concern themselves only with moral and ethical issues and operate independently of external objects and in an impersonalized way. As Sandler (1960) puts it, it is the authority of the parents which is internalized, not the personal elements. The superego acts with the full value that an external love object carries during the preoedipal period. Much has yet to be written about all the complicated processes connected with this epochal event which at one and the same time leads to the resolution of the oedipus complex and to the setting up of the superego as a new, independent psychic agency, "a diffcrcntiated grade in the ego" (Freud, 1921).

That the setting up of the superego is of an epochal nature is testified to by the tremendous upheavals and changes that take place. Some of these are: the intense mounting pressure to neutralize the drives; the urgent need to withdraw libidinal cathexis from the oedipal love object and the aggressive cathexis from the oedipal rival and yet retain those vital object relationships; a shift in that which is most valued away from gratification, power or possessions, or phallic attributes, to moral and ethical issues; the establishment of an independent personal moral code, impersonalized, carrying a neutral energy charge, and operative with little need for an external object; the formation of a similarly independent self-limiting function and a self-punitive and rewarding function, both of which are also impersonalized but use more deneutralized (aggressive and libidinal) energy; the use of an entirely new kind of identification, which we call superego identification.

Superego identification differs from the earlier forms of identification in that it does not *primarily* alter the self representation. Instead, it sets up a new psychic agency which, first of all, helps repress libidinal and aggressive drives. During the oedipal period the child's drives are of greater intensity than ever before and, in order to check them, the child's ego needs the kind of reinforcement which previously was supplied externally by the parental figures. Secondly, the urgency to renounce and decathect the degraded and feared oedipal objects is so great that it threatens a sense of inner object loss, a source of anxiety which can be stemmed by the superego identification precisely because something of the parental values is set up within the individual's psychic apparatus and becomes part of the self.

These two powerful needs—to provide the equivalent of external parental support against powerful drives, and to overcome the fear of inner object loss with the renunciation of the oedipal objects—provide the motivation for the setting up of a new psychic agency with the passing of the oedipus complex. The mechanisms available to the ego are no longer adequate to master these greatly intensified psychic processes and for this reason a new process (superego identification) is called into play, and a new psychic agency (the superego) is formed. Hartmann and Loewenstein (1962) and Jacobson (1954a, 1964) have helped us understand a great deal about these processes. In fact, because of their contributions we can no longer say today, as Anna Freud did in 1936, that the superego can be studied only in a state of conflict. States of high moral self-esteem or moral pride are examples of clinically visible superego functioning without intersystemic conflict. Self-pity and self-comforting similarly are states in which the superego plays a major role and in which, despite the absence of conflict with the ego, it can be studied clinically.

We can observe many superego functions in their earlier formative stages during the preoedipal period of development. When self-object differentiation has progressed sufficiently and re-fusions are no longer readily resorted to, a new substructure begins to form within the ego, the wished-for self image, which is made up of the qualities and attributes that are admired in the object (mainly the rival) and that the child realizes, with the help of his advancing reality testing, are not yet his own (Jacobson, 1964). From then on, the earlier re-fusions of self and object representations, which had magically gratified, shift to a realistic effort to approximate or become one with the wished-for self image. This effort to approximate the wished-for self image is genetically related to the later efforts to approximate the perfectionistic standards of the ego ideal, once the superego is formed. But the qualities of value contained in the wished-for self image are broad, involving strength, speed, possessions, and phallic attributes, whereas the ego ideal is concerned only with standards of moral and ethical perfection. In other words, with the formation of the superego, the ego's wished-for self image extends into the superego, where it takes on the new qualities of concern with moral and ethical issues, and where it becomes relatively independent of external objects and the drives, and where we know it as the ego ideal.

The process extending preoedipal ego functions into the superego, once that psychic structure has been formed, produces functions which have both ego and superego aspects in much the same way as described above. Self-observation is such an ego function which can be observed prior to superego formation. Once that psychic agency is established, the self-observing function of the ego extends into the superego where that portion of it concerns itself with morals and ethics, and where it becomes associated with processes using less neutral energies since it is ready to trigger condemnation or reward (Stein, 1966; Schafer, 1960). Self-critical attitudes also can be observed before superego formation, but only after superego formation do they become connected solely with moral transgressions and independent of support from external objects. Self-pity and self-comforting too can be observed in the preoedipal period where they are most often connected with physical injury or illness and closely associated with a comforting adult love object (Lussier, 1960). After the superego is formed, the stimulus of an unjust narcissistic wound calls the rewarding function of the superego into action, as if such an unjust wound were equivalent to a high ethical virtue, and the process again takes place without the necessary support of parental figures.

Self-Pity and the Role of Aggression

The wound or injury, which is so important in the genesis of self-pity, will under ordinary conditions evoke quite a different response. The usual response would be an active move toward self-protection or a retaliatory attack of some kind. The absence of this expected response, in self-pity, suggests that the expression of aggression has been curbed. In addition, pity is a familar defense against sadism in obsessive-compulsive syndromes, further suggesting that self-pity may serve as a defense against the aggressive drive, in this case self-directed aggression or guilt. People who have prominent self-pitying reaction patterns tend to see themselves as manifestly unaggressive, passive individuals. They indeed often inhibit the direct expression of hostile impulses while remaining surprisingly unaware of their less obvious, indirect or "unintended" hostile behavior.[2] They are equally fearful of arousing angry reactions in others which then might be directed toward themselves. In *The Ego and the Id* (1923), Freud made the well-known statement that "the ego forms its super-ego out of the id" (p. 38), meaning, as he went on to explain, that the superego expresses id drives. He was at the time concerned with the aggressive drive. The more a person controls aggression, the more tyrannical does his superego become. Just as castration anxiety is reinforced by the child's own aggressive drives, so the dread of the superego is reinforced by his own aggression. Hartmann and Loewenstein (1962) enlarged on these ideas and described how the formation of the superego aids the stability of object relations by turning the aggressive component in the ambivalence to the object onto the self.

It is characteristic of patients with prominent patterns of self-pity and self-comforting that just as they inhibit their own open aggression and fear the aggression of others, so they also dread aggression directed from the superego onto the self representation. Self-criticism and self-recrimination must be warded off. The defenses most commonly used for this purpose are self-pity (in effect, comforting the self representation rather than punishing it) ; turning the anger onto an external object rather than the self—a projection of responsibility; and externalizing the criticism meted out by the punitive function of the superego, which then permits the criticism to be experienced as though it came from outside and to be more easily disowned. These processes facilitate the satisfaction of the person's need to see the experience as an unjust one, and

2 For a discussion of the role of self-pity and passivity in the psychology of disabled people see Lussier (1960).

thereby trigger a reaction of self-pity. These patients seem to have a specific ego weakness, namely, an intolerance for that special psychic tension which is caused by an intersystematic conflict between the superego and the ego (Zetzel, 1965). To experience guilt feelings, the ego must be able to tolerate that tension. The defensive maneuvers resorted to keep that psychic tension low and lead these people to suffer more from a dread of social anxiety rather than from a dread of guilt. Another common defense is the employment of a currently justified grievance to ward off deeply rooted feelings of guilt associated with past traumatic experiences. The following clinical examples illustrate these theoretical considerations.

Illustration 3

Mr. C., a young man who had grown up in circumstances of near poverty, as the youngest child in a fairly large family, reported an episode which had made a great impression on him. When he was 15 the family acquired a new piece of furniture for the living room. For his mother this was the fulfillment of a wish she had had as long as the patient could remember. His mother had for many years regularly voiced her frustrated longings for a more attractive home. But as luck would have it, this new piece of furniture was found to be damaged shortly after it was delivered. The patient's older brother discovered that a part of the wooden frame was split in a prominent place. When the patient entered the room, his brother pointed the split out to him. The patient immediately became concerned about how upset his mother would be, promptly fetched some equipment, and repaired the damage in what to him seemed an acceptable fashion. In fact, he felt proud of the results. To his surprise, however, his older brother thereupon accused him of having broken the wood frame in the first place. Why else would he have been so quick to fix it? The brother ignored the patient's strenuous denials; the two began to fight and in the ensuing struggle the older brother easily overpowered the younger one. The patient then retired to his room, feeling grossly misunderstood, wrongly accused, and thoroughly unappreciated.

One could easily empathize with his feeling that an injustice had been done. But his fixation on the incident and the prominent display he made of it raised further questions about his need to portray himself as a victim and to protest his innocence so vigorously. Briefly, further analysis disclosed that the incident was closely related dynamically to the events surrounding his birth, details of which he had heard countless times as it was the part of the family lore which his mother never tired of recounting. He had been an unwanted child, born late in the mother's reproductive life, and she had wanted to abort the pregnancy. In addition, she held the pregnancy and his birth responsible for many of her ailments, organic and hypochondriacal. This formed the basis for the patient's profound sense of guilt, which was woven into his masochistically colored character. The damage to his mother's prized furniture recapitulated the damage he caused her at birth, and his reaction of self-pity to his brother's accusation was a welcome defense against the more deeply repressed guilt over that earlier damage.

Illustration 4

Mrs. A., the patient who referred to herself as Poor Pitiful Pauline, reported that once when her mother was suddenly taken ill, she did not know how to feel or act. She believed she had wished the illness on her mother by being so angry with her at that time, but surprisingly she experienced no guilt feelings. Instead, she became more furious with her mother and was afraid to visit her because she would feel enraged. She said, "I hate her being down and sick and ugly. I would want to smash her if I visited." I pointed out that in place of the expected feeling, "I am terrible for wishing this on her," we saw the opposite reaction, "She is no good for doing this to me." After a thoughtful silence the patient added that she never blamed herself. If she did badly on a test in college, she blamed the professor and felt the test was unfair.

After her mother's operation she did not visit her for a few days. Then she took a weekend trip to the beach with her husband, but only after a period of indecision and after having checked with her husband, her father, and friends whether it would be acceptable to go away. It turned out to be an unhappy weekend during which she and her husband fought most of the time. In talking about it, she said she had felt abducted and had been furious with her husband and sorry for herself. We worked out her defense of projecting the self-directed hostility onto her husband, and then turning self-criticism into self-comforting. At this point this bright college graduate said with obvious surprise, "I just don't know what guilt means." She realized that guilt as an experiential phenomenon was foreign to her, even though she understood it intellectually.[3]

This patient once reported an incident which occurred before Christmas. Loaded down with packages after a shopping trip, she was waiting for a bus. As one full bus after another passed her by, she became increasingly angry; finally, when she got onto a bus, she fell, hit her shin on the step and tore her new and expensive stockings, which, she added, had not yet been paid for. At first she was furious with her husband, who did not want her taking taxis; then she went into a prolonged period of self-pity, during which she felt especially put upon. Pursuing her strange comment about taxis (she had used them freely in the past), I learned that her husband had asked her to be careful with expenditures because he was buying out his partner and cash would be low for a while. She was then able to see the entire shopping trip and her many packages as a defiant reaction to her depriving husband, and spontaneously described the state of ensuing tension she experienced while waiting at the bus stop.

I interpreted this state of tension as the equivalent of a feeling of guilt, the result of her bad conscience, although she was not aware of feeling that she was bad for defying her husband. She was aware only of the many packages. Yet her token gesture of taking the bus was not enough to appease her conscience; she needed further punishment for her wrongdoing and therefore injured herself. At the same time the injury then became the stimulus for self-comforting. The important element here is, I think, the avoidance of any experience of self-directed aggression, its projection onto the husband, and the replacement of conscious, self-directed

---

[3] One should recall here that in exploring regression in relation to the superego (including the role of deneutralization and defusion), Freud (1923, 1924a) indicated that superego functions become sexualized once more (deneutralized) and are replaced by sadomasochistic relations to the ego.

aggression by self-directed libidinal discharge in the form of self-comforting and self-pity.

This patient's avoidance of depression or self-criticism did not always involve superego processes. For example, on one occasion she reluctantly told of her fantasy life, which was intense whenever she was alone. In one fantasy, which she had in the shower, she was the wife of the President, the First Lady of the land. She was an orphan with two rich grandmothers, one in New York and one in Rome. She was sophisticated and well-traveled, a child psychologist, bright and rich, and she drove a Bentley. She was the ultimate woman, a showman with a lot of style of her own. She was different and everybody wanted to talk to her. Being the center of admiration brought back the feeling she had had before her brother was born when she was 7. In reality she usually felt that no one noticed or admired her. Then she added, "My fantasies fill the gap between what I am and what I want to be." [4] She then recalled her first college mixer when she had retired to the ladies' room and spent most of the evening crying.

She began to feel sorry for herself; in answer to my question what depressed her in the shower and triggered the fantasy, she told of a second fantasy in the shower. She was a professor at Princeton lecturing to the young boys about the Irish poets and playwrights. She felt invincible, powerful, and everybody was noticing her. Impressing young college boys was important in the fantasy. She sensed that she seduced them and made them all fall in love with her. Casually she added that it was perhaps related to her brother, whereupon I suggested that it was related to what went on in the bedroom which they shared until she was 14 years old. (Previously this subject had been unapproachable.) These memories were very cloudy, she said. But she recalled her present neighbor's 13-year-old son, of whom she was very fond, as she was of all boys. She almost said to him the evening before the fantasy, "I have a brother your age." (In reality her brother was then 19.) She mused that the neighbor's boy was fond of her because she

---

[4] This is a clear-cut way of describing the distinction between her self image and the wished-for image of herself. The fantasy changed her self image temporarily to conform with her wished-for self image. The filling of the gap also had a deeper unconscious meaning.

must have seduced him. I said she must have done something similar to her brother; moreover, the importance of the shower and the theme of exhibiting in the fantasies suggested exposure. She mentioned then a vague memory of bathing with her brother, then recalled a photograph of both of them in the tub.

Much later in her analysis I learned about the events that had led to an extreme transformation in her attitude toward her brother when she was about 13. Prior to that time she had been outspokenly and cruelly hostile to him, but then she became overly fond, even romantically attached to him. In later years they went out together a great deal rather than having dates with others. Her brother had been enuretic and no parental attempts at solution had helped. When she was 13 (he was 6), unsolicited she took it upon herself to wake her brother and take him to the bathroom to urinate before she would retire. She stood behind him, pressed against him, and held his penis as he urinated. She recalled feeling his penis "stiffen" as he urinated. Significantly, in that same session, when she spoke about what the close relationship with her brother did for her, she said he made her feel "puffed up." He became her penis. It was he who filled "her gap." The primitive identification helped her overcome her depression just as the fantasies did. For this patient even the self-criticism involved in seeing herself as castrated was intolerable and had to be warded off.

This patient had a similar approach to her anal-erotic interests. Her masculine aggressive mother had frequently given her enemas, an activity which eventually became erotized and sought after. But she disliked the idea that she enjoyed it, could not admit it, and spoke of it only with the greatest difficulty in the analysis. Equating the dirty, animalistic quality in herself with a monkey, she wished to disown that part of herself. Whenever anal wishes arose, however, she warded them off by a change of identity; she became a perfect angelic princess who had no anus and to whom bowel movements were unknown.

Jacobson (1964) stressed the importance of the anal phase in fashioning precursors to the formation of the superego, because it is in this phase of development that the child begins to have feelings of disgust about functions and products related to himself. This patient could not tolerate those self-critical feelings and dealt with them not by repression, reaction formation, sublimation, etc., but by disavowing her identity and assuming a new pseudoidentity of an angelic princess. In fact, she made a life style of believing her self image to be as grandiose as her wished-for image of herself. But it meant she had to rely on fantasy and magic and had to avoid as much as possible situations that called for the "cold truth" such as application forms for college or jobs. These were depressing and demoralizing, because they brought her face to face with her real self, closer to the monkey.

The reliance on magical thinking and fantasy and the blurred distinctions between fantasy and reality also were useful in the service of warding off guilt feelings. When she had minimally conscious fantasies of infidelity, or forgot, lost or broke something that her husband valued, she would fantasy her husband tyrannizing her and cruelly ordering her about. By means of these fantasies she avoided any guilt feelings, and in their place experienced only self-pity. In these situations the fantasy assumed reality value for her.

Self-Pity and the Integrity of Self Representation

The unstable self image referred to in the last illustration is not an accidental feature of a single case, but is an important and characteristic feature of many cases involving severe states of self-pity and self-comforting. The narcissistic regression, along with the tendency to project superego-instigated aggression from self onto object representation, implies a looseness of boundaries between self and object images and gives the stamp of a narcissistic object choice to the ambivalently loved object.[5] In other words, these cases frequently show an ego regression to a point prior to a stable state of individuation. As a result, the patient may confuse his own role with that of others, and subjectively he may experience a threat to the integrity of the self.

For example, the woman who thought of herself as Poor Pitiful Pauline on one occasion attended a well-advertised peace rally and became panicky in the mob. She felt she was losing her "identity."

---

[5] Edith Jacobson, in discussing this paper, suggested that projection may be a necessary component in producing the syndrome, and that self-pity may ward off paranoid regressions as well as depressive reactions.

Describing it she said, "I felt I was getting lost. I would be swallowed up." She almost cried there, not for the dead soldiers but for her own shaky self. In order to counteract this frightening loss of identity she turned her full attention to herself; in economic terms, she reversed the decathexis of the self representation. She ignored what was going on around her and thought, "Who am I? What am I doing here? I'm not an organizer or a speaker. In fact, no one is paying attention to me." This led to both feelings of self-pity and arrogant haughty feelings of superiority to the crowd.

In a similar way, on occasions when she traveled abroad, she felt like a tiny speck in a vast primitive world, fearing that if she made a wrong turn, she would disappear and no one would find her. She had similar experiences in relation to her husband. When he told her about something they were going to do especially for her—for example, purchase a painting for her birthday—she reacted with anger. She said one time, "I can't find myself in that. I merely feel controlled. He's pushing me around and putting me down." Then, losing her usual control, she blurted out, "He's keeping me away from my mother." This statement condensed much of her childhood experience: it referred to the old blissful state of union with her mother, a longed-for state with which she felt her husband was interfering, just as her father's return from the war when she was 2 years old had displaced her from her mother's bed and her mother's exclusive attention. She shunned agreeing with her husband on anything because she would cease being herself. To differ made her feel separate and an individual. She said once about her husband, "If I said, 'I'd love to go to Paris with you,' where would *I* be? I would have become him. If I refuse to go, I'm still me. I have to be a rebel. If I serve anyone, I lose myself."

In keeping with her self image of Poor Pitiful Pauline, she felt she was herself when she was unhappy and felt mistreated. If she were joyful, there was no distance between herself and others, and she felt herself being swallowed up. "When I'm happy, I lose something of myself," she said. "It's not me. Being unhappy is a part of me. Being unhappy is the part of me I know and like the best." As a child she had instigated many unhappy crises which had kept her mother close at hand and thus prevented her severe dread of separation from becoming realized. She felt incomplete without her mother and dreaded falling apart if her mother left her. In her adult personality there were clear indications that she had never adequately mastered separation and individuation, that she was fixated at a point of development prior to object and self constancy, and still showed considerable confusion between object and self images. In the transference she eventually spoke of her wish for me to take over responsibilities and decisions for her, to become a part of her in that sense. Voicing this was enough to frighten her, as she realized I was separate and would not feel as she wished me to feel.

In playing off her husband and mother against one another she was very successful in having one or the other take over functions for her. She would tell her mother, for example, that her husband wanted to take a trip, or tell her husband that her mother wanted her to visit, but she never said what she herself wanted, nor was she always sure what she wanted. She said, "There is no me in the middle." She could become one with her mother or with her husband, but never with both. The idea of being separate from everyone else frightened her because it meant they would die and fall away and she would be left with no one caring for her. Thus she clearly equated separation with death, a danger warded off by the fusion of self and object images. This equation also implied that she had failed in sufficiently neutralizing primitive aggressive drives. Her choice of marital partner helped vicariously to provide gratification for these drives, as her husband, often tactless in his manner, was a man given to blunt criticism of others. She could remain outwardly kind and let her husband express hostile ideas, which she eventually realized agreed largely with her own opinions of the people involved.

Her retention of hostile impulses paralleled her constipation and the difficulties she had spending money. Each threatened the integrity of her self image and was related to childhood experiences of forced enemas brought on by anal retention, which in turn was her symptomatic reaction to the loss of her mother when her father returned from the war when she was 2 years old. Fusion was welcomed when the love object benevolently and maternally took over psychic functions for her, thus enhancing her self image. It was threatening if she sensed that she would be swallowed up and lose her identity. For this reason she tended to differ with her husband more than with her mother, and found sex terribly unpleasant.

Self-pity and self-comforting can also be used as a defense against depersonalization. A woman who had a borderline condition experienced frightening feelings of unreality, of "falling apart," "withering away," or "disappearing" when she was walking in the street. These experiences were associated with fantasies of rape. She overcame them by becoming enraged and focusing her attention on herself, telling herself, "Don't let yourself go," or "Get hold of yourself," or "Pull yourself together." These are literal translations of her need to bolster her fading self representation. On these occasions she felt extremely sorry for herself because she was so different from other people; she would be drawn to men who pitied her, which led to a pregenital form of promiscuity. Another patient spoke of her self-pity as a way of overcoming a frightening subjective sense of deadness which she would experience at times of great loneliness and isolation. The self-pity provided a way of recathecting her self representation.

Self-Pity and Resistance to Therapeutic Change

The final question on which I would like to focus is why severe forms of self-pity and self-comforting offer such a powerful resistance to analysis. Freud (1923) said that the superego "appears as the representative of the id" (p. 58), by which he meant that superego formation provides a means of internally continuing the gratifying oedipal relationship on a relatively desexualized basis. In a similar vein Anna Freud (1936) described the adolescent's estrangement from his superego on the basis of its incestuous origins. Although in superego formation the oedipal drives are neutralized to a considerable extent, there are differences in the degree of neutralization, so that the ego ideal operates with more neutral energy than the limiting function of the superego, and that with more neutral energy than the punitive and rewarding function (Hartmann and Loewenstein, 1962; Jacobson, 1964). It would appear that in severe cases of self-pity the neutralization of the drives that occurred in superego formation is reversed and the resexualized libido is invested in the self representation. Self-pity in these cases, then, represents an oedipal gratification from the reinternalized, but now repersonified oedipal object in the superego, usually associated with the mother.[6] The gratification is one important factor making this syndrome so difficult to treat.

Loewenstein (1945) described a syndrome in which the superego utilizes the fulfillment of an id drive for the purpose of self-punishment, for example, an irrepressible urge to compulsive masturbation. The exciting and pleasure-giving impulse is used by the superego in the service of punishment or pain. In self-pity the situation is exactly reversed. Here, pain and suffering which are experienced as unjust are used by the superego in the service of comforting. Loewenstein described the manifestations of the punitive function of the superego, whereas self-pity involves the rewarding function. In the course of development, every child is rewarded and approved of when he masters the delay of gratification, or endures necessary painful experiences, or renounces oedipal wishes. In some respects, then, it is a universal experience to feel a heightened self-esteem and to expect love and approval with deprivation and pain. Self-pity is a result of carrying this normal process too far and seeking out pain in order to enjoy the gratifications of comforting oneself.

The aggressive drive is also involved in the power of this syndrome to resist analysis. As described above, these people have problems with the mastery of aggressive drives, cannot tolerate the open expression of aggression to others, are terrified of other people's anger at them, and are exquisitely sensitive to superego criticism of the self. At the root of this constellation is a conflict over unconscious, primitive, murderous impulses. They fear the superego's self-directed criticism as it carries the same lethal potential as their primitive death wishes toward others. Giving up the defensive protection of self-pity would therefore expose them to the

---

[6] The superego not only serves as an internal barrier to instinctual expression (id drives), but also functions as a mode of expressing powerful id drives. The apparent paradox is resolved if we keep in mind that neutralization of the drives makes them available for the purpose of defense. Regression in the degree of neutralization reduces the availability of the drives for the purpose of defense and increases the degree of direct gratification of instinctual expression.

danger of the self-directed violence contained in their guilt reactions.

Freud has been criticized for treating bisexuality in relation to the superego in a one-sided way, for he usually described the superego as the impersonalized father (Schafer, 1960). When he wrote *The Ego and the Id,* however, his emphasis was on the aggressive drive and the punitive function of the superego. The attempt to highlight the role of the *libidinal* drive in self-pity and self-comforting not only restores its proper place in the rewarding function of the superego, but also restores, through the specific link with the maternal comforting function, a more balanced view of the superego as the impersonalized internal representative of *both* parents.

Summary

Self-pity and self-comforting are affective states which offer a powerful resistance to analysis because they provide libidinized oedipal gratification via the rewarding function of the superego, which is activated by a narcissistic wound viewed by the subject as unjust. In addition, they offer a strong defense against self-directed punitive aggressive drives. Narcissism is heightened and there is an interference with object relationships. The genetic basis seems to be a significant trauma in the anal period which interferes with self-directed aggression (later reflected in an intolerance for guilt feelings) at a time when the stability of the self-representation has not yet been established. In the ensuing regression, the individual retreats to the early oral phase, focusing on maternal comforting and partial fusion of self and object images.

BIBLIOGRAPHY

FREUD, A. (1936), *The Ego and the Mechanisms of Defense.* New York: International Universities Press, rev. ed., 1966.
FREUD, S. (1916), Some Character Types Met with in Psycho-Analytic Work. *Standard Edition,* 14:309–333. London: Hogarth Press, 1957.
— (1921), Group Psychology and the Analysis of the Ego. *Standard Edition,* 18:67–143. London: Hogarth Press, 1955.

— (1923), The Ego and the Id. *Standard Edition*, 19:3–66. London: Hogarth Press, 1961.
— (1924a), The Economic Problem of Masochism. *Standard Edition*, 19:157–170. London: Hogarth Press, 1961.
— (1924b), The Dissolution of the Oedipus Complex. *Standard Edition*, 19:173–179. London: Hogarth Press, 1961.
— (1927), Humour. *Standard Edition*, 21:159–166. London: Hogarth Press, 1961.
FURER, M. (1967), Some Developmental Aspects of the Superego. *Int. J. Psycho-Anal.*, 48:277–280.
HARTMANN, H. & LOEWENSTEIN, R. M. (1962), Notes on the Superego. *This Annual*, 17:42–81.
JACOBSON, E. (1954a), The Self and the Object World. *This Annual*, 9:75–127.
— (1954b), Contribution to the Metapsychology of Psychotic Identifications. *J. Amer. Psychoanal. Assn.*, 5:61–72.
— (1959), The "Exceptions": An Elaboration of Freud's Character Study. *This Annual*, 14:135–154.
— (1964), *The Self and the Object World*. New York: International Universities Press.
JEKELS, L. (1930), The Psychology of Pity. *Collected Papers*. New York: International Universities Press, 1952, pp. 88–96.
— (1936), Mitleid und Liebe. *Imago*, 22:383–388.
KRIS, E. (1951), Some Comments and Observations on Early Autoerotic Activities. *This Annual*, 6:95–116.
LOEWENSTEIN, R. M. (1945), A Special Form of Self-Punishment. *Psychoanal. Quart.*, 14:46–61.
— (1966), On the Theory of the Superego: A Discussion. In: *Psychoanalysis— A General Psychology*, ed. R. M. Loewenstein, L. M. Newman, M. Schur, & A. J. Solnit. New York: International Universities Press, pp. 298–314.
LUSSIER, A. (1960), The Analysis of a Boy with a Congenital Deformity. *This Annual*, 15:430–453.
MALONEY, J. C. (1949), *The Magic Cloak*. Wakefield, Mass.: Montrose Press.
SANDLER, J. (1960), On the Concept of Superego. *This Annual*, 15:128–162.
SCHAFER, R. (1960), The Loving and Beloved Superego in Freud's Structural Theory. *This Annual*, 15:163–188.
STEIN, M. H. (1966), Self Observation, Reality, and the Superego. In: *Psychoanalysis—A General Psychology*, ed. R. M. Loewenstein, L. M. Newman, M. Schur, & A. J. Solnit. New York: International Universities Press, pp. 275–297.
ZETZEL, E. R. (1965), Depression and the Incapacity to Bear It. In: *Drives, Affects, Behavior*, Vol. 2, ed. M. Schur. New York: International Universities Press, pp. 243–274.

Psychoanalysis of a Latency Boy with Neurodermatitis

MARSHALL D. SCHECHTER, M.D.

THE MATERIAL TO BE PRESENTED IS FROM THE ANALYTIC TREATMENT of an 8-year-old boy conducted 20 years ago. The delay in presenting this case was recommended by one of the dermatologists whom I consulted. It was Obermayer's impression that adolescence often presented sufficient stresses to cause a return of the dermatitis, the major presenting symptom. He suggested if nothing occurred before, during, or after this period, we could consider the psychoanalysis a success. Referring to this case in his book (1955), Obermayer said:

> This study by Schechter is of considerable interest. Should the child continue to live his life free of neurodermatitis, this case

---

Professor, Department of Psychiatry and Behavioral Sciences, and Consultant Professor of Pediatrics, University of Oklahoma Health Science Center.

(529)

would constitute a remarkable result of psychoanalysis; permanent cessation of all manifestations of the disease after having been constantly present since his birth—for eight years—would, in my experience, represent a most uncommon observation. Schechter has an opportunity here to make another valuable contribution by careful periodic follow-up studies and publication of their results [p. 223].[1]

In this presentation I hope to set forth, essentially in an hour-by-hour fashion, the psychoanalytic treatment of this case. I shall then describe the contacts I had with the patient on the three occasions when there was a brief flare-up of the dermatitis after the termination of the treatment, as well as the parents' reports on the boy's progress throughout the ensuing 20 years. The presentation of the clinical material will be followed by a brief discussion setting forth my thoughts on what transpired. At the end I shall briefly review the psychoanalytic literature on dermatitis, focusing on specific aspects that are pertinent to this case.

Case Presentation

Background

Jeff was referred to me at the age of 8 years. During the preceding 6 months, he had been unable to attend school. He had been suffering from a dermatitis that covered his entire body and was especially severe on the thighs, the popliteal and anticubital creases, and in the pubic area. He had been treated and given up by seven other physicians (three pediatricians and four dermatologists).

Despite double adult dosages of sedatives, Jeff slept only fitfully, and even during sleep it required two adults to hold his arms to prevent scratching the genital area. No matter how closely he was watched around the clock (for much of the time the family employed a night nurse), he would scratch himself with such ferocity that his flexor surfaces and especially his genital area, according to his father, looked like "raw hamburger."

By the time one of the pediatricians recommended psychiatric

[1] For a discussion of neuralanatomy and physiology of the skin see Wittkower and Russell (1953, pp. 28–38).

consultation, both of Jeff's parents were exhausted from their constant 24-hour vigils. They also felt hopeless and desperate about their son's condition. It was my impression at that time, and even more so in retrospect, that the excessive investment of time, varying treatment modalities, money, and medical people of good intentions and repute which had preceded this psychoanalytic treatment, ultimately eased the therapeutic task. Feeling up against the wall, the parents were willing faithfully to follow suggestions from the psychoanalyst which they might not have accepted so unquestioning otherwise.[2]

Jeff's parents were warm, friendly, well-educated, civic-minded people of Italian descent who involved themselves with interest in Jeff's and his brother Michael's activities. They seemed to derive genuine satisfaction from their family life. The father was a highly successful businessman coming from a well-to-do family. The mother, also from a financially comfortable family, had worked prior to their marriage. After the birth of Michael (6 years older than Jeff), the mother began art classes and became recognized as one of the outstanding local amateurs.

Allergies figured heavily in the family backgrounds of both parents. Michael was described as an outgoing, athletic youngster who was extraordinarily popular with his peers and did well academically. Although he was said to tolerate Jeff at the time of referral, earlier in Jeff's life, Michael dominated, bullied, and directed Jeff constantly. Michael, the parents initially reported, had no physical ailments other than a strabismus, which was corrected before Jeff's birth.

Both parents were aware of their desire for and even expectation of a girl when Jeff was born. Both said that they were not disappointed when they saw what a fat, healthy baby he was. They reported that Jeff was troubled by asthma and eczema from birth on.

---

[2] Anna Freud (1965, p. 48) suggests it is the parents' task to help the child overcome resistances and periods of negative transference. If parents side with the child's defenses, the analyst is helpless. Individual child analysts deal with parents quite differently varying from excluding them entirely from their child's treatment, to keeping them informed, to permitting direct participation with the very young child, to treating them separately but simultaneously, to analyzing the parent in preference to analyzing the child.

He was breast-fed until the age of 5 months, when he was suddenly weaned due to maternal pneumonitis. Both walking and talking occurred at about 14 months. Jeff was bowel and bladder trained by 2 years without any difficulty. When Jeff was 4, the family moved from one house to another. There were fewer children on the new block. Jeff was therefore enrolled in a nursery school, which he did not like. Nightmares were reported to have occurred around age 5. He liked regular school, but the parents reported that he seemed frightened by competitive sports and played mainly with girls. When treatment began, he did not have a single close boyfriend. Academically, he was a C+, B− student. There seemed to be no special learning problems, and the teachers never reported any behavioral difficulties.

Although both parents were affectionate with each other and the children, they felt that Jeff had an inordinate need for visible signs of affection. When the parents were first seen, they were extremely perplexed about the nature and cause of Jeff's dermatitis. They could not understand what had caused a skin reaction of such severity and why so many local and systemic treatments had failed. Throughout Jeff's treatment, his parents were in constant contact with me via phone, letters, and interviews. The analytic treatment added up to 100 hours over a total of 5 months. Occasional visits with the parents are included in the 100 hours. With the exception of holidays and weekends, the child was seen 5 days a week.

Diagnostic Phase

Jeff, a dark-haired, neat-looking boy, came readily to the first interview after he had been introduced by his mother. He was of normal height and weight for his age. His head was narrow in the transverse diameter and relatively longer in the anteroposterior diameter. His face was very narrow. What could be seen of his exposed skin surfaces was red and branny in places and oozing in others. He walked hunched over like an old man with a Strumpel-Marie arthritis and with his legs spread rather widely apart. (It was not until a few weeks later that I found out he was in diapers to keep the medicines in place and to prevent excessive rubbing from his clothes or too direct access to this area for scratching.) His voice was quiet, but his speech distinct and clear; his vocabulary and grammatical construction were decidedly advanced.

It was evident in this initial contact that Jeff knew exactly why he had come to see me. His attitude reflected the insights and intuitions markedly noted in the sporadic interviews after the psychoanalysis was terminated. The dermatitis was clearly a constant source of discomfort pressing for an early solution.[3]

In this first hour, the discussion revolved around Jeff's daytime preoccupation with thoughts of the rash becoming constant and implacable during the night. He mentioned that he frequently dreamed about a fireman who could put him on fire. In this dream he felt as if he were burning up. Later in the hour, after he had investigated all of the office, including the desks, closets, and toys, he spontaneously told me that he liked to play games only if he won. Just before he left that day, he mentioned that he never played with boys. They could beat him in games, and they might attack him physically.

In the next hour, he indicated that his parents very much wanted him to do things their way. If he did not do as they suggested, he worried that they would punish him in a way he anticipated as being intolerable. I suggested to him that when he felt forced to do what other people wanted, he became angry and then felt burned up inside. He thought this made sense and went on to talk about his feelings that his parents' standards were too high. He again stressed his need to do what he was told lest some catastrophe befall him. Jeff then emphasized the importance of doing the same things Michael did and living up to the same standards Michael had set, lest his parents think less of him.

By the 5th hour, Jeff talked about his tremendous need to

[3] A. Freud (1965, p. 220) states, "Despite the fact . . . that suffering from symptoms is not the same diagnostic indicator in children as it is in adults, many neurotic children are motivated for therapy by suffering, i.e., by the bodily discomforts and pains caused by the psychological upsets of stomach and digestion, the skin eruptions, asthma, the headaches, sleep disturbances, etc.; in the phobias of school, street, or animals, by the loss of freedom of action, the inability to do what other children do, and the exclusion from their pleasures; in the rituals and obsessions, by the feeling of being at the mercy of an unknown and compelling force which prescribes senseless actions; etc."

scratch, yet he felt that he really should stop himself or his mother would be forced to restrain him. To him, scratching felt good; but he noted that every time he scratched, it made his mother extremely unhappy. The main itching, he said, occurred particularly on his penis or on the pubic area just above the penis.

Upon consultation with a colleague, Mrs. Margarete Ruben, whose help and understanding in this case were extraordinary, after the diagnostic process, it was my opinion that although Jeff was suffering from an acute and severe dermatitis, the proclivity for which had been present from birth, he had reached the phallic-genital level of development. Jeff's dermatitis was viewed as a reaction to castration anxieties and a failure to settle his oedipal conflict. His ego and superego were quite well organized (better than to be expected in a case where regression had occurred due to the pull of the libidinal drives) and were able to stand relatively firm in the face of repressed drive activity. Because his ego organization was judged to have reached the phallic-oedipal phase, the presenting symptom was seen as being primarily related to an infantile neurosis. Chronologically, skin erotism should have been outgrown; but because of the underlying ever-present skin allergies, this mode of discharge became the primary one as regression occurred during the oedipal phase. The parents were seen after diagnostic interviews. The need for psychoanalytic treatment was described and accepted.[4]

Treatment Phase

At the beginning of the next hour, Jeff made up a story about a sad monkey in the zoo whom nobody liked. Everybody, however,

---

[4] A. Freud (1965, p. 219) suggests that: "None of these difficult decisions [e.g., regarding child analysis as the treatment of choice] come into question with regard to the infantile neuroses . . . , and in this therapeutic field the child analyst can feel at ease. With the conflicts of the oedipus complex as precipitating cause and the neurotic symptomatology explained by the classical formula of danger→anxiety→ permanent regression to fixation point→rejection of reactivated pregenital impulses→defense→compromise formation, the infantile neuroses not only come nearest to the corresponding adult disturbances in metapsychological identity, they also offer the analyst a role within the treatment which is similar to the one he has with adults. He can assume the part of helpmate to the patient's ego, and under favorable conditions is accepted by the child as such."

liked the monkey's mother and gave her peanuts, some of which she gave to the baby monkey. This made the baby extremely sad, and he decided to run away to show everyone how tough he really was. His mother also escaped and happened quite accidentally to find him, bringing him back to the zoo. Everyone felt very sorry for the little monkey, and then they started to like him. As he grew up, he felt people should like him for himself, so he made friends and then people just didn't feel sorry for him, but liked him because he was such a wonderful monkey. This story occupied almost the entire hour.

On the following day when I asked about this story, Jeff said that he really did not feel that it was terribly good. Just prior to this hour his mother had called to say that he had slept the previous two nights and that she and her husband were extremely pleased about it.

In the succeeding hours as Jeff talked about competition and his fear that this could lead to his own death, the dermatitis was extremely severe both day and night. I asked Jeff if it was alright for me to tell the story of the sad monkey to another boy who was depressed because I was certain it would please and might help him. He gave permission joyously and then engaged in a game of Parcheesi. During the Parcheesi game he talked about the competitive sports at home and the competition he felt from his father and brother. That night the itching and scratching were intense and continuous. The father's concern was so great that he called the dermatologist, who prescribed heavy doses of demerol.

The next day, after playing Parcheesi for a while, I asked Jeff what had occurred during the previous day that might have something to do with the itching. He puzzled a great deal and then told me that his cousin had come over and had talked about the death of their grandfather and paternal uncle (neither of whom the patient had ever seen) . As Jeff continued the game, he became more and more excited and used all kinds of tricks to win. The more excited he became, the more anxious he seemed. I wondered whether he himself had been concerned about death. He confessed that a few years prior to the outbreak of the dermatitis he had suffered from constant fears of dying and had repeatedly asked his parents whether young people died as well as old. He was told by his mother that people who were young and took good care of themselves did not die.

In his next hour, Jeff indicated that he had slept poorly. He noted that I did not win frequently in the games we were playing; I gave the game to him and treated him as a child. He was making plans to trick me into losing. He thought that possibly there was some kind of relationship between his rash and not wanting others to give him extra chances.

Later he talked about his sleep and the frequency with which he had a very cold feeling in his chest and stomach when going to sleep. He used a hot water bottle to combat the cold feeling. I said that it sounded as if his anxiety must be terribly great just as he was falling asleep and during the rest of the night (see A. Freud, 1965, p. 157; Nagera, 1966).

The next day he looked considerably better and talked about his father's strength and his father's enormous willpower to do whatever he wanted to do whenever it was necessary. He indicated he was going to start school, half days at this time.

Two days later I received a call from the dermatologist who told me that the cortisone and the day and night sedation were without effect. Jeff himself recognized that during the first day in school he had become increasingly anxious about the other children. He had then become aware of an itch beginning in his genital area. I spoke of a boy who was very sad and wanted to get sick in order to get attention from his parents; when I suggested that it was not necessary to go to school at this time if it was too difficult, he told me other doctors too had told him to stop school. As a matter of fact, he said, some of his former physicians had hospitalized him, given him a great deal of sedation and steroids, and tied his hands and feet to the bed in order to prevent the scratching. Being tied up in bed created enormous fears, which resulted in an increased outbreak of dermatitis and forced a release from the hospital.

In his analytic sessions Jeff's play was self-destructive and at home he often spoke of suicide. He was angry with me (and all other doctors) because he felt I could not be trusted either. But he could not directly express his anger because he thought I was his last hope for a cure; as a consequence, the hostile feelings led to guilt and increased anxiety. When he made innumerable mistakes in the Parcheesi game (see A. Freud, 1965, p. 83), I pointed out his constant expectation of punishment. If the punishment did not come from the outside as expected, he would make it happen himself. This, I suggested, might bring on the rash—a kind of self-punishment for bad thoughts or feelings.[5]

The next day Jeff related his fear of sleeping to his ideas of a fireman putting him on fire. He was certain that because he wanted to be a man so badly, men (e.g., his father or I) would not allow him to. He talked about his genital itching and the desire to scratch, but he knew it was bad for him to do because in the past his parents had forbidden this kind of activity. I told him that there was nothing wrong with the desire to touch himself or the feeling of pleasure he had while playing with his penis. As we talked of this, there was a distinct clearing of some of the redness in his face.

That afternoon Jeff's father called, having remembered an incident just prior to the onset of the dermatitis. Jeff had pulled down a girl's pants. When asked about it, Jeff flagrantly denied any kind of interest or even having done it at all.

The following day I had an interview with Jeff's mother in which I explained to her the probable masturbatory nature of some of Jeff's desires to touch his genitals. She recognized that her past attitudes might have conditioned him against masturbation; but if I was certain it was alright, she would permit it.[6]

A few days later in talking about his mother's visit Jeff wondered what it was that we had talked about. I told him that his mother would be understanding of his pleasure in genital play after our interview. At first Jeff denied any interest in masturba-

---

[5] A. Freud (1965, p. 69) remarks: "Although for the whole of early childhood the child's life will be dominated by body needs, body impulses, and their derivatives, the quantities and qualities of satisfactions and dissatisfactions are determined not by himself but by environmental influence. The only exceptions to this rule are the autoerotic gratifications which from the beginning are under the child's own management and, therefore, provide for him a certain circumscribed measure of independence of the object world."

[6] A. Freud (1965, p. 25f.) suggests that many child analysts feel committed to the same therapeutic principles in treating children as adults are treated. This implies not using the authority of the analyst, thereby eliminating suggestion and keeping environmental manipulation to a minimum except where "demonstrably harmful or potentially traumatic (seductive) influences were at work."

tion, but he kept on coming back with more and more questions which required repeated reassurances that no genital injury would result.

In the following session Jeff indicated that his whole family was constantly watching to see if he was scratching himself. He mentioned fearfully that at home and at school he had frequent erections, making his whole body feel hot and troubled when this occurred. After this piece of information, he insisted on playing a card game of War, manipulating the rules in such a way that he always won.

During the next hour he saw a squirt gun which he used hesitatingly. He talked about the forbidden things that went on at home. I asked him to tell me what kind of things he was referring to. Jeff spoke of his brother coming into his room without his parent's knowledge and telling him dirty stories. He also said his brother and he built fires and took the car out for drives when his parents were away.

A few days later he related having had a dream of being in bed. While dreaming, he became aware of itching in his genitals and in a cut he had on his arm. As far as he recalled, he actually did not scratch too much that particular night. Jeff then associated to his dream: he did not know what to do with his hands at night; remembering the cut on his arm, he recalled that Michael had used the term "cut" for the female genital. I suggested that some boys felt that their mothers at times received far too much attention from their fathers, and since the boys indeed loved their fathers, they very often even might have wished to have been a girl themselves. Jeff was fascinated with this idea and kept asking how a boy might magically transform himself into a female. He told me of a number of times he had placed his penis in between his legs to see whether or not he could look like a girl. He even thought he might want to get rid of his penis; perhaps some of his scratching so hard was an attempt to make it disappear entirely.

In subsequent hours Jeff wondered whether he could have a baby himself. He recognized his fear of genital injury and frequently found himself thinking anxiously that when he grew up, his father would probably die. He was certain castration would be his fate for this thought because of his father's anger.

During the next session, Jeff reported another dream in which he was walking down a street and getting lost. He tried to find a policeman to give him directions, but couldn't find any. He asked a man who was walking on the street. The man told him he would take him home, but instead took him in his car to his own house. The patient realized that he was being kidnapped. A woman came into the house and said she knew what a fine boy he was. Although the woman seemed to be on his side, the man still kept him locked up. Jeff realized during the dream that it was only a dream and his anxiety abated with this recognition. He recalled that the previous day he had been in a store with his mother and had gotten lost there. A man in the store had helped him find his mother. The man reminded him of the man who lived across the street from their house. This neighbor had a dog who attacked Jeff's dog. Jeff wished that they would take the neighbor's dog and put him to death in the pound. While talking about this he began scratching at the pubic area just above his penis. It was evident that he became depressed as well as anxious. I told him he seemed to be concerned about the idea of a man injuring him in order to fulfill his desires to be a female.

The patient said that most of the time he liked his father more than his mother; he thought so much about his wish to be at home with his father that often he was unable to work adequately in school. He again worried that if he began to grow up and get older, this would mean that his father would be nearing death. With some surprise he recalled that his father's parents were still living despite the fact that his father was grown up. Jeff recalled a Biblical story about a man who killed and tortured his own brother. In retaliation God killed the man himself.

In the following hour, he said he had slept relatively well and had awakened only once because of the itching. He put some cream where it itched, and was able to fall back to sleep. He began to play Parcheesi, cheating at every turn. I asked him why it was necessary to play this way when, if he played according to the rules, he still was able to win many times. He became very anxious and said I was just like his father and brother, trying to make him feel small, and that he would never be able to compete successfully in the usual way against me or his family. When it came to physical sports, his brother had everything bigger than he and therefore would be winning all the time. I said I thought this was another one of the areas where he was anxious—even though he would grow up, he feared he might still have the penis of a little boy. Brightening up, he said he recognized this as one of his worries. Following this interpretation he was able to give up cheating at Parcheesi.

In the subsequent session he wanted to play a card game of War. He talked about pressure from his father to speed up his treatment because it was a costly affair. I told him I agreed and suggested he could accomplish this best if he would tell me everything that he thought, recognizing how difficult this might be. He then told me of a story he had read in the newspaper about a boy who put his arm too close to the lion's cage at the zoo and had the arm ripped off. He recognized that the idea of having something torn away from his body was both frightening and fascinating.

His parents told him that during the following night he had repeatedly shouted in his sleep, "No! No!" He could not remember what his dream was about, but he recalled that the previous day he had become preoccupied with maintaining grades at school after his teacher had expressed concern about his ability to catch up after the 6 months' absence. He spoke of the possibility of growing up and having to go into the army. This filled him with terror. The only way he thought he would be able to protect himself and to feel secure in any way would be to have guns all over the place. He would have cannons and bombs extending from all parts of his body. He would carry guns, sharp knives, and swords. He would be so protected that nobody could do anything to him at all. He would learn to fight even with his hands, although if he did this, he might lose them. Yet this might not be too bad; he would really have so much protection from all of the guns, he would not have to be afraid of anything. I said that I agreed it would be wonderful if he could be so protected. Then there would be nothing to fear at all. Besides, the idea of losing his hands would mean he would lose another one of his fears, namely, that of touching his genitals (see Pearson, 1940) .

Jeff indicated a fear of genital excitement while sliding (without benefit of sled) in the snow. He was certain somebody would see his pleasure and become angry with him. This coincided with a visit to the dermatologist during which the doctor suggested he might have to give up his dog because of his allergies. Shortly after this appointment Jeff developed a headache. The headache, he said, seemed to start when he got home and was in the bathtub. His mother also was there, sitting on the toilet. He did not recollect what she was doing other than talking on the telephone while she was seated there. He said he enjoyed having someone in the bathtub or the bathroom with him, but that perhaps there was something about what he saw that distressed him. He did not know whether this was so or whether it had any relationship to the headache or to the rash. At the end of the hour I suggested there was something about which he was mixed up and this was what caused both headache and rash.

For many years prior to the onset of the dermatitis it seemed that each time the parents attempted to go away Jeff would have an asthmatic attack or would become ill. Many times this either prevented the parents' leaving or resulted in their being called back from where they had gone. I suggested to the father that since Jeff at this particular point felt so uncertain about himself, it would probably be better for the parents not to leave on a short planned vacation by themselves. I also suggested that it would be better to discontinue sedatives and specifically leave the problems to be settled by the psychoanalytic work.

The following night there was a considerable amount of scratching. The parents felt that this might have been related to their restricting his watching horror programs on television. There had also been an argument with Michael, the nature of which they were uncertain. Jeff reported having had a bad night. His face was very red. He brought in a comic book for us to read together. Instead of doing this, I said that I thought it would be better to puzzle out what caused the very bad night. In a most adult manner, he sat down and said that perhaps it might have had to do with the argument with his brother, which turned out to have been about television as well. Jeff stated that he was uncomfortable when he heard mystery music. When mysteries were shown on television, the music made him feel very eerie inside. He felt ill at ease and with the discomfort, the itching seemed to increase. I suggested there were other boys who were troubled by nightmares following TV programs, but each of these programs seemed to be related to a specific kind of fear in each of these boys.

To associate to this idea, he played a game similar to 20 questions. He expressed concern about a giantlike man with a beard or a moustache who might kidnap him and do him some physical harm. (At that time I did not have a beard.) He then recalled that the mystery music brought on the same kind of eerie feeling as he had when he and his brother lit fires while their parents were away. He remembered that when he was younger, there had been times when he and his brother had taken money from his parents; subsequently he would worry constantly lest his parents, especially his father, become angry and punish him.

Jeff wondered whether other boys ever did this kind of thing—was it really bad or was it just that he thought it was bad? I said it was true that a lot of the things boys did were just like what he and his brother did, but I wondered why it was so troublesome for him. He thought it might have something to do with the other exciting things he and his brother did which he felt might be bad. I asked him what he was referring to. He said that sometimes while his parents were gone he and his brother would wrestle and his brother would touch Jeff's penis, causing him to have an erection and a desire to urinate.

It was clear that the mystery music brought up anxieties about his relationship with his brother and his concern about the excited sexual feelings he experienced in relation to his brother when his parents were gone. He was anxious for his parents not to leave so that they could protect him against these experiences and feelings.

That night the mother called, stating the itching and the scratching were as bad as ever. It seemed best to cancel the trip they had planned; but I suggested that they let Jeff know that the trip would be rescheduled for a time in the future when he was over his problems. I suggested quite specifically that if he troubled them at night, they should tell him not to bother them anymore, to use the creams he had available, and to discuss the problems with me, when next we met.

Jeff then spoke of his fear of his parents going away on vacation. He indicated that if he were ill, his parents would not leave him.

We discussed this from the standpoint of his fear of being alone with Michael without their protection. He also indicated how sad and lonely he would be without them.

During one of the next nights he awakened crying. When his mother went to find out what was wrong, he stated with considerable anxiety that he was worried about his penis; he had been playing with it and thought he had broken the bone in it. The anxiety was exceptionally intense and the scratching increased markedly. Jeff spoke of his concern of ever getting well. There was so much blood and pus exuding from the wounds, he feared not only permanent injury but also a total loss of strength. He fantasied that if he could drink the blood and pus, perhaps this could conserve his energies.[7] The bleeding flexor surfaces reminded him of menstrual bleeding and the desire to be a girl. To protect against this, he began playing with magic tricks. Then in a counterphobic fashion, he crashed cars and threw toys about the playroom. The scratching became so constant that the dermatologist strongly recommended a marked increased in steroids. Jeff knew I actively opposed this treatment and recommended that he bring his thoughts and feelings into the analysis for help instead of avoiding them by being given medication.

In the next hour, he insisted that we play checkers and refused to talk at all. I told him that he seemed to be upset about something. He agreed that this might be so; but he did not think it was the party they had had at his home the night before. He said the party was for some friends of his parents whom he did not know very well, and then insisted we play checkers some more. I told him I had thought more about the last few analytic sessions in which he had been crashing cars; this reminded me very much of a boy who was afraid to become angry since he felt his ideas would come true and that he would and should be punished for thinking such bad thoughts. Jeff did not respond directly except by saying that during

---

[7] This fantasy is very reminiscent of similar concerns in a patient described by Lefer (1964). This psychotic adolescent girl felt her body was not real, needing to reassure herself of its existence by rubbing herself continuously. As she spoke of this fear of not having a body at all (i.e, penis, body image), she became dyspneic and sucked her open wounds. While I did not at any time feel that Jeff was psychotic, I have had a number of patients who practiced autofellatio with self-conservation and self-perpetuation fantasies accompanying the acts.

the party a little boy had broken Jeff's train set. He was very un-happy about this but did not complain. He said he awakened only once that night. He felt that thinking certain things was just about as bad as doing them, but he never got angry at all. I told him that it was very hard to believe that he never got angry because it was something all people did, but perhaps he was very much afraid of being angry with his parents or with me. Throughout the hour he looked troubled, scratching his face a good deal.

The following night was a very bad night during which he had the idea of having many penises all over his body with each of them itching. If he could only put medicine on each of them, he thought, they would feel better. He felt more comfortable when he wore tight underpants because then he could not feel his penis bounce about as he ran. Throughout this time he remained quite morose, feeling that he would not get rid of the desire to scratch. His mother suggested that he talk to me about his laziness, which she related to his insistence on her dressing him.

I linked his feeling of having multiple penises with the earlier wish to have all the guns on his body and suggested that they might be related to his desire for strength and power. Similarly, it must have made him feel powerful to control his parents (such as forc-ing his mother to dress him, restrain him from scratching, or keep-ing them from vacations) and also not talk to me about his thoughts and feelings. He could not see that this had anything to do with it, but then he remembered our previous conversation about a boy who wanted to be a girl and recalled how he himself had tried to push his penis into his body and had become terribly worried it might stay inside and never come out again. Following this, he mentioned that some of the scratching was a matter of making sure his penis was still out and present rather than being inside and possibly lost.

On the next day, he said he had had a dream: it was raining in the daytime and he was in a car accident, "but it was only a dream and it probably didn't mean too terribly much anyway." As he was talking about this, he turned on a fan in the room and put his foot close to the blades of the fan. He instantaneously withdrew his foot when it touched the blade, looking terribly frightened. With this he immediately put his hand on his genital area. I said this looked like part of the dream insofar as the act of putting his foot in the fan was like the accident in the dream where he might have had his penis cut off. He denied this, but then talked of how he would like to live in an apartment or house by himself. He would be able to do the laundry and cooking himself instead of needing to rely on his mother. He went back into the playroom and began crashing automobiles together. He refused to do any cleaning up, insisting that I do it. At the same time he asked me questions about how many children I had, what their ages were, their names and sex. That night he slept well, as he did the two succeeding nights. His father stated he was acting much more aggressively at home and even had become rather antagonistic and challenging to Michael.

During the next hour he reported a dream in which he was with Michael doing something they weren't supposed to do. He didn't know exactly what it was, but in the dream he, Jeff, was the leader rather than Michael. He said he had been told by his father Michael might be coming to me because of his nail-biting. I told Jeff, as I had his father, that Jeff being my patient, I would refer Michael elsewhere. Jeff was still concerned I might take Michael as a patient and get to like him better than Jeff. I told him this seemed to be what had worried him for a long time—namely, whether his parents could care for him as much as he thought they cared for Michael. I added that since Michael was a boy, Jeff might have thought it would be better if he were a girl to guarantee his parents would like him better.

In subsequent hours he discussed having been in the same room with his parents during past vacations; he was certain he had seen or heard something he didn't understand. He asked me for and received an explanation of sexual intercourse. This concerned him because of his certainty of a dentate vagina. His actions at home seemed far more aggressive. At the same time he often came to his father's bed, wanting to sleep with him. This only seemed to increase the scratching.

Jeff said he was enjoying the scratching even though there was no longer any itching connected with it. He was concerned about when to apply the salve and about possibly really injuring himself. I indicated it seemed the scratching was some sort of substitute pleasure. Any boy who hurt himself so continually and enjoyed it was apparently guilty over thoughts such as wanting to be with his mother and having father out of the way or vice versa. He must also be afraid of both parents punishing him if ever they knew this was what Jeff had in mind. Instead of his parents doing the punishing, he was doing it to and by himself.

The following day I saw the parents who mentioned that Jeff had been very unhappy the night before; he had cried continuously for 5 hours until early morning. He constantly feared he would not get well. During the evening his father went in a few times to tell Jeff he could cry or scratch as much as he liked, but he was not to keep the entire family up. His mother, however, in desperation, said that he was making her sick and that if he continued to carry on this way, she would be ill the following day. She said that the sheets were filled with blood and they turned her stomach. She told Jeff she felt like a washerwoman since their help rebelled against washing blood-stained clothes. After this outburst from his mother, Jeff stopped his carrying on and went to sleep. That morning his legs were swollen. He was so fatigued that he did not go to school or keep his appointment with me.

Jeff's mother indicated there was no modesty in the house whatsoever. She felt that any modesty would be potentially harmful to the children. Therefore, she would change her menstrual pads, take baths or go to the toilet regardless of whether Michael or Jeff were about; when Jeff asked questions about menstrual periods, she told him that a woman gets cleaned out every month. Up to a few weeks prior to his analysis, while the lesions on his body were relatively closed, his mother bathed with him routinely. The parents told me how much they had wanted a girl when the mother was pregnant with Jeff. The story of their picking out only a girl's name, clothing, and furniture was repeated quite often in Jeff's presence. Some 4 years before the analysis the parents decided they would adopt a child, but *only a girl*. I advised considerably more restraint with open displays of body parts and functions and suggested that both mother and Jeff needed privacy.

The dermatologist again recommended removal of the dog. Again I opposed this plan. The games Jeff played at home and in his sessions were filled with aggression and immediate fears of punishment. During the game of Parcheesi he insisted on winning and when he saw that I was likely to win, he made me change sides and took my seat. As soon as the fortunes of the game again seemed to turn, he began scratching his face. I asked him what he was thinking about, but he was not able to say. I told him that from now on, I wanted him to be very certain to remember what he was thinking whenever he began to scratch. Now I felt he might be thinking of wanting to be a girl because this would remove him from competition with me. With this interpretation, the scratching stopped and he was able to play the game without further scratching even while losing.

His play during the next therapy hour consisted of erecting targets, identifying them as me or members of his family. He shot each down unerringly, laughing joyously as he did. When one of the darts came very close to me, he seemed momentarily anxious and said he had to go to the bathroom to have a bowel movement. When he came back, he said going to the bathroom during sessions with me was something new. I asked him if he had thought of something that made the bowel movement occur at this time. He denied any thoughts. I told him I knew of boys who became very anxious when they were very aggressive with me because they were then frightened of what I might do to them in my anger. Some of them felt they had to respond as he had when he put his foot near the fan, when he held on to his penis, or when he had to go to the bathroom to check on its presence.

Jeff's parents then went on a 5-day vacation. Throughout this time Jeff had no asthmatic or dermatologic symptoms at all. He enjoyed winning in games (without cheating) and talked of his pleasure in scratching.[8]

---

[8] Musaph (1964, p. 7f.) states: "Scratching without itching . . . may be an entirely unconscious action. It may be considered an expression of certain autoerotic, aggressive and sexual impulses. Somewhat more differentiated, this would mean that feelings of embarrassment, anger, resentment, joy, tense expectation, sexual excitement, anxiety and fear could be expressed in this motor language. . . . Some people develop a scratching technique by which they can produce a sensation of mild pain, which undoubtedly gives them feelings of pleasure. Such a sensation is the so-called 'after-glow' after violent scratching. Part of these actions may be interpreted as an equivalent of masturbation. In this connection, the element of skin eroticism should be borne in mind. In the genital sphere, scratching and scrabbling in order to evoke a pleasure sensation of itching cannot be divorced from masturbation."

Jeff felt very sensitive to people's reactions about the way he looked and the way he acted. After his parents' return he told me of a dream in which a teacher was looking at him critically and he felt as if he were disappointing her by not performing adequately. He related this to the previous day when he had had some difficulty with one of the boys on the block and had developed a headache. He came into the house where his mother was entertaining some guests and asked, very matter-of-factly, for an aspirin for the headache. The adults thought this was grown up and mature, and they were amused. He interpreted their amusement as their laughing at him. There was some return of scratching, but this stopped after a few minutes.

At this time the cost of treatment was mentioned frequently both by his parents and by Jeff. There were many allusions to the amount of money I must be making as a psychoanalyst and how powerful I was to get his parents and the dermatologist to do as I wished. Yet during the same period Jeff had reached the height of a very positive transference. One day he asked me to go for a walk with him, during which he stayed physically close to me and took my hand in an affectionate way. Shortly after we returned he excused himself to go to the bathroom and have a bowel movement.

I told him that I was seeing a boy who was very very attached to me and who thought that the only way he could really show me how much he liked me was to have a baby for me like my wife did. He responded to this with a description of his brother's operation for an undescended testicle a few years ago and his concern that he, too, would have to undergo this kind of surgery. He feared that such surgery might actually result in making him into a female. He then played a game in which he was the psychiatrist and I became the patient who had headaches. He told me that the reason I had headaches was that I wanted very much to be a woman to avoid getting into the army and that at times I had bad ideas such as wanting to shoot my mother.

His play at home was becoming rougher and more aggressive. He was now openly provocative with Michael. With this went an overt desire to replace his father in his mother's affections. He spoke of crooks in the police force. He indicated that his father was not strict enough with either of the boys; Jeff felt it would be far better if his father would be consistent in his punishments. I suggested that Jeff wanted punishment from his father for his bad thoughts about wanting his mother for himself, as well as wanting to have his father to himself. A partial solution, perhaps, might be by injuring himself so severely around the pubic area that he would literally, as he fantasied about Michael's operation, change himself into a girl. He laughed a great deal at this suggestion, stating it would have been a solution. He also recognized that it might not be an entirely satisfactory one.

Jeff began to hide things all over the office. Hour after hour he insisted on my finding some small object which he had secreted. One day he announced that he had a sliver in his hand, insisting, most anxiously, that I take it out lest he get an infection. Since I could do this with a tweezer without breaking the skin, I took it out, after which he went back to the hiding game. I mentioned that his parents had called and told me he had had a difficult weekend. He thought he was crying out at night because something was bothering him. I suggested he might be interested in getting his father to come into his bedroom, an interpretation to which he agreed quite readily. He felt girls often teased boys and that his actions with me as with the hiding of the objects, insisting I take out the sliver, as well as his crying at home and trying to get his father to come into his bedroom at night might all be related to some desire to be a girl. But, he insisted, he really didn't want to know about such ideas and was loudly and boisterously angry.

The next day when I went to get him in the reception room I found him lying on the couch complaining of scrotal itching. He could not recall anything that happened the previous night or on the day before this interview. He felt he was frightened about learning why he did certain kinds of things. Then he said that when he was at the dematologist, the day before, he saw an X-ray of a boy's head and it looked just like the outside. I said that I thought I now understood why he was frightened and the itching was so bad: boys often are very frightened when they see a skeleton or an X-ray that does not have any penis, like the X-ray of the skull that did not show a nose. While he did not agree directly, he talked about how his scrotum wrinkled up when he was cold or went into the water. He wondered about what happened to food inside the body and about how babies came into being. When I tried to describe something about the nature of conception, he denied any interest. When, at his insistence, we looked through one of the medical books showing a picture of a child in the uterus, he became more anxious.

The following day he threatened he would do much more scratching. At home he had faked crying, which his mother and father ignored. It appeared that his attachment to me was very strong, but he felt, as in the hiding game, that if he did not hide certain thoughts, he might not be able to continue seeing me because I would only see him as long as he was sick.

Again Jeff spent much time on the hiding game. During one of the hours he wanted to take me out to the elevator because he was uncertain about why the doors did not close entirely. He said he was frightened of elevators and the crack between the building and the elevator shaft. He spoke a good deal about how one could lose things there and even fall down and get crushed if the elevator door opened up with the elevator a floor above. I told him about a boy who was concerned about what was between his mother's legs; this boy, too, often hid in play with me, which I thought was his way of asking the question of what was really behind the hair. Jeff said he knew that, but then became increasingly anxious as he reported that he looked all of the time when his mother was undressing; he worried about the insides of the woman and what might be there that could destroy or injure the male genital. I told him there was a vagina that had neither teeth nor anything else that might injure a man. He appeared enormously relieved by this explanation.

The weekend that followed was a very quiet one, with his symptoms in abatement. In the next hour Jeff wanted to go down to the garage to look at my car. He admired it and felt that it was a wonderful automobile, far better than the one his mother drove, with many more advantages. (Parenthetically, the car not only was exactly the same make, but was the same model and year as the one his mother was driving.) When he came upstairs into the office, he decided he would be the doctor and I would be his small boy patient. He shifted quickly from being a kind, understanding, and friendly doctor to being a tough man and a crook. I verbalized for him that with his game of being big and tough, he was perhaps telling me that in reality he was fearful of being small and misused and that his dermatitis was preferable to his ever growing up and having the genital of an adult male. After this interpretation, he insisted on playing checkers with a special variant he invented. This consisted of his giving away most of his men with glee and, without any particular anxiety, losing with the utmost aplomb.

He then expressed his certainty that women (his mother, grandmother, teachers) were opposed to his ever growing up to be a potent productive male. He thought of his wheezing not as equivalent to crying but as a suppression of crying since to cry would be to act like a girl. He wanted to be a man in every way. He recalled a dream he had had some years ago in which a fire came out of one of the light plugs. He asked how I had grown up to become a man, to be as wealthy and as successful as I was. I told him about a boy who was extremely frightened when he saw his mother undress and who worried whether a man having intercourse would not sustain a permanent injury to his penis. Such a bright boy might think that if he could have many penises on his body, just losing one wouldn't be important. Or perhaps he could imagine that they might all be contained within his body like a bowel movement, each day replenishing itself even though the female might injure his genital during intercourse. He asked to go for a walk with me, holding onto my hand in the elevator and outside.

In the subsequent hour he frightened the woman patient who came before him as she was leaving. He was ebullient and effervescent. He said that when he grew up he was going to be a businessman like his father and ultimately would take over his father's business. He recalled how in the past he was worried about thinking of such a thing, since he connected growing up and becoming like his father with his father's death—but this did not concern him anymore.

He wondered whether if anything happened to his parents (e.g., if they died), I would consider adopting him so that he could become an adult male of whom he and I could be proud. He then asked questions about ending the treatment.

One day after this, he came in with an obvious asthmatic wheeze. He felt so filled up with asthma, he said, he could not have a bowel movement. He talked about how difficult it would be not to have me to talk to in case his symptoms returned. I told him of boys being afraid of terminating treatment because they believed they would lose contact completely. The only way they knew how to maintain contact with me was to remain sick. The connection with the bowel movement was the old story of wanting to have a baby inside and in this way he could pretend to carry part of me inside of him all of the time untouched by whether we terminated or not. He became quite furious, but the wheezing stopped. He then asked me whether I knew the cause of his rash. I said that it seemed like it was a terrible conflict inside of him between wanting to be a man with a big penis or a woman without any. He said he had been trying in the past few days to push his penis inside his body. He was very relieved when it wouldn't stay. He went back to the idea of foster parents, indicating that in case anything happened to his parents, he wanted me to adopt him.

He wished he could have for himself the attainments he felt I had. I told him that this reminded me of his request at the beginning of treatment that I give him a present from the office. I told him when he was all ready to stop, he could select anything from the office he wanted; but I felt what he was really asking for was for me to give him the gift of a big penis. He laughed with glee, nodding in agreement. His play indicated an identification with the aggressive male.

A few days later, I received a call from his father who said that Jeff had cried when he was chastised for a minor misdemeanor by his father. It had seemed like a genuine response to a very real situation and there had been no dermatologic symptoms. During the hours, he was aggressive and even somewhat destructive, which I interpreted as his desire to injure me because I was insisting on stopping at some time in the near future. Jeff again felt, as he had when he kept his parents from going on vacation, that if he were still sick, I would not discharge him from treatment. While he recognized his progress and realized that termination would come sooner or later, he still felt sad about interrupting a relationship which he felt was rewarding and satisfying.

In one of the following hours I saw the parents who were delighted with the progress Jeff had made. They noted that he was sleeping well and was doing extremely well in school. He had caught up the entire 6 months he had missed. He was still boisterous and aggressive at home with them as well as at school with the other boys. They described a fight he had had with a boy in class. When they tried to punish him for it, he quoted them the golden rule as he interpreted it: "This boy has been a bully and you've always told me the golden rule is to do unto others what they have done unto you."

In one of the last hours (the family was starting a long vacation) Jeff wanted to select his "going away" present. First, he gave me a big licorice stick he had purchased prior to coming that day. Then, after a long and careful search, he took the gun he had become so fond of in his dart games with me. I told him it seemed as if we were sort of trading penises. This seemed to reflect the whole idea of what he had been worried about for such a long time.

Although he hesitated and delayed his leaving each time, he was very aggressive and demanding in the hours prior to the summer vacation, making certain that I recognized that he was a real tough man and no longer desired to be a girl. This attitude continued very much through the last hour as he again spoke very calmly about the problems he had had when he first came. He recognized that the illness itself at times had been an attempt to force his parents to treat him as a female. If he could assume this position, the threat of castration was no longer present.[9]

A week prior to Jeff's stopping for the summer vacation, the rash had disappeared entirely and there were no asthmatic attacks. He stated he was very sad about stopping treatment. He noticed that he had to hide the gun he had gotten from me because he was afraid somebody would take it away. I indicated that this was part of the old fear and he need not be concerned about that anymore. With this, he told me a dream about a man chasing him with a gun. In the dream Jeff turned a corner, tripped the man who then fell, dropped the gun, and Jeff recovered the gun to hold it over

[9] Schur (1950), quoted in Deutsch (1952, p. 192f.), analyzed two cases where the skin eruption gratified their need for self-punishment. The defense is determined by a magical sacrifice of the penis which the ego endures rather than suffer greater regressive tendencies (*pars pro toto*). Such conditions, Schur discovered, stir basic castration fears which the ego attempts to meet with denials, panic, or attempts at restitution. Periodical menstrual bleeding is such an attempt at restitution.

the man until the police came. During the last hour he reviewed what we had talked over together the past 5 months. He also told me that in the last few days he had been telling his father that if there were a national crisis, he certainly would feel it was his duty and responsibility to join the army in order to be able to fight for his country and defend what he felt was right. He shook my hand both pleasurably and sadly as he left. He said he would call me at the end of the summer.

Posttreatment Contacts

Four months later, 2 months after the start of a new school term, he seemed to be progressing satisfactorily even though he had an extremely strict teacher. There was no asthma or dermatitis throughout the entire summer. He occasionally became a bit disturbed when some of the other children commented about his peculiarly shaped head. This resulted on one occasion in a slight branny kind of rash on his upper lip. The rash, however, also seemed to be associated with an upper respiratory infection and the vigorous use of tissue. The parents decided that Jeff should see me again for re-evaluation.

During the next three interviews which we held at that time he recalled that he also had had a very strict teacher the previous year. He had been frightened of her and of the remarks the children might make if he acted like a "sissy."

A few weeks prior to the current school term he had heard about a German boy who had two mothers—one who was supposedly killed in a concentration camp, and the other, his adopted mother —each of whom legally wanted him as their own son. The idea of possibly losing his own mother and getting a foster mother returned and was magnified by the aloofness and coldness of his "stepmother" teacher and by one of the boys in school calling him a "dirty wop." He reacted first with mild anxiety, then with anger, and finally precipitated a fight with the boy who derogated him, thrashing him thoroughly. The slight wheezing he had had as well as the rash on his face cleared entirely after these three interviews.

The second posttreatment contact, $2\frac{1}{2}$ years after treatment, was related to sexual attraction stimulated by a kissing game. This contact required merely one hour, which was devoted to an explanation to Jeff of his fear of forbidden wishes; the rash, perioral at that time, cleared immediately after this.

The third flare-up, a year later, coincided with his maternal grandfather's death. At this time the mother was exasperated with Jeff, experiencing him as being difficult. Although the dermatologist thought the rash located on his thighs, pubis, and abdomen was a contact dermatitis, Jeff, then 11 years of age, felt the rash was related to his fear of and yet desire to spend more time with girls. He also related his anxiety and the subsequent rash to his mother's threats to send him away, reminiscent of his grandfather's death. The rash disappeared shortly after a single hour's consultation. These were the only times that there was even a hint of recurrence of the original symptom in the entire 20 years after psychoanalytic treatment.

About 8 years ago Jeff himself, at 19 years of age, asked me to see him again because of a problem with determining his vocational future. He had just completed his first year of college and felt uncertain about what course to take. His grades in college were not terribly good as he had invested all of his energy in socializing —becoming the president of his freshman class, joining a fraternity, and engaging in numerous campus activities.

Follow-up

Jeff, now aged 28, is not married although he has dated steadily and is currently engaged. He is in a business somewhat allied to his father's but has no financial connections with his father. During and after college, Jeff maintained a very high level of productivity in many avocations and gained more than just a local reputation in helping with civil liberties. He knew that his parents continued to keep me informed of his progress. He also knew of my shifting from private practice to a full-time academic position. Other than the request for vocational help at the age of 19, Jeff has made no attempts to seek further psychoanalytic help—ostensibly, according to his parents, because he in no way felt he had any problems. Occasionally he was aware of seasonal allergy, primarily nasal, and the only times he had wheezing were during severe respiratory infections. His parents, family, and close familial friends feel that Jeff has been much more successful in his life and accomplishments than Michael.

Discussion

This psychoanalytic treatment raises a number of questions with regard to the fate of the severe, introjected superego; the seeming lack of libidinal regression, the analyst taking such active roles in handling medication, giving advice to the parents and the dermatologist, giving much educational information; whether a genuine transference neurosis developed; and whether treatment was stopped prematurely.

It seems in retrospect that the superego was not as punitive as the original clinical picture led one to expect. The essential point was that Jeff's psychosexual development had progressed to the phallic-oedipal level, making this a case of infantile neurosis rather than a "psychosomatic" disorder. His internal conflict (A. Freud, 1965) had led to a regression to an earlier fixation point and was colored by his allergic diathesis, but he had not regressed to the earliest levels of interaction (Schur, 1955).

Libidinal and aggressive regression (and/or fixation) were apparent in the symptoms of the dermatitis, the compulsive masturbation, the sleep disturbance, and the evidences of bisexuality expressed in the positive and negative oedipal conflicts. Musaph (1968, p. 328) notes that psychoanalytic investigations have demonstrated that itching can be a sign of repressed sexual excitement and that all aspects of sexuality can be observed in the skin. Thus Jeff gave evidence of having progressed to the oedipal phase of psychosexual development prior to the onset of his acute dermatitis.

As mentioned in the background material, the transference was strongly influenced by his prior treatment failures and by the willingness of the parents and the dermatologist to accept direction. A. Freud (1926, p. 17) notes that the factor of power and authority of the experienced analyst tends to the patient's developing less "negative transference" toward him, with fewer indications of hostility and mistrust. The child responds to the analyst not only because he is older and bigger but also because the parents put the analyst's authority beyond their own. In this case I felt it was therapeutically correct to oppose some of the dermatologic recommendations and parental ways of caring for Jeff which were antithetical to the psychoanalytic process. Fortunately, the dermatologist (and the pediatrician) was understanding and eminently cooperative. In this sense Jeff indeed saw me act in an overtly directive way; but, as contrasted with the period of hospitalization when he was tied down, Jeff recognized the need to cope with his conflict through the analysis rather than through medicinal suppression.

The psychoanalytic treatment of Jeff brought about not only a cessation of the acute dermatologic disease which had interfered with normal development. Jeff also gained an emotional understanding of his symptoms and began to show signs of once more progressing in development. For this reason I felt probationary cessation of treatment was in order. The vacation period coincided with this decision, but treatment could have been resumed if any of the symptoms returned. This continuous availability of analytic help both immediately after the termination of treatment and in subsequent years, and Jeff's knowledge that his parents were in contact with me might have allayed some anxiety. This readily available help permitted him and the family to attempt to work out their conflictual interpersonal relationships, knowing that if they did not succeed, they could always return for analytic clarification.

During the years after treatment Michael became much more involved with people and activities outside the home, allowing Jeff to distance himself from the earlier interactions with Michael. To a degree Jeff's activities during his first year in college represented an identification with Michael, who had been so very successful and popular with his peers.

Jeff may have been helped to sustain the gains of treatment by another important factor—a special characteristic which I have observed in several children who have had chronic (and at times incapacitating) physical illnesses or who have been slower in physical development. The drive to discharge energies through motoric and/or sexual routes is delayed, and with this there seems to be a greater tendency toward introspection, insightfulness, empathy, and an internal language system. Restriction of activities or enforced confinement stimulates fantasy formation which, if coupled with good reality testing, can lead to more adequate secondary process thinking. It was this positive developmental action potential which I felt was present in Jeff and which I thought his family would support.

Although the parents had made many errors in Jeff's upbringing, they were enormously supportive during and after his treatment, and acted positively on the analytic recommendations given them. Moreover, Jeff was a child who observed his thoughts and actions as we wish all our adult patients could do. Perhaps this is the reason why he did not develop any further symptoms: his identification with the analyst's functions enabled him to exercise his own capacity for self-analysis, thus preventing renewed regressions.

Revelant Psychoanalytic Literature

Most cases of dermatitis never are referred for psychoanalytic consultation or treatment. Therefore, the literature correlating dermatologic and emotional responses is sparse. This is explained by Sanger (1968, p. 315) who indicates the controversial role of emotions in many cases of dermatitis, suggesting that most authors pay lip service to their importance. Psychoanalysis, suggestions, and hypnosis are advised "when all else fails."

The intensity of scratching resulting in the "raw hamburger" appearance of Jeff's lesions is not unique. Musaph (1964) notes that both the early and late forms of allergic dermatitis are accompanied by itching often disproportionate to the severity of the skin lesions. The children start scratching so violently that the skin is heavily damaged in a few moments. Musaph suggests that the compulsive scratching is indeed primary, the skin lesions being the result of the scratching. The connection with tension states is reflected in the syndrome being called "neurodermatitis."

Different authors, both in the psychoanalytic and in the dermatologic literature, assign different weight to the nature-nurture factors in the causation of this skin disease, a circumstance which results in a bias for one treatment form over another. My own experience parallels that of Marmor et al. (1956) who are convinced that one cannot ignore the importance of the hereditary factors in neurodermatitis. In their studies a very high percentage of the families of children with this disorder not only had allergic reactions but had specifically the same cutaneous disorder. This finding made these authors question the contention that neurodermatitis is causally related to rejection or neglect. They view these cases as "disorders of adaptation" on the basis of a hypersensitivity in which "allergic" responses can be precipitated by emotional or physiological stress or by the presence of certain allergens. Viewing neurodermatitis as a multifactorial disorder, Marmor et al. found no value in attributing specific personality profiles to these child patients. They concluded that the psychological tendencies described in adult patients were the consequences of the disorder rather than its preconditions.

On the basis of individual cases and *post-hoc* theorizing some authors postulated an etiologic connection between life events and the genesis of various dermatologic disorders and subsequently offered various psychodynamic formulations. In many instances (as was originally true in the etiologic and therapeutic philosophies of many authors in cases of early infantile autism), all dermatologic disorders were lumped together, the illness was viewed as a "deficiency" disease, and the search for *the* pathological mother was on. Kahn (1969) notes the emotional conflict between the desire for affection and the fear of rejection in the patient with skin disease. Spitz (1951) feels that the mother of a child with eczema is filled with anxiety because of repressed aggression which prevents her from touching the infant. Since proper identifications are based upon sensory experiences offered by the mother, Spitz believes that in the absence of tactile stimulation, the aggressive and libidinal drives are discharged in the form of the skin reaction.

Saul's views can be cited as representative of this approach. He states (1941):

In all of these studies of symptoms of an allergic nature in which emotional factors were found to play a rôle, the central emotion related to the symptom was a strong longing for love, basically for the mother's. *This suggests that intense, unsatisfied longing for love affects the individual's allergic sensitivity. This longing is of the infantile dependent kind of the child for its mother* [p. 70, my italics].

Whether it is the "chicken or egg," there seems little question about the multidetermined ways in which the skin disorder can be utilized to express hostility—e.g., in turning it against the self. In an excellent research study Miller and Baruch (1950) found that the allergic patients were more prone than the nonallergics to hide and deny hostility or to express it hesitantly and reluctantly. Related to this, they felt, was significant maternal rejection creating greater guilt and conflict in the child for his hostile feelings. These authors indicate that hostility turned against the self occurs far more frequently (than in the normal controls) even when the patients were *not* suffering from the physical illness. Miller and Baruch (1950) conclude:

> In a way then, the allergic child is like a cornered animal. He feels and hates the impact of his mother's rejection as all children do. But he fears to bring out hostility directly to his parents. He tries to bring it out by indirection, but again is apparently too guilty and blocks. He turns to displacing it but even so cannot seem to vent it sufficiently. In short, he cannot get release from the tension of his hostile feelings by expressing them in outgoing fashion. He seeks to punish himself. Still he does not gain absolution or peace, so he goes on trying to shut off the expression of his hostile feelings and to deny them. The inner conflict, however, apparently remains, and so he must draw from other resources within him to solve his dilemma. Here is probably where his allergic constitution comes in. It becomes useful to him. He can muster it to his aid [p. 517].

The meaning of a symptom and the appreciation of how it develops and is perpetuated can be obtained only with analytic techniques exploring and understanding the entire range of metapsychological determinants. Only in this manner can the specific unconscious determinants be discovered, which in Jeff's case were found to be masturbatory equivalents. Similar findings are reported in the literature. Kahn (1969) states:

> . . . an aflammatory lesion may develop as a result of a patient's attempt to solve a difficult emotional problem. Children tend to manipulate an irritating skin condition. It is not unusual for adolescents to rub a part of the body while engaged in mental activity. Not infrequently, handling the skin surface may be a substitute for handling the genitals. Eczematous and urticarial eruptions may be secondarily genitalized so that the rubbing and scratching assume a masturbatory function [p. 152].

Jeff's case also bore out the finding that forcible restriction of the scratching actually leads to an *increase* rather than a *decrease* in the dermatologic response. When Jeff was hospitalized and his hands and feet tied, the dermatitis became so much worse that he had to be discharged from the hospital. Jeff's experience thus verified Musaph's thoughtful reflections:

> Not so long ago we used to tie up the arms and legs of children who had attacks of itch and therefore of scratching, or to put cylinders on them, thus greatly restricting their psychomotor function. The idea was that scratching could be averted in this manner, thus preventing the itching skin from being torn to shreds. I remember that reference was made to "beefsteak à la tartare" in descriptions of the skin after an attack of scratching.
>
> However, imposing restrictions on the psychomotor function of children must have repercussions on their character development. Fundamental research in this respect has been done by biologists [p. 260].

As indicated earlier, the different views with regard to etiology have a bearing on the medical and psychological management of the child. Thus it is not surprising that the concern as to when and whether psychoanalysis is the treatment of choice (and even whose brand of psychoanalysis) has occupied the literature periodically. With cases of psychosomatic disorders the confusion and discord have been especially heated, as is exemplified by the views of the following authors.

Macalpine (1952) indicates that one can always find a recent stimulus that precipitated the outbreak of a psychosomatic illness. But the illness itself, rather than created by the initiating stimulus, is much more rudimentary in that the emotions are somatically displayed rather than felt. It is the purpose of therapy to get the patient to experience the emotion. Macalpine feels that psychosomatic symptoms are similar to psychotic behavior in that the anxiety state is experienced in its preconceptual and preverbal phase. She therefore concludes that classical psychoanalytic technique is unsuited for these patients because their need is not the undoing of faulty defenses, but rather a reduction of the excessive undifferentiated anxiety. She further states that asthma and eczema prove refractory to psychoanalysis.

In contrast to this categoric statement concerning the meaning and treatment of psychosomatic disorders are the views expressed by Schur (1955), whose carefully worded formulations are much more applicable to the case presented in this paper. He sees innate factors in both the mental and somatic spheres which interact with emotional and reactive states to external factors. These vector forces can be responded to with a neurosis or psychosis, or "supply the emotional background of 'psychosomatic disorders'" (p. 158f.). Although Schur undertook the psychoanalytic treatment of cases with dermatoses for their general emotional problems rather than specifically for their skin condition, improvement in the dermatitis did occur. Schur asks:

> What factors account for the therapeutic results? If regressive reactions which accompany affects and instinctual drives can produce symptoms, *anything* counteracting such regression should be beneficial. That patients rarely itch during sessions cannot be explained only with alleviation of anxiety by the analyst. The explanation seems to be that verbalization is, in the scale of ego responses, counteracting ego regression. Verbalized thoughts are closer to the secondary process than fantasies, daydreams, etc. Thus verbalization has more than cathartic value. Any improvement by "organic" methods can also counteract regression and help break a vicious circle [p. 160].

Musaph (1964), utilizing Spitz's construct of coenesthesia (common sensations), which occurs in the first 6 months of life, feels that this early organization tends to continue in the eczematous child without assuming a more diacritical function. This results, Musaph suggests, in a hyperesthesia (or hypoesthesia) in skin contact. In cases in which this fixation is present Musaph believes that psychoanalytic treatment can remove these early conflicts and facilitate abstract thinking and structuralization. My own clinical experience (especially with Jeff) clearly indicates my agreement with Schur and Musaph.

In conclusion, I believe that each patient deserves an evaluation as an individual, irrespective of the theories and case reports presented in the literature. Our most valuable and impressive research data can come from carefully detailed intensive psychoanalytic longitudinal dissections, as I hope this case of Jeff's represents.

BIBLIOGRAPHY

DEUTSCH, F. (1952), Psychoanalysis and Psychosomatic Medicine. In: *The Annual Survey of Psychoanalysis*, 1:179–199. New York: International Universities Press.

FREUD, A. (1926), *The Psycho-Analytical Treatment of Children*. New York: International Universities Press, 1950.

— (1965), *Normality and Pathology in Childhood*. New York: International Universities Press.

KAHN, J. P. (1969), Allergic Children: Their Psyche and Skin. *Post-Grad. Med.*, 45(2):149–152.

LEFER, J. (1964), Psychosis, Somatic Disease and the Perceived Body. *J. Hillside Hosp.*, 13:18–31.

MACALPINE, I. (1952), Psychosomatic Symptom Formation. *Lancet*, 262:278–282.

MARMOR, J., ASHLEY, M., TABACHNICK, N., STORKAN, M., & McDONALD, F. (1956), The Mother-Child Relationship in the Genesis of Neurodermatitis. *A.M.A. Arch. Derm.*, 74:599–605.

MILLER, H. & BARUCH, D. W. (1950), A Study of Hostility in Allergic Children. *Amer. J. Orthopsychiat.*, 20:506–519.

MUSAPH, H. (1964), *Itching and Scratching: Psychodynamics in Dermatology*. New York & Basel: Karger.

— (1968), Psychodynamics in Itching States. *Int. J. Psycho-Anal.*, 49:336–340.

— (1969), Aggression and Symptom Formation in Dermatology. *J. Psychosom. Res.*, 13:257–264.

(564)   MARSHALL D. SCHECHTER

NAGERA, H. (1966), Sleep and Its Disturbances Approached Developmentally. *This Annual*, 21:393–447.
OBERMAYER, M. E. (1955), *Psychocutaneous Medicine*. Springfield: Thomas.
PEARSON, G. H. J. (1940), Some Psychological Aspects of Inflammatory Skin Lesions. *Psychosom. Med.*, 2:22–33.
SANGER, M. D. (1968), Psychosomatic Approach to Allergic Dermatoses. *Ann. Allergy*, 26:314–320.
SAUL, L. J. (1941), Some Observations on the Relations of Emotions and Allergy. *Psychosom. Med.*, 3:66–71.
SCHUR, M. (1950), Case Analyses of Chronic, Exudative, Discoid and Lichenoid Dermatitis (Sulzberger-Garbe's Syndrome). *Int. J. Psycho-Anal.*, 31:73–77.
— (1955), Comments on the Metapsychology of Somatization. *This Annual*, 10:119–164.
SPITZ, R. A. (1951), The Psychogenic Diseases in Infancy: An Attempt at Their Etiologic Classification. *This Annual*, 6:255–275.
WITTKOWER, E. & RUSSELL, B. (1953), *Emotional Factors in Skin Disease*. New York: Hoeber.

The Life Master

A Case of Severe Ego Regression Induced by Combat Experience in World War II

HENRY WEXLER, M.D.

IN THIS PAPER I SHALL PRESENT THE CASE HISTORY OF A PATIENT suffering from a combat neurosis, whom I treated many years ago over a prolonged period of time. The patient presented a great number of diagnostic and therapeutic problems which were not easy to resolve. Similar issues have arisen with the emotional casualties of the current war in Vietnam and, it seems to me, are as puzzling to the therapist today as they were 30 years ago. It there-

Associate Clinical Professor of Psychiatry, Yale University; Training and Supervising Analyst and member of the faculty, The Western New England Institute for Psychoanalysis, New Haven, Connecticut.

Parts of this paper were presented at a scientific meeting of The Western New England Psychoanalytic Society at Austen Riggs Center, Stockbridge, Massachusetts, on September 25, 1954.

fore seemed timely to me to review, in connection with this case, the psychoanalytic literature on traumatic war neuroses.

In addition, this patient's life history illuminates several theoretical issues, only one of which I have singled out for detailed discussion, namely, the general problem of mastery. This case raises an especially interesting question—one that we also encounter in other deeply regressed patients whose functioning in one area of their lives not only has remained intact but is in fact unusually successful. Why this is so, I am unable to answer; but what my case demonstrates is the following: precisely the same ego functions, when applied to the one area of the patient's interest, were highly effective, while in all other areas they failed him.

Clinical History

The patient's birth was uneventful. It was his mother's second pregnancy, the first having terminated in a miscarriage. His mother had been apprehensive throughout her pregnancy with the patient because of this first loss. He was breast-fed for 10 months, weaned quickly and with no apparent difficulty. There were no feeding difficulties. Toilet training was begun at 6 months. His mother had no recollection of when this was completed or whether there were attendant emotional disturbances. Speech and walking developed normally. There were no temper tantrums or excessive crying. When he was 2 years, his sister was born. As far back as he could remember, he had always felt an intense rivalry and hatred for this sister. During these early years his father was absent for many months of each year on business trips. On one occasion during infancy both father and mother were away for 6 weeks and had left him in the care of a nurse.

From the age of 3 to 9 there occurred a series of medical and surgical incidents. The patient's earliest memory of one such incident, which he dated to age 3, but which according to a history from the mother occurred at 5, was that of an ether mask being applied to his face for a tonsillectomy. Prior to the operation a nurse, while giving him a hypodermic injection, broke off the needle in his arm. His mother reported that he had been unusually terrified. Each winter for a number of years he suffered recurrent abscesses of the middle ear which had to be lanced. He had a great deal of anticipatory terror about this procedure, although he behaved like a model patient during it. Again he was the model patient while receiving physiotherapy for a minor fracture of the elbow incurred while playing ball. At age 6 a long splinter of wood was driven accidentally into his leg and was surgically removed. At the age of 8 he was sent to camp, notwithstanding his violent protests. At camp he had an attack of abdominal pain and was rushed to the hospital with a presumed attack of appendicitis, which turned out to be German measles. He recalled the great terror and panic on the ambulance trip to the hospital.

Shortly after this incident his "nervousness" became manifest. Each night he prayed that he would not be afflicted with any more surgical trauma, repeating the prayer over and over again. Each time a friend got sick he worried as much as if it had been himself. He insisted that his parents' bedroom door remain open at night and that a light be kept shining there. At camp he managed to have his cot placed in the doctor's tent. Every night he had to check the gas jets—sometimes as often as 5 or 6 times—especially on nights when his father came home late and the patient was still awake. After his father went to bed he would go to the kitchen and again check the jets. When a cousin got trench mouth, presumably from dirty silverware, the patient insisted on absolute asepsis of all eating utensils. He inspected egg dishes carefully for stray bits of shell, fearing that if he swallowed one his stomach would be lacerated.

He was very much afraid of his father, who spanked him frequently. Yet the boy engaged in constant fights with his sister, provoking his mother to report these to his father, who then would invariably spank him. Nevertheless, hardly a day passed without his teasing and provoking. The daily spankings by the father stopped only when, in his 13th year, he bested him in a "friendly" wrestling match.

Until the age of 15 he was shy, had only remote relationships with his contemporaries, and devoted himself exclusively to athletics and studies. In his 15th year a change occurred with some suddenness. A few of his schoolmates, the athletes and socialites,

invited him to join in their extracurricular social activities. He
was flattered and set himself out to excel in this as he had in athletics and studies. He learned to dance and had dates. He devoted
himself so wholeheartedly to this that his studies suffered badly.
Fifteen was an eventful year for him. A 23-year-old housemaid employed by his family seduced him and he enjoyed sporadic sexual
play and intercourse with her for a number of years.[1] At 18 he was
graduated from a boarding academy where he was outstanding in
athletics, but only an average student.

At college he thought he would study medicine, but gave up this
ambition for journalism after failing chemistry in his freshman
year. Yet he continued to collect medical books and on several occasions posed as a medical student to get into the hospital surgical
amphitheater to watch various operations.

He was inducted into the Army on graduation from college after
a series of anxious incidents. He served for about a year, was
shipped overseas, and after a few days of terror on the battlefield
received a shattering wound to his left arm.

I shall briefly trace the events of his military adventure to the
day of his being wounded by shellfire. It is evident from what has
been said that he was an emotionally disturbed youth with phobias, counterphobias, obsessions and compulsions. The prospect of
military service made him very anxious, but he said he was too
proud to try to evade it. His classmates were entering the Marine
Training School for officer training. Fearing that the Marine Corps
would be dangerous, he decided to enlist in the Coast Guard,
which seemed relatively safe to him. Since he was 65 pounds over-
weight, he went on a strict diet and, aided by thyroid pills and
strenuous exercise, lost this weight in a short time. He was accepted by the Coast Guard on condition that he volunteer for
service at once. He wished to complete his college education, however, and so tried the Navy, but was refused when he told the examining doctor about using thyroid in dieting. As he left the Navy
Recruiting office, he saw, a few doors away, the Marine Recruiting
office, and he impulsively registered there. He omitted telling

[1] Who seduced whom is a moot question. The patient was fantastically seductive
and could give Dale Carnegie pointers on—if not how to win friends—at least on
how to influence people.

about the use of thyroid, was accepted and allowed to complete his college courses, although his anxieties about the military studies for officer rank required by the Marines almost caused him to fail. He continued the training at Parris Island, but hated it. His qualities for leadership were characterized by him thus: "I couldn't lead a marine with a diarrhea to the latrine." He "deliberately" flunked the subsequent military requirements, had his choice of becoming a Pfc. in the Marine Corps or entering another branch of the service. He tried the Navy once again, but found that if accepted he would be inducted immediately, which did not suit his plans. He wanted to see the baseball World Series which was scheduled to begin shortly: enlistment in the Army gave him the desired deferment so that he could see these games. Assignment to the infantry surprised and disappointed him; he expected a non-combat position because of his education and, according to him, his high IQ. He did well in basic training. There were no sick calls or disciplinary defections. His pride forced him to be a "good" soldier. So did his desire for passes. He seldom thought of the future. Until the day he heard the shells dropping about him he never thought he would actually be engaged in combat. "In my mind," he said, "I had put up a kind of protective film." Despite the "protective film" he had to struggle against a constant depression and fatigue.

Overseas, in Italy, he found himself in a replacement depot, from where he was sent to a new combat unit at the Anzio Beachhead. He felt a constant, growing loneliness and apprehension which, under the shelling, turned to terror. There were other terrors, such as those stirred up crawling through a reputed mine field. Just prior to an attack on a town he was too frightened and helpless to clean and oil his gun as the others were doing. The men talked of old buddies who had been killed or wounded. He said some of the soldiers were crying quite openly. The patient constantly fingered a little amulet he wore around his neck; an Army chaplain had given it to him. His bowels moved frequently in a watery diarrhea. He slept hardly at all. His thoughts, when not paralyzed by terror and the certainty that he would be killed, dwelt on home, on his childhood, and on particular foods that he loved. Shells were dropped close and often. He said, "It was like traveling the last mile to the electric chair; the protective film over my mind was gone."

On the third day after his arrival in the zone of combat his unit went forward to the attack and the patient with it, automatically moved by his legs, which seemed disconnected from the rest of his body, a compromise between his pride and his terror. A shell killed the sergeant who was close to him. It took some little time for the realization of this to sink in. Then he was struck by exploding shell fragments which shattered his left arm. He felt the blow and saw the blood. A sudden wave of joy swept through him: "It was the million dollar wound." He started to the rear on advice of nearby soldiers, but did so with such reckless abandon that another shrapnel burst drove some shell fragments into his back over the scapula and into the flesh of his thigh. Medical field personnel placed his wounded arm in a temporary splint. While awaiting surgery, and in the initial phases of anesthesia, he heard the surgeon say to an assistant: "Take it off." The patient, terrified, almost jumped off the table. He thought the surgeon was referring to his arm, but it was only the cast he wished removed. The fractured bones were then set, leaving a small but perceptible shortening of the arm.

There were, during the subsequent time of convalescence, portents of psychic difficulties: he remained bedfast longer than required by ordinary standards; he showed an exaggerated sensitivity to slight pain; he avoided the amputee ward. He had some spells of weakness and dizziness and had to call for help when he saw some soldiers he knew lying in bed with various wounds. Later he became aware of temper outbursts over trifles. He vowed he would never again suffer feelings of insecurity. While overseas he thought of this country as his zone of security. But after his arrival here this zone of security became more and more restricted until finally it coincided with the boundaries of a locked ward.[2]

The florid manifestations of his illness appeared after military discharge while he was working for his father. There was a constant and severe conflict about his job in which he engaged at the bidding of his father, and about his recreation, the latter given

[2] For a thorough and excellent delineation of the sufferings of psychiatric casualties of war, see Lidz (1946a, 1946b).

over chiefly to bridge playing, begun while he had been convalescing. He did poorly in his work, which he disliked intensely, offering the rationalization that in a sense life was over for him: his dreams and ambitions could no longer come true; he had experienced everything and had nothing to look forward to. The only exception to this lay in his bridge playing, of which, when it became excessive, his father disapproved. When his father in exasperation threatened to send him to the most distant and most difficult areas of his business, the panics began. They were associated with anger and the fear of dying of a heart attack.

The patient was then treated by a psychoanalyst using a standard technique, but after 8 months his condition worsened, and his panics became so incapacitating that he had to be hospitalized. He began to drink heavily to relieve his severe anxiety, and he demanded the constant attendance of a personal nurse to watch over him. He spent the day recording his pulse rate and asking for reassurance about his "condition." After a stormy and fluctuating course over 2 years, which ended in a drunken flight home, he was transferred to another hospital and eventually came under my care.

At that time he presented a chaotic clinical picture and had been puzzling to a number of psychiatrists who had seen him. An abundance of infantile neurotic and psychotic manifestations tended to obscure the essential war neurosis, which was further complicated by a severe, chronic ego regression and intense anxiety and secondary gain phenomena, which had a peculiar "quality of malingering." [3]

The Literature on War Neurosis

But what is a war neurosis? A review of the literature reveals the uncertainties of the nosological position of the group of cases described by this designation. With some authors the term is accorded little significance; others feel it has a specific significance. Some use the terms "war neurosis" and "traumatic neurosis" interchangeably. Others attempt a differentiation between the two. "War neuroses" and/or "traumatic neuroses" are equated with the psychoneuroses and also differentiated from them. Some writers in-

[3] In this context see Eissler's (1951) interesting case report.

voke organic factors to explain the manifestations, but use the term "functional" to describe these. And still others broaden the concept of traumatic neurosis to include every neurosis.

Thus, the "war neuroses" pose a number of questions. Are they temporary reactions to catastrophic events? Do they become permanent and chronic? Are they different from the traumatic neuroses of peace and from the psychoneuroses, hence justifying a special diagnostic category?

The literature contained answers to these questions, some ambiguous and some clear, but hedged around with many qualifications, as the following samples demonstrate.

Freud (1920) states that " 'war neuroses' (in so far as that term implies something more than a reference to the circumstances of the illness's onset) may very well be traumatic neuroses" (p. 33), thus making the term synonymous with the precipitating factor. But in his "Introduction to *Psycho-Analysis and War Neuroses*" (1919, p. 208f.) we find: "The war neuroses, in so far as they are distinguished from the ordinary neuroses of peace-time by *special characteristics,* are to be regarded as traumatic neuroses whose occurrence has been made possible or has been promoted by a conflict in the ego" (my italics).

Although Grinker and Spiegel (1945) conclude that neuroses of war are psychoneuroses, the certainty of their equation is vitiated somewhat by qualifying remarks like: "yet there are some quantitative features common to most war neuroses that give them, as a group, an apparent distinction from all other neuroses" (p. 348). They further take issue with those who use the terms "traumatic neurosis" and "war neurosis" interchangeably and offer certain distinguishing criteria, which are, however, not convincing as basic distinctions (being more phenomenological than dynamic).

Glover (1939), writing of the traumatic neuroses, states that "neither the term 'neurosis' nor for that matter 'psychosis' is adapted to describe the clinical manifestations" (p. 178), but he cannot escape the use of these terms in the exposition of the subject.

Fenichel, who in many ways gives the clearest statement of the traumatic neuroses (1945), also adds to the ambiguity of the whole problem. Although he says that the distinction between the traumatic neuroses and psychoneuroses is an "artificial" one, it is useful from a theoretical point of view. In his further discussion he treats "trauma," on the one hand, as an inherent aspect of the psychoneuroses and, on the other, as involved in an entity which deserves separate nosologic classification, thus making a distinction which in some ways appears to belie his use of the term "artificial."

Despite the nosological confusion and uncertainty indicated in the literature, my own clinical impressions lead me to the view that the term "war neurosis" has a specific significance. This clinical entity deserves the special designation not only because it describes the precipitating event but also because of the specific and nonspecific effects of the trauma on ego functioning and the intrinsic dynamics involving what is called "the military ego." War neurosis is a special case of the traumatic neuroses and is to be differentiated from the psychoneuroses and psychoses, which may be superimposed. In addition, the war neuroses may be either temporary or chronic and permanent reactions to war experiences.

Such a categorical statement perhaps begs the question, but I hope that clinical observations yet to be unfolded will give this position some validity.

The Definition of "Trauma"

There is greater accord in the literature with respect to the definition of "trauma" as a sudden, overwhelming influx of external excitation, although here, too, there is no solid agreement, some authors pointing out that the factor of "suddenness" may be absent and reminding us that the term "overwhelming" is a relative one.[4]

In the war neuroses there is often a preparatory period of stress, usually absent or minimal in the traumatic neuroses of peacetime. The traumatic shock consists in the fact that in the original situation because of the suddenness either anxiety could not have developed or, if it did occur, the outer motor discharge adequate to it (i.e., fight or flight) had been blocked (Simmel, 1944b). Thus, a quantity of excitement is built up which the individual cannot master in the usual way. According to Freud (1926), it is not the energy of the trauma, but the internal energy liberated by the

[4] For a recent review, see Furst (1967).

trauma, that is the essential force in creating the traumatic neurosis. The energies so released may be associatively related to the anxieties of castration or separation or to other pregenital anxieties (see also Thorner, 1946).

Historically, the hypotheses which explain the traumatic neuroses most persuasively have been almost wholly the work of Freud. In the *Three Essays on the Theory of Sexuality* (1905) Freud attempted a psychophysiological explanation of these neuroses: "the combination of fright and mechanical agitation produces the severe, hysteriform, traumatic neurosis. It may at least be assumed that these influences, which, when they are of small intensity, become sources of sexual excitation, lead to a profound disorder in the sexual mechanism or chemistry if they operate with exaggerated force" (p. 202). Thus Freud tried to fit these neuroses into his libido theory as a further justification for the latter, an attempt he still made more than a decade later in his "Introduction to *Psycho-Analysis and the War Neuroses*" (1919). Subsequent writers (e.g., Dreyfuss, 1949) described this "hysteriform" neurosis as essentially a narcissistic ego neurosis, notwithstanding the hysterical appearance of its symptoms.

Analysts need hardly be reminded that Freud (1920), aware that the libido theory could not explain all his observations, and in a mood of speculation, started with the traumatic neuroses and the pleasure principle to arrive, via the concept of the repetition compulsion, at a new hypothesis—the death instinct. On the way he also devised in metapsychological terms a hypothesis to explain the concept of "trauma." He postulated the existence of a "protective shield" (*Reizschutz*) which had the function of damping down the inflow of excitation from the outer world, making it impossible for the energies from this source to act with more than a fraction of their intensity on the subjacent layers of the mind. Such external excitations as are strong enough to break through the barrier against stimuli or the "protective shield" are called "traumatic." Thus the concept of trauma involves such a relationship to an otherwise efficacious barrier. In addition, the pleasure principle is put out of action and the individual undergoes a psychic fixation to the traumatic event.

With respect to internal stimuli Freud clearly states that no intervening "barrier" exists which serves in a similar protective capacity. Others, however, have postulated its possible existence (Dreyfuss, 1949).

In addition to the protection offered by this "shield," the ego attempts to deal with external stimuli of traumatic force by certain defenses, one of the most important of which is denial.[5] It was to this mechanism that my patient was referring when he spoke of the "protective film" he placed over his mind. When this failed, he entered a trancelike state, which is based on even more primitive levels of functioning.

Freud (1920) speaks of two other factors which appear to act as protective measures against the development of the traumatic neurosis: (1) "a wound or injury inflicted simultaneously [with the trauma] works as a rule *against* the development of the neurosis," and (2) "I do not believe that anxiety [i.e., a state of expecting the danger or preparing for it, in contrast to fright, for which there is no preparation] can produce a traumatic neurosis" (p. 12f.).[6] Although this is stated quite categorically, he later modified it with the statement that even these mechanisms may be overwhelmed, which I believe took place in my patient. The injury merely served to delay the full-blown appearance of the neurosis.

The Predisposing Factors

The factors predisposing the individual to a traumatic neurosis are constitutional, developmental, and the condition of the mental apparatus at the time of the trauma. The literature lists the

[5] Among the ego's basic functions is the restoration of stability after a disturbance by external stimuli. For this purpose the functions of neutralizing the energies of incoming excitation, of discharging in action excesses of such energies, and of anticipating and preparing for future events are the first line of defense at the ego's disposal. Quantities of excitement unmastered by these functions set in motion other more primitive methods of dealing with it. Automatic discharges occur without the intervention of the ego. Pathological and archaic methods are called into play in the attempt to restore a measure of equilibrium in the mental economy. Constitutional factors, previous repressions which reduce the neutralizing powers, and the immediate mental economics of the individual play their part. The ego also plays a vital role in transforming passive experiences into active mastery (Fenichel, 1945).

[6] Freud also states that a bodily injury sustained at the same time as the trauma binds the surplus excitation by putting in a claim to a narcissistic overcathexis of the injured part.

infantile and narcissistic personality types among the constitutionally prone individuals. Some authors regard latent homosexuality
a predisposing factor. I should like to add, speculatively, that there
are probably constitutional as well as adaptive variations in the
strength of the "protective shield" envisioned by Freud. This
might help account for the variations in the responses of small children to the impact of similar kinds of trauma.

Developmentally, any prior neurotic complex with its infantile
fixations may provide favorable soil. Glover (1939) singles out the
defenses against repressed sadomasochism, which he feels is responsible for the more crippling symptoms.

The immediate condition of the mental apparatus includes such
factors as fatigue, exhaustion, worry, emotional loss, limitation of
motor freedom during the trauma, and especially its unexpectedness and the lack of preparation for it—their specific combinations producing the characteristic variations in symptomatology.

Aside from the very strong evidence of infantile fixations and an
infantile neurosis, other predisposing factors were present in my
patient such as fatigue to the point of exhaustion, worry, a sense
of separation, and the restriction of motor freedom peculiar to infantry combat. One cannot say, however, that lack of preparation
and unexpectedness, two important predisposing factors, were
present, except in the sense that this usually highly apprehensive
man closed off his mind to the possibility of anything happening to
him.

With the onset of the acute manifestations of his illness a host
of symptoms made their appearance. I should like to present the
details of his symptomatology against the general theoretical background reviewed above.

The Symptom Complex

Instinctual and Ego Impairments

One of the patient's outstanding symptoms was his overly demonstrative attitude of helplessness. He wanted to be helped at every
turn of his life, to be told what to do and when to do it. Associated with this passive dependence was the resurgence of an intense

primitive orality by means of which he maintained his contact with the object world. He ate voraciously, especially when lonely. The food filled up what he described as a "great cavern in my stomach—a great emptiness." Eating reduced the loneliness and gave him a sense of well-being. The world of objects came closer. Once in an interview at the noon hour when I asked him if he had had his lunch he replied: "You are my lunch." He tended to "devour" his objects as he did his food and, like the infant, enjoyed a primitive kind of object attachment—usually evanescent and requiring constant renewal. Overeating was often followed by induced and ritualized vomiting.[7] He feared the effects of his voracity, but he also felt very guilty about it. Overeating was often followed by abdominal discomfort: his abdomen felt "tight" and "hardened like a board." He became anxious, developed hypochondriacal fears of a heart attack, and was certain that if he could not get rid of the "gases," he would die. These complaints with the accompanying restlessness and relief after belching were reminiscent of infants with severe colic: writhing about, abdomen hard, acutely uncomfortable, screaming with pain and temper, but suddenly relaxed after eructations and the expulsion of flatus. After the expulsion of "gases" either spontaneously or by induced vomiting, the patient was comfortable and the tension left his body.

Eating is a means of reducing tension. Appetite need not enter the picture with regard to this. The patient would gulp large quantities of food without tasting it; at times, he was even unaware that he was eating so that he would reach for some food that he had already eaten. He had to fill up the "empty cavern" of his stomach which he related directly to his tension. At times fear banished his appetite and hunger. During spells of anger he ate voraciously, sometimes feeling soothed, at other times increasing his anxieties and discomforts.

He dieted periodically and during such times the loss of object interest could be clearly observed. He became indifferent to every-

7 He would stick his finger down his throat a magical 6 times to bring up food and "gases." This ritual was related to his fear of dying of a heart attack from pressure of the distended stomach against his heart. The magic number 6 was explained as follows: the word "heart" has 5 letters which made it bad luck to regurgitate 5 times; 4 times, he felt, were too few to do any good; hence, 6 would serve the purpose.

one and to the things which previously had delighted him. Once during a long spell of complete apathy and indifference I insisted on interrupting the rigid diet he had imposed on himself and ordered a regular meal for him. The change in mood and in interest was instantaneous and striking: he became friendly, gay, talkative, and was once more alert to things about him.

These observations suggest that the patient dealt with the world of objects by the primitive mechanisms of incorporation and ejection (I am using these terms as much in a psychophysiological sense as in a psychological one; the counterparts in the latter sense being introjection and projection).[8] These mechanisms were in evidence during the patient's late childhood and returned with greater intensity after the war experience.

The patient, not surprisingly, made sudden, shifting, and unstable identifications, which all had the qualities of incorporation. The most notable stimulus to such quick identification,[9] easily observed, was his encountering an injury or illness in another person. He put himself in that person's place and suffered severe anxiety and tension. Thus the mechanism of identification came under the aegis of the trauma and served the purpose of mastery by putting into action the ego's powers of anticipation and apprehension.

In the intellectual sphere I observed a blocking of thought processes which distressed the patient a great deal. He would say, "I can't think," and would shake his head vigorously as one shakes a stopped watch to set it in motion again.[10] When his mind "blocked" in this way or when he felt momentarily confused, he feared he was "going crazy."

His intellectual interests and activities were not commensurate with his level of education. He hated to concern himself with or

[8] According to Hartmann, Kris, and Loewenstein (1946), Freud assumed that these processes follow a pattern established by physiological organization of incorporation and ejection; the psychological counterparts are introjection and projection, the basis of the child's ambivalence (endangering the ego's stability).

[9] Kris (1950) states that Freud believed that a more permanent attachment was needed to replace the anaclitic and transient one in order that the control of impulses may be facilitated by identification. In other words, stable identifications are needed for impulse control.

[10] Pious speculated on this as the central clinical event in schizophrenia: a sudden emptying of withdrawal. (In a seminar he conducted which was devoted to the study of this case.)

think about weighty matters. He disliked giving sustained attention to anything—except the game of contract bridge. There was a general diminution and inhibition of his intellectal activity. For the most part, when he was not playing bridge,[11] he spent his time reading cheap literature and seeing Western movies.

His capacity to recall recent events was excellent—superb for bridge hands, which he played out in his mind; but his memory for past events seemed poor, the reason being the ever-present fear of touching on something painful. These painful memories seemed to be close to the surface and, as I thought, constantly needed to be suppressed. This was particularly true for all events associated with his war experiences.

The war trauma also had disturbed his perceptual functioning. He suffered from hyperacusis and was prone to severe startle reactions. Noise disturbed and irritated him. This associatively became connected with certain complexes. For example, during one interview I made a rhythmic popping noise, without the patient's being aware that I had made the noise. He jumped sharply, looked startled, and asked if I had heard anything. He had imagined the noise to be the loud beating of his own heart.[12] Noises also produced other illusions in him. He was hyperalert as if danger lurked everywhere, yet his appraisal of actual danger in reality was very defective.

His speech, under the impact of excitement, tension, and anger, became rapid, loud, explosive, and was accompanied by wild gesticulations. It was a verbal indicator of the difficulties of the ego in the sphere of control.

In their attempts to avoid unbearable reality, persons suffering from traumatic neurosis frequently resort to regressions, which

---

[11] There seems to be a relation between the blocking of thought and the focusing of attention. In normal people, these functions may be disturbed momentarily by an influx of excitation, pleasant or otherwise, specific or nonspecific. Usually the normal person can by composing himself, that is, by reducing the excitation, attend to the task at hand and think about it. Nunberg (1920) observed that in schizophrenia there is an increase in self-observation, combined with compulsive remembering and the urge to interpret symptoms and symbols. My patient was prone to specific kinds of self-observation and remembering—very sharp in certain areas. For a discussion of "focusing," see Pious (1950) .

[12] This would appear to indicate a loosening of ego boundaries when certain unconscious complexes are touched upon.

then make it difficult for them to maintain object cathexis. However, there is no real break with reality. Most authors writing on this subject believe that the partial ego impairments are regressions to the stage at which the infant was completely helpless; that its aim is to achieve a full measure of security, to re-establish the narcissistic equilibrium of the ego, and to maintain a need-satisfying object relation. To this end the ego functions are blocked or diminished, which enables it to concentrate all available mental energy on the one task of building up counterenergies to master the intruding overwhelming excitation (Fenichel, 1945).

Emotional Spells

The patient had frequent anxiety attacks which often developed into panic states, sudden irritable outbursts, and occasional rage reactions, usually triggered by trifling matters or slight frustrations. Short periods of moderate depression and spells of hypomanic excitement occurred. Several times he had a crying spell after some frustration or insult or when he felt he had failed to maintain the gains he had achieved in therapy.

The anxiety attacks were accompanied by the well-known sympathetic nervous system symptoms: palpitation, sweating, pallor, tremors, dizziness, tension headaches, diarrhea, and spells of "weakness" localized in the knees. At other times these phenomena appeared only as anxiety equivalents, the patient having no conscious awareness of his anxiety. In any event, the anxiety attacks and panics were either a mystery to the patient or were associated by him to threats of separation or hypochondriacal fears quite clearly related to the threat of castration. Of his panics he said: "They remind me of the battlefields."

For several years he drank heavily or drugged himself, although he hated the taste of liquor and feared addiction. Alcohol and barbiturates helped relieve his panics and fears and allowed him to face himself and the world with a certain bravado. They relaxed his tension and allowed him to rest and to sleep.

There seemed to be a specific correlation between anxiety and anger. When he was sober or not under the influence of drugs, situations which would ordinarily call forth his anger resulted instead in severe anxiety reactions. Yet, when he was under the influence of drugs or alcohol, the same situation evoked direct anger or rage reactions without anxiety.

These rages and aggressiveness were in sharp contrast to his friendly, polite, submissive, often timid attitude when he was sober. It was a long time before he could tolerate any anger when sober and if this emotion threatened him, he would get intoxicated in a hurry so that he could be "happily angry."

In connection with the emotional spells—or, more specifically, with states of tension, excitement, or exertion—he complained of marked fatigue, which was one of the major symptoms observed in World War II in psychiatric casualties.

Earlier I referred to the fact that several psychiatrists had been puzzled by the anxiety picture presented by this patient. I believe they were perplexed because they did not consider the superimposition of a war neurosis on his basic character disorder. The emotional states in the traumatic (war) neuroses represent more archaic and involuntary emergency discharges. To some degree they are entirely unspecific, that is, unrelated to any dynamic unconscious content. The specific aspect of the emotional reactions can be explained by the immediate (motor and sensory) situation at the time of the trauma and by the pretraumatic history. "A study of the development of anxiety shows that all later spells of anxiety represent repetitions of early traumatic states." My findings are in accord with this statement made by Fenichel (1945),[13] although I believe that in this patient the anxiety was reinforced by the continuing unspecific discharge due to the war trauma.

[13] Fenichel (1945) says further: "The fact that the emotional quality of such spells is most often felt as anxiety or rage is important and should be kept in mind. . . . The objective state of being flooded with unmastered excitation is subjectively felt as being very painful, and the quality of this pain is very similar to anxiety. This is brought about partly by the unmastered inner tension itself and partly by involuntary vegetative 'emergency discharges.' Later states of rage, too, are rooted in situations of frustration, that is, in states where an urgent need is not fulfilled and the available discharges are not adequate" (p. 119) . Note the phrase "*similar* to anxiety" with its implication that the felt emotion is actually not anxiety, although it partakes of the quality of this emotion. This raises an interesting point. I have observed what appeared to be anxiety states in my patient, but from his description of the emotion it was more a state of tension than one of anxiety. However, I believe that for the most part it is an admixture of the two. States of tension may also call forth feelings of anxiety.

Thus, anxiety and rage in the traumatic neurosis represent undischarged excitation aroused by the trauma. Their specific nature can be explained by the emotion felt but inhibited during the trauma as well as by the revival of reactions to earlier neurotic complexes. In this case the anxieties and rages associated with early trauma were intensively revived.

Sleeplessness and Repetition Symptoms

One of the patient's major difficulties and distresses after the onset of the acute phase of his illness was his inability to fall asleep. This was torturing to him and he begged for medication to give him a night's rest. Without it he frequently remained wakeful until 5 or 6 in the morning. The prospect of facing a sleepless night so terrified him that sleeping pills became for him as precious as gold to a miser, and he kept count of the capsules prescribed for this purpose with the same kind of avarice. After a sleepless night the irritability, depression, tension, and worry about himself contrasted very sharply with his cheerful good humor after a night of sleep. Obsessive rumination about the day's events kept him awake, although at times he denied thinking about anything: he just could not relax and compose himself for slumber. He suffered from the anxiety of anticipation, especially if it related to the prospect of an examination of any sort (e.g., by a physician; for a driver's license, etc.) .

He reported his dreams with great reluctance; usually only when I asked about them. These dreams were characteristically anxiety dreams and battle dreams. In the manifest content of one dream he had himself mustered out of the Army and entering civilian life —this 9 years after his discharge from the Army. In another he saw the flash of guns with bursts of light illuminating the battle front and woke to see a hospital attendant flashing his light into the room on his nightly rounds. In all the dreams his intense castration anxiety was clearly betrayed.

The insomnia of the traumatic neurotic was one of his major symptoms and was due to a flooding of the mental apparatus with the unbound quantities of excitation. If he was lucky enough to fall asleep, the function of the dream with regard to protecting the continuation of sleep remained for the most part intact, even though its wish-fulfilling function (in respect to the trauma dream) did not. According to Freud (1920), the dreams in traumatic neuroses behave like the archaic ego before it is capable of anticipating the future and which still masters the world by the active repetition of what it experienced passively. This type of dream is void of wish fulfillment.

Psychoneurotic Complications

The patient's history prior to the war trauma leaves no doubt that he suffered from an emotional disorder during childhood and that elements of it remained with him until his induction into the military.

That the patient conceived of his early medical experiences as a series of severe assaults, a repeated series of traumas to which he had to submit, is clear in the history. At the same time he constantly anticipated possible future trauma for which he felt he needed to prepare himself. His attempts at mastery of these early experiences have been mentioned. During childhood he had phobias,[14] obsessions and compulsions, and many hypochondriacal worries. He had been shy and withdrawn in early youth—very obedient and polite. In some respects he could become quite aggressive, occasionally in an explosive fashion. Many of the overt neurotic symptoms receded as he got older, only to return in full force after the war experience.

The question of psychosis, and more specifically schizophrenia, was often in the forefront of my thinking about this patient during the many years of treatment. The various batteries of psychological tests given at three different periods of treatment failed to reveal any psychopathology that would be conclusive. Clinical ob-

---

[14] The phobic structure of this patient's symptomatology was extremely complex. His fear of death and an agoraphobia were most conspicuous. Lewin (1952) described sensations in agoraphobbes which I observed in my patient, such as a feeling of his legs giving way, fear of losing his mind, and a fear of fear itself, which Weiss (1934) interpreted as a dread of painful changes in consciousness, depersonalization, and half-dream states. To such changes in ego feeling (or other hysterical manifestations) in the initial attack, Weiss attributed an etiological, traumatic significance.

servation certainly aroused suspicion that the basic character disorder might be schizophrenic. The combination of hypochondria-
sis, phobias, obsessions and compulsions in a shy, withdrawn youth
may well be a front for schizophrenia.[15]

Several of the criteria offered by Federn (1952) for indications
of hidden schizophrenia apply to this patient: a history with periods of different kinds of neurosis, prevalence of the narcissistic reaction pattern over that of object libido, deterioration in work,
and isolation in social contacts after puberty or after leaving the
regulated life at home or in school. To this may be added certain
subjective experiences which hint at a loss of ego boundaries, and
the wide weight fluctuations with the accompanying psychological
reactions.

On the other hand, how much of the war neurosis entered the
picture to give the underlying character disorder the flavor of
schizophrenia? What Glover (1939) has to say of the traumatic
neuroses may be relevant to this: "In a number of instances psy-
cho-neurotic symptoms (anxiety phobias and hysterical dissocia-
tions) may make their appearance. In rarer instances the symptoms of confusion, inhibition and retardation may be hard to distinguish from a schizophrenic regression or other psychotic reaction" (p. 179). He speaks of regressions to infantile behavior in
gait, speech, mannerisms, feeding habits, scenes of violence and
rage, etc., and says these are neither psychoneurotic nor psychotic.

In summary one could say that there was (1) an unspecific disintegration of the personality with abolition of fine differentiation in the ego and with regression to a childish dependence; and
(2) a mobilization of a latent neurotic or psychotic disposition. The
trauma acted as precipitating factor. Instinctual drives, particularly aggression, which had been repressed threatened to erupt
(and at times did erupt), increasing anxiety and repression and reviving old conflicts between ego and superego.

The Superego and the Fear of Death

With regard to the complex ego-superego conflicts, I shall single
out only one aspect that is pertinent to one of the patient's outstanding symptoms: the fear of death.

[15] Acting as restitution phenomena in this disease, according to Pious (1950).

In *The Ego and the Id* (1923), Freud speaks of the mechanism concerned with this: "the ego relinquishes its narcissistic libidinal cathexis in a very large measure . . . it gives up itself . . . the fear of death is something that occurs between the ego and superego" (p. 58). Fear of death on the battlefield is a realistic fear. The ego normally meets it by action: by fighting or retreating. In my patient the fear had reached such a degree that he could do neither. He was paralyzed with panic. He said he felt himself "dying rapidly." [16]

Psychically he was ill prepared to meet the dangers of the battlefield. The entire development of his personality as well as his attitude to his military indoctrination was against it. If his ego could not take an active attitude toward what threatened it, it was lost. In his case it could not because the danger was too great and too real. Nor could he summon the inner strength needed to meet it: the strength which in part stems from the healthy superego and the ego ideal. He submitted himself to the enemy without because he had already submitted to the enemy within—the cruel superego image of the father to whom he always had to submit for punishment. The cruelty of the superego derived not only from the punishing father but also from the abandoning mother. His loneliness and sense of isolation and abandonment, even though he was surrounded by fellow soldiers, was intense. Perhaps it was ultimately this sense of being abandoned which made it impossible for him successfully to handle the sadism of the superego. His relief and exhilaration on receiving the wound were, from his standpoint, appropriate reactions and a realistic appraisal of his position: it was an escape from the possibility of death. Paradoxically, however, his unrealistic behavior after he had received the wound —the throwing of caution to the winds by exposing himself to get to the rear lines in a hurry—had in it a further invitation to death. The reactions to the symbolic meanings of the wound did not appear until later when the latent character disorder was revived. He

[16] Pious (in personal communications) offered the interesting speculation that in schizophrenia one observes phenomena which could be explained by an increase in the rate of dying in the individual and which is experienced in certain ways (e.g., a feeling of sudden "emptying"). In this connection I recall a schizophrenic patient's not infrequent complaint of "feeling suddenly and frighteningly empty," accompanied by a fear of dying.

then behaved, on the one hand, as if fit only to consort with "little old ladies" (in his self-demeaning phrase) and, on the other, engaging in violent rage and revenge behavior directed particularly toward his father.

Lewin (1952) quotes a remark made by Fritz Wittels concerning the "devourer" and "castrator" Father Time that further illuminates the reasons for my patient's fear of death. Wittels said: "So Freud was right; death means Castration" (p. 310).

The patient's "military" ego—poorly constituted as we have seen—was made even weaker by its interaction with an even worse "military" ego ideal. He completely lacked any sense of what he was fighting for and showed a great indifference to his country. He seemed to have less comprehension of these things than the average soldier who had had far less education and advantages. Even the smaller ideals of the combat soldier were lacking. He merely submitted to the military discipline, as he had to his father, hating it and fearing the authority figures who ordered and administered it. His hollow and childish sense of duty operated only to bring him the gratification of passes, to avoid punishment, and to insure these to get the good conduct ratings.

His sense of self-esteem was very feeble. It needed constant support from without. Even in retrospect, after winning battle decorations for his wounds and the good conduct ribbon, which he made much of, his superego could give him little else than a sense of uneasy guilt for the part he played in the war.

If he had seen no combat, he would have served uneventfully and been discharged with a good conduct ribbon. The military service with its "infantilization" of the soldier might have been appealing to him under other circumstances. However, if he had not received his wound, he would have been a combat casualty nonetheless—a psychiatric casualty. The wound only covered from view, for the time being, the psychiatric disorder which began to show itself gradually.

The Secondary Gains

This factor plays a most important role in the traumatic neuroses, much more so than in the psychoneuroses. The uses the patient makes of his illness, which have nothing to do with its origin, may be the largest single element with which the therapy has to deal. The driving need for security, love, and appreciation makes the patient exploit his symptoms to the utmost.[17]

It was this factor which impressed one with the "malingering quality" in the patient's anxiety. The extensive and successful exploitation of his environment, by means of his helplessness and other symptoms, contributed to making the clinical picture such a chaotic one. He was unbelievably shrewd and cunning in his methods and would go to great lengths to gain his ends.

Financial arrangements with his father were a constant source of irritation to him. He was determined to live in a certain style to which he had been accustomed, and his father was equally determined to fix the limits of luxury and comfort for this son who earned nothing, but required large sums of money for treatment and hospital care. Both attitudes were understandable, albeit from widely different angles, resulting in a constant battle between father and son: furious exchanges of letters, phone calls, and detailed financial accountings. After 2 years it appeared to be settled, in part at least, in the way the son wished it to be. In the course of this money wrangle the patient wrote his father a letter which was almost an open "hold-up." It was one of the few times he acted with such self-assertion toward his father while sober. He wrote (knowing it to be untrue) that he was "getting well" and that he expected "to be cured in another year." He hoped his father would not jeopardize this by trying to save a few hundred dollars over the year. He insisted on a certain minimum sum to carry him through without worry. Although the father understood this as a "hold-up," he acquiesced with some grace, and as he did so I am sure he had in mind the depredations against self and others of which his son was capable when frustrated and which were a source of great embarrassment and worry to the father. The patient's guilt and self-castigation over these actions seemed momentarily genuine, but were soon forgotten or pushed aside. (Needless to say

[17] The secondary gain factor continued unabated and long after the patient was removed from the war situations when it would have been expected to stop. Apparently, in the war neurosis, the secondary gain factor may operate long after removal from the military danger situation.

his manipulativeness came up for discussion, but it is doubtful that these interpretations had much impact on him.)

The story of how the patient obtained a chauffeur to drive him to various places is instructive of his cunning and the lengths to which he would go to get his wishes fulfilled. After one of his discharges from the hospital he was picked up by the police and charged with driving while intoxicated. He probably would not have been apprehended had he not been driving through the streets in a very conspicuous manner with the hood of his car raised. He claimed it became fixed in this position because of some mechanical failure and that he was looking for a place to have it fixed. When he was stopped, the odor of liquor was detected and he lost his license but gained a chauffeur.[18]

I learned about the deliberate aspects of this maneuver only long after the event. At the time it occurred he was too nervous to drive to various places alone and wanted a companion for these trips. He also liked to prepare himself for the bridge tournaments he traveled to by resting in the back of the car enroute. He could not muster sufficient energy to drive himself. He admitted almost a year after this incident that though he knew he was under the influence of the liquor, he also knew how conspicuous he had made himself and realized he was risking the loss of his license. It was not entirely an unconscious piece of acting out: he denied that the strategy had been planned, but confessed that he had been thinking of ways to get someone to drive him and to act as his companion. At the time obtaining the money needed for this purpose was out of the question. He found the way. Later, when he felt better, he retrieved his license and got rid of the chauffeur.

In the moments of bravado already alluded to he openly prided himself on his ability to get people to do what he wanted them to: by aggressive means, by cunning, by seduction, etc.

The Goal of Mastery

Studying the patient's strivings for achievements throughout the years one gains the impression that these were not so much di-

---

[18] The unconscious need for punishment involved in this maneuver is not discussed. However, this need was strong and when he sobered up afterward, he feared he would be punished (for example, that he might be given shock therapy) .

rected toward an overall purposeful goal as isolated accomplishments motivated by a need for relief and gratification that the sense of mastery over a given situation can bring.[19]

The patient set himself a succession of tasks to master and when he felt he had succeeded, often after a number of failures, he expected me to show my approval. In fact, he was unable to pass judgment himself on whether or not he had succeeded and required this outside approval. The task finished, he would lose interest in it and have nothing more to do with it. For example, he became intensely interested in photography, purchased expensive equipment, and enrolled for a course in an accredited school. The most important aspect of this work was to prove to me that he could finish the course with almost perfect grades. He brought his pictures to me for my praise. When he had completed the course, he lost interest in photography altogether. The voyeuristic element is obvious, but its interpretation would have been meaningless to him.

His dieting, too, was a lesson in mastery. Some of his statements on this subject were in such introspective contrast with his mockingly "babyish" ways and manner of speech that they always surprised me. He said: "Dieting for me is very important. It's like mastering a strict discipline within myself. It is mastering frustration and building up my strength of mind. The same goes for playing bridge. I meet people and learn to get along with them in public. It is learning to stretch the security cord. I can now win tournaments in stiff competition without drinking. It is a compensation because no one feels more embarrassed than I for not doing real constructive work."

He also offered certain rationalizations, which, however, were significant for the subject of mastery; e.g., "I want to be a leader. But unless I can do a good job at this, I must keep away from it [i.e., from work] for the time being." In this connection it should be said that his father was a leader in his community and had great ambitions for his only son.

[19] Eissler (1953) made a statement which I consider significant for this case: "There is undoubtedly a beneficial effect on the therapeutic situation when a schizophrenic patient succeeds in doing something which he has been convinced would transgress his resources" (p. 242).

The patient mastered his panics and the need to drink disappeared. He mastered his fears of driving his car alone and discharged his chauffeur-companion. The counterphobic attitude which caused him to observe surgical procedures while he was in college had its counterpart in the first job he had while still a hospital patient, that of part-time orderly in the general hospital. He seemed driven on at times by counterphobic pressures.[20]

The bridge game, his supreme effort at mastery, became a kind of monomania. It was something he could do very well. Any losing streak upset and depressed him. The game was endowed with an assortment of symbolic meanings. It served his instinctual gratifications. He could "kill" his opponents at the bridge table. It became his sounding board of well-being and achievement. If he played well and won, the whole compact of his satisfactions seemed gratified and he went along in a happy frame of mind. His life was channeled into the bridge game, which he had learned while in the military hospital with his arm propped in a cast. All else was secondary. Nothing could compete with it, and he allowed nothing to interfere with his concentration on the game. Whenever an unpleasantness arose, he barricaded his thoughts and feelings behind images of bridge hands.

This patient showed a phenomenon which I refer to as a "curve of mastery." It was somewhat similar to what one finds in the "circle of orality" in the alcoholic (Knight, 1946). I observed that initially he made a desperate effort to succeed. This was often followed by failure and then by remorse and self-castigation. His renewed efforts would bring him closer to success, and then the cycle would start again. However, each succeeding failure was not as profound as the previous one and his rate of recovery from it was faster.

In the literature the motif of mastery is classified as specific and unspecific and as passive-receptive and active. The specific and unspecific types of mastery were discussed earlier in connection with

[20] In this connection I mention his fear of tension and excitement. Fenichel (1939) claims that this assumes a very painful quality because they cannot be discharged. The patient became a trauma-ridden personality. Some of his attempts to master the excitation by acting out, by striving for various experiences which were in themselves traumatic, were countered by his efforts to avoid any possible traumatic situations.

discharges of affect and the various protective inhibitions of the ego.[21]

With respect to the passive-receptive and active types of mastery, the traumatic experience flooded the organism with stimuli while it was in a relatively passive state. The subsequent repetitive actions represent an active attempt to achieve belated mastery over the stimuli. Abreacting a trauma, according to Freud (1926), is essentially changing from passivity to activity to master the situation. Regressive efforts at mastery also occur after the trauma and lead to the development of a passive-receptive attitude.

While the concept of mastery in the traumatic neuroses of war refers to the attempt to deal with and overcome the psychophysiological effects of the trauma per se, other complexes of a dynamic psychological nature, which in their origins are associated with another order of a traumatic nature, get drawn into the mastery attempts. More specifically, in this patient, the oedipal and pre-oedipal conflicts were directly involved in his compulsive, frenetic attempt to achieve the Life Mastership at the bridge tournament table.

It has been said that most bridge fanatics are not equipped to play the game as it should be played. Among the necessary attributes set down for this are the possession of a monumental narcissism, stamina, endurance, a "killer instinct," intense concentration, ability to calculate, and a certain card sense which includes a prodigious memory for them. Some train to play as if they were athletes, while others bolster their talents by a moderate use of pills or alcohol. In my patient the anxiety was so high, and the necessity so great to keep it within bounds to allow for effective action, that moderation was lost sight of. The bridge game was a fierce challenge, a competitive battle to which he was frenziedly

21 One further item about nonspecific mastery deserves mention: several authors (Simmel, 1944b; Fenichel, 1945) have noted that the ego of the war neurotic seems to be in *search of anxiety*. At times my patient seemed to call it up for no apparent reason. It appeared to be a repetitive discharge phenomenon. Moreover, he often endowed figures with far more authority than their station warranted. The anxiety created by this was sometimes transformed into anger and aggressive action, so that the ego could master the situation by once again fighting the battle of a past reality. In this way the ego felt equal to its enemy—the externalized parental authority. At other times he behaved like the psychoneurotic who is at pains to avoid anxiety (i.e., superego anxiety: clashes with the powerful parental authority).

addicted. The dynamic significance of this involvement became abundantly clear in the course of time.

On his attaining the Life Mastership the moment of joy and triumph was so overwhelming that he grew faint with the exhilaration of it. In the first flush of victory he surrendered all his pills, vowing he never would need them again; and he experienced a sudden generosity toward his father, in great contrast to his usual aloof distance from him, by allowing that his father had an even greater native talent for the game than he had (though his father played bridge only on social occasions). He longed for his father's approval, for an acknowledgment of the greatness of his struggle to win the prize of the Life Master. He did not receive it in the fashion he hoped for.

The day following his victory, it was like ashes in his mouth. He desperately had to impress his private world, which was not the bridge world, and he could not. Without approval of key surrogates of his personal world his feeling of triumph was short-lived. A girlfriend was only politely excited, patients and nurses at the hospital were indifferent, the doctors praised his achievement, but admonished him in the same breath about the dangerous consequences of drugging himself. His egocentricity was not that of the genuine bridge shark: an impervious narcissistic structure sufficient unto itself. His aggressiveness, though powerful, was caught up, like the libido, in an intense neurotic conflict. His stamina and endurance, lacking true native strength, were reduced by the psychic disorder and urgently needful of external supports. The greater the driving passion to master his neurotic conflict and the war trauma, the greater became the necessity for certain props to his ego—be they of a positive nature (therapist, bridge partner, etc.) or negative (the "supportive"—self-destructive—drugs).

The game of bridge represented the drama in symbolic form of the oedipal conflict. His remarks, feelings, associations, attitudes, all revealed this clearly. To play and especially to win meant to possess the potent male genital. He said: "Take away bridge, and you cut off my prick and balls." His mastery of the bridge game with his attainment of the Life Mastership were like a public announcement of his masculine power. He was at least as great as his father, and therefore as deserving. The triumph was short-lived and felt hollow because the real prize was still forbidden him: the love of the cold mother. Thus he spoke of her surrogate, his girlfriend, as having lived through the agony of his struggle to become a Life Master and on the day of his achieving it she refused to see him, which again turned his thoughts to suicide and back to the comfort of his pills. At least in those he could find the embrace of his mother as well as her destructiveness.

Dynamically related to these factors was the expressed thought that becoming a Life Master "was like finally getting to have intercourse with the girlfriend [unattainable to him]; but once you've done it, you have no interest in her any longer," a reference to his dalliance with prostitutes. He never saw the same prostitute twice and each time following intercourse developed a depression. The oedipal guilt was obvious in all he had to say about these experiences. Even the degraded position he ascribed to these women could help little in alleviating his guilt and depression.

In the game of bridge by demolishing his opponent (father) he was able to win for himself the powerful father phallus (Life Mastership) and take his place with mother. But the triumph was brief and guilt and depression supervened at this forbidden success. The mother-prize was downgraded (the prostitute) and defensive regression to the oral phase—in which drugs gave the maternal gratifications—saw the conflict played out at that stage of psychosexual development. The punishment came in the form of depression at the success, a loss of interest in the bridge game that brought him to it, and in thoughts of suicide.

One might almost wish he had never reached the desired goal and that the drive for mastery might have continued to make of his life the exciting, passionate, goal-driven life it had been. He could have continued the father-son relationship with his bridge partner (which was acceptable to him) and carried on in the competitive struggle without clear-cut issue. It is like a fantasied wish that the ancient battle between Oedipus and Laius at the crossroads would have had no final or clear outcome. This is not, of course, what we desire as a therapeutic outcome in our patients, and I only say this retrospectively in view of what did happen. (It also touches on the negative therapeutic reaction which is a chapter in itself.) Put another way, one could say that if he could have lived a full lifetime in the attempt at mastery without reaching his goal, he might have counted it a life worthwhile.

What triggered off the urge to master the bridge game with such intensity? As a youth he had played with his parents, though his interest then was not at all excessive. He did feel that his father had a natural, but undeveloped talent for the game. It was important for the patient to stress his father's talent in that area because it was the only one in which he felt he could compete. While the father was an extremely successful man, he had no particular ambitions in bridge. Perhaps this made it possible for my patient to choose this area to play out the psychic conflicts afflicting him. He had begun to play the game with some regularity while convalescing from his combat experiences. With regard to the question posed above: it is my impression that the psychic war trauma suffered in combat, and the need to master it in the way Freud described, acted as trigger to the urge to master the repressed oedipal forces; it was as if it flowed over into that dynamic field of psychic conflict. The mastery action helped keep at bay those repressed complexes when they threatened to erupt into consciousness. This was related to a fear of a recurring nightmare which prevented sleep. It was a fear of dying on the battlefield and it signified that the "great" game of war was still being played out in his unconscious, but transposed into action in the "lesser" game of bridge. Behind both was the unremitting struggle of his chilhood—the oedipal conflict.

Postscript

During the years of the therapy the patient lived his precarious existence toward the one goal of becoming a Life Master of the bridge game, which he did achieve. Thereafter, and not too unexpectedly, the passion for bridge waned. He then moved to another city and I lost contact with him except indirectly. I learned that he married, that he had some interrupted periods of treatment and several brief hospitalizations, and then, on the verge of another of those, he took an overdose of sleeping pills and died. It was never determined how deliberate that had been. Treatment [22] helped him attain the title he so passionately sought, but it could do little to help him achieve the title of "Master of Life" in what he felt was the grimmest of all "games" called "Everyday Living."

The evidence indicated that following the stress of the combat experience, insufficiently mastered, the trauma remained like a foreign body in the psyche and began to threaten the already precariously put-together ego so that a more serious psychotic disorganization became an ever-present possibility. In part this sense of disintegration was heralded by the panic reactions he suffered. It was experienced as "dying," and to restore himself to the world of the living (at one time he spoke of himself as being transformed "from a constantly dying man" to one who was "living at last") he made use of all the restitutive and mastery powers at his command. He relived in dreams and fantasies the terrifying battle experiences in an attempt to master them; he utilized his psychoneurotic symptoms for restitutive purposes; they also helped stave off the latent psychotic process. Above all, the bridge game became a combined restitutive and mastery attempt, a form of "combat," so to speak, on a far less dangerous battleground. When his meagre psychic resources failed him on the outside, it was necessary to resort to the hospital to help sustain him,[23] but the hospital held its own risks, since for him it was an invitation to a dependence and a curtailment of action that could be equally as threatening as the outside world with its intensified and diversified demands. He was more imperiled there, but more "alive."

As has been emphasized, the focus of the paper was on the traumatic neurosis caused by the combat experience and its interaction with the pre-existing psychopathology. The case demonstrated the significance of the stimulus barrier, one of the primary autonomous functions of the ego, and an important clinical theory for explaining the symptoms of the traumatic neurosis. Whether the stimulus barrier (*Reizschutz*) of the patient's ego was constitutionally weak or had been weakened by the traumatic experiences

[22] The therapeutic problems posed by this patient are beyond the scope of this paper.

[23] There is a growing psychoanalytic literature which considers these reactions in connection with the very early mother-child fusions and separations.

of childhood could not be satisfactorily determined; nor could a conclusion be reached as to the presence of an internal barrier against stimuli which some investigators believe to exist, though Freud is not among them. The patient's injury delayed the appearance of the signs of the traumatic neurosis by binding the surplus excitation, but apparently the "binding" was not of long duration, for with the healing of the wound the traumatic neurosis started. A number of recent articles have been critical of Freud's economic theory and claim to have found it dispensable, but I still regard it as eminently useful, and perhaps in no place more so than in the consideration of the traumatic neurosis, as I believe this case demonstrates.

The tragic outcome of this patient's life was related to the undercurrent of self-destructiveness which he half-sensed in himself and which contributed to his severe panics. The one comforting thought in it all was that he had attained his goal which he so often felt to be beyond his reach: he became a Life Master, not in Life, but in the game of Bridge.

BIBLIOGRAPHY

DREYFUSS, D. K. (1949), Delayed Epileptiform Effects of Traumatic War Neuroses and Freud's Death Instinct Theory. *Int. J. Psycho-Anal.*, 30:75–91.

EISSLER, K. R. (1951), Malingering. In: *Psychoanalysis and Culture.* New York: International Universities Press, pp. 218–253.

— (1953), Notes upon the Emotionality of a Schizophrenic Patient and Its Relation to Problems of Technique. *This Annual*, 8:199–251.

FEDERN, P. (1952), *Ego Psychology and the Psychoses.* New York: Basic Books.

FENICHEL, O. (1939), The Counterphobic Attitude. *Collected Papers*, 2:163–173. New York: Norton, 1954.

— (1945), *The Psychoanalytic Theory of Neurosis.* New York: Norton.

FREUD, S. (1905), Three Essays on the Theory of Sexuality. *Standard Edition*, 7:125–243. London: Hogarth Press, 1953.

— (1919), Introduction to *Psycho-Analysis and the War Neuroses. Standard Edition*, 17:205–210. London: Hogarth Press, 1955.

— (1920), Beyond the Pleasure Principle. *Standard Edition*, 18:7–64. London: Hogarth Press, 1955.

— (1923), The Ego and the Id. *Standard Edition*, 19:3–66. London: Hogarth Press, 1961.

— (1926), Inhibitions, Symptoms and Anxiety. *Standard Edition,* 20:77–175. London: Hogarth Press, 1959.

FURST, S. S., ed. (1967), *Psychic Trauma.* New York: Basic Books.

GLOVER, E. (1939), *Psychoanalysis.* London: Staples Press.

— (1942), Book Review: A. Kardiner, *The Traumatic Neuroses of War. Int. J. Psycho-Anal.,* 23:92–93.

GRINKER, R. & SPIEGEL, J. P. (1945), *Men Under Stress.* Philadelphia: Blakiston.

HARDCASTLE, D. N. (1944), Some Notes on Traumatic Neurosis and Allied Conditions. *Int. J. Psycho-Anal.,* 25:132–142.

KARDINER, A. (1941), *The Traumatic Neuroses of War.* New York: Hoeber, 1947.

KNIGHT, R. P. (1946), Lecture on Alcoholism, Topeka.

KRIS, E. (1950), Notes on the Development and on Some Current Problems of Psychoanalytic Child Psychology. *This Annual,* 5:24–46.

LEWIN, B. D. (1952), Phobic Symptoms and Dream Interpretation. *Psychoanal. Quart.,* 21:295–322.

LIDZ, T. (1946a), Nightmares and the Combat Neuroses. *Psychiatry,* 9:37–44.

— (1946b), Psychiatric Casualties from Guadalcanal. *Psychiatry,* 9:193–214.

NUNBERG, H. (1920), On the Catatonic Attack.. *Practice and Theory of Psychoanalysis,* 1:3–23. New York: International Universities Press, 1965.

PIOUS, W. L. (1950), Obsessive-Compulsive Symptoms in an Incipient Schizophrenic. *Psychoanal. Quart.,* 19:327–351.

RADO, S. (1942), Pathodynamics and Treatment of Traumatic War Neurosis (Traumatophobia). *Psychosom. Med.,* 4:362–368.

RAPAPORT, D. (1951), The Conceptual Model of Psychoanalysis. In: *Collected Papers,* ed. M. M. Gill. New York: Basic Books, pp. 405–431.

SIMMEL, E. (1944a), Self-Preservation and the Death Instinct. *Psychoanal. Quart.,* 13:160–185.

— (1944b), War Neurosis. In: *Psychoanalysis Today,* ed. S. Lorand. New York: International Universities Press, pp. 227–248.

THORNER, H. A. (1946), The Treatment of Psychoneurosis in the British Army. *Int. J. Psycho-Anal.,* 27:52–59.

WEISS, E. (1934), Agoraphobia and Its Relation to Hysterical Attacks and to Traumas. *Int. J. Psycho-Anal.,* 16:59–83, 1935.

Problems of Technique during Latency

MIRIAM WILLIAMS, M.D.

THE LATENCY PHASE HAS GENERALLY ATTRACTED MUCH LESS ATTEN-
tion as an object of research than have the first 5 years of life or adolescence. Developmentally, however, latency can be looked upon
as an essential period of psychic growth, during which the inher-
ited and acquired "raw materials" of the individual undergo vital

Based on a paper presented at the Annual Meeting of the American Association
for Child Psychoanalysis, New Haven, Conn., March, 1969.

Senior Faculty Member and member of Committee for Child Analysis Training,
Los Angeles Psychoanalytic Society-Institute. Member of British Psychoanalytic
Society.

I wish to thank the following colleagues from the Child Analytic Study Group
for their helpful suggestions in preparing the earlier text: Margarete Ruben, Lillian
Weitzner, Heiman Van Dam, and Christoph Heinicke. I also wish to express my
gratitude to Anna Freud for her advice and encouragement to pursue the topic
further.

changes and transformations. This development, as we know, is determined by important phase-specific factors, such as greatly increasing changes in the ego, part of which is the emergence of a powerful defensive system. Shifts occur in drive development, determining the individual's emotional development, especially his object relations. There is a gradual evolution of the autonomous function of the superego, which is of the utmost importance during this phase as well as for the future psychic equilibrium of the individual.

Introducing the concept of latency, Freud (1905a) stressed that it not be taken literally, but rather understood as a period of comparatively lessened drive urgency—relative to the preceding oedipal phase. After the partial resolution of the oedipal complex, the latency period is experienced as a respite from instinctual pressures, permitting the consolidation of ego and superego functions. Opinions are divided on whether the latency period is due primarily to the lessening of biological forces, or whether it is the demands of our civilization and education that encourage this consolidation of ego and superego functions. It is also possible to look upon latency as the outcome of the intrapsychic resolution of the oedipal conflict, in which the ego, representing the reality principle, was aided by the superego's condemnation of the child's oedipal fantasies. Freud's (1905) opinion is that "the lines . . . [of latency development] have been already laid down organically" (p. 178) and that they develop without the influence of education.

In my discussion of the technical problems of analysis during latency, the focus will be on the developmental subphases of that period. Originally, latency was described as one undifferentiated developmental phase. Augusta Alpert (1941) was the first who referred to an "early phase" of latency, in a general way distinguishing it from the upper limit of age 14 when puberty starts. Berta Bornstein (1951), in one of her classic papers on latency, elaborates in detail the psychoanalytic conceptualization of this phase, which she divides into an early phase, extending from $5\frac{1}{2}$ to 8, and a late phase of 8 to 10 years. By way of neurological and physiological findings, Elizabeth Bremner Kaplan (1965) also arrives at the conclusion of a biphasic classification of latency.

When one works with latency children, however, it appears that a *triphasic* division of latency would serve better to describe the vicissitudes of the drives, ego, and superego. A division into early latency, latency proper, and late latency helps in emphasizing the influence of the preceding phase of prelatency on early latency development, and in delineating the impact of the phase that follows latency—namely, prepuberty. Without trying to schematize, one can roughly describe early latency as lasting from 5 to 7, latency proper from 7 to about 9, and late latency from approximately 9 to 11. It should be understood that this scheme does not represent a strict categorization: in some children the prelatency period, chronologically speaking, extends far into what we would regard as latency proper; others show an early thrust into prepuberty.

As mentioned before, latency is a crucial developmental phase in the life of civilized human beings. Describing the vital importance of the development of defenses during latency, Freud (1905) showed how they help to impede the course of the sexual instinct, restricting its flow and thereby aiding in the building up of mental forces such as disgust, feelings of shame, and claims of aesthetic and moral ideals. He asks, "What is it that goes to the making of constructions which are so important for the growth of a civilized and normal individual?" (p. 178), and answers that they are the result of the diversion of a great part of the sexual impulse into energy that is used in the service of cultural achievements—that is, sublimation. Those who question whether or not latency is a necessary step in development do not take into consideration its paramount importance with regard to those integrative powers that are inherent in this phase of development. Some analysts are of the opinion that latency is not a favorable time for analysis, because of the latency child's natural tendency to shut out the past and to employ defenses to excess. However, we recognize that the mental forces at play in the child during this period are still in a state of fluidity and more easily accessible to change than they would be later.

Children who are brought for analysis during the latency period present a variety of clinical pictures, depending on the particular subphase through which they are passing. The child in the early phase is often physically restless, as well as psychologically burdened by the great impact of the oedipal conflict; moreover, he is still subject to the regressive pull of earlier developmental phases (Anna Freud, 1945) . Anxieties, nightmares, fears, and sleeping disturbances frequently are in the foreground of the young latency child's psychic life (Bornstein, 1951) . In early latency, the child's immature ego is only beginning to develop controls over his mental functioning. His struggles against genital impulses on the one hand, and against pregenital conflicts on the other, are well described by Berta Bornstein (1951, 1953a) .

As a rule, we find that the child who enters analysis after the age of 7—that is, during the phase of latency proper—is more composed than the younger latency child, due to physical and psychological maturation. Child patients between 7 and 9 pursue their activities with greater concentration. Their elaboration of a theme, while playing or drawing, shows more cohesion and permits easier access to their defenses, functioning, and interests. Late latency is also characterized by more balanced functioning, although at times one begins to see the slow incursion of prepubertal phenomena and the erection of an elaborate defensive system.

One of the most important aspects of the latency period lies in the achievement of a balance in which the reality principle gradually outweighs the pleasure principle. During this crucial development, the strength of the ego is continually being tested by the id and by the superego. In this "power struggle," the nature of the superego is often decisive for the final outcome. A few examples will illustrate some variations of superego development in its effect on the latency child's frequent intrapsychic struggles.

For instance, when the intense conflicts of early latency continue into late latency, with the superego exerting undue pressures, we get a picture of an early character disorder. In this case, the ego's efforts might remain thwarted. The object world remains invested with the authority that was previously held by the parents of the younger latency child. Anna Freud (1936) describes other important variations of the interplay between the ego and the superego, in which the ego defensively projects and displaces onto the object world its intolerance and guilt feelings toward the self. Among other conditions, she mentions one in which the development of superego function is arrested at an intermediary stage. In such cases, internalization of the superego remains incomplete; it does not get beyond identification with the aggressor. The superego then behaves as cruelly toward others as toward its own ego— which indicates an abortive beginning of the development of melancholic states.

The problems of technique during early latency are dynamically tied up with the influence of the primitive superego which is so characteristic of this developmental stage. Strict superego representations are externalized and relived in the transference, thereby making the child very sensitive to the analyst's interpretations. In our work with young latency children, we become aware that interpretations are frequently experienced as criticism. It is important to be cognizant of the fact that early latency is a phase dominated by the superego. Developmentally, the harsh dictates of the superego serve a necessary function, for, in spite of its severity, or because of it, the early latency child finds in it the support with which he is able to stem and halt the demands of the pleasure principle, and of the oedipal wishes. Unless interpretations are given with consideration of developmental needs, the patient may experience the analyst's "understanding" and "permissive" attitude as a seduction, as permission to do what has been forbidden. This may apply not only to the child in the early phase of latency development, but also somewhat beyond that phase. We always have to consider the latency child's dependence on and sensitivity to the adult's superego attitudes. If this is overlooked, the child might fear and mistrust the analyst, which will impede the analytic work.

One of the technical difficulties throughout latency is the lack of free associations; this has been mentioned and elaborated on by many authors (A. Freud, 1965; Bornstein, 1951). For the same reason, dreams are not often recounted; when they are, free associations are obtained only with difficulty. Moreover, during the early latency phase, the child often and easily slips back into primary process thinking, producing such material as if it were reality. To the child, of course, it is. More often than not, it is only through contact with the parents that we can find the kernel of this thinking that has to do with the reality of the child's life. Such confabulation is governed by wishful thinking and differs from those later communications that are defensively distorted.

These earlier free expressions soon come under the surveillance of the defenses. With the gradual evolution of the autonomous function of the superego, which is aided by the maturing ego, verbal communications of primary process thinking diminish, at least in the presence of adults; now they are being censored and defended against. In the prelatency child, however, we find it natural for the child to express verbally whatever comes into his mind; to talk to himself, to imaginary companions, to toys—or to us. The disappearance of this freedom of expression is most vividly manifested in children whose treatment begins during prelatency; in such cases, it is interesting to witness the emergence of new defenses. Before describing the development during the latency phase, I should like to illustrate such a transition, and the subsequent development, around one theme in the analysis of a boy whose treatment started in the oedipal phase and extended into early latency.

From the Oedipal Phase into Early Latency

Jim, the highly verbal sighted twin of a blind brother, started analysis at the age of 4. He suffered from overwhelming castration anxiety which was augmented by fears of retaliation, for he was convinced that he had made his brother blind. He masturbated compulsively to reassure himself that nothing would happen to his penis. His frequent outbursts of aggressive behavior were subsequently understood as a response to his father's increasing strictness. Identification with the enforced passivity of his blind twin led Jim to ordering me to do things for him that he was actually able to do for himself. At the height of the oedipal phase, his screaming at me was designed to shut out my interpretations. Later, when he was able to tolerate the interpretations of his castration anxiety and oedipal conflict, the screaming was replaced by his showing irritation. Progressively, he became able to verbalize concern about the parents' displeasure with his masturbation. At this point, Jim's castration anxiety shifted to a fear of a monster appearing nightly at his bedroom window. When his play presented displaced and exciting masturbatory activities, it would be followed by anxiety and projected accusations against me, at the same time as he asked for reassurance.

In the second year of Jim's analysis an episode occurred which clearly showed the changes that were taking place in his defensive structure, pointing to the onset of latency development.

Earlier in treatment, at the age of 4, Jim had been curious about a photograph of Freud. He had shown great interest in the explanation that Freud found how unwell people could feel because of the fears they were harboring. A simplified illustration from "Little Hans," about the displacement of his fear from father to the horse, was followed by Jim with great attention and seeming understanding. Eight months later, he asked me to repeat the story about Freud and Little Hans; now he showed disdain toward Little Hans's displacement and fear, calling it "stupid." In order to take his distancing of himself a step further, I mentioned that I knew a boy who experienced his father as a monster. He immediately recognized himself, acknowledging the insight by silence, along with a thoughtful look at me; this was followed by a knowing smile. Not long thereafter he relegated this episode in his life to the distant past.

This ability to recognize himself in an interpretation and to react to it without an impulsive outburst was a new phenomenon in his ego development and ego integration. It signified that he was now capable of controlling impulses and exercising the self-observing and critical functions of the ego. An interpretation was no longer viewed as a threat by an authority; instead, it could be consciously accepted. The present defenses showed the move toward independent functioning of the superego, with the patient becoming aware of his guilt feelings in relation to his oedipal conflict.

The following day he found it necessary to rationalize why he had once believed in the father-monster, which he now also regarded as "stupid." He explained the earlier displacement as a distorted visual observation in his room; he proudly reported that this had been "just thought up."

In the course of the analysis I was able to observe this child's attempt to resolve the oedipal conflict through the use of more varied and stronger defenses. This chatty little boy gradually became a much quieter patient than he had been, thereby indicating the development into latency.

Early Latency

Anna Freud (1945) in her paper on "Indications for Child Analysis," writes: "The latency period is usually in existence for one or two years before the tendencies of the first infantile period fade into the background" (p. 137). As long as these earlier tendencies are present, they exert a powerful regressive pull, as was shown in the case of 6-year-old Jack.

Jack's verbal communications did not show the latency child's usual reserve; rather, they resembled those of a younger child. Despite his advances in some intellectual pursuits and his developing skills in the use of mechanical tools, he continued to demand as much attention from his mother as he had during his earlier development when any frustration of his wishes had provoked temper tantrums. The parents apparently were not aware of Jack's demandingness and dependency when they encouraged him to wake them at any time during his nightly ordeals of bed wetting or stomach upsets. Because of the parents' indulgence, he was unable to express his oedipal aggression to them, displacing it instead onto his younger sister, Betty, whom he attacked frequently. His oedipal love for his mother and the jealousy of his father also were expressed via a displacement: he showed great resentment of his older sisters' boyfriends. His easy acceptance of interpretations at the beginning of treatment revealed the fact that he understood them to constitute a permission to persist in his regressive modes of functioning.

After the parents ceased to cater to Jack's regressive demands, however, a shift in his behavior took place. He gradually identified with the parents' new expectations of him, which led to an increasing internalization of superego demands. As is so characteristic of the young latency child, Jack now perceived interpretations as criticisms. This led to an increasingly negative transference. The interpretative work, therefore, had to take into consideration the great sensitivity of the newly emerging autonomous superego. This early superego, since it has to guard its boundaries with vigilance, can be very punitive. Jack expressed this not only in his criticism of others, but also in many physical hurts, though they were minor. One could look upon the frequent scrapes and hurts of the young latency child as being due as much to self-punishment as to physical immaturity.

It was interesting to observe how a meeting of inner and outer demands helped in the resolution of Jack's oedipal conflict. An unexpected confluence of happenings was experienced by Jack as a female betrayal, symbolizing his disappointment in his mother as an oedipal figure. This occurred when, against Jack's violent protestations, the mother planned a trip with his father. At the same time, his older sisters had little time for him because of their involvement with their boyfriends; and, even worse, the housekeeper, who was a ready mother substitute, planned to leave to get married. These events coincided with Jack's own need for object removal and thus facilitated it. He began to shift his loyalty away from the oedipal figures. The expected change in his transference to me was dramatically proclaimed. Soon after the parents' safe return from their trip, Jack came to his analytic hour announcing that he had a secret which he would not tell me; until then he had shared all his secrets with me. He maintained this new-found freedom from me with the defensive "stubbornness" and fiercely asserted "independence" that are characteristic of the child who is entering the latency phase.

Jack now formed closer friendships with peers and somewhat older boys. He spoke with pride of their adventures, games, and club activities, which evidently permitted them to give vent to their aggression. Jack developed an avid interest in mechanics and a preoccupation with machines and engines. He became quite skillful in reproducing them in drawings, although often with fantasied attributes. The boys sought sexual information from older siblings and magazines. Because of the prohibitive and guilt-producing aspects of these exciting explorations, Jack felt the need to tell me about them, but his accounts had a defensively boastful note. In contrast, he displayed his feelings of shame and secrecy by asking me to "guess" the name of a magazine, writing it in such minute letters that I could decipher it only with his help.

Jack's behavior demonstrates the young latency child's conflict: he feels grown up and confident in the circle of his friends; but when he confronts an adult, who symbolizes rationality and the critical aspect of the child's own ego and superego, he becomes anxious lest he displease the adult and thereby lose his love. This fear leads the young child confronted with his conflicts to institute especially strong defensive behavior. His frequent moodiness and complaining betray the buffeting he experiences when his ego is exposed to the conflicting demands of the superego and the id. The primitive superego's function is by its very nature expressed in simple formulas: the world is divided into good and bad, black and white. During this period, fairy tales and stories of the "good" and "bad" guy are preferred themes. The child looks to the parents for support in his efforts to uphold the primitive superego's regimen, which is often threatened with being overthrown by the pleasure principle. As often as the child welcomes the adults' support of his superego demands, he also fights against such support with the characteristic ambivalence of this developmental phase.

This conflictual situation, which echoes the superego's criticism, leads, in the transference of the analytic situation, to the great sensitivity vis-à-vis interpretations. The still frail intrapsychic balance of the young latency child makes it necessary to couch interpretations in a considerate and thoughtful way. However carefully I had thought out some of the interpretations I gave to Jack, I could tell from his tightly closed lips and averted eyes that he perceived them as criticism.

Latency Proper

During latency proper, the gradually increasing ability of the ego to evaluate reality enhances the intrapsychic equilibrium between ego, id, and superego. Among the "realities" confronting the child who is undergoing analytic treatment are the analyst's interpretations. The way in which the child responds to them gives us a very useful clue to measuring his progression of development. Focusing on this particular area of observation, I shall present further material from Jack's analysis.

During this phase, Jack's reality testing advanced in many different areas, and he showed an increasing ability to distinguish between what was real and what was imagined. For instance, roaming the streets with his friends, he gained a new view of the neighborhood, correcting many of his previously irrational beliefs:

houses that had in the past been pronounced to be "spooky" were found to be ordinary dwelling places, inhabited by ordinary people; "kooky" activities of neighbors were now seen more realistically. The spirit of adventure, which at times had seemed to be "limitless," gradually gave way to more caution and scrutiny. Jack now told me of situations that he felt would be dangerous to pursue. Such communications were often given more as evidence of his trust than out of guilt feelings. On such occasions, one could see that Jack now regarded the analyst less as a critic and more as a helper.

Jack also told his parents about some of his adventures, and the parents learned to understand these accounts as Jack's way of asking for their help in limiting activities that could be injurious to him. It was again instructive to these previously permissive parents to see that their help in setting limits brought relief and a sense of protection to Jack. Although at the beginning of this phase of latency proper Jack still hurt himself frequently during play, he did so progressively less. At the same time, he was also less inclined to take punishment from his playmates, whom he had previously allowed to use him as a whipping boy. During the early part of treatment, Jack had not been able to tell me about the circumstances of his various hurts; it was the parents who had to be the informants. Now, however, Jack was able to tell me about them and to give voice to his anger and thoughts of revenge toward his enemies. He no longer felt that he deserved the punishment, nor was he afraid that his anger, which had previously been explosive, might bring utter destruction to his enemy.

Now, while listening to an interpretation, he no longer tried to distract me in order to shut me out. While his ability to grasp the meaning of interpretations was at times amazing, it was not easy to measure their impact during early latency, but during latency proper this became possible. The following example illustrates this point. When Jack's envy and jealousy of his younger sister were interpreted during early latency, he displayed great sensitivity about this topic. He fought back tears while he was expressing anger toward his mother, whom he accused of treating Betty as a favorite. Indeed, Jack showed irritation and anger with me for opening up the subject at all—especially at a time when he had been reprimanded by his mother for appropriating a present she had intended for Betty. At that moment, he was unaware of the fact that my question had been prompted by his outward show of unhappiness and that it was he himself who had brought up this subject. The very act of my discussing this problem was proof to him in the transference that I favored his little sister.

When, during latency proper, the subject of his jealousy of Betty came up, Jack defensively exaggerated the number of presents each had received on a special occasion because he felt that girls were always favored. Although consciously, in word or deed, his mother had not betrayed any feeling "that boys had everything anyhow," she must have somehow conveyed her envy of males to produce that reaction in Jack. Nevertheless, Jack's primary concern was that his mother had produced another child at all. He was now able to accept my interpretation of his feelings of rejection when his sister was born. After pondering this interpretation in silence for a while, he made the seemingly unrelated remark that he could not remember in which hospital she was born, thus trying to deny her birth. On another occasion, he indicated his defensive acceptance of Betty by turning to humor: he said, amidst laughter, that he would not mind his sister getting more presents than he, if only they would be "no-good" presents, dirty and broken. Shortly thereafter, Jack began to be considerate toward his sister, helping her and showing kindness to others.

This reaction formation, which is so significant during latency development, was not produced under the sudden pressure of superego demands, but instead came about through the influence of the gradually maturing ego in relation to the superego. The parents' protective attitude toward their little daughter, their efforts to shield her against Jack's earlier aggressive attacks, had kept Jack alerted to the undesirability of his behavior. Jack's aggressive outbursts had for a long time been a problem, both at home and in school. During such periods, he would try, in the analytic session, to damage the table with the scissors, or to cut up a whole pad of paper. In the end, he would tie up the scissors with large amounts of scotch tape, thereby stopping himself from further expressing aggression and, at the same time, of course, preventing others from using them.

With the advance into latency proper, Jack was able to acknowledge the interpretation of his anger at feeling controlled and restricted in his aggression and of his wish to hurt and control others. The understanding that he wanted to exercise control in order to counteract his feeling of helplessness by the possession of power— that understanding helped Jack to perceive himself as not so small as he had believed himself to be. With this realization, he started to gain considerably better control over his angry outbursts.

The increasing integration of his ego was perhaps most clearly revealed in his interest in and enjoyment of organized games. The level of participation in an organized game demonstrates the state of the latency child's progressive psychic functioning, for, in addition to the id gratification, it requires an advanced state of ego organization, indicated by the development of new skills. Jack's willingness to abide by rules and his recognition of the idea of "fair play" were the early signs of an ongoing integrative process in superego development. Jack was now able to accept the concept of fairness for himself, as well as to demand it of others.

During the period of latency proper there also occurred a shift in Jack's identifications. Whereas previously his ambivalence conflict was clearly shown by his identification with both "good guys" and "bad guys," he now began to favor the "good" hero. Repeated drawings of battle scenes in which the bad guy was defeated by the good guy bore witness to the internal struggle between his efforts to gain control over his feelings and the onslaught of instinctual demands—the "bad guys." He now also strove to maintain superego control, whereas previously he had engaged in a variety of delinquent acts. This phenomenon, incidentally, occurs more often in boys than in girls. Boys appear to have a stronger tendency than girls to rebel openly against the dictates of the internalized strict and punishing image of the forbidding father. This may be one of the reasons why more boys with behavior problems are referred to child guidance clinics. Another factor may be that as a rule, girls are more anxious and concerned than boys about losing their love object. In order not to incur its displeasure, girls tend to obey rules of discipline more readily.[1]

1 There are other differences between latency boys and girls which have a bearing on technique. In this paper, however, I have focusd primarily on boys, leaving the discussion of girls to another occasion. On the other hand, what I have said about the importance of observing the latency child's reactions to interpretations applies equally to boys and girls.

Jack's fantasies of being all-powerful and all-knowing were displaced onto vehicles, which thereby took on magical powers. For a long time he remained preoccupied with drawing many varieties of cars, later of planes, which performed incredible feats. These drawings served the expression of several conflicts. Initially, Jack began to draw in competition with another boy, whom he envied for his ability to draw. He maintained his admiration even though he knew that his idol was copying his drawings from an older boy. My interpretation of Jack's envy merely spurred his sense of competition, so that he tried to outdo his friend in the designs of the models. These drawings also served the very important function of providing him with an outlet for the expression of aggressive feelings and fantasies in which the "good guys" bombed and killed the "bad guys." The explosion of a bomb was accompanied by newly invented anal sounds and words. I would then give Jack the interpretation that these battle scenes represented his own conflicts, in which good feelings were fighting bad ones. Jack responded by elaborating on such experiences in his life: he spoke of how temptations to do forbidden things presented themselves daily, and of his relief when his parents, particularly his father, stepped in to help him with his decision, by fostering the image of what was good and socially acceptable.

The bombing attacks also depicted elements of Jack's fantasy of the powerful and aggressive mother: "Women Hurt Men." The projection of his own anger toward and envy of women was especially prominent at times when he felt that his mother's demands were unreasonable.

His masturbation fantasies were most vividly depicted in a game with a pencil. A small ruler, which had been made to stand up with the help of another object, was the support of a long pencil; Jack "demanded" that this pencil stand up while it was leaning slightly against the ruler. Eventually, he withdrew all support from the vertically poised pencil, but still expected it to stand up. His perseverance in this game indicated his preoccupation with penile erections and masturbation. While at first he could not overtly accept my interpretation in which I linked his pencil game and masturbation, he showed no signs of feeling criticized, as he would have during the early latency phase. The working through of this conflict resulted in lessening of tension, much greater freedom of verbalization, and increased movement during the analytic session.

Simultaneously, the parents noticed a "dramatic" change in Jack's behavior at home. In this phase of "liberation" from his guilt feeling over masturbation, Jack experimented with making airplanes and flying them, and finally with drawing them. While earlier he had wanted to sketch planes, he had always abandoned his efforts in favor of earthbound vehicles. It seemed as if in his earlier attempts at drawing planes, he could not "get off the ground." The interpretation of his conflict around masturbation not only gave him a sense of sharing his oedipal secret with me, but, as mentioned before, removed the great burden of his guilt feelings. Concomitantly, his work in school improved.

In this connection, it is of interest to note that during early latency Jack had responded very differently to the interpretation of his masturbation fantasies. Whenever his mother had reproached him about his lack of cleanliness, Jack invariably became very angry and rebellious. Unconsciously, he had felt criticized for being a "dirty boy," a connection facilitated by the regressive pull to the anal phase which is still strong in early latency. In Jack's case, however, an additional factor served to fix this meaning: his masturbation was linked with his bed wetting. In Jack's thinking, therefore, his mother's demands for cleanliness during the anal phase were linked with the demands for giving up masturbation/bed wetting. The desirability of tidiness and of "clean hands" was unconsciously equated with the prohibition of masturbation, thereby reviving anal-aggressive responses. These phenomena evoked once again the angry behavior of the toddler who resists toilet training, and the young latency child's regressive behavior which is mainly expressed toward the mother. Thus, during early latency, my interpretation evoked a sense of irritation and hurt; when I went on to interpret the reason for his intense anger with his mother, his ego was not yet sufficiently mature to counteract the critical attitude of the archaic superego, as it was later capable of doing during latency proper.

A statement made by Freud (1923) illuminates this point: "The way in which the super-ego came into being explains how it is that the early conflicts of the ego with the object-cathexes of

the id can be continued in conflicts with their heir, the superego" (p. 38f.).

Late Latency

Patients who have been in analysis prior to the late latency phase
are capable of attaining an intrapsychic equilibrium that is in
abeyance during the preadolescent and adolescent years and is regained only during adulthood. The growing ego is no longer challenged simultaneously by an immature superego and by regressive
instinctual demands. This inner balance is reflected in object relationships that are comparatively free of ambivalent conflicts.
Creativity and scientific curiosity, as well as a striking ability to distinguish between what is right and what is wrong and to accept
painful feelings without denying them, make the late latency child
appear much more adult.

This was true in the case of Jack, who came to analysis during
early latency because of physical symptoms which he used defensively to perpetuate his dependence on his mother, and for his aggressive behavior toward other children. Jack's physical growth
during late latency was paralleled by age-appropriate ego growth.

Previously, his drawings had mainly been a means to express
aggressive fantasies. Now he concentrated on developing his skills,
especially the task of drawing in proper "perspective." His verbalization accompanying these efforts also revealed the ability to view
his past from a new perspective. Thus, he now remarked, "I remember when . . . ," usually referring to past, regressed behavior, i.e., bed wetting, complaints of gastric pain, and sadomasochistic relationships with his friends. He was now conscious of the
absence of regressive behavior, particularly bed wetting, which had
occurred during the phase of latency proper.

The gradual liberation from his oedipal entanglement allowed
for freer interaction within his family. During this phase of late
latency, we saw the emergence of a previously unknown awareness
of and sensitivity to the feelings of others, which were especially
clear in his changed attitude toward his younger sister. When Jack
was rewarded for a good report card, he asked that his father also
reward Betty commensurate with her better grades, emphasizing

fair play. Chores around the house were, as a rule, no longer used as an opportunity to involve his parents in arguments. Formerly, he had used these occasions to express his involvement with both parents, but especially his mother. Now he usually performed the required tasks without conflict.

During late latency an air of relaxation in his relationship with me mirrored the lessening of his anxiety that had been present earlier. This anxiety had been linked to his masturbation and the guilt feelings connected with it. The increased ease that Jack now felt during sessions was a reflection of his greater intrapsychic equilibrium. The wish for independence and object removal was expressed in the transference in the request to handle his affairs on his own.

Child patients who are brought for analysis during this late phase of latency development often present more technical difficulties than do children who begin analysis during the earlier phases. The older latency child who has not had previous treatment has usually built up an elaborate system of defenses. These children frequently have the primitive superego of the early latency period. Among these children who are brought for analysis during late latency, those who are involved in a symbioticlike relationship to their mother (Mahler, 1963) present the greatest technical difficulties.

Ordinarily, the patient in late latency exhibits some of the rebellious attitudes of prepuberty. At times, the desire for independence may prematurely overshadow all other strivings. An overdetermined precocious thrust into adolescent behavior often covers up a deeper developmental disturbance than one would assume from its surface appearance. Such cases may require prolonged treatment. In other cases, which overtly appear to be more difficult, analysis has a far better chance of resolving their problems. I am thinking of those patients who are still locked in a sadistic conflict with their oedipal rival, but whose ego functioning is otherwise not deeply affected. The resolution of their oedipal struggle enables such patients to integrate the gains of latency development, especially in relation to object removal. This, as we know, plays an important role during adolescence, in a more decisive separation from the primary love objects.

Summary

In this paper I have attempted to demonstrate the technical implications arising from the predominant trends of the three subphases of latency.

During the early phase of latency, the rigidity of the superego is in the foreground of mental development. The tension that exists between the superego and the instincts creates the child's ambivalence and his swiftly changing moods. Anna Freud (1936) has called the superego of the early latency phase an "ally" of the ego, in the sense that the still immature ego builds up its primitive defenses under the pressure of the superego. Precisely because of their rigid nature, these defenses support the child's stand against the instincts. The defensive reaction formations during latency initiate the first recognizable character changes. The ego is continually being challenged to take a position toward the id and toward the superego, and these confrontations gradually crystallize out the individual's character formation. Due to the fact that during early latency the superego is still characterized by archaic traits, incomplete internalization, and immaturity, the young latency child has a special sensitivity to interpretations and readily reacts to them as criticism; this is particularly true with regard to masturbation conflicts. The comparative lack of free associations must here be made up by analysis of the ego's defense mechanism and of the affects that accompany the child's defensive measures.

During latency proper, there is a shift in, and a strengthening of, the defensive system. The maturing ego experiences less anxiety than it did during the early phase and can effect a more balanced relationship with the superego. Analysis during latency follows the goal of all analyses: to free the patient of his inhibitions, thereby enabling him to proceed with further ego growth. The tact and patience that are required of a child analyst in the pursuit of this aim are amply illustrated in cases reported in our literature (Bornstein, 1949, 1953b; Ruben, 1957; Fraiberg, 1966; Furman, 1967; Pearson, 1968).

The technical problems encountered in latency proper are still present in late latency, but in addition we encounter other diffi-

(616)   MIRIAM WILLIAMS

culties that are due to specific developmental phenomena. The analytic task is made easier if the child starts his analysis before the late latency phase. The child who begins his analysis during the late phase has carried the burden of faulty development for a longer period, with the result that his difficulties and defensive maneuvers have become more fixed. At times, we find a well-functioning exterior that conceals many conflicts; these may involve impairment of object relationships and vital ego function, often associated with learning difficulties.

Where an elaborate system of defense mechanisms has been developed, the child resembles an adult with a character disorder, and the treatment will present the same technical difficulties as those found in the adult. The outstanding defense mechanism in late latency children is often denial, but during this phase it is far more difficult for the analyst to deal with this mechanism than it is with the frequent denials during the earlier phases. While the use of denial during early latency can be regarded as phase-specific, its extensive use during late latency indicates a pathological character formation. The disruptive influence of prepuberty in late latency is often outweighed by the gratifications the child derives from his achievements gained during latency.

For ego development, latency is a time of integration, a time of building, consolidating, and perfecting the functions of body and mind. It is normal for the latency child to reject anything that to him signifies regression to functioning on lines of earlier development, such as free association. Important shifts take place in the distribution of libidinal attachment, and hence in object relationships. A relative distancing from the oedipal figures which makes its appearance as object removal is phase-specific. The emergence of the superego as an independent agency is the hallmark of this developmental phase.

BIBLIOGRAPHY

ALPERT, A. (1941), The Latency Period: Re-examination in an Educational Setting. *Amer. J. Orthopsychiat.*, 11:126–132.

BORNSTEIN, B. (1949), The Analysis of a Phobic Child. *This Annual*, 3/4:181–226.
— (1951), On Latency. *This Annual*, 6:279–285.
— (1953a), Masturbation in the Latency Period. *This Annual*, 8:65–78.
— (1953b), Fragment of an Analysis of an Obsessional Child: The First Six Months of Analysis. *This Annual*, 8:313–332.
FRAIBERG, S. (1966), Further Considerations of the Role of Transference in Latency. *This Annual*, 21:213–236.
FREUD, A. (1936), *The Ego and the Mechanisms of Defense*. New York: International Universities Press, rev. ed., 1966.
— (1945), Indications for Child Analysis. *This Annual*, 1:127–149.
— (1951), Observations on Child Development. *This Annual*, 6:18–30.
— (1965), *Normality and Pathology in Childhood*. New York: International Universities Press.
FREUD, S. (1905), Three Essays on Sexuality. *Standard Edition*, 7:125–243. London: Hogarth Press, 1953.
— (1923), The Ego and the Id. *Standard Edition*, 19:3–66. London: Hogarth Press, 1961.
FURMAN, E. (1967), The Latency Child as an Active Participant in the Analytic Work. In: *The Child Analyst at Work*, ed. E. R. Geleerd. New York: International Universities Press, pp. 142–184.
KAPLAN, E. B. (1965), Reflections regarding Psychomotor Activities during the Latency Period. *This Annual*, 20:220–238.
MAHLER, M. S. (1963), Thoughts about Development and Individuation. *This Annual*, 18:307–324.
PEARSON, G. H. J., ed. (1968), *A Handbook of Child Psychoanalysis*. New York: Basic Books.
RUBEN, M. (1957), Delinquency: A Defense against Loss of Objects and Reality. *This Annual*, 12:335–355.

PSYCHOANALYSIS

AND THE LAW

The Child As a Person
in His Own Right

ANNA FREUD

CHILDREN ARE PRESUMED BY LAW TO BE INCOMPLETE BEINGS DURING
the whole period of their immaturity. Their utter inability to fulfill their own basic needs, or even to maintain life without extraneous help, justifies their being automatically assigned by birth

This article will form part of a forthcoming book entitled *Beyond the Best Interest of the Child,* planned with Joseph Goldstein and Albert J. Solnit as co-authors.
Since this book is meant to reach a wider and for the most part a nonanalytic audience, much is stated here that will be familiar to analytic readers.

The material used in this essay stems from the author's experiences gained during work in the Hampstead Child-Therapy Clinic, which is at present supported by
the Field Foundation, Inc., New York; the Foundation for Research in Psychoanalysis, Beverly Hills, Calif.; the Freud Centenary Fund, London; the Anna Freud
Foundation, New York; the National Institute for Mental Health, Bethesda, Maryland; the Grant Foundation, New York; the New-Land Foundation, Inc., New
York; and a number of private supporters.

All copyrights retained by the authors.

(621)

certificate to their biological parents or, where this natural relationship fails to function, by later Court proceedings to parent
substitutes. Responsibility for the child, for his survival, for his
physical and mental growth, for his eventual adaptation to community standards thus passes from the jurisdiction of the State to that
of the designated adults to whom the child, in his turn, is responsible for his behavior, his misdemeanors, etc.

This state of affairs on the legal side is matched on the psychological side by a number of tenets, some of old standing, some new,
such as the following:

> that a child's mental reliance on the adult world is as long-lived
> as his physical dependency;
> that each child's development proceeds in response to the envi-
> ronmental influences to which he is exposed;
> that his emotional, intellectual, and moral capacities unfold, not
> in a void, but within his human relationships;
> that his social reactions are determined by them;
> that conflicts arise in the child in the first instance with the pa-
> rental demands and prohibitions before they are internalized
> and may provide the base for later pathology.

There are, by now, many pediatricians, nurses, health visitors,
social workers, probation officers, nursery school workers, school
teachers, and child therapists who agree with these findings and
conclude from them that no child should be approached, assessed,
treated, nursed, taught, corrected, etc., without the parental influences being taken into account, and that without knowledge of
their impact neither the child's developmental successes and failures nor his adjustments and maladjustments will be seen in their
true light.

However, valuable as these insights are if placed within the general context of psychoanalytic child psychology, if used as guides
on their own they are misleading and highlight one side of child
development while they obscure another. Some workers within the
services for children have learned the lesson of environmental influence too well and consequently err by viewing the child as a
mere adjunct to the adult world, as a passive recipient of parental
impact. They tend to ignore that children interact with the latter

on the strength of their individual innate givens, and that it is this interaction, not mere response, which accounts for the countless variations in resulting characters and personalities as well as for the marked differences between siblings in spite of their growing up in the same family, etc. To see children too one-sidedly as mirroring their backgrounds blinds the observer to the vital characteristics of their own specific nature on which their own specific developmental needs are based.

There are a number of respects, such as the following, in which the mental makeup of children differs from that of the parent generation:

Unlike adults, whose psychic functioning proceeds on more or less fixed lines, children *change* constantly: from one state of growth to another; with regard to their understanding of events, their tolerance for frustration, their demands on motherly or fatherly care for stimulation, support, guidance, and restraint, or, according to the degree in which their personalities mature, for increasing freedom from control and for independence. Since, due to these changes, none of their needs remains stable, what serves their developmental interests on one level may be detrimental to progression on another.

Unlike adults, who measure the passing of *time* by clock and calendar, children have their own built-in time sense, based on the urgency of their instinctual and emotional needs. This results in their marked intolerance for postponement of gratification or for frustration, a heightened sensitivity to the length of separations, a shortening of the periods for remaining attached to absent parent figures, etc.

Unlike adults, whose reasonable mind is able to see occurrences in their true perspective, young children experience events in an *egocentric* manner, i.e., as happening solely with reference to their own persons. Thus, they may experience the mere move from one house or location to another as a grievous loss, imposed on them; the birth of a sibling, as an act of parental hostility; emotional preoccupation or illness of a parent, as rejection; death of a parent, as intentional abandonment, etc.

Unlike adults, who are able to deal with the vagaries of life via ego functions such as reason and intellect, immature children are governed in much of their functioning by the primitive parts of their minds, i.e., the *irrational id*. Consequently, they respond to any threat to their emotional security with fantastic anxieties, denial or distortion of reality, reversal or displacement of feelings, i.e., with reactions which are no help for coping but put them at the mercy of events.

Unlike adults, who are capable of maintaining positive emotional ties with a number of different individuals, unrelated or even hostile to each other, children are constitutionally unable to do so. They will freely love more than one adult only if the individuals in question feel positively to one another. Failing this, they become prey to severe and crippling *loyalty conflicts*.

Unlike adults, children have no psychological conception of relationship by blood-tie, whereas in the adult the fact of having engendered, borne, or given birth to a child produces an understandable sense of proprietorship and possessiveness, which underlies the frequent reconsiderations of consent to adoption, the claiming of offsprings after initial abandonment, etc. These considerations carry no weight with the children who are emotionally unaware of the events leading to their births. What registers in their minds are the day-to-day interchanges with the adults who take care of them and who, on the strength of these, become the parent figures to whom they are attached.

It is due to these differences between the adult and the childish mind that children, more often than not, do not react according to expectation. As the discrepancies described are not common knowledge, decisions about a child's custody or placement may proceed wholly on the basis of adult reasoning, regardless of what this means in terms of the child's own emotional language.

Thus, it is not only with regard to *timing* that Courts and welfare agencies are out of step with the children's own requirements. Following an order for *placement,* a young child may be removed from a known environment to an unknown one, with the adults oblivious of the hazards this implies for the child's still shaky sense of orientation. Following *adoption,* the inevitable change of name, which seems merely incidental to the adults, may have repercussions on the child's sense of identity, which is insecure at best. *Returned* to a biological parent after having been fostered, the child may face the traumatic task, not appreciated by the adults, of transferring emotional allegiance from a familiar and trusted adult to an unfamiliar stranger. Following *divorce*, with custody assigned to one parent, children are expected to concur peacefully with the Court's decision, disregarding the fact that they are the prey of their own distorting and unsettling interpretations of the break-up; that they blame the mother for removing the father because of his alleged cruel, male demands on her; that boys fear the same fate awaiting them unless they inhibit their masculinity; that they blame whichever parent they live with and punish him or her by being disobedient; or that they blame themselves for the defection of the absent parent and become dejected and withdrawn. Following *visiting rights* allotted to the absent parent, the child is expected to relate positively to him, regardless of the fact that relations to a parent do not thrive naturally if restricted to pre-scribed days and hours and, even if they should do so, are inter-fered with by the child's conflict of loyalty between warring part-ners. When a child's residence is being divided evenly between the *two parents,* it may not be realized that this prevents both adults from exerting normal parental influence.

What is fair to the adults, their standards and their interests in all these instances, may be far from being in the best interests of the children concerned, or even the least detrimental alternative for them.

What emerges from the foregoing is that children are not adults in miniature but beings per se, different from their elders in their mental nature, their functioning, their evaluation of events, and their reactions to them. It follows from this that children, far from sharing the adults' concerns, are frequently put in direct conflict with them: their needs may contrast with those of their biological parents, their foster parents, or the social agencies concerned with them. For this reason, their rights cannot be represented ade-quately by the advocates of either the adult claimant or the adult defendant. They need party status in any Court proceeding con-cerned with their fate, i.e., to be represented, independently of the adults, as persons in their own right.

It goes without saying that their own advocates need to be knowledgeable about the specific characteristics which govern any child's specific needs for more or less unhampered growth and de-velopment.

Finding the Least Detrimental Alternative

The Problem for the Law of Child Placement

JOSEPH GOLDSTEIN, PH.D., LL.B.

FOR THIS ESSAY I HAVE SELECTED FOR EXAMINATION A NOT UNCOMmon court decision involving the placement of a "foster" child. This material is drawn from a book which I am writing with Anna Freud and Albert J. Solnit. The book, on which Seymour Lustman was to collaborate and which he helped plan, is to be entitled *Beyond the Best Interests of the Child.* In it, we seek to develop psychoanalytic guides which will (1) provide a basis for critically evaluating individual case decisions as well as the varied legal pro-

Walton Hale Hamilton Professor of Law, Science and Social Policy, Yale University.

This essay is taken from material prepared for a book which I am writing with Anna Freud and Albert J. Solnit entitled *Beyond the Best Interest of the Child.* All copyrights have been retained by the authors.

I am indebted to Steven Goldberg, Sonja Goldstein, Hillary Rodham, and Amos Shapira for their assistance.

(626)

cedures concerned with determining who is or should be assigned the opportunity and the task of being "parent" to a child; and (2) constitute a theoretical and conceptual framework, not only for identifying and criticizing unsound precedents, but also for understanding and making secure many sound, but frequently unfollowed precedents—many of which were intuitively developed long before psychoanalysis.

I have chosen to evaluate a New York case, *Rothman v. Jewish Child Care Association,* decided in 1971 by Justice Nadel.[1] This evaluation is presented in the form of an opinion written by a fictitious Judge Analjo. Analjo's opinion is what might have been written had Justice Nadel, the actual trial judge, applied guides from psychoanalysis about child development in determining whom Stacey, age 8 and a "foster" child, should have as parents.

My minutes of one of five meetings held for planning the book during the Spring of 1970 between Drs. Freud, Lustman, Solnit and myself at Yale's Davenport College record that Dr. Lustman set in motion a discussion which led to the observation that a psychological bond frequently develops between child and foster parents despite a child care agency's purpose and the law's interest in providing no more than a "temporary" custodial relationship for the child. He was thinking about a 1959 New York appellate court decision involving the very same Jewish Child Care Association but concerned with another child, Laura.[2] In that case the Association, at the request of the natural mother, placed Laura, an infant of 1 year, in the "temporary" custody of foster parents. Four and a half years later, when the foster parents indicated that they wished to adopt Laura, the Association, in the name of "the child's best interests," thwarted their efforts and convinced the court that Laura should be returned to the custody of her biological mother. Further discussion of this decision, which wrenched Laura from her psychological parents led, as the minutes of April 15, 1970, record, "to the idea that we should develop a set of guides for foster parents. . . . From there, Dr. Lustman turned our attention to another lesson from the Laura case, which is that child agencies ought not to be so specialized that there is one for adoption and

---

[1] 166 *N.Y. Law J.,* p. 17, col. 1 (Nov. 4, 1971).
[2] *In Re* Jewish Child Care Association 5 N.Y. 2nd 222, 156 N.E., 2d 700 (1959).

another one for foster care, but that agencies should be multifunctional so that staff can consider as many alternatives as might be made available in selecting a placement that is least likely to disserve the interests of the particular child involved." Thus, he argued that there should be agencies of general child placement rather than agencies exclusively concerned with either adoption or foster care.

Interestingly, it appears from the *Rothman* case that the Jewish Child Care Association, sometime since its 1959 "victory," may have modified its policy regarding such cases as Laura's.[3] Unfortunately, the same cannot be said for the court, as Justice Nadel's decision, which is first reproduced in full, demonstrates.

I

Rothman v. Jewish Child Care Ass'n.

Supreme Ct. New York County
166 *N.Y. Law Journal*, p. 17, Col. 1 (Nov. 5, 1971)

Justice Nadel
In this proceeding the natural mother seeks a judgment for the return of her eight-year-old daughter, Stacey. Petitioner gave her daughter to respondents for temporary care in December, 1964, when she voluntarily entered a hospital for treatment of a mental illness. Petitioner left the hospital for a period of time and then was readmitted. In December, 1969, the petitioner was released from the hospital and has not been hospitalized since. She is living with her parents, is employed as an executive secretary, and earns $140 per week.

The petitioner has never surrendered the child for adoption. The respondent, Jewish Child Care Association, opposes giving custody to the natural mother on the ground that she is unfit to care for the child by reason of her vast mental illness. However, on the trial they failed to produce any evidence upon which the court could make a finding that the petitioner is unfit to have custody of the child. The burden is upon the non-

---

[3] But see, *New York ex rel: Jewish Child Care Association v. Cahn* Sup. Ct. Nassau County Special Term Part V (April 28, 1972) in which the court upholds the Association's efforts to remove a 9-year-old child from "foster" parents with whom she had been placed for more than 9 years in order to return her to her "natural" parents.

parent respondent to prove that petitioner is unfit to care for her daughter, and that the child's well-being requires separation from her mother. The Court of Appeals has ruled that absent abandonment of the child, statutory surrender of the child or the established unfitness of the mother, a court is without power to deprive the mother of custody (*Spence-Chapin Adoption Service v. Polk, N.Y.L.J., Sept. 27, 1971, p. 1, col. 1*). At best, respondents have shown that the relationship between mother and daughter is not as good as it should be. That this is so, is primarily the fault of the Jewish Child Care Association. Its extra-judicial determination that the child should not be returned, its hindrance of visitation and its failure to encourage the parental relationship were, to a great extent, responsible for the lack of a better relationship. It has been established in the Family Court that the said Association failed to make any real efforts to encourage and strengthen the parental relationship. The petitioner had to commence court proceedings for visitation and custody of her child, which were denied her by the Association.

Not only have respondents failed to sustain their burden of proof, but the evidence submitted amply demonstrates petitioner's fitness to have custody of her child. It was in the interest of the welfare of her daughter that the petitioner gave respondents temporary custody when she was hospitalized and unable to care for the child.

In the period of nearly two years preceding this trial, petitioner has been gainfully employed and she has been active in community, charitable and religious affairs. During the trying period of her hospitalization and separation from her child, petitioner appears to have successfully rehabilitated herself.

The court has observed petitioner during the course of her testimony. After hearing and observing the petitioner, the court finds that she is sincere in her desire to care for her daughter, and that she is able to do so. Petitioner is residing with her parents, and they will be able to care for their grandchild in the interim between the child's return from school and the time when the petitioner comes home from work. Their presence adds two persons to aid petitioner in the care of her daughter.

The request by the attorneys for the respondent Association to reargue the motion to refer this case to the Family Counseling Service is denied. Similar relief was denied respondent by several justices of this court. In any event, there has been a trial of the issues involved, and the court finds no valid reason for any further delay in returning the child to her natural mother.

The petitioner indicated that she realizes that the attitude of her daughter may require a transitional period before acquiring full custody. The parties shall, therefore, confer and shall submit in the judgment to be settled herein, a program for visitation and transfer of custody. Should the parties fail to agree, the court will determine such provisions, giving due consideration to their suggestions.

Settle judgment. Exhibits are with the clerk of the part.

II

Judge Analjo reaches his decision using only the data relied upon by Justice Nadel. Since it is realistic to assume that no more adequate data about the child or the competing adults are generally available to a court, Judge Analjo, to compensate for the data deficiency, develops for general application a number of new legal concepts and presumptions sensitive to our knowledge of a child's developmental needs. Beyond this, Judge Analjo, in order to keep Stacey and her interests in focus, has, in restating the facts, refrained from using such emotionally freighted and conclusion-tending words and phrases as "natural mother" or "mother" in describing Ms. Rothman. In accord with the sound legal tradition of using such neutralizing, not dehumanizing, words as "petitioner" and "respondent" rather than continuously repeating the real names of the parties to the proceeding, Judge Analjo identifies Ms. Rothman only as an adult who gave birth to a female child named Stacey. Enough by way of introduction to the Analjo decision:

Rothman v. Jewish Child Care Ass'n.

Supreme Ct. Hampstead-Haven County
1 *New World Law Journal* p. 1, col. 1 (Nov. 5, 1971)

Justice Analjo
In this proceeding, the petitioner, an adult woman, seeks our judgment to award to her for custody and care an 8-year-old fe-

male child named Stacey. To support her claim, she established
the following uncontested facts:

1. In December of 1963 petitioner gave birth to Stacey and, in
accord with custom, practice, and the law, was initially and automatically assigned parental responsibility for the custody and care
of the infant.

2. Seven years ago petitioner entered the hospital for the treatment of a mental illness. At the same time, she gave Stacey, then
1 year old, to the Jewish Child Care Association, the respondent,
with the intention that she be cared for temporarily.

3. Two years ago, petitioner was released from the hospital
and has not been hospitalized since. She is now living with her
parents, is employed as an executive secretary, and earns $140
per week.

4. Petitioner is sincere in her request to care for Stacey, and her
parents are prepared to assist in this while she is at work.

5. The respondent has refused to disturb Stacey's present relationship with her adult custodians. It has hindered petitioner's
efforts to visit Stacey and to establish a parental relationship.

The respondent, on Stacey's behalf, opposed giving custody to
petitioner. Because of her prior illness, it asserts that she is unfit
to care for the child, to serve as a parent. So far as this case is concerned, petitioner is, as is any other adult, initially presumed in
law to be fit to be a parent. We need not and do not reach that
question.

The real question is: does Stacey need to have a parent assigned
to her by the court. The presumption that petitioner is fit could
have become subject to challenge only had it first been established
that Stacey is currently an unwanted child in need of a parent. Not
until then could the court admit evidence concerning the petitioner either to overcome the presumption or, preferably, to inform the court about petitioner and others in terms of determining
whose custody, among available alternatives, would serve Stacey's
best interests by providing the least detrimental opportunity for
meeting her needs.

What is strangely missing from the evidence is any material on
Stacey's needs. In the absence of such evidence the law must and
does presume that Stacey is a *wanted child* and that her present

custody ought not to be disturbed. It is presumed, therefore, that she is receiving affection and nourishment on a continuing basis from at least one adult and that she feels that she is valued by those who take care of her.[4] The burden is on the petitioner (assuming she had standing to invoke this proceeding) to overcome the presumption that the adult or adults who currently are responsible for Stacey are fit to remain her parents; and to overcome the presumption that Stacey (after living from infancy for such an extended period of time with her foster parents) is a wanted child—not merely in the sense of "want" as expressed by the competing adults, but additionally in her feeling of being wanted by those who have become a continuing source of affection, nourishment and well-being.[5] Another facet of these presumptions is that the relinquishing "parent," here the petitioner, after such a lapse of time, has, from the child's psychological vantage point, abandoned her. The burden then is on petitioner to establish that there is a necessity for altering the now long-standing ongoing relationship between Stacey and whoever may have become her "common-law" parent or parents, as well as between her and whoever may have become her "common-law" siblings, if there be any. The burden in short is to show that Stacey is an *unwanted child* in her present home. If petitioner were to meet the burden (and her attempts to do so do not give her license to invade the privacy of Stacey's "common-law" family [6]), she would not then have to prove her fitness to be a parent. Rather, she would have to establish that among the interested adults, all of whom are presumed fit to be parents, her taking custody would be *least detrimental* (Goldstein and Katz,

---

[4] On the right to be a wanted child and some of its implications for law, see Goldstein and Provence (1970).

[5] See, e.g., Anna Freud (1965), "According to the psychoanalyst's experience, the best interests of an infant are safeguarded under the condition that three needs are fulfilled: the need for *affection* (for the unfolding and centering of the infant's own feelings); the need for *stimulation* (to elicit inherent functions and potentialities); and the need for *unbroken continuity* (to prevent damage done to the personality by the loss of function and destruction of capacities which follow invariably on the emotional upheavals brought about by separation from, death or disappearance of, the child's first love-objects)" (p. 1053).

[6] The law, seeking to safeguard the privacy of family relationships and the private ordering of one's life, has adopted a policy of minimum state intervention consistent, of course, with the state's goal of safeguarding the well-being of children, protecting them from exploitation by adults (Goldstein and Gitter, 1969, p. 82).

1965, p. 4, n. 57) to Stacey's healthy growth and development and to her physical and psychological well-being.

Though not directly in issue here, it is appropriate to digress momentarily in order to suggest that the legislature, in addition to giving statutory recognition to the "right to be a wanted child," consider establishing in its guides to child placement a new standard, "that which is least detrimental among available alternatives for the child" as a substitute for the now traditional "that which is in the best interests of the child." Under such a legislative mandate to use "least detrimental" rather than "best interest," courts as well as child care agencies are more likely to confront the detriments inherent in each child placement decision without getting enmeshed in the hope and magic associated with "best" in a way which often misleads decision makers into believing they have more power for "good" than for "bad" in what they may decide.

Introducing the idea of "available alternatives" should force into focus from the child's vantage point consideration of the advantages and disadvantages of the actual real options to be measured in terms of that which is least likely to preclude the chances of the child becoming "wanted." The proposed standard is less awesome, more realistic, and thus more amenable to relevant data gathering than "best interest." No magic is to be attributed to the new formulation, but there is in any new set of guiding words an opportunity at least for courts and agencies to re-examine their tasks and thus possibly to force into view factors of low visibility which seem frequently to have resulted in decisions actually in conflict with "the best interests of the child."

Further, it is not beyond the capacity of the court, were the legislature not inclined to accept the suggestion, to construe the statutory guide of "in the best interests of the child" to require the court or agency to select that placement which is "the least detrimental available alternative." In any event, whether by legislative or judicial decision, the new standard might permit going beyond the best interest of the child by enhancing the opportunities for each child to have made secure his or her right to be and feel wanted.

Petitioner further argues, returning now to the specific claims in this case, that she never lost custody-in-law of Stacey. She established that she has always considered herself responsible for Stacey's care, that she had made "temporary" arrangements for her with the respondent, that from the outset it was understood that they were to be temporary, and that she had always intended, once her health was restored, to care personally for Stacey. At no time during the last 7 years, she asserts, has she *abandoned* Stacey; has she ever ceased being her "mother." If anyone is at fault, it is, she claims, the respondent Association. It has prevented her from maintaining, or, at least, establishing a parental relationship with Stacey.

These arguments and the supporting facts reflect an understandable, but still mistaken notion of the law,[7] its limits and limitations. Like the wanted child concept, abandonment of a child by an adult, at least for the purpose of determining who is parent, rests, not on the intentions of the adult, but rather on the impact such a leave-taking has on the child. In the absence of specific evidence to the contrary, a child of 1 year, who has been left in "temporary" care for as many years as have elapsed since Stacey had continuous, affectionate, and otherwise nurturing contact with petitioner, must be presumed in law to be wanted by petitioner and to have been *abandoned* for purposes of custody and care. If nothing else, from Stacey's vantage point, there has been a critical break in whatever psychological tie had begun to develop between herself and petitioner. Painful as it must be for this well-meaning woman, her intentions alone are not enough to prevent such psychological abandonment. Those intentions would have had to be accompanied by a carefully designed program with respondent, and then only for a relatively short time span, which did, in fact, maintain petitioner as the primary adult source for Stacey of affection, stimulation, and, most importantly, of a sense of continuity essential to securing healthy growth and development.[8]

[7] Courts have consistently held that for a child to be considered abandoned the natural parents must have a "settled intent to renounce the parental relationship" (*Winnans v. Luppie* 47 N.J. Eq. 302, 305 [1890]) and see, e.g., *In re* Adoption of Branzley 122 So. 2d 423 (Fla. 1960) (abandonment is a "settled purpose to permanently forgo all parental rights"). The problem has generally not been conceptualized, as the original Rothman case demonstrates, in terms of the child's sense of abandonment.

[8] See A. Freud's and D. Burlingham's Monthly Reports of the activities of the Hampstead War Nurseries for descriptions of a variety of efforts to maintain alive the image of the parent during separations (A. Freud, 1973).

So far as Stacey's interests are concerned, it matters not that the implementation of those intentions may have actually been thwarted by the actions of the respondent, or by anyone else, nor does it matter, for purposes of determining custody, whether petitioner's intentions were defeated through her kindness, her misunderstanding, or her ignorance. Whatever the cause, whoever may feel responsible, the psychological fact, which the law must recognize, is that Stacey does not now have in petitioner a parent.

It is impossible to locate precisely the moment in time when a parent's "temporary" relinquishment of a child to the custody of another becomes abandonment for that child. To put it more affirmatively and, hopefully, realistically, it is not possible to determine just when a new parent-child relationship has formed which deserves the recognition and protection of the law. That new relationship, which in the absence of contrary evidence must be presumed to have developed over the past 7 years, may be perceived, not unlike a common-law marriage, as one of *common-law parenthood* or *common-law adoption*. While the process through which a new child-parent status emerges is too complex and subject to too many individual variations for the law to know just when "abandonment" may have occurred, the law can generally verify that the biological tie never matured into an affirmative psychological tie for the child or that a developing psychological tie has been broken or damaged and whether a promising new relationship has developed and is being formed. The law presumes, barring extraordinary efforts to maintain the continuity of a "temporarily interrupted" relationship, that the younger the child, the shorter the period of relinquishment before a developing psychological tie is broken and a new relationship begins—a relationship which must not be put in jeopardy if the primary goal of the state is to safeguard the health and well-being of the child.

The court is mindful that a parent (an adult with primary responsibility for the continuous care of a child) may entrust a child to others for short periods of time (with the length of time amenable to extension for older children) and may make arrangements for maintaining the continuity of existing ties without necessarily jeopardizing the child's health and well-being. But there comes a point, whatever the declared or conscious intent of the "parent" and whatever the nature of the arrangement for as-

(636) JOSEPH GOLDSTEIN

suring continuity, when temporary arrangements are no longer temporary, when separations are so prolonged that the force of the law must be available to protect, not break, already established or even newly developing parent-child relationships. The abandoned child has, hopefully, begun to establish a new tie with an adult or adults who for all purposes are then becoming his or her psychological parents.[9] And such persons are in law recognized as parents by a process we would call *common-law adoption*. Such an adoption carries with it all the legal protections generally available to nurture and secure healthy ties between parent and child. Were the state to intervene, as it often has following "abandonment" and before the hoped-for new tie has begun to develop, the "abandoning" parent, if he or she wished, might be given a preference based on the expectation that the residue of the former relationship would facilitate renewal of the earlier tie and thus provide the least detrimental alternative.

[9] Art Buchwald, the distinguished humorist, who 50 years ago was a foster child, recalled in a speech celebrating the 150th Anniversary of the Jewish Child Care Association in April, 1972:

"The status of a foster child, particularly *for* the foster child, is a strange one. He's part of no-man's land.

". . . The child knows instinctively that there is nothing permanent about the setup, and he is, so to speak, on loan to the family he is residing with. If it doesn't work out, he can be swooped up and put in another home.

"It's pretty hard to ask a child or foster parent to make a large emotional commitment under these conditions, and so I think I was about seven years old, when confused, lonely and terribly insecure I said to myself, 'The hell with it. I think I'll become a humorist.'

"From then on I turned everything into a joke. Starting as the class clown, I graduated to making fun of all authority figures from the principal of the school to the social service worker who visited every month. When a person is grown up and he attacks authority, society pays him large sums of money. But when he's a kid and he makes fun of authority, they beat his brains in.

"Having chosen this dangerous pasttime of getting attention by poking fun at everything, I found I could survive. I had my bag of laughs, and I had my fantasies, which I must say were really great. Would you believe that I dreamed I was really the son of a Rothschild, and I was kidnapped by gypsies when I was six months old, and sold to a couple who were going to America?

"If you believe that, would you believe the Rothschilds had hired France's foremost detective to find me and that it was only a matter of time when he would trace me to the foster home in Hollis, Long Island, and would you believe that once my true identity had been established, I would prevail on my Rothschild father to drop all charges against the people that had kidnapped me, and give them a substantial pension.

"That's the kind of kid my social worker had to deal with."

This decision is not and must not be read to require the assigning of fault to any person or to any child placement agency.[10] By shifting the focus of decision to the problem of meeting the needs of the child, the intent of the leave-taking adult or of the administrative agency is no longer of relevance. The law moves as it should, away from making moral judgments about fitness to be a parent; away from assigning blame; and away from looking at the child and the award or denial of custody as reward or punishment. It becomes unimportant then whether the parent-child relationship grew out of circumstances within or beyond the "control" of an adult claimant.

Though obvious once said, when left unsaid, the limitations of law often go unacknowledged in cases such as this. There is attributed to the law a magical power, a capacity to do what is far beyond its means. While the law may claim the power to establish relationships, it can, in fact, do little more than acknowledge them and give them recognition. It may be able to destroy human relationships, but it cannot compel them to develop. It has taken the law a long time to recognize that the power to deny divorce cannot establish a healthy marriage, preclude the parties from separating, or prevent new "married" relationships from maturing.[11] While the impact of a court decision concerning adult-child relationship is not necessarily quite so limited as with adult-adult relationships in divorce proceedings, the court still does not have the power to establish meaningful relationships. Here it can destroy or protect such relationships and can facilitate their growth. But it cannot compel them, even though the child, unlike the adult in the denial-of-divorce situation, has less freedom to establish new relationships on his own. The child is far more vulnerable to exploitation by the adult who is recognized in law as parent or custodian. By decreeing that Stacey be returned to her biological "mother," no court could establish a real relationship between them. Yet such a decision cannot be assumed to be a hollow or meaningless one for either of them or for the adopting foster par-

[10] Of course, an agency may lose its license or be liable for damages if it is negligent in carrying out responsibilities it undertakes. What is important here is that the child not become the award for damages.

[11] See generally Goldstein and Gitter (1969).

ents. It would have greater potential for damage and pain for all than for the health and well-being of any of them.

There will, of course, as in all human situations, be the hard case. But more than likely the law can resolve such cases, if it has clarified for itself and the participants the function and purpose of the proceeding and the limitations of the legal process. In so doing, it is less likely to obscure the problem by a mistaken concern for the person whose only special claim to the child rests on a biological tie. Such a tie deserves and receives an initial acknowledgment in law by making it the basis for determining who will first be "parent." But the status of parent, once a child has left the chemical exchange of the womb for the social exchange, where law has a role to play, rests on maintaining a continuous nurturing, affectionate, and stimulating relationship essential to the physical and psychological health and development of the child.

Though the status of parent is not easily lost in law, it can exist only so long as it is real in terms of the health and well-being of the child. It is a relationship from birth, whether legitimate or illegitimate, or from adoption, whether statutory or common-law, which requires a continuing interaction between adult and child to survive. It can be broken by the adult parent by "chance," by the establishment of a new adult-child relationship, which we call common-law adoption, or by "choice," through a more formal legal process we have come to call adoption.

It must be realized that the tie of adoption is no more nor less significant than the biological tie. It is the real tie—the reality of an ongoing relationship—that is crucial to this court's decision and that demands the protection of the state through law. The court must not, despite its sympathetic concern for the petitioner, become a party to tearing Stacey away from the only affectionate parents she knows. Stacey must be presumed to be, in her present surroundings, a wanted child.

Finally, it must be observed that this decision does not constitute a break with the past. Rather, the past is future. There is in law, as psychoanalysis teaches that there is in man, a rich residue which each generation preserves from the past, modifies for the now, and in turn leaves for the future. Law is, after all, a continuous process for meeting society's need for stability by providing authority and precedent and, at the same time, meeting its need for flexibility and change by providing for each authority a counterauthority and for each precedent a counterprecedent. The living law thus seeks to secure an environment conducive to society's healthy growth and development.

That this decision is not incompatible with legal decisions of the last century will come as no surprise then, either to students of law who constructively resist sharp breaks with the past or to students of child development who have made us understand man's need for continuity. In 1824, for example, the distinguished American jurist and justice of the United States Supreme Court, Joseph Story, had no psychoanalytic theory of child development to draw upon, yet acting as circuit judge he could write in *U.S. v. Green* (3 Mason 482 Fed. Cas. No. 15256 [1824]) :

> As to the question of the right of the father to have the custody of his infant child, in a general sense it is true. But this is not on account of any absolute right of the father, but for the benefit of the infant, the law presuming it to be for its interests to be under the nurture and care of his natural protector, both for maintenance and education. When, therefore, the court is asked to lend its aid to put the infant into the custody of the father, and to withdraw him from other persons, it will look into all the circumstances, and ascertain whether it will be for the real, permanent interests of the infant and if the infant be of sufficient discretion, it will also consult its personal wishes.

Far less vague and in language often sounding psychoanalytic, yet written more than a decade before Freud published *The Interpretation of Dreams,* are the words of Justice Brewer speaking for the Supreme Court of Kansas in 1889 in the child placement case of *Chapsky v. Wood* (26 Kan. Reports, pp. 650–658 [2nd ed. annotated, 1889]) :

> [When a] child has been left for years in the care and custody of others, who have discharged all the obligations of support and care which naturally rest upon the parent, then, whether the courts will enforce the father's right to the custody of the child, will depend mainly upon the question whether such custody will promote the welfare and interest of such child. This distinction must be recognized. If, immediately after

[giving up the child] reclamation be sought, and the father is not what may be called an unfit person by reason of immorality, etc., the courts will pay little attention to any mere speculation as to the probability of benefit to the child by leaving or returning it. In other words, they will consider that the law of nature, which declares the strength of a father's love is more to be considered than any mere speculation whatever as to the advantages which possible wealth and social position might otherwise bestow. But, on the other hand, when reclamation is not sought until a lapse of years, when new ties have been formed and a certain current given to the child's life and thought, much attention should be paid to the probabilities of a benefit to the child from the change. *It is an obvious fact that ties of blood weaken, and ties of companionship strengthen, by lapse of time; and the prosperity and welfare of the child depend on the number and strength of these ties, as well as on the ability to do all which the promptings of these ties compel* [my italics].

[T]hey who have for years filled the place of the parent, have discharged all the obligations of care and support, and especially when they have discharged these duties during those years of infancy when the burden is especially heavy, when the labor and care are of a kind whose value cannot be expressed in money—when all these labors have been performed and the child has bloomed into bright and happy girlhood, it is but fair and proper that their previous faithfulness, and the interest and affection which these labors have created in them, should be respected. Above all things, the paramount consideration is, what will promote the welfare of the child? These, I think, are about all the rules of law applicable to a case of this kind.

. . . What the future of the child will be is a question of probability. No one is wise enough to forecast or determine absolutely what would or what would not be best for it; yet we have to act upon these probabilities from the testimony before us, guided by the ordinary laws of human experience. . . .

[T]he child has had, and has today, all that a mother's love and care can give. The affection which a mother may have and does have, springing from the fact that a child is her offspring, is an affection which perhaps no other one can really possess; but so far as it is possible, springing from years of patient care of a little, helpless babe, from association, and as an outgrowth from those little cares and motherly attentions bestowed upon it, an affection for the child is seen in Mrs. Wood that can be found nowhere else. And it is apparent, that so far as a mother's love can be equaled, its foster-mother has that love, and will continue to have it.

On the other hand, if she goes to the house of her father's family, the female inmates are an aunt, just ripening into womanhood, and a grandmother; they have never seen the child; they have no affection for it springing from years of companionship. . . .

Human impulses are such that doubtless they would form an affection for the child—it is hardly possible to believe otherwise; but to that deep, strong, patient love which springs from either motherhood, or from a patient care during years of helpless babyhood, they will be strangers.

In acknowledging Stacey's adoption by affirming the respondent Association's assertion of her right to remain with her "foster" but real parents of the past 8 years, the court takes the position of Justice Brewer in the *Chapsky* case:

It is a serious question, always to be considered, whether a change should be advised. "Let well enough alone" is an axiom founded on abundant experience [at p. 656].

So ordered.

BIBLIOGRAPHY

BUCHWALD, A. (1972), Speech to Jewish Child Care Association (Perie Hotel, New York, April 19; unpublished).

FREUD, A. (1965), Cindy. In: *The Family and the Law* by J. Goldstein & J. Katz. New York: Free Press, pp. 1051–1053.

— & BURLINGHAM, D. (1973), Monthly Reports [of the Activities of the Hampstead War Nurseries]. In: *The Writings of Anna Freud*, Vol. III. New York: International Universities Press (in press).

GOLDSTEIN, J. (1968), Psychoanalysis and Jurisprudence. *This Annual*, 23:459–478.

— & GITTER, M. (1969), On the Abolition of Grounds for Divorce: A Model Statute and Commentary. *Family Law Quart.*, 3:75–99.

— & KATZ, J. (1965), *The Family and the Law*. New York: Free Press.

— & PROVENCE, S. (1970), The Rights of Children. *Memorandum Prepared for Forum 22 of the White House Conference on Children* (unpublished).

Index

Contents of Volumes 1-26

(665)

Contents of Volumes 1–26 (699)